Dreamweaver® MX Extensions

Laura Gutman

www.newriders.com

201 West 103rd Street, Indianapolis, Indiana 46290
An Imprint of Pearson Education
Boston • Indianapolis • London • Munich • New York • San Francisco

Dreamweaver MX Extensions

FIRST EDITION: September 2002

International Standard Book Number: 0-7357-1182-8

Library of Congress Catalog Card Number: 2001095778

Printed in the United States of America

06 05 04 03 02 7 6 5 4 3 2 1

Interpretation of the printing code: The rightmost double-digit number is the year of the book's printing; the rightmost single-digit number is the number of the book's printing. For example, the printing code 02-1 shows that the first printing of the book occurred in 2002.

Trademarks

Warning and Disclaimer

Publisher
David Dwyer

Associate Publisher
Stephanie Wall

Production Manager
Gina Kanouse

Managing Editor
Kristy Knoop

Senior Acquisitions Editor
Linda Anne Bump

Acquisitions Editor
Deborah Hittel-Shoaf

Development Editor
Audrey Doyle

Senior Marketing Manager
Tammy Detrich

Publicity Manager
Susan Nixon

Senior Editor
Lori Lyons

Copy Editor
Nancy Sixsmith

Indexer
Angie Bess

Manufacturing Coordinator
Jim Conway

Book Designer
Louisa Klucznik

Cover Designer
Aren Howell

Proofreader
Julia Prosser

Composition
Jeff Bredensteiner

Media Developer
Jay Payne

Dedication

To Janie, for all her professional and emotional support, and for being willing to bring me lattes at midnight when deadlines loomed. And for Murphy, who was always there to help me drink the latte. And to all my students, for teaching me so much and letting me experiment on them for all these years. Little did they know.

Contents At a Glance

Introduction xvii

Part I Objects and Behaviors: Learning the API 1

1 Dreamweaver Configuration and the API 3

2 Creating Custom Objects 11

3 Creating Custom Behaviors 55

Part II Commands, Inspectors, Floating Panels: Working with the DOM 57

4 The Dreamweaver DOM 101

5 Creating Custom Commands and Menu Commands 135

6 Creating Custom Property Inspectors 229

7 Creating Custom Floating Panels 273

8 Mixing Extension Types 311

9 Server Behaviors 333

10 Into the Great Beyond 363

Part III Appendixes 411

A JavaScript Primer 413

B Macromedia User Interface Guidelines 437

C Packaging Extensions for Use with the Extension Manager 455

D Submitting Extensions to the Macromedia Dreamweaver Exchange 477

E Online Resources for Dreamweaver Extensibility 487

F Contents of the Dreamweaver MX Extensions Book Companion Web Site 493

Index 501

Table of Contents

Part I Objects and Behaviors: Learning the API

1 Dreamweaver Configuration and the API 3

How Dreamweaver Is Configured 4

The Configuration Folder 4

The Structure of Configuration Files 5

Multiple Configuration Folders 6

The Dreamweaver API 8

Parts of the API 8

Working with the API 10

Ready, Set, Go! 10

2 Creating Custom Objects 11

How Objects Are Constructed 12

Object Files in the Configuration Folder 12

Objects in the Insert bar (insertbar.xml) 14

Objects in the Insert Menu 14

Structure of an Object File 14

The API Procedure for Objects 19

Making Objects: Practice Session 20

Workshop #1: Creating a Simple Object 27

Sample Object: Inserting a Single-Celled Centering Table 27

Creating the Table Object 27

Workshop #2: Creating a Simple Object with User Input 32

Sample Object: Inserting a Netscape Spacer Tag 32

Creating the Spacer Object 33

Workshop #3: Creating a More Complex Object 39

Sample Object: Inserting a Custom Horizontal Rule 39

Creating the Custom HR Object 39

Summary 53

3 Creating Custom Behaviors **55**

How Behaviors Are Constructed 56

Behaviors in the Configuration Folder 57

Behavior Files 57

Structure of a Behavior File 58

API Procedure for Behaviors 60

API Procedure for Inspecting Behaviors 61

Making Behaviors: Practice Session 62

Workshop #1: Creating a Simple Behavior 67

Sample Behavior: Adding "Back" and "Forward" Controls to a Document 68

Creating the Back/Forward Behavior 68

Workshop #2: Creating a Full-Featured Behavior 75

Sample Behavior: Set Page Properties 75

Creating the Set Page Properties Behavior 75

Inspecting Behaviors 90

The inspectBehavior( ) Function and How it Works 90

Inspecting Behaviors: Practice Session 90

Using the Shared Files to Help Inspect Behaviors 94

Workshop #3: Inspecting the Set Properties Behavior 96

Summary 98

Part II Commands, Inspectors, Floating Panels: Working with the DOM

4 The Dreamweaver DOM **101**

What Is a DOM? 101

The DOM in JavaScript 101

The Dreamweaver DOM 103

DOM Basics 107

Document (DOCUMENT_NODE) 107

HTML Elements (ELEMENT_NODE) 108

HTML Comments (COMMENT_NODE) 110

Text Objects (TEXT_NODE) 110

Nodes and Document Structure 111

Extensibility and the DOM 112
DOM Object *112*
Enhancing Objects and Behaviors Using the DOM *122*
Working with the DOM: Practice Session 123
Summary 134

5 Creating Custom Commands and Menu Commands **135**
How Commands Are Constructed 137
Commands in the Configuration Folder *137*
Structure of a Command File *137*
API Procedure for Commands *140*
Workshop #1: A Command That Uses Object Access 141
Sample Command: Automatically Adding the alt Parameter to All Images in a Document *142*
Wrapping Up the Automatic Alt Command *167*
Workshop #2: A Command That Uses String Access 167
Sample Command: Converting Selected Text to Uppercase *168*
Commands and Menus 180
Working with menus.xml *180*
Controlling a Command's Appearance in the Menus *187*
Passing Parameters to Commands Using receiveArguments( ) *187*
Workshop #3: Manipulating the Menu Entry for a Command 189
Menu Commands 193
Menu Commands in the Configuration Folder *193*
Structure of a Menu Command File *194*
The API Procedure for Menu Commands *198*
Making Menu Commands: Practice Session 200
Workshop #4: Creating a Menu Command 214
Sample File: Creating a Menu Command that Displays the Images in a Document *214*
Summary 228

6 Creating Custom Property Inspectors **229**
How Property Inspectors Are Constructed 230
Property Inspectors in the Configuration Folder *230*
Property Inspector Files *231*

The Structure of an Inspector File 232
The API Procedure for Property Inspectors 236
Making Inspectors: Practice Session 238
Workshop #1: A Simple Property Inspector 248
Sample Inspector: Netscape Block Spacer 248
Workshop #2: Replacing a Default Inspector 255
Sample Project: Custom Horizontal Rule 256
Summary 272

7 Creating Custom Floating Panels **273**
How Floating Panels Are Constructed 274
Floating Panels in the Configuration Folder 275
Floating Panel Files 275
The Structure of a Floating Panel File 276
API Procedure for Floating Panels 279
Making Floating Panels: Practice Session 280
Workshop 1: A Floating Panel Utility 295
Sample Floater: Table Helper 296
Challenge! 308
Summary 309

8 Mixing Extension Types **311**
Why Mix Extension Types? 312
Rollovers, Jump Menus, and Navigation Bars, Oh My! 312
Coloring Outside the Lines 312
API Functions for Mixing Extension Types 313
Running Commands 313
Inserting Objects 314
Inserting Behaviors 315
Accessing Inspectors and Floaters 318
Mixing Extension Types: Practice Session 319
Summary 331

9 Server Behaviors **333**
Server Behavior API 334
Server Behavior Builder *334*
Some Basic Server Behavior Concepts *335*
Building Server Behaviors: Practice Session *336*
Beyond the SBB: How Server Behaviors Are Constructed *341*
Workshop #1: Inserting Conditional Page Content with an If-Then Statement 348
Workshop #2: Inserting Dynamically Determined Images 356
Summary 361

10 Into the Great Beyond **363**
The Nature of Class Files 364
ListControl Items 364
Specifications *365*
ListControl Practice *369*
ImageButtons 380
Specifications *381*
ImageButton Practice *383*
Layered Interfaces 388
Specifications *390*
Layered Interface Practice *399*
Other Custom Classes 406
Summary 409

Part III Appendixes

A JavaScript Primer **413**
How JavaScript and HTML Work Together 414
Practice Session #1 *414*
Variables and Expressions 416
Practice Session #2 *417*

Functions 418
Functions and Function Calls 418
Function Parameters 419
Practice Session #3 420
Logical Structures (Conditionals and Loops) 423
Conditional Statements 423
Practice Session #4 424
For-Loops and Arrays 425
Practice Session #5 426
Working with Form Elements 428
Form 428
Text Fields 429
Checkboxes 429
Radio Buttons 430
Popup Menus 431
Buttons 433
Form Elements and Event Handlers 433
JavaScript and Objects 434
Linking JS and HTML Files 435
Summary 436

B Macromedia User Interface Guidelines 437
Fonts and Colors 438
Graphics 438
Inserting Images 438
File Formats 438
Navigational/Illustrative Images (Icons) 439
Branding Images (Logos) 440
Layout 441
Dialog Box Layout 441
Property Inspector Layout 444
Form Elements 444
Text Fields 444
Checkboxes and Radio Buttons 445

Lists and Popup Menus 445
Color Buttons 447
Tree Controls 447
Buttons 448
Buttons in Objects and Behaviors 448
Buttons in Commands 449
Buttons in Property Inspectors/Floating Panels 450
Online Help 450
Short Help 450
Tabbed Help Layer 450
Help Button 451
Error-Checking, Default Values, and More 451
Focus and Selection 452
Error-Checking 452
Default Values 453
Summary 454

C Packaging Extensions for Use with the Extension Manager 455
Packaging Extensions 456
Summary 474

D Submitting Extensions to the Macromedia Dreamweaver Exchange 477
Guidelines for Submission 478
Recommended Test Plan 479
All Extensions: Preparing to Test 479
All Extensions: Testing Installation 479
Testing Objects 480
Testing Property Inspectors 481
Testing Commands 482
Testing Behaviors 483
Testing Floating Panels 484
Testing Site-Wide Extensions 486

E Online Resources for Dreamweaver Extensibility 487

Web Sites 488

Forums 489

Tools 489

F Contents of the Dreamweaver MX Extensions Book Companion Web Site 493

Chapter 2: "Creating Custom Objects" 494

Workshop #1: Centering Table 494

Workshop #2: Block Spacer Tag 494

Workshop #3: Custom Horizontal Rule 494

Chapter 3: "Creating Custom Behaviors" 494

Workshop #1: Back/Forward Behavior 494

Workshop #2: Set Page Properties 494

Chapter 4: "The Dreamweaver DOM" 495

Test Files 495

Chapter 5: "Creating Custom Commands and Menu Commands" 495

Workshop #1: Automatic Alt Text 495

Workshop #2: Make Uppercase 495

Workshop #3: Change Case 495

Menu Commands Practice 496

Workshop #4: Select Images 496

Chapter 6: "Creating Custom Property Inspectors" 496

Inspector Practice 496

Workshop #1: Block Spacer Inspector 496

Workshop #2: Custom Horizontal Rule Inspector 497

Chapter 7: "Creating Custom Floating Panels" 497

Sample and Resource Files 497

Workshop 1: Table Helper 497

Chapter 8: "Mixing Extension Types" 497

Chapter 9: "Server Behaviors" 498

Workshop #1: If-Then Statement (Conditional Content) *498*

Workshop #2: Dynamically Determined Image *498*

Chapter 10: "Into the Great Beyond" 499

Practice Files *499*

Resource and Framework Files *499*

Appendixes 499

Index **501**

About the Author

Laura Gutman

Laura works as a multimedia, web application developer, and educator in the fields of multimedia, programming, and design. Her first experience in computer science was at an IBM training school in 1983, where she learned how to punch cards, dissect mainframes, and program in COBOL. In the intervening years, Laura earned her Ph.D. in English from the University of St. Andrews (Scotland) and has worked as a graphic designer and illustrator (for print and multimedia), technical writer, and multimedia developer. Currently, she lives with her dog, parakeets, and hundreds of computer toys in Albuquerque, New Mexico. In addition to her development and consulting work, Laura teaches a range of courses in multimedia and graphic design at the University of New Mexico. You can visit her online at `http://www.rocketlaura.com`.

About the Technical Reviewers

These reviewers contributed their considerable hands-on expertise to the entire development process for *Dreamweaver MX Extensions*. As the book was being written, these dedicated professionals reviewed all the material for technical content, organization, and flow. Their feedback was critical to ensuring that *Dreamweaver MX Extensions* fits our reader's need for the highest-quality technical information.

Julie Hallstrom

Julie is a team lead for Macromedia's Dreamweaver technical support team. She came to her love of Dreamweaver after hand-coding HTML for a year, designing web sites for small companies. She sees her job of supporting Dreamweaver users as an opportunity to share her enthusiasm for a really wonderful product.

Matt Zimmerman

Matt has spent the last five years living on the web, from personal projects to freelance sites to working professionally in the industry. In the winter of 1999, he joined Omega Design Studio, a web development company in Indianapolis. While at Omega, he has had the opportunity to further develop his skills in Flash, JavaScript, and ColdFusion. Matt's work was also included in a multimedia gallery opening entitled "Evidence Manifest" where he showed an HTML/Flash-based piece on interfacing and interface design. In the summer of 2001, Matt earned his BFA in Visual Communication from Herron School of Art, IUPUI.

About the Technical Contributor

Drew McLellan

Drew has been involved in web design and development since 1996. Starting originally as a hand coder, Drew quickly saw the great productivity benefits that could be brought by a visual editor with the arrival of Dreamweaver 1.2. Since then, he has been pushing the boundaries of Dreamweaver through its solid HTML-based methodology and powerful extensible architecture.

With literally tens of thousands of his Dreamweaver extensions in use around the globe, Drew has established a firm seating within the center of the online Dreamweaver community and can be found on a daily basis teaching and aiding fellow developers in Macromedia's news forums. His online tutorials from his DreamweaverFever.com web site are recognized as one of the more valuable Dreamweaver resources available, due to their clear and "non-assuming" use of language.

Drew also helps out at the Web Standards Project (`http://www.webstandards.org/`) as a Dreamweaver expert, focusing on the issues surrounding web standards in Macromedia's flagship HTML editor.

As a Team Macromedia volunteer, he is a committed Dreamweaver user and enjoys nothing more than being able to share his knowledge and experience of the product with fellow developers. Drew has a wide knowledge of both web design and development, and is currently working for a design, marketing, and IT agency in London, UK. Drew is also the author of *Dreamweaver MX Web Development*, published by New Riders.

Acknowledgments

Many thanks to those who have provided technical knowledge, feedback, and support throughout the conceiving and writing of this book. My colleagues at Caliente Media Center and the University of New Mexico, and the Girl Geeks, have all offered critiques and suggestions. Those wonderful, anonymous programmers at Macromedia have provided an invaluable learning laboratory in the files of Dreamweaver itself. The community of extension authors has also been a great source of information and good examples. And my thanks to the editors at New Riders, for believing in this project and helping make it the best it can be.

Tell Us What You Think

As the reader of this book, you are the most important critic and commentator. We value your opinion and want to know what we're doing right, what we could do better, what areas you'd like to see us publish in, and any other words of wisdom you're willing to pass our way.

As the Associate Publisher for New Riders Publishing, I welcome your comments. You can fax, email, or write me directly to let me know what you did or didn't like about this book—as well as what we can do to make our books stronger.

Please note that I cannot help you with technical problems related to the topic of this book, and that due to the high volume of mail I receive, I might not be able to reply to every message.

When you write, please be sure to include this book's title and author as well as your name and phone or fax number. I will carefully review your comments and share them with the author and editors who worked on the book.

Fax: 317-581-4663

Email: stephanie.wall@newriders.com

Mail: Stephanie Wall
Associate Publisher
New Riders Publishing
201 West 103rd Street
Indianapolis, IN 46290 USA

Introduction

This is a book about extending Macromedia Dreamweaver. If you are reading it, you're probably an intermediate to advanced Dreamweaver user, you've visited the Macromedia Exchange, and you've downloaded and installed various extensions. You have probably also discovered the many powerful additions available for this already powerful program—and you want to try it yourself. You've been working away, turning out web pages and managing web sites with Dreamweaver, and you find yourself saying, over and over again, "Gee, my life would be so much easier if only the program did xxx." Or "How come I always have to hand-code xxx? I could really use an extension to help with that." You're comfortable writing HTML code, you've worked with JavaScript, and you're ready to open up Dreamweaver, look under the hood, and see how you can soup this baby up! That's what we're going to do in the following chapters. We'll cover some basic groundwork; set up shop; and get to work writing custom objects, behaviors, commands, inspectors, and floating panels. Along the way, we'll discuss how best to analyze your own workflow needs and determine where custom extensions can help you. So, let's get started!

What Is Extending Dreamweaver?

Extending Dreamweaver means adding custom interface elements, and the extended functionality that goes along with them, to the program. If you've been to the Macromedia Exchange, you know all about this. On the Exchange, you'll find custom objects, behaviors, commands, Property inspectors, panels, and more for every purpose under the sun. You download them, you use the Extension Manager to install them, and your copy of Dreamweaver is transformed—extended.

note

You've never used the Exchange? Check it out at `http://www.macromedia.com/exchange/dreamweaver`. You can also read all about it in Appendix D, "Submitting Extensions to the Macromedia Dreamweaver Exchange."

If you're like me, though, the Macromedia Exchange isn't enough. I often find myself unable to find the perfect extension that will make my work life easier, or my job more efficient and productive. I don't want to be limited by what other people write; I want to create my own extensions. However, I don't have years to dedicate to learning and doing that. I just want to do it as part of my real job, which is designing for the web.

Macromedia Dreamweaver is possibly the most easily and powerfully extensible piece of commercial software in common use today. The reason there is such a thriving community of extension authors submitting to the Exchange is that it doesn't take a rocket scientist to create Dreamweaver extensions, nor does it take any special software. This means that with Dreamweaver, software users can become software authors. Everyday users with a certain amount of scripting knowledge and a stout heart can author their own extensions. You aren't limited to what you can find on the Exchange. You can build custom interface elements that will meet your particular workflow needs. You can even submit them to the Exchange and become part of the extension-sharing community. My purpose in this book is to show you how to do that.

Who's On First? Confusing Terminology

One of the tricky things about starting to write software extensions is keeping track of who's doing what and for whom.

If you're used to using Dreamweaver to create web pages, you know how to create code that will become part of a web page, to be viewed in a browser and appreciated by visitors to your web site.

When you author extensions, most of what you create will never see the inside of a browser, and will never be appreciated (or underappreciated) by anyone surfing the Net.

In its documentation, Macromedia uses a strict terminology to keep confusion out of these matters. This book also uses that terminology, as follows:

- **Authors** write Dreamweaver objects, behaviors, commands, and so forth to customize how the program does its job.
- **Users** use Dreamweaver to create web pages.
- **Visitors** go online and view the finished web pages.

Now, you personally may be an author and a user and a visitor—but you won't be all three at the same time. When you're an author, you're creating things for users; when you're a user, you're creating things for visitors. When you're doing the exercises in this book, you're an author. When you're testing your extensions to see if they work and if they're useful, you're a user.

Get it? Got it? Good!

How to Use This Book

Here are some tips about approaching this particular book.

Who Should Read This Book

This book is not intended to teach you how to use Dreamweaver. There are plenty of good books for that. (*Inside Dreamweaver MX*, published by New Riders, is a great all-around information source; *The Dreamweaver Bible*, published by Wiley, is another.) You should read this book if you're already using Dreamweaver successfully; have worked with prepackaged extensions; and want to start creating your own objects, behaviors, commands, and panels.

You should be comfortable working with HTML and have some knowledge of JavaScript. Maybe you're a busy web designer and can see all sorts of opportunities to streamline your workflow. Maybe you're part of your company's web team, and you want to write extensions to make everyone's jobs easier. Maybe you just love learning how things work and how to make them better, and you're all set to become the next star author on the Macromedia Exchange.

If you think you fit these criteria but aren't sure if your JavaScript skills are up to it, start by reading Appendix A, "JavaScript Primer." Although this appendix isn't intended as a complete teach-yourself-JavaScript kit, it offers a crash course on the basic concepts of JavaScript with an emphasis on those language features that will be used throughout this book. Use it as a refresher or a quick reference. If you understand everything in the appendix, you know enough to start extending Dreamweaver.

How the Book Is Structured

This book should be a teaching source for you first, and a reference source after you've learned its topics. When you're first learning how-to, it's best to go through the book from front to back because the topics are presented in order of difficulty, and some of the more advanced projects build on earlier projects.

The book is divided into three main parts:

- **Part I: Objects and Behaviors: Learning the API.** Part I covers the Dreamweaver Application Programming Interface (API) and how to work with it to script simple extension types that insert HTML or JavaScript code into the user document.
- **Part II: Commands, Inspectors, Floating Panels: Working with the DOM.** Part II covers the Dreamweaver Document Object Model (DOM) and how to use it to create extension types that alter existing code in user documents. You also delve into problem solving and strategizing.

- **Part III: Appendixes**. The appendixes include a quick tour of JavaScript, user interface guidelines, the procedure for creating an MXP file for easy sharing, guidelines for submitting extensions to Macromedia's Dreamweaver Exchange, online resources, and information on the companion web site.

How the Tutorials Work

For each new topic that is introduced, we'll start with an explanatory section or chapter. You will probably refer to these sections after you have read the book to learn how-to, and just want some reference material.

The explanatory section is followed by one or more tutorials:

- **Practice tutorials** are very simple, hands-on explorations to get you used to the underlying architecture of how each extension type works. Practice tutorials are divided into tasks that encourage you to experiment. Every extension type includes a practice tutorial.
- **Workshop tutorials** go step-by-step through the creation of usually simple, but potentially useful extensions. Every extension type includes at least one workshop tutorial.

What This Book Isn't

This book isn't the be-all and end-all ultimate resource for everything anyone ever wanted to know about Dreamweaver extensions. A book like that would be many times bigger than what you're now holding in your hands—especially if there were tutorials all along the way—because there's such a lot to learn! Not every single extension type is covered; not every single tip, tool, and technique known to man is in here. What you'll get from reading this book and working through the tutorials is a good, solid foundation in extensibility and how the major kinds of extensions work, as well as lots of hands-on practice creating simple and useful extensions. You'll also learn how and where to find out more when you need to know more.

Setting Up Shop

Before you start extending, you need to collect your materials and prepare your work environment.

Choosing a Text Editor

Extending Dreamweaver involves a lot of hand coding, for which you'll need a text editor. Various text editors are available on each computer platform, from the no-frills variety to full-featured commercial applications.

Text Editors (Windows)

The full Windows version of Dreamweaver ships with Macromedia HomeSite+, an excellent text editor with all sorts of bells and whistles. (Note that HomeSite+ doesn't install automatically as you install Dreamweaver. You have to find it on the application CD and install it separately.) There are also a variety of other commercial, shareware, and freeware text editors available for Windows, including TextPad, CuteHTML, and others. Go to `www.download.com` and search for "text editor"—you'll be overwhelmed with text editors available for download. Or, if you prefer, there's always good old NotePad.

Text Editors (Mac)

For the Mac, the most popular text editor is BareBones' BBEdit. The Mac version of Dreamweaver ships with a copy of BBEdit, but unfortunately it's only a demo version that expires after 24 uses. If you want to keep things free, you can try BBEdit Lite instead (downloadable from `www.barebones.com`). For Mac OS X users, a popular shareware alternative is Pepper (`www.hekkelman.com`). And of course, there's always SimpleText (OS 9) or TextEdit (OS X).

Dreamweaver As a Text Editor

Don't forget, though, that Dreamweaver itself includes a handy text editor with lots of nice features such as line numbers, auto completion, code hints, syntax coloring, and even debugging. Although it may seem strange to use Dreamweaver to edit its own extensions, you can do it. With a few exceptions, Dreamweaver accesses extension files only when it's launching, so it's not trying to access the extensions as you're writing them.

You may, however, find it confusing using Dreamweaver to create extensions, and then using Dreamweaver to test and use those same extensions. Working like this, it's easy to get lost and confused and forget which part of the process you should be focusing on. Using a separate text editor (even a simple one like NotePad) makes it easier to maintain a sense of when you're developing and when you're testing.

Assembling Reference Materials

Because extending Dreamweaver involves lots of JavaScript coding, it's a good idea to have a good general JavaScript reference book handy while working. Danny Goodman's *JavaScript Bible* or David Flanagan's *JavaScript: The Definitive Guide* and *JavaScript Pocket Reference* are good resources; or you may have your favorite. If you'd rather use an online reference than a printed book, the Dreamweaver Reference panel is a good resource.

note

To access the Reference panel's JavaScript help, choose Window > Reference to open the panel and choose O'Reilly JavaScript Reference from the Book popup menu (see Figure 1). The information in this panel is organized by JavaScript object, so you need to know something about how JavaScript's predefined objects, methods, and properties work before you can use it efficiently.

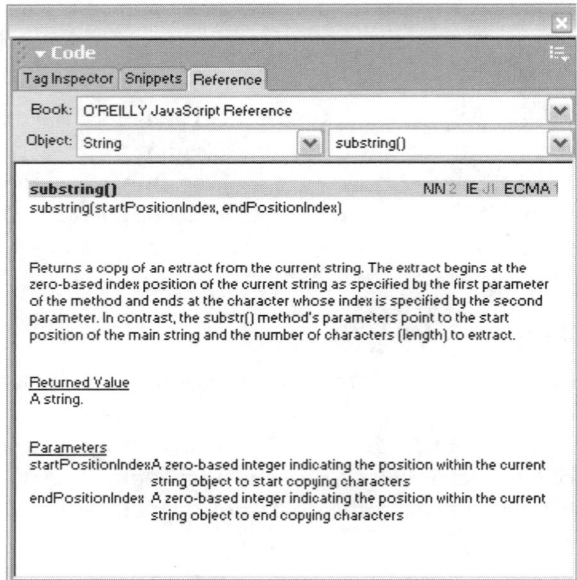

FIGURE 1 *The Reference panel, part of the Dreamweaver online help system.*

The most important reference source—one you can't do without—is Macromedia's *Extending Dreamweaver* manual. This 550-page book includes explanations of the API and the DOM, and a complete dictionary of custom objects, methods, and properties. It comes in PDF form on the Dreamweaver application CD. If you like online references, copy the PDF file to your hard drive, and keep it open in the background as you're working. If you'd rather work with a printed reference, you can order a printed copy from the Macromedia web site, or you can print the PDF file and pop it in a three-ring binder (or two). Mine always sits right next to my chair as I work.

Backing Up

Extending Dreamweaver involves making some serious changes to the program. It's possible to goof things up so that the program won't function at all. Of course, you can always reinstall the software if this happens. A simpler solution, however, is to make a backup copy of the Configuration folder (found inside the Dreamweaver application folder). If in the middle of extending, you need your original untouched Dreamweaver back in action, just remove the altered Configuration folder from the Dreamweaver application folder and replace it with your backup.

note

Warning: Never replace the Configuration folder while Dreamweaver is running. Quit the program first!

note

When restoring the original Configuration folder, make sure you're really eliminating the problem. First, delete or move the damaged Configuration folder; then put the backup copy in place. Just copying the backup over the damaged copy doesn't necessarily delete problematic files.

Setting Up Files and Folders

For efficient working, set up the following:

- Somewhere outside the Dreamweaver application folder, create a folder called "**Working**" for storing test files, disabled extensions, and other working files. (This is a good place to keep your backup Configuration folder, as well.)
- Create a shortcut/alias for the active Configuration folder (that is, not the backup copy), and place it in an easily accessible place—on the desktop, for instance, or in the "**Working**" folder. You'll need to access this folder frequently, and don't want to have to navigate to it repeatedly.

Conventions Used in This Book

This book also follows a few typographical conventions:

- A new term is set in *italic* the first time it is introduced.
- Program text, functions, variables, and other "computer language" are set in a monospaced, fixed-pitch font—for example:

```
var myFile = dw.browseForFileURL("select");
```

- During the exercises, when the text instructs you to add or change existing code, the new code will appear in **`boldface`** so that you can easily distinguish it from the surrounding code.

Are you excited about writing your own extensions? Do you have the lay of the land, knowing which parts of the book to tackle first? Do you have your text editor and working folders in place, and your Configuration folder backed up? If so, you're ready to rumble.

Part I

Objects and Behaviors: Learning the API

1 Dreamweaver Configuration and the API 3

2 Creating Custom Objects 11

3 Creating Custom Behaviors 55

CHAPTER 1

Dreamweaver Configuration and the API

Dreamweaver possesses amazing extensibility because of how the program is configured. In this chapter, we'll see an overview of the Dreamweaver configuration, learning how all the pieces of the program are constructed and how they fit together to create the software user's experience. We'll also be introduced to the Dreamweaver API (Application Programming Interface), which provides the set of tools and procedures allowing us extension authors to change the configuration as needed.

How Dreamweaver Is Configured

Like other commercial applications, the core of the Dreamweaver application is written in the C programming language. Unlike other programs, however, the Dreamweaver core allows the application to call on external files to construct much of its interface and execute its various functions. These external files are written in a combination of HTML, JavaScript, and XML. They are stored in the Dreamweaver application folder, in a subfolder called Configuration. Unlike the core application, the configuration files are easily and fully editable within a text editor, so they are open to examination and alteration.

note

Why can't we open and edit most commercial programs or the core Dreamweaver application? Programming languages such as C are compiled languages, which means that programs written in those languages must be compiled into non-editable packages called executables. JavaScript, on the other hand, which creates the functionality of Dreamweaver extensions, is an interpreted language. Script files that are created in JavaScript remain in editable text format and are processed at runtime by an interpreting application, such as a browser or the Dreamweaver core application.

The Configuration Folder

Open the Dreamweaver application folder, and you'll find the Configuration folder. This is the heart of Dreamweaver extensibility. Open up the Configuration folder and you'll see subfolders representing each major interface element (as well as other folders whose purpose may not be as immediately evident). You'll see folders for Menus, Objects, Behaviors, Commands, Inspectors, Floaters—each one contains the functionality for that part of the interface. (In case you were wondering, "inspectors" are Property inspectors; all other panels are "floaters," or floating panels. Objects are items in the Insert bar and Insert menu.) If you examine the files within the folders, you'll see a combination of XML, HTML, and JS files whose names match Dreamweaver commands and other functions. Inside the Objects folder, for instance, you'll find a folder corresponding with each tab in the Insert bar—Common, Forms, Media, Frames, and so on. In the Common folder, you'll find Table.htm, Navigation Bar.htm, E-Mail Link.htm, all of which should be familiar to you as the items found in the Common tab of the Insert bar. Figure 1.1 shows the Configuration folder and its contents.

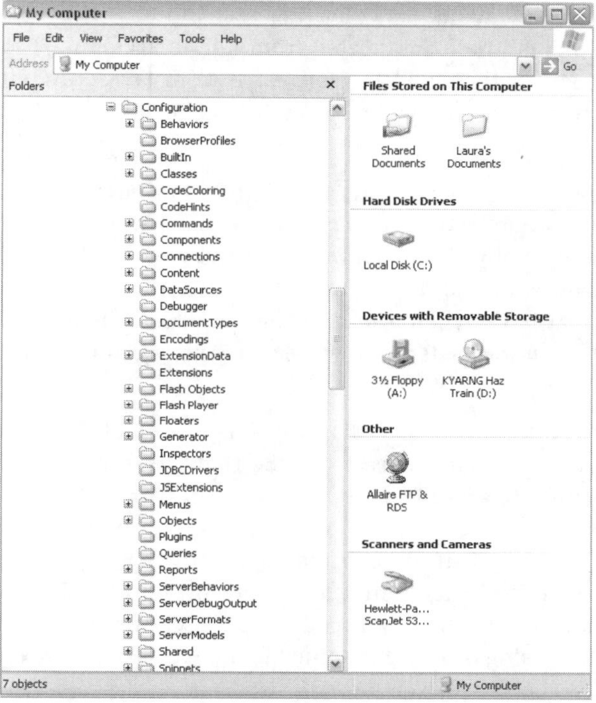

FIGURE 1.1 *The Configuration folder showing its subfolders.*

note

Actually, the structure of the Configuration folder is not always that straightforward. If you look in the Commands folder, for instance, you'll see files representing things that you might not think of as Dreamweaver Commands—Jump Menu or Insert Nav Bar, for instance. For the most part, though, it's easiest (and perfectly safe) to think of each folder containing elements related to its name.

The Structure of Configuration Files

The Configuration folder contains four main kinds of file: HTML, JS (JavaScript), GIF, and XML. Each has a specific purpose in how Dreamweaver looks and works.

Each different thing Dreamweaver can do—each object or behavior to be inserted, command to be executed, inspector to be displayed, and so forth—is coded into an HTML extension file. The visual components of that element—dialog boxes and panel interfaces—are built from the `<body>` content of the HTML file, including a form and form elements for collecting user input. If the visual interface uses any graphic elements, these are created from GIF images linked to the HTML file. The functional part of the extension is created from JavaScript, either written into the HTML file or saved in a separate JS file that is linked to the HTML file.

How the Dreamweaver interface ties all these extensions together is determined by the Configuration folder's XML files. For instance, the menus.xml file (found in Configuration/Menus) determines which menus will appear, which items each menu will hold, and what will happen when a menu item is selected. The insertbar.xml file (Configuration/Objects) determines what buttons will appear in the Insert bar and how they'll behave when clicked. The various XML files in the Configuration/ExtensionData folder determine what code the Dreamweaver Live Data objects will insert.

A simple example of how this works is the Table.htm file, which is in the Objects/Common folder. This is the file that Dreamweaver launches every time a user clicks the Table object in the Insert bar or chooses Insert > Table. Open Table.htm in a text editor and you'll see that it contains the standard code for an HTML page. This HTML page contains a form that creates the dialog box we see whenever we insert a table in Dreamweaver. The file's functionality—the bit that makes Dreamweaver insert table code into a user's page when the user clicks the OK button in the dialog box—is contained in an external JS file, to which this document links.

If you open the Table.js file to examine that JavaScript code, you'll see some JavaScript functions you're probably not familiar with, such as `objectTag()` and `isDomRequired()`. These are part of The Dreamweaver JavaScript API; we'll be learning about them in the course of this book.

Multiple Configuration Folders

How many Dreamweaver Configuration folders are there on your computer? If you're working with Dreamweaver MX (and not one of the earlier versions of the program), you may have two, three, or more Configuration folders. To successfully extend your Dreamweaver application, you need to know your way around them.

Previously Installed Versions

If you already had Dreamweaver installed on your computer when you installed Dreamweaver MX—for instance, if you upgraded from an earlier version or if you've re-installed Dreamweaver MX—your Dreamweaver application folder will include an extra Configuration folder called Configuration-1, containing the configuration files from the previous installation. If you've upgraded or re-installed a number of times, you might even have a Configuration-2 and even a Configuration-3 folder.

These are inactive folders. They're present in case you want to access any special configuration information, such as custom extensions, from your previous installation. For purposes of doing the exercises in this book, you can ignore these folders.

User-Specific Configuration Files

If your computer's operating system supports multiple user setups (Windows, Mac OS X), Dreamweaver creates two sets of configuration files: In addition to the main Configuration folder located in the Dreamweaver application folder, it also creates a Configuration folder for each user that contains a personalized set of files that will be used only when that user launches Dreamweaver. For Dreamweaver/Windows, each user's personal Configuration folder is stored in:

c:\documents and settings*username*\application data\macromedia\dreamweaver mx\configuration\

For Dreamweaver/Mac OS X, they're stored in:

/users/*username*/library/application support/dreamweaver mx/configuration

(For each user, substitute the correct user name for `username`.) This folder is created the first time the user launches Dreamweaver.

Examine one of these extra folders, and you'll see that it isn't a complete duplicate of the main Configuration folder. It contains only certain files, representing interface elements that individual users may want to customize only for their own use. Application preferences such as code coloring, menus that can be customized with keyboard shortcuts, commands recorded using the History panel, and objects that save their dialog box settings from one work session to another, are all saved as files in the individual user's Configuration folder.

How does Dreamweaver determine which configuration files to use? It always begins by checking to see whether a certain file is present in the user's Configuration folder. If not, it looks for the file in the main Configuration folder.

How does this affect you as an extension developer? If your extension project involves editing menus.xml or some other user-customizable extension file, you'll need to know which version of the file to open and edit. You can also create your own extensions that include user-specific features by telling Dreamweaver to save them to the user's Configuration folder. If you like, you can also isolate your extension files in progress by storing them in a user-specific Configuration folder. If you create a special Dreamweaver Developer user for your computer, you can log on as that user to do your developing and then log on as another user when you need to use Dreamweaver for your day-to-day web authoring jobs. That way, you won't risk compromising your program's stability as you develop your extensions.

For the exercises in this book, it's assumed you're working on the main Configuration folder unless otherwise specified.

The Dreamweaver API

The Dreamweaver API is a set of custom JavaScript functions and objects that can be used to communicate with the program and extend its functionality, and a set of procedures for processing those instructions.

Parts of the API

The API puts three kinds of entities at your disposal for working with extensions, each with its own rules for use and purpose within the whole. They are extension-specific functions and procedures; custom JavaScript objects for use with all extensions; and custom form elements for creating dialog box and panel interfaces.

Extension-Specific Functions and Procedures

Each kind of extension (object, behavior, and so on) has its own procedures and functions, some required and some optional. Some of these functions are called automatically and need be defined only in the extension file. The first thing you'll need to know about creating any extension is how to work with its required functions and procedures. In this book, we'll cover that information for each extension type as we come to it.

Custom Dreamweaver Objects

In addition to these custom functions, the API includes several custom objects, providing hundreds of methods and properties. Usually, these must be explicitly called on and can be used with any extension type. (The *Extending Dreamweaver* manual devotes 300 of its 500 pages to a dictionary reference of these objects.) The most generally useful of these objects are the `dreamweaver` object, the `site` object, and the object representing the current document's DOM. Other objects include the `MMHttp` object (for working with Web servers), the `DWFile` object (for working with file input and output operations), the `MMNotes` object (for working with design notes), and the `FWLaunch` object (for working with Fireworks). Some sample methods will give you the idea of what these objects can accomplish:

```
dw.quitApplication()

dw.openDocument()

dw.setUpFindReplace()

site.checkLinks()

site.recreateCache()

site.defineSites()
```

```
dom.loadTracingImage()

dom.setRulerUnits()

dom.setSelection()
```

If you examine the source code for any of the files in the Configuration folder, you'll see these and other object methods used extensively to control the program.

Custom Form Input Tags

All user input, whether through dialog boxes, inspectors, or floating panels, is handled by HTML forms. In addition to the standard form input tags (text, button, checkbox, and so on), the Dreamweaver API includes two custom input types: a color control button and a tree control structure. Color control is provided through the `<mmcolorbutton>` tag, which creates a color swatch and pop-up color palette like that seen in various inspectors and dialog boxes throughout Dreamweaver (see Figure 1.2). Tree structures are provided through `<mm:treecontrol>`, `<mm:treecolumn>`, and `<mm:treenode>` tags, and create an expandable data hierarchy such as that found in the Edit: Keyboard Shortcuts dialog box and the Tag Inspector's tree view (see Figure 1.3). We'll be using both of these custom input elements in the course of the exercises in this book.

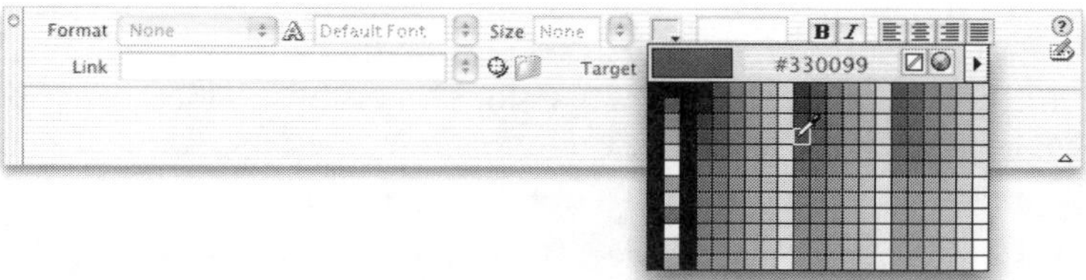

FIGURE 1.2 *The Property inspector, showing the color button and popup color swatches palette.*

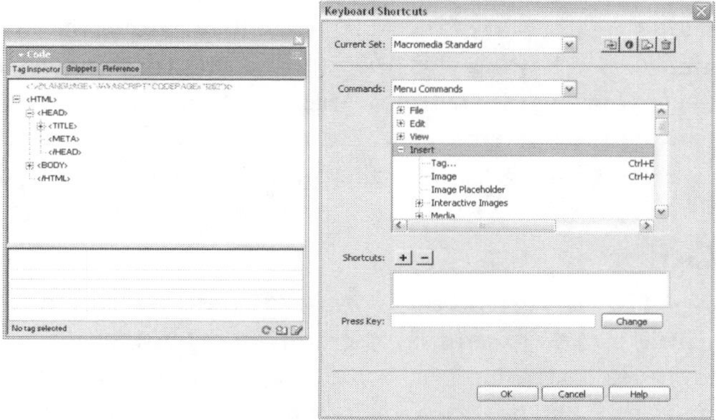

FIGURE 1.3 *The Tag Inspector and Keyboard Shortcut Editor, both of which use tree control structures.*

Working with the API

Every extension-writing task you perform will involve working with the API. The main purpose of this book is to familiarize you with it. Extending Dreamweaver means writing JavaScript and putting all of your scripting knowledge to work, but the particular requirements and possibilities of the Dreamweaver API may be confusing if you're used to writing scripts for browsers to use. In particular, be aware of the following:

- **Procedures are important.** As mentioned earlier, each extension type has its own procedures. These procedures often involve functions that are automatically called without function calls, and forms that are automatically processed without requiring event handlers or submit buttons. It's important to know which actions to specify and which to leave to the Dreamweaver automatic procedures.
- **Extensions can include local as well as API functions.** In addition to the supplied functions and objects of the API, extensions may also include "local" functions that are not part of the API. These functions won't be called in any API procedure, so they must be explicitly defined and called, as in any JavaScript file. The standard extension files include many local functions created by the Macromedia engineers; most have "MM_" affixed to the beginning of the function name. When you're writing extensions, you can create any local function you need, as long as you explicitly define and call it. You are also free to copy and re-use Macromedia's local functions as local functions in your own code, although if you alter them Macromedia asks that you remove the "MM" from the function name.
- **Take advantage of shared files.** Dreamweaver ships with a variety of JS files that are called on as external JavaScript source links in different extensions. (These files are stored in the Shared folder, inside the Configuration folder.) You are free to link to these files as you write your own extensions. The contents of these files are not part of the API; rather, they're tools that the Macromedia programmers used to work with the API, and that you can also use. You're also free to create your own shared files; Macromedia recommends that you store those files inside the Shared folder, in a folder with your company name. We'll be accessing and creating shared files in the course of the exercises in this book.

Ready, Set, Go!

Are you ready to start extending? Then it's time to get started. The following chapters will introduce you to scripting the simplest extension types—objects and behaviors. Both of these extension types insert code into user documents, and so require a less intimate working knowledge of Dreamweaver extensibility than extensions that change existing code. As you proceed through the next two chapters, you'll see the API at work and get used to thinking like an extensions author.

CHAPTER 2

Creating Custom Objects

Objects are the little guys you find in the Insert bar and Insert menu. They represent items users might want to insert into their documents. More specifically, each object represents a snippet of HTML code. When the user selects an object from the panel or the menu, the relevant code is inserted into the current document, usually at the insertion point. Some objects simply insert code; others provide a dialog box that allows the user to customize the code that will be inserted. In this chapter, we'll learn how the object extension type works, how to work with the API to create custom objects, and what sorts of tasks custom objects can be good for.

How Objects Are Constructed

Each Dreamweaver object is created from two or three files stored in one of the subfolders in the Configuration/Objects folder. Exactly where and how the object will appear in the Dreamweaver interface is determined by two XML configuration files: insertbar.xml (in Configuration/Objects) determines the object's placement in the Insert bar; and menus.xml (in Configuration/Menus) determines its placement in the Insert menu.

Object Files in the Configuration Folder

If you open the Configuration/Objects folder, you'll see that object files are not stored directly inside this folder; instead, they're stored in various subfolders. The subfolder names are probably familiar to you because most of them match the names of the categories in the Insert bar: Common, Forms, Frames, Head, and so on (see Figure 2.1).

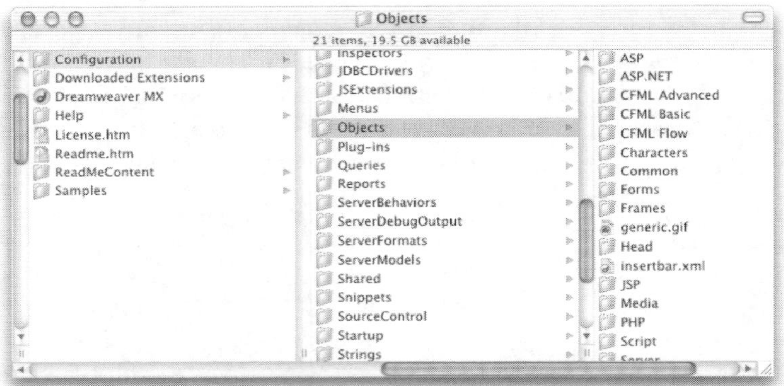

FIGURE 2.1 *The Objects folder and its subdirectories.*

Within the Configuration folder, if you open one of the subfolders (such as Common, for instance) and examine its contents, you'll see that each object that normally appears in that category of the Insert bar is represented by two or three files. These files, taken together, form the object. The files that make up each object are:

note

If you've already customized your copy of Dreamweaver by using the Extensions Manager, you may have more subfolders in your Objects folder than those shown in Figure 2.1.

- **HTML file (required).** This is the main object file. Without it, there is no object! The `<head>` section of the file may contain JavaScript functions for constructing and inserting the object code, or it may contain a link to an external JS file that contains those functions. If the object includes a dialog box for user input, the dialog box will be created as an HTML form in the `<body>` section of the file. As an HTML file, the filename must have an extension of .htm or .html (either will work, although Macromedia extensions all use .htm). Unlike files intended for use on Web servers, the filename may include spaces or special characters for easier reading.
- **JS file (optional).** The JavaScript functions for constructing the object code may be placed in this separate file instead of embedding them in the `<head>` section of the main object file (the HTML file). For easier access during editing and updating, Macromedia recommends creating separate JS files for all but the simplest objects. It's customary, although not required, to match this file's name with the filename of the HTML file.
- **GIF file (optional).** This file contains an 18×18-pixel GIF image that will be displayed in the Insert bar to represent the object. This file isn't required for an object to function; if it isn't present, Dreamweaver will use the object's name to represent it in the Insert bar. The filename must include the .gif extension. It's customary to match this file's name with the filename of the HTML file.

Figure 2.2 shows the files that constitute two typical Dreamweaver objects.

FIGURE 2.2 *The Date object (top) consists of two files. The more complex E-Mail Link object (bottom) consists of three files.*

Objects in the Insert bar (insertbar.xml)

The insertbar.xml file, located in the Configuration/Objects folder, controls the appearance and functionality of the Insert bar. If you open this XML file in a text editor, you'll see that it contains a `<category>` tag for each tab, or category, of the Insert bar, and a `<button/>` tag for each object within a category. A typical entry looks like this:

```
<category id="DW_Insertbar_Common" folder="Common">
     <button id="DW_Hyperlink"
          image="Common\Hyperlink.gif"
          enabled=""
          showIf=""
          file="Common\Hyperlink.htm"/>
     ...
</category>
```

As this example shows, each category is identified with a certain folder within the Objects folder—in this case the Common folder. Each button is linked to a specific object file and image.

Objects in the Insert Menu

By default, the Insert menu contains an item for every object file within the Objects folder, with item names determined by the object filename (minus its .htm or .html extension) and the order of items determined alphabetically. The menus.xml file, however, located in the Configuration/Menus folder, can be used to override these defaults (changing names, controlling the order of entries, creating submenus). (See Chapter 5, "Creating Custom Commands and Menu Commands," for a more in-depth discussion of working with menus.xml.)

Structure of an Object File

Like anything else in life, Dreamweaver objects can be simple or they can be complex. Simple objects just insert code—the same code, every time, without allowing for user customization. Fancier, more full-featured objects include such niceties as help screens, context-sensitivity, and dialog boxes that allow users to customize what code the object inserts.

Simple Object Files

At its simplest, an object file must contain the basic framework for an HTML page and should include a recognizable filename, a `<title>` tag containing a recognizable object title, and an `objectTag()` function. Let's take a moment to look at these individual requirements.

Recognizable Filename

As mentioned in the previous section, by default the filename appears in the Insert menu to represent the object, so in creating your own objects it's a good idea to take advantage of the Dreamweaver program's flexible approach to filenames to make your object's entry in the Insert menu as easily understood as possible. "Copyright Statement" makes a much better menu item than "copy_st", don't you think? The filename's capitalization will also be carried into the menu item, so capitalize nicely.

Title

The information in the object file's `<title>` tag becomes the ToolTip that appears when the user hovers over the object in the Insert bar. It's standard practice, although not required, to use the object's name for the title.

objectTag() function

The code that makes the object actually work—in other words, the code that tells Dreamweaver what HTML to insert in the user's document when the object is chosen—is the `objectTag()` function. This function can exist inside a `<script>` tag in the object file's `<head>`, or it can exist in a JS file linked to the object file. This function needn't be explicitly called (Dreamweaver will do this automatically). It should include a `return` statement that contains the HTML you want the object to insert. A good `objectTag()` function might look like any of these:

```
function objectTag() {
return "Copyright John Smith, 2001.";
}
function objectTag() {
return '<font face="Arial, Helvetica, sans-serif" size="1">Copyright
John Smith, 2001</font>';
}
function objectTag() {
var username = "John Smith";
return "Copyright " + username + ", 2001.";
}
```

Listing 2.1 shows the code for a very simple object file. The object shown will insert the text "This is my simple object" into the user's document.

Listing 2.1 Code for a Very Simple Object File

```
<html>
<head>
<title>My Simple Object</title>
<script language="JavaScript">
function objectTag() {
```

continues

```
return "My object inserted this text.";
}
</script>
</head>
<body>
</body>
</html>
```

note

It is possible to create simpler objects than this without any scripting. Any file residing in the correct place in the Objects folder, and containing only a code snippet with no HTML framework, can be used as an object. When Dreamweaver encounters a file like this, it simply inserts the file's contents into the user's document. This kind of file does not offer much flexibility, though, and the object created by this file is not a full-featured object. This book covers only standard scripted objects.

Full-Featured Object Files

Fancier object files can include all sorts of additional elements, building on the basic framework shown in Listing 2.1.

Form

If an object file contains a `<form>` tag in its `<body>` section, Dreamweaver displays a dialog box when the object is inserted. The contents of the form become the contents of the dialog box. Any information collected by the form can be processed by the `objectTag()` function and built into its `return` statement—which is how user-customized objects are created. The form shouldn't include OK or Cancel buttons because Dreamweaver adds these automatically. A plain and simple form will work fine:

```
<form name="myForm">
Enter your name: <input type="text" name="username">
</form>
```

However, using a table for layout will create a nicer looking form (and is recommended by Macromedia):

```
<form name="myForm">
<table border="0">
<tr align="baseline">
<td align="right">Enter your name:</td>
<td align="left"><input type="text" name="username"></td>
</tr>
</table>
</form>
```

note

Macromedia has created a full set of User Interface Guidelines for extensions. See Appendix C, "Packaging Extensions for Use with the Extension Manager," for more about these guidelines.

If you want your object to call up a dialog box that provides information about your object, but don't need to ask for user input, you can even omit input fields altogether—but you still need the `<form>` tag:

```
<form name="myForm">
This object will insert a copyright statement for John Smith, 2001. The
text will appear in a small, sans-serif typeface.
</form>
```

displayHelp() function

If an object that calls up a dialog box also includes a `displayHelp()` function in its `<head>` section (or in a linked JS file), Dreamweaver adds a Help button to the dialog box. This function is called when the user clicks on the Help button. The `displayHelp()` function can contain instructions for opening an alert window that contains brief help information, launching a browser and going online to display a remote HTML page, or launching the user's OS help application to display a locally stored help page. The code for `displayHelp()` might look like any of the following:

```
function displayHelp() {
window.alert("How much help can you put in an alert window, anyway?");
}

function displayHelp() {
dw.browseDocument("http://www.mywebdomain.com/dreamweaverhelp/copyright.
➥html");
}

function displayHelp() {
var myURL = dw.getConfigurationPath();
myURL += "/Shared/MySharedFiles/CopyrightHelp.html";
dw.browseDocument(myURL);
}
```

Building and displaying help pages is covered in more detail in Chapters 5 and 6.

isDomRequired() function

The `isDomRequired()` function determines whether Code view and Design view need to be synchronized before the new object's code can be inserted. Dreamweaver calls it automatically, so it needn't be called in the object file. It should return `true` or `false`. If it's not present, Dreamweaver assumes Code view and Design view don't need to by synchronized—so the only reason to include it, really, is if you want it to return `true`.

Local Functions

In addition to the standard functions already listed, which are part of the object API, you can add any other functions you want to further refine your object. The Macromedia documentation refers to these as local functions. Common uses for local functions include initializing the dialog box and adding special functionality to individual form input elements. Local functions must be explicitly called, usually by adding an `onLoad()` event handler to the object file's `<body>` tag, or adding `onChange()` or `onBlur()` handlers to `<input>` tags.

> **note**
>
> See Appendix A, "JavaScript Primer," for more information on calling functions from form elements.

Listing 2.2 shows a more full-featured object file.

Listing 2.2 A More Full-Featured Object File

```
<html>
<head>
<title>My Fancier Object</title>
<script language="JavaScript">
function objectTag() {
var myName=document.myForm.username.value;
return "This document was created by "+myName+".";
}
function isDomRequired() {
return true;
}
function displayHelp() {
window.alert("This is a brief help statement for my object.");
}
function initializeUI() {
      document.myForm.username.focus();
      document.myForm.username.select();
}
</script>
</head>
<body onLoad="initializeUI()">
<form name="myForm">
<table>
<tr valign="baseline">
<td align="right" nowrap>Your name:</td>
<td align="left"><input type="text" name="username"></td>
</tr>
</table>
</form>
</body>
</html>
```

The API Procedure for Objects

Not only does the object API specify certain functions, but it also determines the procedure that Dreamweaver will use to process the object. Every time a user clicks an icon in the Insert bar or chooses an object from the Insert menu, Dreamweaver executes a sequence of events that form the API procedure for this type of extension. The main events in this procedure are as follows:

1. Dreamweaver scans the object file (the HTML file) for a `<form>` tag.
   - If it finds a `<form>` tag, it displays the form as a dialog box with OK and Cancel buttons, and waits for the user to enter information and click OK. If it finds a `displayHelp()` function in the object file, it adds a Help button to the dialog box. If any functions are called from the `<body>` tag using the `onLoad` event handler, they're executed before the form is loaded. If any functions are called from event handlers (such as `onChange` or `onBlur`) added to form elements, they're executed as those events occur—as the user changes text in a text field, chooses from a popup menu, and so forth.
   - If there isn't a `<form>` tag, it moves on to the next step.
2. Dreamweaver scans the `<head>` section of the object file for an `objectTag()` function and executes it. Whatever code the `objectTag()` function returns is inserted into the user's document at the insertion point.

Figure 2.3 shows a flowchart diagramming this process.

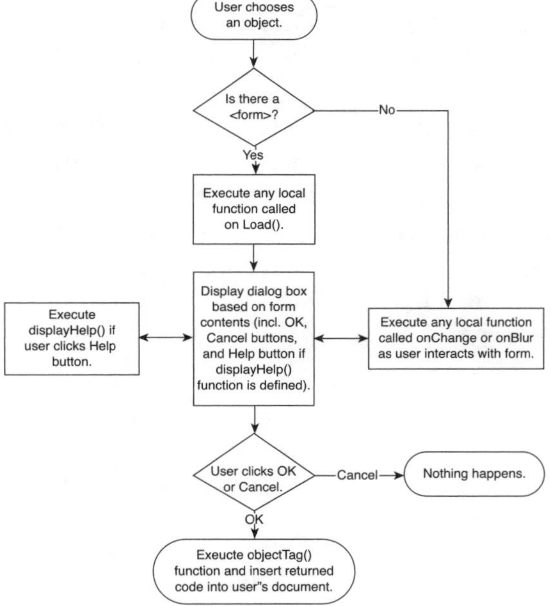

FIGURE 2.3 *The API process for objects.*

note

The *Extending Dreamweaver* manual mentions one other automatically called API function, the `windowDimensions()` function. This optional function can be used any time you ask Dreamweaver to display a dialog box; its purpose is to specify dimensions for the dialog box. If it isn't present, Dreamweaver will size the dialog box automatically based on its contents. Macromedia doesn't recommend using the `windowDimensions()` function, however, unless the contents are so extensive that they would otherwise result in the dialog box being automatically sized larger than 640×480 pixels. Because that's hardly ever the case, I haven't included it in the samples or discussion here. For more information, see the *Extending Dreamweaver* manual.

Making Objects: Practice Session

Start with a little experimenting, just to get your feet wet and make sure your working setup is just the way you like it. (See "Setting Up Shop" in the Introduction for more information.)

Task 1: Create a custom objects category

Before creating custom objects, you want to create a special place to put them. You also want a custom category, or tab, to appear in the Insert bar to hold your objects. This first practice task will set you up to create all the objects in this chapter.

1. Dreamweaver normally configures its interface and extensions when it starts up, so it's standard procedure to quit the program, make any desired configuration changes, and then launch Dreamweaver again (see the sidebar "Reloading Extensions"). Therefore, start your practice task by quitting Dreamweaver if it's running.
2. Find and open the Configuration folder. Then open the Objects folder. (Remember: It is easier to work if you create a shortcut or alias of the Configuration folder and place it where you can easily get at it.)
3. In the Objects folder, create a new folder. Call it **Development**. It's always a good idea to put your objects-in-progress in one folder until they're complete so that they don't get in your way when you try to get actual work done in Dreamweaver.

4. Now, to make that folder show up as a category in the Insert bar, open the insertbar.xml file in your text editor. Find the `</insertbar>` tag at the end of the file and enter this code immediately before it:

```
<category id="DW_Insertbar_Development" folder="Development">
</category>
```

   Because you added this element below all other categories in the file, you're telling Dreamweaver to add a new tab after all other tabs in the Insert bar. When you've done this, save insertbar.xml and close it.

5. Launch Dreamweaver.
6. Check out the Insert bar. If the panel is in its standard horizontal position, you'll see a new tab called Development. If the panel is in its classic vertical position, click on the popup list of categories to see a new category called Development. (Of course, if you choose that category, it's empty—but not for long!) See Figure 2.4 for a picture of the newly extended Insert bar.

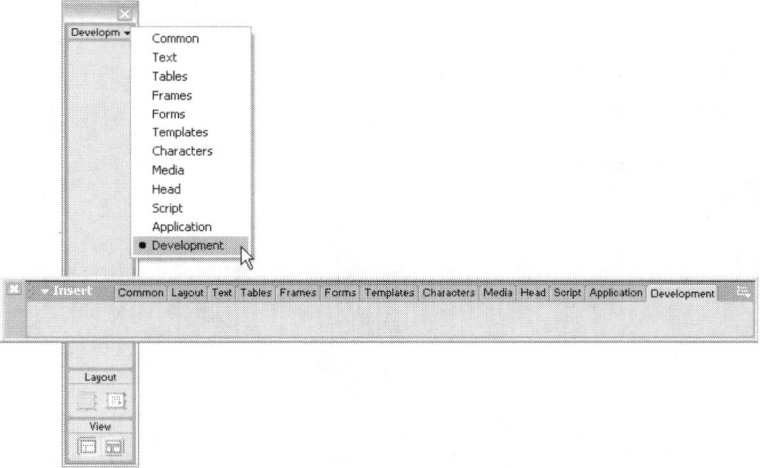

FIGURE 2.4 *The Insert bar (shown in vertical and horizontal modes), with a new Development category.*

Reloading Extensions

Dreamweaver checks its configuration files, and configures its extensions, when starting up. This means that, for most extension types, it's safe to edit the extension files when Dreamweaver is running. It also means that whenever you make a change to any configuration file, Dreamweaver will not notice your change until you quit and relaunch.

There is a shortcut, however. A quicker way to update the configuration, without having to quit Dreamweaver, is to Ctrl-click (Windows) or Option-click (Mac) the Insert bar's Options menu icon—the little icon at the upper-right corner of the Insert bar. Clicking this icon normally shows the panel's Options menu. Ctrl-clicking (Opt-clicking) shows the Options menu with a Reload Extensions command showing at the bottom. Choosing this command forces Dreamweaver to reload its configuration files without quitting and relaunching. Figure 2.5 shows this happening.

FIGURE 2.5 *Ctrl-clicking (Opt-clicking) to access the Reload Extensions command in the Insert bar's options menu.*

If you're working in the classic workspace, with the Insert bar in its vertical arrangement, Ctrl-click (Opt-click) the category name at the top of the panel to access the list of other categories. The Reload Extensions command will appear at the bottom of this menu.

Note that there are a few kinds of configuration changes that won't be updated using this shortcut method: Adding new categories to the Insert bar, adding new behaviors, changing Property inspectors and floaters, and some other changes will not be reloaded unless the program is actually quit and relaunched. (These special cases will be noted in the appropriate chapters throughout the book.)

Task 2: Create a basic object file

The best way to see how objects work is to create one and try it out.

1. Launch your text editor of choice, or bring Dreamweaver to the front in Code view if you plan to write your extensions there.
2. Create a new file. Save it in your new Configuration/Objects/Development folder. Call it **My Object.htm**.
3. Type in the basic code for a simple object, as shown in Listing 2.1. Okay, it's not a very exciting object, but it has all the required elements: The title will become the ToolTip, the function will insert the code, and all will be right with the world.

4. Save your file and close it.
5. That creates your object. To add the object to the Insert bar, open insertbar.xml. Add the following lines to your Development <category> tag (new code is in bold):

```
<category id="DW_Insertbar_Development" folder="Development">
     <button id="DW_Development_MyObject"
             image=""
             enabled=""
             showIf=""
             file="Development\My Object.htm" />
</category>
```

6. If Dreamweaver isn't running, launch it. If Dreamweaver is running, you could quit and relaunch to make it notice your new object. But try the shortcut method for reloading extensions (see the sidebar on "Reloading Extensions"). In the Insert bar, Ctrl-click (Windows) or Opt-click (Mac) the icon for the panel's popup options menu. When the menu appears, choose Reload Extensions.
7. In the Insert bar, find your Development tab and bring it to the front. There's your new object, represented by a text button (see Figure 2.6). Congratulations!

FIGURE 2.6 *The Insert bar, showing the brand-new My Object object in the Development tab.*

8. Try out the ToolTip. Let your cursor hover over the object. The ToolTip says My Simple Object (the same as your object file's <title>).
9. Try out the Insert menu entry. Somewhere near the bottom of the menu, you should find My Object (the same as your object's filename, minus its extension).

note

If you haven't used the Extension Manager to add any custom extensions, your new object probably appears at the very bottom of the Insert menu. If you have a lot of custom extensions, you probably have a very long Insert menu; your new object will appear somewhere in there.

10. Try out your object. Choose it from the Insert bar or the Insert menu. It should insert the text This is my simple object. into your document. There you go!

note

Troubleshooting
What if your object doesn't work? If the object doesn't appear in the Insert bar, check insertbar.xml to make sure you don't have any typos in your entry; check the Configuration folder to make sure your object file is in the right place, and has the .htm or .html filename extension. If you get an error message when you click the object, or if you get an error message when you reload extensions, it means there's a syntax error in your `objectTag()` function, probably just a typo. Check your code against the code in Listing 2.1.

Task 3: Add a simple form

Now, see how HTML forms are used to create dialog boxes in objects. You won't do any fancy coding here; you are just trying out the `<form>` tag. You also see how object code can easily include HTML tags as well as text.

1. Back in your text editor, open My Object.htm again.
2. Revise the `<head>` section of the file to look like this (new code is in bold):

```
<head>
<title>My Fancy Object</title>
<script language="JavaScript">
function objectTag() {
     return "<h1>My fancy object inserted this text</h1>";
}
</script>
</head>
```

3. Revise the `<body>` section of the file to look like this (new code is in bold):

```
<body>
<form name="myForm">
This is the dialog box for my very first object.
</form>
</body>
```

4. Save the file and close it. Then go back to Dreamweaver and reload extensions. (Quit and relaunch the program, or Ctrl-click/Opt-click on the Insert bar's Options menu icon and choose Reload Extensions from the menu.)
5. Open a new document and try out your object. Choosing the object in the Insert bar opens a dialog box that looks something like the one in Figure 2.7. Ugly, but functional. And see how the OK and Cancel buttons were added for you? Click OK, and your newly formatted `<h1>` statement should be inserted into your document. (If you want to see exactly how the code is getting inserted, try switching to Code view and inserting the object. The code in your `objectTag()` function's `return` statement is inserted into the code of your document.)

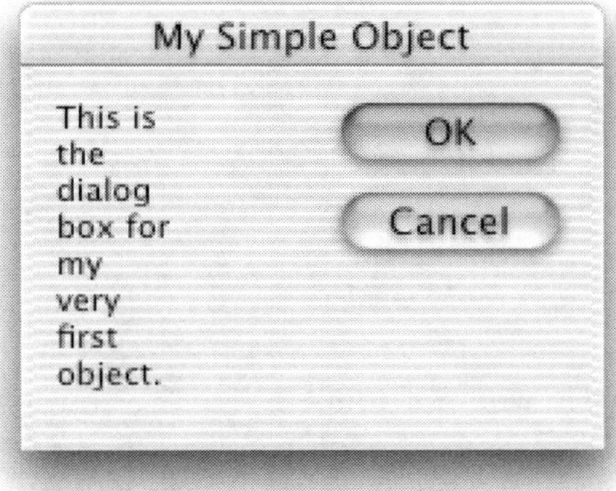

FIGURE 2.7 *A basic dialog box for My Object.*

6. Go back to your text editor and open the object file again. You can make a more attractive dialog box by putting a very simple table in your form. Change the form code to look like this (new code is in bold):

```
<form name="myForm">
<table border="0">
      <tr>
          <td nowrap>
                  This is the form for my very first object.
          </td>
      </tr>
</table>
</form>
```

   When you're done, save the object file and close it, and then return to Dreamweaver.

7. Back in Dreamweaver, reload extensions and try the object again. Your dialog box is much nicer looking—like the one shown in Figure 2.8. Macromedia recommends that you put your forms into tables like this to create attractive dialog boxes. Notice also that the dialog box has been automatically sized to fit your form's content, even if you didn't specify a width for the table. (For more information on user interface issues, see Appendix B.)

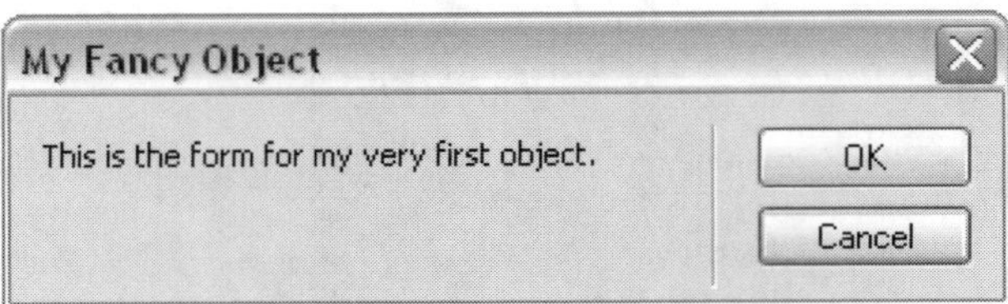

Figure 2.8 *An improved dialog box for My Object.*

8. When the file is working properly, save a copy of it somewhere outside the Dreamweaver Configuration folder for future use. A working object file makes a great template for building future objects (such as the ones you will do next). If you followed the setup instructions in the Introduction chapter (see the section on "Setting up Files and Folders"), you have a Working folder somewhere on your computer for just this purpose. You might also take a minute to comment the code for future reference. Listing 2.3 shows how your final, commented code might look.

Listing 2.3 Final Code from the Object-Making Practice Session, with Comments for Reference

```
<html>
<head>
<!--the title will become the ToolTip-->
<title>My Fancy Object</title>
<script language="JavaScript">
//this function is called automatically
function objectTag() {
//this code will be inserted
return "<h1>My fancy object inserted this text</h1>";
}
</script>
</head>
<body>
<!--presence of a form tag tells Dreamweaver to display a dialog box-->
<form name="myForm">
<table border="0">
      <tr>
          <td nowrap>
                  This is the form for my very first object.
          </td>
      </tr>
</table>
</form>
</body>
</html>
```

Workshop #1: Creating a Simple Object

The purpose of creating objects is to make your work life a little easier. An object that inserts `My object inserted this text` into every document certainly isn't going to do that! But is there any little chunk of coding that you find yourself adding repeatedly that you want to insert with the click of a mouse? For this workshop, you create an object that doesn't require any form input, but uses the principles you learned in the practice tasks to insert a useful piece of code into a document. If you have some code in mind that you want to insert, feel free to use your own. Or, you can follow the sample code here and insert an object that I find quite helpful.

Sample Object: Inserting a Single-Celled Centering Table

For one reason or another, I find myself creating single-celled tables every so often. A one-celled table, set to 100% width and 100% height, with the cell alignment set to center its contents horizontally and vertically, and placed on an empty page with a picture or chunk of text inside it, is a lovely way to create a vertically and horizontally centered layout. I use this kind of table to create splash screens, little announcement windows—all sorts of things. And to create it, I always have to spend several minutes using the Dreamweaver Table object. I have to set all the options in the Insert Table dialog box, then add the height dimension from the Property inspector, and then select the cell and set its alignment properties. What a perfect opportunity for a simple object!

Creating the Table Object

Creating the object involves several main tasks: deciding what code you want it to insert, putting that code into an object file, testing, and refining. This workshop takes you through each of those tasks. Each task has been broken down into numbered steps to help you through them.

Task 1: Create the HTML code you want to insert

The first step in creating any object is to figure out—and, ideally, to create and even test—exactly what code you want it to insert. Especially with code that's more extensive than a few words or characters, it's important to have it typed out in a temporary file for you, ready to insert into the object file when the time comes.

If you don't mind doing a little bit of typing, launch your text editor, create a new file, and type the following code:

```
<table width="100%" height="100%" cellpadding="0" cellspacing="0"
border="0">
      <tr>
            <td align="center" valign="middle"> </td>
      </tr>
</table>
```

After you've done that, you're done with this task. Leave this file open and go on to Task 2.

If you'd rather let Dreamweaver do the typing for you, launch Dreamweaver and follow these steps:

1. Create a new document, and then go to Design view.
2. Using the Insert bar, insert a table. When the Insert Table dialog box appears, choose to create a table with 1 row and 1 column, with cellpadding, cellspacing, the border all set to 0, and width set to 100%. Click OK to insert the table and close the dialog box.
3. When the table has been inserted, use the Property inspector to set its height to 100%.
4. Click inside the table's one cell and use the Property inspector to set its horizontal alignment to center and its vertical alignment to middle.
5. Go to Code view. There's the code for your table! That's what your new object will insert. Leave this file open and go on to Task 2.

Task 2: Put that code into an object file framework

The next step in creating the simple object is to fit that ideal code into the `return` statement of an `objectTag()` function, inside an object file.

1. In your text editor, open My Object.htm and save it in your Configuration/Objects/Development folder as **Centering Table.htm**.
2. Change the `<title>` to **Centering Table**.
3. Go back to the file containing your table code (either in your text editor or in Dreamweaver Code view). Before you can put this code in the `objectTag()` function, it must have all hard returns removed. Revise the code so that it looks like this (➥ indicates soft-wrapping):

```
<table width="100%" height="100%" cellpadding="0" cellspacing="0"
➥border="0"><tr><td align="center" valign="middle">
➥ </td></tr></table>
```

note

The printed page can fit only a limited number of characters on each line. Throughout the printed code samples in this book, code that should be typed on one line may have to be shown here wrapped onto two or more lines. Whenever it might not be obvious that the wrapped code line is part of the line above it, the ➥ symbol is used to indicate that this is only soft-wrapping and you should not reproduce it in your code.

4. When you're sure your code is hard-return free, select it and Edit > Copy.
5. Go back to the new Centering Table.htm object file you just created. From the objectTag() function, delete the return statement and replace it with a new, shorter statement that looks like this:

   ```
   function objectTag() {
   return '  ';
   }
   ```

   Note that the statement now includes two single quotes (not double quotes).

6. Place the cursor between the two single quotes and Edit > Paste your table code. (Can you see why you surrounded the return statement with single quotes? Because the code contains double quotes. Double quotes can't be nested inside other double quotes in JavaScript.) Your objectTag() function should now look like this (newly pasted code in bold):

   ```
   function objectTag() {
   return '<table width="100%" height="100%" cellpadding="0"
   cellspacing="0" border="0"><tr><td align="center"
   valign="middle"> </td></tr></table>';
   }
   ```

7. Finally, because there's no reason for this object to include a dialog box, select the <form> tag and its contents and delete them.
8. When you've finished, save and close the object file.

Listing 2.4 shows the final code for the Centering Table object.

Listing 2.4 Final code for Centering Table.htm

```
<html>
<head>
<!--the title will become the ToolTip-->
<title>Centering Table</title>
<script language="JavaScript">
//this function is called automatically
function objectTag() {
//this code will be inserted
return '<table width="100%" height="100%" cellpadding="0"
cellspacing="0" border="0"><tr><td align="center"
valign="middle"> </td></tr></table>';
}
</script>
</head>
<body>
</body>
</html>
```

Task 3: Add an entry for the object to insertbar.xml

To make sure your object appears properly in the Insert bar, you need to add an entry for it in the insertbar.xml file. Just follow these steps:

1. In your text editor, open insertbar.xml.
2. Find the code for the Development category you created earlier.
3. Revise the entry to look like this:

```
<category id="DW_Insertbar_Development" folder="Development">
     <button id="DW_Development_MyObject"
             image=""
             enabled=""
             showIf=""
             file="Development\My Object.htm" />
  <button id="DW_Development_CenterTable"
             image=""
             enabled=""
             showIf=""
             file="Development\Centering Table.html" />
</category>
```

4. When you're done, save and close the file.

Task 4: Test and troubleshoot the new object

It's time for the rubber to meet the road! Are you ready? In Dreamweaver, reload extensions and open a new file.

1. Check out the Insert bar and make sure your new object appears there. It should show up as a button called Centering Table. If no button shows up, double-check your entry in insertbar.xml. Are there any typos? Did you spell the filename correctly?
2. Click the object to insert a centering table. If the object works, Dreamweaver will insert a lovely centering table in your test file. If Dreamweaver gives you a JavaScript syntax error when you click the object, you probably have a typo in your `objectTag()` function—or you may not have removed all of the hard returns from your table code. Read the Dreamweaver error message carefully and examine your object file to find and fix the problem. If you don't get an error message, but you also don't get a centering table, check your test page in Code view to see whether the object inserted any code at all, or just the wrong code. Accidentally deleting one of the double quotes inside the `objectTag()` `return` statement, for instance, or one of the <> characters, may have turned your inserted code into invalid code. Go back to your object file and tweak the `return` statement as needed.

3. If you encountered problems and adjusted the object file, reload extensions in Dreamweaver and try again. Keep doing this until the object works correctly.

Task 5: Create an icon for the object

As discussed earlier in the chapter, objects can use GIF images as icons for display in the Insert bar. Objects without associated GIF files (like the Centering Table object) display as names only. Adding a custom icon to an object involves making (or borrowing) an 18×18-pixel GIF image and saving it in the Objects folder, and updating insertbar.xml so that it associates the GIF with the object.

1. The centering table is just a variation on the table object, so why not use (and maybe adapt) the table icon? In the Configuration/Objects folder, open the Common folder and find the files for the table object.
2. Make a copy of Table.gif and put it in your Development folder. Rename it **Centering Table.gif**.
3. (optional) If you have access to a graphics program and know a little bit about painting pixels, you can customize this icon to really look like a centering table. Open Centering Table.gif in your favorite graphics editor. Zoom in close to see how the icon creates an illusion of a 3D table with just a few colored pixels.
4. Using the tools in your graphics program, paint over the center row and column lines so the new icon looks like a one-cell table. (Most graphics programs offer a pencil tool that is perfect for this job when set to paint one pixel at a time.) All done! Figure 2.9 shows a before-and-after shot of the altered graphic.

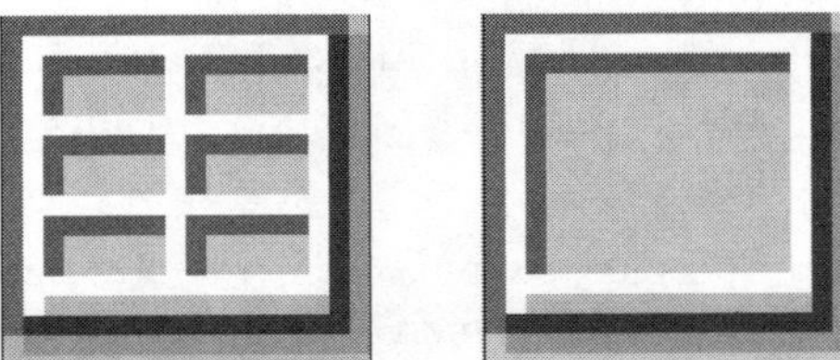

FIGURE 2.9 *The standard table object icon (left), and the altered version for the Centering Table object (right).*

5. To make sure Dreamweaver recognizes your new image, open insertbar.xml in your text editor. Change the code for the Centering Table's `<button/>` tag to look like this (new code is in bold):

```
<button id="DW_Development_CenterTable"
           image="Development\Centering Table.gif"
           enabled=""
           showIf=""
           file="Development\Centering Table.html" />
```

note

The companion Web site for this book has icon files for all objects created in this chapter. (See Appendix F for more information about the Web site contents.)

6. When you're all done, reload extensions in Dreamweaver and see how your new icon looks in the Insert bar. Figure 2.10 shows the finished result.

FIGURE 2.10 *The Centering Table object in the Insert bar, represented by a custom icon.*

Workshop #2: Creating a Simple Object with User Input

In this next workshop, we'll take our object-building skills one level higher, creating an object that uses a form to collect user input. Along the way we'll see how to create a nice layout for the dialog box and how to collect user input and build it into the `return` statement for the `objectTag()` function.

Sample Object: Inserting a Netscape Spacer Tag

The `<spacer>` tag creates a little block of empty white space on a page—a handy item, but one that works only in Netscape Navigator (all versions including 6). Internet Explorer completely ignores this tag. In its admirable effort to encourage users to use only cross-browser, cross-platform HTML code, Dreamweaver has no `<spacer>` tag in its standard set of objects.

I like to use `<spacer>` tags for two purposes: First, they are perfect when I design web pages for corporate intranets in which Netscape is the only browser in use; and second, they help Netscape to stabilize layout tables on complex pages. It's a well-known problem that some browsers (especially Netscape) will sometimes shrink empty table cells, even if those cells have specified width or height attributes, resulting in a distorted page layout. The commonly accepted solution to this problem is to tuck little transparent GIF images throughout layout tables to "prop" cells open. But the same stability can often be achieved, without having to fiddle with spacer images, by inserting `<spacer>` tags instead.

Creating the Spacer Object

Like any project that involves creating an object, the Netscape `<spacer>` tag project can be broken down into three main components: determining what code the object will insert, building the object file, and testing and refining. This object is a bit more complex to create than the Centering Table because it requires user input to determine the various attributes of the `<spacer>` tag. It also includes the additional task of designing the form.

Task 1: Determine the HTML code you want the object to insert

The `<spacer>` tag takes three properties: `type` (horizontal, vertical, or block), `width`, and `height`. Horizontal spacers have only a `width` parameter; vertical spacers have only a `height` parameter; block spacers have both. To make things easy as you start out, assume that your object will create only block spacers; thus, there will always be two parameters to collect from the user (`width` and `height`). The code you have to insert will look like this:

```
<spacer type="block" width="?" height="?">
```

The question marks (`?`) represent numbers that the user will supply. The form/dialog box will collect those numbers.

Task 2: Design a form to collect user input

As forms go, yours will be simple. It needs two input elements, both of which can be text fields, and a descriptive label for each. Following the Macromedia UI guidelines, this becomes a two-column dialog box with right-aligned labels and left-aligned text fields, as shown in Figure 2.11. For this task, don't worry about coding the form—you just want to know what it's going to look like and what input elements it will include.

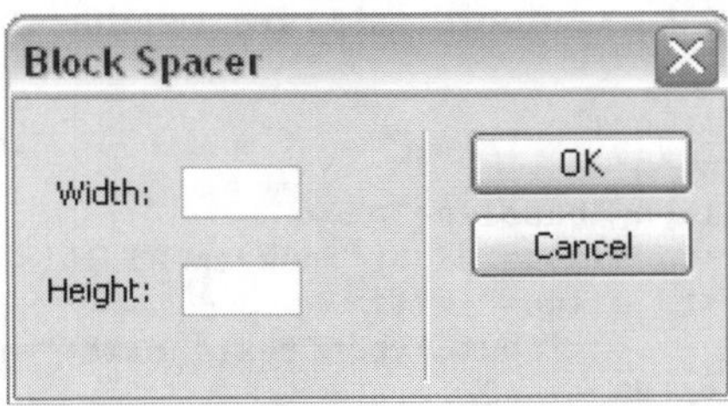

FIGURE 2.11 *The desired layout for the Block Spacer object's dialog box.*

Task 3: Create a basic object file

How you proceed in turning the previous elements into an object file depends largely on how comfortable you are with JavaScript coding and what your scripting habits are. My preference is to start simple and add complexity one step at a time. (I always like to start from what I know I can do, and work toward what I'm not sure I can do.) So that's how you will work here. You'll start by creating an object that inserts a spacer with no user input and make sure that works properly; then you'll add the form and revise the `objectTag()` function so it makes use of the information collected.

1. To start, open My Object.htm and save it in your Development folder as **Block Spacer.htm**.
2. Change the `<title>` to **Block Spacer**.
3. Revise the `objectTag()` function so that it inserts a spacer tag with set values (don't worry yet about collecting user input). Because you want your inserted spacer code to include double quotes, make sure to change the quotes around the `return` statement to single quotes. The code for your `<head>` section should now look like this (new code in bold):

```
<head>
<title>Block Spacer</title>
<script language="JavaScript">
function objectTag() {
      return '<spacer type="block" width="50" height="50">';
}
</script>
</head>
```

4. For the object's dialog box, create a form that looks like the one shown earlier in Figure 2.11. Name the two text fields `width` and `height`. The code for the object file's `<body>` section should now look like this (new code in bold):

```
<body>
<form name="myForm">
<table border="0" >
      <tr valign="baseline">
            <td align="right" nowrap>Width:</td>
            <td align="left">
                  <input type="text" name="width" size="8">
            </td>
      </tr>
      <tr valign="baseline">
            <td align="right" nowrap>Height:</td>
            <td align="left">
                  <input type="text" name="height" size="8">
            </td>
      </tr>
</table>
</form>
</body>
```

When you've created the form, save and close the object file.

Task 4: Add an entry for the object to insertbar.xml

To make sure the new object displays properly in the Insert bar, open insertbar.xml in your text editor and add the following `<button/>` tag to your Development category:

```
<button id="DW_Development_BlockSpacer"
  image=""
  enabled=""
  showIf=""
  file="Development\Block Spacer.htm" />
```

When you've entered the code (and double-checked for typos!), save and close the file.

Try it out! In Dreamweaver, reload extensions and make sure the Block Spacer object appears in the Insert bar. Create a new document and choose the object. It should create a dialog box like that shown in Figure 2.11 and (regardless of user input into the form) should insert the following line of code into your document:

```
<spacer type="block" width="50" height="50">
```

(Note that Dreamweaver doesn't display spacers in Design view. You'll need to check Code view to make sure the proper code has been inserted.) If the object doesn't work, check your code against that shown previously, and troubleshoot until it does.

Task 5: Add form interactivity

Now that you have the object and you have the form, it's time to revise the `objectTag()` function so that it collects the information the user has entered into the form and uses that information to construct the string of code that it returns.

1. To collect the information from the form, define two variables whose names match the names you gave your two form text fields. Add these variable declarations at the beginning of your `objectTag()` function, like this (new code is in bold):

   ```
   <script language="JavaScript">
   function objectTag() {
   var width=document.myForm.width.value;
   var height=document.myForm.height.value;
   return '<spacer type="block" width="50" height="50">';
   }
   ```

2. Next, you have to rewrite the `return` statement so that it uses those variable names instead of the hard-coded width and height values it previously held. This is tricky. Start by removing the numbers from the code:

   ```
   return '<spacer type="block" width="   " height="   ">';
   ```

Then break quoted text string into smaller chunks by entering single quotes on either side of each hole where you removed a number. Like this (new code in bold):

```
return '<spacer type="block" width="'  '" height="'  '">';
```

Then put plus signs (+) on either side of each hole, to indicate that you'll be adding a variable there (new code in bold):

```
return '<spacer type="block" width="'+  +'" height="'+  +'">';
```

Finally, fill in the holes with the names of the variables (new code in bold):

```
return '<spacer type="block" width="'+width+'" height="'+height+'">';
```

Your revised `objectTag()` function should look like this:

```
function objectTag() {
var width=document.myForm.width.value;
var height=document.myForm.height.value;
return '<spacer type="block" width="'+width+'" height="'+height+'">';
}
```

Putting strings of text and variable values together like this is called *concatenating*, and it can be one of the most difficult tasks in creating your Dreamweaver objects because of the single and double quotes that must be balanced. If you follow a procedure like the one above whenever you have to do this, you'll save yourself a lot of grief. Figure 2.12 shows a graphic representation of what happens when you replace values with variables.

width = "50"

width = " '+ width +' "

FIGURE 2.12 *Inserting a variable in place of a property. See how a new set of quotes always gets inserted with the variable?*

3. Finally, in Dreamweaver, reload extensions and try the object again. When the dialog box appears, enter numbers into the text fields and click OK. The code that gets inserted should include your numbers. If you get an error message, or if the right code doesn't get inserted correctly, go back to your object file. Carefully compare your code to the code shown here. Be on the lookout for typos! Make sure the names of your form and your text fields exactly match the names you call on in the `objectTag()` function. Make sure your double and single quotes balance (no opening quotes without closing quotes to match).

note

For a quick tutorial on using HTML forms and JavaScript together, see the section "Working with Form Elements" in Appendix A.

note

The most common mistakes in creating objects with dialog boxes are misaligning the quotation marks and not referring to the form field names correctly.

Task 6: Add some spit-and-polish

To tidy up, let's add a few last items. Wherever there's a dialog box that includes text fields, you want it to appear with the first text field active and its contents (if any) selected. To do that, use a local function (one that's not part of the API) that most standard Dreamweaver objects use.

1. In your text editor, open the Block Spacer.htm object file and add the following function to your `<script>` tag (new code in bold):

```
<script language="JavaScript">
function objectTag() {
var width=document.myForm.width.value;
var height=document.myForm.height.value;
return '<spacer type="block" width="'+width+'" height="'+height+'">';
}
function initializeUI() {
      document.myForm.width.focus();
      document.myForm.width.select();
}
</script>
```

   The first statement of this function puts the insertion point in the specified field (notice that this function specifies the text field called `width`); the second selects any contents.

2. Because the function you've just defined is a local function, not part of the API procedure, it must be explicitly called. You want it to execute as soon as the dialog box appears, so you'll call it `onLoad`. Add the following code to your object file's `<body>` tag (shown in bold):

```
<body onLoad="initializeUI()">
```

   Make sure you spelled the function name exactly the same in this line as you did when you defined the function (step 1). There you go!

note

If you test your extensions using Dreamweaver for Windows, you may notice that you don't need the `initializeUI()` function—your object's dialog box opens with the width text field active even without the function. Dreamweaver for Macintosh requires the function to place the focus in the proper text field. Even if you're not developing for any Mac users, though, it's a good idea to get used to the concept of initializing dialog boxes as you open them—and initializing the text field focus is also part of the UI requirements for extensions that are submitted to the Dreamweaver Exchange.

Listing 2.5 shows the complete code for the Block Spacer object.

Listing 2.5 Code for the Finished Block Spacer Object, Commented for Reference

```
<html>
<head>
<!--the title will become the ToolTip-->
<title>Block Spacer</title>
<script language="JavaScript">
function objectTag() {
//collect information from form/dialog box
var width=document.myForm.width.value;
var height=document.myForm.height.value;
//insert this code into document
return '<spacer type="block" width="'+width+'" height="'+height+'">';
}
//put focus in first text field of form
function initializeUI() {
      document.myForm.width.focus();
      document.myForm.width.select();
}
</script>
</head>
<body onLoad="initializeUI()">
<form name="myForm">
<table border="0" >
      <tr valign="baseline">
            <td align="right" nowrap>Width:</td>
            <td align="left">
                  <input type="text" name="width" size="8">
            </td>
      </tr>
      <tr valign="baseline">
            <td align="right" nowrap>Height:</td>
            <td align="left">
                  <input type="text" name="height" size="8">
            </td>
      </tr>
</table>
</form>
</body>
</html>
```

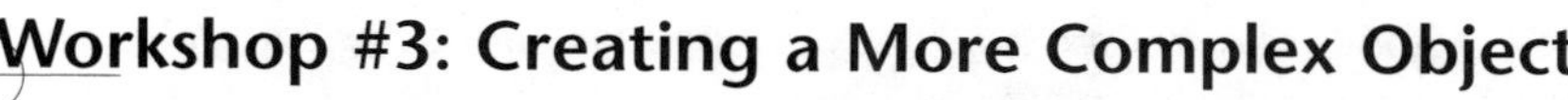

Workshop #3: Creating a More Complex Object

By now, you should be feeling at least a little bit comfortable with the API for creating Dreamweaver objects. So, it's time to get into some serious object scripting. This last workshop builds the most complex object yet—one that requires a variety of form elements in its dialog box and requires a more complex `return` statement. You also add some short online help.

> **note**
>
> **Warning**
> This object includes some fairly advanced concepts. If you're new to scripting, you might want to skip this workshop for now and come back to it when you've had some more JavaScript practice.

Sample Object: Inserting a Custom Horizontal Rule

This is a case in which Dreamweaver already provides an object to insert certain code, but you may not like the options the program gives you. Again, I start from my own workflow needs. The Dreamweaver Horizontal Rule object calls up no dialog box, although I can always use the Property inspector to set its properties. More important for me, though, the Property inspector won't let me set a color property for the tag. This wasn't an oversight on Macromedia's part; it was good, sound practice because only Internet Explorer supports this property, and, as noted previously, Dreamweaver encourages you to stick with cross-platform, cross-browser coding.

But when I design web pages for intranets in which all the site visitors are using Internet Explorer, I want to be able to use colored rules. If I use the regular Horizontal Rule object, I have to use Code view or the Edit Tag command to enter the color property every time. It's definitely time for a custom object!

Creating the Custom HR Object

Creating this object follows the same basic procedure as the first two object workshops, but with the added complexity that the code inserted must be much more customizable and the dialog box interface will use more than just text fields for input.

Task 1: Decide on the code to insert and how customizable it should be

Where there's user input, there are lots of possibilities that have more to do with strategy than scripting. The `<hr>` tag can take several parameters in addition to `color` (`width`, `height`, `align`, `noshade`, `id`). Do we want to include all of them in our dialog box, or only some? If we include them all, and the user specifies only one or two, do we let the others revert to a default value, or do we eliminate them entirely? (Note that the `<hr>` tag has no required properties.)

In keeping with good clean coding practice, thoroughness and a dose of probability, for the sample code here we'll include all the properties in the dialog box except `id`, which can be added later from the Property inspector if desired. All dialog box fields start out empty or at their default values. Unless the user enters a value for a property, the inserted code won't include that property. Thus, our custom object needs to be flexible enough to insert any code from `<hr>` to `<hr width="50%" height="3" noshade align="center" color="#FF0000">`.

Task 2: Design the form that collects the user input

As well as determining what code should be inserted, it's always a good idea to know approximately what user interface (the dialog box) an object will have. For the new `<hr>` object, each possible property that users can add to the `<hr>` tag should be represented in the dialog box by a descriptive statement or label and an appropriate form input element to collect it: `width` (text field), `height` (text field), `align` (popup menu), `noshade` (checkbox), and `color`. If this were a regular HTML form, we'd probably use a text field for collecting color information. But the Dreamweaver API includes a custom form element: the color button. We'll follow the Dreamweaver program's own interface example in this, and use the color button along with a text field to allow users to enter the information however they choose. The desired layout for the dialog box is shown in Figure 2.13.

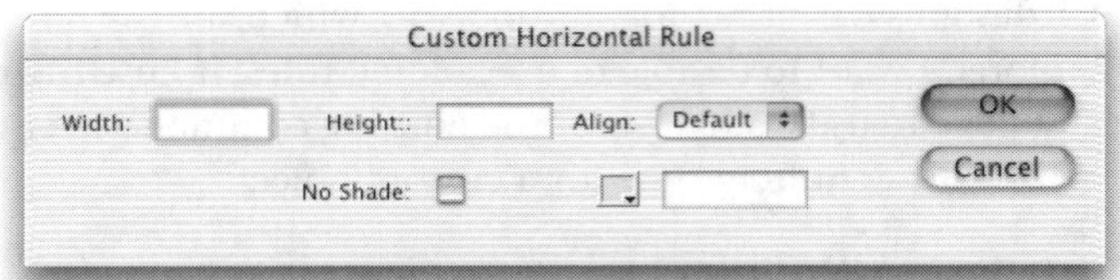

FIGURE 2.13 *The desired layout for the Custom HR object's dialog box.*

Task 3: Create the basic object file

As with the Block Spacer, creating this object is easiest if you start simple and add complexity as you go. Follow these steps:

1. In your text editor, open My Object.htm and save it in your Development folder as **Custom HR.htm**.
2. Change the title to **Custom Horizontal Rule**. Revise the `objectTag()` function so it returns a simple `<hr>` tag. The code for your object file's `<head>` section should now look like this (new code in bold):

```
<head>
<title>Custom Horizontal Rule</title>
<script language="JavaScript">
function objectTag() {
return '<hr>';
}
</script>
</head>
```

(Note that single quotes have been substituted for double quotes around the `return` statement. That's because eventually the `<hr>` tag will include some attributes, with their values specified using double quotes.)

3. For the form, build a table-based layout that re-creates the dialog box design shown in Figure 2.13. Name the form elements `width`, `height`, `align`, `noshade`, and `color`. For those of you creating your form in Dreamweaver Design view, Figure 2.14 shows an annotated diagram (note that the color button form element is recognized by the Dreamweaver Property inspector). The code for the revised `<body>` section of the object file should look like this (pay particular attention to the way the color button form element is coded):

```
<body>
<form name="myForm">
  <table border="0">
    <tr valign="baseline">
      <td align="right" nowrap > Width:</td>
      <td align="left" nowrap>
        <input type="text" name="width" size="8">
          </td>
      <td align="right" nowrap>Height::</td>
      <td align="left" nowrap>
        <input type="text" name="height" size="8">
      </td>
      <td nowrap align="right"> Align:</td>
      <td nowrap>
        <select name="align">
          <option selected value="default">Default</option>
          <option value="left">Left</option>
          <option value="right">Right</option>
          <option value="center">Center</option>
        </select>
      </td>
    </tr>
    <tr valign="baseline">
      <td align="right"> </td>
      <td align="left">  </td>
      <td nowrap align="right">No Shade:</td>
      <td align="left">
        <input type="checkbox" name="noshade" value="noshade">
```

```
          </td>
          <td  align="right">
            <input type="mmcolorbutton" name="colorswatch">
          </td>
          <td >
            <input type="text" name="colorfield" size="10">
          </td>
        </tr>
      </table>
      </form>
    </body>
```

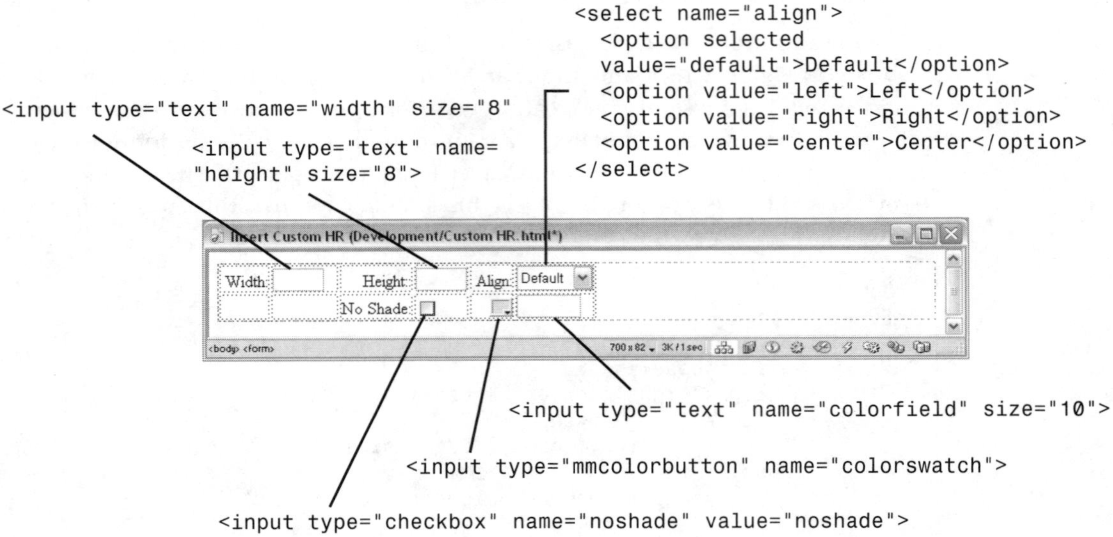
<select name="align">
<option selected
value="default">Default</option>
<option value="left">Left</option>
<option value="right">Right</option>
<option value="center">Center</option>
</select>
<input type="text" name="width" size="8"
<input type="text" name=
"height" size="8">
Width:
Height:
Align:
Default
No Shade:
<body> <form>
700 x 82
<input type="text" name="colorfield" size="10">
<input type="mmcolorbutton" name="colorswatch">
<input type="checkbox" name="noshade" value="noshade">

FIGURE 2.14 *The Custom Horizontal Rule form being created in Dreamweaver Design view.*

Task 4: Add an entry for the object to insertbar.xml

So that the new Custom Horizontal Rule object displays properly in the Insert bar, open insertbar.xml in your text editor and add the following `<button/>` tag to your Development category:

```
<button id="DW_Development_CustomHR"
  image=""
  enabled=""
  showIf=""
  file="Development\Custom HR.htm" />
```

Before proceeding to the next step, test the object out in Dreamweaver to make sure the dialog box displays properly. Of course, the dialog box is not functional yet. But it should display correctly—and clicking on the color button should even bring up the Dreamweaver color palette (see Figure 2.15).

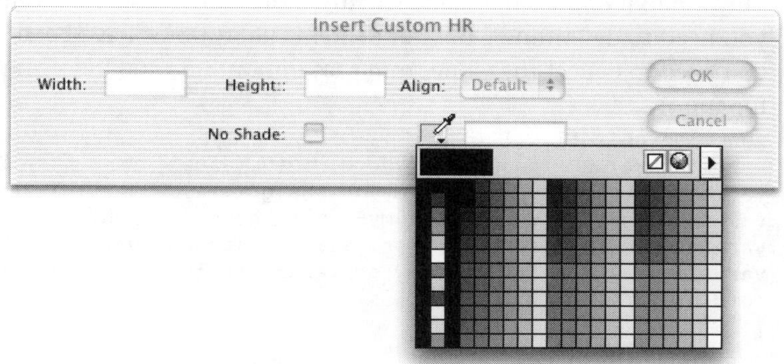

FIGURE 2.15 *The dialog box for the Custom Horizontal Rule object, with working color button.*

Task 5: Revise the *objectTag( )* function to collect user input

The tricky part about the Custom Horizontal Rule object is that, unlike the Block Spacer object, it contains conditional code—attributes for the `<hr>` tag that shouldn't be included unless the user enters values into the dialog box. This makes the task of constructing the `objectTag()` function's `return` statement a little bit different than it was in the previous workshop. This task is a challenge! Don't be frustrated if it takes you several tries to get it right.

1. Open the Custom HR.htm file in your text editor.
2. As you did with the Block Spacer object, you need to start by creating variables to collect user input from the form. Start by collecting values from the two text fields (`width` and `height`). Add the following code to your `objectTag()` function (new code is in bold):

```
function objectTag() {
var widthValue = document.myForm.width.value;
var heightValue = document.myForm.height.value;
return '<hr>';
}
```

   Don't worry about the color button form element just yet; you'll be adding that into the mix later.

3. The checkbox form element (`noshade`) returns true or false, depending on whether it's checked or not. To collect this value, add the following line to your code (new code is in bold):

```
function objectTag() {
var widthValue = document.myForm.width.value;
var heightValue = document.myForm.height.value;
var noshadeValue = document.myForm.noshade.checked;
return '<hr>';
}
```

4. The popup menu (align) takes slightly more work to collect a value from. First, you need to determine which of its items, or options, have been selected; then you need to collect the value from that option. Add the following code to your function:

```
function objectTag() {
var widthValue = document.myForm.width.value;
var heightValue = document.myForm.height.value;
var noshadeValue = document.myForm.noshade.checked;
var selected = document.myForm.align.selectedIndex;
var alignValue = document.myForm.align.options[selected].value;
return '<hr>';
}
```

(If you're not sure what's happening in these two lines of code, remember that the items in a popup menu create an options array. Each option in the array has an index number, by which it can be identified and accessed.)

5. Finally, collect the value from the color button. This is easy. Although the color button may have an unusual interface, for scripting purposes it behaves just like a text field. So, you can collect its value just like you collected the width and height fields, like this:

```
function objectTag() {
var widthValue = document.myForm.width.value;
var heightValue = document.myForm.height.value;
var noshadeValue = document.myForm.noshade.checked;
var selected = document.myForm.align.selectedIndex;
var alignValue = document.myForm.align.options[selected].value;
var colorValue = document.myForm.colorswatch.value;
return '<hr>';
}
```

Task 6: Use collected input to build the *objectTag( )* function's *return* statement

Now for the fun part: turning all this collected input into a complete <hr> tag for the return statement. The trick of creating an object like this, where the attributes are all optional and the user may or may not provide values for them, is that you don't want the code to include any properties not specified in the dialog box. After all, you don't want your <hr> tag to look like this:

```
<hr width="" height="" color="" align="">
```

To ensure that only properties with values appear in the code, think of the code you're going to insert as a bunch of building blocks, like the illustration in Figure 2.16. Each attribute/value combination is a block; the opening and closing parts of the tag itself are blocks. The opening and closing blocks must always be present, but the interior blocks can be included or excluded based on which attributes you want to use. You're going to revise the `objectTag()` function so that it builds the `<hr>` tag one block at a time. You'll start with the opening block. Then, for each attribute, you'll determine whether the user has entered a value for that attribute and if he has, you'll add that block. When you're done, you'll tack on the closing block.

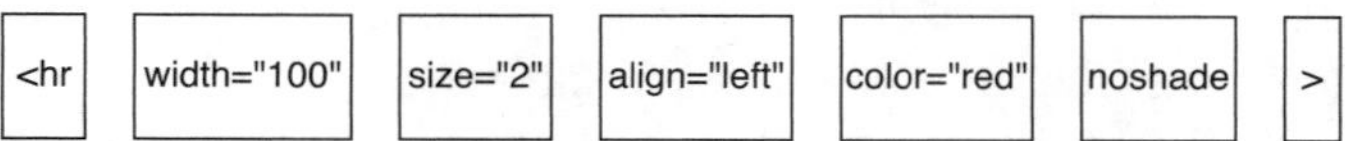

FIGURE 2.16 *The <hr> tag and its attributes, seen as individual building blocks of code.*

1. Start by creating the opening and closing blocks. Define two variables, `openingTag` and `closingTag`, and revise your `return` statement so that it concatenates the two (puts them together), like this (new code is in bold):

```
function objectTag() {
var widthValue = document.myForm.width.value;
var heightValue = document.myForm.height.value;
var noshadeValue = document.myForm.noshade.checked;
var selected = document.myForm.align.selectedIndex;
var alignValue = document.myForm.align.options[selected].value;
var colorValue = document.myForm.colorswatch.value;
var openingTag="<hr";
var closingTag=">";
return openingTag+closingTag;
}
```

At its most basic, then, the function will return `<hr>`. (You can try it out with just this much code in place to check this out. You still aren't processing any form input, but the `objectTag()` function should successfully insert a plain vanilla `<hr>` tag.)

2. Next, for each additional building block (attribute), you need to determine whether the user has entered a value for that attribute; and if he has, you need to construct that block and add it to the code. You do it with a conditional statement and bit of concatenation. To add the `width` building block, add the following lines of code:

```
function objectTag() {
var widthValue = document.myForm.width.value;
var heightValue = document.myForm.height.value;
var noshadeValue = document.myForm.noshade.checked;
var selected = document.myForm.align.selectedIndex;
var alignValue = document.myForm.align.options[selected].value;
```

```
var colorValue = document.myForm.colorswatch.value;
var openingTag="<hr";
var closingTag=">";
if (widthValue) {
   openingTag += ' width="' + widthValue + '"';
   }
return openingTag+closingTag;
}
```

Can you see how this works? If the width form element contains any value, the conditional statement changes the `openingTag` variable from `<hr` to `<hr width="value"`. If it doesn't contain a value (if the user hasn't entered any value), the conditional statement doesn't execute and the property is not added. The form elements that don't use text fields will require slightly different syntax—but the principle remains the same. If you're confused by the quotes in the concatenation part of the statement, refer back to the diagram in Figure 2.8. Note that the first quoted segment starts with a space. If that space isn't present, the opening turns into `<hrwidth`, which is not good HTML.

3. Go ahead and add the remaining conditional statements and building blocks to your code. When you're done, your revised `objectTag()` function will look like this (new code is in bold):

```
function objectTag() {
var widthValue = document.myForm.width.value;
var heightValue = document.myForm.height.value;
var noshadeValue = document.myForm.noshade.checked;
var selected = document.myForm.align.selectedIndex;
var alignValue = document.myForm.align.options[selected].value;
var colorValue = document.myForm.colorswatch.value;
var openingTag="<hr";
var closingTag=">";
if (widthValue) {
   openingTag += ' width="' + widthValue + '"';
   }
if (heightValue) {
   openingTag += ' size="' + heightValue + '"';
   }
if (alignValue != "default") {
   openingTag += ' align="' + alignValue + '"';
   }
if (colorValue) {
   openingTag += ' color="' + colorValue + '"';
   }
if (noshadeValue) {
   openingTag += ' noshade ';
   }
return openingTag+closingTag;
}
```

Can you see how this works? Assuming the user assigns a value for every attribute, by the end of the function the `openingTag` variable will look something like this:

```
<hr width="100" size="2" align="center" color="red" noshade
```

All it will need is the closing > to finish it off.

4. Try it out! In Dreamweaver, reload extensions and see how many different kinds of horizontal rules you can insert. If you choose the object and then click OK to close the dialog box without entering any values, it should insert a plain `<hr>` element. If you enter values in all fields, it should insert a fully packed tag. If you enter only some values, it should add only those attributes. (Note that the color text field has not been accounted for yet, so you will only be able to choose colors using the color button.)

Now all you need is some refining.

Task 7: Refine the color input

To follow the Dreamweaver interface standard for choosing colors, we should let our users choose whether to use the color button or the color text field to choose the color for the horizontal rule. We do this by linking the two fields so that no matter which entry method is used, both input elements will register the user's choice. (If the user types in a color name, the color button should display a swatch of that color; if he chooses a color from the button, the text field should display the name or hex number of that color. No matter which he chooses, the `objectTag()` function should collect the information.)

To do this, we create two new functions and function calls for our object: a function that copies the value of the color text field into the color button, to be executed when the user has entered text in the text field; and a function that copies the value of the color button into the color text field, to be executed when the user chooses a color using the button.

1. Start by adding the functions. Inside the `<script>` tag in your document's `<head>` section, after the closing curly brace of the `objectTag()` function, add the following code:

```
function setColorField() {
document.myForm.colorfield.value = document.myForm.colorswatch.value;
}

function setColorButton() {
document.myForm.colorswatch.value = document.myForm.colorfield.value;
}
```

Pretty simple code, eh? It just copies the value from one form element to another.

2. Now these functions need to be triggered by function calls attached to the appropriate form elements. You want to set the color field when the user has changed the color of the color button; so add an `onChange` event handler to the color button calling the `setColorText()` function, like this (new code is in bold):

```
<input type="mmcolorbutton"
➥name="colorswatch"
onChange="setColorField()">
```

Now do the same thing, going the other way. You want to set the color of the color button when the user has finished typing a color name or hexadecimal number into the text field; so add an `onBlur` event handler to the color text field calling the `setColorButton()` function (new code is in bold):

```
<input type="text" name="colorfield" size="10"
onBlur="setColorButton()">
```

In case you were wondering, the `onBlur` event happens when the user's cursor has been in the text field and then the user clicks somewhere else—which is presumably what he will do after he has finished typing.

> **note**
>
> The `setColorField()` and `setColorButton()` are both local functions—that is, they're not part of the Dreamweaver API. Unlike the `objectTag()` function, they must be called or they will not execute.

3. Try it out. In Dreamweaver, reload extensions and try inserting a Custom Horizontal Rule. When the dialog box appears, see what happens when you use either of the color controls. If you choose from the color button, the text field automatically fills in; if you enter a name or hexadecimal number in the text field, the color button changes color automatically.

   And that's not all! If you think back to how you coded the `objectTag()` function, you'll remember that the script collects the value of the color button to use in constructing the `<hr>` tag. But what happens if you type color information into the text field instead? The `setColorButton()` function updates the value of the color button. So, no matter which entry method you use, the `objectTag()` function still processes your input and adds your color choice to the code it inserts.

Task 8: Refine the dialog box, and add some online help

The Custom Horizontal Rule object is now fully functional and something to be proud of. It just needs a few extra touches on its interface to make it presentable to the world. Like the Block Spacer object in the previous workshop, this new object's dialog box should open with its focus in the first text field—it needs initializing, in other words. And it could also use a sentence or two of online help, which can be added at the bottom of the dialog box.

1. To properly initialize the dialog box, add an `initializeUI()` function to the `<script>` tag in your document head, after the closing curly brace of the last function you defined:

   ```
   function initializeUI() {
         document.myForm.width.focus();
         document.myForm.width.select();
   }
   ```

   This puts the focus in the width text field, which is normally where the user will want to start typing.

2. Because `initializeUI()` is a local function, not called as part of the API process, you must also include a function call for it. Add the following code to your `<body>` tag:

   ```
   <body onLoad="initializeUI()">
   ```

3. Now for the online help. According to the Macromedia UI guidelines, any short online help messages should be added in a new table cell at the bottom of the dialog box, and that table cell should have a light gray (#D3D3D3) background color—as shown in Figure 2.17. To create the Custom Horizontal Rule help message, add the following code to the bottom of your `<table>` tag (new code shown in bold):

   ```
       <tr valign="baseline">
         <td align="right"> </td>
         <td align="left" colspan="5" bgcolor="#D3D3D3">
           <p>To set width as percent, enter a percent sign in the width
           ➥field; to set width as pixels, enter a number only. </p>
           <p>Note that the color property is recognized by MSIE
           ➥only.</p>
         </td>
       </tr>
   </table>
   ```

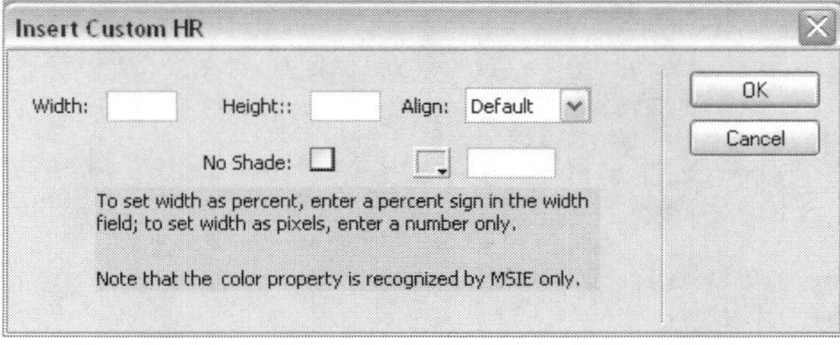

FIGURE 2.17 *Dialog box for the Custom Horizontal Rule object, showing added Help text.*

Listing 2.6 shows the completed code for the Custom Horizontal Rule object, with all refinements in place.

Listing 2.6 Code for the Custom Horizontal Rule Object, Commented for Reference

```
<html>
<head>
<!-- title shows in dialog box title bar -->
<title>Custom Horizontal Rule</title>
<script language="JavaScript">

function objectTag() {

//collect information from form/dialog box
var widthValue = document.myForm.width.value;
var heightValue = document.myForm.height.value;
var noshadeValue = document.myForm.noshade.checked;
var selected = document.myForm.align.selectedIndex;
var alignValue = document.myForm.align.options[selected].value;
var colorValue = document.myForm.colorswatch.value;

//start with two building blocks
var openingTag="<hr";
var closingTag=">";

//if user has entered a width, add the code for this attribute
if (widthValue) {
   openingTag += ' width="' + widthValue + '"';
   }

//if user has entered a height, add the code for this attribute
if (heightValue) {
   openingTag += ' size="' + heightValue + '"';
   }

//if user has chosen an alignment other than default, add the code for
this attribute
if (alignValue != "default") {
   openingTag += ' align="' + alignValue + '"';
   }

//if user has entered a color, add the code for this attribute
if (colorValue) {
   openingTag += ' color="' + colorValue + '"';
   }

//if user has selected the noshade checkbox, add the code for this
attribute
```

```
if (noshadeValue) {
   openingTag += ' noshade ';
   }

//assemble the building blocks
return openingTag+closingTag;
}

//copy input from color text field to color button
function setColorField() {
document.myForm.colorfield.value = document.myForm.colorswatch.value;
}

//copy input from color button to color text field
function setColorButton() {
document.myForm.colorswatch.value = document.myForm.colorfield.value;
}

//put cursor in first text field when dialog box opens
function initializeUI() {
document.myForm.width.focus();
document.myForm.width.select();
}

</script>
</head>
<body onLoad="initializeUI()">
<form name="myForm">
  <table border="0">
    <tr valign="baseline">
      <td align="right" nowrap > Width:</td>
      <td align="left" nowrap>
        <input type="text" name="width" size="8">
          </td>
      <td align="right" nowrap>Height:</td>
      <td align="left" nowrap>
        <input type="text" name="height" size="8">
      </td>
      <td nowrap align="right"> Align:</td>
      <td nowrap>
        <select name="align">
          <option selected value="default">Default</option>
          <option value="left">Left</option>
          <option value="right">Right</option>
          <option value="center">Center</option>
        </select>
      </td>
    </tr>
    <tr valign="baseline">
      <td align="right"> </td>
      <td align="left">  </td>
```

continues

Listing 2.6 Continued

```
      <td nowrap align="right">No Shade:</td>
      <td align="left">
        <input type="checkbox" name="noshade" value="noshade">
      </td>
      <td  align="right">
<!-- if user chooses a new color, calls a function to copy color to text
field -->
        <input type="mmcolorbutton" name="colorswatch"
onChange="setColorField()">      </td>
      <td >
<!-- if user types in a new color name, calls a function to copy value
to color button -->
        <input type="text" name="colorfield" size="10"
        onBlur="setColorButton()">      </td>
    </tr>
    <tr valign="baseline">
      <td align="right"> </td>
      <td align="left" colspan="5" bgcolor="#D3D3D3">
      <p>To set width as percent, enter a percent sign in the width field;
         to set width as pixels, enter a number only. </p>
      <p>Note that the &lt;color property is recognized by MSIE only.</p>
    </td>
  </tr>
  </table>
  </form>
</body>
</html>
```

Task 9: Split the code into separate HTML and JS files

Your Custom Horizontal Rule is finished! And what a lot of JavaScript code went into that object. If you want to follow the Macromedia example, for all but the simplest objects you'll separate your code into an HTML file and a linked JS file. In this task, you'll do that, so you can see how the HTML/JS file linking setup works.

1. In the `<head>` section of the object file, select and cut all the code between the `<script>` tags (but not the tags themselves). This should include the `objectTag()`, `setColorField()`, `setColorButton()`, and `initializeUI()` functions.
2. Create a new text document, paste the code into it, and save it in your Configuration/Objects/Development folder as **Custom HR.js**.
3. Now link the HTML file to the JS file. In the HTML document (Custom HR.htm), change the `<script>` tag to read like this:

```
<script src="Custom HR.js"></script>
```

4. Save the HTML file and close it.
5. Reload extensions in Dreamweaver and try it out. If you moved your code and added the link correctly, the Custom Horizontal Rule objects will behave exactly as they did before you separated the code.

note

Troubleshooting
What could go wrong? If you didn't link the two files correctly, Dreamweaver will report an error as soon as you try to choose the object, because it won't be able to find `initializeUI()` to initialize the dialog box. If you didn't quite copy and paste all the JavaScript code, Dreamweaver will report a JavaScript syntax error as soon as a function that wasn't moved successfully tries to execute. What can you do if this happens? Double-check the filename you entered as the `src` for the `<script>` tag. In the new JS file, double-check every function to make sure each ends with its very own curly brace.

Summary

Congratulations! That last project was a tough one. By now, you should feel your JavaScript muscles flexing. You are now well on the road to becoming the next object-writing guru of the Dreamweaver world. We'll revisit objects in Part II of this book, in which we'll look at more refinements, such as creating dialog boxes that remember previous settings and strategies for handling error checking. We'll also see our friends—the `<spacer>` tag and the custom `<hr>` tag—again in Chapter 6, when we learn how to create custom Property inspectors.

CHAPTER 3

Creating Custom Behaviors

In terms of how they're constructed and what they do, Dreamweaver behaviors are very similar to objects. Like an object, a behavior inserts code into the user's document. But although objects generally insert chunks of HTML code, behaviors insert JavaScript functions and function calls.

How Behaviors Are Constructed

Like objects, behaviors are constructed from HTML and JavaScript, and are either located in one HTML file or created as an HTML file and linked JavaScript (JS) file. The Application Programming Interface (API) requirements for behaviors are stricter than those for objects. In particular, behaviors must insert a generic (non-customizable) function in the head of a user's document and a customizable function call with an event handler elsewhere in the document (see Figure 3.1). All behaviors must present dialog boxes, even if there are no user input options to collect. Behavior files also include several required API functions, as opposed to the single required function for objects.

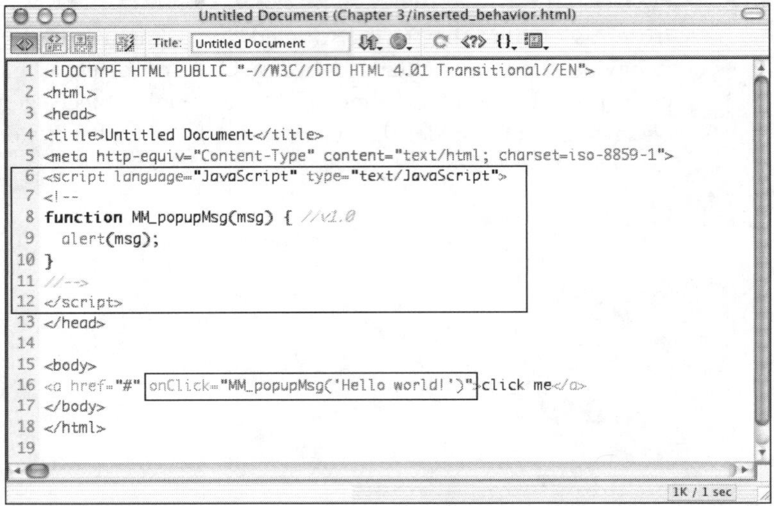

FIGURE 3.1 *A Dreamweaver document with behavior code inserted.*

note

Because of the restrictions imposed by the behavior API, there are all kinds of scripting setups you cannot create using behaviors. You can't, for instance, use a behavior to insert a `<script>` tag into a document's body, and the code inserted by a behavior can't declare global variables, and so on. To extend Dreamweaver so that it performs these kinds of tasks, you need to use other extension types, such as commands. (See Chapter 8, "Mixing Extension Types," for more on this.)

Behaviors in the Configuration Folder

The HTML and JavaScript files that make up a behavior are stored in the Configuration/Behaviors/Actions folder or in one of its subfolders. The structure of the Actions folder relates directly to the structure of the actions menu that appears in the Behaviors panel when users click the plus (+) button. Behavior files that are stored loose in the Actions folder appear in the main actions menu; subfolders in the Actions folder appear as submenus, with their contents appearing as submenu items (see Figure 3.2).

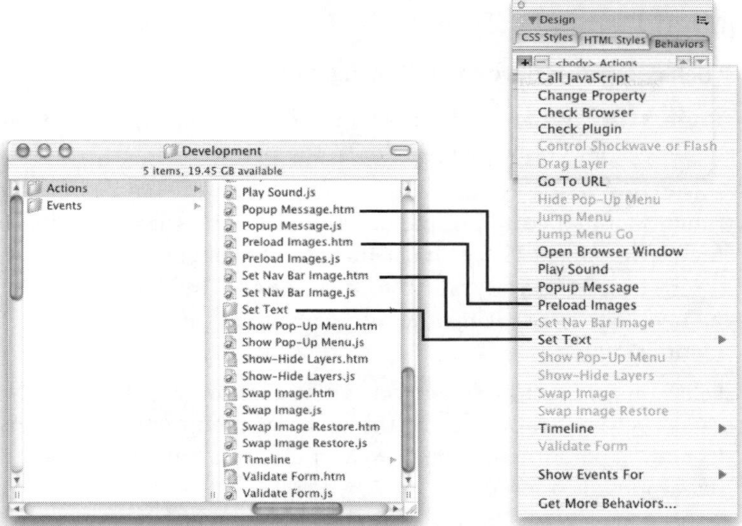

FIGURE 3.2 *The Behavior/Actions folder structure, as it corresponds to the Behaviors panel's actions menu structure.*

Behavior Files

A behavior consists of the following files:

- **HTML file (required).** This is the main behavior file. Just as with objects, the section of the file contained in the `<head>` tag may contain JavaScript functions for constructing and inserting the object code, or it may contain a link to an external JS file. Any contents of the behavior file's `<body>` tag become the contents of the behavior's dialog box. If the `<body>` tag is empty, the dialog box is empty, too! If the behavior does not require user input, there is no need for a `<form>` tag.

- **JS file (optional).** As with objects, the JavaScript functions for constructing the behavior code may be placed in this separate file, instead of embedding them in the `<head>` section of the main file. It's customary to match this file's name with the filename of the main object file.

Structure of a Behavior File

Like objects, behaviors can be simple—containing only the required elements—or they can be refined with a number of features. The next two sections discuss the elements in both simple and more full-featured behavior files.

Required Elements (Simplest)

Every behavior must have the following basic elements:

- **Page title.** Whatever appears in the document's `<title>` tag becomes the name of the actions menu item for the behavior.
- **Function to be inserted.** Remember: every behavior must insert a generic function and a customizable function call. The `<head>` section of the behavior file (or its linked JS file) must include the function you want the behavior to insert, exactly as you want it to be inserted. This function must have a unique name (that is, two Dreamweaver behaviors can't both insert functions with identical names).
- **`behaviorFunction()` function.** This function, which is part of the API and is called automatically, returns the name of the function to be inserted, without its ending parentheses. Dreamweaver uses this function to identify the function it's supposed to insert.
- **`applyBehavior()` function.** This function, also part of the API and also called automatically, returns the function call to be inserted. If the function call depends on user input to customize its parameters, this return statement needs to be constructed from form input, just as we did with the `objectTag()` function in the previous chapter.
- **`<body>` content.** Any content in the `<body>` section becomes the behavior's dialog box.

Listing 3.1 shows the basic structural elements required for a behavior file.

Listing 3.1 A Basic Behavior File, Containing Only Required Elements and Commented for Reference

```
<html>
<head>
<!-- title becomes actions menu item name -->
<title>My Behavior</title>
<script language="JavaScript">
```

```
//this is the function the behavior will insert into the user's document
function myBehavior() {
    alert('Hello world!')
}

//this returns the name of the function to be inserted, minus its
➥parentheses
function behaviorFunction() {
    return "myBehavior";
}

//this returns the function call, which will be inserted as part of the
➥user's selected object
function applyBehavior() {
    return "myBehavior()";
}
</script>
</head>
<body>
<!-- Everything in the body will be displayed in the dialog box. -->
This is the dialog box for my behavior.
</body>
</html>
```

Optional Elements (Fancier)

In addition to these required elements, the following elements are recommended for the behavior file:

- **`canAcceptBehavior()` function.** This function determines whether or not the behavior is grayed-out (unavailable) in the actions menu. It can also be used to determine the default event handlers that will be used in the function call when the behavior is inserted into the user's document. Behaviors for controlling layers, for instance, should be unavailable in the menu if there are no layers to control in the user's current document. This function is called automatically as part of the API procedure.
- **`inspectBehavior()` function.** After a behavior has been inserted into a user's document, it appears in the Behaviors panel whenever the page element it's attached to is selected. The user expects to be able to double-click here to open the behavior's dialog box and edit its settings. The `inspectBehavior()` function allows Dreamweaver to fill the dialog box with the currently chosen settings. If this function is not present in the behavior file, when the user double-clicks to edit her behavior, she will see a default (blank) dialog box. This function is called automatically as part of the API procedure.

- **`displayHelp()` function.** This function works in behaviors exactly as it does in object files. If this function is defined, a Help button appears in the behavior's dialog box. The function can be used to call an online or offline help document, or to create a popup window containing help information. (See the description of `displayHelp()` in the section "Full-Featured Objects" in Chapter 2.)
- **Local functions.** As with object files, behavior files can include any number of custom or "local" functions, as long as they are explicitly defined and called.

API Procedure for Behaviors

After reading the previous descriptions of behavior file elements, you can see that the Dreamweaver procedure for handling behaviors is more complex than that for handling objects.

The procedure starts when the user clicks the + menu in the Behaviors panel. For each file in the Actions folder, Dreamweaver calls the `canAcceptBehavior()` function to determine which behaviors should be available in the actions popup menu. If the function returns `false`, the behavior is grayed-out. If the function returns a list of event handlers, Dreamweaver determines whether any of the events listed are valid for the currently selected HTML element and for the target browser; if none is valid, the command is grayed-out. Otherwise, the behavior is available.

After the user selects an available behavior from the menu, the following events occur:

1. Dreamweaver displays a dialog box containing the contents of the behavior file's `<body>` tag.

- If the `<body>` tag contains an `onLoad` event handler, its function is executed now.
- Dreamweaver supplies the OK and Cancel buttons. If the program finds a `displayHelp()` function in the behavior file, it also displays a Help button.
- Any local functions attached to individual form elements using `onBlur` or `onChange` execute as the user proceeds through the dialog box. Other than responding to these functions, the program waits for the user to click OK.

2. After the user clicks the OK button, Dreamweaver calls the `behaviorFunction()` and `applyBehavior()` functions, and inserts the specified function and function call into the user's document. (Note that Dreamweaver is pretty smart about this. If the function already exists in the user's document, it is not inserted twice; in such a case, only the new function call is inserted.)

   Figure 3.3 shows a flowchart diagramming this process.

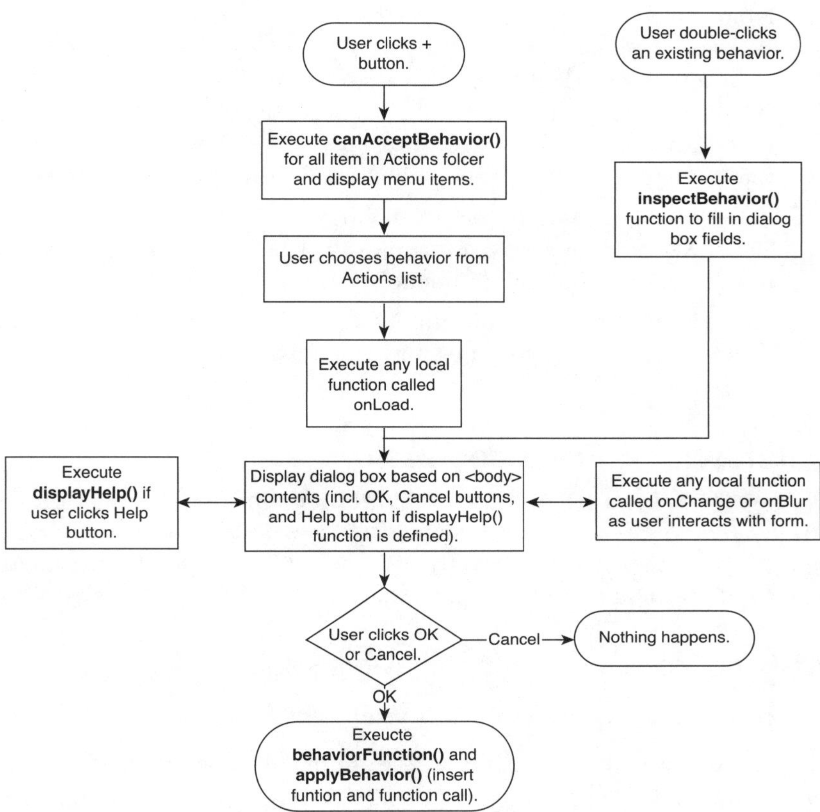

Figure 3.3 *The API procedure for inserting behaviors.*

API Procedure for Inspecting Behaviors

After the behavior is inserted into a user's document, the user can inspect and edit it at any time by double-clicking on it in the Behaviors panel. The Dreamweaver procedure for what happens at this point is as follows.

1. Dreamweaver looks for the `inspectBehavior()` function in the behavior file. If this function is defined, it is executed and its return value is used to fill in the form fields of the dialog box with the appropriate values. Otherwise, the dialog box appears in its default state (that is, the same way it appeared when the behavior was first chosen, with blank form fields or default values present).

2. From this point on, the API process is the same as when the behavior was first inserted. Dreamweaver supplies the OK and Cancel buttons for the dialog box; local functions called by `onChange` and `onBlur` events are executed as called. When the user clicks OK, the `behaviorFunction()` and `applyBehavior()` functions are called, but instead of inserting a new instance of the behavior, they update the behavior that has already been inserted into the document.
3. If the user later selects the action in the behavior inspector and deletes it, Dreamweaver removes the function call. The function itself is removed only if it is not called elsewhere in the document.

   The flowchart shown earlier in Figure 3.3 shows how the inspection process relates to the process for inserting behaviors.

Making Behaviors: Practice Session

Confused? There's a lot to learn in the API for behaviors. It will all become much clearer after you've actually had some practice with behaviors. This practice session will get you used to the behaviors API and will leave you with some framework behavior files to build on in the workshops.

Task 1: Create a custom behaviors folder

Your first task is to create a special Development folder for your custom behaviors.

1. If you already have Dreamweaver running, quit the program.
2. In the Configuration folder, find and open the Behaviors/Actions folder.
3. Create a new subfolder in this folder. Call it **Development**.
4. Relaunch the program and check out the actions popup menu in the Behaviors panel. You should have a new submenu called Development, like the one shown in Figure 3.4 (it's an empty submenu for now, of course).

note

Dreamweaver can be a little fussier about reloading behaviors than about other extensions. You must always quit the program and relaunch it to get new items in the actions menu to appear. Items that have already been created, that you're just editing, generally update with the Reload Extensions command from the Insert bar.

FIGURE 3.4 *The Development submenu (empty) in the Behaviors panel actions popup menu.*

Task 2: Create a basic behavior file

It's time to build the world's simplest behavior! When you're done, you will be able to see how the architecture of these files works, as well as having a handy file to use as a template for building future behaviors.

1. Launch your text editor of choice, or bring Dreamweaver to the front in Code view.
2. Create a new file. Save it in your new Configuration/Behaviors/Actions/ Development folder. Call it **My Behavior.htm**.
3. Type in the basic code for a simple behavior, as shown earlier in Listing 3.1.
4. Save your file and close it.
5. If Dreamweaver is currently running, quit. (Remember that simply reloading extensions doesn't work with new behaviors.)
6. Launch Dreamweaver. Create a new Dreamweaver document if you need to, and in that document create a simple text link. (Type a few words such as **click me** and link them to #, as is shown in Figure 3.5). Leave the link selected so that you can assign a behavior to it.

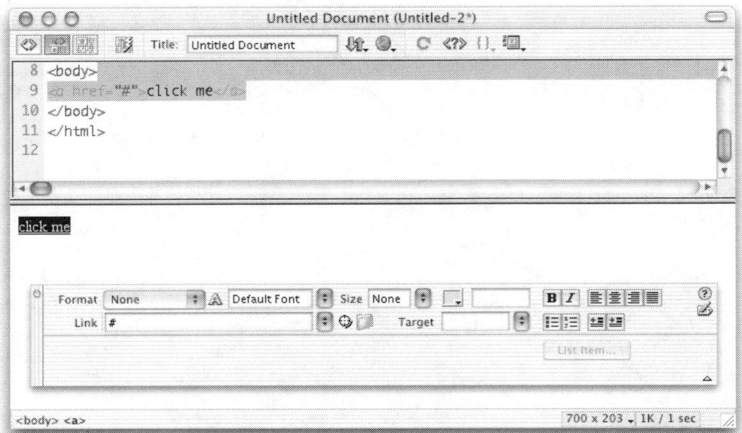

FIGURE 3.5 *Creating a simple text link, preparatory to testing a custom behavior.*

7. Open the Behaviors panel and click the + button. (Dreamweaver might take a minute to load the actions popup menu—be patient!) If there's a JavaScript error in your behavior file, you get an error message at this point. Otherwise, you should be able to choose the Development submenu and find your behavior. Figure 3.6 shows what it should look like.

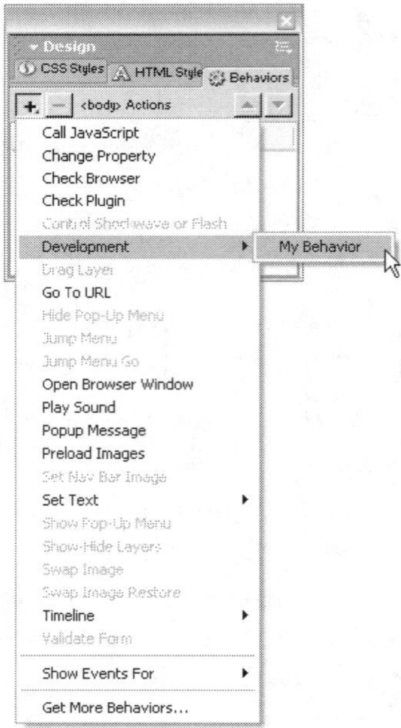

FIGURE 3.6 *The Development submenu and My Behavior, ready for action.*

8. Choose the behavior. Your bland, basic dialog box should pop up (see Figure 3.7). Click OK to insert your behavior.

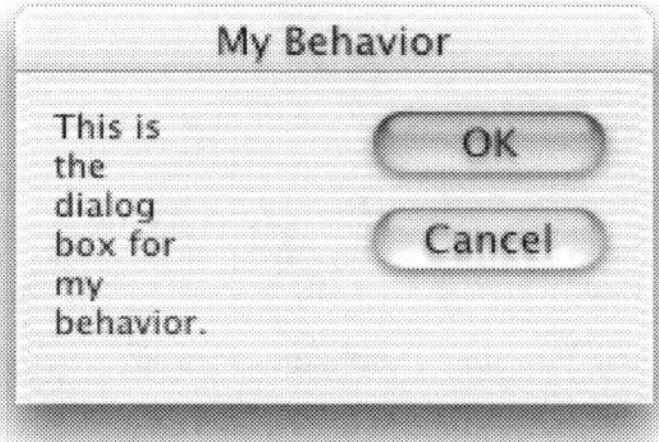

FIGURE 3.7 *The dialog box for My Behavior.*

9. Check your code! As shown in Figure 3.8, you should have a new function and function call in your document.

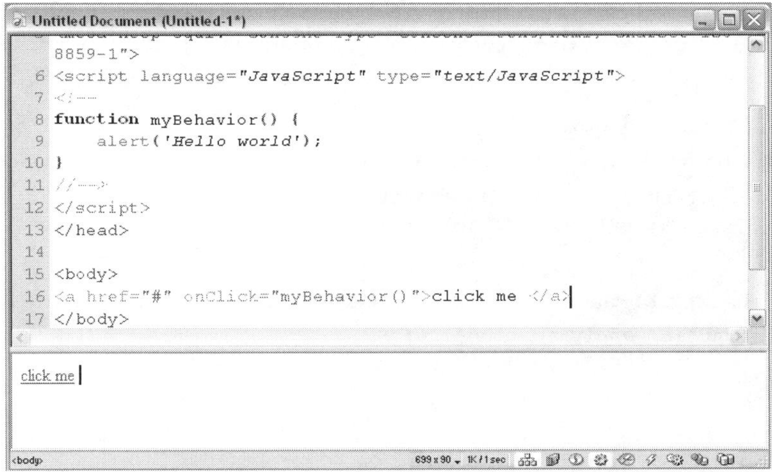

FIGURE 3.8 *A test document with My Behavior applied to a text link.*

note

When Dreamweaver inserts the `<script>` tag into your document <head>, it surrounds the tag's contents with comment lines (`<!--`and `//-->`). This coding nicety keeps browsers that don't understand JavaScript from displaying the script as text in the browser window.

10. Try it out in a browser! Clicking the click me link should open up a popup window with your exciting message inside (see Figure 3.9). If you have problems, check your code against that shown earlier in Listing 3.1 and troubleshoot.

FIGURE 3.9 *The test document previewed in a browser, showing My Behavior in action.*

Task 3: Create a behavior with a passed parameter

To see how Dreamweaver lets you customize the function call (but not the function) you insert, you can tweak your practice behavior just a little. You'll be rewriting the defined function to accept a passed parameter; then you'll rewrite the `applyBehavior()` function to insert a function call that passes a parameter.

1. Open My Behavior.htm in your text editor.
2. Change the defined function to accept a passed parameter (new code is in bold):

```
function myBehavior(myParameter) {
      alert(myParameter)
}
```

3. Change the `applyBehavior()` function to pass a parameter (new code is in bold):

```
function applyBehavior() {
      return 'myBehavior("This is my parameter. ")';
}
```

4. Save the file and close it.
5. In Dreamweaver, reload extensions using the popup options menu in the Insert bar. (Because this behavior isn't new, only changed, you don't need to quit and relaunch.)
6. In your test file, select the text link you made earlier and remove the behavior from it. (With the link selected, click the – button in the Behaviors panel.) Then add the behavior to the link again (see Figure 3.10). If you examine your code, you will see that the statement returned by the `applyBehavior()` function has become the function call. The inserted function appears exactly as you entered it in your behavior file. That's it!

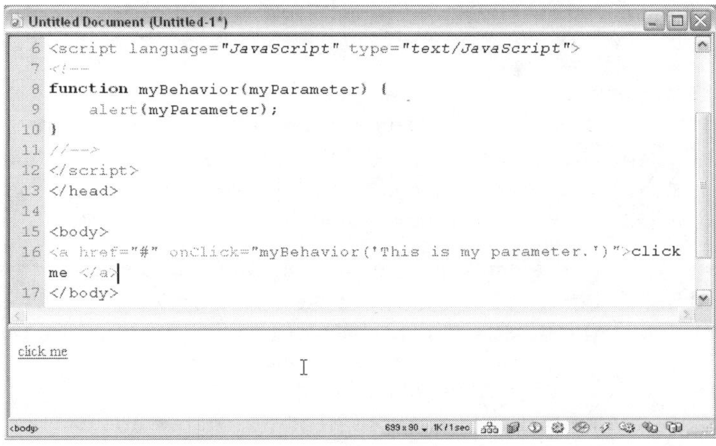

FIGURE 3.10 *The test file showing the revised My Behavior being inserted.*

7. When the behavior is working properly, save a copy of it outside the Configuration folder for future reference. (If you have created a Working folder, save it there.) You can use this file as a template for creating future behaviors. If you haven't commented the code yet, you might want to add comments now, for future reference.

Workshop #1: Creating a Simple Behavior

It might take a bit of thought to wrap your brain around this, but you're about to write a JavaScript that instructs Dreamweaver to write some JavaScript in the user's document. Why would you want to do this? You (as an author) write behaviors for scripting tasks that you (as a user) need repeatedly, but don't want to have to manually script over and over again. You also might want to write behaviors to share with your less scripting-savvy colleagues so that they can put them in their documents with the click of a + button. Are there any bits of JavaScript you find yourself always entering by hand, either because Dreamweaver doesn't provide them or because you don't like the way the Dreamweaver versions are scripted? Do you always end up using Dreamweaver behaviors and then tweaking the code by hand to make it just the way you want it? If so, you should start making your own behaviors.

Sample Behavior: Adding "Back" and "Forward" Controls to a Document

With a short chunk of JavaScript, web page creators can put text links or buttons on their pages that will navigate through the visitor's browser history, mimicking the functionality of the browser's Back and Forward buttons. Why would someone want to do this? It can be a nice added element in a web site's navigation controls, and it doesn't rely on the visitor using the browser's built-in controls.

In this workshop, you create a behavior that causes Dreamweaver to add a Back or Forward link to a piece of text or an image. The behavior includes a dialog box that asks which way the link should go—back or forward. Nice and simple, eh?

Creating the Back/Forward Behavior

Because the API for behaviors contains so many required and optional elements, creating even a fairly simple behavior like this one involves many tasks: creating and testing the JavaScript code to insert, building the basic behavior file, collecting and processing user input, revising and testing. This workshop takes you through each of those tasks. Complex tasks are broken down into steps for you.

Task 1: Create the JavaScript code insert

A behavior is only as good as the JavaScript it inserts. Our first task, therefore, is to create the properly formatted function and function call that you want the behavior to insert. We'll do this in a test file.

1. In your text editor or in Dreamweaver, create two new files. Call them **fwd_test.html** and **back_test.html**, and be sure each contains the basic HTML framework code. Because these are test files and not extension files, you don't want to make them part of your Dreamweaver configuration—don't save them in the Configuration folder! Instead, save them in your Working folder.
2. In fwd_test.htm, create two text links. One should say `Start` and should be linked to back_test.htm. The other should say `Forward`, and should be linked to the pound sign (#). The first link is just to get the test started; the second link will hold the function call for your JavaScript control. Figure 3.11 shows what fwd_test.htm should look like at this point.

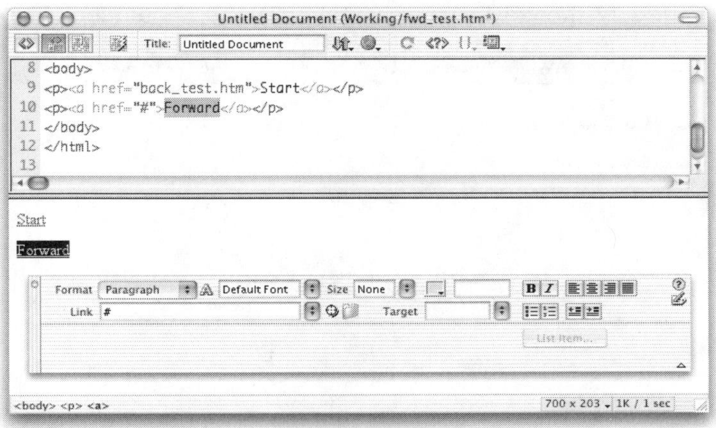

FIGURE 3.11 *The fwd_test.htm test file, with links in place.*

3. Still in fwd_test.html, add a `<script>` tag and a JavaScript function to the document `<head>` that will navigate forward in the browser history. The code should look like this:

```
<script language="JavaScript">
function goThere(page) {
     window.history.go(page);
}
</script>
```

   This function uses the `page` parameter to determine which direction it should send the browser.

4. Now, add a function call to the `Forward` link, passing it the proper parameter. Your code for the two links should now look like this (the new event handler and function call is shown in bold):

```
<p><a href="back_test.html">Start.</a></p>
<p><a href="#" onMouseUp= "goThere(1);">Forward</a></p>
```

5. Open back_test.htm. In this file, create one text link: It should say `Back`, and it should be linked to the pound sign (#).
6. In the `<head>` section of back_test.htm, add the same `<script>` tag and JavaScript function you added to the other file. (You can copy and paste it, or type it from scratch.)
7. Add a function call to the `Back` link, passing it the proper parameter, like this (event handler and function call are in bold):

```
<p><a href="#" onMouseUp= "goThere(-1);">Back</a></p>
```

Figure 3.12 shows what the back_text.htm file should look like at this point.

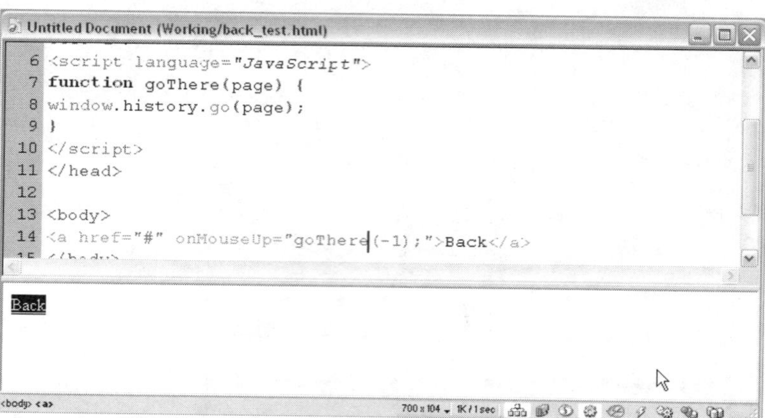

FIGURE 3.12 *The back_test.htm file with links and JavaScript function and function call in place.*

8. Save both files and try them out in a browser. If you start from fwd_test.htm by clicking the `Start` link, you should then be able to use the `Back` and `Forward` links to hop back and forth between the two pages. If the scripts don't work as expected, of course, troubleshoot and tweak them until they do.

Task 2: Insert the code into a behavior file framework

Okay, the script works. It's structured as a function and function call. It's time to turn this puppy into a Dreamweaver behavior.

1. In your text editor, open the behavior framework file you created in the practice session. Save it in your Actions/Development folder as **Back or Forward.htm**.
2. Change the `<title>` to whatever you want to appear in the + menu—**Go Back/Forward** works fine, unless you'd rather see something else show up there.
3. Replace the defined function—the entire `myBehavior()` statement—with the function you created in Task 1:

note

If you're an expert JavaScript writer and are used to having lots of choices in how you structure your scripts, you might be asking yourself a few questions here. Why did you create a generic function and pass it different parameters each time, instead of creating two different functions? And why did you link to # and use an event handler instead of linking directly to `"javascript: goThere(1);"`? Why did you need to use a function at all for such a short line of code? You could have written `<a href="javascript: window.history(-1); ">Back</a>`. You did it this way because Dreamweaver applies these restrictions when you turn this script into a behavior. All behaviors create generic functions and user-customizable function calls.

```
function goThere(page) {
      window.history.go(page);
}
```

4. Change the behaviorFunction() function to point to your new defined function name:

```
function behaviorFunction() {
      return "goThere";
}
```

5. Change the applyBehavior() function to use the new function call (without using any user input just yet):

```
function applyBehavior() {
      return "goThere(-1)";
}
```

6. For now, you can leave the <body> contents as they are. You will add a form as soon as you know the behavior will basically work.
7. Save the file and close it. If Dreamweaver is running, quit and relaunch.
8. In Dreamweaver, create a new document to use as a test file. Because you'll be using this file throughout this workshop, save it in your Working folder as **test.htm**.
9. In test.htm, enter a simple text link, such as the words **click me**, linked to #. With this text link selected, try to apply the Go Back/Forward behavior. You should be able to choose the behavior and apply it. If everything got inserted correctly, the <script> tag in the document's <head> and the <a> tag surrounding your text link should look exactly like the corresponding elements in fwd_test.htm. Figure 3.13 shows what the test document should look like with the behavior correctly inserted.

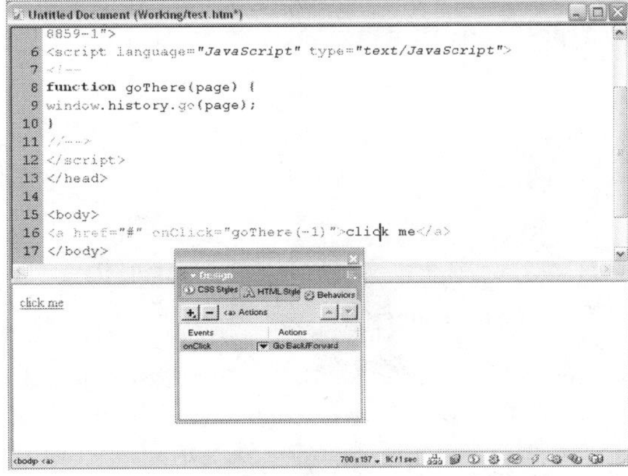

FIGURE 3.13 *The test.htm test document with its simple text link, showing the Go Back/Forward behavior applied.*

Task 3: Create a form to collect user input

Of course, if you always want the behavior to send the browser back to the previously visited page, you don't need a form. But you want your behavior to be a little more versatile than that, allowing the user to specify for each instance of the behavior whether it should send the browser window back or forward. This requires adding a form. Because the user needs to choose only between back and forward, the form needs to contain only a few text labels and a pair of radio buttons. The completed form might look something like the one shown in Figure 3.14.

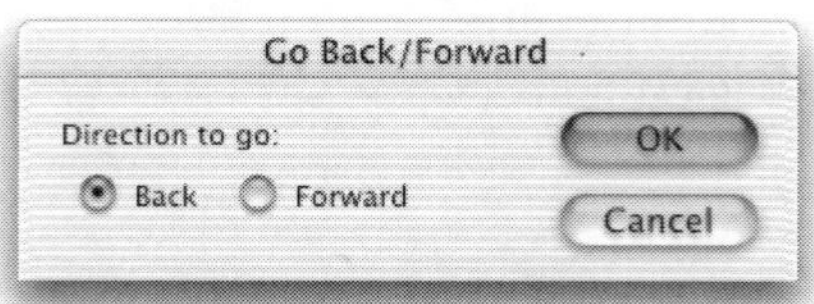

FIGURE 3.14 *The desired layout for the Go Back/Forward behavior's dialog box.*

To create the form, open the Back or Forward.htm behavior file in your text editor and change its `<body>` code to look like this:

```
<body>
<form name="myForm">
<table>
  <tr>
    <td nowrap colspan="2">Direction to go:</td>
  </tr>
  <tr valign="baseline">
    <td nowrap align="left">
      <input type="radio" name="direction" value="-1"
      ➥checked>Back </td>
    <td nowrap align="left">
      <input type="radio" name="direction" value="1">
Forward </td>
  </tr>
</table>
</form>
</body>
```

Task 4: Rewrite the *applyBehavior( )* function so that it builds the function call from user input

The `applyBehavior()` function, like the `objectTag()` function in the last chapter, must return a string of code that will be inserted in the user's document. Any user input collected from the behavior's dialog box must be built into this code string by concatenation (putting variables and text strings together, like you did to create object code in the previous chapter). For the Go Back/Forward behavior, the function call must include either 1 or -1, depending on whether the user selects the top or bottom radio button.

1. First, create a variable to hold the 1 or -1 value, like this (new code is in bold):

```
function applyBehavior() {
var whichWay;
return "goThere("+whichWay+")";
}
```

2. Determine which radio button has been selected and assign a 1 or -1 to whichWay based on this:

```
function applyBehavior() {
var whichWay;
if (document.myForm.direction[1].checked) {
      whichWay = 1;
      } else {
      whichWay = -1;
      }
return "goThere("+whichWay+")";
}
```

3. When this code is in place, reload extensions in Dreamweaver and try it out. (You shouldn't need to quit and relaunch because the behavior isn't new, only altered.) Open test.htm and select the click me link you created in the previous step. Use the – button in the Behaviors panel to remove the Go Back/Forward behavior, and then apply the behavior again.

   This time, the behavior inserts a function call that passes a parameter of -1 if you choose the Back radio button, or it passes a parameter of 1 if you choose the Forward radio button.

4. If you really want to see the behavior in action, you can even set up a full test. Just repeat "Task 1: Create the JavaScript code insert" to create a fwd_test.htm and back_test.htm file. But instead of adding the JavaScript code by hand, apply the behavior to the links in each document.

note

If you open either fwd_test.htm or back_test.htm in Dreamweaver and select one of the back or forward text links, the Behaviors panel will tell you that this link has the Go Back/Forward behavior applied to it. Even though you coded these files by hand, you used the same function name and structure (the goThere() function with one passed parameter) in the hand-coded version as you later used in creating the behavior. This causes Dreamweaver to interpret the function as an instance of the behavior.

If you've come this far, you've created a completely functional behavior. Congratulations! Listing 3.2 shows the final code for the Go Back/Forward behavior.

Listing 3.2 Code for the Finished Go Back/Forward Behavior, with Comments Added for Reference

```
<html>
<head>
<!-- title becomes actions menu item name -->
<title>Go Back/Forward</title>
<script language="JavaScript">

//this is the function the behavior will insert into the user's document
function goThere(page) {
      window.history.go(page);
}

//this returns the name of the function to be inserted, minus its only
➥parentheses
function behaviorFunction() {
      return "goThere";
}

//this returns the function call, which will be inserted as part of the
➥user's selected object
function applyBehavior() {
var whichWay;
//this if-statement sets the variable based on which radio button has
➥been selected
if (document.myForm.direction[1].checked) {
      whichWay = 1;
      } else {
      whichWay = -1;
      }
//this statement constructs the function call
return "goThere("+whichWay+")";
}

</script>
</head>
<body>
<form name="myForm">
<table>
  <tr>
    <td nowrap colspan="2">Direction to go:</td>
  </tr>
  <tr valign="baseline">
    <td nowrap align="left">
      <input type="radio" name="direction" value="-1"
      ➥checked>Back </td>
```

```
      <td nowrap align="left">
        <input type="radio" name="direction" value="1">
Forward </td>
  </tr>
</table>
</form>
</body>
</html>
```

Workshop #2: Creating a Full-Featured Behavior

Okay, it's time to pull out all the stops and create the world's most incredible do-it-all-for-you behavior—okay, not quite yet. But you're on your way.

Sample Behavior: Set Page Properties

Have you ever wanted to click a button to change the color scheme of a Web page? Maybe you just don't like neon pink backgrounds, or maybe you like bright yellow text on black just fine, but want to print the page in regular old black-on-white? In this workshop, we'll write a JavaScript function that changes the default colors on the page (background, text, and links) when the visitor clicks a button; and we'll turn that function into a behavior so that Dreamweaver users can easily insert the function into their documents.

Creating the Set Page Properties Behavior

To create this behavior, you'll again start by creating and testing the JavaScript code the behavior should insert. Then you'll build the behavior file, design and implement a form to collect user input, and add various other bells and whistles.

Task 1: Write the JavaScript function and function call to be inserted

As usual, start by creating the JavaScript code (function and function call) that the behavior should insert. Do this in a test file, with your aim being to create a working script that meets the Dreamweaver requirements for behavior structuring. It must be in the form of a function and function call, and the function ideally should be as generic as possible so that changes in the function call can create a variety of different effects from the same function. (This is because, in Dreamweaver behaviors, only the function call can be customized by the user. The user will have no opportunity to alter the function call.)

1. In your text editor or in Dreamweaver, create a new HTML file, containing the basic HTML framework code. Because this is a test file (not an extension file), save it in your Working folder. Call it **property_test.htm**.
2. Change the `<title>` to **Set Page Properties Test**.
3. In the new document's `<body>` section, enter the text **`Click here to change properties`**. Link the words `Click here` to the pound sign (#). Figure 3.15 shows what the document should look like at this point.

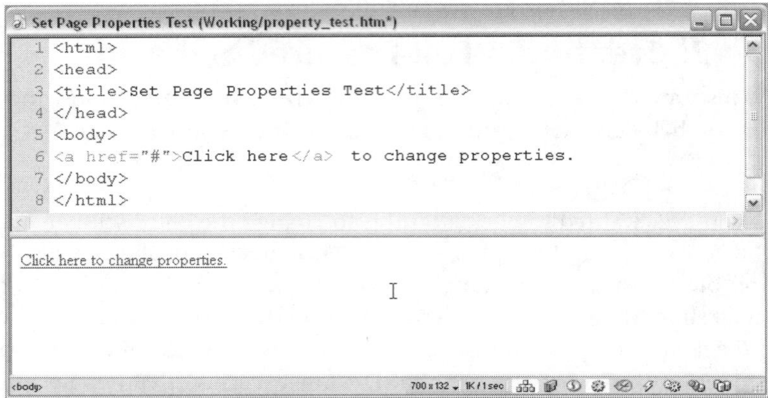

FIGURE 3.15 *The property_test.htm file, with text link in place.*

4. Add a `<script>` tag to the document `<head>`. Inside this tag, enter a JavaScript function that will change several page properties to predetermined values:

```
<script language ="JavaScript">
function setProperties() {
document.bgColor="black";
document.fgColor="white";
document.linkColor="red";
document.vlinkColor="green";
document.alinkColor="blue";
}
</script>
```

When this function is executed, it will change the page background to black, the page text to white, links to red, visited links to green, and active links to blue. Because these specific colors are being built into the function, black/white/red/green/blue is the only color scheme this function will ever be able to perform. It's not yet a flexible function.

note

In the interests of easy typing, color names have been used here. The function works equally well when hexadecimal values are specified for the colors, for example, `document.bgColor= "#000000"`.

5. Now add a function call to the text link, triggering the `setProperties()` function. Your code for the text link should look like this (new code is in bold):

```
<a href="#" onClick="setProperties()">Click here</a> to change
properties.
```

6. After both the function and its function call are in place, try the page out in a browser. Clicking the link should turn the page background black, the non-linked text white, and the linked text bright red. If necessary, troubleshoot until the code works properly before proceeding.

7. So, there you go! You got the code to work. But it's not yet suitable to become a Dreamweaver behavior, because it's not yet generic. Remember, a function in a behavior must be generic; the user won't be able to change anything about it.

   To fix this, revise the `setProperties()` function so that it uses a set of parameters to determine what colors it will create in the document. Like this (new code is in bold):

```
function setProperties(bg,fg,links,vlinks,alinks) {
document.bgColor=bg;
document.fgColor=fg;
document.linkColor=links;
document.vlinkColor=vlinks;
document.alinkColor=alinks;
}
```

   Each color to be set is now being passed into the function. The statements in the function now set the page properties based on externally specified colors.

8. Now revise the function call so that it passes a series of color choices to the function (new code is in bold):

```
<a href="#"
onClick="setProperties('black','white','red','green','blue')">Click
here</a> to change properties.
```

   Now the code is getting flexible. After this function and function call are turned into a Dreamweaver behavior, a dialog box can be used to collect color choices from the user, and those colors can be passed to the function.

   Before proceeding any further, try the page in your browser to make sure your revised code works. If it doesn't, troubleshoot until it does. (Tip: Make sure the parameter names specified in line 1 of the function exactly match the names that appear in subsequent lines. And watch the quotes and commas in the function call!)

9. How about adding one more bit of flexibility? The way the function is currently written, it must set all five default page colors every time it is executed. A truly flexible function would be ready to set one, two, or all five colors when executed, depending on how many parameters are passed from the function call.

The trick to adding this flexibility is to make each statement within the function a conditional (if-statement) that will execute only if the relevant parameter has been specified. Add the following code to the `setProperties()` function (new code is in bold):

```
function setProperties(bg,fg,links,vlinks,alinks) {
if (bg) {
   document.bgColor=bg;
   }
if (fg) {
   document.fgColor=fg;
   }
if (links) {
   document.linkColor=links;
   }
if (vlinks) {
   document.vlinkColor=vlinks;
   }
if (alinks) {
   document.alinkColor=alinks;
   }
}
```

If any particular parameter has been left out of the function call, that property won't be set. Now, that's a flexible function!

10. To take the function through its paces, try it with a variety of function calls. First, try the page out in a browser using the function call that's already in place. If you entered the revised function code correctly, clicking the text link should have the same effect it had before you changed the function. Because your function call currently specifies all five parameters, all five conditional statements should execute, and all of the page's colors should change.

11. After you know the function is working properly, experiment a bit with the function call. Change the text link by removing all values from the function call, leaving only empty quote marks in their place.

```
<a href="#" onClick="setProperties('','','','','')">Click here</a> to
change properties.
```

Be careful, as you're deleting, to leave the quotes and commas in place, and not to add any extra spaces. After you've done that, try the page in a browser again. If you deleted correctly, you shouldn't get any JavaScript error messages—but of course, the page properties won't change because none of the function's conditional statements execute.

12. Finally, try adding just a few parameters—maybe text and link color only, like this (new code is in bold):

    ```
    <a href="#" onClick="setProperties('','orange','green','','')">Click
    ➥here</a> to change properties.
    ```

    This function call changes the text and link colors by including the second and third parameters. (Check the function definition to remind yourself what order the parameters must be specified in.) Try it out in a browser. Assuming you typed your new color names between the correct quotes, clicking the link will change the non-linked text orange and the linked text aqua.

    Can you see how rewriting the function to include conditionals has made it more flexible? Depending on the parameters included in the function call, some or all of the page properties can be changed. Now this function is ready to be turned into a decently flexible behavior. Listing 3.3 shows what the final property_test.htm file should look like.

Listing 3.3 The Finished Code for the *setProperties( )* Function and its Function Call, Ready to Be Made into a Behavior

```
<html>
<head>
<title>Set Page Properties Test</title>
<script language="JavaScript">
function setProperties(bg,fg,links,vlinks,alinks) {
if (bg) {
   document.bgColor=bg;
   }
if (fg) {
   document.fgColor=fg;
   }
if (links) {
   document.linkColor=links;
   }
if (vlinks) {
   document.vlinkColor=vlinks;
   }
if (alinks) {
   document.alinkColor=alinks;
   }
}
</script>
<body>
<a href="#" onClick="setProperties('','orange','green','','')">Click
➥here</a> to change properties.
</body>
</html>
```

Task 2: Put the code into a basic behavior file framework

When you know what JavaScript code you want your behavior to insert, turning that code into a behavior is your next task. Keep the property_test.htm file handy as you work so that you can just copy and paste the relevant code into your behavior file.

1. In your text editor, open the My Behavior.htm framework file. Save it in your Actions/Development folder as **Set Page Properties.htm**.
2. Change the `<title>` to **Set Page Properties**.
3. Open property_test.htm (if it's not already open) and copy the `setProperties()` function. In the new behavior file, delete the `myBehavior()` function and paste the `setProperties()` function into its place.
4. Revise the `behaviorFunction()` function so that it returns the name of the new function:

```
function behaviorFunction() {
     return "setProperties";
}
```

> **note**
>
> If you want the user's document to include comments as part of the function, just add them as part of the defined function; Dreamweaver inserts your function exactly as you specify it—comments and all.

5. Revise the `applyBehavior()` function so that it returns a function call that specifies all parameters the function can set. Eventually, of course, you'll want to rewrite this function so that it processes user input; but for now, just enter a set function call. The revised `applyBehavior()` function should look like this (new code is in bold):

```
function applyBehavior() {
    return "setProperties('black','white','red','green','blue')";
}
```

At this point, the `<head>` section of your new behavior file should look like this:

```
<head>
<!-- title becomes actions menu item name -->
<title>Set Page Properties</title>
<script language="JavaScript">

//this is the function the behavior will insert into the user's document
function setProperties(bg,fg,links,vlinks,alinks) {
if (bg) {
   document.bgColor=bg;
   }
if (fg) {
   document.fgColor=fg;
   }
if (links) {
   document.linkColor=links;
```

```
      }
   if (vlinks) {
      document.vlinkColor=vlinks;
      }
   if (alinks) {
      document.alinkColor=alinks;
      }
   }
```

6. Try the behavior out before proceeding any further to make sure the basic structure works. Save and close the behavior file. Quit and relaunch Dreamweaver to make it recognize the new behavior. Create a new test file with a text link in it (something similar to the link in property_test.htm). Save the new file in your Working folder as **property_test2.htm**.

   Apply the Set Page Properties behavior to the text link. As Figure 3.16 shows, the code that the behavior inserts should be identical to the code you entered by hand in property_test.htm. It should behave identically in the browser.

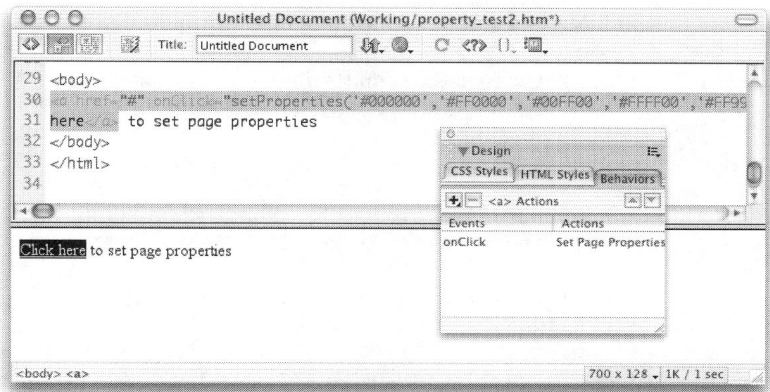

FIGURE 3.16 *The Set Page Properties behavior, being used in a Dreamweaver document.*

note

Caution: What if it doesn't work? The most common error at this point is a problem copying and pasting (or retyping) the wrong code—even missing a quote or curly brace at the end of something will cause problems. These mistakes will all cause Dreamweaver to report syntax errors. Read the error message carefully. It will point you right to the problematic line of code.

Task 3: Design and create the form to collect user input

We need to give the user opportunities to change five different properties (`bgcolor`, `fgcolor`, `link`, `vlink`, `alink`), using a color button and text field for each. Figure 3.17 shows what your completed form should look like. The code for the form looks like this:

```
<form name="myForm">
<table>
      <tr valign="baseline">
            <td align="right" nowrap>Background color:</td>
            <td align="left" nowrap>
            <input type="mmcolorbutton" name="bg_button">
            <input type="text" name="bg_label" size="10"></td></tr>
      <tr valign="baseline">
            <td align="right" nowrap>Text color:</td>
            <td align="left" nowrap>
            <input type="mmcolorbutton" name="fg_button">
            <input type="text" name="fg_label" size="10"></td></tr>
      <tr valign="baseline">
            <td align="right" nowrap>Link color:</td>
            <td align="left" nowrap>
            <input type="mmcolorbutton" name="link_button">
            <input type="text" name="link_label" size="10"></td></tr>
      <tr>
            <td align="right" nowrap>Visited link color:</td>
            <td align="left" nowrap>
            <input type="mmcolorbutton" name="vlink_button">
            <input type="text" name="vlink_label" size="10"></td></tr>
      <tr>
            <td align="right" nowrap>Active link color:</td>
            <td align="left" nowrap>
            <input type="mmcolorbutton" name="alink_button">
            <input type="text" name="alink_label" size="10"></td></tr>
</table>
</form>
```

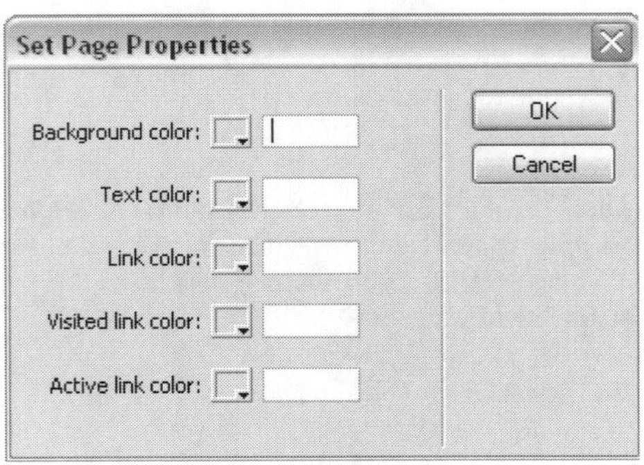

FIGURE 3.17 *The desired layout for the Page Properties behavior's dialog box.*

Task 4: Rewrite the *applyBehavior( )* function to construct the function call from user input

As in previous exercises, creating the function call is a simple matter of collecting the form information and concatenating it into variables and concatenating those variables into a return statement.

1. To collect the form information, add the following code to your `applyBehavior()` function (new code is in bold):

```
function applyBehavior() {
var bg=document.myForm.bg_button.value;
var fg=document.myForm.fg_button.value;
var links=document.myForm.link_button.value;
var vlinks=document.myForm.vlink_button.value;
var alinks=document.myForm.alink_button.value;
return "setProperties('black','white','red','green','blue')";
}
```

2. Now the hard part—rewriting the `return` statement to account for all those variables. Figure 3.18 shows a diagram of how the concatenation will work. Using that diagram as a guide, revise your `return` statement to leave holes for the variables (new code is in bold):

```
return "setProperties('"+ +"','"+ +"','"+ +"','"+ +"','"+ +"')";
```

Then fill in the variable names, like this:

```
return
"setProperties('"+bg+"','"+fg+"','"+links+"','"+vlinks+"','"+alinks+"
')";
```

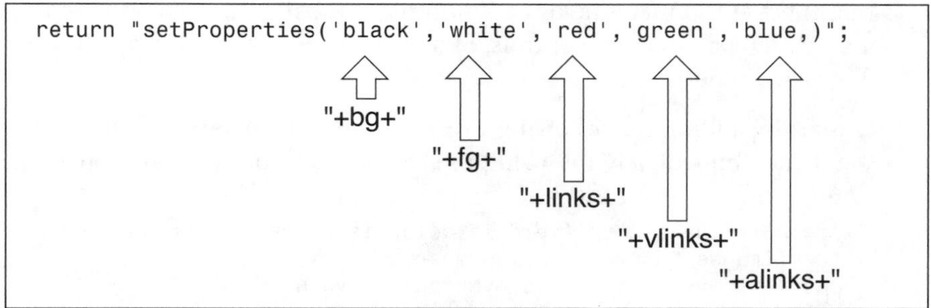

FIGURE 3.18 *Diagram showing concatenation of the* `setProperties()` *function call for the* `applyBehavior()` *function.*

Your completed `applyBehavior()` function should look like this:

```
function applyBehavior() {
var bg=document.myForm.bg_button.value;
var fg=document.myForm.fg_button.value;
var links=document.myForm.link_button.value;
var vlinks=document.myForm.vlink_button.value;
```

```
var alinks=document.myForm.alink_button.value;
return
➥"setProperties('"+bg+"','"+fg+"','"+links+"','"+vlinks+"','"+alinks+"')";
}
```

3. At this point, the behavior should be basically functional. The `behaviorFunction()` function tells Dreamweaver to insert the `setProperties()` function in the user's document; the form collects information for the function call; and the `applyBehavior()` function processes that information to construct and insert the function call.

   Try it out. In Dreamweaver, open property_test2.htm. Remove the Set Page Properties behavior from the text link and re-apply it to see the behavior in action. The dialog box will appear and should allow you to set the parameters for the behavior. It won't yet recognize color information entered into the text fields of the form yet, but colors chosen from the color buttons should work fine.

Task 5: Add local functions to make the color buttons and color text fields reciprocal

You did this in the Custom Horizontal Rule workshop (Workshop #3) in Chapter 2. You need to define a function that puts the chosen color value in a text field when the user chooses a color using the related color button—and a function that does the opposite, updating the color button if the user enters information into the related text field. Then you call each function using the `onChange` and `onBlur` event handlers attached to each form element. The only aspect of this procedure that's trickier here is that there are so many fields and buttons; you either have to write separate functions for each pair of color controls, or use parameters to specify which fields should change each other.

1. Start by adding the following two functions to the `<script>` tag in the behavior file, immediately following the closing curly brace of the `applyBehavior()` function:

```
//update the swatch field if color is chosen using the text field
function setColorButton(myNumber) {
document.myForm.elements[myNumber-1].value =
➥document.myForm.elements[myNumber].value;
}

//update the color text field if the color is chosen using the swatch
function setColorField(myNumber) {
document.myForm.elements[myNumber+1].value =
➥document.myForm.elements[myNumber].value;
}
```

How does this system of parameters work? All input elements within a form are considered to be members in an array of form elements and are assigned an array number based on the order in which they appear in the form. The first element in a form named `myForm` can be addressed as `document.myForm.elements[0]`; the second element can be addressed as `document.myForm.elements[1]`; and so on.

note

For a refresher on using JavaScript with forms and form elements, see Appendix A, "JavaScript Primer."

Because each color button in the form is followed immediately by its paired text field, if a color button's array number is 1, the array number of its text field must be 2 (1 + 1); if a text field's number is 2, the number of its related color button must be 1 (2 – 1).

Therefore, if a color button passes its own array number to the `setColorField()` function as a parameter, the function just needs to add 1 to that number to access the button's paired text field because the text field always immediately follows the button in the form. And conversely, if a text field passes its own array number to the `setColorButton()` function as a parameter, subtracting 1 from that parameter will access the field's paired color button because the related button always immediately precedes the text field in the form.

2. To see how this parameter passing works in practice, locate the first pair of color controls in the document's form (the `bg_button` and `bg_label` form input elements). Because these two elements are the first two input elements in the form, their array numbers are 0 and 1 respectively. Add the following function calls to these controls (new code is in bold):

```
<input type="mmcolorbutton" name="bg_button"
➥onChange="setColorField(0)">
<input type="text" name="bg_label" size="10"
onBlur="setColorButton(1)">
```

With this code in place, try the behavior in Dreamweaver again. The first color button/text field in the dialog box should now work. Choosing a color from the color button should update the text field, and vice versa. After you have chosen a color, clicking OK should successfully insert the `setProperties()` behavior with the first color parameter correctly set.

3. After you have the first set of color controls working correctly, you only need to add similar `onChange` and `onBlur` event handlers to the other elements in the form. Repeat the process you went through in the previous step for each of the other color buttons and text fields. You can even copy and paste the code you added in the previous step; just increment the numbers that get passed as parameters each time (new code is in bold):

note

I have not included the entire code for the form here, but I do want to show all the added code throughout the form. What I have here instead is just the selected lines, with changes shown in bold.

```
<input type="mmcolorbutton" name="bg_button"
➥onChange="setColorField(0)">
<input type="text" name="bg_label" size="10"
➥onBlur="setColorButton(1)">
...
<input type="mmcolorbutton" name="fg_button"
➥onChange="setColorField(2)">
<input type="text" name="fg_label" size="10"
➥onBlur="setColorButton(3)">
...
<input type="mmcolorbutton" name="link_button"
➥onChange="setColorField(4)">
<input type="text" name="link_label" size="10"
➥onBlur="setColorButton(5)">
...
<input type="mmcolorbutton" name="vlink_button"
➥onChange="setColorLabel(6)">
<input type="text" name="vlink_label" size="10"
➥onBlur="setColorButton(7)">
...
<input type="mmcolorbutton" name="alink_button"
➥onChange="setColorLabel(8)">
<input type="text" name="alink_label" size="10"
➥onBlur="setColorButton(9)">
```

As you can see from the code shown here, the numbers in parentheses in the function calls (the parameters) simply increase by one for each new form element.

4. When you're done, be sure to test the revised behavior in Dreamweaver. (You can use property_test2.htm for this, like you did in the previous task—just remove the existing Set Page Properties behavior from the text link and re-apply it to see the behavior in action.) Make sure that, for every pair of color controls, you can select a color in the button or enter its name in the text field and have both color controls properly respond to your change. Figure 3.19 shows the Set Page Properties dialog box with reciprocal values showing in the color controls.

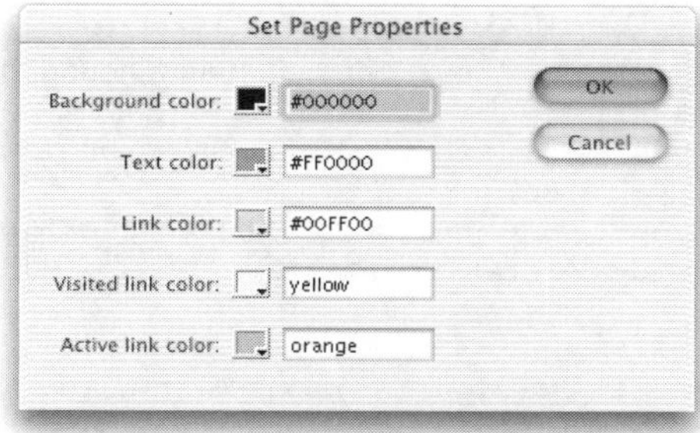

FIGURE 3.19 *The Set Page Properties dialog box, showing color fields and color buttons updated to show reciprocal values.*

Task 6: Split the code into HTML and JS files

Your code will only get more complex from here on, so now is a good time to put the JavaScript functions in their own file. Do it this way:

1. Open the behavior file in your text editor. Select all the JavaScript code between the `<script>` tags in the document head, and then Edit > Cut.
2. Create a new text file and Edit > Paste. Save the file in the Actions/Development folder. Call it **Set Page Properties.js**.
3. In the original Set Page Properties.htm file, change the `<script>` tags to link to the new JS file. Like this (new code in bold):

   ```
   <script src="Set Page Properties.js"></script>
   ```

4. Save both files. Reload extensions in Dreamweaver, and try the behavior again to make sure it still works. Listing 3.4 shows what the code for the HTML file should look like at this point. Listing 3.5 shows the code for the linked JS file.

Listing 3.4 Complete Code for Set Properties.htm, Commented for Reference

```
<html>
<head>
<!-- title becomes actions menu item name -->
<title>Set Page Properties</title>
<script src="Set Properties.js"></script>
</head>
<body>
<form name="myForm">
<table>
      <tr valign="baseline">
```

continues

Listing 3.4 Continued

```
            <td align="right" nowrap>Background color:</td>
            <td align="left" nowrap>
      <input type="mmcolorbutton" name="bg_button"
      ➥onChange="setColorField(0)">
      <input type="text" name="bg_label" size="10"
      ➥onBlur="setColorButton(1)">
</td></tr>
      <tr valign="baseline">
            <td align="right" nowrap>Text color:</td>
            <td align="left" nowrap>
            <input type="mmcolorbutton" name="fg_button"
            ➥onChange="setColorField(2)">
            <input type="text" name="fg_label" size="10"
            ➥onBlur="setColorButton(3)">
            </td>
            </tr>
      <tr valign="baseline">
            <td align="right" nowrap>Link color:</td>
            <td align="left" nowrap>
            <input type="mmcolorbutton" name="link_button"
            ➥onChange="setColorField(4)">
            <input type="text" name="link_label" size="10"
            ➥onBlur="setColorButton(5)">
            </td>
            </tr>
      <tr>
            <td align="right" nowrap>Visited link color:</td>
            <td align="left" nowrap>
            <input type="mmcolorbutton" name="vlink_button"
            ➥onChange="setColorLabel(6)">
            <input type="text" name="vlink_label" size="10"
            ➥onBlur="setColorButton(7)">
            </td>
            </tr>
      <tr>
            <td align="right" nowrap>Active link color:</td>
            <td align="left" nowrap>
            <input type="mmcolorbutton" name="alink_button"
            ➥onChange="setColorLabel(8)">
            <input type="text" name="alink_label" size="10"
            ➥onBlur="setColorButton(9)">
            </td>
            </tr>
</table>
</form>
</body>
</html>
```

Listing 3.5 Complete Code for Set Properties.js, Commented for Reference

```
//this is the function the behavior will insert into the user's document
function setProperties(bg,fg,links,vlinks,alinks) {
if (bg) {//if this parameter is specified
   document.bgColor=bg;//change this property
   }
if (fg) {
   document.fgColor=fg;
   }
if (links) {
   document.linkColor=links;
   }
if (vlinks) {
   document.vlinkColor=vlinks;
   }
if (alinks) {
   document.alinkColor=alinks;
   }
}

//this returns the name of the function to be inserted, minus its
➥parentheses
function behaviorFunction() {
    return "setProperties";
}

//this returns the function call, which will be inserted as part of the
➥user's selected object
function applyBehavior() {
//collect user input from the form
var bg=document.myForm.bg_button.value;
var fg=document.myForm.fg_button.value;
var links=document.myForm.link_button.value;
var vlinks=document.myForm.vlink_button.value;
var alinks=document.myForm.alink_button.value;
//concatenate into a text string containing a function call
return
➥"setProperties('"+bg+"','"+fg+"','"+links+"','"+vlinks+"','"+alinks+"')";
}

//update the swatch field if color is chosen using the text field
//each field passes the function its own number in the form elements
➥array
function setColorButton(myNumber) {
//the preceding form element (the color button) gets this element's
➥value
document.myForm.elements[myNumber-1].value =
➥document.myForm.elements[myNumber].value;
}
```

continues

Listing 3.5 Continued

```
//update the color text field if the color is chosen using the swatch
//each button passes the function its own number in the form elements
➥array
function setColorLabel(myNumber) {
//the next form element (the text field) gets this element's value
document.myForm.elements[myNumber+1].value =
document.myForm.elements[myNumber].value;
}
```

Inspecting Behaviors

After a user has inserted a behavior into a document, how can he edit it? By opening up the Behaviors panel and double-clicking on the behavior, which reopens the behavior's dialog box and lets him see and change all the parameters assigned to it.

Have you tried doing that with any of the behaviors you created here? It doesn't work! Double-click an existing instance of the Go Back/Forward or Set Page Properties behavior, and the dialog box reopens, but without any of the values you had previously set for it. That's because your behaviors don't have an `inspectBehavior()` function.

The *inspectBehavior( )* Function and How it Works

The purpose of this function is to fill in the form elements of the behavior's dialog box based on the parameters Dreamweaver finds in the document's inserted function call. It works like this: Whenever the user double-clicks a behavior in the Behaviors panel, Dreamweaver looks in the appropriate behavior file for the `inspectBehavior()` function and executes that function, automatically passing the inserted function call to it as a text string. It's your job to script the `inspectBehavior()` function so that it parses that text string to extract the various parameters, and tells Dreamweaver which pieces of information should go into which form fields. Not an impossible job, or even that difficult—but it can be very, very fiddly.

Inspecting Behaviors: Practice Session

To see how the inspection process works, create a very simple practice file and do some inspecting.

Task 1: Create a practice file

The first task is to create a practice file with a passed parameter, and test it.

1. In your text editor, open My Behavior.htm. Save a copy of it as **My New Behavior.htm** in the Actions/Development folder. So that neither Dreamweaver nor you get confused between the two My Behaviors, also change the `<title>` to **My New Behavior**, and change the defined function name to **`newBehavior()`**. (You'll need to change references to the defined function in the `behaviorFunction()` and `applyBehavior()` functions as well.)
2. If you remember, the script inserted by this behavior causes an alert window to open when the function is called. Change the behavior so that Dreamweaver asks the user what message the window should hold; this information should be passed to `newBehavior()` as part of the function call. This will require adding a form to the `<body>` and changing the `applyBehavior()` function so that it constructs the function call based on user input. Listing 3.6 shows the code for the revised behavior file.

Listing 3.6 The Code for My New Behavior.htm, before Inspection Functions Have Been Added

```
<html>
<head>
<title>My New Behavior</title>
<script language="JavaScript">
function newBehavior(myParameter) {
  alert(myParameter)
}
function behaviorFunction() {
  return "newBehavior";
}
function applyBehavior() {
  var message = document.myForm.messageField.value;
  return "newBehavior('"+message+"')";
}
</script>
</head>
<body>
<form name="myForm">
<table>
  <tr>
    <td><input type="text" name="messageField"></td>
  </tr>
</table>
</form>
</body>
</html>
```

3. Try the behavior out in Dreamweaver to see how it works—and how it doesn't work. (Don't forget, you'll have to quit and relaunch Dreamweaver to make it recognize the new behavior.) Create a test document with a simple text link and add the behavior to that link (just like you did when testing My Behavior earlier in this chapter). A dialog box should appear, asking for a message. Enter a message and click OK to close the dialog box.
4. Preview the page in a browser. Clicking the text link opens an alert window containing your custom message.
5. Now go back to Dreamweaver and try to edit the behavior by double-clicking its entry in the Behaviors panel. The dialog box reopens, but with no message in place (see Figure 3.20).

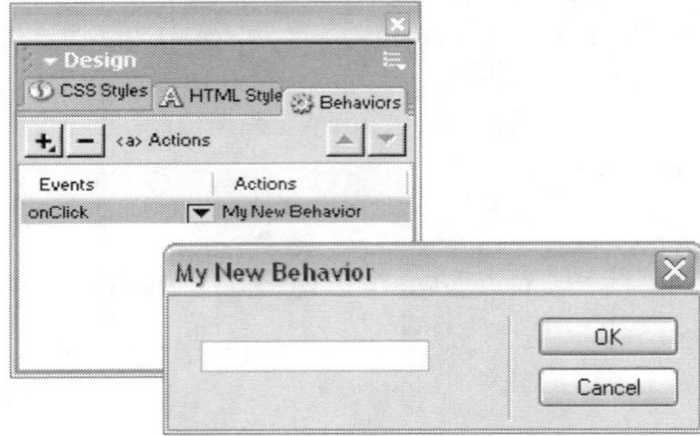

FIGURE 3.20 *Trying to inspect and edit a behavior in the Behaviors panel when there is no* `inspectBehavior()` *function defined.*

Task 2: Add the *inspectBehavior( )* function

Now add the `inspectBehavior()` function and test it to ensure that it works properly.

1. In your text editor, add the framework code for the `inspectBehavior()` function to the `<script>` tag of your behavior file. It should look like this:

```
function inspectBehavior(fnCall) {
//collect information from fnCall
//put information into form fields
}
```

   The `fnCall` parameter is what Dreamweaver automatically passes to `inspectBehavior()` when it's called, as part of the API procedure. This parameter holds a text string that will look something like this:

```
"newBehavior('Hello world!')"
```

In the body of inspectBehavior(), you need to pull out the relevant portion of that passed string and use it to refill your dialog box field.

2. Because the fnCall parameter is a text string, you can do this by using the substring method. The substring method requires that you know the first and last character of the substring you want to remove from the main string, which you should be able to figure out by counting characters: The function call string will always begin with newBehavior(', which is thirteen characters, and the message will always start after that—so you want your substring to begin at the fourteenth character. You don't know how many characters the substring itself will contain (because you can't know what messages the user will enter into the dialog box each time he inserts the behavior). But you do know that the function call will always end with '), which is two letters long—so the last letter of the substring will always be the third character from the end. With this knowledge, you can add a variable to your function that collects the proper information, like this (new code is in bold):

```
function inspectBehavior(fnCall) {
//collect information from fnCall
var myMessage=fnCall.substring(13,fnCall.length-2);
//put information into form fields
}
```

(If you're wondering why you didn't enter 14 as the starting number, remember that computers always count from 0, not 1, so the fourteenth character is character 13.)

3. After you have collected the message in a variable, you just need to feed this information into the proper field in the form, which in this case is a text field named messageField. So you add one more line to your function (new code is in bold):

```
function inspectBehavior(fnCall) {
//collect information from fnCall
var myMessage=fnCall.substring(12,fnCall.length-2);
//put information into form fields
document.myForm.messageField.value=myMessage;
}
```

4. After you enter this code, reload extensions in Dreamweaver and try again to edit the behavior. As long as your character counting was accurate when you calculated your substring, double-clicking the behavior in the Behaviors panel should open a fully populated dialog box (a dialog box with your message showing in its text field). Figure 3.21 shows this happening. When the behavior's dialog box is open again, you change the contents of the message Dreamweaver goes back through the API process of calling the behaviorFunction() function and applyBehavior() function to insert the updated behavior into your document. (Refer back to the API procedure diagram in Figure 3.3 to see how this works).

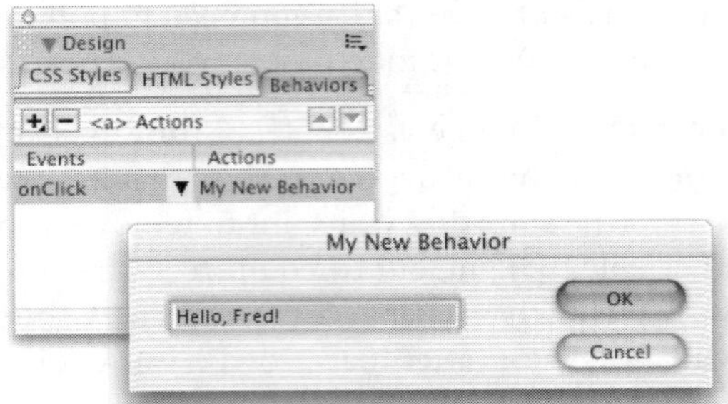

FIGURE 3.21 *Inspecting and editing a behavior in the Behaviors panel after the* `inspectBehavior()` *function has been defined.*

Using the Shared Files to Help Inspect Behaviors

What's wrong with this picture? Nothing, as long as all your function calls are as simple as the one in your practice file. But when you get calls with multiple parameters, character counting isn't efficient. You need to set up loops that can break text strings down into substrings separated by delimiters like commas and quotation marks, and your scripting life just gets a lot more complicated.

Luckily for you, the Macromedia software engineers have already been here and done that. They've solved this problem for you. Dreamweaver ships with a collection of JS files that contain utility scripts for a variety of purposes. All of the standard behaviors that ship with the program use these scripts for tedious tasks such as refilling dialog boxes. None of them is part of the API, but you can use them just as you have been using your own local functions, simply by linking to the relevant JS file.

Finding and Examining dwscripts.js

The most commonly used shared files are stored in the Configuration folder, in the Shared/Common/Scripts folder. The most generally useful shared file is dwscripts.js. This file defines a new object class called `dwscripts`. The methods of `dwscripts` include functions for performing many common extension-writing tasks.

Find dwscripts.js, and open it in your text editor. It's a good idea to see what's in there that you might want to use in future extension projects.

The *dwscripts.extractArgs( )* Methods

The key to happy behavior inspecting is the `dwscripts.extractArgs()` method. This method loops through a text string, pulling out substrings and assigning them to slots in an array. Assuming you pass it a function call as the string to be parsed, the first substring it pulls out is always the function call itself, the next substring is the first parameter that was included in the function call, the following substring is the second parameter, and so on.

Linking to dwscripts.js

Before you can take advantage of `dwscripts.extractArgs()`, you need to link to the shared file. Do this by adding another `<script>` tag to the head section of your behavior file, including a relative path to dwscripts.js, like this:

```
<script src="../../../Shared/Common/Scripts/dwscripts.js"></script>
```

This code shows the relative address to dwscripts.js from a file within Behaviors/Actions/Development. If your behavior is not stored in a subfolder within the Actions folder, you need to amend the address accordingly.

note

Remember the rules of relative addressing! A relative address describes the path from one file to another, navigating the hierarchy of the folder structure as it goes. If the two files are in different folders, the path must move up the hierarchy until it reaches a common parent folder before it can move down the hierarchy into the other folder. In writing the path, the characters `../` indicate moving up one folder. When linking from an extension file to a shared file like string.js, the common parent folder is usually the Configuration folder itself. How many folder levels must you traverse up the hierarchy from your extension file to the Configuration folder? That's the number of `../` elements your relative address must include.

The *inspectBehavior( )* Function, Using *dwscripts.extractArgs()*

With the help of `dwscripts.extractArgs()`, you can now revisit `inspectBehavior()` and create a simple script for repopulating (re-filling) the dialog box. All you need to do is revise the `inspectBehavior()` function so that it calls `dwscripts.extractArgs()`, passing the `fnCall` parameter as a string, and feed the results to a new array. Then access the array, one item at a time, assigning each item to a field in your form. Here's how the code would look for the My New Behavior file you practiced on (new code is in bold):

```
function inspectBehavior(fnCall) {
var argArray = new Array;
argArray = dwscripts.extractArgs(functionCall);
document.myForm.messageField.value = argArray[1];
}
```

note

Warning

Anxious to try this out in the My Behavior 2.html practice file? Here's a word of warning: You may have trouble getting Dreamweaver to recognize the linked JS file, unless you first split your code into My Behavior 2.html and My Behavior 2.js.

Workshop #3: Inspecting the Set Properties Behavior

Now that you know all about inspecting behaviors, you can add that functionality to your Set Page Properties behavior.

Task 1: Link to dwscripts.js

In your text editor, open Set Page Properties.htm. You should already have a `<script>` tag in the head section, linking to Set Page Properties.js. Now add another one, like this (new code is in bold):

```
<script src="Set Page Properties.js"></script>
<script src="../../../Shared/Common/Scripts/dwscripts.js"></script>
```

With this code in place, save the file and close it.

Task 2: Add the *inspectBehavior( )* function

Now that the main behavior file has been linked to string.js, your behavior has access to `dwscripts.extractArgs()`. This includes your JS file, Set Page Properties.js.

1. Open Set Page Properties.js. Add the framework code for the `inspectBehavior()` function to the bottom of the file, using `dwscripts.extractArgs()`:

   ```
   function inspectBehavior(fnCall) {
   var argArray = new Array;
   argArray = dwscripts.extractArgs(fnCall);
   }
   ```

   Remember, the `fnCall` parameter will be passed to this function automatically. For the Set Page Properties behavior, that function call will be a string that looks something like this:

   ```
   setProperties('black','white','red,'green','blue');
   ```

By putting the code shown here into the `inspectBehavior()` function, you're passing this text string to `dwscripts.extractArgs()`. What you'll get back is an array of values, which you're collecting into `argArray`. The elements of `argArray` will look something like this:

```
argArray[0] = setProperties
argArray[1] = 'black'
argArray[2] = 'white'
argArray[3] = 'red'
argArray[4] = 'green'
argArray[5] = 'blue'
```

2. After you have `argArray` at your disposal, the hard work of inspecting this behavior is done! All that remains is feeding the right array element into the right form field. Remember the order in which you told the `setProperties()` function to collect its parameters when you defined it:

```
function setProperties(bg,fg,links,vlinks,alinks)
```

For your function call, then, `argArray[1]` is `bg`, `argArray[2]` is `fg`, and so forth. Therefore, you can add the following lines to your function to finish it off (new code is in bold):

```
function inspectBehavior(fnCall) {
var argArray = new Array;
argArray = dwscripts.extractArgs(fnCall);
document.myForm.bg_button.value = argArray[1];
document.myForm.bg_label.value = argArray[1];
document.myForm.fg_button.value = argArray[2];
document.myForm.fg_label.value = argArray[2];
document.myForm.link_button.value = argArray[3];
document.myForm.link_label.value = argArray[3];
document.myForm.vlink_button.value = argArray[4];
document.myForm.vlink_label.value = argArray[4];
document.myForm.alink_button.value = argArray[5];
document.myForm.alink_label.value = argArray[5];
}
```

(Note that because you had a color button and a color text field, each representing the same color property, each argument is being fed into two fields.)

3. Try it out. In Dreamweaver, reload extensions. Then open your test file, property_test2.htm. Select the text link so that the Set Page Properties behavior appears in the Behaviors panel. Double-click the behavior to open its dialog box.

   If your code is all entered correctly, the dialog box will open with form fields filled in. If you have any problems with your code, either the information won't appear properly or Dreamweaver will report a JavaScript error. Troubleshoot until it works.

note

What if it doesn't work? You know the drill. Check for typing mistakes. Read any error messages carefully. The most common problem in a big script like this (aside from good old typos) is incorrect references to form fields and variables. Make sure you haven't started calling something in your script by a name that doesn't exist.

Summary

Now you know how to create behaviors. If you've been working your way through the exercises in the last two chapters, you're also getting pretty familiar with the idea of API requirements and procedures, and the whole concept of authoring and testing extension code. And if you've been thinking about all the different ways you want to extend Dreamweaver, you may be chomping at the bit when you realize how much you don't know, and how much you can't do with just what you have learned so far. You can't create custom inspectors for the custom objects you made; you can't insert JavaScripts in any formation other than function/function call; you can't do anything that involves examining and altering existing user code—all you can do so far is insert new user code.

All that is about to change. Put your propeller hats on, fasten your seatbelts, and get ready to learn all about the Document Object Model (DOM) and what you can do with it.

Part II

Commands, Inspectors, Floating Panels: Working with the DOM

4 The Dreamweaver DOM 101

5 Creating Custom Commands and Menu Commands 135

6 Creating Custom Property Inspectors 229

7 Creating Custom Floating Panels 273

8 Mixing Extension Types 311

9 Server Behaviors 333

10 Into the Great Beyond 363

CHAPTER 4

The Dreamweaver DOM

Objects and behaviors are the simplest kinds of extensions to create because their main purpose is to insert new code into a user's document, not to interact with code that's already there. But the real power of Dreamweaver extensibility is just that—the capability to interact with, examine, and modify existing code. In order to do that, we have to learn how to navigate and manipulate the Dreamweaver DOM.

What Is a DOM?

DOM is an acronym for Document Object Model. If you're an experienced JavaScripter, and especially if you've worked with coding for Dynamic HTML, you're probably already familiar with using the DOM to script web pages for browser display. If you're not familiar with the DOM, you soon will be! Let's start with a little fundamental information.

The DOM in JavaScript

The DOM in JavaScript is a description of the hierarchy of the scriptable objects in an HTML document. Using the DOM, we can write scripts that access and manipulate specific elements on a page. For example, the following expression

```
document.myForm.username.value
```

accesses the value property of a form input object (named `username`), which is part of a form object (named `myForm`), which is part of the document. The document object contains one or more form objects, which in turn contain various input objects, and so forth. We could also access the value of that particular object by referring to the following, assuming that the object is the fourth input element in the document's first form:

```
document.forms[0].elements[3].value
```

As with all computer languages, JavaScript has developed over time. The first incarnation of the DOM, called the Level 0 DOM or Netscape Navigator DOM, contains the basic hierarchical structures listed in the previous examples and is used by older versions of JavaScript and is supported by older browsers. Figure 4.1 shows part of the Level 0 DOM. Figure 4.2 shows a sample of how this structure would be implemented in a simple document. All page elements that are defined as objects in this model (images, forms, form elements) can be controlled by scripting.

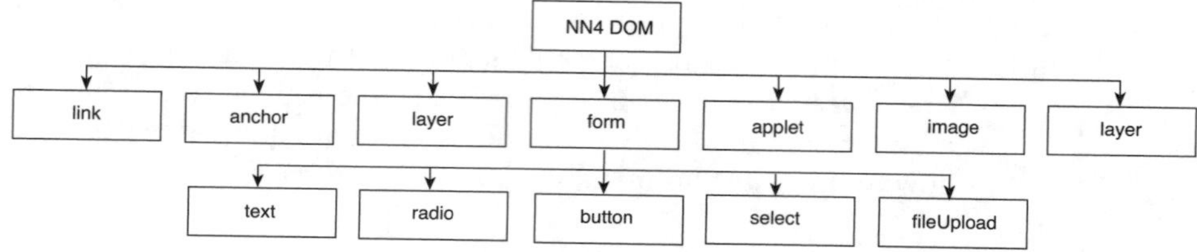

FIGURE 4.1 *The Level 0 (Netscape) DOM structure.*

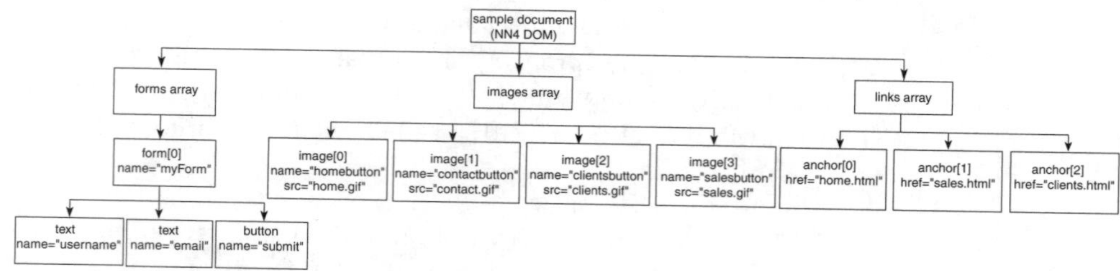

FIGURE 4.2 *Chart showing the DOM structure of a simple document.*

The Level 0 DOM is widely supported by browsers and is considered a standard in JavaScripting. A more extensive version of the DOM, called Level 1, is currently being developed by the World Wide Web Consortium (W3C), although the browsers' lack of consistent support makes it impossible to call the Level 1 DOM a standard. The Level 1 DOM attempts to define every element of an HTML document as an object, and thus opens the entire page to scripting control. (This is an important cornerstone of DHTML.)

The Dreamweaver DOM

The DOM used by Dreamweaver to access user documents is based on a subset of the Level 0 DOM (see Table 4.1 for a list of supported elements and their specifications). But Dreamweaver also includes extensive use of Level 1 DOM scriptability. Thus, Dreamweaver JavaScript-based extensions can gain access to all aspects of users' documents for editing purposes. (The wonderful thing about writing JavaScript for Dreamweaver is that you can take advantage of Level 1 DOM scriptability without worrying about browser compatibility—because no browser will ever see the scripts you create.) To work with this level of control in your extensions, you first need to learn how Dreamweaver implements the Level 1 DOM.

Table 4.1 Level 0 (Netscape) DOM Specifications, As Implemented in Dreamweaver

Object	*Properties (* indicates read-only)*	*Methods*	*Events*

window	document*
	navigator*
	innerWidth*
	innerHeight*
	screenX*
	screenY*
		`alert()`
		`confirm()`
		`escape()`
		`unescape()`
		`close()`
		`setTimeout()`
		clearTimeout( )
		setInterval( )
		clearInterval( )
		resizeTo( )
			`onResize`

navigator	platform*	(none)	(none)
document	forms* [array] images* [array] layers* [array] child objects by name* nodeType* parentNode* childNodes* documentElement* body* URL* parentWindow*	`getElementsByTagName()` `hasChildNodes()`	`onLoad`

continues

Table 4.1 Continued

Object	*Properties (* indicates read-only)*	*Methods*	*Events*

all tags (HTML elements)	nodeType*
	parentNode*
	childNodes*
	tagName*
	attributes by name
	innerHTML
	outerHTML
		`getAttribute()`
		`setAttribute()`
		`removeAttribute()`
		`getElementsByTagName()`
		`hasChildNodes()`
			(none)

form	(In addition to properties available to all tags) elements* [array] mmcolorbutton child objects by name*	(Only those available to all tags)	(none)
layer	(In addition to properties available to all tags) visibility left top width height z-index	(Only those available to all tags)	(none)

image	(In addition to properties available to all tags)
	src
		(Only those available to all tags)	`onMouseOver`
			`onMouseOut`
			`onMouseDown`
			`onMouseUp`
			`onClick`

button
reset
submit
	(In addition to properties available to all tags)
	form*
		(In addition to methods available to all tags)
		`blur()`
		`focus()`
			`onClick`

Object	*Properties (* indicates read-only)*	*Methods*	*Events*

checkbox
radio
	(In addition to properties available to all tags)
	checked
	form*
		(In addintion to metods available to all tags)
		`blur()`
		`focus()`
			`onClick`

password
text
file
hidden
image (field)
textarea
	(In addition to properties available to all tags)
	form*
	value
		(In addition to methods available to all tags)
		`blur()`
		`focus()`
		`select()`
			`onBlur`
			`onFocus`

select	(In addition to properties available to all tags) form* options* [array] selectedIndex	(In addition to methods available to all tags) `blur()` [Windows only] `focus()` [Windows only]	`onChange` `onFocus` [Windows only]
option	(In addition to properties available to all tags) text	(Only those methods available to all tags)	(none)
mmcolorbutton	(In addition to properties available to all tags) name value	(none)	`onChange`
array Boolean date function math	(matches NN4)	(matches NN4)	(none)

continues

Table 4.1 Continued

Object	*Properties (* indicates read-only)*	*Methods*	*Events*
number object string regexp			
text	nodeType* parentNode* childNodes* data	`hasChildNodes()`	(none)
comment	nodeType* parentNode* childNodes* data	`hasChildNodes()`	(none)
nodeList	length*	`item()`	(none)
Named NodeMap	length*	`item()`	(none)
mm:treecontrol	name size multiple style noheaders		
mm:treecolumn	name value width align state		
mm:treenode	name value state selected icon		

note

All specifications for Dreamweaver implementation of the DOM are taken from the *Extending Dreamweaver* manual. See that reference for more detail, if necessary. (See the Introduction for more on this manual.)

DOM Basics

The Level 1 DOM introduces the concept of nodes to describe the content on a page. Every element on the page, every object, is an instance of a node. Each page element returns, among its various properties, a `nodeType` property that tells what kind of node, or object, it is (and, therefore, what kinds of methods and properties it has). There are four node types: document, element, comment, and text. The following sections take a look at each of these in detail.

Document (DOCUMENT_NODE)

This type of node contains the document itself. Therefore, every document has exactly one instance of this node type, and this instance is at the top of the document hierarchy, containing all the other page elements. Table 4.2 and Table 4.3 show the properties and methods of document node objects.

Table 4.2 Properties for DOCUMENT_NODE Objects

Property Name	*Return Value*	*Description/Notes*
`nodeType`	`9`	(read only)
`parentNode`	`null`	(read only) The document is at the top of the hierarchy, and therefore has no parent.
`parentWindow`	An object representing the document's parent window	(read only)
`childNodes`	A `NodeList` containing all children (see Table 4.1 for properties of `NodeList`)	(read only) The document usually has only one child, the `<HTML>` tag element.
`documentElement`	The <HTML> tag element	(read only) Using this property is a shorthand method for calling the `<HTML>` tag element.
`body`	The `<BODY>` tag element	Using this property is a shorthand method for calling the `<BODY>` tag element.

continues

Table 4.2 Continued

Property Name	Return Value	Description/Notes
URL	The absolute address of the document	Working within Dreamweaver, this will return an address beginning with the `"file://"` protocol. If a document hasn't been saved, it will return an empty string.

Table 4.3 Methods for DOCUMENT_NODE Objects

Method Name	Return Value	Description/Notes
`getElementsByTagName(tagName)`	A `NodeList containing` all instances of a certain HTML tag	This list can be stepped through to access a particular tag instance in the document.
`hasChildNodes()`	`true`	This method always returns a Boolean, and the document always has children; so it will always return `true`.

HTML Elements (ELEMENT_NODE)

All HTML elements in the document—all HTML tags, in other words—are instances of this node type. The hierarchical nesting structure of HTML tags translates into `parentNode/childNode` relationships so that a `<table>` element is the parent of all `<tr>` elements it contains, and those in turn are parents of all `<td>` tags they contain. The `<html>` element itself exists at the top of this hierarchy. The `<html>` object is the parent of all tags within it and is the child of the document object. Table 4.4 and Table 4.5 show the properties and methods of element node objects.

Table 4.4 Properties for ELEMENT_NODE Objects

Property Name	Return Value	Description/Notes
`nodeType`	1	(read only)
`parentNode`	The `parent tag`	(read only) For the `<HTML>` tag object, this property returns the document object.

`childNodes`	A `NodeList` containing all immediate children (see Table 4.1 for properties of `NodeList`)	(read only) Any HTML tag completely contained within the opening and closing tags of the current element will be considered its child; text and comment objects can also be children of HTML elements.
`tagName`	The HTML name for the tag (`TABLE`, `A`, `IMG`, and so forth)	(read only) This property always returns its value in uppercase.
`attrName`	A string containing the value of the specified tag attribute	This property can't be used if the string it will return is a reserved word, such as `class`.
`innerHTML`	A string consisting of the HTML code contained within the opening and closing tags of the element	(none)
`outerHTML`	A string consisting of the HTML code contained within the tag, and the opening and closing tags	(none)

Table 4.5 Methods for ELEMENT_NODE Objects

Method Name	*Return Value*	*Description/Notes*
`getAttribute(attrName)`	The value of the `attrName` attribute	If the element doesn't include the `attrName` attribute, the method returns `null`.
`getTranslatedAttribute (attrName)`	The translated value of the `attrName` attribute	
`setAttribute(attrName, attrValue)`	(none)	Sets the specified attribute to the specified value.
`removeAttribute (attrName)`	(none)	Removes the specified attribute.
`getElementsByTagName (tagName)`	A `NodeList` of children of the current element that are of the `tagName` specified in the method's parameters	This `NodeList` can be stepped through to access individual members.
`hasChildNodes()`	`true/false`	
`hasTranslatedAttributes()`	`true/false`	

HTML Comments (COMMENT_NODE)

Any chunk of text enclosed in comment tags (`<!-- -->`) is an instance of the comment node type. Comments never have children; they are the children of whatever HTML tag they are within. Tables 4.6 and 4.7 show the properties and methods of comment node objects.

Table 4.6 Properties for COMMENT_NODE Objects

Property Name	*Return Value*	*Description/Notes*
`nodeType`	`8`	(read only)
`parentNode`	The `parent` tag	(read only)
`childNodes`	An empty `NodeList`	(read only) Comment objects have no children.
`data`	The string of text between the opening and closing comment tags	

Table 4.7 Method for COMMENT_NODE Objects

Method Name	*Return Value*	*Description/Notes*
`hasChildNodes()`	`false`	Comment objects have no children.

Text Objects (TEXT_NODE)

Any piece of text that is not part of an HTML tag or comment is a text object, an instance of the text node type. Text objects are essentially strings for scripting purposes. A text object never has children; its parent is the HTML tag that encloses it. Table 4.8 and Table 4.9 show the properties and methods of text node objects.

Table 4.8 Properties for TEXT_NODE Objects

Property Name	*Return Value*	*Description/Notes*
`nodeType`	`3`	(read only)
`parentNode`	The parent tag	(read only)
`childNodes`	An empty `NodeList` (see Table 4.4.1 for properties of `NodeList`)	(read only) Text objects have no children.
`data`	The string of text that comprises the current text object	

Table 4.9 Method for TEXT_NODE Objects

Method Name	*Return Value*	*Description*
`hasChildNodes()`	`false`	Text objects have no children.

Nodes and Document Structure

Confused yet? The concepts become clearer after you see them in action, so take a look at them that way. Figure 4.3 shows a fairly simple web page as it might look in Dreamweaver visual editing mode. Figure 4.4 shows a diagrammatic breakdown of the object structure behind this page. You can see that each page element is a parent, child, and/or sibling of another page element, although there is a mixture of node types throughout the hierarchy.

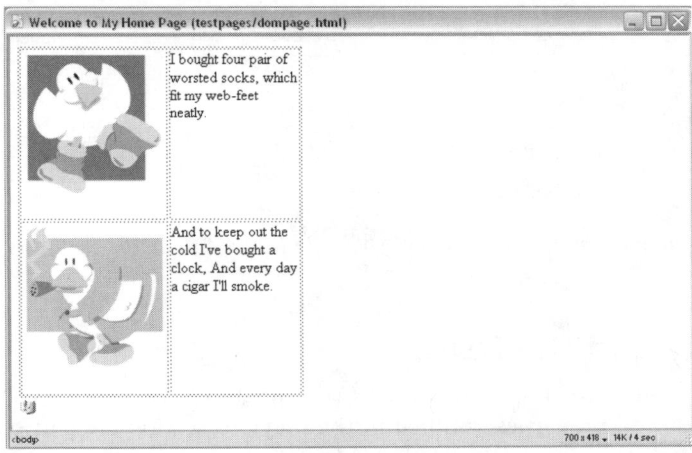

Figure 4.3 *A simple HTML document, as seen in Dreamweaver Design view.*

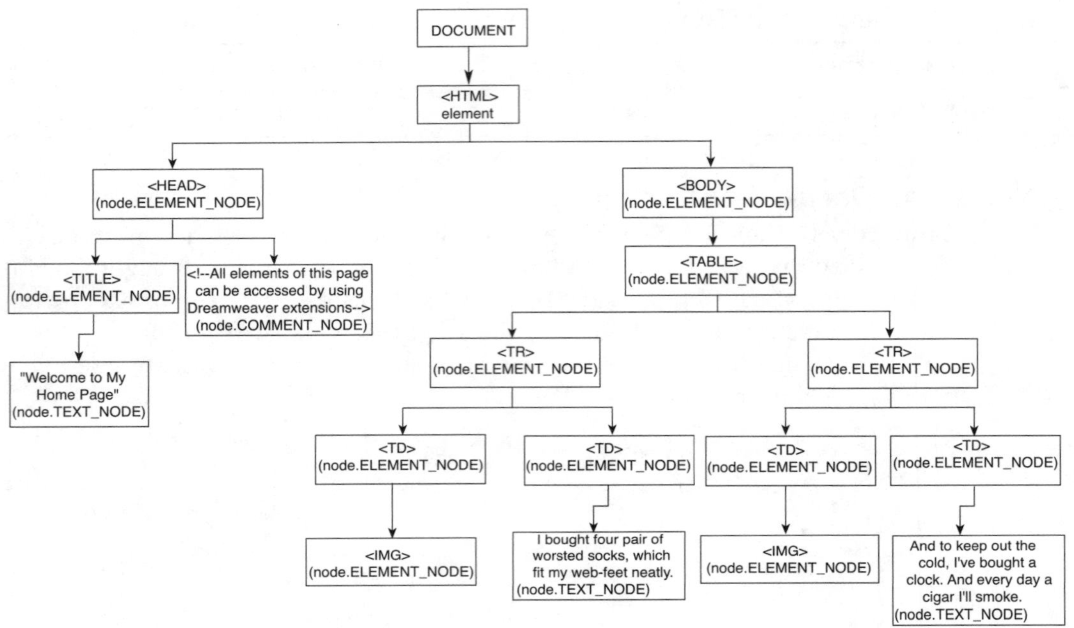

FIGURE 4.4 *Diagram of the HTML document shown in Figure 4.3.*

Extensibility and the DOM

So far, what we've described of the DOM's functionality is fairly generic—most of the methods and properties outlined in the previous section are part of the W3C's proposed standard for the Level 1 DOM. (The *Extending Dreamweaver* manual details which items are non-standard.) How do we employ all this scripting power to write Dreamweaver extensions?

DOM Object

In the discussion of the Dreamweaver Application Programming Interface (API) in Chapter 1, "Dreamweaver Configuration and the API," we saw that the API includes a number of custom objects. One of those objects is the DOM for the user's current document. This object contains many crucial methods and properties for working with user documents.

Accessing the DOM Object

Before the DOM object's methods and properties can be used, we must officially access the target document's DOM. We do this by calling another function—`dw.getDocumentDOM()`—to give the DOM object a name and open it to scripting control. In scripting terms, we call this instantiating the DOM object. The syntax for the instantiation statement looks like this:

```
var myDOM = dw.getDocumentDOM();
```

Any references to DOM object methods or properties for the current document can then access the DOM object by referring to its name, like this:

```
myDOM.setSelection();
myDOM.pageUp();
```

And so forth. In general, DOM objects can only be named for open documents; although if there are multiple open documents (as when working with frames, for instance), multiple DOM objects can exist. Table 4.10 lists the specifications of the `dw.getDocumentDOM()` function.

Table 4.10 Specifications for *dw.getDocumentDOM()*

Specification	*Details*
Syntax	`dw.getDocumentDOM() dreamweaver.getDocumentDOM()` (The `dreamweaver` object can be referred to as `dw` or `dreamweaver`. Throughout this book, we'll use `dw`.)
Description	This function creates a DOM object, giving access to the contents of a document's object structure.
Arguments	No arguments are required. If no arguments are present, the currently active document will be used as the source of the DOM object. Optional arguments: `"document"`, `"parent"`, `"parent.frames[number]"`, `"parent.frames['framename']"`, or a URL. (URLs must be absolute or relative to the extension file.)
Returns	The document object at the top of the DOM hierarchy (DOCUMENT_NODE type).

The DOM Object at Work

After we have our instantiated DOM object, we have access to the document's hierarchy of nodes, and we can use the hundreds of DOM object methods that are part of the Dreamweaver API. No wonder the Macromedia documentation calls this "the most important function"!

Using the DOM to Work with Objects

Using the DOM, we can gain access to all objects in the user's document. After we have access, we can make determinations about document content, change object properties, and perform other editing operations.

Use the charts shown in Table 4.1 through Table 4.9 to determine what properties of objects can be changed. Based on the listings in those charts, you should understand what these code samples can do:

```
//change the background color and default text color of the user's page
var myDOM = dw.getDocumentDOM();
myDOM.body.bgcolor = "#000000";
myDOM.body.text = "#FFFFFF";

//determine the absolute file address of the user's page
var myDOM = dw.getDocumentDOM();
var myURL = myDOM.URL;

//determine the number of elements in the document's body section
var myDOM=dw.getDocumentDOM();
var myBODY=myDOM.body;
var myCONTENTS=myBODY.childNodes.length;

//if the first item on the page is a table, change its border to "3"
var myDOM=dw.getDocumentDOM();
var myBODY=myDOM.body;
var myFIRST=myBODY.childNodes.item(0);
if (myFIRST.tagName == "TABLE") {
   myFIRST.border="3";
}
```

You also have access to the hundreds of DOM methods in the Dreamweaver API, to make working with objects easier. This book isn't long enough to list and discuss every one of those; check out the *Extending Dreamweaver* manual for that. Table 4.11 details some useful functions for working with objects in a document.

Table 4.11 General purpose API functions for working with objects

Function	*dom.insertHTML()*
Description	Inserts the specified HTML code at the insertion point.
Syntax	`dom.insertHTML('`*`code to insert goes here`*`')`
Arguments	The code to insert.
Returns	nothing

Example	`//inserts the code for a spacer image,`
	`//using relative URL`
	`myDOM = dw.getDocumentDOM();`
	`myDOM.insertHTML('<img src="shim.gif" width="10"`
	`height="10">');`

Function	*dom.insertText()*
Description	Inserts the specified text at the insertion point.
Syntax	`dom.insertText('`*`text to insert goes here`*`')`
Arguments	The text to insert.
Returns	nothing

Example	`//inserts a text string into the text portion of the document`
	`//including the proper HTML coding for the ampersand`
	`myDOM = dw.getDocumentDOM();`
	`myDOM.insertText('Hello & good-bye.');`

Function	*dom.insertObject()*
Description	Inserts the specified Dreamweaver object at the insertion point.
Syntax	`dom.insertObject(`*`objectName`*`)`
Arguments	The name of the object file (minus its filename extension) to insert.
Returns	nothing

Example	`//inserts an image object, as though it were`
	`//chosen from the Objects panel`
	`myDOM = dw.getDocumentDOM();`
	`myDOM.insertObject('Image');`

Function	*dom.wrapTag()*
Description	Wraps the specified tag around the current selection. The selection must be able to accept a tag wrapped around it without generating invalid HTML, or Dreamweaver will report an error.
Syntax	`dom.wrapTag(`*`startTag`*`)`
Arguments	The name of the tag to wrap around the selection (as it appears in its opening tag).
Returns	nothing

continues

Table 4.11 Continued

Function	*dom.wrapTag()*

Example	//if the current selection is an image,
	//wraps a link around the image tag
	myDOM = dw.getDocumentDOM();
	myObject = myDOM.getSelectedNode();
	if (myObject.nodeType == "1" && myObject.tagName == 'IMG') {
	myDOM.wrapTag('<a href="mypage.html">');
	}

Function	*dom.stripTag()*
Description	Removes the tag from around the current selection. If the tag has contents, it'll remain. If the selection contains more or less than one tag, Dreamweaver will report an error.
Syntax	dom.stripTag()
Arguments	none
Returns	nothing

Example	//if the current selection is a link,
	//the link is removed
	myDOM = dw.getDocumentDOM();
	myObject = myDOM.getSelectedNode();
	if (myObject.nodeType == "1" && myObject.tagName == 'A') {
	myDOM.stripTag();
	}

Using the DOM to Work with Selections

Working with selections is an important part of using the DOM. We may need to know what the user has selected, move the insertion point, expand or contract the current selection, or select new page elements. We may need to gain access to selected objects, or create selections from certain objects. The DOM object includes a variety of powerful functions for working with selections. These are detailed in Table 4.12 through Table 4.14.

Table 4.12 API Functions for getting information about the current selection

Function	*dom.getSelectedNode()*
Description	Gets access to the node that contains the current selection or insertion point.
Syntax	*variableName* = dom.getSelectedNode()
Arguments	None
Returns	The document object at the top of the DOM hierarchy (DOCUMENT_NODE type).

Table 4.12 Continued

Function	*dom.getSelectedNode()*

Example	`//returns true if the current selection is part of a text node`
	`myDOM = dw.getDocumentDOM();`
	`var currentNode = myDOM.getSelectedNode();`
	`if (currentNode.nodeType == "3") {`
	`return "true";`
	`} else {`
	`return "false";`
	`}`

Function	*dom.getSelection()*
Description	Gets access to the current selection, expressed as character offsets into the current document.
Syntax	`variableName = dom.getSelection()`
Arguments	None
Returns	An array consisting of two numbers. The first item in the array represents character offset at the start of the selection. The second item represents the offset value at the end of the selection. If the current selection is an insertion point, the two items in the array are the same.

Example	`//determine if the selection is an insertion point`
	`myDOM = dw.getDocumentDOM();`
	`var mySelection = myDOM.getSelection();`
	`if (mySelection[0] == mySelection[1]) {`
	`window.alert("The current selection is an insertion point.");`
	`}`

Table 4.13 API functions for using selection offsets to work with objects

Function	*dom.nodeToOffsets()*
Description	Gets the position of a specified object (node) in the document, expressed as character offsets into the document.
Syntax	`variableName = dom.nodeToOffsets(objectName)`
Arguments	An object (node)
Returns	An array consisting of two numbers. The first item in the array represents character offset at the start of the node. The second item represents the offset value at the end of the node. (Once we have these values, we can select the node.)

continues

Table 4.13 Continued

Function	*dom.nodeToOffsets()*

Example	`//finds the offsets for the first image in a document`
	`//and uses them to select the image`
	`var myDOM = dw.getDocumentDOM();`
	`var firstImage = myDOM.images[0];`
	`imageOffsets = myDOM.nodeToOffsets(firstImage);`
	`myDOM.setSelection(imageOffsets[0], imageOffsets[1]);`

Function	*dom.offsetsToNode()*
Description	Gets access to the object (node) in the document that completely surrounds the current selection.
Syntax	*variableName* = `dom.nodeToOffsets(`*offsetBegin*,*offsetEnd*`)`
Arguments	Two numbers, representing the character offsets of a selection.
Returns	The object (node) that contains the selection.

Example	`//determines the node containing the current selection,`
	`//and returns true if it's a text node`
	`var myDOM = dw.getDocumentDOM();`
	`var mySelection = myDOM.getSelection();`
	`var currentObject = myDOM.offsetsToNode(mySelection[0],`
	`mySelection[1]);`

Notes	Using this function with `dom.getSelection()`, as in the example here, is the same as using `dom.getSelectedNode()`.

Table 4.14 API Functions for setting and manipulating the selection

Function	*dom.selectAll()*
Description	Selects all, as if the user had chosen Edit > Select All. In most cases, this selects all the content in a document. Other times (for instance, if the current insertion point is inside a table), it selects all of some element in the document.
Syntax	`dom.selectAll()`
Arguments	none
Returns	nothing
Notes	To ensure that all contents of the active document are selected, use `dom.setSelection()` instead of this command.

Function	*dom.selectTable()*
Description	Selects a table.
Syntax	`dom.selectTable()`
Arguments	none
Returns	nothing
Enabler	`dom.canSelectTable()`(Returns `true` if the current selection is within a table.)

Example	`//determines if the insertion point is within a table,`
	`//and if so, selects the table`
	`var myDOM = dw.getDocumentDOM();`
	`if (myDOM.canSelectTable()) {`
	`myDOM.selectTable();`
	`}`

Function	*dom.setSelectedNode()*
Description	Selects the specified object (node).
Syntax	`dom.setSelectedNode(node,`*`[bSelectInside],[bJumpToNode]`*`)`
Arguments	An object (node)—Required. `bSelectInside` (Boolean)—If the specified node is an element node, this determines if the selection includes the `innerHTML` (the contents but not the outer tags) or the `outerHTML` (the contents and the surrounding tags). Optional. Defaults to false, if omitted. `bJumpToNode` (Boolean)—If this option is set to `true`, the document window will scroll to show the selection. Optional. Defaults to `false` if omitted.
Returns	nothing

Example	`//selects the first image in the document,`
	`//and scrolls the document window to show the selection`
	`var myDOM = dw.getDocumentDOM();`
	`var firstImage = myDOM.images[0];`
	`myDOM.setSelectedNode(firstImage,0,1);`

Notes	Using this function is equivalent to calling `dom.nodeToOffsets()` and passing the return value to `dom.setSelection()`.

Function	*dom.setSelection()*
Description	Sets the selection based on two numbers representing character offsets into the document.
Syntax	`dom.setSelection(`*`offsetBegin,offsetEnd`*`)`
Arguments	Two numbers, representing the desired beginning and ending of the selection expressed as character offsets into the document.

continues

Table 4.14 Continued

Function	*`dom.setSelection()`*
Returns	nothing

Example	`//finds the current selection, and changes it`
	`//to an insertion point at the end of the selection`
	`var myDOM = dw.getDocumentDOM();`
	`var mySelection = myDOM.getSelection();`
	`myDOM.setSelection(mySelection[1],mySelection[1]);`

Notes	If the newly set selection would not be a valid HTML selection, Dreamweaver automatically expands the selection to include the nearest valid selection.

Function	*`dw.selectAll()`*
Description	Selects all in the active document, or in the site window, or (Mac only) in the edit field that has focus in a dialog box or floating panel.
Syntax	`dw.selectAll()` or `dreamweaver.selectAll()`
Arguments	none
Returns	nothing
Enabler	`dw.canSelectAll()` (Returns `true` if Dreamweaver can perform the Select All operation.)

Example	`if (dw.canSelectAll()) {`
	`dw.selectAll();`
	`}`

Notes	To ensure that all contents of the active document are selected, use `dom.setSelection()` instead of this command.

Function	*`dom.selectChild()`*
Description	Selects a child of the current selection.
Syntax	`dom.selectChild()`
Arguments	none
Returns	nothing
Notes	For better control over which child to select, use `dom.getSelectedNode()` and access the `childNodes` property.

Function	*`dom.selectParent()`*
Description	Selects the parent object of the current selection.
Syntax	`dom.selectParent()`

Function	`dom.selectParent()`
Arguments	none
Returns	nothing
Notes	This is similar to using `dom.getSelectedNode()` and accessing the `parentNode` property.

A few notes about selections are in order. Selections can be accessed or set in two ways: by object or by character offsets. Generally, we need to work with both methods to accomplish our goals.

Object-based selection commands should be familiar to you by now. The `dom.getSelectedNode()` function gains access to whatever object is currently selected; `dom.setSelectedNode()` selects a specified object.

Using character offsets may be a little more unfamiliar. The `dom.getSelection()` function always returns an array of two numbers. The first number represents the beginning of the selection—it's the number you would get if you switched to Code view and counted characters from the beginning of the HTML code to where the selection starts. The second number represents the end of the selection. Some examples of character offsets:

- In any document, the HTML element starts at character 0 and ends at the last character in the document.
- In any document, the head element will start at character 7—immediately after the six characters of the `<html>` tag, in other words.
- Any time the current selection is only an insertion point; the beginning and ending offsets will be the same.

After we understand this, we can see how to combine the selection functions to perform useful tasks:

To select a particular object in the document:

```
//get access to the object
var myObject = myDOM.body.childNodes.item(0);
//select the object
myDOM.setSelectedNode(myObject);
```

To delete a particular object:

```
//get access to the object
var myObject = myDOM.body.childNodes.item(0);
//select the object
myDOM.setSelectedNode(myObject);
//delete the current selection
myDOM.deleteSelection();
```

To determine what kind of object the user has selected:

```
//get access to the selected object
var myObject = myDOM.getSelectedNode();
//use conditionals to determine the node type and properties
if (myObject.nodeType == "3") {
window.alert("You have selected text.");
}
```

To place the insertion point after the currently selected object:

```
//get access to the selected object
var myObject = myDOM.getSelectedNode();
//determine the offsets of the selected object
mySelection = myObject.nodeToOffsets();
//set the selection to an insertion point that matches the final offset
myDOM.setSelection(mySelection[1],mySelection[1]);
```

Using the DOM to Work with Strings of Code

Another way to access and work with page contents is by treating the document and its elements as strings of HTML code, and performing string operations on them. As Table 4.4 showed earlier in this chapter, objects of the ELEMENT_NODE type include two properties—`innerHTML` and `outerHTML`—that return strings. This is a different way of accessing the object code. This script, for instance, will return an object with properties that can be set and functions that can be performed on it:

```
var myDOM = dw.getDocumentDOM();
var myObject = myDOM.body.childNodes.item(0);
if (myObject.nodeType == "1" && myObject.tagName == "IMG") {
myObject.alt = "This is an image.";
}
```

This script accesses the same code, but as a string subject to string methods:

```
var myDOM = dw.getDocumentDOM();
var myObject = myDOM.body.childNodes.item(0);
var myString = myObject.outerHTML;
window.alert(myString.toUpperCase());
```

Why would you use this method? It's often the best way to pull a section of code or text out of a document, edit it, and put it back into the document. (We'll see how this works in the next chapter.)

Enhancing Objects and Behaviors Using the DOM

Being able to work with the DOM is most important when we're doing work that involves more than just inserting new code into documents. Therefore, objects and behaviors rely on the DOM less than other extension types. But there are tasks within objects and behaviors that require DOM access and knowledge.

isDomRequired()

As part of the API for objects, this function determines whether an object can be inserted if Code view and Design view have not been synchronized. If the HTML code of a user's document contains invalid markup instructions (incomplete tag pairs, for instance), the DOM is not valid, and certain objects should not be inserted. The function itself only requires a return value of `true` or `false`; but when you are determining how to apply the function, you need to know whether the code you are inserting will work properly without a valid DOM.

canAcceptBehavior()

We've already had a little experience with this function. As part of the API for behaviors, it controls whether a behavior will be grayed out in the behaviors inspector menu, usually based on whether a required element of the behavior is present on the page. Behaviors that control images are useless unless there are images on a page, for instance. To implement this level of functionality for `canAcceptBehavior()`, we need to be able to step through the code to see if any IMG tags are present. After a DOM object has been instantiated, as we've seen above, we can do this:

```
function canAcceptBehavior() {
var myDOM = dw.getDocumentDOM();
if (myDOM.images[0]) {
return true;
} else {
return false;
}
}
```

(If you're curious—and you probably are, or you wouldn't be reading this book—try it out! Open up one of the behaviors we created in the previous chapter, and add the preceding `canAcceptBehavior()` function. Then reload extensions and try the behavior out, first in a document with images and then in a document with no images.)

Working with the DOM: Practice Session

Learning how to manipulate the Dreamweaver DOM is an important part of learning extensibility. If you're already an old hand at working with the Level 0 and Level 1 DOM, you can skip this practice session. If not, roll up your sleeves and let's get tinkering.

Task 1: Create a command file to practice with

For this practice session, you'll create a very simple command file that you use to experiment with the Dreamweaver DOM. (You also get your first taste of working with the API for commands.)

Start by using the History panel to record a command:

1. Launch Dreamweaver and create a new file. There's no need to save the file because you use it only temporarily.
2. Open the History panel (Window > Others > History). The history list should be empty so far because you haven't done anything.
3. In the document window, type a few random words—something like **"This is a test."** The History panel should now show your typing activity as a history step.
4. In the panel, select that step. In the upper-right corner of the History panel, click the icon to access the panel's options menu and choose Save as Command. When the dialog box appears asking you to name your command, call it **Test Command**. Figure 4.5 shows the various steps of this process.

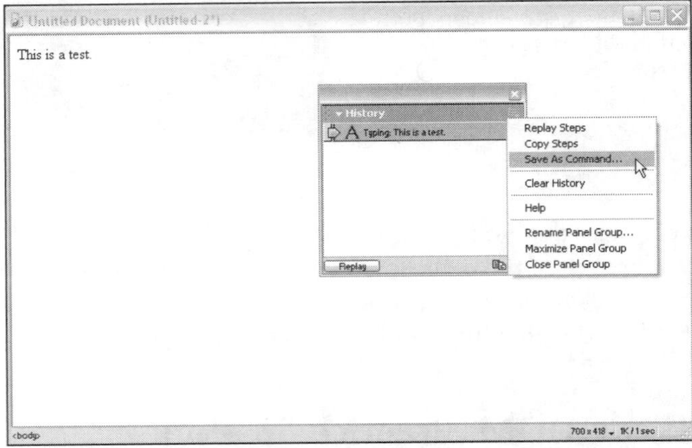

FIGURE 4.5 *Using the History panel to record a test command in Dreamweaver.*

5. Check out your new command. Look in the Command menu—your command should show at the bottom of the menu. Choose the command from the menu. Your sample text is inserted into the open document.

Task 2: Examine the practice command file

Commands exist as HTML files in the Configuration/Commands folder. When you record a command in Dreamweaver, the program creates a new command file in that folder. In this task, you find and open the file you just created, and use it to practice with.

1. Start by minimizing, hiding, or quitting Dreamweaver. You'll be exploring your hard drive for this task.
2. In multiuser environments, Dreamweaver stores recorded commands in the user's Configuration folder, not the main Dreamweaver/Configuration folder. If you're using Windows 98 or Mac OS 9, open the Configuration folder that is stored in your Dreamweaver application folder. If you're using any other Windows OS or Mac OS X, find and open your user-specific Configuration folder. (For Windows users, look in `c:\documents and settings\`*`username`*`\application data\macromedia\dreamweaver mx\configuration\`. For Mac OS X users, look in `/users/`*`username`*`/library/application support/dreamweaver mx/configuration`.)
3. Within the appropriate Configuration folder, find and open the Commands folder. Look in the list of files for a file called Test Command.htm.
4. In your text editor, open Test Command.html and examine its contents. It probably looks like the file shown in Listing 4.1.

note

Refer to the section "Multiple Configuration Folders" in Chapter 1 for more on Dreamweaver in multiuser operating systems.

Listing 4.1 Test Command.html

```
<HTML>
<HEAD>
<!-- Portions Copyright 1999-2002 Macromedia, Inc. All rights reserved.
-->
<TITLE>Test Command</TITLE>
<SCRIPT LANGUAGE="javascript">
<!--
   // This command was recorded by Dreamweaver MX
   function runCommand()
   {
      // Typing: This is a test.
      dw.getDocumentDOM().insertText('This is a test.');
   }
// -->
</SCRIPT>
</HEAD>
<BODY onLoad="runCommand()" >
</BODY>
</HTML>
```

The functionality of the command is contained in the `runCommand()` function, which is defined in the document `<head>` and called as part of the `<body>` tag. The single statement in the function is a shorthand presentation of two statements:

```
dw.getDocumentDOM().insertText('This is a test.');
```

In its standard form, the code would look like this:

```
var myDOM = dw.getDocumentDOM();
myDOM.insertText('This is a test.');
```

The first statement officially gains access to the DOM object (as discussed previously); the second statement uses a method of the DOM object to insert text at the user's insertion point. Can you see how the command works?

5. Strip out the file's comments and the statement inside the `runCommand()` function. Your test command is now ready for action!

Task 3: Practice gaining access to different document elements

For this task, you'll alter the Test Command you just created to make it perform various DOM-related activities on a Dreamweaver document. Before you can go through the steps in this task, you'll need a Dreamweaver document to examine. Any file will do, although more complex files might be confusing to work with. The examples here use the dompage.html file (the same document shown in Figure 4.3 and Figure 4.4). If you want your results for this task to match the examples exactly, you can download dompage.html and its images from the companion web site to this book (`www.newriders.com`), or you can create a file with the same page structure (a table with two rows and two columns) containing your own text and images.

1. In Dreamweaver, open dompage.html or whatever other test file you want to practice on. In your text editor, open Test Command.htm. For the practice session, you can leave both files open, switching between them to try new commands and check them out.

2. Access the `<html>` tag. In your text editor, bring the Test Command file to the front. Rewrite the `runCommand()` function to access the document's `<html>` tag, like this (new code is in bold):

```
function runCommand() {
var myDOM = dw.getDocumentDOM();
var myHTML = myDOM.documentElement;
window.alert(myHTML);
}
```

3. Try it out. Save the file. In Dreamweaver, reload extensions and choose your test command from the Commands menu. You end up with a dialog box like that shown in Figure 4.6, indicating that you have access to an object on the page.

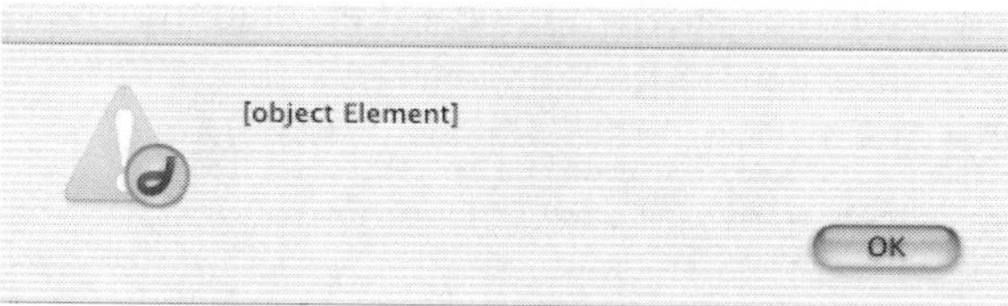

FIGURE 4.6 *Alert window showing that a command has accessed an object element.*

Now it's time to gain some information about the accessed object.

As an object in the DOM, the `<html>` tag is an instance of a node, so it has various node properties. You can, for instance, ask what the object's node type is.

4. Change the code in your test command to look like this (new code is in bold):

```
function runCommand() {
var myDOM = dw.getDocumentDOM();
var myHTML = myDOM.documentElement;
var myNodeType = myHTML.nodeType;
window.alert(myNodeType);
}
```

Reload extensions in Dreamweaver, and try out the revised test command. The alert window reports a `1`. Do you know why?

5. The `<html>` tag is an instance of the `ELEMENT_NODE` node type, so it partakes of all the properties listed in Table 4.4. Change the code in your test command to look like this (new code is in bold):

```
function runCommand() {
var myDOM = dw.getDocumentDOM();
var myHTML = myDOM.documentElement;
var myTagName = myHTML.tagName;
window.alert(myTagName);
}
```

Can you tell, even before trying it out, what this command will cause to appear in the alert window? After you've made your guess, reload extensions in Dreamweaver and try the command.

Next, try to access a child node. According to the Level 1 DOM, the `<html>` has two children (that is, tags nested directly under it): `<head>` and `<body>`. You can access the `<body>` directly by using the DOM object's `body` property (refer to Table 4.2). But to access the `<head>`, you need to do a little more work. Do it this way, building on what you already have:

6. First, get a list of the <html> tag's children, like this (new code is in bold):

```
function runCommand() {
var myDOM = dw.getDocumentDOM();
var myHTML = myDOM.documentElement;
var myChildren = myHTML.childNodes;
}
```

7. The childNodes property returns a nodeList, which is an array of objects. As you can see by checking Table 4.1, nodeLists have one property, length, which reports the number of items in the array; and one method, item(), which allows access to each item in the array. So add another line to your function (new code is in bold):

```
function runCommand() {
var myDOM = dw.getDocumentDOM();
var myHTML = myDOM.documentElement;
var myChildren = myHTML.childNodes;
var myHEAD = myChildren.item(0);
}
```

8. These statements give you access to the <head> tag. To make use of that access, ask the child object for its tag name (new code is in bold):

```
function runCommand() {
var myDOM = dw.getDocumentDOM();
var myHTML = myDOM.documentElement;
var myChildren = myHTML.childNodes;
var myHEAD = myChildren.item(0);
window.alert(myHEAD.tagName);
}
```

Try the command out! The alert window should look like the one shown in Figure 4.7.

Figure 4.7 *Alert window, showing that a command has accessed the tag name of an object.*

note

Note that the code shown here could also have been written in abbreviated form—for instance:

```
function runCommand() {
var myHTML =
dw.getDocumentDOM().documentElement;
var myHEAD = myHTML.childNodes.item(0);
window.alert(myHEAD.tagName);
}
```

Finally, try searching for a specific type of element. Using the Level 0 DOM, you can access certain types of element, like forms and images, by using the document's built-in array of those items. A more thorough way of searching for a specific type of item in Level 1 DOM is with the `getElementsByTagName()` method. This function also returns a nodeList of objects that can be stepped through and accessed.

9. Rewrite your function to gain access to all the table cells on the page (new code is in bold):

```
function runCommand() {
var myDOM = dw.getDocumentDOM();
var allCells = myDOM.getElementsByTagName('TD');
}
```

10. To test out your access, ask for some information from one of the table cells (new code is in bold):

```
function runCommand() {
var myDOM = dw.getDocumentDOM();
var allCells = myDOM.getElementsByTagName('TD');
myCell = allCells.item(0);
window.alert("My alignment is " + myCell.align);
}
```

11. From here, gain access to the cell's contents and ask a few questions about them:

```
function runCommand() {
var myDOM = dw.getDocumentDOM();
var allCells = myDOM.getElementsByTagName('TD');
myCell = allCells.item(0);
myContents = myCell.childNodes.item(0);
window.alert("My alignment is '" + myCell.align +".'\nMy contents are
node type '" + myContents.nodeType + ".'");
}
```

Figure 4.8 shows the resulting alert window this function will generate if you're using dompage.html as your test document.

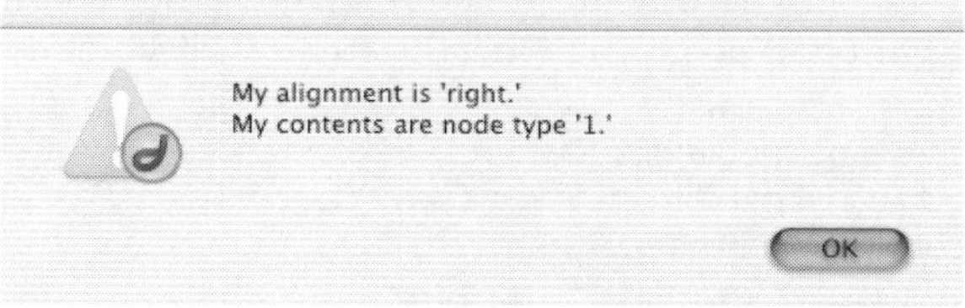

FIGURE 4.8 *Gaining access to the first table cell on the page, and determining its alignment and contents.*

Task 4: Practice Altering Page Elements

Now that you know how to get access to different page elements, it's a small step forward to alter those elements.

1. To change the default colors of your document, rewrite your function like this:

```
function runCommand() {
var myBODY = dw.getDocumentDOM().body;
myBODY.bgcolor = "#000000";
myBODY.text = "#FFFFFF";
}
```

   Can you see how the function first gains access to the `<body>` element and then changes its properties?

2. To add a border to the table in the document, rewrite your function like this:

```
function runCommand() {
var myDOM = dw.getDocumentDOM();
var allTables = myDOM.getElementsByTagName('TABLE');
allTables.item(0).border="2";
}
```

3. To change the alignment of all table cells within the document, rewrite your function to step through the document's array of TD tags, like this:

```
function runCommand() {
var myDOM = dw.getDocumentDOM();
var allCells = myDOM.getElementsByTagName('TD');
for (var a=0;a<allCells.length;a++) {
   allCells.item(a).align="right";
   }
}
```

Task 5: Practice selecting page elements

Now let's try manipulating the document based on user selections, and get some practice using the selection functions detailed in Tables 4.12–4.14.

1. To start, practice getting information about the selection. Change the function code in your command to report the current selection as offsets:

```
function runCommand() {
myDOM = dw.getDocumentDOM();
mySelection = myDOM.getSelection();
window.alert(mySelection);
}
```

To try this out in Dreamweaver, first select something in the practice document and then run the command. The alert window will always report two numbers. These are the offsets measuring the number of characters from the beginning of the document to the beginning of the selection (first number), and the number of characters from the beginning of the document to the end of the selection (second number). Try the command with various things selected, and see how the offset values change. See how the command responds when your selection is only an insertion point.

2. Now try getting information about the selected node (in other words, the object that contains your selection). Rewrite your function to look like this:

```
function runCommand() {
myDOM = dw.getDocumentDOM();
myObject = myDOM.getSelectedNode();
window.alert(myObject.nodeType);
}
```

   Try this out in Dreamweaver by selecting different items in the document and then running the command. Instead of offset values, Dreamweaver returns numbers (1,3,8,11) that represent the node type of the selected object. These numbers indicate that Dreamweaver has given you scripting access to the object. If the selection is a chunk of text, note that the command accesses the entire `TEXT_NODE` object, whether or not the entire text element has been selected.

3. After you can get the selection, try setting the selection. This involves gaining access to an object and then setting the selected node. To select the first image on the page, rewrite your function to look like this:

```
function runCommand() {
myDOM = dw.getDocumentDOM();
myObject = myDOM.images[0];
myDOM.setSelectedNode(myObject);
}
```

   Try the command out in Dreamweaver to make sure it works.

4. After you have the object selected, try changing it. Delete the image by adding one more line to your function:

```
function runCommand() {
myDOM = dw.getDocumentDOM();
myObject = myDOM.images[0];
myDOM.setSelectedNode(myObject);
myDOM.deleteSelection();
}
```

Add a link to the image by changing that last line:

```
function runCommand() {
myDOM = dw.getDocumentDOM();
myObject = myDOM.images[0];
myDOM.setSelectedNode(myObject);
myDOM.wrapTag('<a href="#">');
}
```

5. Now try altering the image and then putting the insertion point after the image. You do this by collecting the object's selection offsets and setting the selection to begin and end at the ending offset value. Rewrite your function call to look like this (new code is in bold):

```
function runCommand() {
myDOM = dw.getDocumentDOM();
myObject = myDOM.images[0];
myDOM.setSelectedNode(myObject);
myDOM.wrapTag('<a href="#">');
objectOffsets = myDOM.nodeToOffsets(myObject);
myDOM.setSelection(objectOffsets[1],objectOffsets[1]);
}
```

Can you see how the offsets and node selections work? Keep tinkering and experimenting until you do.

Task 6: Practice using string functions on page elements

Working with the code as a string is different from working with the code as a hierarchy of objects. In this task, you'll see how that works.

1. To see the difference between accessing the code as a string and accessing the objects, try a comparison. First, rewrite your function to access the document's HTML object and report the result:

```
function runCommand() {
myDOM = dw.getDocumentDOM();
myHTML = myDOM.documentElement;
window.alert(myHTML);
}
```

   Try this command out, and you get an alert window that looks like the one shown earlier in Figure 4.6.

2. Now revise the function to access the HTML object's code as a string (new code is in bold):

```
function runCommand() {
var myDOM = dw.getDocumentDOM();
var myHTML = myDOM.documentElement;
var myHTMLstring = myHTML.outerHTML;
window.alert(myHTMLstring);
}
```

Try this command out and you'll get an alert window that looks like the one shown in Figure 4.9. You just accessed the document as one big fat text string!

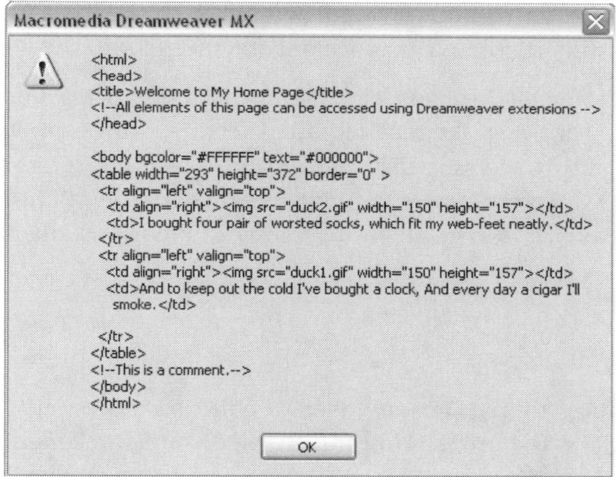

FIGURE 4.9 *Alert window showing that a command has accessed the* `outerHTML` *string of the HTML element.*

3. To see the difference between `innerHTML` and `outerHTML`, revise your function like this (new code is in bold):

```
function runCommand() {
var myDOM = dw.getDocumentDOM();
var myHTML = myDOM.documentElement;
var myHTMLstring = myHTML.outerHTML;
window.alert(myHTMLstring);
}
```

Try this out. Can you see how the results in the alert window are slightly different? The <html> tags are missing from the returned code string.

4. By combining regular object-based access and string access methods, you can easily investigate and alter specific portions of a document's code. Try rewriting your function like this:

```
function runCommand() {
var myDOM = dw.getDocumentDOM();
var allCells = myDOM.getElementsByTagName('TD');
var temp1 = allCells.item(0).innerHTML;
var temp2 = allCells.item(1).innerHTML;
allCells.item(0).innerHTML = temp2;
allCells.item(1).innerHTML = temp1;
}
```

Can you tell, even without trying it out, what this revised function will do? If not, run the command on your practice document and see.

Had enough practice? If you have the time and the inclination, practice some more. Set yourself various tasks that require selecting things, moving around the document, and getting access to different objects. The more comfortable you are working with the DOM, and the more familiar you are with the API functions that call on the DOM, the easier it is to create more complex extensions, like those in the upcoming chapters.

Summary

Using scripting to get Dreamweaver to edit user documents depends on learning about the DOM the program uses to access document elements. In this chapter, you learned the specifications for the Dreamweaver DOM and got some practice using it. In the following chapters, you'll be using the DOM and the API commands associated with it to create custom commands, inspectors, and panels. By the end of this book, you'll be climbing around inside the DOM like a regular DOM-monkey, and creating much more sophisticated extensions than you've been attempting up to this point. Have a blast!

CHAPTER 5

Creating Custom Commands and Menu Commands

Commands are the things we choose from menus. Unlike objects and behaviors, which are limited to performing the specific tasks of adding HTML and JavaScript code to user documents, commands can be used for almost any editing task—inserting code, removing code, editing code, even opening and closing documents, connecting to servers, and launching external applications.

The Dreamweaver Application Programming Interface (API) includes two kinds of commands: regular commands and menu commands. The difference between them is subtle and doesn't involve the functionality of what they can do, but of how and where they appear in the Dreamweaver menu system. Regular commands appear in the Commands menu by default, although this default can be overridden by editing the menus.xml file. The menu items representing regular commands are static, meaning that the name and appearance of the menu item does not change based on document context or other conditions.

Figure 5.1 shows some regular commands as they appear in the Commands menu. Menu commands don't appear in the menu system at all by default; their presence in the menu system is determined solely by menus.xml. In addition to this, menu commands have the ability to generate dynamic menu items—for instance, the menu item can include a toggling checkmark as a program feature is turned on or off, or the item name might read differently depending on what documents are open or what page elements are selected. Figure 5.2 shows a selection of dynamically generated menu commands in various menus.

FIGURE 5.1 *The Commands menu, showing entries for regular commands.*

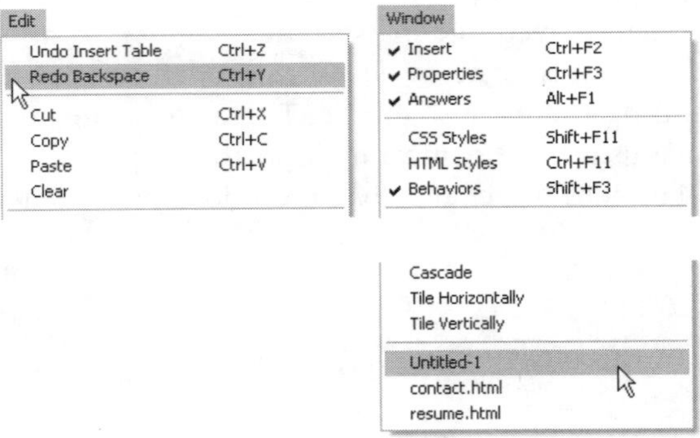

FIGURE 5.2 *The Window and Edit menus, showing dynamic menu entries generated from menu commands.*

In this chapter, we'll start by familiarizing ourselves with the API for regular commands; then we'll examine the added functionality of menu commands.

How Commands Are Constructed

The basic API for regular commands is remarkably simple and flexible. Unlike the API for objects or behaviors, there are few required elements and few required procedural steps. We also have more control over the appearance of dialog boxes in commands than in other extension types, including the ability to specify what buttons will appear (OK, Cancel, and so on) and exactly what functionality each will have.

Commands in the Configuration Folder

Command files are stored in the Configuration/Commands folder. There are no subfolders within the Commands folder. By default, each file in the Commands folder appears in the Dreamweaver Commands menu, although special coding can be added to any file in the folder to prevent it appearing there. Figure 5.3 shows a typical Commands folder.

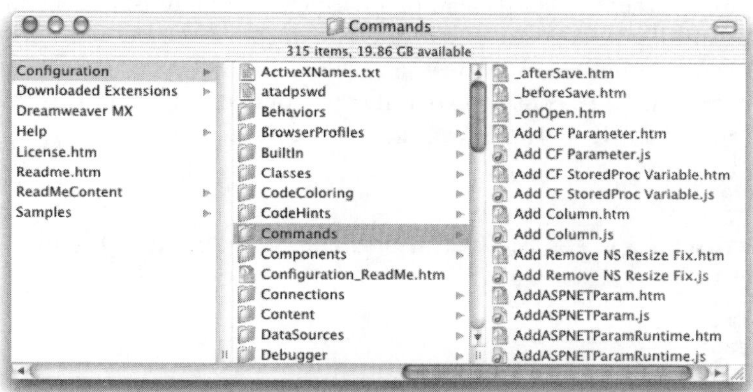

FIGURE 5.3 *The Configuration/Commands folder, showing files representing the contents of the Commands menu as well as a variety of other files. (Only partial contents are visible.)*

Structure of a Command File

As with objects and behaviors, commands are constructed from a combination of HTML and JavaScript, either located in one HTML file or created as an HTML file and linked JavaScript (JS) file. The following sections describe the required and optional elements for command files.

Required Elements (Simple Command)

A command file requires very little. It must be an HTML file with the proper HTML framework, of course. Beyond that, required elements include the following:

- **Filename.** Unless otherwise specified in menus.xml, the filename becomes the menu entry for the command. (Customizing menus.xml is discussed in the section "Working with menus.xml" later in this chapter.)
- **Page Title.** The page title shows in the title bar of any dialog box the command calls up. If there is no dialog box, the page title is not called on.
- **Function and Function Call.** The functionality of the command is provided by a function in the `<head>` section of the document, which is then called from the `<body>` tag using the `onLoad` event handler. What this function is called and what is in it are entirely up to you. Commands have no equivalent to `objectTag()` or `applyBehavior()`, functions that must be present and will automatically be called to insert or edit a document. If desired, this main function can call on other functions, also defined in the `<head>`. Listing 5.1 shows a basic command file, consisting of only the required elements. (This exciting function inserts the text "Hello, World!" at the insertion point.)

Listing 5.1 A Basic Command File, Containing Only Required Elements

```
<html>
<head>
<title>Hello, World</title>
<script language="JavaScript">

function runCommand() {
var myDOM = dw.getDocumentDOM();
myDOM.insertHTML("Hello, world!");
}

</script>
</head>
<body onLoad="runCommand()">

</body>
</html>
```

Optional Elements

Fancier commands use dialog boxes for user input and can interact with the program in other ways as well. A number of custom API functions can help dress up your command files, including the following:

- **`canAcceptCommand()` function.** Like the `canAcceptBehavior()` function for behaviors, this function returns `true` or `false` and determines whether a command will be available to the user or will be grayed out in the menu. A command for editing tables, for instance, should be grayed out if the user's current selection isn't a table. This function is called automatically as part of the API procedure, so it needn't be explicitly called.
- **`isDomRequired()` function.** Another function that doesn't need to be explicitly called, `isDomRequired()` determines whether Code view and Design view need to be synchronized before the new object's code can be inserted. The function should return `true` or `false`.
- **form, or other `<body>` content.** Any content placed in the `<body>` tag causes the command to generate a dialog box. To collect user input, use a form. Important: If your command includes a form, you must also use the `commandButtons()` function, described next.
- **`commandButtons()` function.** Dialog boxes called as part of a command are not automatically supplied with OK and Cancel buttons. Instead, we specify what buttons appear and what functionality they have by using the `commandButtons()` function. (If this function isn't present, the user has no way to get out of the dialog box after it comes up.)

  This function must return an array containing two elements for each button you want in the dialog box: The first element specifies the button's name; the second specifies the action to be taken if the button is clicked. Figure 5.4 shows a typical `commandButtons()` function and the dialog box buttons that it creates. Note that if the user clicks OK or its equivalent, the button executes the `runCommand()` function, which is the function called in the `<body>` section of the command file. (If `commandButtons()` is used like this to execute the command's function, that function shouldn't be called in the `<body>` tag.) All buttons must also execute the `window.close()` function to close the dialog box.

```
function commandButtons(){
 return new Array("Go for it","runCommand();window.close();","Cancel","window.close()");
}
```

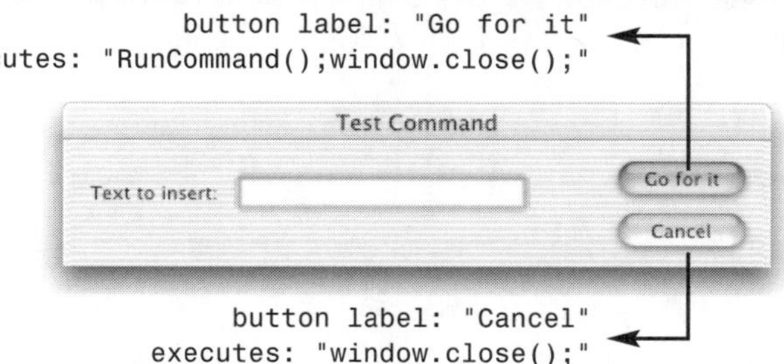

FIGURE 5.4 *The* `commandButtons()` *function in action, and the dialog box buttons it creates.*

- **`receiveArguments()` function.** This function allows for passing parameters to the command, which allows command files to be reused for different purposes in the interface. For instance, the same command file might be used to align text left, right, or center, depending on which menu item the user selected. (This function is discussed in-depth in the "Commands and Menus" section, later in this chapter.)

API Procedure for Commands

The API procedure for commands begins when the user clicks on a menu that contains commands. At that point, Dreamweaver looks through the command files for all items in the menu. For each command file, if the `canAcceptCommand()` function is present, Dreamweaver executes this command. If the function returns `false`, the menu item for that particular command is grayed out in the menu. If the function returns `true` or if there is no `canAcceptCommand()` function, the item is not grayed out.

After the user chooses a command from a menu, the following events occur:

1. Dreamweaver looks in the command file for the `receiveArguments()` function. If the function is present, it's executed.
2. Dreamweaver looks for and calls the `commandButtons()` function, then scans the file for a form.

   If a form exists:

   - Dreamweaver creates a dialog box. If the `commandButtons()` function is defined, it's used to create the buttons in the dialog box.
   - Dreamweaver waits for the user to click one of the buttons in the dialog box and executes the instructions coded into that button by the `commandButtons()` function.

   If no form exists, Dreamweaver loads the `<body>` and executes any functions called in the `onLoad` event handler.

As you can see, a lot of flexibility is built into this procedure because commands include so many optional elements. Commands can be very simple (like the Test command created in the previous chapter) or very sophisticated. The flowchart in Figure 5.5 diagrams the API procedure for commands, with the various optional elements in place.

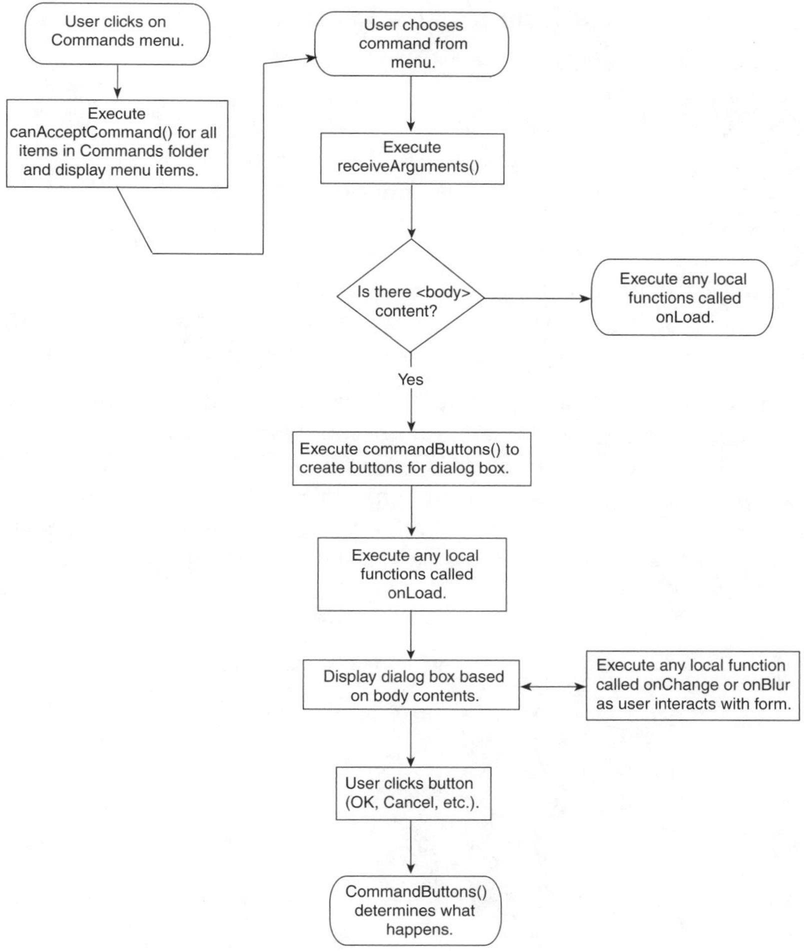

FIGURE 5.5 *The API procedure for commands.*

Workshop #1: A Command That Uses Object Access

Working with commands is all about working with the Document Object Model (DOM). If you have read Chapter 4, "The Dreamweaver DOM," and gone through the Practice Session in that chapter, you already know a little bit about navigating and manipulating user documents with DOM-related functions, and about the basics of working with very simple command files. This workshop builds on that, giving you more experience with the DOM and also with the optional elements of commands. We'll start nice and simple, and add complexity and features as we go.

Sample Command: Automatically Adding the *alt* Parameter to All Images in a Document

> If you haven't gone through the Practice Session in Chapter 4, do so now! All projects in this chapter assume that you have a basic familiarity with the DOM as it operates in the Dreamweaver API.

It's good manners to give all the images on your Web pages alternate text labels for visitors who don't have access to images. (Actually, if you work on government-related web sites, it's more than good manners—it's required by Section 508 of the Federal Rehabilitation Act.) For maximum site usability, nothing beats manually going through your pages and adding the most appropriate labels. But when quick-and-dirty is all there's time for, a command that automatically generates the `alt` parameter is just the thing.

In this exercise, we'll create a command that creates `alt` labels for all images in a document. For images that are not also links, the `alt` text will be constructed from the image filename (minus its extension) for the label text. For images that are links, `alt` text will be generated based on the link address. Images that already have `alt` text will be excluded from the command, on the assumption that the user won't want this text overwritten. Figure 5.6 shows what we want this command to accomplish in a typical document.

FIGURE 5.6 *A sample user document, showing an image's filename being used to generate an alt parameter.*

Task 1: Create the command file document

In your text editor, create a standard command file document with framework elements in place. The code should look like this:

```
<html>
<head>
<title>Automatic Alt Text</title>
<script language="JavaScript">
function addAlt() {
//statements will go here
}
</script>
</head>
<body onLoad="addAlt()">
</body>
</html>
```

Save the command file in the Dreamweaver Configuration/Commands folder. The filename appears in the Commands menu, remember, so give the file a descriptive name such as Automatic Alt Text.htm.

Task 2: Create the basic code for the *addAlt( )* function

This command involves navigating the DOM to access each image object and add an `alt` property. The command's main function—`addAlt()`—is responsible for doing this. In this task, you'll fill in this function.

1. In terms of the DOM, adding `alt` text means accessing each image object and setting an `alt` attribute. Breaking that down to its simplest level, start by adding code to your main function that will access one image, and set its `alt` attribute to a preset value. Revise the `addAlt()` function to look like this (new code is in bold):

   ```
   function addAlt() {
   var myDOM=dw.getDocumentDOM();
   var myImages=myDOM.getElementsByTagName('IMG');
   myImages[0].alt = "Sample Alt Text";
   }
   ```

   Can you see what the code is doing? Using the `dom.getElementsByTagName()` method, it gains access to a node list containing all images in the document. It then selects the first image in the node list and assigns it an `alt` property.

   Before proceeding, try out the command to make sure it works so far. Reload extensions in Dreamweaver and open a document that contains at least one image (the command looks for the first image on the page). Then choose Commands > Automatic Alt Text. Figure 5.7 shows what should happen to your document when you do this.

note

What's the difference between a node list and an array? For scripting purposes, node lists use slightly different syntax. To access the first item in an array, the correct syntax is `myArray[0]`. To access the first item in a node list, the syntax is `myNodeList.item(0)`. For specifications of node lists, see Table 4.1 in Chapter 4.

FIGURE 5.7 *Setting the `alt` attribute for one image in a document to a preset value.*

2. If you can set `alt` text for one image in the document's node list of image objects, you can add a `for` loop to step through the entire node list and add `alt` attributes to all of them. Revise your function to look like this (new code is in bold):

```
function addAlt() {
var myDOM = dw.getDocumentDOM();
var myImages = myDOM.getElementsByTagName('IMG');
for (var a=0;a<myImages.length;a++) {
   myImages.item(a).alt = "Sample Alt Text";
   }
}
```

   To test the code, save the file, reload extensions in Dreamweaver, and try it out on a Dreamweaver document that contains more than one image.

3. The next step is to revise the function so that it uses each image's filename as its `alt` text. The filename is included as part of every image's `src` attribute—the attribute that specifies the relative or absolute path to the image file. Because the `src` attribute is a text string, extracting the desired filename is a simple matter of using the JavaScript substring method to get results like this:

`src` *attribute*	*desired* `alt` *text*
scheherezade.gif	scheherezade
Images/blinky.gif	blinky
../../../images/housepix/diningroom.jpg	diningroom
http://www.domain.com/images/home.gif	home

   You need to extract everything after the final / and before the final period (.). To accomplish this, revise your function to look like this (new code is in bold):

```
function addAlt() {
var myDOM = dw.getDocumentDOM();
var myImages = myDOM.getElementsByTagName('IMG');
var mySrc = "";
var myName = "";
for (var a=0;a<myImages.length;a++) {
   mySrc = myImages.item(a).src;
   myName = mySrc.substring(mySrc.lastIndexOf("/")+1,mySrc.lastIndexOf("."));
   myImages.item(a).alt = myName;
   }
}
```

The new code declares two variables (mySrc and myName) that are then used in the for loop. The first variable holds the complete src attribute; the second is passed a substring of the src attribute that contains only the filename.

To test the command's thoroughness, try it on a variety of files with different paths listed in the src parameter. Try to stump the command by giving it a filename or path that it won't report correctly. If you find a problem path, see if you can rewrite the code so that the command deals with it correctly.

note

If you're unclear on how to use the substring() method, read all about it in the Dreamweaver Reference panel. Set the panel to display the O'Reilly JavaScript Reference, and look up the String object and its methods. See the section on "Assembling Reference Materials" in the Introduction for more about the Reference panel.

Task 3: Refine the *addAlt( )* function

The command is fine, as far as it goes. Now it's time to ask yourself how it might be more flexible and useful.

1. It would be nice, for one thing, if the command didn't overwrite any existing alt text. To accommodate this, rewrite the function to include a conditional statement so that it looks for existing alt tags and adds the alt property only if one doesn't already exist (new code is in bold):

```
function addAlt() {
var myDOM = dw.getDocumentDOM();
var myImages = myDOM.getElementsByTagName('IMG');
var mySrc = "";
var myName = "";
for (var a=0;a<myImages.length;a++) {
   if (!myImages.item(a).alt) {
      mySrc = myImages.item(a).src;
      myName = mySrc.substring(mySrc.lastIndexOf("/")+1,mySrc.lastIndexOf("."));
      myImages.item(a).alt = myName;
      }
   }
}
```

Try this version of your command in Dreamweaver. Be sure to test it out on a Dreamweaver document that has several images, some with and some without existing `alt` text. It should ignore the images that already have an `alt` attribute and add `alt` text only to those without.

2. Another refinement you can make is to improve how it handles images that are being used as links. If an image is functioning on the page as a button, information about the link provides a more useful `alt` label than information about the image.

   How will you identify which images in the user's document are linked? The HTML code for a linked image has the `a` tag wrapped around the `img` tag, like this:

   ```
   <a href="index.html"><img src="dog.jpg"></a>
   ```

   Therefore, for each image in the array you can check to see whether it's a link by checking its parent element to see whether it's an `a` tag.

   What will you do with linked images? Instead of using the image's own `src` attribute to generate the `alt` text, you'll use the parent link's `href` attribute (this property specifies the destination of the link).

   To add this new criteria to your function, you'll need to add another conditional statement. Revise your code like this (new code is in bold):

   ```
   function addAlt() {
   var myDOM = dw.getDocumentDOM();
   var myImages = myDOM.getElementsByTagName('IMG');
   var mySrc = "";
   var myName = "";
   for (var a=0;a<myImages.length;a++) {
      if (!myImages.item(a).alt) {
         if (myImages.item(a).parentNode.tagName == 'A') {
            myName = "Visit "+myImages.item(a).parentNode.href;
            }else{
            mySrc = myImages.item(a).src;
            myName =
            ➥mySrc.substring(mySrc.lastIndexOf("/")+1,mySrc.lastIndexOf("."));
            }
         myImages.item(a).alt = myName;
         }
      }
   }
   ```

What's happening here? Line 8 of the code adds a conditional statement that checks for an <a> tag wrapped around the image. If that condition is true, line 9 sets the `myName` variable to reflect the <a> tag's `href` attribute. The code that was already in place for creating `alt` text based on the image's `src` attribute has been moved into the `else` portion of the conditional, to be executed only if there isn't a link.

3. But wait! What about images that are linked only for scripting purposes? You don't want # or `javascript:myFunction()` to show up as part of your `alt` text, yet both of these are often used in HTML construction. If an image is linked to one of these pseudo-destinations, you want its `alt` text to display the standard `src` information that non-linked images display.

   To accomplish this, you need to refine the conditional statement in line 8 so that it will return `true` only if three conditions are met: an image's parent element must be an <a> tag, and that <a> tag must not have # for its `href` value, and that <a> tag also must not have an `href` that begins with `javascript:`. This all adds up to a pretty packed conditional statement, requiring three parts. Revise line 9 of your function to look like this:

```
if (myImages.item(a).parentNode.tagName == 'A' &&
➥myImages.item(a).parentNode.href != "#" &&
➥myImages.item(a).parentNode.href.substring(0,10) != "javascript") {
```

   Try this out—the Automatic Alt Text command is now cognizant of links, pseudolinks, and filenames.

note

How fancy do you want to get? Before you spend a lot of time and effort making the biggest, baddest extension on the block, ask yourself what you're going to use it for. If you'll be the only person using a command, and you know the limited circumstances you'll be working in, you don't have to accommodate all possible permutations of circumstance that might break your code. If you're planning to share your extension with others, however, it's a good idea to be as comprehensive as you can be.

Task 4: Add the *canAcceptCommand()* function

As noted earlier in this chapter, the `canAcceptCommand()` function determines whether a command is available or grayed out in the menu. If the function returns `true` (or if it isn't present), the command is available. If it returns `false`, the command is grayed out.

When would you want the Automatic Alt Text command to be unavailable? Well, it's a pretty useless command if the document doesn't contain any images—although running the command under those circumstances wouldn't cause any problems. It's also useless—and will generate errors—if there's no open document at all.

To make the Automatic Alt Text command unavailable under these circumstances, add the `canAcceptCommand()` function to your command file, coded so that it returns `false` if there's no DOM or if the array of `<img>` tags in the document is empty:

```
function canAcceptCommand() {
var myDOM = dw.getDocumentDOM();
if (!myDOM) return false;
var myImages = myDOM.getElementsByTagName('IMG');
if (myImages.item(0)) {
    return true;
    } else {
    return false;
    }
}
```

Can you see how the command works? If there is no DOM it returns `false`; otherwise, it gains access to a node list of all images in the document using the `dom.getElementsByTagName()` function. Then it tries to find the first item in the node list, `item(0)`. If it can't find that item, then there are no images, and it returns `false`.

Try the command out now. In Dreamweaver, reload extensions and open a file that doesn't contain any images. Then try to choose the Automatic Alt Text command. It should be grayed out in the Commands menu (see Figure 5.8). Open a file that does contain images and try again. The command should be available (not grayed out) in the menu.

note

What if it doesn't work? There's not much that can go wrong with this simple `canAcceptCommand()` function, except typos. Compare your code to the code printed here, and make sure there are no misspellings or mistypings.

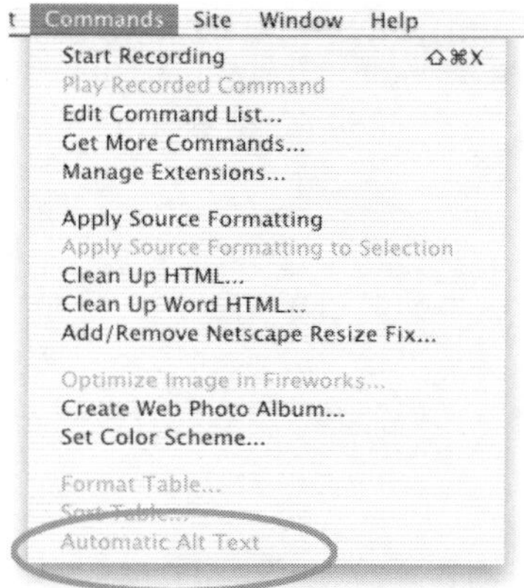

FIGURE 5.8 *The Automatic Alt Text command, available for use.*

Task 5: Add a dialog box and the *commandButtons()* function

It's a common technique in web page layout to use small, invisible shim images to stabilize tables and add white space to a page. These images don't need `alt` text; in fact, having `alt` text for every shim can be a distraction for visitors. This is especially true if the visitor's browser is set to show little popup ToolTips based on `alt` text. The standard way to avoid an overload of `alt` text when shim images are used is to assign empty `alt` labels (`alt = " "`) to those images.

Expanding on the preceding techniques for accessing DOM objects, it should be easy enough to alter the function to identify and deal with shim images. But we'll need a way to ask the user which images in the current document are shims. This requires that our command have a dialog box. The dialog box requires some extra coding; equally importantly, it requires some strategizing.

1. Start by designing the form for the dialog box. It needs one input field to collect the source (`src`) information for shim files. There are several ways to collect this information. You could ask the user to type in the filename or path; allow the user to browse to the file and derive the path from that; present the user with a list of images already in the document and ask him to select one (or more) to be treated as shims; or present a checkbox list of common filenames and allow the user to check all that apply. The solution we'll use here is to present a text field and a browse button, as this follows the approach used elsewhere in Dreamweaver.

In your command file, create the form, remembering not to include any OK or Cancel buttons (Dreamweaver supplies those). Figure 5.9 shows the proposed dialog box design. The code for the form should look like this:

```
<form name="myForm">
<table border="0">
   <tr valign="baseline">
      <td align="right" nowrap>Shim image:</td>
      <td align="left" nowrap>
         <input type="text" name="shimfile">
         <input type="button" value="Browse">
      </td>
   </tr>
</table>
</form>
```

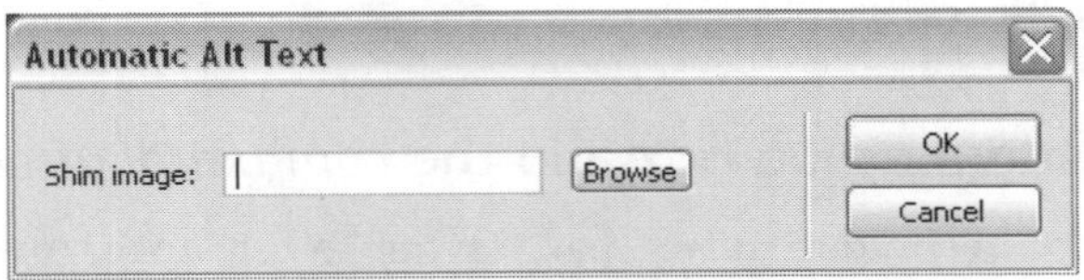

FIGURE 5.9 *The desired layout for the Automatic Alt Text command's dialog box.*

2. Unlike the API for behaviors and objects, the commands don't automatically add OK and Cancel buttons to dialog boxes. Now that the form code is in place, you need to add the `commandButtons()` function to the file to tell Dreamweaver what buttons to include and what actions to associate with each button. This function must return an array consisting of a pair of items for each button. The first item in each pair is the name of the button, and the second item is the action to take if the button is clicked.

   For the Automatic Alt Text command, you want an OK button, which causes the `addAlt()` function to execute and close the dialog box window; and a Cancel button that just closes the window. To create these buttons, add the following code to the command file:

```
function commandButtons() {
return new
Array("OK","addAlt();window.close();","Cancel","window.close()");
}
```

   To remind yourself how this function creates its buttons, refer back to Figure 5.3.

3. Now that you have an OK button to execute the main function, remove the `onLoad` event handler from the `<body>`. (If you don't remove it, the command will execute before the dialog box even opens.

   To check the button functionality, try out the revised command. The dialog box should look like the one in Figure 5.9. Note that the command file's `<title>` becomes the title of the dialog box.

4. Now you want the dialog box to actually do something. Whenever the `addAlt()` function encounters an image whose `src` attribute matches whatever file path the user has entered in the dialog box, it should assign that image an `alt` label consisting of an empty space.

   Adjusting the `addAlt()` function so that it does this involves collecting the form data and then adding yet another conditional statement, this one checking the `src` attribute of each image. Because the `src` is first examined in line 11 of the function (in the `else` portion of the conditional that tests for links), this seems like a logical place to add the new code. Revise your `addAlt()` function like this (new code is in bold):

```
function addAlt() {
var myDOM = dw.getDocumentDOM();
var myImages = myDOM.getElementsByTagName('IMG');
var mySrc = "";
var shimfile=document.myForm.shimfile.value;
var myName = "";
for (var a=0;a<myImages.length;a++) {
   if (!myImages.item(a).alt) {
if (myImages.item(a).parentNode.tagName == 'A' &&
➥myImages.item(a).parentNode.href != "#" &&
➥myImages.item(a).parentNode.href.substring(0,10) != "javascript") {
            myName = "Visit "+myImages.item(a).parentNode.href;
            }else{
            mySrc = myImages.item(a).src;
            if (mySrc==shimfile) {
                  myName=" ";
                  }else{
                  myName = mySrc.substring(mySrc.lastIndexOf("/")+1,
                  ➥mySrc.lastIndexOf("."));
                  }
            }
       myImages.item(a).alt = myName;
      }
   }
}
```

With this code, line 6 collects the dialog box input into a variable called `shimfile`. In line 14, the `src` is compared to `shimrfile`. If the condition is met, an empty space is used for the `alt` text; if not, the original code using a truncated version of `src` for the `alt` text is executed instead.

Try this out and see how it works! Open a Dreamweaver file that contains regular images and at least one or two spacer images. Note that because the Browse button is not functional yet, you'll need to type the relative address of the shim image into the text field.

note

What if it doesn't work? Aside from typos, the most common problem when dealing with this many nested conditionals is balancing the curly braces. Make sure you have an opening brace for every closing brace, and that they're in the right places. One trick is to comment lines that contain closing braces, indicating which opening brace is being closed, like this:

```
if (a==b) {
    alert("Hello");
    }//end if (a==b)
```

Task 6: Add browsing capability to the dialog box

Making users type in filenames and paths isn't very good interface design. That's why you created the Automatic Alt Text dialog box with a Browse button. Following Macromedia's UI practices, you want the user to be able to manually enter information in the text field, but you also want the user to be able to click the Browse button, choose a file, and have that information automatically fill in the text field. In scripting terms, this means adding an `onClick` event handler to the button that triggers a new browse-for-file function, and having that function return a filename and path into the `shimfile` text field. Sounds simple, eh? Guess what? It is simple!

1. Start by adding the framework code for a new function to the `<script>` tag in the `<head>` section of your command file. For now, don't add any statements within the code, but you can remind yourself what the function will eventually do by adding comment lines:

   ```
   function browseForShim() {
   //open Browse dialog box and allow user to choose file
   //store the chosen file address in the text field
   }
   ```

2. Because the `browseForShim()` function needs to be called when the Browse button is clicked, also add a function call to the button in your form:

   ```
   <input type="button" value="Browse" onClick="browseForShim()">
   ```

3. In case you're wondering how on earth you're going to write the code that will let users browse for a file, you can relax! The Dreamweaver API has a method for just that—`dw.browseForFileURL()`. Calling this method opens a standard Dreamweaver Select File dialog box, allows the user to select a file, and returns the file path for the chosen file. Table 5.1 lists the specifications of this method.

Table 5.1 Specifications of the *dw.browseForFileURL( )* Function

Function	*dw.browseForFileURL()*
Description	Opens a browse dialog box to allow users to choose files of varying types.
Syntax	`variableName = dw.browseForFileURL(openSelectOrSave, [titleBarLabel], [bShowPreviewPane], [bSuppressSiteRootWarnings], [arrayOfExtensions])`
Arguments	`openSelectOrSave`: Indicates which type of browse dialog box to bring up. Accepted values: `open`, `select`, `save`. `[titleBarLabel]`: The label that should appear at the top of the dialog box. If this parameter is not defined, the operating system default is used. Accepted value: a string. `[bShowPreviewPane]`: A Boolean value that indicates whether to display the image preview pane as part of the dialog box. If this parameter is not defined, it defaults to `true` if browsing for image files, and `false` if not. `[bSuppressSiteRootWarnings]`: A Boolean value indicating whether to suppress warnings about selected files being outside the site root. If this parameter is not defined, it defaults to `false`. `[arrayOfExtensions]`: An array of strings for specifying the Files of Type popup menu that appears at the bottom of the dialog box. Accepted syntax for each entry in the array: `menuEntryText|.xxx[;.yyy;.zzz]|CCCC|`. The name specified in place of `menuEntryText` appears in the popup list. The extensions can be specified as `.xxx[;.yyy;.zzz]` or `CCCC`; where `.xxx` specifies the file extension for the file type (optionally, *.yyy* and `.zzz` specify multiple file extensions), and `CCCC` is the four-character file type constant for use on the Macintosh.
Returns	A string containing the file path (for example, `../../images/myfile.gif`)
Examples	`myVar = browseForFileURL("select", "Find an image", true, false)` opens a "select" dialog box, with a custom title at the top, the preview pane turned on regardless of file type, and site root warnings turned off. `myVar = browseForFileURL("open", "", false)` opens an "open" dialog box, with the default title at the top, and the preview pane turned off regardless of file type. `myVar = browseForFileURL("save")` opens a "save" dialog box, with all other options at their defaults.

Add the following code to your `browseForShim()` function (new code is in bold):

```
function browseForShim() {
//open Browse dialog box and allow user to choose file
var myFile = dw.browseForFileURL();
//store the chosen file address in the text field
document.myForm.shimfile.value = myFile;
}
```

This code is still incomplete, lacking the parameters that you'll need to pass the `dw.browseForFileURL()` method. But you should be able to see how it uses the method to collect a file path into a variable, and then puts that variable into the `shimfile` text field in the form.

4. Look at the syntax requirements in Table 5.1. The `dw.browseForFileURL()` method takes one required and four optional parameters. For the required parameter, the purpose of this Browse button is to let the user select a file, not open or save a file, so the function should call up a select dialog box. Rewrite line 3 of your `browseForShim()` function to look like this (new code is in bold):

```
var myFile = dw.browseForFileURL("select");
```

5. At this point, all required parameters are present, and the code is technically complete. But do you want to add any optional parameters? How about determining what title appears in the title bar of the dialog box? That would be a nice touch. Rewrite the code to look like this:

```
var myFile = dw.browseForFileURL("select","Select Shim File");
```

Try it out! When you choose the Automatic Alt Text command and its dialog box appears, you should now be able to click the Browse button to open a Select Shim File dialog box. Choosing a file in that dialog box, and clicking OK to close that dialog box, should put the file path of the chosen image in your dialog box's text field. Figure 5.10 shows the functional browsing interface at work.

FIGURE 5.10 *Using the Browse feature in the Automatic Alt Text command.*

Task 7: Create a fancier dialog box

Instead of asking the user to choose a shim file from among all the files on his system, wouldn't it be helpful to let him choose from just the images that are actually in the document? That's what we'll tackle next. To accomplish this, we must replace the Browse button and text field with a popup menu that displays the filenames for all images in the document. Because the contents of the popup menu must be determined when the command is called and the dialog box opens, we must also add a new local function to the command file, to be executed `onLoad`, which will collect the filenames of all images in the document and use those names to fill the menu.

1. Start by redesigning the form so that it uses a popup menu instead of a Browse button. For now, give the popup menu only one choice—`**no images found**`. Your redesigned form should look like the one shown in Figure 5.11. The revised form code looks like this (new code is in bold):

```
<form name="myForm">
<table border="0">
   <tr valign="baseline">
      <td align="right" nowrap>Shim image:</td>
      <td align="left" nowrap>
         <select name="shimfile">
            <option>**no images found**</option>
         </select>
      </td>
   </tr>
</table>
</form>
```

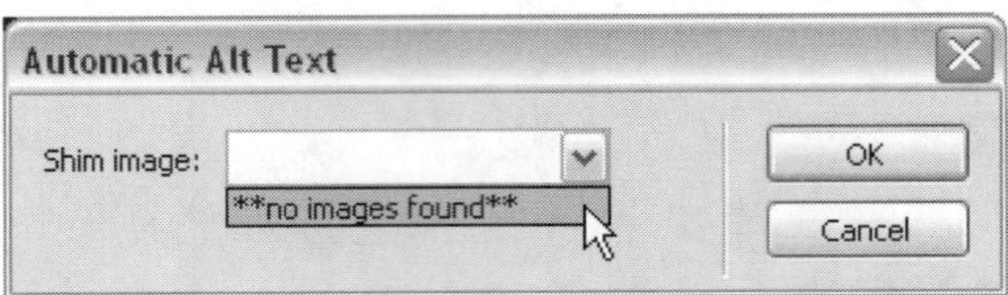

FIGURE 5.11 *The Automatic Alt dialog box, showing a popup menu with default option.*

2. While you're at it, you no longer need the `browseForShim()` function that you created in the previous task. Delete that code from the command file's `<head>` section.

3. Next, start building the function that will initialize the dialog box by filling in the popup menu entries. Start by adding the framework code for the function, like this:

```
function initializeUI(){
//gain access to the document's images
//put each image's src into a new menu item
}
```

4. Because this is a non-API function that must be executed when the dialog box loads, revise your `<body>` tag to include a function call (new code is in bold):

```
<body onLoad="initializeUI()">
```

5. Now start filling in the code framework for the function. As the first comment line says, the function must start by accessing the document's images. Revise the `initializeUI()` function like this (new code is in bold):

```
function initializeUI(){
//gain access to the document's images
var myDOM=dw.getDocumentDOM();
var myImages=myDOM.getElementsByTagName('IMG');
//put each image's src into a new menu item
}
```

6. After the images can be accessed, you need to create a popup menu item (or `<option>` element, in HTML terms) for each one. Menu items require two pieces of information: a label, to be displayed in the menu; and a value, to be used if that menu, item is chosen. For the current project, the value should be the image's file path. The file path could also be used for the label, but for a more readable menu, you'll use the image's filename only (minus any other path information). Both of these pieces of information can be obtained from each image's `src` attribute.

Add the following code to your function:

```
function initializeUI(){
//gain access to the document's images
var myDOM=dw.getDocumentDOM();
var myImages=myDOM.getElementsByTagName('IMG');
//put each image's src into a new menu item
var imageLabel, imageValue;
imageValue=myImages.item(0).src;
imageLabel=imageValue.substring(imageValue.lastIndexOf('/')+1,
imageValue.length);
}
```

The added code creates two variables (`imageLabel` and `imageValue`) to store the label and value information for the popup menu entry. Then, for the first image in the document, it collects the `src` into one variable and creates a truncated version of the `src` for the other. (The substring method used here is very similar to that used in Task 2 of this workshop to generate `alt` labels from `src` properties.)

7. Now use JavaScript's `Option()` constructor to create a new `<option>` (new menu item) using the information collected (new code is in bold):

```
function initializeUI(){
//gain access to the document's images
var myDOM=dw.getDocumentDOM();
var myImages=myDOM.getElementsByTagName('IMG');
//put each image's src into a new menu item
var imageLabel, imageValue;
imageValue=myImages.item(0).src;
imageLabel=imageValue.substring(imageValue.lastIndexOf('/')+1,
imageValue.length);
document.myForm.shimfile.options[0]=new Option(imageLabel,imageValue);
}
```

Because all menu items in the popup menu are part of an options array, by referring to `options[0]` this code creates a new menu item replacing the single menu item (`**no images found**`) that has been coded into the HTML.

note

To learn more about the `Option()` constructor, look up the Option object in the Dreamweaver JavaScript Reference panel.

8. Before proceeding any further, test the command to make sure it works so far. When the command is called and the Automatic Alt Text dialog box opens, it should display a popup menu containing one item—not the default item but the name of the first image in the document (see Figure 5.12).

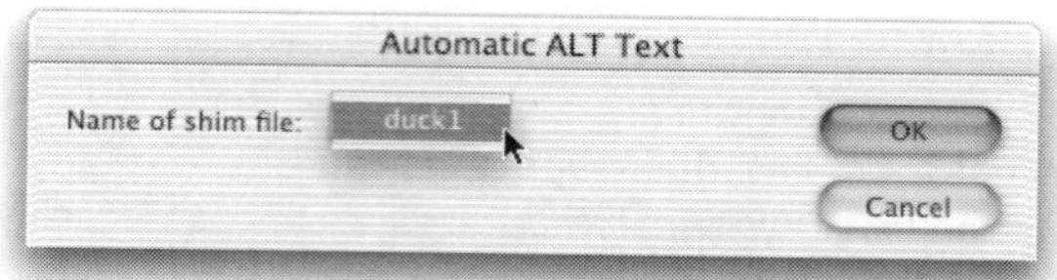

FIGURE 5.12 *The Automatic Alt Text dialog box, showing one dynamically generated menu item.*

9. Why does the popup menu contain only one item? Because the `initializeUI()` function collects information from only the first image in the document's node list. Revise the function by adding a `for` loop to step through every image in the list, creating a menu item for each, like this:

```
function initializeUI(){
//gain access to the document's images
var myDOM=dw.getDocumentDOM();
var myImages=myDOM.getElementsByTagName('IMG');
//put each image's src into a new menu item
var imageLabel, imageValue;
for (var a=0;a<myImages.length;a++) {
   imageValue=myImages.item(a).src;
   imageLabel = imageValue.substring
   ➥(imageValue.lastIndexOf('/')+1,imageValue.length);
   document.myForm.shimfile.options[a]=new
   ➥Option(imageLabel,imageValue);
   }
}
```

The `for` loop surrounds all the code for collecting image information and creating menu items. Within the loop, the references to the image node list (line 8) and the options array (line 10) have been revised to reference the counter variable, `a`, instead of `0`. This allows the function to add popup menu items for all images in the document.

10. Try the command again. When the dialog box appears, the popup menu should contain a full list of all images in the document (see Figure 5.13).

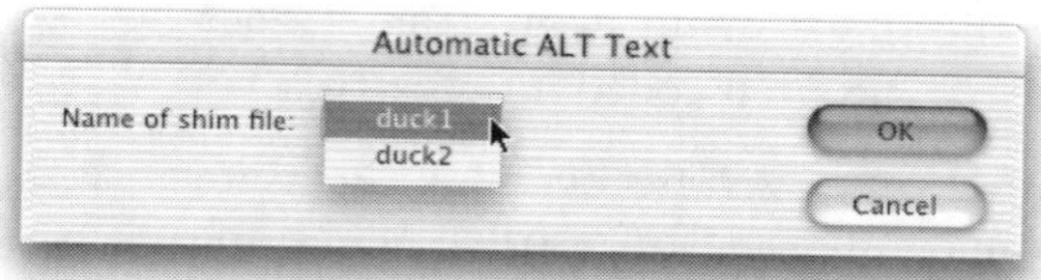

FIGURE 5.13 *The Automatic Alt Text dialog box, with dynamically generated popup menu displaying the filenames of all document images.*

11. Now that the dialog box is working properly, another problem remains. The `addAlt()` function has been written to collect a value from a text field, ike this:

```
shimfile = document.myForm.shimfile.value;
```

It must be revised to collect information from a popup menu. Revise the opening portion of the `addAlt()` function to look like this (new code is in bold):

```
function addAlt() {
var myDOM = dw.getDocumentDOM();
var myImages = myDOM.getElementsByTagName('IMG');
var mySrc = "";
var myName = "";
var choice = document.myForm.shimfile.selectedIndex;
var shimfile = document.myForm.shimfile.options[choice].value;
[etc]
```

Line 6 of the function determines which option the user has chosen from the menu; line 7 collects the value of that selected option. As long as the rest of your function refers to the variable `shimfile`, as the sample code here does, no other changes need to be made.

note

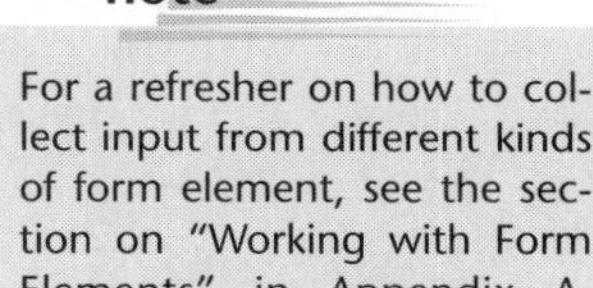

For a refresher on how to collect input from different kinds of form element, see the section on "Working with Form Elements" in Appendix A, "JavaScript Primer."

12. Try your command out and see how it works. Choosing the command should generate a dialog box that looks like the one shown in Figure 5.14. Choosing an image from the popup menu should identify that image as the shim for the document, exactly as if you had browsed to it using the dialog box you defined earlier. When you click OK, `alt` labels should be added to all images in the document except your chosen shim images, which should have empty `alt` labels.

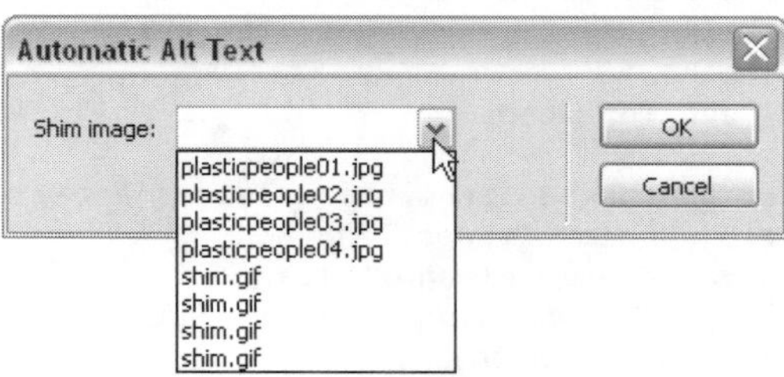

FIGURE 5.14 *The Automatic Alt Text dialog box, showing the populated popup menu. Repeated images in the document appear multiple times in the list.*

13. One interface problem you could complain about in this dialog box is that any image that appears more than once in the document also appears more than once in the popup list. (If the test document used to try out your command didn't have multiple instances of images, you may not have noticed this problem.) A better solution is for the popup menu to list each image only once, even if it appears in the document multiple times. This requires some revision of the `initializeUI()` function.

    How can you make this happen? Instead of using the document's node list of images to create your popup menu (the node list may have repeated occurrences of images in it), you need to create a special array of unique images in the document and build the popup menu from that. You need to create this special array by stepping through the node list and adding images to it only if they haven't already been added. This requires some complex `for` loops and if-statements.

    Start by changing your code so that it puts all images into an array called `uniqueImages` and creates the popup menu from that array (new code is in bold):

    ```
    function initializeUI(){
    //gain access to the document's images
    var myDOM=dw.getDocumentDOM();
    var myImages=myDOM.getElementsByTagName('IMG');
    //put each image's src into a new menu item
    var imageLabel, imageValue;
    var uniqueImages = new Array();
    var ctr=0;

    //feed node list of images into uniqueImages array
    for (var b=0;b<myImages.length;b++) {
          uniqueImages[ctr]=myImages.item(b);
          ctr++;
          } // end for loop b

    //construct popup menu from uniqueImages array
    for (var a=0;a<uniqueImages.length;a++) {
          imageValue=uniqueImages[a].src;
          imageLabel=imageValue.substring(imageValue.lastIndexOf('/')+1,
          ➥imageValue.length);
          document.myForm.shimfile.options[a]=new
          ➥Option(imageLabel,imageValue);
          } //end for loop a
    }
    ```

    You've defined a new array in line 7, with its own counter variable (`ctr`, defined in line 8). Then you added a second `for` loop (this one using the variable `b` as a counter), which steps through the document's images node list and moves every image into the `uniqueImages` array.

Note that you also added comments to the end of each of your two `for` loops, in lines 14 and 21. This is simply to help you keep track of the closing curly braces so that you can tell at a glance where each loop starts and ends.

14. After you have this new code in place, reload extensions in Dreamweaver and try your command again. The resulting dialog box and popup menu should be identical to the ones created earlier, because you haven't changed any functionality here. All you did was add an intermediate step so that the script now uses an intermediate `uniqueImages` array.

15. You've created the intermediate array because you don't necessarily want to put all of the images in the node list into your popup menu. Weeding out the unwanted images requires a conditional statement, so only certain images get fed into the `uniqueImages` array. To prepare the ground for that, add the following new code (shown in bold):

```
function initializeUI(){
//gain access to the document's images
var myDOM=dw.getDocumentDOM();
var myImages=myDOM.getElementsByTagName('IMG');
//put each image's src into a new menu item
var imageLabel, imageValue;
var uniqueImages = new Array();
var ctr=0;
var found=0;

//feed node list of images into uniqueImages array
for (var b=0;b<myImages.length;b++) {
      if (found==0) {
      uniqueImages[ctr]=myImages.item(b);
            ctr++;
            }//end if (found==0)
      }//end for loop b
[etc]
```

What did you do here? You created a variable called `found` and used it as part of a conditional statement that determines whether or not each image will be fed into the `uniqueImages` array. Only if `found` is set to `0` will the image in question be added. Of course, this is a very simple setup, in which `found` will always be set to `0` because that's how you initialized it, and your script never changes that. This bit of code is just an easy way of getting the if-statement syntax in place without disturbing the functionality of your script.

16. Can you tell how the new conditional will change what appears in your popup menu? Try it out and see. Because `found` is always equal to `0`, the condition will always be `true`, and the image will always be added to the `uniqueImages` array. So your resulting popup menu should still display all images, just as it did before. (If you test the script, and it doesn't work, make sure the syntax of your conditional is correct.)

17. Now that the conditional is in place, see how it works. Change line 9 of your code by initializing `found` to `1` instead of `0`, like this:

```
var found = 1;
```

    Now when you try your command, what will show in the popup menu? Nothing except the default entry, because no images are moved into the `uniqueImages` array.

18. Finally, make your conditional do something useful. Each image in the `myImages` node list should be added to the `uniqueImages` array only if an entry with that `src` doesn't already exist there. This means adding yet another `for` loop and conditional, to set `found` before moving the images. To do this, don't initialize the `found` variable right away. Instead, add the following the lines to your code (shown in bold):

```
function initializeUI(){
//gain access to the document's images
var myDOM=dw.getDocumentDOM();
var myImages=myDOM.getElementsByTagName('IMG');
//put each image's src into a new menu item
var imageLabel, imageValue;
var uniqueImages = new Array();
var ctr=0;
var found;

//feed node list of images into uniqueImages array
for (var b=0;b<myImages.length;b++) {
   //test to see if this image is in the uniqueImages array
   found=0;
   //step through the uniqueImages array, comparing each entry to
   ➥this image
   for (var c=0;c<uniqueImages.length;c++) {
      //if a match is found, set found to 1 and stop looking
      if (myImages.item(b).src==uniqueImages[c].src) {
         found=1;
         break;
         }//end if
      }//end for loop c
   if (found==0) {
      uniqueImages[ctr]=myImages.item(b);
      ctr++;
   }//end if (found==0)
   }//end for loop b
[etc]
```

What's happening here? Within `for loop b`, before adding an image to the `uniqueImages` array, the image's `src` value must be compared to all `src` values already in the `uniqueImages` array. The process starts by setting `found` to `0` (because at the beginning of the process, no match has been found in the `uniqueImages` array). Then another `for` loop (indicated by the `c` counter variable) steps through the entries already in the `uniqueImages` array. Within that loop, another conditional compares the `src` value of the image to each entry in the `uniqueImages` array. If a match is found, `found` is set to `1`, and a break statement stops the loop from continuing. Can you see why it helps to comment the closing curly braces for each loop and conditional?

19. After you have this latest code revision in place, try the command out in Dreamweaver. You should get a dialog box with a much tidier popup list, like the one shown in Figure 5.15.

FIGURE 5.15 *The Automatic Alt Text dialog box, with non-redundant popup list.*

20. Are you done yet? Not quite! Here's one last problem you may run into: If, when you're testing your command, you don't choose anything from the popup menu and then click OK, you'll generate a JavaScript error. This is because the `addAlt()` function tries to pull a value from the selected popup menu option, but there isn't one.

    To eliminate this error, add the following code to your function (new code is in bold):

```
function addAlt() {
//gain access to the images in the document
var myDOM = dw.getDocumentDOM();
var myImages = myDOM.getElementsByTagName('IMG');
//variables to store info for new menu options to be created
var mySrc = "";
var myName = "";

//collect name of selected image in popup menu (shim)
var choice = document.myForm.shimfile.selectedIndex;
if (choice>=0) {//if user has made a choice
   var shimfile = document.myForm.shimfile.options[choice].value;
   }
```

    If the user doesn't make any choice from the popup menu, the `selectedIndex` property fed into the `choice` variable will be `-1`. So, by adding a conditional that only tries to collect a `shimfile` value only if the choice is `0` or larger, you eliminate this error.

Task 8: Adding online help

Adding online help to commands is basically the same as adding help to any extension type: The help can be in the form of a short paragraph in the dialog box itself, a link to a web page, or a link to an HTML page stored within the Configuration folder. Just as you must explicitly add OK and Cancel buttons to command dialog boxes, however, you must also explicitly add Help buttons. In this step, you create an HTML document containing help information, and create a Help button that links to it.

1. Macromedia requests that help documents, along with any other support files your extensions may need, be stored in subfolders in the Configuration/Shared folder. So, start by navigating to the Configuration/Shared folder and creating a new folder. Call the folder **MyShared**. Figure 5.16 shows the new MyShared folder in place.

note

If you're going to share your extensions, especially if you may want to submit them to the Dreamweaver Exchange, it's a good idea to name your shared folder something that reflects you or your company. A generic name is used in the exercises here, but for your own use you'll want something more descriptive.

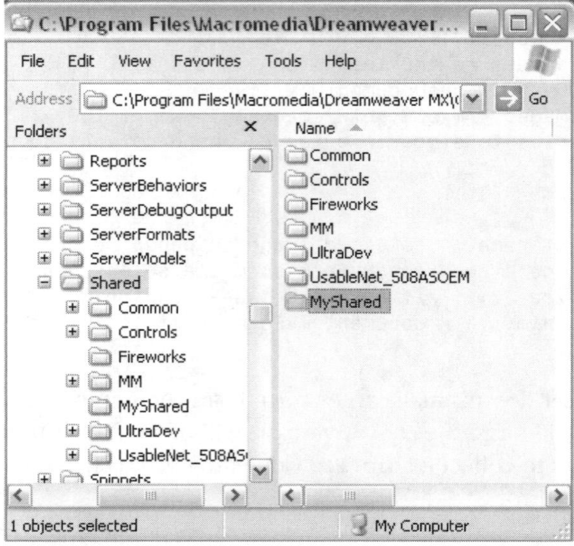

Figure 5.16 *The Configuration/Shared folder, with the MyShared folder added.*

2. Next, create the HTML help document for your command. Call it **AutomaticAltHelp.htm** and store it in the MyShared folder.

   You can do this in Dreamweaver or in your text editor. You can make the document as simple or as extensive as you like. Macromedia recommends that the document include information about where the item can be found in the interface and how it works. Figure 5.17 shows a sample of a simple help file for Automatic Alt Text.

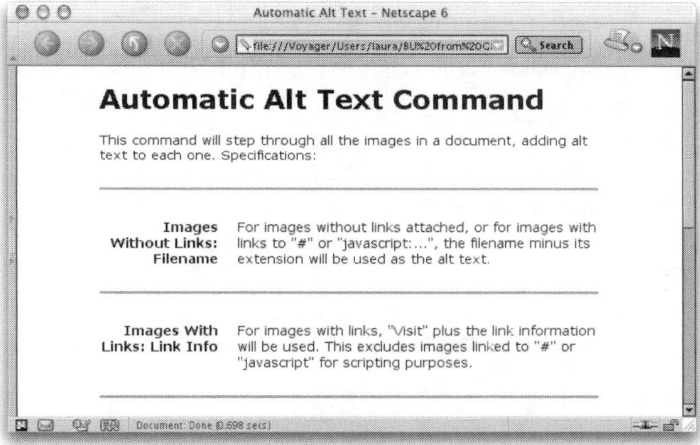

FIGURE 5.17 *The Help document for Automatic Alt Text.*

Now you create the Help button in the command's dialog box. This is a two-step process: first, you write a function that launches the help document; second, you use the `commandButtons()` function to create a new button to call that function.

3. In your text editor, open the command document, and add the following function (new code is in bold):

```
function launchHelp() {
var myURL = dw.getConfigurationPath();
myURL += "/Shared/MyShared/AutomaticAltHelp.htm";
dw.browseDocument(myURL);
}
```

   What's happening here? To open the help document, you need its absolute address on the user's computer. The `dw.getConfigurationPath()` function gets the absolute address of the Configuration folder. Then you concatenate that information with the path from the Configuration root to the file itself. Finally, you use the `dw.browseDocument()` function, feeding it the absolute address, to open the file.

Table 5.2 shows the specifications for these two functions. Note that because both functions are methods of the `dreamweaver` object, you don't need to get DOM access before calling them.

Table 5.2 Specifications and Examples for the Functions Used in Calling Help Documents

Function	*`dw.getConfigurationPath()`*
Description	Gets the absolute address of the Configuration folder on a user's computer.
Syntax	`variableName = dw.getConfigurationPath()`
Arguments	None
Returns	A string containing the file path (for example, `file://MyComputer/ProgramFiles/Macromedia/Dreamweaver/Configuration`)
Function	*`dw.browseDocument()`*
Description	Launches the default browser and opens a specified file.
Syntax	`dw.browseDocument(`*`absoluteURL`*`)`
Arguments	`absoluteURL`: a string representing an absolute path to an HTML document
Returns	Nothing

Examples	`//launches the default browser, connects to the Internet, and opens the Macromedia home page`
	`dw.browseDocument("http://www.macromedia.com")`
	`//launches the default browser and opens a locally stored file var myURL="file://MyComputer/WebFiles/index.html"`
	`dw.browseDocument(myURL);`
	`//launches a file in the Configuration folder`
	`var myURL=dw.getConfigurationPath();`
	`myURL += "/Shared/MyShared/myfile.html";`
	`sdw.browseDocument(myURL);`

4. Now you need to add the Help button that calls this function. In your command document, find the `commandButtons()` function and add the following code (new code is in bold):

```
function commandButtons() {
return new
➥Array("OK","addAlt();window.close();","Cancel","window.close()","Help","
➥launchHelp()");
}
```

Note that the instructions for the Help button do not include closing the dialog box. Normally, when a user asks for help while in a dialog box, he wants to come back to the same dialog box after reading the help document.

With all of this new code in place, try your command out again. If you entered the correct code in the `commandButtons()` function, the dialog box will include a Help button, like that shown in Figure 5.18. If you created your help document and entered the correct path for it in the `launchHelp()` function, clicking the Help button will open it in the browser. When you return to Dreamweaver from the help page, the dialog box will still be open.

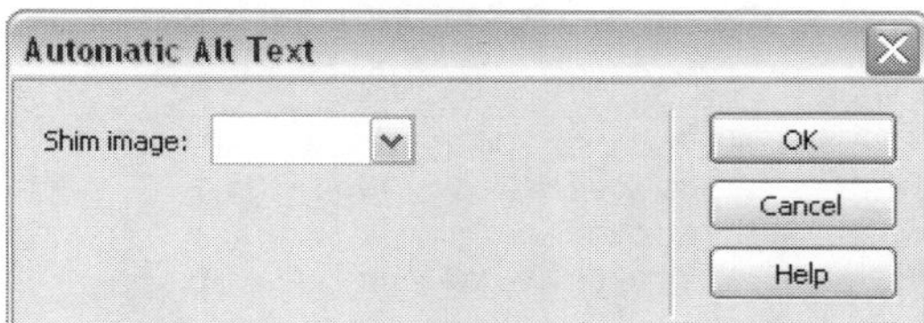

FIGURE 5.18 *The Automatic Alt Text dialog box, with the Help button in place.*

Wrapping Up the Automatic Alt Command

There has been a lot to learn in this one command. You learned how to use the commands API. In the course of building the main `addAlt()` function, you got some good experience working with the DOM to access images and their properties. You learned how to make some sophisticated interface elements, and how to add more substantial online help to an extension. And you learned a whole selection of useful API methods along the way, including `dw.browseForFile()` and `dw.getConfigurationPath()`. As a bonus, you ended up with a potentially useful command for future Dreamweaver projects.

Workshop #2: A Command That Uses String Access

In this workshop, you create another command that starts simple and adds complexity. The command you create here shows that accessing the DOM as a string can be used to great effect when object access is inappropriate. This includes any time the user may want to perform operations on objects that are only partially selected (such as only one word of a text chunk) or when the editing task involves pulling selected text out of a document, performing edits on it, and putting it back in the document.

Sample Command: Converting Selected Text to Uppercase

Have you ever wanted to convert selected text to uppercase in Dreamweaver? It seems straightforward, and in a way it is—but only if you use string access.

A little explanation is in order here. The goal of this command is to take exactly the text the user has selected and convert it to uppercase. If you refer back to the discussion of nodes and node types in Chapter 4 (see the section on "DOM Basics"), you'll remember that each chunk of text in a document constitutes an object of the `TEXT_NODE` type. So one way to accomplish this task would be to access the text object (using `dom.getSelectedNode()`), access the text within the object by accessing its `data` property, and apply the JavaScript `toUpperCase()` string method, like this:

```
function ChangeCase() {
       myDOM = dw.getDocumentDOM();
       myObject = myDOM.getSelectedNode();
       myText = myObject.data;
       myObject.data = myText.toUpperCase();
}
```

The limitation of using this approach, however, is that it assumes an entire text object (with no surrounding objects) has been selected. Life—and user selections—are seldom that simple. For example, here are a few samples of what users might have selected in the document at the time they choose this command (in each case, the user's selection is shown in bold):

- `<p>It was a` **`dark and stormy`** `night.</p>`. A simple selection consisting of text only, which is part of a larger text node object. You need to access the selection offsets, compare them to the node offsets, and create a substring of the node data.
- **`<p>It was a dark and stormy night.</p>`**. The selection is an element node containing text. You need to determine that the selected object is not text, but has a text node as a child.
- **`<p><font size="2">It was a dark and stormy night.</font></p>`**. The selection is an element node containing an element node that contains a text node. This involves climbing down through two generations of childNodes.
- **`<p>It was a <b>dark</b> and stormy night.</p>`**. The selection is an element node containing two text nodes and another element node, which then contains another text node. This involves some fancy maneuvering, sorting out childNodes.
- `<p>It was a <b>`**`dark</b>`** `and stormy night.</p>`. The selection is a text node and part of an element node—this can happen when the user double-clicks to select a single word. This selection is very difficult to isolate.

Can you see that trying to determine the selection by accessing nodes is going to get very complicated very quickly? A much more straightforward approach is to assume that the entire HTML code for the user's document is one large string, and then use the Dreamweaver `dom.getSelection()` method, along with the JavaScript `substring` method, to isolate exactly the text to be changed.

Task 1: Create the command file document

In your text editor, create a new document containing the command file framework (use the code from Listing 5.1 to start with). Save it in the Commands folder as **Make Uppercase.htm**.

Task 2: Create the basic code for the main function

Here's the idea: You access the entire HTML string (`outerHTML`) and assign it to a variable. Then access the selection as character offsets into the HTML string (`dom.getSelection()`), which means you can now use the JavaScript `substring` method on the HTML string to gain access to the individual characters in the selection. Using the `substring` method, divide the HTML string into three smaller strings: all the code before the selection, all the code in the selection, and all the code after the selection. Convert the selected string into uppercase; using the JavaScript `toUpperCase()` method, then join the three substrings back together using concatenation, and feed them back into the document as the new HTML string. Ready?

1. Start by setting up your command file's main function. Change the name of the generic `runCommand()` function to a more appropriate name, like `changeCase()`. Then fill in comment lines indicating what the command needs to do (new code is in bold):

```
function changeCase() {
//gain access to the HTML element node object
//collect the document's entire code as a string
//collect the character offsets of the current selection
//break the document string into three substrings
//change the substring representing the selection to upper case
//concatenate the three substrings back into one big string
//replace the document's HTML string with the new string
}
```

2. Next, add the code that will access the document as an HTML string (new code is in bold):

```
function changeCase() {
//gain access to the HTML element node object
var myDOM = dw.getDocumentDOM();
var myHTML = myDOM.documentElement;

//collect the document's entire code as a string
var myHTMLstring = myHTML.outerHTML;
```

```
//collect the character offsets of the current selection
//break the document string into three substrings
//change the substring representing the selection to upper case
//concatenate the three substrings back into one big string
//replace the document's HTML string with the new string
}
```

3 Using the `dom.getSelection()` method, find the first and last character of the user's selection, and use that information to collect the three substrings (`beforeSelection`, `mySelection`, `afterSelection`):

```
function changeCase() {
//gain access to the HTML element node object
var myDOM = dw.getDocumentDOM();
var myHTML = myDOM.documentElement;

//collect the document's entire code as a string
var myHTMLstring = myHTML.outerHTML;

//collect the character offsets of the current selection
var myOffsets = myDOM.getSelection();

//break the document string into three substrings
var beforeSelection = myHTMLstring.substring(0,myOffsets[0]);
var mySelection = myHTMLstring.substring(myOffsets[0],myOffsets[1]);
var afterSelection =
myHTMLstring.substring(myOffsets[1],myHTMLstring.length);

//change the substring representing the selection to upper case
//concatenate the three substrings back into one big string
//replace the document's HTML string with the new string
}
```

4. So far, you're doing a lot of typing without seeing any results. As a diagnostic procedure, try adding a few `window.alert` statements to the end of your function code, which will tell you what's being collected in your three variables:

```
//change the substring representing the selection to upper case
//concatenate the three substrings back into one big string
//replace the document's HTML string with the new string
//examine the contents of the variables
window.alert(beforeSelection);
window.alert(mySelection);
window.alert(afterSelection);
}
```

5. After you've added this last bit of code, try out your extension. Reload Dreamweaver extensions and open a document within Dreamweaver that contains various page elements you can select. Select something and run your command. Three alert windows should appear, one after the other, displaying all the HTML code up to your selected code, your selected code, and all the code after your selection. Figure 5.19 shows a typical result.

The `window.alert()` statement was used throughout the Practice Session in the previous chapter as a quick way of getting feedback from Dreamweaver about DOM access. As you can see here, it's also a simple way to test the progress of variable assignments and calculations as you're developing projects.

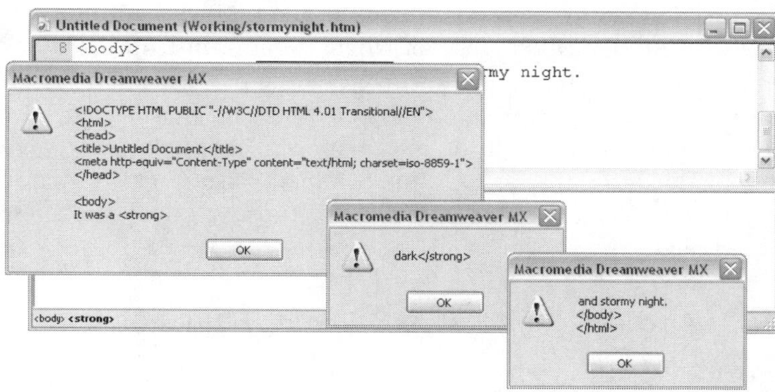

FIGURE 5.19 *Running the Make Upper Case command with three* `window.alert()` *statements to display different portions of the HTML code string.*

6. Now that you have isolated the selection and run a test to see that the code string is being properly subdivided, all you need to do is convert the text in the `mySelection` variable to uppercase and then concatenate the three substrings back together.

   To accomplish this, remove the `window.alert()` statements and change the end of your function to look like this (new code is in bold):

```
function changeCase() {
//gain access to the HTML element node object
var myDOM = dw.getDocumentDOM();
var myHTML = myDOM.documentElement;

//collect the document's entire code as a string
var myHTMLstring = myHTML.outerHTML;

//collect the character offsets of the current selection
var myOffsets = myDOM.getSelection();
```

```
//break the document string into three substrings
var beforeSelection = myHTMLstring.substring(0,myOffsets[0]);
var mySelection = myHTMLstring.substring(myOffsets[0],myOffsets[1]);
var afterSelection =
➥myHTMLstring.substring(myOffsets[1],myHTMLstring.length);

//change the substring representing the selection to upper case
var newSelection = mySelection.toUpperCase();

//concatenate the three substrings back into one big string
var newHTMLstring = beforeSelection + newSelection + afterSelection;

//replace the document's HTML string with the new string
myHTML.outerHTML = newHTMLstring;
}
```

Take this code for a test drive. Can you see any problems with it? Are there any situations where it just won't work, or where it does something you don't want it to? As written, the script has the following potential problems: The command can't distinguish between selected text and selected tags, so that if your selection includes elements other than text, all the information in those elements (tag names, attributes) is changed to uppercase. Or, the command also can't distinguish special characters (entities) such as ` `, and converts those to uppercase. These problems are addressed next.

Task 3: Add the *canAcceptCommand( )* function

Some of the problems you may be experiencing after completing Task 2 can be dealt with by making the command unavailable if there is no open document or if the selection isn't appropriate. This means adding a `canAcceptCommand()` function to your command file.

1. Start with a very simple solution, adding this code to your command file's `<script>` tag:

```
function canAcceptCommand() {
var myDOM = dw.getDocumentDOM();
if (!myDOM) return false;
var myOffsets = myDOM.getSelection();
var myObject = myDOM.getSelectedNode();
if (myOffsets[0] < myOffsets[1] && myObject.nodeType == "3") {
      return true;
      } else {
      return false;
      }
}
```

Can you see what's happening here? After gaining DOM access in line 2, line 3 gains access to the beginning and ending position of the selection in the document's HTML string. Line 4 gains access to the object (node) that contains the user's current selection. In line 5, a conditional statement tests for two conditions: If the two numbers stored in `myOffsets` are not the same number, then the beginning of the selection is not the same as the ending of the selection, which means there is actually something selected in the document. (Remember from Table 4.12 in the previous chapter that if the two offset numbers are the same, this means the selection is an insertion point.) That's the first condition that must be met. Then, if the object is of nodeType 3, which is the type for text objects, the selection must be part of a text object and therefore must consist of text. If both conditions are true, the function returns `true`, and the Make Uppercase command will be made available in the Command menu. If not, the function returns `false`, and the command will show as grayed out.

2. This is a very strict standard, though, that doesn't allow any selections that include anything other than text. To see how limiting it is, create a practice document in Dreamweaver that contains the following lines of HTML:

   ```
   <p>It was a dark and stormy night.</p>
   <p>It was a <b>dark</b> and stormy night.</p>
   ```

   Triple-click in the first paragraph to select it. Then try to choose the Make Uppercase command. The command will be grayed out in the menu because the selection includes the entire `<p>` element, which is technically not an object of the text node type. (It's an object of the element node type).

   Now double-click the word `dark` in the second paragraph and try to choose the command. Again, double-clicking also selects part of the `<b>` element, which is not a text object.

   Finally, drag across portions of both paragraphs to select them and then try to choose the command. It will still be grayed out because in this case your selection includes more than one text object.

   You probably don't want your `canAcceptCommand()` function to be this strict.

3. A better criterion is to make the command unavailable only if the selection contains absolutely no text. The code for this is substantially harder to write because you need to start from the user's selection, and then navigate as far as necessary down the DOM hierarchy until you either find text or hit bottom.

Start by adding the following code—which includes a revised `canAcceptCommand()` function and two new items—to your document's `<script>` tag:

```
var gTesting = 0;
function canAcceptCommand() {
var myDOM = dw.getDocumentDOM();
if (!myDOM) return false;
var myOffsets = myDOM.getSelection();
var myObject = myDOM.getSelectedNode();
if (myOffsets[0] < myOffsets[1] && (myObject.nodeType ==
➥"3" || testGeneration(myObject))) {
      return true;
      } else {
      return false;
      }
}

function testGeneration(thisGen) {
var myChildren = thisGen.childNodes;
for (var a=0;a<myChildren.length;a++) {
      thisChild = myChildren.item(a);
      if (thisChild.nodeType == 3) {
            gTesting = 1;
            break;
      }
      if (thisChild.hasChildNodes()) {
            testGeneration(thisChild);
      }
}
return gTesting;
}
```

What does this code do? First, it declares a global variable, `gTesting`, that all functions in the command file will be able to access. This variable will eventually be assigned a value of `1` (for `true`) if a text object has been found, or a `0` (for `false`) if no text object has been found. As a global variable, `gTesting` is automatically established as soon as the command file loads.

The `canAcceptCommand()` function has been rewritten so that its test of acceptability is more complex. As before, the selection must be more than an insertion point (`myOffsets[1]` must be a larger number than `myOffsets[0]`.) In addition to this, one of two conditions must be met:

- The selection must be contained within a text object (of node type 3); or
- If the selection is not contained within a text object, its containing object must be passed to a function called `testGeneration()`, which will determine if it any text elements are present.

What does the testGeneration() function do? It takes an object (such as a <p> tag or a text chunk) as a parameter. In line 2 of the function, it gains access to all of that object's child objects. Starting in line 3, it uses a for loop to examine each child object in turn. For each child, the conditional statement in line 5 asks whether the object is a text object; if so, the gTesting global variable is set to 1, and the loop ends. (There's no need to keep looking, because the goal of this whole set of functions is to determine whether even one text object exists.) If the child object is not a text object, a second conditional in line 9 asks whether the child object has any children of its own; and if so, the testGeneration() function calls another incarnation of itself to examine the child object.

Calling itself like this makes testGeneration() recursive. It hunts through all sibling nodes and calls itself for each of these nodes that has child nodes. If it finds a text node, it stops (breaks). If it doesn't find a text node but finds child nodes, it calls itself to test each of those children. When it runs out of generations, it stops.

When all the different instances of testGeneration() have finished running, the global variable gTesting is passed back to the canAcceptCommand() function. If any text element has been found, the gTesting variable will have been set to 1, which canAcceptCommand() will interpret this as true. If no text elements have been found, the gTesting variable will still be set to its initial value of 0, which canAcceptCommand() will interpret as false.

Task 4: Refine the command to skip over entities and tag elements

Unless you were very strict in implementing canAcceptCommand(), you still have the challenge of telling the command to ignore tags and entities. One way to deal with this is to use a for loop to examine and change one special character at a time; when a < or & is found, skip all subsequent characters until finding > or ;. Can you see how this works? If a < character is found, it marks the beginning of an HTML tag. The script should ignore all characters until the end of the tag is indicated by finding a > character. Using the same logic, when a & is found, that indicates the beginning of an HTML entity such as   or “. On seeing this character, the script should ignore all characters until the end of the entity is indicated by finding a ; character.

1. To implement this refinement, start by changing the `changeCase()` function so that it processes one character at a time instead of the entire `mySelection` substring at once (new code is in bold):

   ```
   function changeCase() {

   [etc]

   //change the substring representing the selection to upper case
   var newSelection="";
   var thisLetter="";
   for (var a=0;a<mySelection.length;a++) {
      thisLetter=mySelection.charAt(a);
      thisLetter=thisLetter.toUpperCase();
      newSelection+=thisLetter;
      }

   [etc]
   }
   ```

   In the previous version of the command, you changed the case of all the characters in `mySelection` and put them into `newSelection` all at once. In this version, you're creating a variable called `thisLetter` and adding one character at a time to it. Then you change the case of `thisLetter` tack its contents onto the existing contents of `newSelection`.

2. To see how you'll proceed from here, add some comment lines to your code. Also add two variables (you'll see what they do by examining the comment lines):

   ```
   function changeCase() {

   [etc]

   //change the substring representing the selection to upper case
   var newSelection="";
   var thisLetter="";
   var toggle=1;
   var endChar;
   for (var a=0;a<mySelection.length;a++) {
      thisLetter=mySelection.charAt(a);
      //if thisLetter is < then turn toggle to 0 and turn endChar to >
      //if thisLetter is & then turn toggle to 0 and turn endChar to ;
      //if thisLetter is endChar then turn toggle to 1
      //if toggle is 1 then change to upper case
      thisLetter=thisLetter.toUpperCase();
      newSelection+=thisLetter;
      }

   [etc]
   }
   ```

Can you see how the logic you're framing will work? The toggle variable will always have a value of `1` (true) or `0` (false). Capitalization of the current character will take place only if the toggle is set to `1`. For every character the `for` loop encounters, if the character is the beginning of a tag (<) or entity (&), the toggle will be turned off (set to `0`), and the `endChar` variable will be set to the appropriate ending character for that element (> or ;). If the loop encounters the character specified by `endChar`, the toggle will be set back to `1` and capitalization will resume.

3. Now all you need to do is add the code that will make each of these comments happen. It's all done with a series of simple conditionals. Add the following code to your function (new code is in bold):

```
function changeCase() {

[etc]

//change the substring representing the selection to upper case
var newSelection="";
var thisLetter="";
var toggle=1;
var endChar;
for (var a=0;a<mySelection.length;a++) {
   thisLetter=mySelection.charAt(a);
   //if thisLetter is < then turn toggle to 0 and turn endChar to >
   if (thisLetter=="<") {
      toggle=0;
      endChar=">";
      }
   //if thisLetter is & then turn toggle to 0 and turn endChar to ;
   if (thisLetter=="&") {
      toggle=0;
      endChar=";";
      ;
   //if thisLetter is endChar then turn toggle to 1
   if (thisletter==endChar) {
      toggle=1;
      }
   //if toggle is 1 then change to upper case
   if (toggle==1) {
      thisLetter=thisLetter.toUpperCase();
      }
   newSelection+=thisLetter;
   }

[etc]
}
```

That's it! Try your command! You should be able to select all sorts of different text chunks and make them upper case. And you did it all by accessing the HTML code of the document as a string. Listing 5.2 shows the complete code for the command.

Listing 5.2 The Finished Code for the Make Upper Case Command, Commented for Reference

```
<html>
<head>
<title>Make Upper Case</title>
<script language="JavaScript">

//to be used by canAcceptCommand() and testGeneration()
var gTesting = 0;

//determines if the command will be grayed-out in the menu
function canAcceptCommand() {

//gain access to object containing user's selection
var myDOM = dw.getDocumentDOM();
if (!myDOM) return false;
var myOffsets = myDOM.getSelection();
var myObject = myDOM.getSelectedNode();

//if user has text object selected, or selection contains a text object,
➥return true
if (myOffsets[0] < myOffsets[1] && myObject.nodeType == 3 ||
➥testGeneration(myObject)) {
      return true;
      } else {
      return false;
      }
}

//tests the children of an object to see if they're text objects
function testGeneration(thisGen) {

//gain access to children of current object
var myChildren = thisGen.childNodes;

//test each child to see if it's a text object
for (var a=0;a<myChildren.length;a++) {
      thisChild = myChildren.item(a);
      if (thisChild.nodeType == 3) {
            gTesting = 1;
            break;
      }
```

```
//if the child has children, run another instance of this function to
➥test them
      if (thisChild.hasChildNodes()) {
            testGeneration(thisChild);
      }
}
//if any child is a text object, this variable will be 1
return gTesting;
}

//main function of command
function changeCase() {

//gain access to the object created by the <html> tag and its contents
var myDOM = dw.getDocumentDOM();
var myHTML = myDOM.documentElement;

//collect the document's entire code as a string
var myHTMLstring = myHTML.outerHTML;

//collect the character offsets of the current selection
var myOffsets = myDOM.getSelection();

//break the document string into three substrings
var beforeSelection = myHTMLstring.substring(0,myOffsets[0]);
var mySelection = myHTMLstring.substring(myOffsets[0],myOffsets[1]);
var afterSelection =
➥myHTMLstring.substring(myOffsets[1],myHTMLstring.length);

//change the substring representing the selection to upper case
var newSelection="";
var thisLetter="";
var toggle=1;
var endChar;

//step through each character in the selection
for (var a=0;a<mySelection.length;a++) {
   thisLetter=mySelection.charAt(a);
   //if thisLetter is < then turn toggle to 0 and turn endChar to >
   if (thisLetter=="<") {
            toggle=0;
            endChar=">";
            }
   //if thisLetter is & then turn toggle to 0 and turn endChar to
   if (thisLetter=="&") {
            toggle=0;
            endChar=";";
            }
   //if thisLetter is endChar then turn toggle to 1
   if (thisLetter==endChar) {
            toggle=1;
```

continues

Listing 5.2 Continued

```
            }
    //if toggle is 1, set thisLetter to upper case
    if (toggle==1) {
        thisLetter=thisLetter.toUpperCase();
        }
    newSelection+=thisLetter;
    }

//concatenate the three substrings back into one big string
var newHTMLstring = beforeSelection + newSelection + afterSelection;


//replace the document's HTML string with the new string
myHTML.outerHTML = newHTMLstring;
}


</script>
</head>
<body onLoad="changeCase()">
</body>
</html>
```

Commands and Menus

The API for commands allows you a great deal of control over how commands work in the menus. Although all commands appear in the Commands menu by default with names determined by their filenames, you can override these defaults and place the commands wherever in the menu system you like. Using the `receiveArguments()` function, you can also make a given command document behave differently by passing it various parameters. The following sections describe how all this works.

Working with menus.xml

The functionality of Dreamweaver menus is determined by another file in the Configuration folder, menus.xml. This file determines what menus appear, what items each menu contains, and what will happen when a user chooses any of these items. This includes menus in the main application menu bar and, for Dreamweaver/Windows, those in the Site window menu bar. It also includes all contextual menus (those that appear when a user right-clicks/Ctrl-clicks) and all panel options menus (those that appear when a user clicks on the popup options menu icon in the upper-right corner of the panels).

menus.xml in the Menus Folder

The menus.xml file is located in the Configuration/Menus folder, along with various other menu-related files (see Figure 5.20). Note that menus.xml is a user-customizable file, which means that if your OS supports multiuser configurations, the copy of it stored in the Dreamweaver main Configuration folder may not be the active copy. Instead, you may find another copy of menus.xml in your user-specific Configuration folder. This is the active copy of the file that you should use in your development work.

note

Windows users, look for your menus.xml in c:\Documents and Settings\username\Application Data\Macromedia\Dreamweaver MX\Configuration\Menus\. Mac OS X users, look in /Users/username/Library/Application Support/Macromedia/Dreamweaver MX/Configuration/Menus/. (Substitute your user name for username.) For more on extending Dreamweaver in a multiuser environment, see the section on "User-Specific Configuration Files" in Chapter 1.

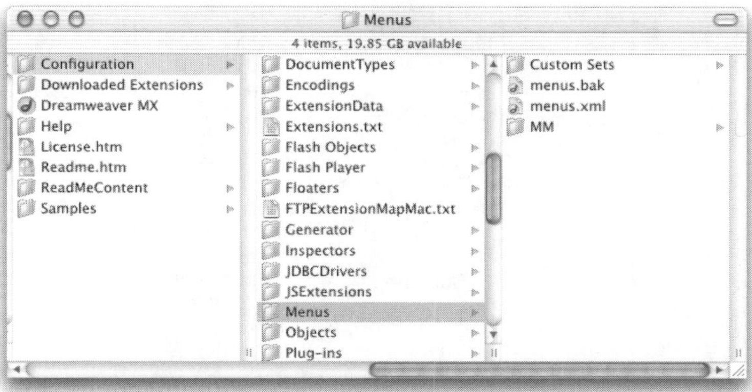

Figure 5.20 *The Configuration/Menus folder, showing menus.xml.*

Another item of interest in the Menus folder is the Custom Sets folder. This folder stores the custom shortcut key definitions that appear when a user accesses the Dreamweaver Edit > Edit Shortcut Keys command. (Again, if you're working in a multiuser environment, the active copy of the Custom Sets folder is stored in your user-specific Configuration folder.)

The Structure of menus.xml

note

menus.xml is a long, possibly confusing file with long lines of markup code. Turn off soft-wrapping in your text editor to get a better sense of how the file structure works.

Before opening the menus file, quit Dreamweaver. It's not good to open the menus file while the application is still running because, unlike most other extension files, the menus file needs to be continually accessed.

After you quit Dreamweaver, go to your text editor and open menus.xml. Snoop around in there until you get a handle on what's stored in there.

As an XML file, menus.xml is built from a series of custom tags that describe menus and menu items. In fact, the entries in this file create the menus and menu items in Dreamweaver, and assign each entry its functionality. Figure 5.21 shows a diagram of the main elements of the file; Table 5.3 shows a list of attributes used in the `<menuitem/>` tag.

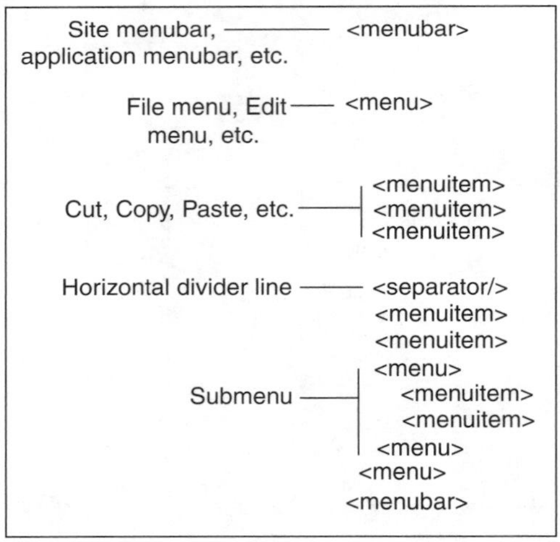

FIGURE 5.21 *Diagram of entries in menus.xml.*

Table 5.3 Elements of *<menuitem>* entries in menus.xml

Parameter Name	*Accepted Values*	*Examples*	*Description*
`name`	String containing a name.	`name="Edit _Query"`	This is the name that appears in the menu. Underscores create Windows-OS shortcuts (those activated by typing the Windows key on a PC keyboard).
`dynamic name`	String containing a placeholder or default entry for a name to be dynamically determined at runtime.	`dynamic name="xxx"` `dynamic name= "No Browsers Selected"`	This parameter can be used with menu commands instead of the `name` parameter. (One or the other must be present, but not both.)
`key` (optional)	Reference to a key and modifiers, formatted as a string. Modifiers are "Cmd" (refers to Cmd/Mac and Ctrl/PC), "`Shift`", and "`Option`"; and are separated by "+".	`key="Cmd+Shift+Q"`	This parameter creates the shortcut key that appears in the menu. Shortcuts specified here are overridden by the shortcut files found in Configuration/ Menus/Custom Sets, and specified under the Dreamweaver Edit: Edit Shortcuts interface.
`enabled` (optional)	String containing a conditional statement that must resolve to `true`.	`enabled="dw. getDocumentDOM ().getSelectedNode(). nodeType=='3' "`	This parameter is generally used when the code to be executed is specified in the command parameter. When code is specified in the file parameter, the file can contain the `canAcceptCommand()` parameter instead.

continues

Table 5.3 Continued

Parameter Name	*Accepted Values*	*Examples*	*Description*
`command`	String containing one or more of JavaScript statements to be executed when the menu item is chosen.	`command="dw.getDocumentDOM().insertHTML('Hello world') "`	The menu entry gets its functionality from either the code in this parameter or the code in a file called by the file parameter. One of these two, but not both, is required.
`file`	String containing a link to a file containing JavaScript code to be executed when the menu item is chosen.	`file="Commands/"Query.html"`	Any link specified here must be root-relative to the Configuration folder. Files used can be stored in the Commands folder, the Menus folder, or elsewhere.
`platform` (optional)	String containing `"Mac"` or `"Win"`.	`platform="Win"`	This parameter indicates that a menu item should appear only on one platform or another. (For instance, only the Mac platform has the "Edit with BBEdit" menu item.) If the parameter is not present, the item appears in all platforms.
`app` (optional)	String containing `"dreamweaver"` or `"ultradev"`.	`app="ultradev"`	This parameter indicates that a menu item should appear only in a particular application: Dreamweaver or UltraDev. If the parameter is not present, the item appears in both programs.

Parameter Name	*Accepted Values*	*Examples*	*Description*
domRequired (optional)	String containing `"true"` or `"false"`, representing whether the command requires a valid DOM.	`domRequired="true"`	If a valid DOM is required, the command can be executed only if the Design and Code views have been synchronized. This parameter is most important when the menu's executable code is specified in the command parameter. When the file parameter is used to link to code, the file contains the `isDomRequired()` function instead.
`arguments` (optional)	String containing any parameters to be passed to the executable code.	`arguments="value1, value2, value3"`	Arguments are passed to executable code in a file using the `receiveArguments()` function in the file. Arguments are passed as an array called `arguments`.
`checked`	String containing a conditional statement.	`"dw.getDocumentDOM().getTextAlignment() == 'center'"`	Checkmarks are generally used as toggles, determined by some condition in the user's document (whether a particular floating panel is showing, for instance). If the statement resolves to `true`, the menu item shows with a checkmark next to it.

continues

Table 5.3 Continued

Parameter Name	*Accepted Values*	*Examples*	*Description*
`id`	String containing a unique, one-word identifier code.	`id="MyStuff_QueryCommand"`	The ID must be present, and must be unique. Macromedia recommends affixing your company name to the beginning of the ID to avoid possible conflicts with other developers' IDs. All Macromedia IDs start with `"MM_"`.

note

XML is a more rigidly structured language than HTML. Its syntax must be followed carefully, and it is case-sensitive.

Customizing the Menus

You can extensively customize the menus in Dreamweaver, without any scripting, by tinkering with the menus.xml file.

- **Rearrange menu items.** To make a menu item appear in a different position in a menu or in a different menu altogether, find the line of code that creates that item in the menus file, and cut and paste it into its new location.
- **Add items to contextual menus.** All Dreamweaver contextual menus are also controlled by this file. To put a menu item into a contextual menu, find the line of code that creates it, and paste a copy into the appropriate contextual menu.
- **Add separator lines.** Separators are the horizontal dividing lines that break menus up into logical groupings for easier reading. To add a separator, just add this line of code between two menu items:

  ```
  <separator/>
  ```

  Note that, in keeping with XML syntax requirements, tags like this that don't occur in pairs must include a forward slash before the closing tag.
- **Add shortcut keys.** Although it is possible to add shortcuts by altering the code in the menus file, it's much simpler to use the Dreamweaver Edit > Edit Shortcuts command (not available prior to Dreamweaver 4).

Controlling a Command's Appearance in the Menus

Although newly added commands appear by default at the bottom of the Commands menu, you can override those defaults by tweaking the menus file and the command file. This is a two-step process:

1. Remove the command from the Commands menu.

   To do this, put the following code in the very first line of the command document:

   ```
   <!-- MENU-LOCATION=NONE -->
   ```

   This comment must be the first line in the document, above the `<html>` tag. If you have separated your command document into separate HTML and JS files, the preceding statement must appear in the HTML file, not the JS file.

2. Add the command to the desired menu.

   To do this, add a properly formatted `<menuitem/>` entry in the menus file. For instance, to add the Automatic Alt Text command to the top of the Modify menu, the following entry should be added to menus.xml immediately following the entry creating the Modify menu and immediately preceding the entry for the Page Properties command:

   ```
   <menuitem name="Automatic Alt Text" file="Commands/Automatic Alt
   ➥Text.html" id="MyStuff_AltText"/>
   ```

   After you've done this, the command file's filename no longer determines the menu item entry, and the command file's location (in the Commands folder) no longer determines its location in the menu system.

Passing Parameters to Commands Using *receiveArguments( )*

After a command has an entry in the menus file, you can pass parameters to the command file to govern exactly how it works. The Import Word HTML and Clean Up Word HTML commands, for instance, both use the same command file document, Clean Up Word HTML.htm, with only a difference in passed parameters to distinguish them.

This process requires two steps: adding an argument to the menus file and receiving the argument in the command file. Because these steps are a bit more complicated than those for controlling a command's appearance in the menus, each step is discussed separately in the following sections.

Menu File: Adding the Arguments Parameter

Within the menus file, you pass parameters to a command by adding an arguments property to the `<menuitem/>` tag (see Table 5.3 for details). In the menus.xml entries for the two Word HTML commands, for instance, the first one passes an argument, and the second one doesn't:

```
<menuitem name="Import _Word HTML..." file="Commands/Clean Up Word
➥HTML.htm" arguments="'import'" id="DWMenu_File_Import_WordHTML" />

<menuitem name="Clean _Up Word HTML..." file="Commands/Clean Up Word
➥HTML.htm" id="DWMenu_Commands_CleanUpWordHTML" />
```

Command File: Using the *receiveArguments( )* Function

Within the command file, you receive the passed arguments and process them by using the `receiveArguments()` function. This function is called automatically as part of the API procedure for commands (refer back to Figure 5.5). Items specified as arguments in the menus file are passed to this function as an array called `arguments`.

Within the `receiveArguments()` function, you can call on the elements in the `arguments` array to set global variables for the main command function to act on, or you can cause actions to happen independently of the command function. In the Clean Up Word HTML command file, for instance, the main command function cleans up Word HTML. But if `arguments[0] == "import"` is passed then, before the main function executes, the `receiveArguments()` function creates a new document and copies the contents of the specified Word file into it, as dictated by the function's code:

```
var curDOM, newDOM;
        // Select the word file to be imported, don't show images,
        ➥supress not in root warnings.
        var HTMLfileTypes = new Array("Word HTML Files (*.htm;
        ➥*.html)|*.htm;*.html|TEXT|");
        var fileName = browseForFileURL("open", MSG_Word_Import, false,
        ➥true, HTMLfileTypes);  //returns a local filename
        if (fileName) {
            // Check for name may not exist.
            curDOM = dw.getDocumentDOM(fileName);
            if (curDOM) {
            newDOM = dw.createDocument();
              if (newDOM) {
                   newDOM.documentElement.outerHTML =
                   ➥curDOM.documentElement.outerHTML;
              }
            }
        }
```

Workshop #3: Manipulating the Menu Entry for a Command

In this workshop, we'll make the Make Upper Case command a bit fancier. First, we'll make the command disappear from the Commands menu and appear in the Text menu (much more logical placement). Then we'll add a new, related command to the Text menu—Make Lower Case—and use a passed argument to allow us to use the same command document for both commands.

Task 1: Change the menu placement of the Make Upper Case command

This is a fairly simple operation. Often, the most challenging part of moving menu entries is determining where to move them to. To make life easier and to avoid disturbing the existing interface, this workshop shows you how to tuck your command in at the bottom of the Text menu, below the Check Spelling menu item.

1. Open the Make Uppercase.htm file and put the following line of code at the very top of the document:

```
<!-- MENU-LOCATION=NONE -->
```

   When this is done, save the file and close it. Now, if you reload Dreamweaver extensions and check your Commands menu, you'll see that the Make Upper Case command no longer appears there.

Task 2: Add an entry for Make Upper Case to the menus.xml file.

Now that the command no longer appears in the menus automatically, we need to explicitly add it by adding an entry to menus.xml. (Remember, if you're working in a multiuser environment, use the menus.xml file in your user-specific Configuration folder.)

1. Quit Dreamweaver. It's best not to edit menus.xml while Dreamweaver is running.
2. In your text editor, open menus.xml. Here comes the tricky part! Find the lines of code that control the Text menu, and in particular the line that creates the Check Spelling entry. To make this job easier, use your text editor's Find command to search for **Spelling**. Unless you've installed other extensions that change menus.xml, the entry should be at line 2468.
3. Directly under the `menuitem` for Check Spelling, create a new line, and enter this code:

```
<menuitem name="Change to Upper Case" file="Commands/Make Uppercase.htm"
➥id="MyStuff_Make_Uppercase"/>
```

Feel free to substitute your own ID if you like, specifying your own company or personal name. Make sure that the file attribute matches the filename you used for the command file.

4. When you're all finished, launch Dreamweaver, and look in the menus for your new command. Figure 5.22 shows the menu item in its new home, at the bottom of the Text menu. Try the command on a test document to make sure it still works.

Figure 5.22 *The Text menu, showing the Change to Upper Case menu item.*

Task 3: Add the Change to Lower Case command to the Text menu

It's time to leverage all the hard work you put into developing the `changeCase()` function by making it work for two commands instead of one. We'll do this by creating an argument in the menus file, and setting it to `upper` for one command and `lower` for another. This is done in the menus file.

1. Quit Dreamweaver. Then open the menus.xml file and find your command's menu item. (Here's a tip: To find the proper menu entry, search for whatever you assigned as the ID property of your custom menu item.)
2. Add the arguments property to your entry, assigning it a value of `upper`, like this (new code is in bold):

```
<menuitem name="Change to Upper Case" file="Commands/Make
➥Uppercase.html" arguments="'upper'" id="MyStuff_Make_Uppercase"/>
```

Note that the argument must appear in two sets of quotation marks, single quotes inside double quotes. The argument must be passed as a string, and you need it to contain a string as well.

3. To create the new menu entry for converting text to lowercase, select and copy the `<menuitem/>` tag for your command, and paste it into the next line of the menus file. Change the code to create a lowercase command and to pass the argument `lower`, like this (new code is in bold):

```
<menuitem name="Change to Lower Case" file="Commands/Make
➥Uppercase.html" arguments="'lower'" id="MyStuff_Make_Lowercase"/>
```

Make sure you change the ID! Remember, every command must have its own unique ID, and you are creating a new command (but without creating a new command file).

5. When you're done, save and close the menus file.

6. Launch Dreamweaver and check the Text menu. You'll see both of your commands present, as shown in Figure 5.23. Of course, they won't be fully functional yet. Because the command file doesn't have a way of processing arguments, at this point both commands will make text uppercase.

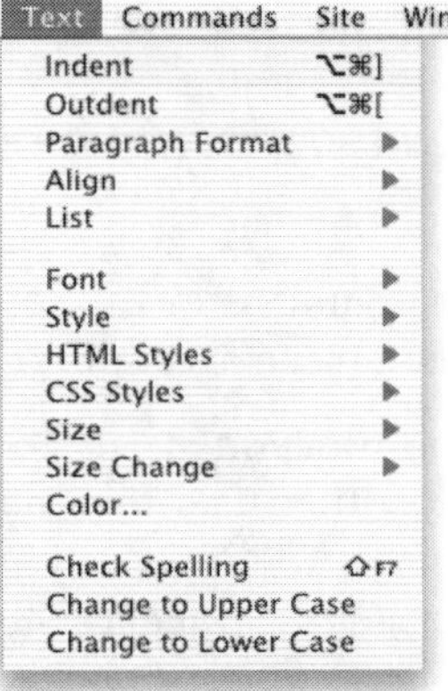

FIGURE 5.23 *The Text menu, showing the Make Upper Case and Make Lower Case commands in place.*

Task 4: Add the *receiveArguments( )* function to the command document

Now we need to set up the command document to receive and process this new argument. We'll do this by creating a global variable to store the argument, and adding the `receiveArguments()` function to feed the `upper` or `lower` argument into the variable.

1. Open the Make Upper Case.htm command file in your text editor. Add the following code to the document's `<script>` tag:

```
var gCase;

function receiveArguments() {
gCase = arguments[0];
}
```

When the user chooses Text > Make Upper Case or Text > Make Lower Case, Dreamweaver will access this file, passing it the appropriate argument (`upper` or `lower`) as specified in the menus.xml entry. The `receiveArguments()` function you just defined feeds that argument into the `gCase` variable. Because you have defined `gCase` as a global variable, the command's other functions (such as the `changeCase()` function) will have access to it as well.

Task 5: Revise the *changeCase( )* function to accommodate the argument

After you've collected the argument in the `gCase` variable, you only need to tweak the `changeCase()` function a bit to account for it.

1. Only one line of the function needs to be changed. Find the line of your `changeCase()` function that uses the `toUpperCase()` method, and change it from this

```
//if toggle is 1, set thisLetter to upper case
if (toggle==1) {
   thisLetter=thisLetter.toUpperCase();
   }
```

to this (new code is in bold):

```
//if toggle is 1, set thisLetter to upper case
if (toggle==1) {
   if (gCase=="upper") {
      thisLetter=thisLetter.toUpperCase();
      }else{
      thisLetter=thisLetter.toLowerCase();
      }
   }
```

Can you see how this works? If `toggle` is set to `1`, some kind of capitalization change will occur. Within that conditional, if the `gCase` argument is set to `upper`, that change will be to capitalize the character in question. Otherwise, the change will be to uncapitalize the character.

2. Save the file and close it. Then try your two commands out in Dreamweaver.

note

Troubleshooting

Assuming your command worked before you added the argument, the only problems you're likely to encounter at this point are typing mistakes. Make sure you've entered the `receiveArguments()` function and the `gCase` variable inside the command file's `<script>` tag but not inside any other functions. Make sure that, in menus.xml, your arguments are nested inside two sets of quotes. In the `changeCase()` function, make sure you added the proper number of curly braces for the nested `if-else` statement.

Menu Commands

Menu commands are commands that have enhanced control over how they will appear in the menu. In particular, menu commands can create dynamic menu entries, including custom menu item names, checkmark toggles, and complete submenus of dynamically generated options.

Menu Commands in the Configuration Folder

Menu commands are not stored in the Commands folder, but in a subfolder within the Configuration/Menus folder. All the standard Macromedia menu commands are stored in the Configuration/Menus/MM folder. Macromedia requests that developers not store their own commands there. Instead, create a custom folder with whatever name you choose, and store custom menu commands there. Because all menu commands are given their place in the menu system by using the menus.xml file, this folder name is not something the user will see. Figure 5.24 shows the Menus folder and its subfolders.

Figure 5.24 *The Configuration/Menus folder, showing the MM subfolder (where the Macromedia standard menu command files are stored). Only partial contents of the MM folder are shown.*

Structure of a Menu Command File

Structurally, menu command files are just like command files, but with added API functions to create their dynamic menu presence. All these extra API functions are optional, and all are called automatically.

setMenuText()

If this function is present in a command file, it determines what text will appear in the menu as this command's menu entry, overriding whatever name is specified in the `<menuitem/>` tag's `name` attribute. For instance, the command document `LaunchExternalEditor.htm` utilizes this function:

```
var MENU_strLaunch = "_Edit with ";

function setMenuText()
{
return MENU_strLaunch + dw.getExternalTextEditor();
}
```

The `dw.getExternalTextEditor()` method gathers the user's specified external editor (chosen in Edit > Preferences and saved in another Dreamweaver configuration file) and concatenates it after the text string `Edit with` to create the menu entry, as shown in Figure 5.25.

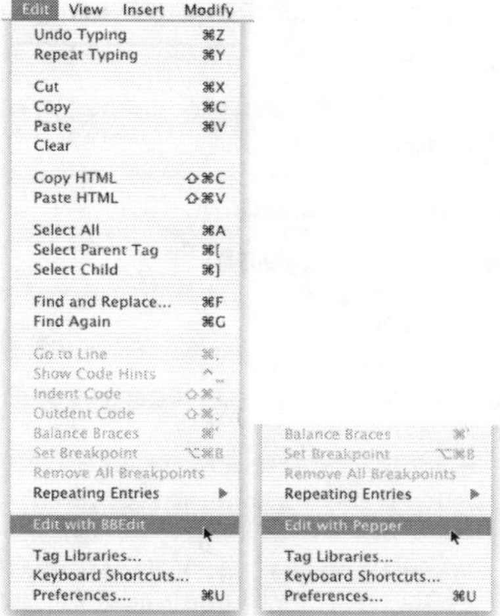

FIGURE 5.25 *The Edit menu, showing different dynamically generated menu text for the Launch External Editor command.*

Although `setMenuText()` does not require any parameters, if the `<menuitem/>` tag in the menus file includes an `arguments` attribute, this function will accept them as parameters. This is useful for distinguishing between two commands that call on the same command file.

*getDynamicContent(*menuID*)*

This function retrieves content to be used in dynamically generating an indeterminate number of menu items to add to a menu. This function may not be used in conjunction with the `setMenuText()` function—only one of the two functions may be used for a given command.

When a user clicks on a menu, Dreamweaver examines the menus.xml file, preparatory to displaying a menu. If any of the `<menuitem/>` entries for that menu contain a `dynamic name` attribute in place of the standard `name` attribute, Dreamweaver looks through that menu item's command file to see if the `getDynamicContent()` function is present. If that function is present, Dreamweaver calls it, passing it the `<menuitem/>`'s unique ID as a parameter. The function must return a `null` value or an array of text strings, each containing the name of a menu item and a unique ID for that menu item, separated from the name by a semicolon. If the function returns `null`, no change is made to the menu—in other words, the menu will display with no dynamically generated items added. If the function returns an array of strings, the first part of each string in the array will become the name of an item in the menu; the second part of each string will become that item's ID, and will be passed to that item's command file as an argument.

As an example of `getDynamicContent()`, the Window menu's list of open windows is generated by this `<menuitem/>` tag:

```
<menuitem dynamic name="(No Open Documents)"
➥file="Menus/MM/Window_Titles.htm" id="DWMenu_MainSite_Window" />
```

And this `getDynamicContent()` function in the Window_Titles.htm file:

```
function getDynamicContent(itemID) {
      var windowList = null;
      var i;
      windowList = new Array();
      var dwWindowNames = dw.getDocumentList();
      if (dwWindowNames.length > 0)
      {
            for (i=0; i<dwWindowNames.length; i++)
            {
                  windowList[i] = new
                  ➥String(dwWindowNames[i].getWindowTitle());
                  windowList[i] += ";id='"+i+"'";
                  windowList[i] = windowList[i].replace(/_/g,"%_");
            }
      }
      return windowList;
}
```

If no windows are open when the command is chosen, the `windowList` variable remains `null`. When the function returns this variable, Dreamweaver displays the Window menu with one entry named (`No Open Documents`)—determined by the dynamic name entry of the `<menuitem/>` entry. If one or more windows are open, the `getDynamicContent()` function uses the dw.`getDocumentList()` method to collect information about all open documents and uses that information to put an array of strings in `windowList`. When the function returns this array, the menu will display an entry for each window.

Figure 5.26 shows the dynamically generated menu entries created by this code.

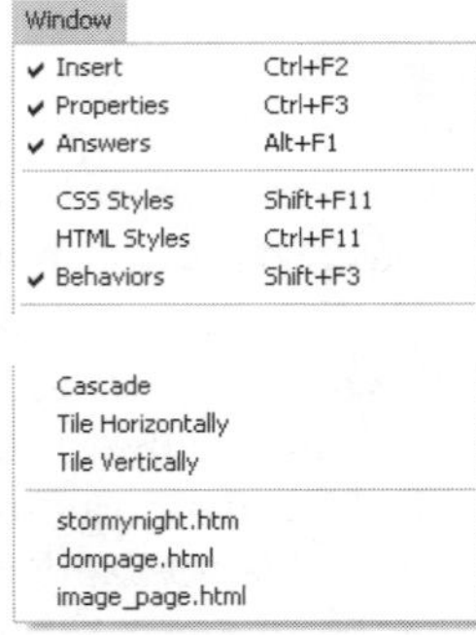

FIGURE 5.26 *The list of open windows generated by the Window_Titles.htm command document, using* `getDynamicContent()`.

isCommandChecked( )

This function determines whether the command's menu item should display with a checkmark next to it or not. It must return a Boolean (`true/false`) value. If it returns `true`, a checkmark appears next to the command's menu item; if it returns `false`, no checkmark appears. The `isCommandChecked()` function doesn't require any parameters, although—as with `setMenuText()`—if the argument's attribute is present in the `<menuitem/>` tag that calls this command file, Dreamweaver passes the arguments to the function as parameters.

The Text_List.htm menu command file is an example of how `isCommandChecked()` works with arguments passed from the menus.xml entry to determine which item in the Text > List submenu will display with a checkmark. This command file is called by the following code in menus.xml:

```
<menuitem name="_None" file="Menus/MM/Text_List.htm" arguments="'None'"
id="DWContext_Table_Text_List_None" />
<menuitem name="_Unordered List" file="Menus/MM/Text_List.htm"
➥arguments="'UL'" id="DWContext_Table_Text_List_UL" />
<menuitem name="_Ordered List" file="Menus/MM/Text_List.htm"
➥arguments="'OL'" id="DWContext_Table_Text_List_OL" />
<menuitem name="_Definition List" file="Menus/MM/Text_List.htm"
➥arguments="'DL'" id="DWContext_Table_Text_List_DL" />
```

The relevant portion of the `isCommandChecked()` function looks like this:

```
function isCommandChecked(){
[etc]
    var textList = dw.getDocumentDOM().getListTag();
    var what = arguments[0];

    if (what == "None")
       return (textList == "");
    if (what == "UL")
       return (textList == "ul");
    if (what == "OL")
       return (textList == "ol");
    if (what == "DL")
       return (textList == "dl");
    else
       return false;
[etc]
}
```

What's happening here? Each submenu item that uses this command passes it a tag name (`UL`, `OL`, `DL`) as a parameter. The function collects that parameter as the `what` variable. It also tests the user's selection to determine whether a list tag is selected, collecting the name of the tag in the `textList` variable. It then uses a series of `if` statements to determine if the tags match. For the Unordered List menu entry, for instance, the parameter collected is what will be `OL`. The relevant `if` statement asks if the user's tag (`textList`) equals `"ol"`. If it does, the command returns `true` and the Unordered List menu entry will appear with a checkmark.

Figure 5.27 shows the Text > List submenu, showing that the user currently has an unordered list selected.

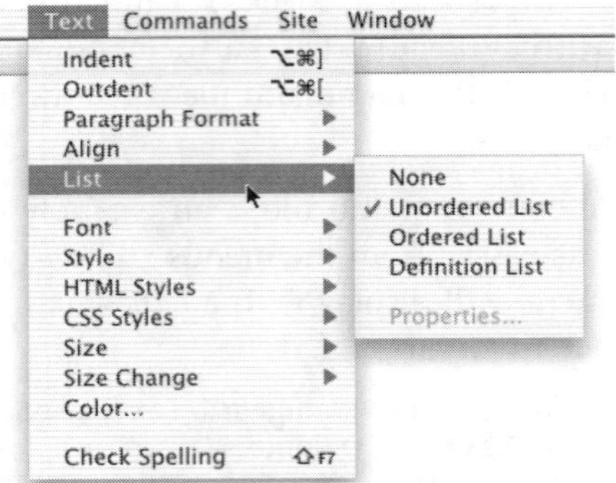

FIGURE 5.27 *The Text > List submenu, which uses the* `isCommandChecked()` *function to determine which item will appear with a checkmark.*

The API Procedure for Menu Commands

The Dreamweaver procedure for handling menu commands is basically the same as its procedure for handling regular commands, but with extra steps at the beginning of the process for the automatic calls to the special menu-related functions just described.

The menu commands API procedure starts when the user clicks a menu that contains a menu command. At that point, the following events occur:

1. If any `<menuitem/>` tag in the menu contains the `dynamic name` attribute, Dreamweaver looks in the associated command file for the `getDynamicContent()` function, and if it's present, executes it. The array of strings returned by `getDynamicContent()` is used to populate the menu, replacing whatever text was specified as the `dynamic name` attribute's value. If the `getDynamicContent()` function is not available, or if it returns a `null` value, the dynamic name is used in the menu.
2. For each menu item, Dreamweaver looks in the associated command file for the `canAcceptCommand()` function, and if it's present, executes it. If this function is present and returns `false`, the menu item is grayed out and the API process for this item stops here. If it's not present, or if it returns `true`, the following events occur.

3. For each menu item, Dreamweaver looks for the `isCommandChecked()` function, and if it's present, executes it. If this function returns `true`, Dreamweaver displays a checkmark next to the menu item.
4. For each menu item, Dreamweaver looks for the `setMenuText()` function and executes it if it's present. Whatever text string is returned by this function becomes the text of the menu item. If this function isn't present, the default text specified in the `<menuitem/>` name attribute is used. (Note that this command should not be present if the `getDynamicContent()` function is present.)
5. Dreamweaver then displays the menu and waits for the user to choose a specific item from the menu. At that point, the API procedure continues, following the same steps as the standard command API procedure.

   Figure 5.28 shows a diagram of the API procedure for menu commands. Compare it to the diagrammed procedure for standard commands, as seen in Figure 5.5.

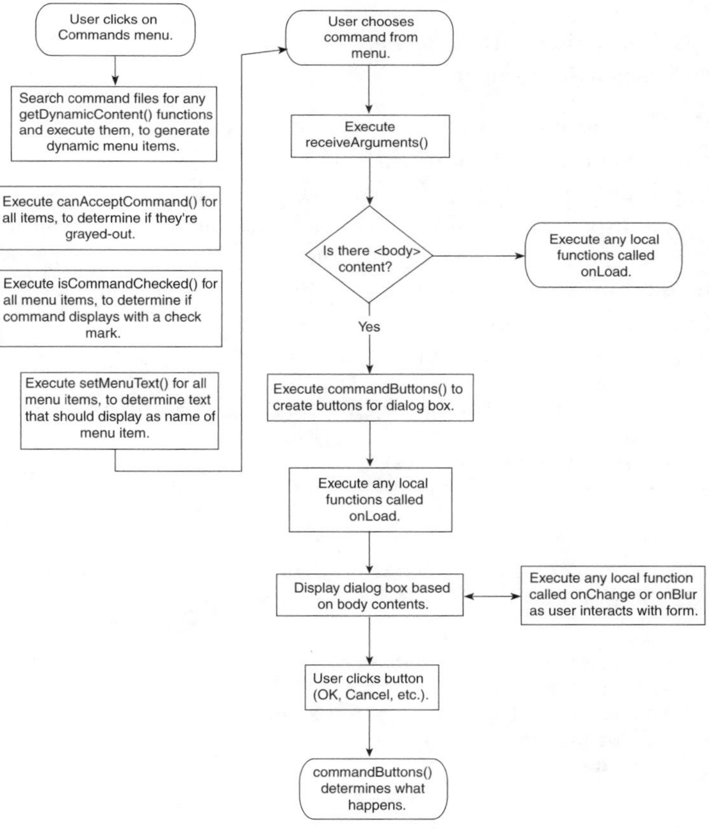

Figure 5.28 *The API procedure for menu commands.*

Making Menu Commands: Practice Session

Ready for some hands-on work with menu commands? In this practice session, we'll explore menus.xml and create samples of the three menu command functions just described.

Task 1: Create a custom folder to hold your menu commands

Menu commands should be stored inside the Configuration/Menus folder, within a folder you create. So, to start, find the Menus folder and create a new folder. Call it **Development**. (If you're working in a multiuser environment, you can create this folder within the main Configuration folder or within your user-specific Configuration folder.)

Task 2: Set up a development submenu to hold your test commands

We'll start by adding a Development submenu at the bottom of the Modify menu, to hold our practice exercises.

1. Quit Dreamweaver if it's running.
2. Open menus.xml in your text editor. Find the part of the file that controls the bottom of the Modify menu. You want to add your new submenu at the bottom of this menu, so find the `</menu>` tag that closes the Modify menu and add a new blank line immediately preceding that tag. The relevant section of menus.xml should now look like this (with a comment in place of the blank line you have added):

```
        <menuitem name="Add _Timeline" enabled="dw.getFocus() etc />
        <menuitem name="Remove Time_line" enabled="dw.getFocus() etc />
        <menuitem name="Rename T_imeline..." enabled="dw.getFocus() etc />
   </menu>
<!--your new menu code will go here -->
</menu>
```

3. You want to add a new submenu, which is created by adding a pair of `<menu>` tags inside the Modify menu. Add the following code to your new blank line (shown in bold):

```
   </menu>
   <!--your new menu code will go here -->
   <separator/>
   <menu name="Development1" id="DWMenu_Modify_Development1">
      <menuitem />
   </menu>
</menu>
```

The `<separator/>` tag creates a horizontal line that nicely separates your play area from the business areas of this menu. The `<menu>` tag creates a new submenu identified by the name Development1. For the moment, your menu has one (empty) menu item, indicated by the empty `<menuitem/>` tag. Filling it is the next task!

note

Leave the menus file open as you go through the next task; otherwise, you'll have to find this part of the file again when you reopen it later.

Task 3: Use *setMenuText( )* to create a dynamically named menu item

The goal for this task is to create a menu entry that says "Edit [whatever kind of text the user has selected]," determined dynamically. To do this, you'll work back and forth between the menus.xml file and your command file.

1. In your text editor, create a new HTML document. (Remember that you shouldn't use Dreamweaver for this and keep the menus.xml file open at the same time.) Save this file in your custom Menus/Development folder as **Set_Menu_Test.htm**. Enter the basic code for a command file in it:

    ```
    <html>
    <head>
    <title>My Dynamic Command</title>
    <script language="JavaScript">
    function myCommand() {
    //command statements go here
    }
    </script>
    </head>
    <body onLoad="myCommand()">
    </body>
    </html>
    ```

2. To dynamically generate the text for this command's menu item, add the following `setMenuText()` function to the `<script>` tag:

    ```
    function setMenuText() {
    return "This name will show";
    }
    ```

    This function must return the string to be inserted in the menu, remember. For now, you are just giving it a simple string to return. Remember, also, that you don't have to call `setMenuText();` Dreamweaver calls it automatically when preparing to display the menu that contains this command.

3. Now add a very simple statement to the `myCommand()` function, so this menu command will have something to do (new code is in bold):

```
function myCommand() {
//command statements go here
window.alert("This is my command.");
}
```

When it's chosen from the menu, this command will cause an alert window to open up, with the message `This is my command` showing in it.

4. Go back to menus.xml and find the code for the Development submenu that you created in the previous task. It's time to add your command to the Dreamweaver menus by creating a `<menuitem/>` element for it. Do it by adding the following code (new code is in bold):

```
<menu name="Development1" id="DWMenu_Modify_Development1">
   <menuitem name="(this name won't show")
   ➥file="Menus/Development/Set_Menu_Test.htm" id="Development_SetMenu" />
</menu>
```

When you have this code in place, save and close the menu and your command file.

5. Launch Dreamweaver and check out your command. The Modify menu should look like the one shown in Figure 5.29. Congratulations! There's your first dynamic menu item.

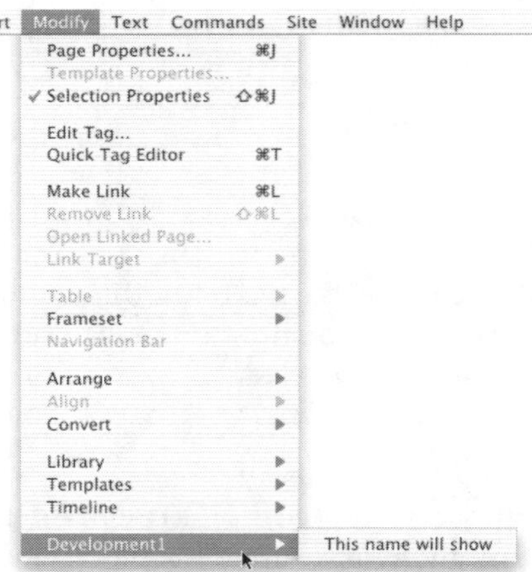

FIGURE 5.29 *The Modify menu with its Development1 submenu and dynamically set menu item.*

6. Next, revise the function so that it returns one string if text is selected, and another if the selection isn't text. Do this by opening the command file and rewriting the `setMenuText()` function like this (new code is in bold):

```
function setMenuText() {
      var myDOM = dw.getDocumentDOM();
      var myObject = myDOM.getSelectedNode();
      if (myObject.nodeType == 3) {
            return "Edit Text";
            } else {
            return "(no text selected)";
            }
}
```

   Can you see what this code is doing? Line 2 gains access to the DOM of the user's document. Line 3 accesses the selected object. Starting in line 4, a conditional statement tests to see whether the selected object is of node type 3, which is a text node. If the test is true, the words `Edit Text` are returned; otherwise, the words `(no text selected)` are returned.

   Try this out in Dreamweaver—in a document with text and some other page elements. Select different elements, and choose the command to see how it changes. If you have, say, a table, image, or even a formatting tag such as `<h1>` selected, you should see the `(no text selected)` menu entry.

7. Finally, make the function respond differently depending on the formatting tag the user might have selected: `<h1>`, `<p>`, `<b>`, and so on. To accomplish this, rewrite the `setMenuText()` function like this (new code is in bold):

```
function setMenuText() {
var myDOM = dw.getDocumentDOM();
var myObject = myDOM.getSelectedNode();
if (myObject.nodeType == 3) {
      return "Edit Text";
      } else {
      myTag = myObject.tagName;
      if (myTag == "P") {
            myTag = "Paragraph";
            } else if (myTag == "IMG") {
            myTag = "Image";
            } else if (myTag=="H1" || myTag=="H2" || myTag=="H3" ||
            ➥myTag=="H4" || myTag=="H5") {
            myTag = "Heading";
            }
      return "Edit " + myTag;
      }
}
```

Can you see what this new code is doing? If the selected object is a text node, the function still returns "Edit Text." But if the selected object is a `<p>`, `<img>`, or `<h1>`–`<h6>` tag, the function will return the word `Edit` plus `Paragraph`, `Image`, or `Heading`, as appropriate. So if you have an `<h1>` tag selected, the menu item for this command will read `Edit Heading`. This code is still pretty crude—it accounts for only a few of the possible tags that might be selected in a document. But this is only a practice session, right? If you feel the urge to be more thorough than this, go do it!

8. When you have it all coded, try it out on a document with a choice of tags that might be selected. Depending on your selection, you should see a menu displaying `Edit Text`, `Edit Paragraph`, `Edit Image`, or `Edit Heading`. Figure 5.30 shows the practice command at work.

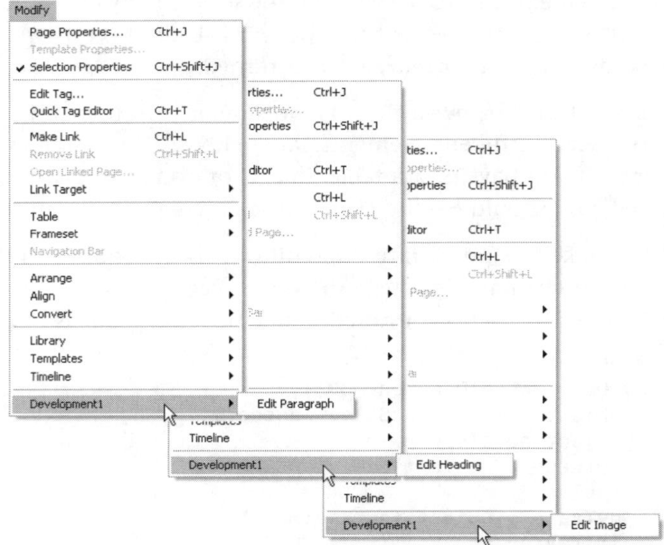

FIGURE 5.30 *Possible menu entries resulting from the practice* `setMenuText()` *function*

Task 4: Use *isCommandChecked( )* to create a command with a checkmark toggle

There are two different ways to use checkmarks in menus. You can have the checkmark report whether a certain condition is on or off. (Are floating panels showing or hidden? Is the current document a frameset or not?) Or, you can have a series of several menu items that function as alternate choices, only one of which can have a checkmark at any given time (the choices in the Type > Size submenu, for example). In this task, you create a simple on/off menu display.

1. Start by creating the menu entry. Quit Dreamweaver, if it's running, and open menus.xml in your text editor. Find the development submenu you created earlier, and add the following new <menuitem/> (new code is highlighted):

   ```
   <menu name="Development1" id="DWMenu_Modify_Development1">
      <menuitem name="(this name won't show") file =
      ➥"Menus/Development/Set_Menu_Test.htm" id="Development_SetMenu" />
      <menuitem name="Check Me"
      ➥file="Menus/Development/Toggle_Check.htm"
      ➥id="DWMenu_CommandChecked_Test" />
   </menu>
   ```

2. Now create a new HTML file to hold this. Save it in the Menus/Development folder as **Toggle_Check.htm**. Enter the basic HTML framework for a command file, like this:

   ```
   <html>
   <head>
   <title>Toggle Check Command</title>
   <script language="JavaScript">
   function myCommand() {
   //command statements go here
   }
   </script>
   </head>
   <body onLoad="myCommand()">
   </body>
   </html>
   ```

3. Now add the following isCommandChecked() function to the <script> tag in your command document's <head>:

   ```
   function isCommandChecked() {
   return true;
   }
   ```

   This code simply returns a value of true, which will cause Dreamweaver to display the menu item for this command with a checkmark next to its name.

4. Save and close your menu and command files, and try them out by launching Dreamweaver and accessing the Modify > Development submenu. Your submenu should display a new menu item called Check Me, which should appear with a checkmark next to its name.

5. Now you'll revise your menu command to display a checkmark if the user's selection is text, and not to display a checkmark if it is not. Do it by revising your isCommandChecked() function to look like this (new code is in bold):

```
function isCommandChecked() {
var myDOM = dw.getDocumentDOM();
var myObject = myDOM.getSelectedNode();
if (myObject.nodeType == 3) {
      return true;
      } else {
      return false;
      }
}
```

In lines 2 and 3, the command accesses the DOM and the selected object. A conditional statement then determines whether the selected object is of node type 3 (the text node), and returns `true` only if it is.

6. Try this command out. In Dreamweaver, reload extensions. Then open or create a test file that contains text and non-text items. Select some of the text in your document and examine the Modify > Development submenu—the Check Me command should have a checkmark next to its name. Select a non-text element and examine the submenu again—the Check Me command should appear with no checkmark.

Task 5: Use *isCommandChecked( )* to create an options submenu

To see what this task is all about, examine the Text menu's Font, Size, and Align submenus. Each of these menus presents a series of alternatives as menu items, with a checkmark indicating the currently active option (currently chosen font group, size, or alignment).

For this task, you'll create a submenu of three choices, one of which should be checked, depending on which of three images the user has selected when the menu is displayed.

1. Start by creating the menu items for your new command. Open menus.xml and find the code controlling your Development submenu. Add the following code (new code is in bold):

```
<menu name="Development1" id="DWMenu_Modify_Development1">
   <menuitem name="(this name won't show")
   ➥file="Menus/Development/SetMenu_Test.htm" id="Development_SetMenu" />
   <menuitem name="Check Me" file="Menus/Development/Toggle_Check.htm"
   ➥id="Development_CommandChecked_Test" />
</menu>
<menu name="Development2" id="DWMenu_Modify_Development2">
   <menuitem name="First" file="Menus/Development/Select_Check.htm"
   ➥arguments="'one'" id="Development2_Check_One" />
   <menuitem name="Second" file="Menus/Development/Select_Check.htm"
   ➥arguments="'two'" id="Development2_Check_Two" />
   <menuitem name="Third" file="Menus/Development/Select_Check.htm"
   ➥arguments="'three'" id="Development2_Check_Three" />
</menu>
```

With this code, you're creating a new `<menu>` that will appear in the Modify menu as Development2. All three `<menuitem/>` elements in this submenu call your Select_Check.htm command file, each time passing a different argument (`'one'`, `'two'` and `'three'`). What you want to have happen is this: Assuming a user has a document containing three images, if he has one of the images selected, the relevant menu item (`First`, `Second`, or `Third`) should have a checkmark by its name. If no images are selected, no checkmarks are present. (Remember that `isCommandChecked()` accepts arguments just like `receiveArguments()`—so you don't have to use the latter function to explicitly collect the arguments specified in the menus file.)

2. Now create the command file. Save it in the Menus/Development folder as **Select_Check.htm** and add the basic HTML framework for a command. Like this:

```
<html>
<head>
<title>My Dynamic Command</title>
<script language="JavaScript">
function myCommand() {
//command statements go here
}
</script>
</head>
<body onLoad="myCommand()">
</body>
</html>
```

Launch Dreamweaver and try the command right now. You should see a menu set up like that shown in Figure 5.31.

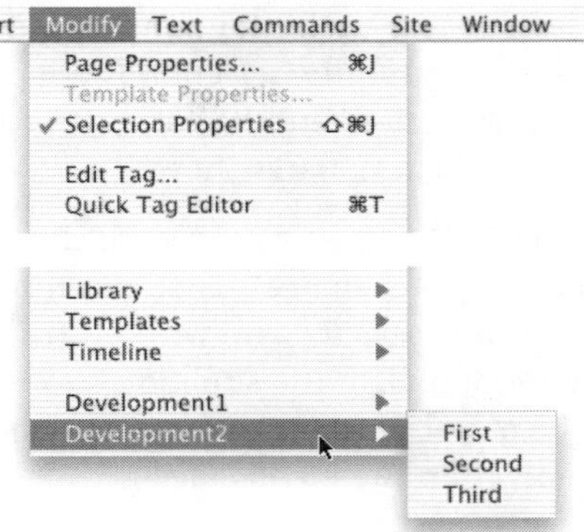

FIGURE 5.31 *The Development2 submenu.*

3. Now it's time to write the `isCommandChecked()` function. The function itself isn't hard—just a conditional statement or two returning `true` or `false`. But the logic behind its use in this situation might be a little puzzling. Here's the idea: When Dreamweaver is ready to display the `First` command with an argument of `'one'`, you want to test whether the current selection includes the first image in the document. So, if `arguments[0] == 'one'`, return the answer to the following question: Is the currently selected object the first image on the page? When Dreamweaver is ready to display the `Second` command, this function is called again, but this time with an argument of `'two'`. So, if `arguments[0] == 'two'`, return the answer to the following question: Is the currently selected object the second image on the page? And so on.

   To do this, open the Select_Check.htm command file and add the following function to your `<script>` tag:

```
function isCommandChecked() {
what = arguments[0];
myDOM = dw.getDocumentDOM();
myObject = myDOM.getSelectedNode();
if (myObject.nodeType == 1 && myObject.tagName == "IMG") {
   if (what == "one") return (myObject == myDOM.images[0]);
   if (what == "two") return (myObject == myDOM.images[1]);
   if (what == "three") return (myObject == myDOM.images[2]);
      else return false;
   } else {
   return false;
   }
}
```

   The function starts by collecting the arguments and gaining access to the selected object (node). The first `if` statement, in line 5, determines whether the selection is an image. If the selection is an image, then each possible argument gets its own `if` statement. If the selection is not one of the first three images on the page, or if the selection isn't an image, the function returns `false` for all three options, and no checkmarks show.

4. Try it out and see! In Dreamweaver, reload extensions. Then open a document that contains at least three images. Try examining the Modify > Development2 submenu with nothing selected and with one of the first three images selected. Your results should look like the situation shown in Figure 5.32. This exercise demonstrates the power not only of `isCommandChecked()`, but also the power of passing arguments from the menus file.

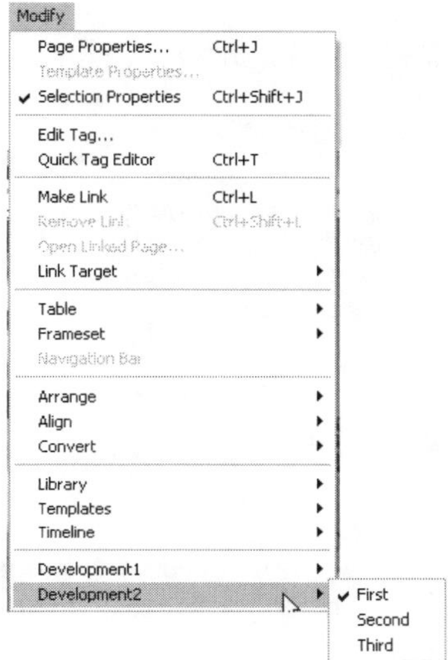

FIGURE 5.32 *Testing the Development2 submenu, with its three submenu commands.*

Task 6: Use *getDynamicContent( )* to dynamically create a submenu

For this practice session, you'll create a dynamically generated submenu at the bottom of the Modify menu. All entries in the submenu will be determined by code in a command file's `getDynamicContent()` function.

1. As in previous tasks, start by creating the menu item Quit Dreamweaver. In menus.xml, find the code for your Development submenus and add the following code immediately below it:

```
<menu name="Development3" id="DWMenu_Modify_Development3">
      <menuitem dynamic name="(nope, this won't show)"
      ➥file="Menus/Development/Dynamic_Test.htm" id="Development_DynamicTest" />
</menu>
```

   Note that the `<menuitem/>` tag includes a `dynamic name` attribute in place of the `name` attribute.

2. Now create a command file. Save it in your Menus/Development folder as **Dynamic_Test.htm** and add the HTML framework for a basic command, like this:

```
<html>
<head>
<title>Another Dynamic Command</title>
<script language="JavaScript">
function myCommand() {
//command statements go here;
}
</script>
</head>
<body onLoad="myCommand()">
</body>
</html>
```

3. In the command file, you now need to define the `getDynamicContent()` function. This function can be tricky because it must return a very specific kind of array. The array must consist of strings, each of which is made up of a menu item name, a semicolon, and a menu item ID.

   To get used to the syntax required here, start with a hard-coded array used for the `return` statement. Add a new function to your `<script>` tag, with the following code:

```
function getDynamicContent(itemID) {
var testList = new Array();
testList[0] = new String("Item 1;id='Development_Dynamic_1'");
testList[1] = new String("Item 2;id='Development_Dynamic_2'");
return testList;
}
```

   First, note that the function accepts a parameter called `itemID`. Dreamweaver automatically passes the correct ID from the `<menuitem/>` element that calls the command. (For this exercise, Dreamweaver passes `Development_DynamicTest` as a string.)

   Next, notice the syntax of each item in the `return` array. The item as a whole will automatically be returned surrounded by quotes, because it's a string. Within this main set of quotes, the menu name (`Item 1` or `Item 2` for the array elements shown here) is not in quotation marks, but the ID name is. A semicolon separates the two parts of the string, with no spaces on either side.

4. With this code in place, launch Dreamweaver and try out the menu command. If you coded correctly, the Dreamweaver Modify menu should contain a Development3 submenu that looks like the one shown in Figure 5.33.

FIGURE 5.33 *The Modify menu, showing a dynamic submenu generated by the* `getDynamicContent()` *function in the command file.*

5. Remember, if `getDynamicContent()` returns `null`, the dynamic menu items aren't generated, and the default `menuitem` name specified in the menus file appears instead. Revise your `getDynamicContent()` function to make that happen, by commenting out the current statements and adding a new statement, like this (new code is in bold):

```
function getDynamicContent(itemID) {
//var testList = new Array();
//testList[0] = new String("Item 1;id='Development_Dynamic_1'");
//testList[1] = new String("Item 2;id='Development_Dynamic_2'");
return null;
}
```

Now reload extensions in Dreamweaver and examine the Modify menu again. The resulting Dynamic submenu should look like the one shown in Figure 5.34.

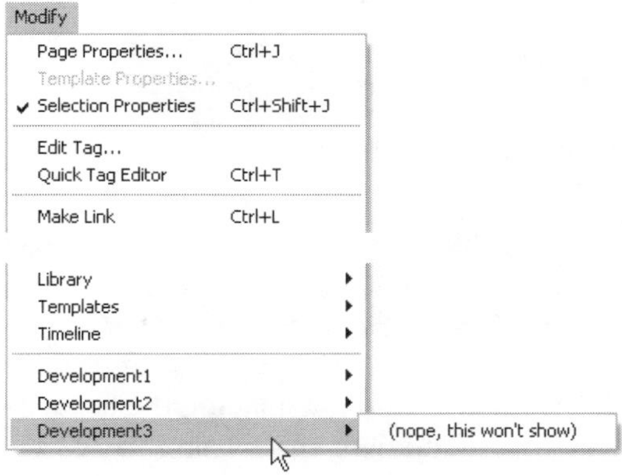

FIGURE 5.34 *The Modify menu, showing the dynamically generated Development3 submenu when the* `getDynamicContent()` *returns null.*

6. Now revise the function so that it returns a value only if the document contains images. Do it by un-commenting your original code statements and adding a new conditional statement framework. Like this (new code is highlighted):

```
function getDynamicContent(itemID) {
myDOM = dw.getDocumentDOM();
if (myDOM.images[0]) {
   var testList = new Array();
   testList[0] = new String("Item 1;id='Development_Dynamic_1'");
   testList[1] = new String("Item 2;id='Development_Dynamic_2'");
   return testList;
   } else {
   return null;
   }
}
```

   Try this out! In Dreamweaver, open a document that contains no images and access the Modify > Dynamic submenu to view the items there. Your menu should look like the one shown in Figure 5.33. Then open a document that contains images and access the submenu. It should look like the one shown in Figure 5.34.

7. The dynamically generated menu items automatically have one argument, which for each item is the same as its unique ID. To test this out, try a little experiment.

   In your command file, add a global variable and the `receiveArguments()` function to your `<script>` tag, like this:

```
var gWhat;
function receiveArguments() {
gWhat = arguments[0];
}
```

   Then add a new statement to the main command function (new code is in bold):

```
function myCommand() {
//command statements go here
window.alert(gWhat);
}
```

   What does this code do? The `receiveArguments()` function collects the argument for the menu item that has activated this command file, storing that argument in the global variable `gWhat`. Then the command's main function, which is called `onLoad` and which will execute when the user chooses the menu item, opens an alert window displaying the `gWhat` variable. This code enables you to see exactly what argument is being passed to each command in the Modify > Dynamic submenu.

In Dreamweaver, reload extensions and try it out. Open a Dreamweaver document that contains images and access Modify > Development3. From the submenu, choose either of the two menu items that appear (`Item 1` or `Item 2`). Figure 5.35 shows what should happen.

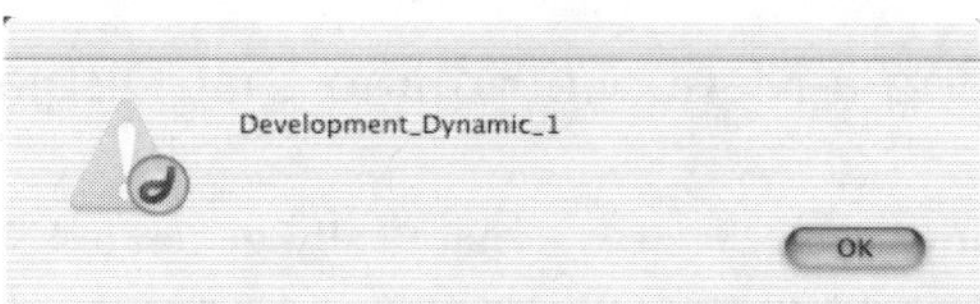

FIGURE 5.35 *Choosing a dynamically generated menu item, and receiving its argument in a popup window.*

8. You most commonly see dynamically generated menu items in submenus, but they don't need to live there. They can exist in a main menu as well. To see this, open menus.xml (be sure to quit Dreamweaver first) and change the code for your Development3 submenu so that the dynamic menu item sits directly in the Modify menu like this (deleted code is shown in bold with strikethrough):

```
<menu name="Dynamic" id="DWMenu_Modify_DynamicTestMenu">
     <menuitem dynamic name="(nope, this won't show)"
     ➥file="Menus/MyStuff/Dynamic_Test.html" id="MyStuff_DynamicTest" />
</menu>
```

This change deletes the submenu and makes the `<menuitem/>` element a child of the Modify menu's `<menu>` tag.

Launch Dreamweaver and examine the Modify menu now. It should look like the one shown in Figure 5.36. The dynamic menu item should behave exactly as it behaved when there was a submenu.

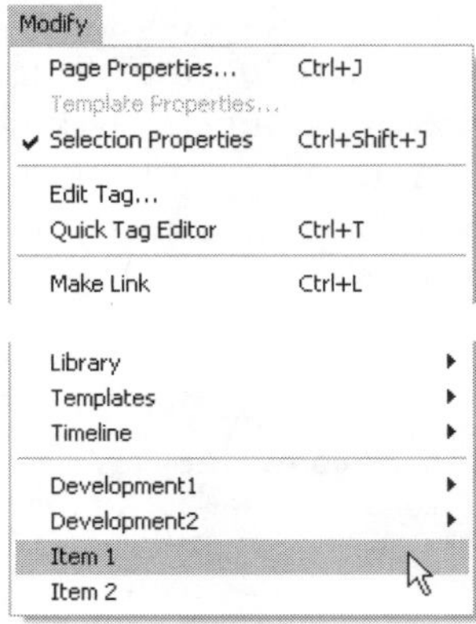

FIGURE 5.36 *Dynamically generated menu items showing in the Modify menu itself, rather than in a submenu.*

Workshop #4: Creating a Menu Command

We've already built quite a lot in the practice sessions. In this workshop, we'll put all the pieces together, using `isCommandChecked()` and `getDynamicContent()`, as well as other command API options, to create something robust and useful.

Sample File: Creating a Menu Command that Displays the Images in a Document

For this workshop, we'll create a dynamically generated submenu that lists all the images in the current document, includes a checkmark if one of those images is selected, and selects the appropriate image if the user chooses it from the submenu. We'll even tell Dreamweaver to scroll, if necessary, to display the newly selected image in the Document window.

Task 1: Create the menu entry

Quit Dreamweaver and open menus.xml. Navigate to your menu entries at the bottom of the Modify menu. Add another `<menu>` entry, containing the following code:

```
<menu name="Select Image" id="DWMenu_Modify_SelectImage">
      <menuitem dynamic name="(no images)"
      ➥file="Menus/Development/Select_Images.htm"
      ➥id="Development_SelectImages" />
</menu>
```

This code creates another submenu in the Modify menu, this one named Select Image. The Select Image submenu is set to contain at least one menu item, and possibly more, generated by the `getDynamicContent()` function in the Select_Images.htm command file—although the menu entry won't work yet, because the Select_Images.htm file hasn't yet been created. You may already have figured out that the coding for the `getDynamicContent()` function in Select_Images.htm must be written to return an array of strings containing names of images in the user's document; or, if no images are present in the user's document, code must be written to return `null`, which will result in the Select Image submenu displaying with one menu item only, named `(no images)`.

note

If you don't want your Modify menu cluttered up with Development entries, you can take this opportunity to strip out all the custom `<menu>` and `<menuitem/>` elements you added in the Practice Session.

Task 2: Create the command file

Start with the basic command file framework. In your text editor, create a new HTML file. Save it in the Menus/Development folder as Select_Images.htm. Enter the following basic command file framework code:

```
<html>
<head>
<title>Select Image</title>
<script language="JavaScript">
//determine if command is available in the menu
function canAcceptCommand() {
//return true if images are present in the user's document
return true;
}

//generate dynamic submenu
function getDynamicContent(itemID) {
//return an array of strings to create menu items for all images in
➥document
//or return null
}
function receiveArguments(itemID) {
//collect argument from menu item that accesses this command file
return null; //temporary
}

//hold argument collected by receiveArguments()
var gWhat;

function isCommandChecked() {
//if an image is selected, put a check mark by corresponding menu item
return false; //temporary
}

function selectImage() {
//this is the main function
//it selects an image in the user's document
}
</script>
</head>
<body onLoad="selectImage()">
</body>
</html>
```

Can you see what all the pieces of this command file are for? Because the command is for working with the images in a document, you need `canAcceptCommand()` to make it unavailable in the menu (grayed out) if the current document contains no images. Because you want to generate a dynamic submenu with multiple entries, you need the `getDynamicContent()` function. Because you may want one of the menu items to have a checkmark, you need `isCommandChecked()`. And because the main command function, `myCommand()`, will need to know which dynamically generated menu item is being used, you need `receiveArguments()` and its related global variable, `gWhat`. The comments in the code indicate approximately what needs to be accomplished within each function. The functions that must return values have been given very simple `return` statements, so the command file is syntactically and logically correct.

At this point, you should be able to launch Dreamweaver and see your Modify > Select Image submenu in place, though it will contain only the default menu item.

Task 3: Fill in the *getDynamicContent( )* function

Your goal is to collect a list of all the images in the current document and create a menu item for each image. To do this, you must fill in the `getDynamicContent()` function to return an array of strings if the user's document includes images, and a `null` value if there are no images.

1. Open your command file, Select_Images.htm. Revise the `getDynamicContent()` function by adding a framework of comments, like this (new code is in bold):

   ```
   function getDynamicContent(itemID) {
   //access the DOM so the document can be examined
   //if the document contains images
   //create an array to be returned
   //for each image in the document, add a text string to the array
   //or return null
   return null;
   }
   ```

   As these comments indicate, if the document contains images, the function needs to step through the document's node list of images, creating a text string for each one.

2. To access the DOM (the first commented task), add the following code:

   ```
   function getDynamicContent(itemID) {
   //access the DOM so the document can be examined
   var myDOM=dw.getDocumentDOM();
   //if the document contains images
   //create an array to be returned
   //for each image in the document, add a text string to the array
   //or return null
   return null;
   }
   ```

3. Then add a conditional statement to test whether the document contains images:

```
function getDynamicContent(itemID) {
//access the DOM so the document can be examined
var myDOM=dw.getDocumentDOM();
//if the document contains images
if (myDOM.getElementsByTagName('IMG').item(0) {
   //create an array to be returned
   //for each image in the document, add a text string to the array
   } else {
   //or return null
   return null;
   }
}
```

4. Within the conditional, create an array to hold the return string:

```
function getDynamicContent(itemID) {
//access the DOM so the document can be examined
var myDOM=dw.getDocumentDOM();
//if the document contains images
if (myDOM.getElementsByTagName('IMG').item(0) {
   //create an array to be returned
   var imageList = new Array();
   //for each image in the document, add a text string to the array
   return imageList;
   } else {
   //or return null
   return null;
   }
}
```

5. And, finally, the trickiest part—add a `for` loop within the conditional, to construct the array of text strings from the document's images:

```
function getDynamicContent(itemID) {
//access the DOM so the document can be examined
var myDOM=dw.getDocumentDOM();
//if the document contains images
if (myDOM.getElementsByTagName('IMG').item(0)) {
   //create an array to be returned
   var imageList = new Array();
   var imageName;
   //for each image in the document, add a text string to the array
   for (var a=0;a<myDOM.getElementsByTagName('IMG').length;a++) {
      imageName = myDOM.getElementsByTagName('IMG').item(a).src;
      imageList[a] = new String(imageName+";id='"+itemID+"_"+a+"'");
      }
   return imageList;
   } else {
   //or return null
   return null;
   }
}
```

What's happening here? The `imageName` variable is created in line 8 to hold the `src` attribute for each image that is processed. Then the `for` loop in lines 10–13 steps through the node list of images in the document, accessed using the `dom.getElementsByTagName()` method. For each image in the node list, a string is constructed from the `imageName`, the `itemID` (the parameter Dreamweaver passes automatically to this function, and which holds the unique ID for the Select Image `<menuitem/>` element), and the counter variable `a`.

For instance, assuming that the first image in your document has a `src` attribute of `images/myImage.gif`, and remembering that the menu item for this dynamic command has an `id` attribute of `Development_SelectImage`, the concatenation in line 12 would create `images/myImage.gif;id='Development_SelectImage_0'` as the first string to go into the `imageList` array. Assuming that the second image in the document has a `src` attribute of `images/otherImage.gif`, the string to be created for that dynamic menu item would be `images/otherImage.gif;id='Development_SelectImage_1'`. Figure 5.37 shows a diagram of how the concatenation works. (Why add the number from the counter variable a to the end of the ID? Because it guarantees that the ID for each dynamically generated menu item is unique. The first time through the `for` loop, `a = 0` and the ID generated will be `Development_SelectImage_0`; the second time through the loop, the ID will be `Development_SelectImage_1`; and so on.)

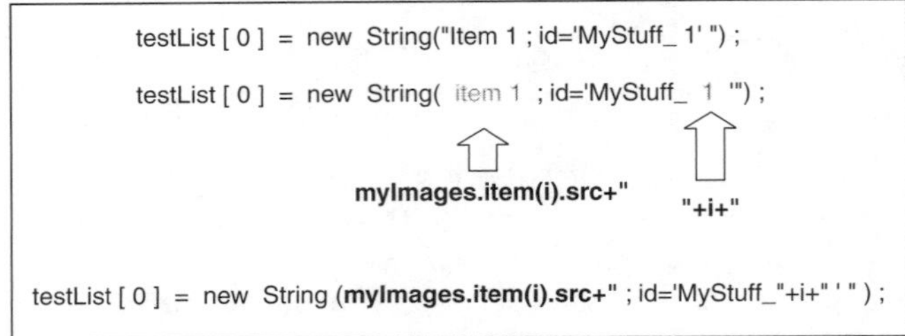

FIGURE 5.37 *Concatenating dynamic elements into a properly formatted return string for* `getDynamicContent()`.

6. At this point, your command contains enough information to correctly display the dynamic Modify > Select Image submenu. Launch Dreamweaver and try it out by opening an HTML document containing several images. When you choose Modify > Select Image, the dynamic menu that Dreamweaver generates should contain the name of every image in the document, as shown in Figure 5.38.

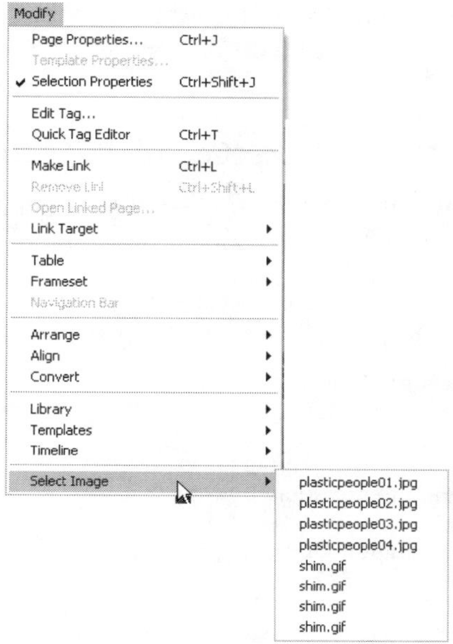

FIGURE 5.38 *A dynamically generated submenu showing path information for all image files in the current document.*

7. One problem remains with `getDynamicContent()` in this command. If the images in the user's document have long, complex file paths (such as `../../images/myImage.gif`), the menu items will be cumbersome and long. To alleviate this, truncate the `imageName` like this (new code is in bold):

```
function getDynamicContent(itemID) {
//access the DOM so the document can be examined
var myDOM=dw.getDocumentDOM();
//if the document contains images
if (myDOM.getElementsByTagName('IMG').item(0)) {
   //create an array to be returned
   var imageList = new Array();
   var imageName;
   //for each image in the document, add a text string to the array
   for (var a=0;a<myDOM.getElementsByTagName('IMG').length;a++) {
      imageName = myDOM.getElementsByTagName('IMG').item(a).src;
      imageName = imageName.substring(imageName.lastIndexOf('/')
      ➥+1,imageName.length);
      imageList[a] = new String(imageName+";id='"+itemID+"_"+a+"'");
      }
   return imageList;
   } else {
   //or return null
   return null;
   }
}
```

This new code statement uses the JavaScript substring method to isolate just the filename of the image in question, removing all folder paths and other URL information.

Task 4: Revise the *canAcceptCommand( )* function to gray the command out if there is no document open, or if there are no images present

There's nothing new about this one by now. In your command file, revise the `canAcceptCommand()` function to look like this (new code is in bold):

```
function canAcceptCommand() {
//return true if images are present in the user's document

//access the user's document
var myDOM = dw.getDocumentDOM();

//if there's no open document, return false
if (!myDOM) return false;

//if there are any <img> tags, return true
if (myDOM.getElementsByTagName('IMG').item(0)) {
   return true;
   } else {
   return false;
   }
}
```

What's happening here? The `dom.getElementsByTagName()` method is used to access the node list of images for the current document. If the node list contains at least one item (`item(0)`), the function returns `true`; otherwise, it returns `false`.

Task 5: Collect arguments with *receiveArguments( )*

Why are you doing this? Remember that all dynamically generated items in the Select Images submenu access this same command file. In essence, a separate instance of the Select_Images.htm command file will be run for each submenu item. In the main function, which you will write next, you need to determine which of the submenu items is calling each particular instance of the command file. Remember also that the dynamically generated menu items automatically pass their ID values to the command file as arguments. All you need to do is collect them.

note

Because the Select Image menu item will be grayed out if no images are present, the Select Image submenu will never appear unless images are present. So it isn't really necessary to test for the presence of images in the `getDynamicContent()` function, or to return a `null` value if no images are present. If no images are present, `getDynamicContent()` will never be executed because `canAcceptCommand()` will return `false` and stop the whole API procedure.

You've already created a global variable—gWhat—to store the argument being passed to the command. The function receiveArguments() just needs to collect the argument and put it in that variable. Add the following code to your document:

```
function receiveArguments() {
//collect argument from menu item that accesses this command file
gWhat = arguments[0];
}
```

note

As you may remember, some functions such as isCommandChecked() and setMenuText() are automatically passed these arguments. Because the main function is locally created by you and is not part of the API, however, you must collect the arguments to use them.

Task 6: Create the main function

What do you want to happen when the user clicks on one of the submenu items? You want the image to be selected in the document. You also want Dreamweaver to scroll to the image if it needs to so that the user can examine it. That functionality needs to be built into the command's main function.

1. In scripting terms, what you need to do is collect the argument (to determine which menu item the user has clicked on), and from that, determine which image to select. The argument is the ID, remember, but exactly what does the ID contain? To find out, revise your main function to look like this:

   ```
   function selectImage() {
   window.alert(gWhat);
   }
   ```

2. Try the command out now. Choosing one of the submenu items brings up an alert window with the message Development_SelectImage_*n*—that's the argument you constructed in getDynamicContent().
3. How do you determine the correct image to select based on the argument? The last character in the argument string is the item number of an image in the node list created using getElementsByTagName(). If you can isolate that character and convert it back from a substring into a number, you can reconstruct the image array, and determine which image name the user just clicked on. To do this, change your main function code to look like this (new code is in bold):

   ```
   function selectImage() {
   var what = new String(gWhat);
   what = what.substring(what.lastIndexOf("_")+1,what.length);
   var myDOM = dw.getDocumentDOM();
   var myImages = myDOM.getElementsByTagName('IMG');
   var myObject = myImages.item(parseInt(what));
   }
   ```

Can you see what's happening here? In line 2, you collect the global variable `gWhat`, converting it into a string object so that you can perform string operations on it. In line 3, you extract the portion of the string that contains the image's node list number. You then gain access to the DOM (`myDOM`) and to the node list of images (`myImages`). And finally, in line 6, you parse the `what` substring as an integer and use it to specify the correct image in the node list. You now have access to the image, stored in the `myObject` variable.

note

You could also have approached the problem from another way, and included the image's `src` name in the unique ID generated by `getDynamicContent()`. Then, you could use a `for` loop to step through the `image` array in the document until you found a match of `src` values.

4. What do you do with the image, now that you have access? You select it, of course! Revise your function to look like this (new code is in bold):

```
function runCommand() {
var what = new String(gWhat);
what = what.substring(what.lastIndexOf("_")+1,what.length);
var myDOM = dw.getDocumentDOM();
var myImages = myDOM.getElementsByTagName('IMG');
var myObject = myImages.item(parseInt(what));
myDOM.setSelectedNode(myObject,false,true);
}
```

What does this code do? As you learned in Chapter 4, `dom.setSelectedNode()` selects an object. If you look at the table shown in Table 4.14 in Chapter 4, you'll see that this method has two optional parameters, both Booleans: `bSelectInside` and `bJumpToNode`. You don't want to use the first of these, so you set it to `false`. But you do want Dreamweaver to scroll to the selected object, if it needs to, to display the selected image in the Document window; so you set `bJumpToNode` to `true`.

5. Try it out! To see it working, use a test document that has lots of images and requires some scrolling. Choosing an image from the submenu should scroll to the image and leave it selected.

Task 7: Revise the *isCommandChecked( )* function so that it puts a checkmark by a menu item if its associated image is selected

This is very similar to what you did in Task 5 of the practice session, earlier in this chapter. When the user chooses Modify > Select Images and causes its submenu to display, if there's already an image selected, you want that menu entry to have a checkmark next to it.

1. The function must determine which of the submenu items was chosen, which image is associated with that item, and if the image is selected in the document. To start, add the following set of comment lines to the `isCommandChecked()` function in your command file:

```
function isCommandChecked() {
//collect the argument, and isolate the item number at its end
//get access to the image node list, and the current selection
//if the selection is an image, and if its number in the node list
➥matches the argument,
//return true
//otherwise, return false
return false;
}
```

2. To fill in the code for the first commented task, remember that each menu item that calls this command file will have a name that specifies an image and an ID that looks like this: `Development_SelectImage_1`, where the number at the end corresponds with the image's number in the document's node list of images. This information is passed automatically to `isCommandChecked()` as `arguments[0]`. To determine which image this instance of the command file is referring to, you need to isolate the number at the end of this parameter. Revise your `isCommandChecked()` function to look like this (new code is in bold):

```
function isCommandChecked() {
//collect the argument, and isolate the item number at its end
var what = new String(arguments[0]);
what = what.substring(what.lastIndexOf('_')+1,what.length);
var myNumber = parseInt(what);
//get access to the image node list, and the current selection
//if the selection is an image, and if its number in the node list
➥matches the argument,
//return true
//otherwise, return false
return false;
}
```

By feeding `arguments[0]` into a specifically created String object (`what`), you guarantee that the substring method will work on it. By parsing the truncated `what` string as an integer, you then guarantee that you will be able to use it to access numbered items in the document's images node list.

3. To access the appropriate image, add the following code:

```
function isCommandChecked() {
//collect the argument, and isolate the item number at its end
var what = new String(arguments[0]);
what = what.substring(what.lastIndexOf('_')+1,what.length);
var myNumber = parseInt(what);
//get access to the image node list, and the current selection
```

```
var myDOM=dw.getDocumentDOM();
var myImages=myDOM.getElementsByTagName('IMG');
var myObject=myDOM.getSelectedNode();
//if the selection is an image, and if its number in the node list
➥matches the argument,
//return true
//otherwise, return false
return false;
}
```

In these three lines of code, you access the DOM (`myDOM`), access the node list of images for the document (`myImages`), and finally access the selected object (`myObject`)—whether it's an image or not.

4. To determine whether the selected object is the same image referenced by `arguments[0]`, add the following code:

```
function isCommandChecked() {
//collect the argument, and isolate the item number at its end
var what = new String(arguments[0]);
what = what.substring(what.lastIndexOf('_')+1,what.length);
var myNumber = parseInt(what);
//get access to the image node list, and the current selection
var myDOM=dw.getDocumentDOM();
var myImages=myDOM.getElementsByTagName('IMG');
var myObject=myDOM.getSelectedNode();
//if the selection is an image, and if its number in the node list
➥matches the argument,
if (myObject.nodeType=="1" && myObject.tagName=="IMG" &&
➥myObject==myImages.item(myNumber)) {
   //return true
   return true;
   //otherwise, return false
   }else{
   return false;
   }
}
```

In line 11, you're asking if the selected object (`myObject`) is of node type 1 (HTML tag); if the selected object has a `tagName` attribute of `IMG`; and if the selected object is the same object as that found in item (`myNumber`) of the document's node list of images. For instance, if the `arguments[0]` parameter contains the string `Development_SelectImage_4`, is the selected object the same object also referred to as `item(4)` in the node list of images? If so, return `true` (and add a checkmark to this menu item). If not, return `false` and add no checkmark.

5. You might think you're done at this point, but not quite. What if there are no images? What if the user has nothing selected? To take care of these possible situations, you need to wrap the entire set of statements in a few conditionals (new code is in bold):

```
function isCommandChecked() {
//window.alert(arguments[0]);
//collect the argument, and isolate the item number at its end
var what = new String(arguments[0]);
//if there are any arguments
if (what) {
   what = what.substring(what.lastIndexOf('_')+1,what.length);
   var myNumber = parseInt(what);
   //get access to the image node list, and the current selection
   var myDOM=dw.getDocumentDOM();
   var myImages=myDOM.getElementsByTagName('IMG');
   var myObject=myDOM.getSelectedNode();
   //if there is a selection
   if (myObject) {
      //if the selection is an image, and if its number in the node
      ➥list matches the argument,
      if (myObject.nodeType=="1" && myObject.tagName=="IMG" &&
      ➥myObject==myImages.item(myNumber)) {
         //return true
         return true;
         } //end if (myObject)
      } //end if (what)
   //otherwise, return false
   }else{
   return false;
   }
}
```

6. Reload Dreamweaver extensions and try it out! Open a Dreamweaver document containing several images and select one. Then access the Modify > Select Image submenu. All images in your document should be represented by menu items, and the menu item corresponding to the selected image should appear with a checkmark next to its name.

   Try the command with no images selected. Try the command in a document with no images. How does your command fare? If you have problems, troubleshoot to identify and eliminate them. Then congratulate yourself on a command well done. Listing 1 shows the final, working version of this command.

Listing 5.3 Final Code for the Select Image Menu Command, Commented for Reference

```
<html>
<head>
<title>Select Image</title>
<script language="JavaScript">

//determine if command is available in the menu
//return true if images are present in the user's document
function canAcceptCommand() {

//access the user's document
var myDOM = dw.getDocumentDOM();

//if there's no open document, return false
if (!myDOM) return false;

//if there are any <img> tags, return true
if (myDOM.getElementsByTagName('IMG').item(0)) {
   return true;
   } else {
   return false;
   }
}

//determine if a check mark should appear next to the menu item
function isCommandChecked() {

//collect the argument, and isolate the item number at its end
var what = new String(arguments[0]);
if (what) { // if there are no images, there will be no argument
   what = what.substring(what.lastIndexOf('_')+1,what.length);
   var myNumber = parseInt(what);

   //get access to the image node list and the current selection
   var myDOM=dw.getDocumentDOM();
   var myImages=myDOM.getElementsByTagName('IMG');
   var myObject=myDOM.getSelectedNode();

   //if the selection is an image, and if its number in the node list
   ➥matches the argument,
   //return true
   if (myObject.nodeType=="1" && myObject.tagName=="IMG" &&
   ➥myObject==myImages.item(myNumber)) {
      return true;
      }
   //otherwise, return false
   }else{
   return false;
   }
}

//generate dynamic submenu
```

```
function getDynamicContent(itemID) {

//access the DOM so the document can be examined
var myDOM=dw.getDocumentDOM();

//if the document contains images
if (myDOM.getElementsByTagName('IMG').item(0)) {
   //create an array to be returned
   var imageList = new Array();
   var imageName;
   //for each image in the document, add a text string to the array
   for (var a=0;a<myDOM.getElementsByTagName('IMG').length;a++) {
      //put src path in imageName
      imageName = myDOM.getElementsByTagName('IMG').item(a).src;
      //truncate imageName for display
      imageName = imageName.substring
      ➥(imageName.lastIndexOf('/')+1,imageName.length);
      //construct return string consisting of name and ID
      imageList[a] = new String(imageName+";id='"+itemID+"_"+a+"'");
      }
   //if there is an array of strings to return, return it
   return imageList;
   //otherwise, return null and no submenu entries will be generated
   } else {
   return null;
   }
}

//determine which of the dynamic entries has called this instance of the
➥command
function receiveArguments() {
//collect argument from menu item that accesses this command file
gWhat = arguments[0];
}

//global variable to hold argument collected by receiveArguments()
var gWhat;

//main function, called and executed onLoad
function selectImage() {

//collect argument to determine which dynamic menu item user has chosen
var what = new String(gWhat);

//isolate node list number from end of argument, to determine which
➥image to process
what = what.substring(what.lastIndexOf("_")+1,what.length);

//access the image in question
var myDOM = dw.getDocumentDOM();
var myImages = myDOM.getElementsByTagName('IMG');
```

continues

Listing 5.3 Continued

```
var myObject = myImages.item(parseInt(what));

//and select the image, scrolling to show it if needed
myDOM.setSelectedNode(myObject,false,true);
}
</script>
</head>
<body onLoad="selectImage()">
</body>
</html>
```

note

Troubleshooting

What if it doesn't work? Logic errors can be the bane of commands as complex as this one, though if you followed the code written here, your logical bases should be covered. If you run into syntactical errors, make sure your code matches the code in Listing 1 exactly. Watch out for typos!

If you are experiencing problems, at what point in the API procedure are they happening? Can you tell which function is executing improperly? Here's a trick if you think one of the API functions is causing problems: Add an alert statement to each API function—`getDynamicContent()`, `isCommandChecked()`, `receiveArguments()`—so that you can tell when each is function is being executed. The code for the alert message can be simple, like `window.alert("The getDynamicContent() function is running.")`. Then try to run the command, paying attention to when the alerts appear in relation to when the command runs into problems.

note

Commands versus menu commands, revisited: In terms of functionality, menu commands have special menu-related API elements that commands don't have. There's nothing, however, to stop you adding your regular commands to your folder within the Configuration/Menus folder. It makes for a tidier Configuration folder if all your custom commands are in that one folder, rather than having half of them in the Commands folder. To move the Automatic Alt text command to the Menus folder, move Automatic Alt Text.htm to Configuration/Menus/Development, and add a `<menuitem/>` tag to the proper place in the menus.xml file.

Summary

Ideally, you're feeling fairly comfortable working with the DOM, the commands API, and the Dreamweaver menu system by now. If your brain isn't full of ideas for how you want to expand Dreamweaver horizons, take some time to snoop through the JavaScript API section in the *Extending Dreamweaver* manual—and you'll soon be inspired. In the next chapter, you revisit objects, but this time to inspect them rather than insert them.

Chapter 6

Creating Custom Property Inspectors

The Property inspector is the most familiar of the Dreamweaver floating panels. You can use it to view the properties of selected HTML elements in your documents, and to add, remove, and change those properties. The Property inspector is actually many different Property inspectors, all of which appear in the same panel framework on users' screens. Depending on what the user has selected, or where the cursor is placed, Dreamweaver shows a different inspector—created from a different inspector file—in the panel interface.

Several Property inspectors in Dreamweaver are built-in, coded into the program itself instead of being programmed as extensions. You can't access or alter their code. An example would be the default Property inspector for editing text. Other Property inspectors are written as extensions, using the standard HTML/JavaScript combination. Following the Application Programming Interface (API) requirements of these inspectors, you can create your own custom inspectors, and even tell Dreamweaver to use your inspectors instead of its own built-in alternatives. In this chapter, you learn how to do just that.

How Property Inspectors Are Constructed

Property inspectors that are coded as extensions share the following API structure and functional procedure.

Property Inspectors in the Configuration Folder

In the Configuration folder, Property inspector extensions live in the Inspectors folder. All inspectors are at the root level of this folder; there are no subfolders. Figure 6.1 shows the default Inspectors folder, with only Macromedia's standard inspectors showing. Note that Property inspectors and objects often go together, so if you have used the Extension Manager to add objects to your copy of Dreamweaver, you may see extra items in this folder.

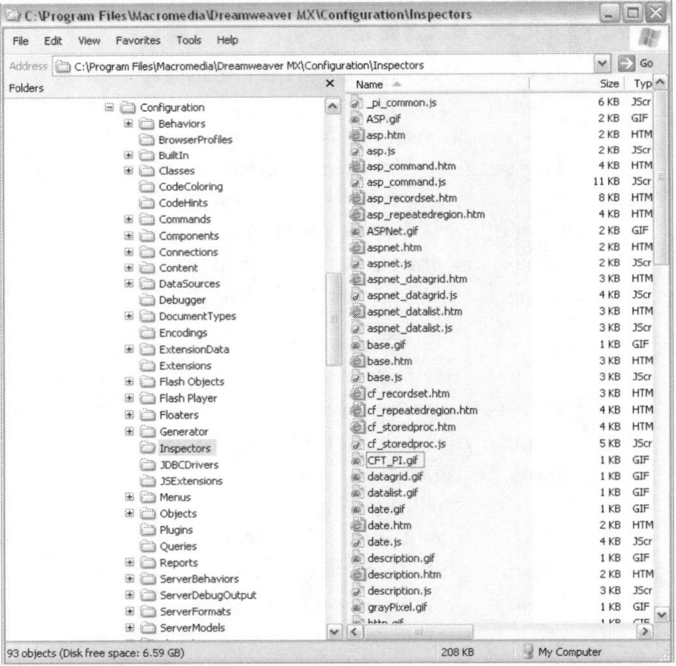

FIGURE 6.1 *The Configuration/Inspectors folder, as it appears in its default state (no third-party extensions added).*

Property Inspector Files

Each Property inspector is created from one, two, or three files in the Inspectors folder. These files are discussed in the following sections.

HTML File (Required)

As usual, the HTML file is the inspector file itself. Without this file, there is no inspector. The filename will never be seen by the user, but it can be important in determining priority. (Dreamweaver sometimes uses alphabetical sorting of names to determine which inspector to use in a given situation. This is discussed in more detail in the later section "The API Procedure for Property Inspectors.")

JavaScript File (Optional)

Again as usual, the JavaScript portion of the inspector can be saved in the HTML file, or it can saved separately in a linked JS file. It's customary, though not required, to match this file's name with the filename of the HTML file (for example, My Inspector.htm and My Inspector.js).

GIF File (Optional, but Usually Present)

This file contains a 36×36-pixel icon to be used in the upper-left corner of the inspector, to identify the object being inspected. Figure 6.2 shows some sample icons. The icon isn't required, but it is important for good user interface design. The Macromedia standard icons all have a "depressed button" frame and a transparent background, so they blend in well with the inspector. It's customary, though not required, to match this file's name with the filename of the main object file.

FIGURE 6.2 *Some GIF icons from the Macromedia standard Property inspectors.*

Other Image Files

Depending on the complexity of your Property inspector's layout, you may want to use additional images to enhance it. You can use your own custom images, or take advantage of the handy image files already stored in the Inspectors folder or in the Configuration/Shared/MM/Images folder.

The Structure of an Inspector File

At their simplest, inspector files are indeed simple, with few required elements. At their fanciest, they can get pretty detailed.

Required Elements

Each Property inspector file requires at least these elements:

- **Opening line/comment.** The first line of every inspector file above the `<HTML>` tag must be a comment in this format:

  ```
  <!-- tag:tagNameOrKeyword,priority: 1-10,selection:exactOrWithin,hline,vline -->
  ```

  Without this line, Dreamweaver won't recognize the file as an inspector. The values entered into the comment refer to the following:

  - **`tagNameOrKeyword` (required).**This is the tag to be inspected, or one of the following keywords: `*COMMENT*` (for comments), `*LOCKED*` (for locked regions), `*ASP*` (for ASP tags).
  - **`1-10` (required).** This rates the priority Dreamweaver should give the inspector (`1` is lowest; `10` is highest). Any time Dreamweaver has a choice between using two or more inspectors to inspect a user selection, the higher-priority inspector wins. (You can use this to force the program to override its own built-in inspectors.)
  - **`exactOrWithin` (required).** This indicates whether the user's selection must exactly contain the tag named above (`exact`), or whether it can be within that tag (`within`).
  - **`hline` (optional).** If this parameter is present, a gray horizontal line is used to divide the upper and lower halves of the expanded Property inspector.
  - **`vline` (optional).** If this parameter is present, a gray vertical line is used to divide the tag name field from the rest of the properties in the inspector. This line is used as a visual cue for the user, in order to organize the interface clearly.

Here are some sample opening tags for inspectors:

```
<!--tag:LINK,priority:5,selection:within,vline,hline-->
(from "link.htm")

<!--tag:META,priority:6,selection:within-->
(from "keywords.htm")

<!--tag:*LOCKED*,priority:5,selection:within,vline,hline-->
(from "date.htm")
```

- **`canInspectSelection()` function.** This function returns `true` or `false`, determining whether the inspector is appropriate for the current user selection. This is usually done by using the `dom.getSelectedNode()` function to access the currently selected object, and comparing that to the allowable tags for this inspector. This function is part of the API, and is called automatically. A simple example of this function is found in title.js (one of the more straightforward inspector files):

```
function canInspectSelection(){
var titleObj = getSelectedObj();
//accept if the selected node is text or if it is the title tag
return (titleObj.nodeType==Node.TEXT_NODE ||
(titleObj.nodeType=Node.ELEMENT_NODE && titleObj.tagName=="TITLE"));
}
```

- **Body/Form Elements.** The content in the `<body>` tag becomes the interface for the inspector—it's what will show up in the Property inspector floating panel. In order for the inspector to process user input and display values, the `<body>` must contain a `<form>` and form elements, as well.
- **Event Handlers.** The `inspectSelection()` function allows the inspector to display only the current settings for the selection. If the inspector is to process user input, changing the document as the user enters changes into the inspector, each form field must have an event handler that calls a local function. The `<title>` Property inspector, for instance, includes one text input field, which calls a local function, `onBlur`:

```
<input type="text" name="Title" size="57" onBlur="setTitleTag()">
```

After the user has typed in a title and left the input field, the `setTitleTag()` function then changes the `innerHTML` property of the `<title>` tag:

```
function setTitleTag(){
var titleObj = getSelectedObj();
//while an element node (the title one) is not selected
while (titleObj.nodeType!=Node.ELEMENT_NODE )
      titleObj=titleObj.parentNode; //traverse up the tree
if (titleObj.innerHTML != findObject("Title").value){
      titleObj.innerHTML = findObject("Title").value;
      }
}
```

Listing 6.1 shows the HTML code for a very simple Property inspector.

Listing 6.1 Framework Code for a Basic Property Inspector, Containing Required Elements Only

```
<!-- tag:MYTAG,priority:10,selection:within,hline -->
<html>
<head>
<title>MYTAG Inspector</title>
<script language="JavaScript">
function canInspectSelection() {
return true;
}
</script>
</head>
<body>
This is the body.
</body>
</html>
```

Semi-Required Element

If you want your Property inspector to collect and display any values from the user's selection, one more element is required:

- **`inspectSelection()` function.** This function populates the input fields of the Property inspector form based on an inspection of the current selection. Dreamweaver automatically feeds one argument into the function: `max` (if the Property inspector is in its expanded state, with both halves visible, when the inspector is called) or `min` (if the Property inspector is abbreviated, with only the top half visible). This function is part of the API, and is called automatically.

  Most examples of this function are fairly extensive because this is one-half of the functionality of the inspector. One of the simplest examples is from title.js, for creating the <title> inspector:

  ```
  function inspectSelection(){
  var titleObj = getSelectedObj();
  while (titleObj.nodeType!=Node.ELEMENT_NODE ) //while an element node
  (the title one) is not selected
        titleObj=titleObj.parentNode; //traverse up the tree
  findObject("Title").value = titleObj.innerHTML
  showHideTranslated();
  }
  ```

note

The preceding code calls the `findObject()` function, a handy utility function for use with inspectors. It's found in the shared file `_pi_common.js`, and is discussed in more detail later in this chapter.

A few Property inspectors, however—the Date inspector, for instance—don't display attribute information about the selected object and therefore don't use the `inspectSelection()` function. They still work as inspectors—that is, they show up when the specified page element is selected and they present functional form elements—without the `inspectSelection()` function.

Optional Elements

An inspector with only the preceding elements will function just fine, but it will probably be fairly crude to look at. Consequently, most inspectors use at least some of these optional elements to dress themselves up:

- **Layers.** All the Macromedia standard inspectors, and probably all inspectors you will download from the Exchange as well, use CSS layers to define the layout of the form elements. Either the `<div>` or `<span>` tag can be used for these layers. Figure 6.3 shows a standard Property inspector as it appears in the Dreamweaver interface and as its file appears in the Dreamweaver design and code views.

note

Why use layers? You may decide not to. Their presence certainly complicates the HTML and JavaScript coding for your inspector. Layers are covered in this chapter as a way of introducing you to these special requirements, and because they are commonly used in inspectors.

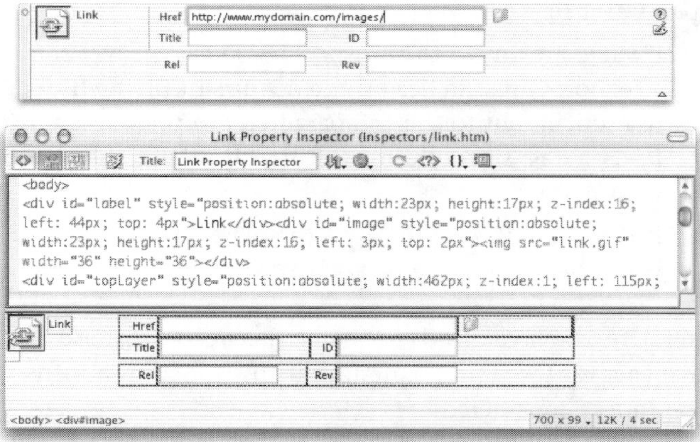

FIGURE 6.3 *The Link Property inspector, shown as a functioning part of the Dreamweaver interface and as a document in the Dreamweaver Design/Code view.*

- **`findObject()` function (`_pi_common.js`).** Of course, if the inspector includes form elements that are in layers, the `<form>` tag ceases functioning, so user input must be collected in some other way. The `findObject()` function allows scripts to access named form elements as objects rather than as form elements, and collect their values for processing in scripts. For instance, this code

  ```
  myVariable = document.myForm.userchoice.value
  ```

  can be re-coded as

  ```
  myVariable = findObject("userchoice").value
  ```

  Any Property inspector that uses layers to control its layout almost certainly uses `findObject()` to process form elements.

  The `findObject()` function is not part of the API. Rather, it's a local function defined in the `_pi_common.js` file, which is located in the Configuration/Inspectors folder. To use this function, the inspector file must link to `_pi_common.js`.

- **Icons and other images.** We've already discussed the GIF icon file. Using it isn't required, but it is recommended for good interface design. Use other images as well, if your interface calls for them. To include an image in your inspector, save the image file in the Inspectors folder, and link to it using a relative URL. To keep your inspector's visual interface compact and efficient, don't use images larger than about 36×36.

The API Procedure for Property Inspectors

The procedure for inspectors begins when the user makes a selection or moves the insertion point in a document. Every time this happens, the following events occur:

1. Dreamweaver looks through the valid inspector files for any file with a selection type of `within`.
   - If there are any `within` inspectors, Dreamweaver starts from the current selection and searches up the document hierarchy, comparing tags in the user document to the `tag` parameter in the `within` inspector file until it finds a tag surrounding the selection that has an inspector associated with it.
   - If there are no `within` inspectors, Dreamweaver looks for an inspector file with a selection type of `exact`.

2. After Dreamweaver finds a match between `tag` and inspector, it calls the `canInspectSelection()` function. If this function returns `false`, the inspector is no longer considered.

If only one inspector returns `true`, Dreamweaver moves on to the next step. If, however, more than one potential inspector returns `true`, the following occurs:

- Dreamweaver compares the priority values for each candidate. The inspector with the highest priority rating (10 is highest) is chosen.
- If the priority ratings are equal, Dreamweaver chooses an inspector alphabetically by filename.

3. After an inspector file has been chosen, its `<body>` content appears in the Property inspector floating panel. If a `displayHelp()` function is defined, the "?" icon is displayed in the panel's upper-right corner. Dreamweaver calls the `inspectSelection()` function to populate the input fields of the form.
4. From this point on, event handlers attached to individual input fields in the inspector form call local functions that edit the document in response to user input.

Figure 6.4 shows a diagram of this procedure.

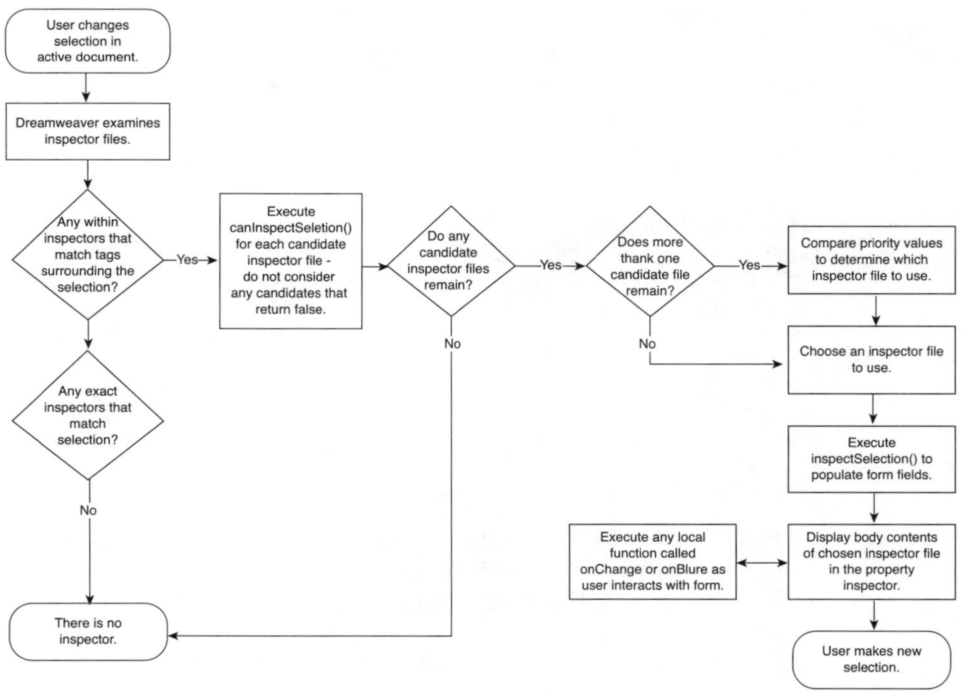

FIGURE 6.4 *The API procedure for Property inspectors.*

Making Inspectors: Practice Session

Let's roll up our sleeves and get some practice making inspectors. As usual, as we practice we'll also be building framework files that we can save and build on later.

For most of the practice session, you'll be creating an inspector for a fake HTML tag—the `<mood>` tag, for marking up text that describes a mood. Why a fake tag? Dreamweaver has all the standard HTML and XHTML tags covered already, and you don't want to be getting in its way with your practice. After you learn the ropes of designing and implementing inspectors, you'll practice using priority settings and other methods to override the default Dreamweaver inspectors.

Task 1: Create a bare-bones *<mood>* inspector

We'll start simply, with only the required elements that an inspector needs: the opening comment line, the `canInspectBehavior()` function, and some `<body>` content.

1. In your text editor, create a new file. Save it in the Configuration/Inspectors folder as **mood.htm**.
2. Add the framework inspector code shown in Listing 6.1, changing a few key elements to make this a mood inspector, like this (code altered from the code in Listing 6.1 is shown in bold):

```
<!-- tag:MOOD,priority:10,selection:within,hline -->
<html>
<head>
<title>Mood Inspector</title>
<script language="JavaScript">
function canInspectSelection() {
return true;
}
</script>
</head>
<body>
This is the body.
</body>
</html>
```

3. Try it out! Launch Dreamweaver and create a practice document. (If you've been using Dreamweaver to create your inspector file, quit the program and relaunch it.) Using Code and Design view, enter the following tag into the `<body>` of the practice document:

```
<mood>Happy!</mood>
```

You have to use Code and Design view for this because the fake tag can only be added in Code view, but you can see the inspector at work only in Design view.

note

Because Dreamweaver checks the Inspectors folder for valid Property inspectors when it first starts up, forcing extensions to reload may not cause new inspectors to be recognized. It's safest to quit Dreamweaver, and then relaunch it when adding new inspectors. Reloading extensions is, however, usually sufficient when you're editing an existing inspector.

4. After you have typed in the tag in Code view, use the tag selector in Design view to select it. Open the Property inspector, if it isn't currently showing. Your custom Property inspector should come up, looking like the one in Figure 6.5.

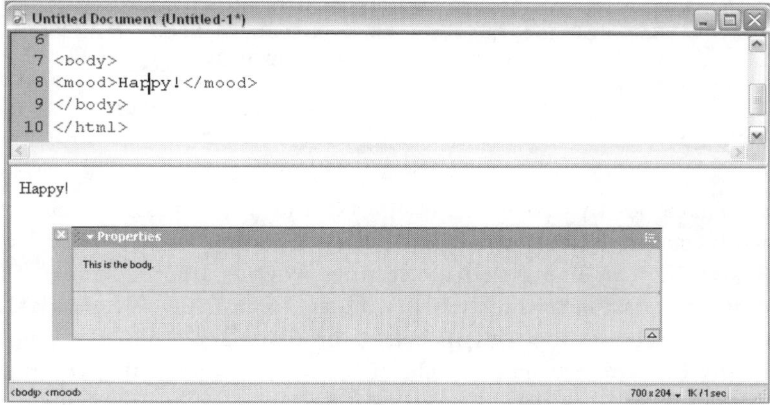

FIGURE 6.5 *The* <mood> *tag being used and inspected in a practice document.*

Congratulations! You've made your first (albeit pretty basic) inspector.

Task 2: Add a form and *inspectBehavior( )* function

Our next goal is to get the inspector to display the current value for `mood`—which we'll assume to be the text within the opening and closing `<mood>` tags. We'll do this by putting a `<form>` in the `<body>` section, and using the `inspectBehavior()` function to collect data from the selection and pass it into the form.

1. In the mood.htm file, replace the <body> content with a simple form consisting of one text field, like this (new code is in bold):

```
<body>
<form name="myForm">
      What mood are you in?
      <input type="text" name="myMood">
</form>
</body>
```

2. In the <head> section, add the following inspectBehavior() function to your <script> tag:

```
function inspectSelection() {
var myDOM = dw.getDocumentDOM();
var myObject = myDOM.getSelectedNode();
if (myObject.nodeType == 1 && myObject.tagName == 'MOOD') {
    document.myForm.myMood.value = myObject.innerHTML;
    } else {
    document.myForm.myMood.value = myObject.data;
    }
}
```

What does this code do? In lines 2 and 3, it accesses the currently selected object (presumably this will be the <mood> tag or its child). The conditional statement in line 4 then determines whether the selection is the <mood> tag itself or its child, which must be a text object. If the selection is the <mood> tag, line 6 accesses the tag's innerHTML property, and feeds the value of that property into the myMood text field. If the selection is the text child, line 8 accesses the text object's data property and feeds that property's value into the myMood text field.

(For the purposes of this exercise, assume that no tag can exist within the <mood> tag, only text. Thus the user's selection can only be the contained text or the tag itself.)

3. Try it out! Reload extensions in Dreamweaver (because there's no new inspector being added, you shouldn't need to relaunch), open your practice document, and click inside the <mood> tag.

   Your revised inspector should come up with the current mood showing in its text field, as shown in Figure 6.6. Changing the text in the document should automatically change the text that shows in the inspector. That's half of your inspector's functionality.

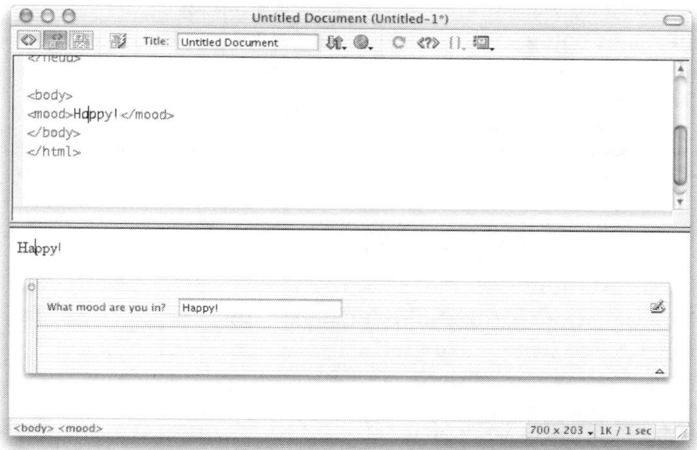

FIGURE 6.6 *The mood inspector, with populated form field. The mood is happy!*

Task 3: Add a local function and event handler

None of the API functions allow your inspector to change the document; for that, we need to define a local function. Because the user expects changes to be made as soon as information has been entered into the inspector, we'll call the function with an `onBlur` event handler attached to the `myMood` text field. The new function performs actions very similar to those in `inspectBehavior()`—namely, determining whether the tag or its text is the current object, and accessing the data in the text. The only difference is that instead of collecting information from the document and feeding it to the form, the local function must do the opposite.

1. In the mood.htm file, add a local function to your `<script>` tag, like this:

```
function makeMeHappy() {
var myDOM = dw.getDocumentDOM();
var myObject = myDOM.getSelectedNode();
if (myObject.nodeType == "1" && myObject.tagName == 'MOOD') {
      myObject.innerHTML = document.myForm.myMood.value;
      } else {
      myObject.data = document.myForm.myMood.value;
      }
}
```

   Compare this code to the code for `the inspectSelection()`, and you'll see that it accesses the selected object and sets either the `<mood>` tag's `innerHTML` or the text objects' `data` property to the value found in the `myMood` text field.

2. Now add an event handler with a function call to the form code, like this (new code is in bold):

```
<body>
<form name="myForm">
      What mood are you in?
      <input type="text" name="myMood" onBlur="makeMeHappy()">
</form>
</body>
```

3. That's it! Reload Dreamweaver extensions, go back to the practice file, and try it out. Everything should look the same as before, but changing the information in the form field changes the `<mood>` of the document to `<mood>Thrilled!</mood>`.

Task 4: Re-create the interface using layers

Our `<mood>` inspector works. Now let's make it look like a real inspector, with layers and an icon.

note

See Appendix F, "Contents of the Dreamweaver MX Extensions Book Companion Web Site," for a full list of the contents on the web site.

To start with, you need a 36×36 GIF icon for your `<mood>` enhancer. The standard icons have some similar features (transparent background, beveled frame around the edge), so you might find it easiest to copy one of the GIF files from the Inspectors folder, delete its icon, and insert your own. You can also download the already made mood.gif file from the companion web site to this book. (The web site also includes inspector_icon.gif, a blank template file with only the beveled frame in place for quickly making your own icons.)

1. Get the icon file in whichever way you choose, and save it as **mood.gif** in the Inspectors folder.
2. Now add the layers. The hardest part about this step is visualizing what the finished inspector should look like, inside the Property Inspector floating panel. Figure 6.7 shows a diagram of the floating panel framework, with measurements in place.

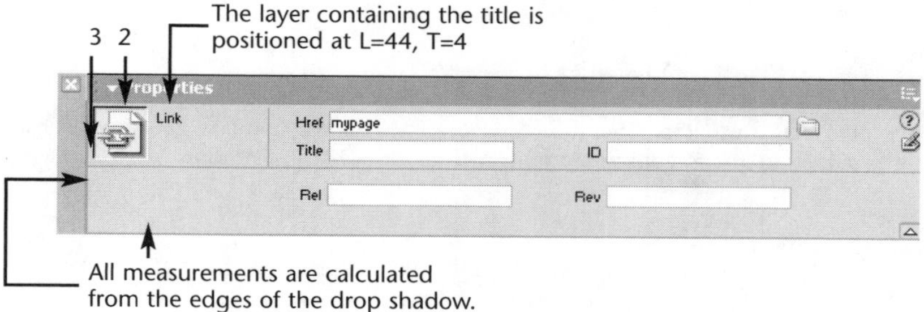

FIGURE 6.7 *The Property Inspector floating panel interface, with measurements for calculating layers' absolute positioning.*

Unless you're a true coding fiend, you'll probably find it easiest to do this part of the job in the Dreamweaver Design view. You may want to open existing inspector files and see where their layers are positioned. Figure 6.7 shows some key measurements taken from these other files. Your author likes to use a blank template Property inspector (like the one shown in Figure 6.6) as a tracing image. Figure 6.8 shows a Dreamweaver document with a tracing image in place, along with the `left` and `top` offsets to position the tracing image for accurate measurements. (You can download a copy of the template file, `blank_inspector.png`, from this book's companion web site.) If you use a tracing image, remember to remove it from your code when you're finished with it.

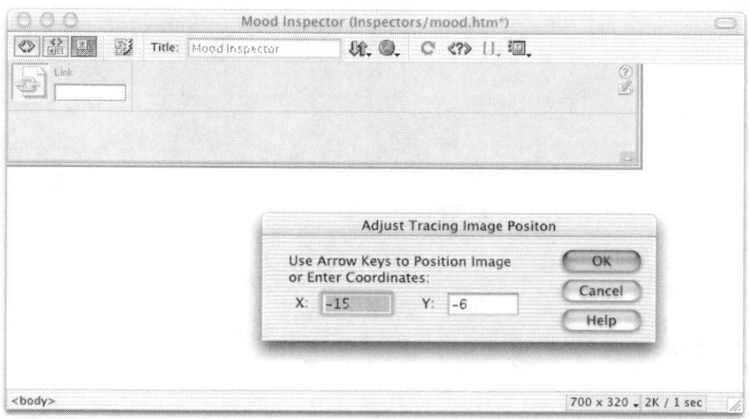

FIGURE 6.8 *Using a blank picture of a Property inspector as a tracing image in Dreamweaver.*

note

To create your own blank inspector, take a screenshot of any of the standard Dreamweaver inspectors and paint out the details in an image-editing program such as Fireworks or Photoshop.

Figure 6.9 shows a good layers-based layout for the `<mood>` inspector. You can use the `<div>` or `<span>` tags to create your layers.

note

If you use the Dreamweaver design tools to draw your layers, you may end up with an extra `<script>` tag containing the `MM_reloadPage()` function. (This function helps layers draw properly in Netscape; because no browser will ever see your inspector file, however, it's a useless function for you.) To stop this from happening every time you draw a new layer, go to Edit > Preferences > Layers and turn off the Netscape 4 Compatibility option.

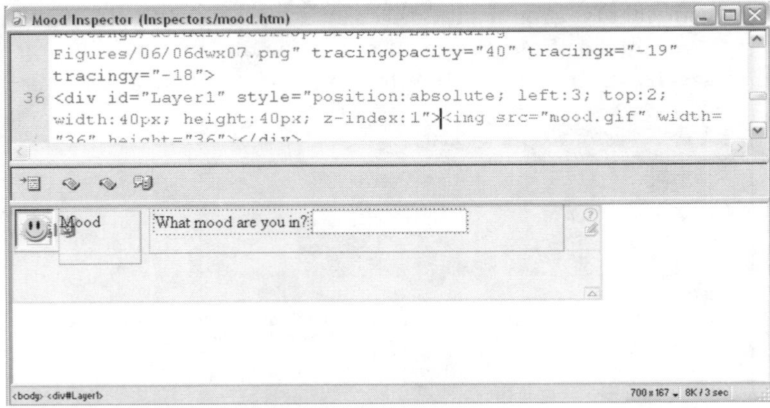

FIGURE 6.9 *Creating the mood inspector in the Dreamweaver Design view.*

3. Are you finished? Not yet! If you try the revised inspector out now, Dreamweaver gives you an error because it can no longer find the form element in your `<body>` section. That's because it's in a layer! You need to change how you access the `myMood` field—accessing it not through the `<form>` but as an object on the page, using Level 1 DOM access.

Solving this problem could involve some complex scripting, but luckily Macromedia has done all the hard work for you by placing the `findObject()` function in `_pi_common.js` for you to access. All you have to do is access the file and call on the function. (Interestingly enough, now that you're not using the form to gain access to the form element, you no longer need the `<form>` tag at all. The `<input>` tag functions perfectly well without it.)

Add a new `<script>` tag to your `<head>` section, linking to the JavaScript file:

```
<script src="_pi_common.js"></script>
```

(This is a relative link to the JS file in the Inspectors folder.)

4. Next, change all references in your code from `document.myForm.myMood.value` to **`findObject("myMood").value`** , like this (new code is in bold):

```
function inspectSelection() {
var myDOM = dw.getDocumentDOM();
var myObject = myDOM.getSelectedNode();
if (myObject.nodeType == 1 && myObject.tagName == 'MOOD') {
   findObject("myMood").value = myObject.innerHTML;
   } else {
   findObject("myMood").value = myObject.data;
   }
}

function makeMeHappy() {
var myDOM = dw.getDocumentDOM();
var myObject = myDOM.getSelectedNode();
if (myObject.nodeType == 1 && myObject.tagName == 'MOOD') {
   myObject.innerHTML = findObject("myMood").value;
   } else {
   myObject.data = findObject("myMood").value;
   }
}
```

There you go—try it out! The inspector should work just as well as it did before you introduced the layers, and it looks a lot better—just like the one in Figure 6.10. The code for the finished `<mood>` inspector is shown in Listing 6.2.

Listing 6.2 Final Code for *mood.htm,* Commented for Reference

```
<!-- tag:MOOD,priority:10,selection:within,hline -->
<html>
<head>
<title>Mood Inspector</title>

<!-- link to this file so findObject() function is available -->
<script src="_pi_common.js"></script>
```

continues

Listing 6.2 Continued

```
<script language="JavaScript">

//return true or inspector won't be used
function canInspectSelection() {
return true;
}

//determine tag attributes and put them in form fields
function inspectSelection() {

//access the selected object
var myDOM = dw.getDocumentDOM();
var myObject = myDOM.getSelectedNode();

//if the <mood> tag itself is selected
if (myObject.nodeType == 1 && myObject.tagName == 'MOOD') {
   //set form field to its innerHTML
   findObject("myMood").value = myObject.innerHTML;
   //if the text inside the tag is selected
   } else {
   //set form field to its data
   findObject("myMood").value = myObject.data;
   }//end if
}

//called when form's text field is changed
//to update <mood> tag in document
function makeMeHappy() {

//access selected object
var myDOM = dw.getDocumentDOM();
var myObject = myDOM.getSelectedNode();

//if <mood> tag itself is selected
if (myObject.nodeType == 1 && myObject.tagName == 'MOOD') {
   //collect info from form and put it in the tag's innerHTML
   myObject.innerHTML = findObject("myMood").value;
   //if text inside tag is selected
   } else {
   //collect info from form and change the text object's data value
   myObject.data = findObject("myMood").value;
   }//end if
}

</script>
</head>
<body>

<!-- icon -->
<div id="iconLayer" style="position:absolute; left:3; top:2; width:40px;
```

```
height:40px; z-index:1"><img src="mood.gif" width="36"
height="36"></div>

<!-- name -->
<div id="nameLayer" style="position:absolute; left:44px; top:4px;
width:75px; height:50px; z-index:2">Mood</div>

<!-- label and form field -->
<div id="inputLayer" style="position:absolute; left:128px; top:0px;
width:383px; height:44px; z-index:3">
<table width="60">
   <tr>
      <td align="right" nowrap>What mood are you in?</td>
      <td><input name="myMood" type="text" id="myMood"
onBlur="makeMeHappy()"></td>
   </tr>
</table>
</div>

</body>
</html>
```

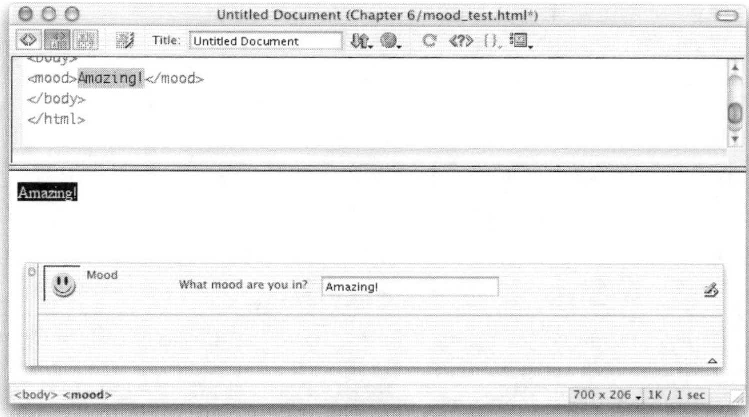

Figure 6.10 *The completed mood inspector in action.*

note

Sometimes, links to shared files don't work if the JavaScript and HTML portions of the inspector code are in one file. If this happens, Dreamweaver tells you it can't find the `findObject()` function. To fix the problem, split your inspector into mood.htm and mood.js. The link should then work fine.

Task 5: Create a competing inspector, and play with priorities

You know Dreamweaver doesn't have any other inspectors capable of handling <mood> disorders, so it doesn't matter what priority level you assign your inspector. But with most real tags, there will always be competition. You have to let Dreamweaver know when you want to override the default inspectors to use yours. In this task, you'll experiment by creating your own competing mood inspector.

1. In your text editor, create another inspector file. Save it in the Inspectors folder as **othermood.htm**. You don't care if it's functional, just that it looks significantly different from the original—for this purpose, you can just enter the bare-bones code shown in Task 1.
2. In the opening comment line, give the new inspector a priority of 10. Then open the original inspector (mood.htm) and change its priority to 8.
3. Try it out! Save both files and close them. Then quit Dreamweaver, if it's running, and relaunch it. (Changes in priority won't show up if you just reload extensions.) When you try to inspect a <mood> tag, the new (bare-bones) inspector should appear instead of the old one. That's because the new inspector now has a higher priority.

   Experiment with this all you like. Reverse the priority settings, set them to the same values, change the filenames, and see what happens each time. (Just remember, because you're working with priorities, you'll have to quit Dreamweaver and relaunch it each time you make a change.)

You now know the basics of property inspecting. Now let's put that knowledge to use!

Workshop #1: A Simple Property Inspector

If you understood everything in the practice session, you should be able to finish this workshop exercise with no difficulty. You'll be creating an inspector for a tag that always uses the same number of attributes, and has no competition from the Dreamweaver default inspectors.

Sample Inspector: Netscape Block Spacer

You created the block spacer object in Workshop #2 in Chapter 2, "Creating Custom Objects." Remember? You may have noticed, if you've ever tried using this object, that there's no way to inspect or edit it except by using the source code. That's because there's no inspector! Creating a fully functional object often involves creating an inspector to go with it.

note

Before you can inspect a Netscape block spacer, you will need to insert one. If you didn't create the spacer object back in Chapter 2, you can download the finished object file from the companion web site. (See Appendix F for more information about the web site.)

Task 1: Create the basic inspector file

If you went through the preceding practice exercise, you already have a framework file to start from—the mood inspector file. If not, you have to create a file from scratch as you go.

note

To make the mood inspector more flexible as a template file, you might want to strip out all mood-specific code and save the gutted file as a template.

1. Duplicate the mood.htm file, or create a new text file containing the HTML framework from Listing 6.2. Save it in the Inspectors folder as **Block Spacer.htm**.

   This is the same name you gave the object file back in Chapter 2. The names don't need to match, but using similar names for corresponding files makes it easier to keep track of files later. This is the way many of the standard extension files are named.

2. Change the opening comment to reflect the new tag being inspected, like this (new code is in bold):

   ```
   <!-- tag:SPACER,priority:10,selection:within,hline -->
   ```

3. Change the document's <title> to reflect the new tag's identify. Like this:

   ```
   <title>Block Spacer Inspector</title>
   ```

Task 2: Create the new layout and form

How you revise the inspector's layout depends on whether you're working in your text editor or in Dreamweaver Design view.

If you're coding your inspector by hand, change the <body> tag of the file to look like this (new code is in bold):

```
<body>
<div id="iconLayer" style="position:absolute; left:3; top:2; width:40px;
height:40px; z-index:1"><img src="blockspacer.gif" width="36"
height="36"></div>
<div id="nameLayer" style="position:absolute; left:44px; top:4px;
width:75px; height:50px; z-index:2">Spacer</div>
<div id="widthLayer" style="position:absolute; left:128px; top:0px;
```

```
width:134px; height:40px; z-index:3">
  <table>
    <tr>
      <td align="right" nowrap>Width:</td>
      <td><input type="text" name="width" size="6"></td>
    </tr>
  </table>
</div>
<div id="heightlayer" style="position:absolute; left:286px; top:0px;
width:140px; height:41px; z-index:4">
  <table>
    <tr>
      <td align="right" nowrap>Height:</td>
      <td><input type="text" name="height" size="6"></td>
    </tr>
  </table>
</div>
</body>
```

If you're working in Dreamweaver, change your layout to look like the one shown in Figure 6.11. Make sure to name your form fields `width` and `height`.

For the inspector's icon, you can download blockspacer.gif from the companion web site, or make your own graphic.

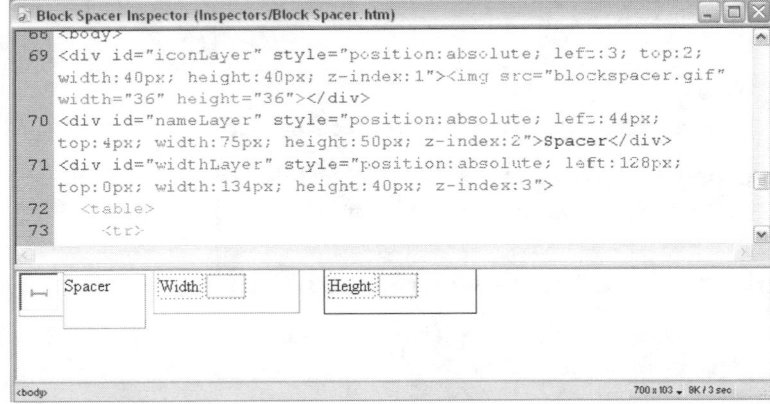

FIGURE 6.11 *Layout for the Block Spacer Property inspector, as seen in Dreamweaver Code and Design view.*

note

If you don't like stopping to create icons when you're ready to design a new inspector, keep a blank or generic icon around to use as a placeholder while the inspector is in development. You can even save a copy of the blank icon with the proper name (for example, blockspacer.gif) in the Inspectors folder, so you don't have to change the file's code when you do eventually create a custom graphic for that file.

Task 3: Double-check the *canInspectSelection( )* function

In the practice session, you created the simplest of all `canInspectSelection()` functions; it just returned `true`, no questions asked. When would you *not* want to do this? Remember, Dreamweaver calls this inspector only when the cursor is within a `<spacer>` tag. Can you think of any times when you wouldn't want this inspector called, given this situation? There are no alternative methods of inspecting spacers—Dreamweaver hasn't provided one, and it's much too simple a tag to warrant you creating multiple inspectors. Therefore, you always want this function to return `true`. So leave it the way it is.

Task 4: Revise the *inspectSelection( )* function

The purpose of inspecting a selection, remember, is to copy any attribute values from the selected object to the relevant form fields in the inspector. To accomplish this for the Block Spacer inspector, revise your `inspectSelection()` function to look like this (new code is in bold):

```
function inspectSelection() {
myDOM = dw.getDocumentDOM();
myObject = myDOM.getSelectedNode();
findObject("width").value = myObject.width;
findObject("height").value = myObject.height;
}
```

Task 5: Create a *setDimensions( )* function

In addition to inspecting properties, your inspector needs to change the document based on user input. For that, you need a local function. (If you're adapting the mood inspector code, you can remove the `makeMeHappy()` function—you no longer need to make anyone happy.)

1. Write a function that will change two properties, `width` and `height`, and pass it a parameter. Call the function `setDimensions()`. The code should look like this:

```
function setDimensions(dim) {
myDOM = dw.getDocumentDOM();
myObject = myDOM.getSelectedNode();
if (dim == "width") {
      myObject.width = findObject("width").value;
      }
if (dim == "height") {
      myObject.height = findObject("height").value;
      }
}
```

Can you tell what this code is doing? The passed parameter can be either `width` or `height`. The function gains access to the selected object (lines 2 and 3) and, depending on which of those two values is passed in the function call, sets either the `width` (line 5) or the `height` (line 8) attribute of the selected `<spacer>` tag to the value entered in the appropriate form field.

2. Now, add function calls to the two text fields in the form, making sure each one passes the correct parameter, like this (new code is in bold):

```
<input type="text" name="width" size="6" onBlur =
➥"setDimensions('width')">

<input type="text" name="height" size="6" onBlur =
➥"setDimensions('height')">
```

3. Try it out! You've built a simple but complete inspector. Launch (or re-launch) Dreamweaver, create a new document, and insert a `<spacer>` element using your Block Spacer object or coding it by hand. When you select it, your Block Spacer inspector should appear. Changing either value in the inspector should change the spacer. (Because Dreamweaver doesn't display spacers in Design view, you'll have to work in Code and Design view to see the results of your inspection.) Figure 6.12 shows the Block Spacer inspector in action.

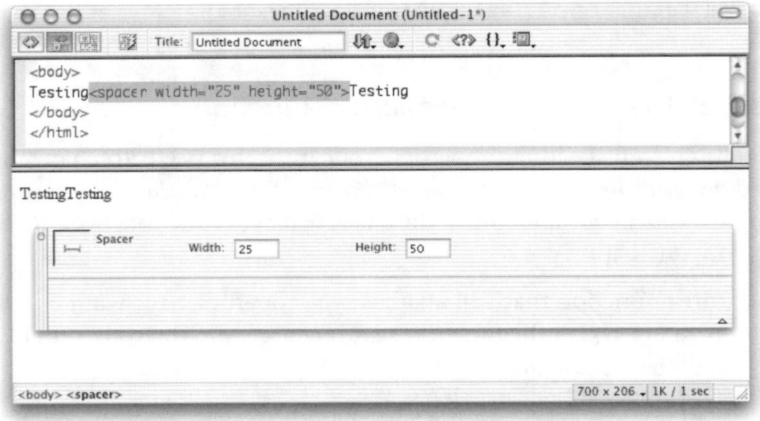

FIGURE 6.12 *The Block Spacer inspector, inspecting a* `<spacer>` *tag surrounded by some sample text.*

Task 6: Refine and bulletproof!

In a perfect world, in which no one ever makes unusual demands, tinkers with the code when Dreamweaver isn't looking, or imports code from other programs, your object and inspector would now work nicely hand in hand. Right. But what if a user didn't want to insert a block spacer, and so hand-coded the spacer to be vertical or horizontal only? What if…

1. What if a user, faced with your inspector, decides to delete the `width` attribute and leave only the `height` attribute? You could always rewrite the `canInspectSelection()` function to return `true` only if the spacer has a type of `block`, but that would cause more problems than it solves.

   Instead, revise the `setDimensions()` function to detect whether both `width` and `height` values are present; and if not, to change the type to `horizontal` or `vertical` and remove the unused attribute. And vice versa, if a user adds a `width` or `height` where there was none before, the function adds the attribute and changes the type accordingly.

   Create a new function, `errorChecking()`, to take care of this. The code for the new function should look like this:

   ```
   function errorChecking() {
   var myDOM = dw.getDocumentDOM();
   var myObject = myDOM.getSelectedNode();
   if (!myObject.height) {
      myObject.removeAttribute("height");
      }
   if (!myObject.width) {
      myObject.removeAttribute("width");
      }
   if (myObject.height && myObject.width) {
         myObject.type = "block";
         } else if (myObject.width && !myObject.height) {
         myObject.type = "horizontal";
         myObject.removeAttribute("height");
         } else if (myObject.height && !myObject.width) {
         myObject.type = "vertical";
         myObject.removeAttribute("width");
         }
   }
   ```

   What's happening here? As in other functions, lines 2 and 3 gain access to the selected object, so it can be inspected. Lines 4–6 determine if there is no `height` value specified in the object, and if so remove the `height` attribute; this is to eliminate code like this:

   ```
   <spacer width="50" height="">
   ```

Lines 7–9 do the same error-checking for the `width` attribute, removing it from the code if there is no value for it.

Starting in line 10, an `if-else` statement sets the object's `type` attribute to `block`, `vertical`, or `horizontal`, based on the presence or absence of width and height attributes in the code.

Now, what if a pesky user insists on removing both the `width` and `height` values? A `spacer` isn't a `spacer` without some dimensions. How you treat such a problem is partly scripting and partly strategic interface design. What do you want to happen in such a case? The least-intrusive solution is to ignore the problem, and let the invalid code stay on the page. A broken spacer doesn't break the web page; it just doesn't function as a `spacer`. A more hands-on solution is to insert default values, and bring up an alert window to let the user know what's happening.

2. Take care of this by adding another conditional to the end of the `errorChecking()` function (new code is in bold):

```
function errorChecking(dim) {

[etc]

if (!myObject.height && !myObject.width) {
   window.alert("Spacers must have at least one dimension.\nDefault
➥values have been inserted.");
   myObject.height = 10;
   myObject.width = 10;
   myObject.type = "block";
   }
}
```

3. You now have your `errorChecking()` function all set, but it won't be able to catch any errors unless you call it! To do this, add the following statement of the `setDimensions()` function:

```
function setDimensions(dim) {
myDOM = dw.getDocumentDOM();
myObject = myDOM.getSelectedNode();
if (dim == "width") {
      myObject.width =
findObject("width").value;
      }
if (dim == "height") {
      myObject.height = findObject("height").value;
      }
errorChecking();
}
```

tip

Here's a tip from this last bit of code: The Dreamweaver alert windows do not wrap text unless you tell them to. Notice that the alert statement here uses a new line character to force a line break between the two sentences.

4. Finally, the preceding error-checking function catches any strange input the user puts into the inspector, but what if a user starts out with a `<spacer>` that's missing something—a `width` or `height` parameter, or both? You can detect such problems as soon as the inspector appears, using `inspectSelection()`—but you can't fix them at this point. (The `inspectSelection()` function isn't allowed to make document edits.) What you don't want is for the inspector to show up with `undefined` as one of its values. That would definitely be bad interface design.

   Eliminate that potential problem by tweaking the `inspectSelection()` function (new code is in bold):

   ```
   function inspectSelection() {
   myDOM = dw.getDocumentDOM();
   myObject = myDOM.getSelectedNode();
   if (myObject.getAttribute('width')) {
      findObject("width").value = myObject.width;
      }
   if (myObject.getAttribute('height')) {
      findObject("height").value = myObject.height;
      }
   }
   ```

   What does this code do? The form fields for width and height will be filled in with a value only if the `<spacer>` object has the specified attribute. (For more information on the `getAttribute()` method, see Table 4.5 in Chapter 4.)

5. That's it! Try out your revised inspector. Go ahead—try to break it. Insert a `<spacer>` tag in a document with information missing. How does the inspector respond? Once you've got the `<spacer>` selected, try deleting the information from either the `width` or `height` form input field. If you can get the inspector to break, see if you can fix it. Keep doing that until you can't break it anymore. Congratulations! You're *probably* bulletproof.

Workshop #2: Replacing a Default Inspector

For this workshop, we'll create a more complex inspector, again building on a custom object from Chapter 2. We'll also see how to use `priority` values and the `canInspectSelection()` function to dictate exactly when an inspector will override the default.

Sample Project: Custom Horizontal Rule

Remember the Custom Horizontal Rule object you created back in Workshop #3 of Chapter 2? This object allows users to set all sorts of attributes, including color, as they insert the `<hr>` tag. As with the `<spacer>` object, however, after a user has a colored `<hr>` in the document, there's no way to use the Property inspector to check, change, or remove the color property. We can't simply add a color button to the default `<hr>` inspector, because that inspector is hard-coded into Dreamweaver, not written as an extension. We'll have to replace it.

Task 1: Create the basic inspector file

Start by creating or copying the basic framework for an inspector file.

1. If you completed the Mood inspector earlier in this chapter, open mood.htm. If not, create a new file in your text editor and enter the code framework from Listing 6.2. Save the file as Custom HR.htm in the Configuration/Inspectors folder.
2. To officially turn the file into an HR inspector, revise the opening comment line like this (new code is in bold):

   ```
   <!--tag:HR,priority:10,selection:within,hline,vline-->
   ```

   By assigning a `priority` of `10`, you guarantee that your inspector will overrule the Dreamweaver default `<hr>` inspector. Working with this value is discussed later in this workshop.
3. Change the `<title>` of the inspector file, like this:

   ```
   <title>Custom Horizontal Rule Inspector</title>
   ```

Task 2: Create the layout and form elements

This, of course, involves design and technical issues. What do you want your inspector to look like? Because it's replacing the default `<hr>` inspector, you can adapt the layout of the default, adding and subtracting elements as needed.

Figure 6.13 shows the original Dreamweaver `<hr>` inspector and a proposed layout for your inspector. The new inspector is missing the ID field, and has added a color button and color field. Although the pixel/percent popup menu is present in both of these layouts, if you don't want to code it, you can eliminate it and let the user simply type the percent sign in the width field instead. (Some of the standard Dreamweaver inspectors follow this strategy.)

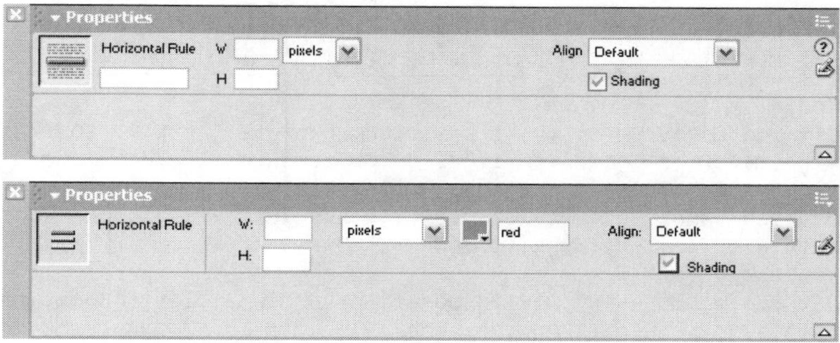

FIGURE 6.13 *The default Dreamweaver <hr> inspector (top) and the revised layout for your new inspector (bottom).*

1. Create the layers and form elements for your inspector, following the design shown in Figure 6.13 or one of your own.

   Figure 6.14 shows the new layout in the Dreamweaver Design view. Listing 6.3 shows the code for the layout. (Remember, it may seem odd, but you won't need a `<form>` tag—just the tags for the individual form elements.) The icon is created by a file called customhr.gif, saved in the Configuration/Inspectors folder. You can create your own customhr.gif file, or download it from the book's companion web site. You may need to adjust the layer positions from what is shown here.

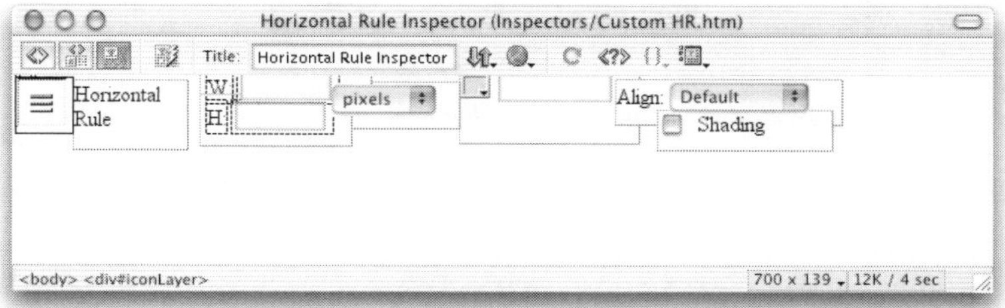

FIGURE 6.14 *The custom <hr> inspector layout, seen in Dreamweaver Design view.*

Listing 6.3 The *<body>* Code for the Custom *<hr>* Inspector, Showing Its Various Form Fields in a Layered Layout

```
<body>
<div id="iconLayer" style="position:absolute; left:3; top:2; width:40px;
height:40px; z-index:1"><img src="CustomHR.gif" width="36"
height="36"></div>
<div id="nameLayer" style="position:absolute; left:44px; top:4px;
width:81px; height:50px; z-index:2">Horizontal
  Rule </div>
<div id="widthLayer" style="position:absolute; left:135px; top:-8px;
width:121px; height:28px; z-index:9">
  <table>
    <tr>
      <td>W:</td>
      <td><input name="width" type="text" size="8"
onBlur="setWidth()"></td>
    </tr>
  </table>
</div>
<div id="unitsLayer" style="position:absolute; left:228px; top:5px;
width:91px; height:33px; z-index:8">
  <select name="units" onChange="setWidth()">
    <option selected>pixels</option>
    <option>percent</option>
  </select>
</div>
<div id="heightLayer" style="position:absolute; left:135px; top:14px;
width:107px; height:37px; z-index:10">
  <table>
    <tr>
      <td>H:</td>
      <td><input name="height" type="text" size="8"></td>
    </tr>
  </table>
</div>
<div id="colorLayer" style="position:absolute; left:320px; top:-3px;
width:127px; height:52px; z-index:4">
  <input type="mmcolorbutton" name="colorswatch"
onChange="setColorField();setColor()">
  <input type="text" name="colorfield"  size="10"
onBlur="setColorSwatch();setColor()">
</div>
<div id="alignLayer" style="position:absolute; left:431px; top:3px;
width:161px; height:32px; z-index:5">
  Align:
  <select name="alignHR" style="width:100px" onChange="setAlign()">
    <option selected>Default</option>
    <option value="left">Left</option>
    <option value="center">Center</option>
    <option value="right">Right</option>
```

```
  </select>
</div>
<div id="shadeLayer" style="position:absolute; left:461px; top:25px;
width:124px; height:29px; z-index:11">
  <input name="shade" type="checkbox" value="checkbox"
onClick="setShading()">Shading</div>
</body>
```

Task 3: Set up the *canInspectSelection( )* function

For development purposes, you always want this inspector to come up as the inspector for <hr> tags.

To do this, make sure the `canInspectSelection()` returns `true`:

```
function canInspectSelection() {
return true;
}
```

Task 4: Revise the *inspectSelection( )* function

An <hr> tag can have all the attributes specified in this inspector, or none of them. For each item, you need to test for the attribute's presence. If an attribute is present, change the form element to reflect its value; if not, set the form field to blank.

1. Now that the layout is in layers, it can take some hunting to find form field names. To make them easier to find, put some comment lines at the top of your <script> tag, listing the form fields and what they're used for, as follows (new code is in bold):

```
<script language="JavaScript">
//Form Field Names//
//"width"  – width attribute (numbers only)
//"units"  – pixels/percent popup; [0]=pixels, [1]=percent
//"height"  – size attribute
//"colorfield"  – color text field
//"colorswatch"  – color button
//"alignHR"  – alignment popup; [0]=default
//"shade"  – noshade checkbox
////////////////////
[etc]
```

2. Now that your fields are easy to refer to, it's time to start inspecting the selected <hr> object and filling those fields with values. Start by gaining access to the object, revising your `inspectSelection()` function to look like this:

```
function inspectSelection(){
var myDOM = dw.getDocumentDOM();
var myObject = myDOM.getSelectedNode();
}//end function
```

3. Collect the horizontal rule's height (size), by adding the following code to your function:

```
function inspectSelection(){
var myDOM = dw.getDocumentDOM();
var myObject = myDOM.getSelectedNode();
//set height (size) field
if (myObject.getAttribute("size") {
findObject("height").value=myObject.size;
    } else {
    findObject("height").value="";
    }//end if (size)
}//end function
```

> **note**
>
> Some of the code samples in this and subsequent chapters include line numbers to help identify specific lines in complex functions. The line numbers aren't part of the code—they're for your reading reference only.

4. The same code structure can be adapted to collect the object's color value for the `colorfield` and `colorswatch` form fields. To collect this information, add the following to your code:

```
function inspectSelection(){
var myDOM = dw.getDocumentDOM();
var myObject = myDOM.getSelectedNode();
//set height (size) field
if (myObject.getAttribute("size")) {
    findObject("height").value=myObject.size;
    } else {
    findObject("height").value="";
    }//end if (size)
//set color field and colorbutton
if (myObject.getAttribute("color")) {
    findObject("colorfield").value=myObject.color;
    findObject("colorswatch").value=myObject.color;
    } else {
    findObject("colorfield").value="";
    findObject("colorswatch").value="";
    }//end if (color)
}//end function
```

   Note that although the `colorswatch` field isn't a text field, it collects information as though it were. Note also all the comments being added, including comments identifying the closing curly braces. This code is going to get long—you want to be able to find your way around it!

5. The `width` attribute is also represented by a text field, but has the added complication of the unit value that may be present in the code. A horizontal rule may have a `width` attribute that looks like either of these two options:

```
<hr width="100">
```

```
<hr width="100%">
```

If the percent sign is present in the `width` attribute, it must be subtracted from the end of the `width` value. Its presence or absence can also be used to determine the state of the `units` popup menu. To handle the possibilities for `width`, add the following code to your function:

```
1 function inspectSelection() {
[etc]
18 if (myObject.getAttribute("width")) {
19    var myWidth = myObject.width;
20    var myUnits = findObject("units");
21    //look for the % and set the popup accordingly
22    if (myWidth.search(/%/) >= 0) {
23       myUnits.selectedIndex = 1;
24       //if there's a %, remove it from the value
25       myWidth = myWidth.substring(0,myWidth.length-1);
26       } else {
27       myUnits.selectedIndex = 0;
28       }//end if-else
29    //put the value in the width field
30    findObject("width").value = myWidth;
31    //if there's no width attribute, blank out both form elements
32    } else {
33    findObject("width").value = "";
34    findObject("units").selectedIndex = 0;
35    }//end if (width)
36 }//end function
```

What's happening in this code? The first conditional, of course, looks for a `width` attribute—if none is present, none of the code here executes. If the `width` attribute is present, its value is searched for a `%` character. If that character is present, line 27 sets the `units` popup to its second listed option (percent) by setting its `selectedIndex` value to 1; and line 30 puts the `width` attribute, minus its `%`, in the `width` text field. If the `%` is not present, line 34 sets the `units` popup to its first option (pixels) and line 33 puts the `width` attribute value in the `width` text field.

6. Now you need to set the alignment. Because alignment information is stored in a popup menu, setting it is similar to setting the `units` popup. The strategy is to determine whether the `align` attribute is present, and what its value is, and use that information to choose a menu option by setting the `selectedIndex` property. To do this, add the following code to your function:

```
function inspectSelection() {
[etc]
if (myObject.getAttribute("align")) {
   var myAlign = findObject("alignHR");
   var myValue;
```

```
39    //step through possible alignments
40    for (var a=0;a<myAlign.options.length;a++) {
41       myValue = myAlign.options[a].value;
42       //test to see if this is the align attribute's value
43       if (myValue == myObject.align) {
44          //if it is, set the popup menu
45          myAlign.selectedIndex = a;
46          //and stop searching
47          break;
48          }//end if (alignment matches)
49       }//end for loop
50    } else {
51    findObject("alignHR").selectedIndex = 0;
52    } //end if (align)
53} //end function
```

What's happening here? If the align attribute is present (line 36), a `for` loop (line 40) looks at each of the possible values it can have—`left`, `center`, `right`—checking each against the actual value of the `align` attribute (line 43). If the values match, line 45 sets the popup menu to the correct option (by setting its `selectedIndex` property). Finally, if there is no `align` attribute (line 50), the popup menu is set to its first option, Default.

7. The last attribute to inspect is `noshade`. Because this attribute is represented by a checkbox, you only have to set its checked value to `true` or `false`. The tricky bit here, though, is getting your brain around some backward logic: If the `noshade` attribute is present, there is no shading, so the checkbox should be off (`false`). If the `noshade` attribute is not present, the checkbox should be on (`true`), like this:

```
function inspectSelection() {
[etc]
 if (myObject.getAttribute("noshade")) {
      findObject("shade").checked=false;
      } else {
      findObject("shade").checked=true;
      }//end if (noshade)
}//end function
```

8. That's your inspection code! Before proceeding any further, check your inspector out to make sure the inspection process is working correctly. Figure 6.15 shows the Custom HR inspector correctly inspecting a slightly unusual `<hr>` page element.

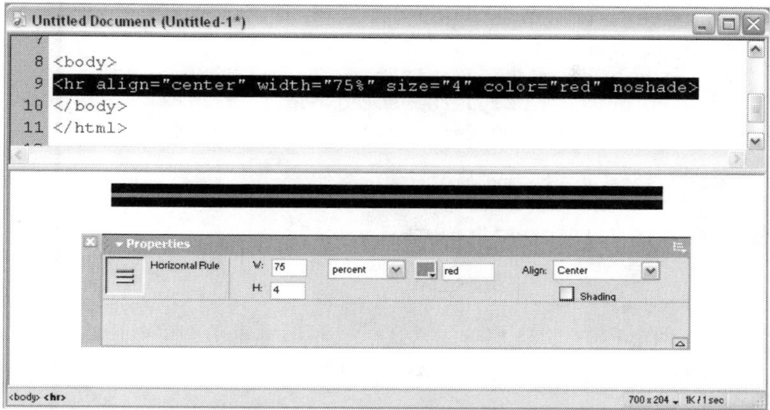

FIGURE 6.15 *The Custom HR inspector, with form fields correctly filled in based on the attribute values of an <hr> in the user's document.*

Task 5: Create local functions and calls so that the inspector can edit the document

For this task, you need to create a separate local function for each attribute. Each function will be called using an event handler attached to the relevant form field so that as soon as the user finishes entering information into a field, his document's code will be updated.

1. The `size` text field is the simplest, so start there. If there's a height value in the inspector, your inspector should set the `size` attribute to match it; if there's no value, the inspector should remove the attribute. To accomplish this, add the following function to your inspector file:

```
function setHeight() {
var myDOM = dw.getDocumentDOM();
var myObject = myDOM.getSelectedNode();
var myHeight = findObject("height").value;
if (myHeight) {
   myObject.size=myHeight;
   } else {
   myObject.removeAttribute("size");
   }//end if
}//end setHeight() function
```

2. This function should be called every time the user leaves the size text field, so add the following function call to the relevant portion of your `<body>` section (new code is in bold):

```
<input name="width" type="text" size="8" onBlur="setHeight()">
```

3. Now create a similar function to handle the colorfield and colorswatch:

```
function setColor() {
var myDOM = dw.getDocumentDOM();
var myObject = myDOM.getSelectedNode();
var myColor = findObject("colorfield").value;
if (myColor) {
   myObject.color=myColor;
   } else {
   myObject.removeAttribute("color");
   }//end if
}//end setColor() function
```

4. Add a function call to the colorfield form element, like this:

```
<input type="text" name="colorfield"  size="10" onBlur="setColor()">
```

And add a function call to the colorswatch form element, like this:

```
<input type="mmcolorbutton" name="colorswatch" onChange="setColor()">
```

5. Note that the colorfield and colorswatch don't need to be independently set if you have functions in place so that each automatically updates the other. You created functions like this for the <hr> object in Chapter 2. For the inspector, add the following two reciprocal functions:

```
//call from colorswatch, to update colorfield
function setColorField() {
findObject("colorfield").value = findObject("colorswatch").value;
}
//call from colorfield, to update colorswatch
function setColorSwatch() {
findObject("colorswatch").value = findObject("colorfield").value;
}
```

6. Calling these two functions is a little bit different from what you've done before, because both the colorfield and colorswatch form elements already have event handlers attached to them. Instead of adding more event handlers, just add more function calls to the existing handlers. Like this:

```
<input type="mmcolorbutton" name="colorswatch"
onChange="setColorField();setColor()">

<input type="text" name="colorfield"  size="10"
onBlur="setColorSwatch();setColor()">
```

7. Now tackle the width attribute. As before, the units popup menu adds a bit of complexity to this function. If the popup menu value is %, a percent sign must be appended to the end of the width value before it's inserted into the document. Accomplish this by adding the following new function to your file:

```
1 function setWidth() {
2 var myDOM = dw.getDocumentDOM();
3 var myObject = myDOM.getSelectedNode();
4 var myWidth = findObject("width").value;
5 var myUnits = findObject("units").selectedIndex;
6 if (myWidth) {
7   if (myUnits == 1) {
8      myWidth+= "%";
9      }//end if (myUnits)
10   myObject.width = myWidth;
11   } else {
12   myObject.removeAttribute("width");
13   }//end if (myWidth)
14 }//end setWidth() function
```

Can you see what's happening here? If the width field has a value (line 6), another `if` statement tests to see whether the units popup is set to its second option, which is percent (line 7). If so, a percent sign is added to the `width` value (line 8). The `width` value is then used to create a `width` attribute for the `<hr>` tag (line 10). As with other attributes, if the `width` field is empty, the `<hr> width` attribute is removed (line 12).

8. What form element should activate the `setWidth()` function? Two elements: the width text field and the units popup menu. After all, the user might want to change his `<hr>` width from pixels to percent without changing the number of pixels or percentage points. To accommodate this, add the following two function calls to your form elements (new code is in bold):

```
<input name="width" type="text" size="8" onBlur="setWidth()">

<select name="units" onChange="setWidth()">
```

9. Alignment is next. Because this attribute is collected using a popup menu that is never without a value, the align attribute is slightly trickier to discern. Do it by adding this function to your code:

```
1 function setAlign() {
2 var myDOM = dw.getDocumentDOM();
3 var myObject = myDOM.getSelectedNode();
4 var myIndex = findObject("alignHR").selectedIndex;
5 if (myIndex == 0) {
6    myObject.removeAttribute("align");
7    }else{
8    myObject.align = findObject("alignHR").options[myIndex].value;
9    }//end if (myIndex)
10 }//end setAlign() function
```

What's happening here? First, line 4 determines which menu option has been selected, by collecting the `selectedIndex` value. Then, if the popup menu is set to its first option (Default), the `align` attribute is removed from the code (line 6). If the menu is set to one of the other options, that option's value is fed into the `align` attribute (line 8).

10. You need to call the setAlign() function every time the user changes the selection in the popup menu. To do this, add the following event handler to the alignHR form element:

```
<select name="alignHR" style="width:100px" onChange="setAlign()">
```

11. The last attribute to deal with is shading (noshade). You must set this attribute differently from the others because it doesn't follow the standard attribute=value format. Instead, the mere presence of the word noshade in the <hr> tag is what creates this attribute. If you just named the attribute and set it (myObject.noshade)—as you've been doing for the other form fields and attributes in this workshop—you would need to give it a value (myObject.noshade=yes), and that would create invalid HTML, like this:

```
<hr noshade="yes">
```

Instead, you need to use string access to append the word noshade to the end of the <hr> code string. To accomplish this, add the following function to your inspector:

```
1 function setShading() {
2 var myDOM = dw.getDocumentDOM();
3 var myObject = myDOM.getSelectedNode();
4 //removing the attribute works as normal
5 if (findObject("shade").checked) {
6    myObject.removeAttribute("noshade");
7    } else {
8    //adding the attribute is done with string access
9    var myHTML = myObject.outerHTML;
10   var openingString = myHTML.substring(0,myHTML.length-1);
11   myObject.outerHTML = openingString + " noshade>";
12   }//end if (shade checked)
13 }//end setShading() function
```

Can you see how this function works? If the shade checkbox is checked (line 5), the noshade attribute should be removed (line 6), which is just like removing any normal attribute. If the checkbox is not checked (line 7), the selected <hr> tag is collected as a string (line 9). Its final character, the closing >, is stripped off (line 10); and a longer string (noshade>) is put in its place (line 11).

12. And, of course, you need to call the setShading() function whenever the user clicks on the checkbox (new code is in bold):

```
<input name="shade" type="checkbox" value="checkbox"
onClick="setShading()">
```

Task 6: Determine priority and refine the *canInspectSelection()* function

Now that you have created an inspector that duplicates much of the functionality of a Dreamweaver default inspector, you need to determine when you want which inspector to be called. The two determining factors in this equation are the priority setting and the `canInspectSelection()` function.

1. You already know that, with a priority setting of 10, your inspector will replace the default. Experiment with lower values to see when the default inspector kicks in. (Remember, you have to quit Dreamweaver between each test because priority values are analyzed only at startup.) You'll discover that any value (1–10) overrides the default inspector. So it doesn't matter too much which priority level you choose, unless some other custom `<hr>` inspector is introduced into the mix.

2. You may decide, though, that the only reason to use the custom inspector is to access the color property. So maybe the standard inspector should appear unless the horizontal rule in question has a color. This sort of functionality is controlled with the `canInspectSelection()` function.

   Rewrite this function to return `true` only if there is a `color` property, like this (new code is in bold):

   ```
   function canInspectSelection() {
   var myDOM = dw.getDocumentDOM();
   var myObject = myDOM.getSelectedNode();
   if (myObject.color) {
      return true;
      } else {
      return false;
      }//end if
   }//end function
   ```

3. Quit and relaunch Dreamweaver. Then try this out! If you create a `<hr>` with no `color` property, the traditional inspector appears. As soon as you add a color (you have to do it in Code view, or by using the Modify > Edit Tag command or the Tag inspector), the new inspector appears. Delete the `color` property, and the old inspector is back. Is this a good division of labor? It depends on how much you like the traditional inspector. What if, for instance, you have a rule with no color, and want to add color? It's easiest to use the Property inspector for this. Therefore, it might be better to leave `canInspectSelection()` returning `true` all the time so that this situation doesn't occur.

That's all there is to the Custom HR Property inspector. If you've come this far, congratulations again! The API for inspectors is complex, and there are plenty of opportunities to go astray. Listing 6.4 shows the finished code for the Custom HR.htm inspector file.

Listing 6.4 Finished Code for Custom HR.htm

```
<!-- tag:HR,priority:1,selection:within,hline,vline -->
<html>
<head>
<title>Horizontal Rule Inspector</title>
<script src="_pi_common.js"></script>
<script language="JavaScript">
//Form Field Names//
//"width" — width attribute (numbers only)
//"units" — pixels/percent popup; [0]=pixels, [1]=percent
//"height" — size attribute
//"colorfield" — color text field
//"colorswatch" — color button
//"alignHR" — alignment popup; [0]=default
//"shade" — noshade checkbox
////////////////////

function canInspectSelection() {
var myDOM = dw.getDocumentDOM();
var myObject = myDOM.getSelectedNode();
if (myObject.color) {
   return true;
   } else {
   return false;
   }//end if
}//end function

function inspectSelection(){
var myDOM = dw.getDocumentDOM();
var myObject = myDOM.getSelectedNode();
//set height (size) field
if (myObject.getAttribute("size")) {
   findObject("height").value=myObject.size;
   } else {
   findObject("height").value="";
   }//end if (size)
 //set color field and colorbutton
 if (myObject.getAttribute("color")) {
    findObject("colorfield").value=myObject.color;
    findObject("colorswatch").value=myObject.color;
    } else {
    findObject("colorfield").value="";
    findObject("colorswatch").value="";
    }//end if (color)
```

```
  if (myObject.getAttribute("width")) {
    var myWidth = myObject.width;
    var myUnits = findObject("units");
    //look for the % and set the popup accordingly
    if (myWidth.search(/%/) >= 0) {
       myUnits.selectedIndex = 1;
       //if there's a %, remove it from the value
       myWidth = myWidth.substring(0,myWidth.length-1);
       } else {
       myUnits.selectedIndex = 0;
       }//end if-else
    //put the value in the width field
    findObject("width").value = myWidth;
    //if there's no width attribute, blank out both form elements
    } else {
    findObject("width").value = "";
    findObject("units").selectedIndex = 0;
    }//end if (width)
  if (myObject.getAttribute("align")) {
    var myAlign = findObject("alignHR");
    var myValue="";
    //step through possible alignments
    for (var a=0;a<myAlign.options.length;a++) {
       myValue = myAlign.options[a].value;
       //test to see if this is the align attribute's value
       if (myValue == myObject.align) {
          //if it is, set the popup menu
          myAlign.selectedIndex = a;
          //and stop searching
          break;
          }//end if (alignment matches)
       }//end for loop
    } else {
    findObject("alignHR").selectedIndex = 0;
    } //end if (align)
   if (myObject.getAttribute("noshade")) {
       findObject("shade").checked = false;
       } else {
       findObject("shade").checked = true;
       }//end if (noshade)
}//end function

function setHeight() {
var myDOM = dw.getDocumentDOM();
var myObject = myDOM.getSelectedNode();
var myHeight = findObject("height").value;
if (myHeight) {
   myObject.size=myHeight;
   } else {
   myObject.removeAttribute("size");
   }//end if
}//end setHeight() function
```

continues

Listing 6.4 Continued

```
//call from colorswatch, to update colorfield
function setColorField() {
findObject("colorfield").value = findObject("colorswatch").value;
}
//call from colorfield, to update colorswatch
function setColorSwatch() {
findObject("colorswatch").value = findObject("colorfield").value;
}

function setColor() {
var myDOM = dw.getDocumentDOM();
var myObject = myDOM.getSelectedNode();
var myColor = findObject("colorfield").value;
if (myColor) {
   myObject.color=myColor;
   } else {
   myObject.removeAttribute("color");
   }//end if
}//end setColor() function

function setWidth() {
var myDOM = dw.getDocumentDOM();
var myObject = myDOM.getSelectedNode();
var myWidth = findObject("width").value;
var myUnits = findObject("units").selectedIndex;
if (myWidth) {
  if (myUnits == 1) {
     myWidth+= "%";
     }//end if (myUnits)
   myObject.width = myWidth;
   } else {
   myObject.removeAttribute("width");
   }//end if (myWidth)
}//end setWidth() function

function setAlign() {
var myDOM = dw.getDocumentDOM();
var myObject = myDOM.getSelectedNode();
var myIndex = findObject("alignHR").selectedIndex;
if (myIndex == 0) {
   myObject.removeAttribute("align");
   }else{
   myObject.align = findObject("alignHR").options[myIndex].value;
   }//end if (myIndex)
}//end setAlign() function
```

```
function setShading() {
var myDOM = dw.getDocumentDOM();
var myObject = myDOM.getSelectedNode();
//removing the attribute works as normal
if (findObject("shade").checked) {
   myObject.removeAttribute("noshade");
   } else {
   //adding the attribute is done with string access
   var myHTML = myObject.outerHTML;
   var openingString = myHTML.substring(0,myHTML.length-1);
   myObject.outerHTML = openingString + " noshade>";
   }//end if (shade checked)
}//end setShading() function

</script>
</head>
<body>
<div id="iconLayer" style="position:absolute; left:3; top:2; width:40px;
➥height:40px; z-index:1"><img src="CustomHR.gif" width="36"
➥height="36"></div>
<div id="nameLayer" style="position:absolute; left:44px; top:4px;
➥width:81px; height:50px; z-index:2">Horizontal
  Rule </div>
<div id="widthLayer" style="position:absolute; left:135px; top:-8px;
➥width:121px; height:28px; z-index:9">
  <table>
    <tr>
      <td>W:</td>
      <td><input name="width" type="text" size="8"
      ➥onBlur="setWidth()"></td>
    </tr>
  </table>
</div>
<div id="unitsLayer" style="position:absolute; left:228px; top:5px;
➥width:91px; height:33px; z-index:8">
  <select name="units" onChange="setWidth()">
    <option selected>pixels</option>
    <option>percent</option>
  </select>
</div>
<div id="heightLayer" style="position:absolute; left:135px; top:14px;
➥width:107px; height:37px; z-index:10">
  <table>
    <tr>
      <td>H:</td>
      <td><input name="height" type="text" size="8"
      ➥onBlur="setHeight()"></td>
    </tr>
  </table>
</div>
<div id="colorLayer" style="position:absolute; left:320px; top:-3px;
➥width:127px; height:52px; z-index:4">
```

continues

Listing 6.4 Continued

```
  <input type="mmcolorbutton" name="colorswatch"
  ➥onChange="setColorField();setColor()">
  <input type="text" name="colorfield"  size="10"
onBlur="setColorSwatch();setColor()">
</div>
<div id="alignLayer" style="position:absolute; left:431px; top:3px;
➥width:161px; height:32px; z-index:5">
  Align:
  <select name="alignHR" style="width:100px" onChange="setAlign()">
    <option selected>Default</option>
    <option value="left">Left</option>
    <option value="center">Center</option>
    <option value="right">Right</option>
  </select>
</div>
<div id="shadeLayer" style="position:absolute; left:461px; top:25px;
➥width:124px; height:29px; z-index:11">
  <input name="shade" type="checkbox" value="checkbox"
  ➥onClick="setShading()">
  Shading</div>
</body>
</html>
```

Summary

Custom objects and custom Property inspectors are natural partners. A custom object is often only as good as the inspector supporting it. In this chapter, you saw how to create inspectors, lay them out, and use them to analyze and edit document contents. As a bonus, you also learned how to process form elements without forms.

Chapter 7

Creating Custom Floating Panels

Floating panels, or floaters, are what Dreamweaver calls all of its panels other than the Property inspector—the Layers panel, the Behaviors panel, the CSS Styles panel, the Code inspector, and so on. They're all floaters. Floaters don't have the layout restrictions of Property inspectors, because they don't have to fit in the Property inspector panel framework. They can be any shape and do anything. Do you remember the "Welcome!" message window that popped up, the first time you launched Dreamweaver 4? A floater. The helpful window that comes up to tell you about using Layout view? Yep, that's a floater, too. Floaters can be tabbed and docked together, or not; they can contain text, form elements, graphics; they can interact with the document and reflect user edits or not. They're pretty flexible and potent little guys. Macromedia recommends using Property inspectors when possible, instead of clogging up the interface with more floating panels than the program already has; but when you need one, there they are. Figure 7.1 shows a selection of diverse floaters in action. In this chapter, we'll learn how the floater API works and how to strategize, create, and use floaters for various purposes.

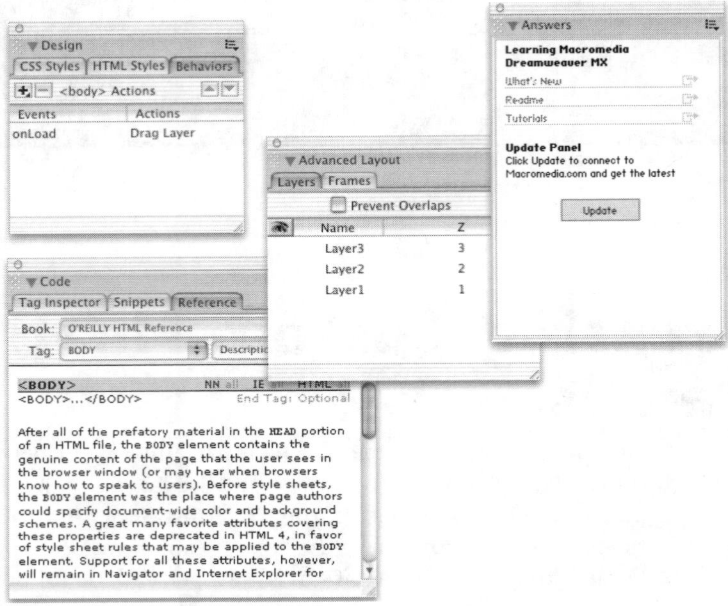

FIGURE 7.1 *A selection of Dreamweaver floaters, showing the variety of size, shape, layout, and purpose they're capable of.*

How Floating Panels Are Constructed

As with Property inspectors, we don't have access to the code for most of the Dreamweaver standard floaters. All of the floating panels listed in the Window menu are coded into the program at C-level, and so are inaccessible to us.

There is, however, a documented API for creating floaters as extensions. Floater extensions are different from C-coded floaters in two ways that will impact us:

- Floaters coded as extensions always float on top of the current document or go behind it, depending on the user setting for "all other panels" in the Edit > Preferences > Panels dialog box.
- Floaters coded as extensions cannot have icons in their title tabs. Their title bars always display a name, determined by the page title.

Floating Panels in the Configuration Folder

Floater extensions live in the Configuration folder at the root level of the Floaters folder. Supporting files called on by floaters can live in subfolders within the Floaters folder. Figure 7.2 shows a list of the contents of the Floaters folder, in its default state. (There's not much in there, because the standard Dreamweaver floaters are not coded as extensions.)

FIGURE 7.2 *The Configuration/Floaters folder. Supporting files can be stored in subfolders, but all main floater files must be stored at the root level.*

Floating Panel Files

Each floating panel is created from one or more files:

- **HTML file (required).** This is the main floater file. Without this file, there is no floating panel.
- **JS file (optional).** As usual, the JavaScript portion of the floater can be saved in the HTML file or separately in a linked JS file. It's customary, though not required, to match this file's name with that of the main file (for example, MyFloater.htm and MyFloater.js).
- **Supporting media files (optional).** Floaters can contain graphics or even SWF (Flash) movies, as desired. These can be stored in the Floaters folder, preferably in a subfolder. Macromedia recommends, however, that multiple support files be stored in a custom folder in the Configuration/Shared folder. (This can be the same custom folder you create for help documents, shared JavaScript files, and any other support files for any extensions you develop.)

The Structure of a Floating Panel File

Because the possible purposes of floaters are so varied, the API is simple and open-ended. At their simplest, floater files require very little—just a few API functions to help display and process information, and some kind of method to hide and show the floater. At their most complex, they can include API functions that watch the user's document for editing changes, and constantly collect and process information.

Required Elements

Not much is required to create a floater. A floater file must exist at the root level of the Floaters folder. Beyond that, the API requires just the following:

- **Filename.** The floater filename (obviously a required element!), minus its .htm or .html extension, becomes the floater's official name for scripting purposes. It's therefore safest, though not required, to avoid spaces and special characters. The filename must also not be one of the reserved floater names that Dreamweaver uses for its own built-in floaters. These names are `behaviors`, `css styles`, `data bindings`, `frames`, `history`, `html`, `html styles`, `launcher`, `layers`, `library`, `objects`, `properties`, `server behaviors`, `site files`, `site map`, `templates`, and `timelines`.
- **Means of hiding and showing the floater.** Because floating panels are not visible by default, each floater must have its opening (and closing) triggered by some other element in the Dreamweaver interface. The API provides two methods for this: `dw.toggleFloater()` and `dw.setFloaterVisibility()`.

  The first of these methods, `dw.toggleFloater()`, toggles the visibility of a floater—opening it if it's closed and closing it if it's open. It takes one parameter, the name of the floater (as specified in the previous section), like this:

  ```
  dw.toggleFloater("myFloater");
  ```

  The second method, `dw.setFloaterVisibility()`, can be used to hide or show a floater. It takes two parameters, the floater name and true/false, to open or close the floater—like this to open a floater:

  ```
  dw.setFloaterVisibility("myFloater",true);
  ```

  or like this to close the floater:

  ```
  dw.setFloaterVisibility("myFloater",false);
  ```

Either of these methods can be placed anywhere—command, menu command, object, behavior, you name it—but the most common method of opening and closing floaters is to place one of them in a `<menuitem/>` entry in the menus.xml file. The following line, for instance, entered in menus.xml, would open `MyFloater`:

```
<menuitem name="My Floater" enabled="true"
command="dw.toggleFloater('MyFloater')"
➥checked="dw.getFloaterVisibility ('MyFloater')"
id="MyStuff_MyFloaterOpener"/>
```

What does this code do? If placed in the Window menu, it creates a My Floater menu item in that menu. The `checked` parameter uses a related API method, `dw.getFloaterVisibility()`, to determine if the floater named `MyFloater` is currently open; if it is, the menu item will display with a checkmark next to its name. (Note that this method gets the visibility, rather than setting it.) Instead of a `file` parameter, which would specify a command file for Dreamweaver to process when the user chooses the menu item, the `command` parameter instructs Dreamweaver to execute the `dw.toggleFloater()` method when the user chooses the menu item, opening or closing the floater named `MyFloater`.

- **Page title.** The floater file's `<title>` appears in the title bar of the floating panel. (As noted previously, there is no way to show image icons in the title bar the way that the Dreamweaver built-in floaters do.)
- **Body content.** No scripting or `<form>` elements are required, unless you want the floater to actually be interactive. Any content placed inside the `<body>` tags becomes the body of the floating panel. Note, however, that Dreamweaver does not process `onLoad` event handlers placed in floater file `<body>` tags. Use `initialTabs()` or `initialPosition()` to get around this. (This is discussed in more detail later in this chapter.)

Optional Elements

Okay, so a floater doesn't *need* much. But it can take advantage of various optional elements, if they're defined:

- **`<form>`.** Form elements are used in floaters just as they're used everywhere else in the API—to allow user input and interactivity.
- **`initialPosition()` function.** The first time a user calls up a floating panel, this function determines where on the screen the panel appears. If the function is not defined, the panel appears in the center of the screen. The function should return a string representing `"leftPositionPixels, topPositionPixels"`. It takes one optional parameter, `platform`, which can accept `Mac` or `Win` as values. Thus, the following code places the floater at coordinates of 60,60 on Macintosh and 100,100 on Windows:

```
function initialPosition(Mac) {
return "60,60";
}

function initialPosition(Win) {
return "100,100";
}
```

The `initialPosition()` function is called automatically, but it is only called once in the floater's lifetime because after that Dreamweaver remembers the panel's position so it will always appear where the user last left it.

- **`isDockable()` function.** This function, called automatically as part of the API process every time the floater appears, determines whether or not the floater appears with a docking bar at its top, allowing it to be docked with other panels. The function should return `true/false`. The absence of this function is the same as returning `true`.
- **`getDockingSide()` function.** This function determines how the floater will integrate with the Dreamweaver MX integrated workspace (Windows only). Assuming that the user is working in the integrated workspace (not the classic workspace), it specifies where in the integrated application window the panel will be docked. It takes no parameters and should return a string containing either the word *left* or *right*, and either the word *top* or *bottom*. For instance, the following code creates a floater that docks at the upper left of the application window (below the Insert bar, in other words):

  ```
  function getDockingSide() {
  return "left top";
  }
  ```

  This function has no effect unless the integrated workspace is being used, so it is inactive for Dreamweaver/Mac and for Dreamweaver/Windows in classic workspace.
- **`isAvailableInCodeView()` function.** This function determines whether the panel will be grayed-out when the user is working in Code view. The function takes no parameters and should return `true/false`.
- **`displayHelp()` function.** Dockable floating panels all appear with the standard Options menu icon in the upper-right corner. Clicking on that icon displays the panel's Options menu, which includes—among other items—a Help command. If the `displayHelp()` function is defined in the floater's HTML or JS file, this function is executed when the user clicks the chooses Help from the panel's Options menu. Without this function, the Help command is nonfunctional—and probably confusing to users, who will wonder why it doesn't work. (Note that if the `isDockable()` function returns `false`, there is no docking bar or options menu icon at the top of the floater window.)

- **`selectionChanged()` function.** As long as the floater is visible onscreen (that is, open), this function is called every time the user changes the insertion point, selection, or focus. It returns nothing, but can be used to make the floater responsive to user focus as he works. Examples of this functionality include the frames panel, which changes its display depending on which part of the frameset has focus; the behavior panel, which changes its title bar, depending on what tag the user has selected; and so on.

  Because `selectionChanged()` is called so frequently, it can impact Dreamweaver performance. Therefore, this function should be used only if absolutely necessary.

- **`documentEdited()` function.** As long as the floater is visible onscreen (that is, open), this function is called every time the document is edited. It returns nothing, but can be used to make the floater responsive to document changes as they happen. Examples of this functionality include the code inspector, in which changes made in the design window are immediately reflected in the panel's code display; the layers panel, in which changes in layer name, visibility and z-index are immediately registered; and so on.

  Because `documentEdited()` is called so frequently, it can impact Dreamweaver performance. Therefore, this function should only be used if absolutely necessary.

API Procedure for Floating Panels

The procedure for floating panels begins when one of the floater-opening commands is called (`dw.setFloaterVisibility()`, `dw.toggleFloater()`, `dw.getFloaterVisibility()`). At that point, the following events occur:

1. Dreamweaver searches the Configuration/Floaters folder for a filename matching the floater name plus the .htm or .html extension. If this file is found, it's now loaded.
2. If the floater is being loaded for the first time, Dreamweaver looks for and calls the `initialTabs()` and `initialPosition()` functions.
3. If `documentEdited()` and `selectionChanged()` are defined, Dreamweaver calls them now, on the assumption that both document and selection have probably changed since the panel was last open.
4. The `documentEdited()` and `selectionChanged()` functions continue to be called as needed, as long as the panel is open. Event handlers attached to form elements in the floater are also called as needed.
5. When the user quits Dreamweaver, the program saves all panels' current position, visibility, dimensions, and tab groupings. These will be restored the next time the program is launched.

Figure 7.3 shows a diagram of this process.

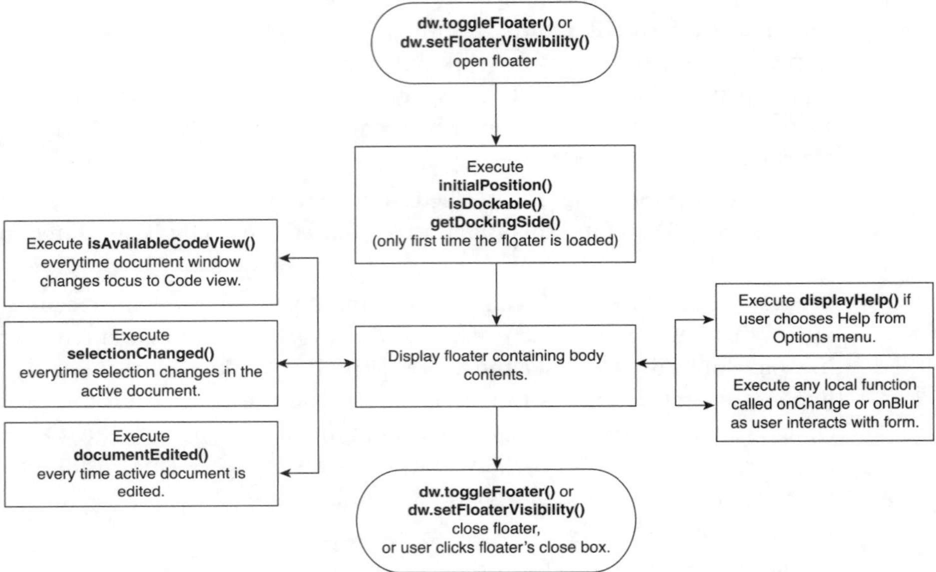

FIGURE 7.3 *The API procedure for floating panels.*

Note that after Dreamweaver loads a floater file, it doesn't load the file again until the user quits and relaunches the program. When you're testing extensions, simply reloading extensions from the Insert bar won't reload floaters; you need to quit the program and start it up again.

Making Floating Panels: Practice Session

It's time to start floating! As in other chapters, we'll experiment with basic settings and, along the way, create some nice framework code to build on in the workshops.

Task 1: Create a really basic floater

We're talking really basic here—it will amaze you how very little there can be to a floating panel.

1. Create the file first. In your text editor, create a new file with the basic HTML framework. Because you have to modify the menus.xml file, use a text editor other than Dreamweaver for this (remember, you should keep Dreamweaver closed when editing the menus.xml file). For adornment, add only a `<title>` and a sentence or two in the `<body>`, like this:

```
<html>
<head>
<title>Test Floater</title>
</head>
<body>
This is a test.
</body>
</html>
```

Save the file in the Configuration/Floaters folder. Call it **floatme.htm**.

2. Next, add a menu entry so you can access your floater. In your text editor, open menus.xml and navigate to the section controlling the Window menu.

   The last entry in the Window menu is a dynamically generated list of open windows. You want to add your items above this, so add the following lines of code directly above the `<separator/>` that marks off the open window list (new code is in bold):

> **tip**
>
> Perform a find operation on `DWMenu_Window_Default`, which is the ID of the last command in the menu.

```
<menuitem name="Previous Document" platform="mac"
key="Ctrl+Shift+Tab"enabled="dw.getFocus() == 'textView' ||
dw.getFocus() == 'document'" command="dw.goToPrevDocument()"
id="DWMenu_Window_PrevDocument"/>

<separator />
<menuitem name="Float Me" enabled="true"
command="dw.toggleFloater('floatme')"
checked="dw.getFloaterVisibility('floatme')" id="MyStuff_FloatMe" />

<separator />
<menuitem dynamic name="(No Open Documents)"
file="Menus/MM/Window_Titles.htm" id="DWMenu_Window_Default" />
</menu>
```

This code adds your menu item, with a separator line above it. There should already be a separator line below it. By using the `"floatme"` parameter, you're using your floater file's name minus its extension as its floater name. With the command attribute, you're accessing `dw.toggleFloater()` to alternately open and close your floater. With the `checked` attribute, you're using `dw.getFloaterVisibility()` as a test whether your floater is currently open; if it is open, your menu item will display with a nice little checkmark next to it.

3. Try it out! Relaunch Dreamweaver. Your Window menu and new floating panel should look like the one shown in Figure 7.4.

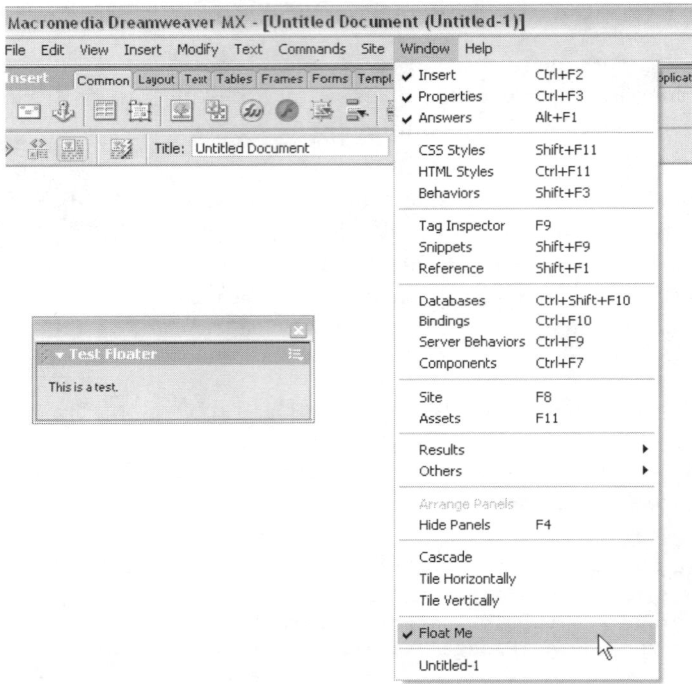

FIGURE 7.4 *A very basic floater (floatme), up and running in the Dreamweaver interface. Note the checkmark in the menu, indicating that the floater is currently open. Choosing the command again toggles it closed.*

As you examine your new floater, pay attention to its default characteristics, including where the floater first appears onscreen and what its dimensions are. The title bar shows a tab with your page `<title>`, in its own group named the same thing; and the background is gray, but the text displays with formatting, even though you didn't add text formatting to your floater code.

Resize your floater. Move it around the screen. Then, quit Dreamweaver and relaunch it. You'll see that the settings for size and position have been remembered for you. Dreamweaver even remembers whether your floater was open or closed when the program quit.

Task 2: Experiment with the API functions

We want to see how some of the other API functions for floaters work, but we can't do it with `floatme` because it's already been opened. So in this task, we'll create two new floaters—`tabfloat1` and `tabfloat2`.

1. Open menus.xml and add two new `<menuitem/>` entries directly below the "Float Me" entry you just added:

```
<separator />
<menuitem name="Float Me" enabled="true"
command="dw.toggleFloater('floatme')"
checked="dw.getFloaterVisibility('floatme')" id="MyStuff_FloatMe" />

<menuitem name="Tabbed Floater 1" enabled="true"
command="dw.toggleFloater('tabfloat1')"
checked="dw.getFloaterVisibility('tabfloat1')" id="MyStuff_TabFloat1" />

<menuitem name="Tabbed Floater 2" enabled="true"
command="dw.toggleFloater('tabfloat2')"
checked="dw.getFloaterVisibility('tabfloat2')" id="MyStuff_TabFloat2" />

<separator />
```

2. In your text editor, save floatme.htm as **tabfloat1.htm** (still in the Configuration/Floaters folder). Make the following changes to the code (new code is in bold):

```
<html>
<head>
<title>Tab 1</title>
<script language="JavaScript">
function initialTabs() {
window.resizeTo(300,400);
return "tabfloat2";
}
function initialPosition() {
return "50,50";
}
</script>
</head>
<body>
Tab One
</body>
</html>
```

3. Now create a new file. Save it as **tabfloat2.htm** and enter the following to the code:

```
<html>
<head>
<title>Tab 2</title>
<script language="JavaScript">
function initialTabs() {
return "tabfloat1";
}
</script>
</head>
<body>
Tab Two
</body>
</html>
```

4. Quit and relaunch Dreamweaver, and try it out. Note the position and size of this new floater. Your new pair of floaters probably looks like the ones shown in Figure 7.5.

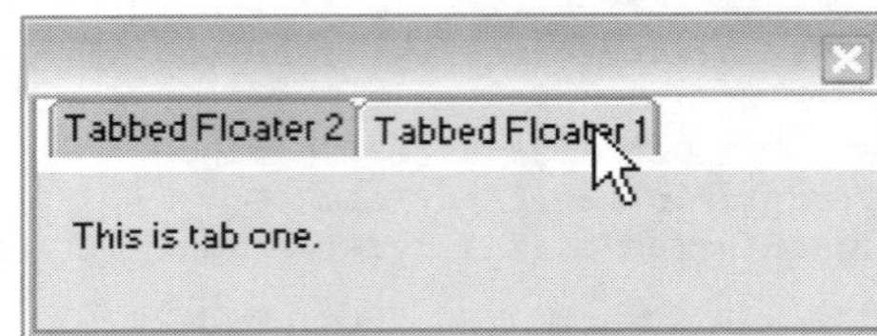

FIGURE 7.5 *A pair of tabbed floaters, with dimensions and position set.*

Task 3: Fancy up the layout with images and layers

For this task, use floatme.htm, adding items to the `<body>` content to experiment with floater interface elements. Feel free to use your own images and SWF files in the steps below. You can also download sample files from this book's companion web site: `www.newriders.com`.

1. In the Configuration/Floaters folder, create a new folder called **MyImages**. Place whatever images you want to work with in this folder; you'll be linking to them there.

2. Try inserting a simple table and GIF image, altering the floater file's code like this:

```
<html>
<head>
<title>Test Floater</title>
</head>
```

```
<body>
<table>
   <tr>
      <td align="right">
         Welcome to <br>my floater!
      </td>
      <td align="left">
         <img src="MyImages/duck2.gif" width="150" height="157">
      </td>
   </tr>
</table>
</body>
</html>
```

If you use the sample files from the book's web site, use duck2.gif—otherwise, any non-animated GIF image will do. Rebuild the floater layout using this image. (As always, you can use Dreamweaver or your text editor to code the fancier layout.) Figure 7.6 shows the test floater with image and text in a table.

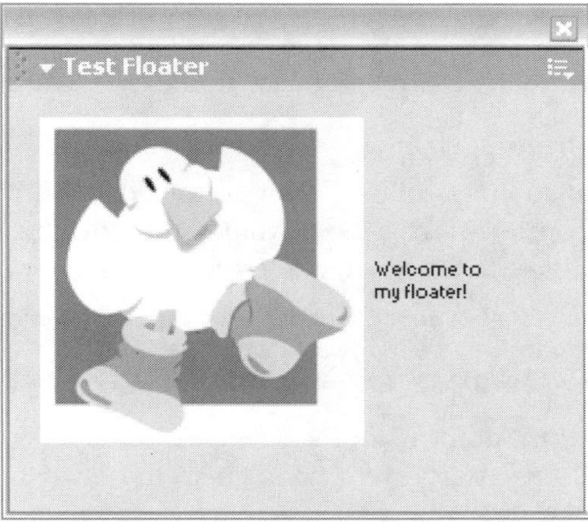

FIGURE 7.6 *The test floater with a simple layout and image.*

If you like, you can experiment putting an animated GIF in the floater—from the sample files, smiley.gif is animated. You'll find that the animation doesn't work. (That's probably for the best. What havoc we could wreak with animated GIFs in all of our floating panels!)

note

Remember, layers-based layouts may not display the same on Mac and Windows platforms. Always check for cross-platform compatibility when designing with layers.

3. Floater layouts work in layers as well as tables. To see how this works, redo your layout in layers, including a layer for the image and one for the text, like this:

```
<body>
<div id="duckLayer" style="position:absolute; left:25px; top:25px;
width:134px; height:110px; z-index:2">
   <img src="MyImages/duck2.gif" width="150" height="157">
</div>
<div id="textLayer" style="position:absolute; left:182px; top:188px;
width:91px; height:73px; z-index:3">
   Welcome to my floater!
</div>
</body>
```

   Try out the floater again and to see that everything still works just fine.

Task 4: Add a rollover image

Now, how about adding a rollover effect to the floater's image? Normally, in creating rollover effects on HTML pages, we would add a link to an image and add one or more event handlers to the <a> tag to create the rollover effect, like this:

```
<a href="#" onMouseOver="document.myImage.src='over.gif'";
onMouseOut="document.myImage.src='normal.gif'"
onMouseDown="down.gif"><img src="normal.gif"></a>
```

Unfortunately, links don't work inside extension layouts (dialog boxes, inspectors, floaters). But we can attach event handlers to the `<img>` tag itself:

```
<img src="normal.gif" onMouseOver="document.myImage.src='over.gif'";
onMouseOut="document.myImage.src='normal.gif'" onMouseDown="down.gif">
```

We can do this by writing the code ourselves, or we can take advantage of the Dreamweaver Swap Image behavior to do it for us. Figure 7.7 shows various stages in the process of using Dreamweaver to add a rollover to a floater. Refer to it as necessary when performing the following steps.

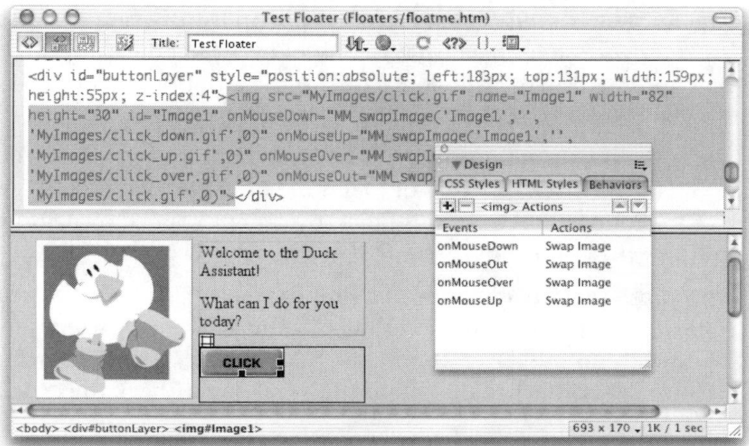

Figure 7.7 *Adding a rollover to a floating panel layout. Note that the code is added to the* `<img>` *tag, and there is no* `<a>` *tag.*

1. In your graphics editor, create several images to represent various stages of an image, or use the click.gif, click_over.gif, and click_down.gif sample files from the book's companion web site. Put the image files in the Configuration/ Floaters/MyImages folder. (Figure 7.8 shows the sample GIF images to give you an idea what you're after here.)

Figure 7.8 *The images to use for the rollover effect. If you're making your own images, you need an up, over, and down state.*

2. In Dreamweaver, open floatme.htm. Create a new layer to hold your image, and use the `Image` object to insert click.gif. Leave the image selected for the next step.

3. Open the Behaviors panel. From the popup list of event handlers, choose IE 5 (this browser supports a wide variety of event handlers attached to `<img>` tags, so choosing it here gives you access to these options). After you do this, take a look at the list of event handlers. It's long!
4. From the popup actions list, choose Swap Image. In the dialog box, choose not to Preload the images and not to Restore on mouseOut (you'll see why shortly). For the rollover image, choose click_over.gif or your equivalent image. Click OK to close the dialog box.

   Dreamweaver may have added a link to your image and attached the function call for the behavior to the `<a>` tag. If this happened, select the behavior and choose the mouseOver command that isn't in parentheses from the list of choices. This attaches the call to the `<img>` tag. (Check the code and see!)
5. Repeat step 4 until you have these behaviors in place:

Event	*Required Actions*
onMouseOver	swapImage to click_over.gif
onMouseDown	swapImage to click_down.gif
onMouseUp	swapImage to click_over.gif
onMouseOut	swapImage to click.gif

   All event handlers should appear in the Behaviors panel without parentheses, and should be added to the `<img>` tag. If Dreamweaver added an `<a>` tag, you can go to Code view and remove it, if you like. It's useless. If Dreamweaver added the `MM_preload` function to the document `<head>`, you can delete that as well. You don't need this function because the images won't ever be downloaded into a browser cache.

note

You have to tell Dreamweaver not to automatically restore onMouseOut, and do it manually, or all the other stages won't be entered correctly.

6. Try it out! The cursor may not change to a pointing finger when it's over the button, but the image should change color when it's rolled over and when the mouse is down on it. Figure 7.9 shows the final effect.

note

This rollover trick works in any Dreamweaver extension layout, although we generally don't use fancy effects like this in inspectors and dialog boxes.

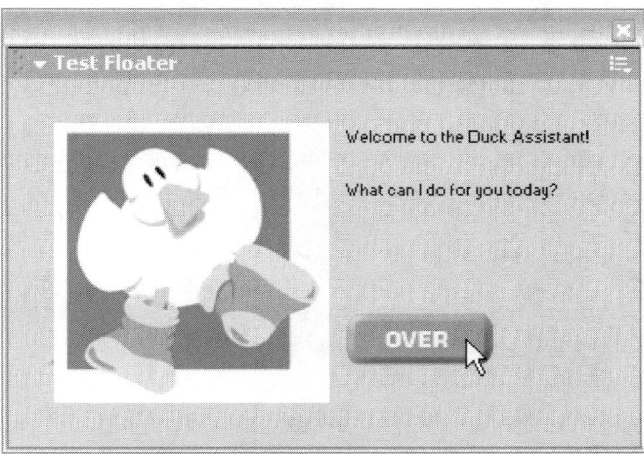

FIGURE 7.9 *A very decorative floater, indeed, complete with rollover in action.*

Task 5: Put a SWF (Flash) movie in a floater

This task shows a nice simple way to get a flashy (ahem) guided tour, promotional intro, or other special message into Dreamweaver. Use Flash! Create an SWF movie that's not too processor-intensive, and place it in the floater file using the `<object>` tag.

1. Create your own Flash SWF file, or use the **workshop.swf** file from the book's companion web site. If you create your own file, here are some tips:
   - Complex animations don't always play smoothly when placed in floaters, so keep it simple.
   - Dreamweaver MX supports Flash MX SWF files.
   - Flash interactivity comes through, though maybe a bit sluggishly if your file is complex.
2. Wherever you get your SWF file from, put it in Configuration/Floaters/MyImages.

3. The simplest procedure is the placement in the Dreamweaver Design view, nice and quick. Open floatme.htm in Dreamweaver and remove all of its contents. Use the Flash object to insert the SWF movie. Some tips on this part of the process:

   - If you want the movie to snuggle up against the upper-left corner of the floater, set the borders to "0" by changing the `<body>` tag or using Modify: Page Properties like this:

     ```
     <body leftmargin="0" topmargin="0">
     ```

   - To make the Flash movie resize as the user resizes the floater window, set the width and height of the Flash object to 100%.
   - Dreamweaver automatically adds `<object>` and `<embed>` tags for the movie. You can remove the `<embed>` tag if you like—Dreamweaver doesn't require it.

   Figure 7.10 shows the Flash movie being inserted and formatted, using Dreamweaver Design view.

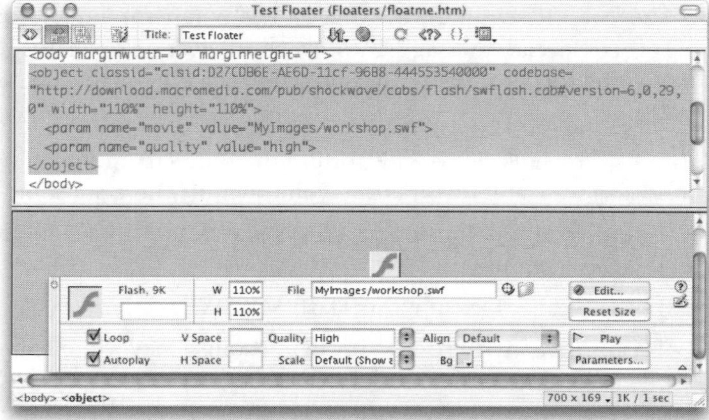

FIGURE 7.10 *Adding the workshop.swf Flash movie to a floater file, using Dreamweaver Design view.*

4. Try it out! If you used the workshop.swf file, your results will look like Figure 7.11.

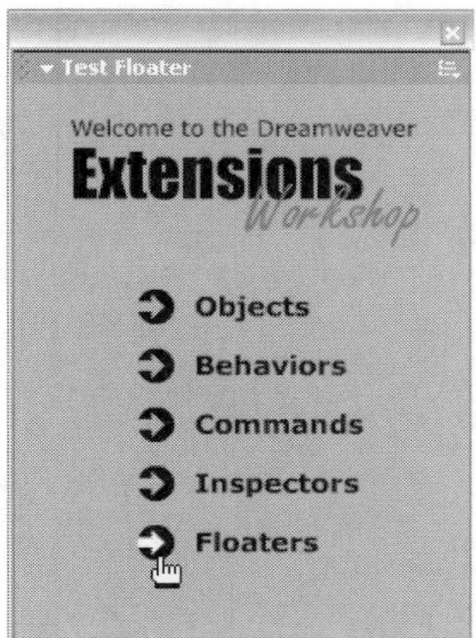

FIGURE 7.11 *A floater containing a Flash SWF movie*

Task 6: Add form elements for interactivity

So far, we have looked at the decorative things we can do with floaters. But of course, we can also use floaters as document editing helpers and inspectors. For this practice task, we'll get rid of all the fancy stuff and go back to a simple Dreamweaver-esque interface. We'll create a selection inspector that reports what kind of object the user has selected.

1. In your text editor or in Dreamweaver, open floatme.htm (or create a new floater file).
2. Enter the following code in the <body> section:

```
<body>
<form name="myForm">
<table>
   <tr valign="baseline">
      <td align="right" nowrap>The current selection is:</td>
      <td align="left">
         <input type="text" name="theSelection">
      </td>
   </tr>
   <tr valign="baseline">
      <td> </td>
      <td align="left">
         <input type="button" value="Check Selection">
      </td>
   </tr>
</table>
</form>
</body>
```

Figure 7.12 shows the proposed layout created by this form.

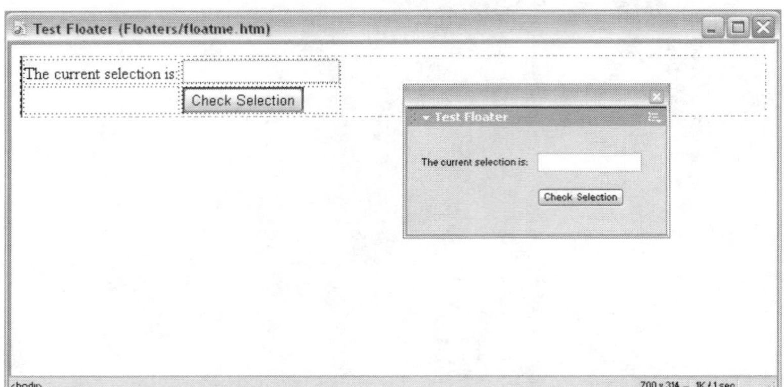

FIGURE 7.12 *The selection editor layout, shown in the Dreamweaver Design view, and in its incarnation as a floater.*

3. You want to create a function that determines the currently selected object's node, and (if applicable) its tag name, and reveals that information in the text field. The function should be called using an `onClick` event handler attached to the Check Selection button. To do this, add the following code to your floater file's `<head>` section:

```
<head>
<title>Test Floater</title>
<script language="JavaScript">
function whatAmI() {
//access the selected object
var myDOM = dw.getDocumentDOM();
var myObject = myDOM.getSelectedNode();
//determine node type
var myType="";
if (myObject.nodeType==Node.TEXT_NODE) {
   myType="TEXT";
   }else if (myObject.nodeType==Node.COMMENT_NODE){
      myType="COMMENT";
   }else{
      myType=myObject.tagName;
   }
//fill in form field
document.myForm.theSelection.value=myType;
}
</script>
</head>
```

What's happening here? After gaining access to the selected object, the `whatAmI()` function creates a variable called `myType` to hold the information that will eventually be fed into the floater's form field. It then uses a series of conditionals to enter the value `TEXT`, `COMMENT`, or a tag name into the variable. And finally, it feeds that variable into the form field.

4. Don't forget to call the function after you define it! Add the following event handler and function call to your form's button:

```
<input type="button" value="Check Selection" onClick="whatAmI()">
```

5. After you're finished, try the floater out and tinker until it's inspecting properly, as shown in Figure 7.13). Remember, you'll need to restart Dreamweaver every time you change the floater file, to make sure Dreamweaver is registering your altered code.

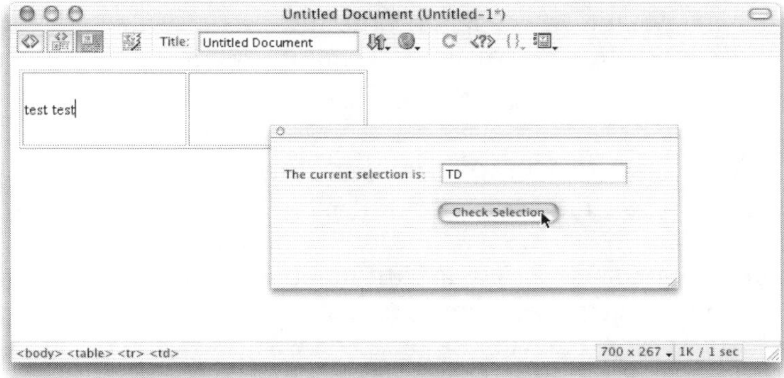

FIGURE 7.13 *The Inspect Selection floater at work.*

Task 7: Add *selectionChanged( )* so that the form works automatically

Now we'll set the floater to continuously report the selection information, not just when the user clicks a button.

1. In the `<head>` section of your floater file, rename the function you just created `selectionChanged()`. In the `<body>` section, delete the button. Why are you doing this? The `selectionChanged()` function is part of the API, and will be called automatically as long as the floater is open. So it no longer needs a form button with event handler and function call to trigger it.
2. After you make these changes, try out the floater. Leave the floater open onscreen as you work in a sample document, changing selections and editing code. Figure 7.14 shows this happening.

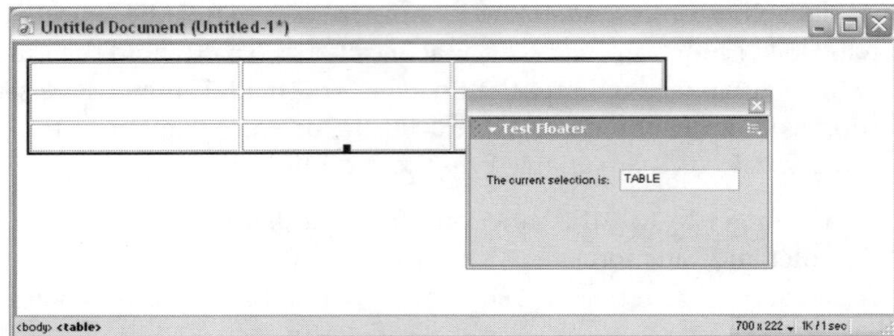

FIGURE 7.14 *The Inspect Selection floater in action, being called automatically as the user works.*

The floater should automatically report your selection, but it may lag slightly behind you if you work quickly. Dreamweaver may also be a little more sluggish than you're used to. That's the performance hit. Can you see why you might want to avoid this lag?

Task 8: Add the *documentEdited( )* function

For this task, we'll experiment with another automatically called function for floaters, `documentEdited()`. We'll revise the floater so that, in addition to detecting the current selection, it also counts the number of edits the user makes to the current document, and reports them. This is a handy way to tell how often the `documentEdited()` command is called, and what user actions will trigger it.

1. Add the following code to your floater's `<body>` section (altered code is in bold):

```
<body>
<form name="myForm">
<table>
   <tr valign="baseline">
      <td align="right" nowrap>The current selection is:</td>
      <td align="left">
         <input type="text" name="theSelection">
      </td>
   </tr>
   <tr valign="baseline">
      <td align="right">The number of edits:</td>
      <td align="left"><input name="myEdits" type="text"
      ➥id="editCount"> </td>
   </tr>
</table>
</form>
</body>
```

This creates a revised layout like that shown in Figure 7.15.

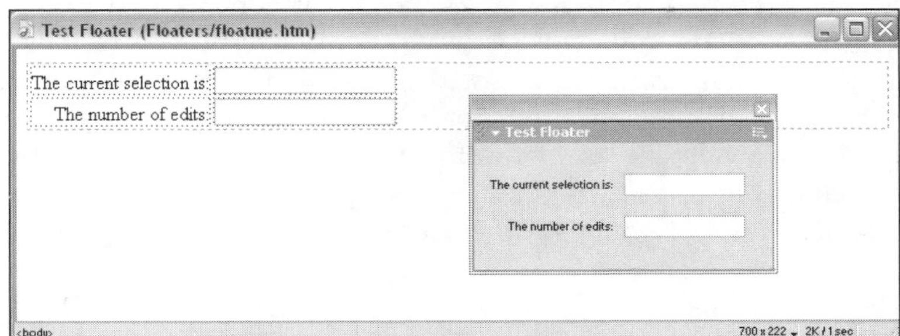

FIGURE 7.15 *The revised layout for the test floater, ready to count edits as well as inspecting user selections.*

2. Now add the following code to the floater's `<script>` tag:

```
var gHowMany = 0;

function documentEdited() {
gHowMany++;
document.myForm.myEdits.value = gHowMany;
}
```

What's happening here? The global variable `gHowMany` is created, to hold the number of edits. The `documentEdited()` form increments `gHowMany` and feeds it into the `myEdits` form field. Each time this function is automatically called, `gHowMany` will be incremented and the floater's form field updated.

3. Launch Dreamweaver and try it out! Work on a sample document with the test floater open onscreen. Keep an eye on what triggers the edit count to increase. The count may lag slightly behind you if you work quickly. Depending on the speed of your computer and the complexity of what you're doing, Dreamweaver may also seem a bit more sluggish than usual.

Workshop #1: A Floating Panel Utility

It's time to put some of this knowledge to work. Why would you want to create a custom floater? Floating panels provide a good opportunity to create utility interfaces, to help users perform common tasks without being restricted by the confines of the standard Property inspector. Watch yourself analytically as you use Dreamweaver. Watch your colleagues as they work. Are there any tasks that could be accomplished much more efficiently or intuitively with the aid of a different interface? That's the time to make a custom floating panel.

Sample Floater: Table Helper

I admit it—I'd rather create my tables the old-fashioned way than use new-fangled toys such as the Dreamweaver Layout View or Convert Layers to Table. I like knowing exactly what structural elements are going into my tables, so I can better second-guess what's going to happen to them in a browser display. But I find myself limited by not being able to see all the widths, heights, rowspans, and colspans at once. I want a table-editing utility that presents me with all that information in one handy visual interface—something like the one shown in Figure 7.16.

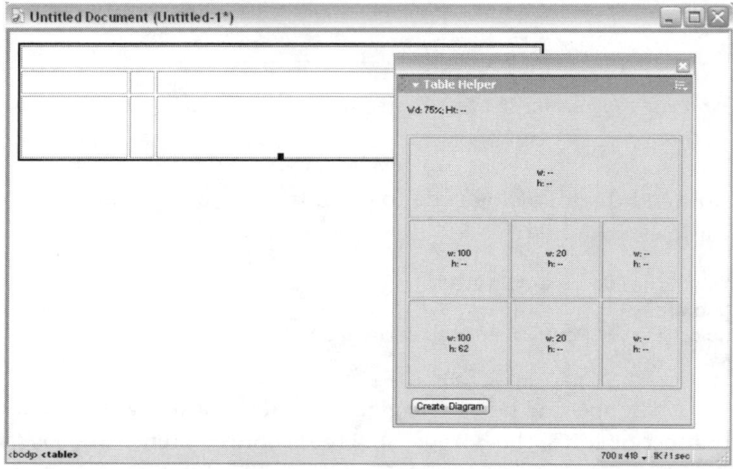

FIGURE 7.16 *The proposed Table Helper utility interface. The diagram reports widths, heights, rowspans, and colspans to help diagnose possible table problems.*

This is the floater we'll be creating in this workshop. Given a user-selected table in a document, the floater reports table dimensions; diagrams how many rows and columns are in the table; and presents information on width, height, rowspan, and colspan for each cell.

Task 1: Create the basic floater

To get started, you need a floater file and a menu entry to launch it.

1. In your text editor, create a new HTML document (you can use framework code from the practice session or create a new document). Call it TableHelper.htm, and save it in the Configuration/Floaters folder. The basic code framework should look like this:

```
<html>
<head>
<title>Table Helper</title>
<script language="JavaScript">
function initialTabs() {
window.resizeTo(300,400);
return "";
}
</script>
</head>
<body>
</body>
</html>
```

The `initialTabs()` function sets up the initial size of the floater window, but doesn't group it with any other floaters.

2. In menus.xml, find the bottom of the Window menu, and enter or change a line of code to launch the new floater:

```
<menuitem name="Table Helper" enabled="true"
command="dw.toggleFloater('TableHelper')"
checked="dw.getFloaterVisibility('TableHelper')"
id="MyStuff_TableHelper_Floater"/>
```

If you're the cautious sort, take a moment to launch Dreamweaver and test the new floater, just to make sure it's been created correctly. (It should launch an empty floater window.)

Task 2: Enable the floater to rewrite its own contents

If you examined the projected floater shown in Figure 7.15, you noticed that its contents are dynamically determined, based on the structure of the user's selected table. The idea behind this floater is to re-create the user's table structure in the floater, stripped of its cell contents and decoration. If you were scripting JavaScript destined for a browser, you would probably use the `document.write()` method to accomplish this. Unfortunately, the Dreamweaver API doesn't support `document.write()`. But you can accomplish your goal by using that most handy of functions: `dw.getDocumentDOM()`.

note

See Tables 4.2 and 4.3 in Chapter 4, "The Dreamweaver DOM," for a list of properties and methods supported by the document object in Dreamweaver. See Table 4.10 for `dw.getDocumentDOM()` specifications, including optional arguments and their uses.

We've been using `dw.getDocumentDOM()` without any arguments to refer to the current user document. By supplying a document name as an argument, however, we can gain access to the DOM of any document—including the floater document itself. To communicate between floater and user document, we can gain access to two DOMs at once like this:

```
//the user's document
var myDOM = dw.getDocumentDOM();

//the floater
var floaterDOM = dw.getDocumentDOM('TableHelper.htm');
```

1. To avoid the penalties that are associated with `documentEdited()` and `selectionChanged()`, you want the floater to appear with a button that activates it. To begin with, that's the only visible element it needs. Create a simple form in the `<body>` section of the floater file:

```
<form name="myForm">
<input type="button" value="Create Diagram" onClick="displayDiagram()">
</form>
```

2. Now create a function to call from it:

```
function displayDiagram() {
//access the floater's DOM
var floaterDOM = dw.getDocumentDOM('TableHelper.htm');
var floaterBody = floaterDOM.body;
//rewrite its contents
var contentString = "This is a test.";
floaterBody.innerHTML = contentString;
}
```

This function tests DOM access by altering the contents of the floater window, replacing the button with the words `This is a test.`

3. Try it out! The resulting floater should look and behave like the one shown in Figure 7.17.

FIGURE 7.17 *The Table Helper floater, scripted to rewrite its own contents when the Create Diagram button is clicked. This is made possible by gaining access to the floater file's DOM.*

4. One problem with the floater so far is that once you've clicked the button and the contents have changed, the button disappears. Closing and re-opening the floater won't even bring it back. To fix this problem, make sure you re-create the button when you rewrite the floater's contents. Revise your `diagramTable()` function to look like this:

```
function displayDiagram() {
//access the floater's DOM
var floaterDOM = dw.getDocumentDOM('TableHelper.htm');
var floaterBody = floaterDOM.body;
//rewrite its contents
var contentString = "<p>This is a test.<\/p>";
contentString += '<input type="button" value="Create Diagram"
➥onClick="displayDiagram()">';
floaterBody.innerHTML = contentString;
}
```

Now that's a handy addition! The `displayDiagram()` function re-creates the form button, complete with a function call to call the `displayDiagram()` function.

Task 3: Make the floater re-create the code for a selected table in the user's document

If the user has a table selected, the floater should reproduce that table in itself. You use your dual DOM access to make this happen. String access is the easiest way to accomplish this.

1. Revise the `diagramTable()` function so it collects a string representing the selected table like this:

```
function displayDiagram() {
//access user's selection
var myDOM = dw.getDocumentDOM();
var myObject = myDOM.getSelectedNode();
//if selection is a table
if (myObject.nodeType == 1 && myObject.tagName == "TABLE") {
//collect it as a string for manipulation
   var myHTML = myDOM.documentElement;
   var myHTMLstring = myHTML.outerHTML;
   var myOffsets = myDOM.nodeToOffsets(myObject);
   var myString = myHTMLstring.substring(myOffsets[0],myOffsets[1]);
//otherwise, don't go any further
   }else{
   return;
   }//end if-else
//access the floater's DOM
var floaterDOM = dw.getDocumentDOM('TableHelper.htm');
var floaterBody = floaterDOM.body;
```

```
19 //rewrite its contents
20 var contentString = myString;
21 contentString += '<input type="button" value="Create Diagram"
   ➥onClick="displayDiagram()">';
22 floaterBody.innerHTML = contentString;
23 }
```

What's happening here? Lines 3–4 access the selected object. In line 6, a conditional statement tests to see if the selected object is a `<table>` tag. If the condition is true, several new variables are declared, gaining access to the selected table as a string (`myString`). If the conditional isn't true, the function stops without doing anything (line 14).

Why collect the selected table as a string? Remember, the second part of the function uses a string (`contentString`) to rewrite the floater's contents. The table must be collected as a string and fed into `contentString`.

2. Launch Dreamweaver, and try out the result. Create a new Dreamweaver document and put a simple table in it. Make sure the table has a border, so its structure is clearly visible. Then open the Table Helper floater and click the Check Table button. Your result should look and behave like the one shown in Figure 7.18.

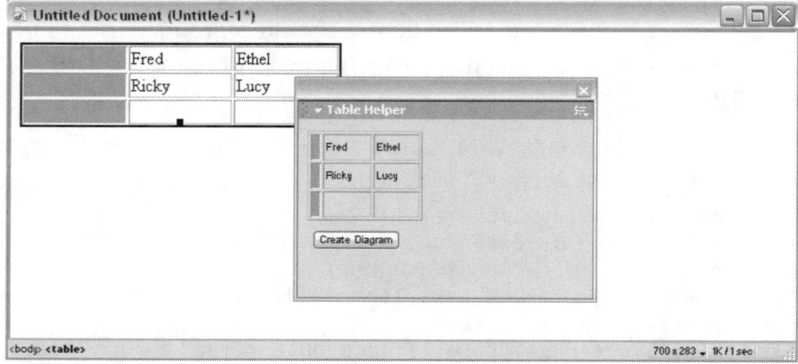

FIGURE 7.18 *The Table Helper floating panel, collecting and reproducing a selected table (contents and all) from a user document.*

3. To make the interface look a little nicer, dress up the code that gets placed in the floater, like this:

```
function displayDiagram() {
etc
//access the floater's DOM
var floaterDOM = dw.getDocumentDOM('TableHelper.htm');
var floaterBody = floaterDOM.body;
//rewrite its contents
var floaterIntro = "<p>Current table structure:<\/p>";
var floaterReset = '<input type="button" value="Create Diagram"
➥onClick="displayDiagram()">';
var contentString = floaterIntro+myString+floaterReset;
floaterBody.innerHTML = contentString;
}
```

You're creating an introductory line of text for the floater (`floaterIntro`). And, because the items to be written into the floater are getting more complex, you've created another variable to hold the form button (`floaterReset`) as well. The resulting interface looks like the one shown in Figure 7.19.

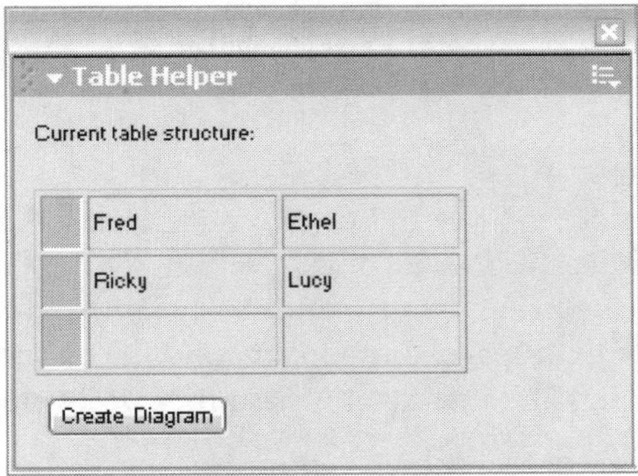

FIGURE 7.19 *The Table Helper floating panel with a friendlier interface.*

Task 4: Remove contents and decoration from the table that appears in the floater

You don't need the floater to show you the user's table as is. You need to keep the table structure but without its formatting, and you need to replace the contents with a reporting of width, height, and so on. The simplest way to do this is with object access after the table code is inside the floater.

What do you want the table to look like as it appears in the floater? It should have a border, to make it visible. It should resize itself to fit nicely inside the floater window. It doesn't need a background color, cell padding, or other niceties.

1. Start by gaining access to the table, once it's in the floater, like this (new code is in bold):

```
1 function displayDiagram() {
etc
23 floaterBody.innerHTML = contentString;
24 //get access to the first (and only) table in the floater file
25 var tableDiagram = floaterDOM.getElementsByTagName("TABLE").item(0);
26 }
```

2. Now adjust the table's attributes for better display in the floater window:

```
1 function displayDiagram() {
etc
23 floaterBody.innerHTML = contentString;
24 //get access to the first (and only) table in the floater file
25 var tableDiagram = floaterDOM.getElementsByTagName("TABLE").item(0);
26 //reset or remove attributes
27 tableDiagram.border = "1";
28 tableDiagram.width = "100%";
29 tableDiagram.height = "75%";
30 tableDiagram.removeAttribute("cellpadding");
31 tableDiagram.removeAttribute("cellspacing");
32 tableDiagram.removeAttribute("bgcolor");
33 tableDiagram.removeAttribute("background");
34 etc
}//end function
```

   What are you doing here? In line 27, you're giving the table a border, so it shows up in the floater. In lines 28 and 29 you're setting the table width to 100%, so it adjusts to the panel's width, and the height slightly smaller (75%), to make room for the extra page contents at top and bottom. Finally, in lines 30–33, you're removing all other attributes so they don't clog up the floater's display.

3. Next, you need to access each cell in the table, determine its width and height, and rewrite the cell's `outerHTML` to display these values, like this:

```
1 function displayDiagram() {
etc
23 floaterBody.innerHTML = contentString;
24 //get access to the first (and only) table in the floater file
25 var tableDiagram = floaterDOM.getElementsByTagName("TABLE").item(0);
26 //reset or remove attributes
27 tableDiagram.border = "1";
28 tableDiagram.width = "100%";
29 tableDiagram.height = "75%";
30 tableDiagram.removeAttribute("cellpadding");
31 tableDiagram.removeAttribute("cellspacing");
32 tableDiagram.removeAttribute("bgcolor");
33 tableDiagram.removeAttribute("background");
34 //collect a list of rows (child nodes of table)
35 var myRows=tableDiagram.childNodes;
```

```
36 var myCells, openTag, cellContents, closeTag;
37 //for each row:
38 for (var a=0;a<myRows.length;a++) {
39    //collect a list of cells (child nodes of row)
40    myCells=myRows.item(a).childNodes;
41    //for each child:
42    for (var b=0;b<myCells.length;b++) {
43       //create new <td> string
44       openTag='<td align="center" valign="middle" nowrap>';
45       closeTag='<\/td>';
46       cellContents='w: ';
47       cellContents+=(myCells.item(b).width)?myCells.item(b).width:'--';
48       cellContents+='<br>';
49       cellContents+='h: ';
50       cellContents+=(myCells.item(b).height)?myCells.item(b).height:'--';
51       //replace outerHTML of TD with new <td> string
52       myCells.item(b).outerHTML=openTag+cellContents+closeTag;
53       }//end for each cell
54    }//end for each row
55 }//end function
```

What's happening here? Line 35 collects all of the `<tr>` tags of the table as a node list (`myRows`). Starting in line 38, a `for` loop steps through each row. Within each row, line 40 collects all `<td>` tags in a node list (`myCells`). Starting in line 42, another `for` loop steps through each cell. For each cell, lines 44–45 create text strings containing the code for the opening and closing `<td>` tags (`openTag` and `closeTag`). Lines 46–47 add a line of text to the cell's contents, indicating the cell's width (if any). Lines 49–50 add a line indicating the cell's height (if any). Finally, line 52 puts the opening tag, closing tag, and contents together into a string (`openTag + cellContents + closeTag`) and substitutes that string for the current cell's `outerHTML` property.

4. For one more refinement, collect the overall width and height of the table itself, and change the opening line of the panel so it displays those values:

```
1  function displayDiagram() {
etc
6  if (myObject.nodeType == 1 && myObject.tagName == "TABLE") {
7  //collect it as a string for manipulation
8     var myHTML = myDOM.documentElement;
9     var myHTMLstring = myHTML.outerHTML;
10    var myOffsets = myDOM.nodeToOffsets(myObject);
11    var myString = myHTMLstring.substring(myOffsets[0],myOffsets[1]);
12    if (myObject.width) {
13       var tableWidth=myObject.width;
14       }else{
15       var tableWidth="--";
16       }//end if (width)
```

```
17    if (myObject.height) {
18       var tableHeight=myObject.height;
19       }else{
20       var tableHeight="--";
21       }//end if (height)
22 //otherwise, don't go any further
23   }else{
24   return;
25   }
26 //access the floater's DOM
27 var floaterDOM = dw.getDocumentDOM('TableHelper.htm');
28 var floaterBody = floaterDOM.body;
29 floaterIntro = "<p>Wd: "+tableWidth+"; Ht: "+tableHeight+"<\/p>";
etc
```

The new pair of conditional statements (lines 12 and 17) create two new variables, `tableWidth` and `tableHeight`, each holding the width/height value or the alternate text string `--`.

5. Try it out! At this point, the floater should work with any table that doesn't use colspans or rowspans, to create a result like that shown in Figure 7.20.

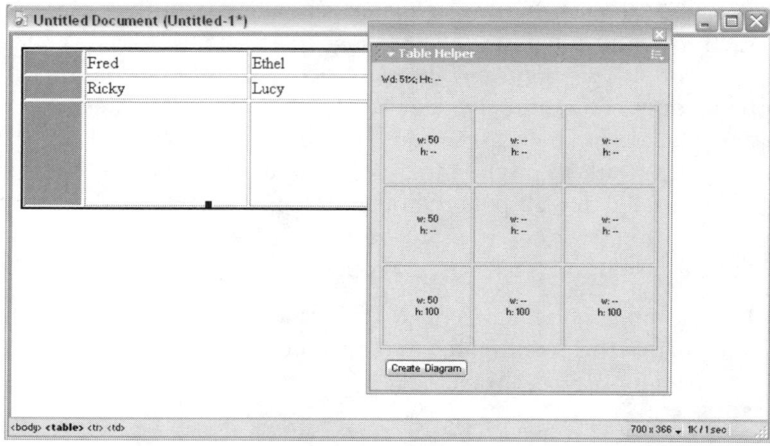

FIGURE 7.20 *The Table Helper floating panel, reporting widths and heights in a generic table diagram.*

Task 5: Refine the floater to work with *rowspan* and *colspan* in tables

The panel, as it is currently scripted, works just fine with plain vanilla tables. But we can make it more robust in all sorts of ways. First and foremost, if it's going to be useful for layout tables, it needs to be able to handle `rowspan` and `colspan` attributes.

1. Because `rowspan` and `colspan` are cell attributes, they must be added to the code string for each cell as it is being created. This means adding a bit of complexity, and a few conditionals, to the portion of your code where you create the `openTag` variable. Revise your code like this:

```
1 function displayDiagram() {
etc
45 //for each row:
46 for (var a=0;a<myRows.length;a++) {
47    //collect a list of cells (child nodes of row)
48    myCells=myRows.item(a).childNodes;
49    //for each child:
50    for (var b=0;b<myCells.length;b++) {
51       //create new <td> string
52       openTag='<td align="center" valign="middle" nowrap';
53       if (myCells.item(b).rowspan) {
54          openTag+=' rowspan="'+myCells.item(b).rowspan+'"';
55          }//end if (rowspan)
56       if (myCells.item(b).colspan) {
57          openTag+=' colspan="'+myCells.item(b).colspan+'"';
58          }//end if (colspan)
59       openTag+=">";
60       closeTag='<\/td>';
```

   Can you see what's going on here? In line 52, the initialization of the `openTag` variable has changed slightly—the text string fed into this variable no longer ends with a > character. A conditional in lines 53–55 determines if the current cell has a `rowspan` attribute, and if so, adds `rowspan="`*`value`*`"` to `openTag`. A conditional in lines 56–58 does the same for `colspan`. Finally, line 59 finishes the code for the opening tag by adding > to openTag.

2. Try your Table Helper out again. It should be able to diagram tables with and without `colspan` and `rowspan` values, like the ones shown in Figures 7.21 and 7.22.

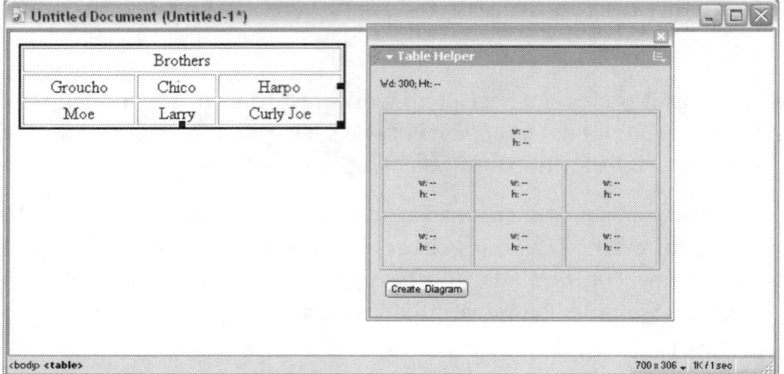

FIGURE 7.21 *The Table Helper, analyzing and reporting on a table that uses the* `rowspan` *attribute.*

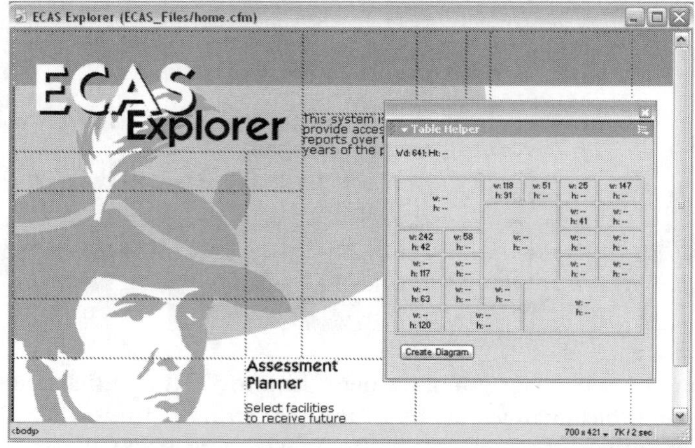

FIGURE 7.22 *Table Helper reporting on a complex layout table (generated by Fireworks).*

That's it! Your Table Helper is now finished. Listing 7.1 shows the finished code, with all comments in place.

Listing 7.1 Final Code for the Table Helper Floating Panel

```
<html>
<head>
<title>Table Helper</title>
<script language="JavaScript">
function initialTabs() {
window.resizeTo(300,400);
return "";
```

Listing 7.1 Continued

```
}
function displayDiagram() {
//access user's selection
var myDOM = dw.getDocumentDOM();
var myObject = myDOM.getSelectedNode();
//if selection is a table
if (myObject.nodeType == 1 && myObject.tagName == "TABLE") {
//collect it as a string for manipulation
   var myHTML = myDOM.documentElement;
   var myHTMLstring = myHTML.outerHTML;
   var myOffsets = myDOM.nodeToOffsets(myObject);
   var myString = myHTMLstring.substring(myOffsets[0],myOffsets[1]);
   if (myObject.width) {
      var tableWidth=myObject.width;
      }else{
      var tableWidth="--";
      }//end if (width)
   if (myObject.height) {
      var tableHeight=myObject.height;
      }else{
      var tableHeight="--";
      }//end if (height)
//otherwise, don't go any further
   }else{
   return;
   }
//access the floater's DOM
var floaterDOM = dw.getDocumentDOM('TableHelper.htm');
var floaterBody = floaterDOM.body;
floaterIntro = "<p>Wd: "+tableWidth+"; Ht: "+tableHeight+"<\/p>";
var floaterReset = '<input type="button" value="Create Diagram"
onClick="displayDiagram()">';
var contentString = floaterIntro + myString + floaterReset;
floaterBody.innerHTML = contentString;
//get access to the first (and only) table in the floater file
var tableDiagram = floaterDOM.getElementsByTagName("TABLE").item(0);
tableDiagram.border="1";
tableDiagram.width="100%";
tableDiagram.height="75%";
tableDiagram.removeAttribute("cellpadding");
tableDiagram.removeAttribute("cellspacing");
tableDiagram.removeAttribute("bgcolor");
tableDiagram.removeAttribute("background");
//collect a list of rows (child nodes of table)
var myRows=tableDiagram.childNodes;
var myCells, openTag, cellContents, closeTag;
//for each row:
for (var a=0;a<myRows.length;a++) {
   //collect a list of cells (child nodes of row)
```

continues

```
    myCells=myRows.item(a).childNodes;
    //for each child:
    for (var b=0;b<myCells.length;b++) {
       //create new <td> string
       openTag='<td align="center" valign="middle" nowrap';
       if (myCells.item(b).rowspan) {
            openTag+=' rowspan="'+myCells.item(b).rowspan+'"';
            }
       if (myCells.item(b).colspan) {
            openTag+=' colspan="'+myCells.item(b).colspan+'"';
            }
       openTag+=">";
       closeTag='<\/td>';
       cellContents='w: ';
       cellContents+=(myCells.item(b).width)?myCells.item(b).width:'--';
       cellContents+='<br>';
       cellContents+='h: ';

cellContents+=(myCells.item(b).height)?myCells.item(b).height:'--';
       //replace outerHTML of TD with new <td> string
       myCells.item(b).outerHTML=openTag+cellContents+closeTag;
       }//end for each cell
    }//end for each row
}
</script>
</head>
<body>
<form name="myForm">
<input type="button" value="Create Diagram" onClick="displayDiagram()">
</form>
</body>
</html>
```

Challenge!

The Table Helper is now a handy-dandy diagnostic tool for reporting on table construction. But it's not quite as powerful as it could be. Can you revise the floater to add the following functionality?

- Tables do not display correctly in browsers if their width, height, rowspans, and colspans don't add up. Can you make Table Helper display a warning if, for instance, all the widths in a row add up to more or less than the table width allows?
- Because of the way you scripted it, Table Helper can be slow in diagramming complex tables or tables with many images in them. You could increase the speed by using string access to rewrite the table code before it's ever displayed in the floating panel.

- Can you make Table Helper respond to user clicks in the floater by selecting particular cells in the main document? How about responding to users selecting individual table cells in the main document by highlighting particular cells in the floater diagram?

Summary

Floating panels are our friends. With them, we can add all sorts of varied utility, tutorial, and informational interfaces to Dreamweaver. Floaters can interact with documents or simply present information. They can be splashy and flashy, or transparent pieces of the Dreamweaver user interface. Because floaters can have such different interfaces, and can require drastically different skill sets than the other more typical interface elements in Dreamweaver, we have to be careful with them. As a rule, users aren't looking for new and drastically different experiences when they open Dreamweaver—they just want to be productive and build on the skills they already have. As long as we remain sensitive to our users' needs, however, we can go far with floaters.

This chapter completes our tour of the basic extension types in Dreamweaver. In the following chapter, we'll see how different kinds of extensions can be used together, how their functionality overlaps, and how to strategize which kind of extension will work best for which jobs.

CHAPTER 8

Mixing Extension Types

If you have worked through all seven preceding chapters, you should now have a good understanding of the major extension types, what each requires, and what sort of tasks each is best at. In this chapter, we'll see how to go beyond the restrictions of individual extension types to access the functionality of one extension type from within the structure of another. Menu commands and floaters can insert objects and behaviors, object files can run commands, and so forth. All of this is possible within the Dreamweaver Application Programming Interface (API).

Why Mix Extension Types?

Why would we want to mix extension types? There are all sorts of reasons, but they break down into considerations of interface usability versus extension functionality.

Rollovers, Jump Menus, and Navigation Bars, Oh My!

Sometimes the "correct" way to code an extension isn't the most logical one for the user. For instance, users intuitively expect items that insert things into documents to be part of the Insert bar and Insert menu—Insert > Table, Insert > Image, Insert > Flash, and so forth. But not all insertion tasks are as easy as that. When a user chooses the Insert Rollover object, for instance, what's happening? Dreamweaver is inserting the code for a linked image into the document at the insertion point, but the program is also inserting a Swap Image function in the head of the document and the relevant function call in the body. Those tasks can't all be performed by the lowly `objectTag()` function. The Rollover "object" should really be an object plus a behavior, or maybe some of each combined into a command.

Take a look at the files behind Insert Rollover, and you'll see the following happening:

- The Insert Rollover object file (Rollover.htm in Objects/Common) contains no `<body>` content at all to generate the dialog box you see when this object is activated.
- The `objectTag()` function found in the object file's linked JavaScript file (Rollover.js in Objects/Common) calls a command file called Rollover.htm to create the content it will insert into the user's document.
- The related command file (Rollover.htm in Commands) contains the `<form>` that will become the dialog box.
- The command file's linked JavaScript file (Rollover.js in Commands) is what actually builds the rollover code.

In other words, you have an object file that calls on a command file to help it perform its function.

If you examine the contents of the Commands file, you'll recognize several other files that are obviously linked to objects: Tabular Data.htm, Jump Menu.htm, LayoutCell.htm, LayoutTable.htm, Navigation Bar.htm, and Date.htm.

Coloring Outside the Lines

You might want to mix the functionality of extension types for similar reasons. When you were reading through Chapter 3, "Creating Custom Behaviors," for instance, were you struck by how many JavaScripts you couldn't turn into behaviors because they didn't fit the mold of generic function/function call? If you created a command that inserted the proper JavaScript code instead of a behavior, you could overcome those limitations—but for intuitive interface presentation, you still might want the command to show up in the Behaviors panel's actions list. The moral of the story is to never feel limited by extension types. Determine the best way to create the result you want—insert code, manipulate code, whatever—and then determine how you can mix and match extension types to make this work intuitively for your users.

API Functions for Mixing Extension Types

The Dreamweaver API offers methods for invoking the functionality of almost all extension types from within other extensions. Take a look at these in the following sections, based on extension type.

Running Commands

Commands are the most flexible of the extension types, giving you access to every aspect of the user's document. Did you ever want to execute the code in a command file without the user having to choose the command from a menu? The API function that allows you to do this is `dw.runCommand()`. Table 8.1 lists the specifications for this function, and shows some examples of its use.

Table 8.1 The *dw.runCommand( )* Function Specifications

Function	`dw.runCommand()`
Description	Executes the specified command. This function provides the capability to call a command from another extension file, exactly as if the user had chosen the command from a menu.
Syntax	`dw.runCommand(`*`commandFile`*`,[`*`commandArg1, etc`*`])`
Arguments	`commandFile`—The name of a file in the Configuration/Commands folder.
	`commandArg1`, and so on—Any arguments that need to be passed to the command file.
Returns	Nothing.
Notes	Only items in the Commands folder can be accessed from this function. This means that dynamic menu commands (that is, those stored in Configuration/Menus) cannot be accessed using `dw.runCommand()`.

continues

Table 8.1 Continued

Function	dw.runCommand()

Examples	`//This code, in the body of a floater or property inspector, creates a button that causes the Automatic Alt Text command to run:`
	
	`<form name="myForm">`
	`<input type="button" value="Insert ALT text" onClick="dw.runCommand('Automatic Alt Text.html')">`
	`</form>`
	
	`//This objectTag() function, in the head of an object file, runs the Automatic Alt Text command when the user chooses the object from the objects panel:`
	
	`function objectTag() {`
	`dw.runCommand('Automatic Alt Text.html');`
	`return "";`
	`}`

What can `dw.runCommand()` do for you? It lets you reuse the code that's already present in the Commands folder or create special command files and put them in the Commands folder specifically to be called on. Maybe you want to create an object that inserts Microsoft Word-generated HTML code into your document and then automatically cleans it up. Just use `dw.runCommand()` in your object file, passing it Clean Up Microsoft Word HTML.htm as an argument.

note

Note that `dw.runCommand()` works only on files actually in the Commands folder. This means menu commands (those stored in the Menus folder) aren't eligible.

Inserting Objects

Would you like your commands, behaviors, inspectors, or floaters to automatically insert objects? The API function that allows you to do this is `dom.insertObject()`. Table 8.2 lists the specifications for this function.

Table 8.2 Specifications of the *dom.insertObject( )* Function

Function	dom.insertObject()
Description	Inserts a specified object into the user's document. This allows other extension types to insert object code into a document, as if the user had chosen the object from the Insert bar.
Syntax	`dom.insertObject(`*`objectName`*`)`

Function	`dom.insertObject()`
Arguments	`objectName`—The name of an object in the Configuration/Objects folder. This is the name of the object file minus its filename extension. No subfolder path (that is, Common/Table) need be included.
Returns	Nothing.

Example	`//This function, placed in the head of a command file and called onLoad, accesses the Table.htm file in the Objects folder, and causes that file to run its objectTag() function:`
	
	`function insertMyTable() {`
	`var myDOM = dw.getDocumentDOM();`
	`myDOM.insertObject("Table");`
	`}`

This function can be used any time we want Dreamweaver to respond as if the user had clicked on an icon in the Insert bar or chosen a command from the Insert menu. Commands, inspectors, and such may not be able to use the `objectTag()` function, but they can call on object files that use that function. With `dom.insertObject()`, we also have access to the functionality of all the standard objects—Image, Table, and so on—for exploitation in your extensions. Because we can even call `dom.insertObject()` from within another object file, we can create custom objects that build on standard Dreamweaver objects.

Inserting Behaviors

There are two API methods for inserting behaviors from other extensions, each with its own unique functionality: `dw.popupAction()` and `dom.addBehavior()`. The specifications for both of these methods are shown in Tables 8.3 and 8.4.

Table 8.3 Specifications for the *dw.popupAction( )* Function

Function	`dw.popupAction()`
Description	Inserts a behavior, exactly as if the user had chosen the behavior from the + menu in the behaviors panel. This function can only be called from within `objectTag()`, or from any script within a command or inspector file.
Syntax	`dw.popupAction(`*`actionName`*`, [`*`functionCall`*`])`
Arguments	`ActionName`—A string representing the name of a file in the Configuration/Behaviors/Actions folder that contains a JavaScript action. The filename must include the relative path from the Actions folder, including any subfolder names (for example, Development/Set Page Properties.html).

continues

Table 8.3 Continued

Function	`dw.popupAction()`
	[`functionCall`]—A string representing the function call for the action specified in the previous parameter. This is the same code that would be returned by the `applyBehavior()` function if the behavior were chosen using the + menu (for example, `"MM_popupMsg('Hello world')"`).
Returns	The function call for the behavior action (for example, `MM_popupMsg('Hello world')`).
Notes	When the user clicks OK to exit the behavior's dialog box, the function is added to the document, but not the function call. That value is returned. It must be added separately, and must be inserted into the user document separately (see the example below).
Example	`//This object file inserts a text link with user-specified text that already has the Set Page Properties behavior applied to it.`

```
<html>
<head>
<title>Insert Link to Change Page Properties</title>
<script language="JavaScript">
function objectTag() {
linkname = document.myForm.linkname.value;
myCall = dw.popupAction("Development/Set Page
➥Properties.html");
returnString = '<a href="#"
onClick="'+myCall+'">'+linkname+'<\/a>';
return returnString;
}
</script>
</head>
<body>
<form name="myForm">
<input type="text" name="linkname">
</form>
</body>
</html>
```

Table 8.4 Specifications for the *dom.addBehavior()* Function

Function	dom.addBehavior()
Description	Inserts a behavior into the user's document, but without calling up a dialog box; instead, any parameters must be set in the function itself.
Syntax	dom.addBehavior(*event, action, [event-based index]*)
Arguments	event—A string representing the event handler to be used in creating the function call (for example, onClick) action—A string representing the complete function call, as it would be returned from the applyBehavior() function if the user had chosen the behavior from the + menu (for example, MM_popupMsg('Hello world')). [event-based index]—A number indicating the position among other function calls that this one should take. If the selected object already has the specified event handler applied to it, but specifying a different function call, this determines the order in which the function calls are placed (for example, onClick="MM_popupMsg('Hello world'); setProperties('#000000','#ffffff')"). This is a zero-based index. In the previous example, the Popup Message call would be index 0, and the Set Page Properties call would be index 1. If this argument is not present, the action is added after all other actions.
Returns	Nothing.

Examples	//This command, placed in the head of a command file and called onLoad, inserts the Popup Message behavior into the user's document, with the function call attached to the currently selected item:
	
	function insertMyBehavior() {
	var myDOM = dw.getDocumentDOM();
	myDOM.addBehavior("onClick","MM_popupMsg('Hello world')");
	}
	
	//This objectTag() function, placed in an object file, inserts the Set Page Properties behavior with parameters set to black and white, and attaches the event handler to the selected object, when the user chooses the object from the Insert bar:
	<html>
	<head>
	<title>Insert Page Properties</title>
	<script language="JavaScript">
	function objectTag() {
	myDOM = dw.getDocumentDOM();

continues

Table 8.4 Continued

Function	`dom.addBehavior()`

	`pagecolor = document.myForm.pagecolor.value;`
	`textcolor = document.myForm.textcolor.value;`
	`myDOM.addBehavior("onClick","setProperties('#000000',`
	`➥'#FFFFFF') ");`
	`return "";`
	`}`

Notes	Various commands are available to work with inserted behaviors. In the *Extending Dreamweaver* manual, check out `dom.getBehavior()`, `dom.reapplyBehaviors()`, `dom.removeBehavior()`, `dw.getBehaviorElement()`, and `dw.getBehaviorTag()`.

What's the difference between these two? Neither one completely re-creates the experience of a user choosing and configuring a behavior.

With `dom.addBehavior()`, you can tell Dreamweaver to insert a behavior, but the standard behavior dialog box doesn't appear. Instead, your script must create the function call, with all of its arguments. If you want to ask for user input, you have to create your own `<form>` for processing input.

With `dw.popupAction()`, you can tell Dreamweaver to call up the behavior's dialog box and create the function call, but this function does not cause the behavior function to be inserted in the document. You have to use other scripting to do that.

Accessing Inspectors and Floaters

Although there is no mimicking the functionality of an inspector or floater, you can use scripting to show and hide them. For this, you use the `dw.setFloaterVisibility()` API method (introduced in Chapter 7 "Creating Custom Floating Panels"). The specifications for this function are listed in Table 8.5.

Table 8.5 Specifications for the *dw.setFloaterVisibility( )* function.

Function	*`dw.setFloaterVisibility()`*
Description	Opens or closes a floating panel or properties inspector, as if the user had chosen it from the Window menu to access it.
Syntax	`dw.setFloaterVisibility(`*`floaterName`*`, `*`bIsVisible`*`)`
Arguments	`FloaterName`—A string representing the name of the floating panel or inspector to be opened or closed. Built-in panels are accessed with these keywords: `objects`, `properties`, `launcher`, `site files`, `site map`, `library`, `css styles`, `html styles`, `behaviors`, `timelines`, `html`, `layers`, `frames`, `templates`, `history`. To access custom floaters, use the floater's name (filename minus extension).

Function	`dw.setFloaterVisibility()`
	`BIsVisible`—A Boolean value, indicating whether to open or close the specified floater or inspector.
Returns	Nothing.

Examples	`//This function, placed in the head of a command file and called onLoad, inserts a table into the user's document, and opens the Table Helper floating panel (as if the user had used the Table object and the Window > Table Helper command):`
	`function insertMyTable() {`
	`var myDOM = dw.getDocumentDOM();`
	`myDOM.insertObject("Table");`
	`dw.setFloaterVisibility('TableHelper',true);`
	`}`

With this and the other API methods described here, you can start programming the way Dreamweaver interface elements interact and share resources with each other. Your extension-writing skills won't be ready for prime time until you learn to go beyond individual extension types.

Mixing Extension Types: Practice Session

For our practice session, we'll play with some of the previous workshops to give the above functions a test drive.

Task 1: Create an object that inserts Alt text

To try out the `dw.runCommand()` method, copy the functionality of your Automatic Alt Text command (refer to Workshop #1 in Chapter 5, "Creating Custom Commands and Menu Commands") into an object, thus creating an `Insert Alt Text` object.

1. Start by creating an HTML containing the basic framework code for an object file. The code should look like this:

```
<html>
<head>
<title>Alt Text</title>
<script language="JavaScript">
function objectTag() {
return "";
}
</script>
</head>
<body>
</body>
</html>
```

The <title>, remember, will become the ToolTip for the Insert bar. The objectTag() function must be present and must have a return statement. The object doesn't need any <body> content—that will be supplied by the command the object will run.

2. Save the file in the Objects > Development folder you created back in Chapter 2, "Creating Custom Objects." Call it Alt Text.htm.
3. To make sure the object displays properly in the Insert bar, open Insertbar.xml (in the Configuration/Objects folder) and add the following <button/> entry to your Development category:

```
<button id="DW_Development_AltText"
image=""
enabled=""
showIf=""
file="Development\Alt Text.htm" />
```

4. Save insertbar.xml and close it.
5. In the API procedure for object files, remember, the objectTag() function is called automatically. Its purpose is to return the chunk of HTML code to be inserted into the user's document at the insertion point. For this object, you use objectTag() to call Automatic Alt Text.htm. Because you don't want it to actually insert any code at the insertion point, you have it return an empty string.

   To accomplish this, add the following code to your objectTag() function (new code is in bold):

```
function objectTag() {
dw.runCommand('Automatic Alt Text.htm');
return "";
}
```

   (Of course, if you called your Automatic Alt Text command file something else, use that name instead in your code. If you didn't complete the Automatic Alt Text project, you can download the finished project file at this book's companion web site.)
6. In Dreamweaver, reload extensions and try it out. Open a file containing some images (and no Alt text) and then choose the Alt Text object. The command should run exactly as if you had chosen it from the Commands menu. Figure 8.1 shows the Alt Text object in action. Listing 8.1 shows the finished code for the Alt Text object file.

Listing 8.1 Complete Code for Alt Text.htm, with Comments for Reference

```
<html>
<head>
<!--ToolTip-->
<title>Alt Text</title>
<script language="JavaScript">
function objectTag() {
//call any file in the Commands folder
dw.runCommand('Automatic Alt Text.htm');
//return an empty string, so the object inserts no code
return "";
}
</script>
</head>
<body>
<!--the dialog box is provided by the command, so no body content is
needed-->
</body>
</html>
```

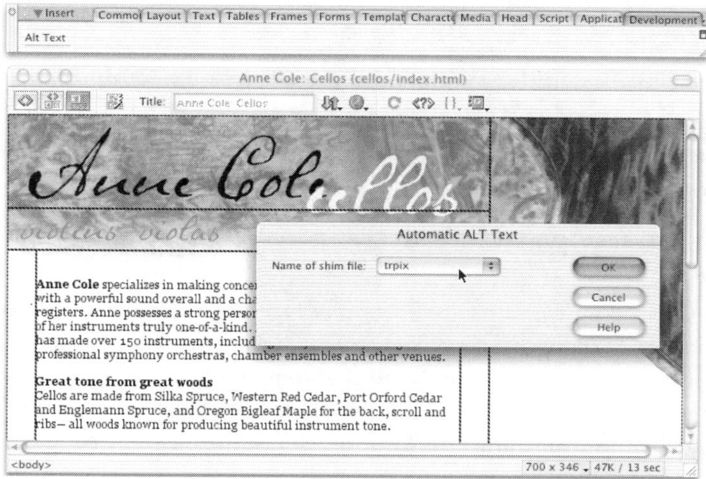

FIGURE 8.1 *The Alt Text object, calling the Automatic Alt Text command in a user document.*

Task 2: Create a command that inserts an object and opens a floating panel

In this task, we'll create a command that inserts a table (just like choosing the Table object) and simultaneously opens the Table Helper floater (refer to Workshop #1 in Chapter 7. We'll use `dom.insertObject()` and `dw.setFloaterVisibility()` to do this.

1. In your text editor, create a new HTML file, consisting of the basic framework code for a command:

   ```
   <html>
   <head>
   <title>Create Table</title>
   <script language="JavaScript">
   function insertMyTable() {
   //command code goes here
   }
   </script>
   </head>
   <body onLoad="insertMyTable()">
   </body>
   </html>
   ```

2. Save the file in the Commands folder as **Create Table.htm**.

3. For the command's main function, use the `dom.insertObject()` method to access the Dreamweaver Table object. Your function code should look like this:

   ```
   function insertMyTable() {
   var myDOM = dw.getDocumentDOM();
   myDOM.insertObject("Table");
   }
   ```

   Don't forget that `dom.insertObject()` must refer to the object's name, not its complete filename. Create the name by starting with the filename of the object file (Table.htm) and removing the filename extension. Also, because this function is a method of the DOM object, it doesn't work unless you access the DOM first.

4. Next, add another statement to this same function to open the Table Helper floating panel. Revise your function code so it looks like this:

   ```
   function insertMyTable() {
   var myDOM = dw.getDocumentDOM();
   myDOM.insertObject("Table");
   dw.setFloaterVisibility("TableHelper", true);
   }
   ```

Again, `dw.setFloaterVisibility()` must refer to the floater's name, which is generated from the floater file's filename minus its extension. (Obviously, if you didn't complete the Table Helper floating panel, you won't be able to perform this step as written. If this is the case, you can choose another floater to open.)

5. That's all there is to it! In Dreamweaver, reload extensions and try the new command out in a new file. When you choose the command, the Insert Table dialog box should appear, exactly as if you had chosen this object from the Insert bar. When you have created your table, the Table Helper should automatically open to help you work with this table. Figure 8.2 shows the new Create Table command in action. Listing 8.2 shows the finished code for the Create Table command file.

Listing 8.2 Complete Code for the Create Table.htm Command File, Commented for Reference

```
<html>
<head>
<title>Create Table</title>
<script language="JavaScript">
function insertMyTable() {
var myDOM = dw.getDocumentDOM();
//duplicate functionality of Insert > Table command or object
myDOM.insertObject("Table");
//duplicate functionality of Window > Table Helper
dw.setFloaterVisibility("TableHelper", true);
}
</script>
</head>
<body onLoad="insertMyTable()">
</body>
</html>
```

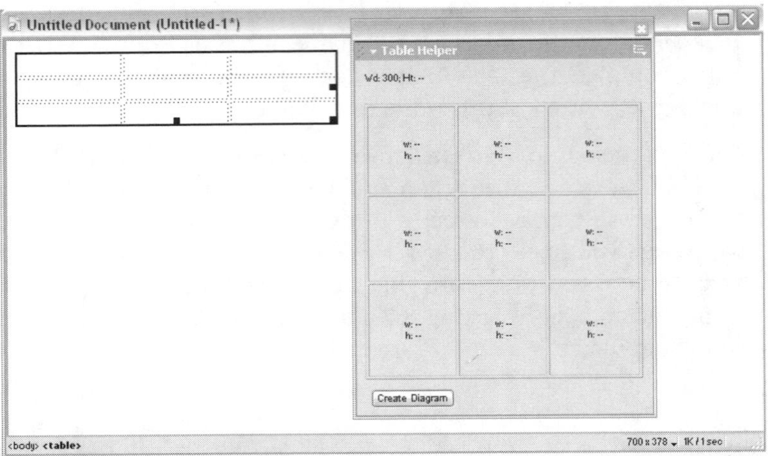

FIGURE 8.2 *The Create Table object, inserting a table and opening the Table Helper floating panel.*

Task 3: Make a floater updatable from outside itself

The previous task may have started you wondering about another possibility in extension-writing. In that task, you automatically opened a floater from a command. But wouldn't it also be nice if the command could interact with the floater? In the case of the Create Table command, wouldn't it be nice if the command could insert a table, open the Table Helper floater, and then automatically generate a table diagram without the user having to click the form button?

To perform tasks like this, you need to be able to access the floater's functions from outside the floater—in the case of the Create Table command, you need to call the `displayDiagram()` function from the Create Table command file.

Unfortunately, you can't control floater files externally; but you can control command files externally, using `dw.runCommand()`. The solution, therefore, is to move the function that the floater normally executes—`displayDiagram()`, in this case—to a command file of its own, and use `dw.runCommand()` to execute that command file from the floater or from anywhere else in the interface. The following steps take you through that process.

1. To start with, create a new command file. Save it in the Configuration/ Commands folder as Table Helper Command.htm. Enter a basic code framework like this:

```
<!--MENU-LOCATION=NONE-->
<html>
<head>
<title>Table Helper Command</title>
<script language="JavaScript">
```

```
function myCommand() {
//command statements go here
}
</script>
</head>
<body onLoad="myCommand()">
</body>
</html>
```

This code creates a command with no dialog box (because the `<body>` is empty) and no menu entry (because of the opening comment line).

2. Next, open the TableHelper.htm floater file. Select all command statements within the `displayDiagram()` function and Edit > Cut. In the place of this code, enter the following as your `displayDiagram()` code:

```
function displayDiagram(){
dw.runCommand('Table Helper Command.htm');
}
```

Save this file and close it.

3. Now go back to the Table Helper Command.htm file, and Edit > Paste the original function code in between the curly braces of the `myCommand()` function. Make the following change to the code:

```
function runCommand() {
etc
//move to floater
var myConfig=dw.getConfigurationPath();
var myFloater=myConfig+"/Floaters/TableHelper.htm";
var floaterDOM = dw.getDocumentDOM(myFloater);
floaterDOM.body.innerHTML=emptyDOM.body.innerHTML;
}
```

What's this change for? Because the function is no longer being executed from within the floater file, you need to be more specific about identifying that file.

4. Finally, open the Create Table.htm command file and add the following code, to control the floater externally:

```
function insertMyTable() {
var myDOM = dw.getDocumentDOM();
myDOM.insertObject("Table");
dw.setFloaterVisibility("TableHelper", true);
dw.runCommand("TableHelper.htm");
}
```

5. Now that you have all of your modules in place, you're ready to rock and roll! Quit Dreamweaver and relaunch (because you're updating a floater). Try using the Table Helper floater on a table you've already created. Then try the Create Table command. If everything is coded properly, this do-it-all-for-you command should now insert a table, open the Table Helper floater, and generate a table diagram.

note

You can find the code for this modularized version of the Table Helper floater on the book's companion web site at www.newriders.com

Task 4: Create a floater that inserts a behavior

For this task, you'll use a floating panel to insert a behavior. This involves creating the floater file and adding a corresponding `<menuitem/>` to menus.xml and adding a form button to the floater that calls the `dom.addBehavior()` function.

1. Start by creating a floater file, with no special functions but including a form button in its layout. The code should look like this:

```
<html>
<head>
<title>Add Behavior Floater</title>
</head>
<body>
<form name="myForm">
<input type="button" value="Insert Behavior">
</form>
</body>
</html>
```

2. Save this file in the Configuration/Floaters folder as AddPopup.htm.
3. Next, add the menu item to hide and show this floater. Open menus.xml and find the `<menuitem/>` entries you created in previous chapters for Float Me and Table Helper. Immediately following those entries, add the following code:

```
<menuitem name="Add Popup Behavior" enabled="true"
command="dw.toggleFloater('AddPopup')"
checked="dw.getFloaterVisibility('AddPopup')"
id="MyStuff_AddPopup_Floater"/>
```

4. Now experiment with the `dom.addBehavior()` API method by adding the following `<script>` tag to your floater file's `<head>` section:

```
<script language="JavaScript">
function insertHelloMessage() {
var myDOM = dw.getDocumentDOM();
myDOM.addBehavior("onClick", "MM_popupMsg('Hello world')");
}
</script>
```

This method adds a function and its function call into the user's document, without bringing up the behavior's dialog box. The code you've entered here inserts the Popup Message behavior, using the `onClick` event handler. (The `dom.addBehavior()` function must return the event handler and the function call, remember.)

> **note**
>
> Before you can insert a behavior using this command, obviously you need to know exactly what a valid function call for that behavior looks like. You may need to use a test file to insert the behavior the normal way and examine the code it creates before proceeding with your extension development.

5. The function you just created is local (not part of the API procedure), so you need to call it when the user clicks the form button. Add the function call to your floater file's form button, like this:

```
<form name="myForm">
<input type="button" value="Insert Behavior"
onClick="insertHelloMessage()">
</form>
```

6. Try out your floater. Remember that you need to quit Dreamweaver and relaunch it to get the new floater code to implement. Then create a test file to insert the behavior into, and enter a simple text link, like that shown in Figure 8.3.

7. Select the text link, choose Window > Add Popup Behavior to open your floater, and click the Insert Behavior button.

   Your test document should look like the one shown in Figure 8.3.

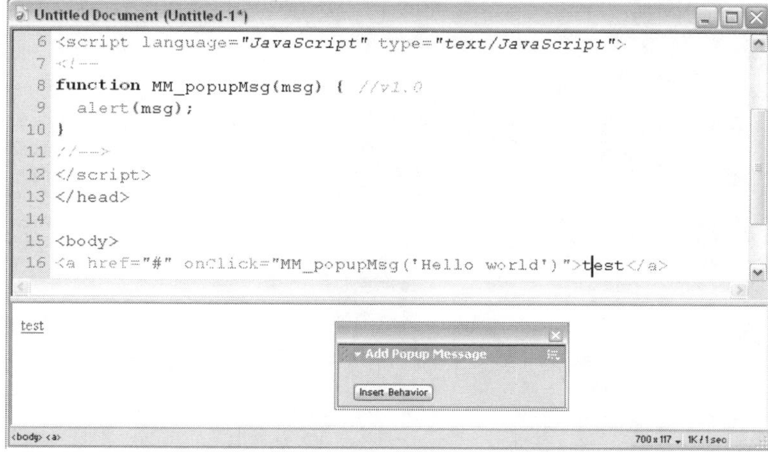

Figure 8.3 *Using a simple floater to insert the Popup Message command.*

8. If you want to give the user a chance to customize the behavior as it's being inserted, you need to collect that information in the floater and feed it to `dom.addBehavior()` to be used in constructing the return statement.

   To try that out, in your text editor, add a text field to the floater file's `<form>` named `message`, like this:

```
<form name="myForm">
<input type="text" name="message">
<input type="button" value="Insert Behavior">
</form>
```

9. Then change your function to collect information from the text field and process it:

```
1 function insertHelloMessage() {
2 myDOM = dw.getDocumentDOM();
3 var message = document.myForm.message.value;
4 message = message.replace(/'/g,"\\'");
5 myDOM.addBehavior("onClick","MM_popupMsg('"+message+"')");
6 }
```

   What's happening here? In line 3, the message is collected from the form. Line 4 escapes any apostrophes the message might contain. Line 5 feeds the revised message into the `addBehavior()` function.

10. Try out the revised floater. Your results should look like those shown in Figure 8.4.

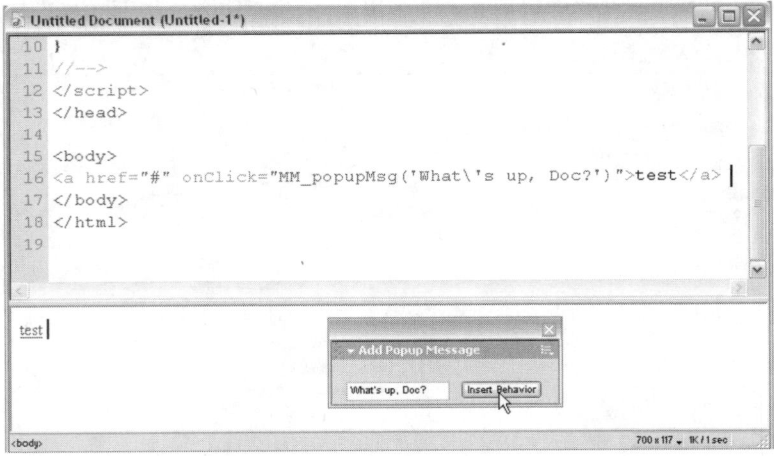

FIGURE 8.4 *Floater that asks for user input, and uses it to create and insert the Popup Message behavior.*

Task 5: Create an object that inserts a behavior and some HTML code

In this task, we'll create an object that inserts a text link into the user's document with the Set Page Properties behavior (or another behavior, if you like) already attached to it. To accomplish this, we'll use `dw.PopupAction()`.

1. Create a new HTML file containing the basic object file framework:

```
<html>
<head>
<title>Interactive Page Properties</title>
<script language="JavaScript">
function objectTag() {
return "";
}
</script>
</head>
<body>
</body>
</html>
```

2. Save this file in the Objects/Development folder as Interactive Page Properties.htm.

3. To make sure the object displays properly in the Insert bar, open Insertbar.xml and add a **<button/>** entry to your Development category:

```
<button id="DW_Development_PageProp"
image=""
enabled=""
showIf=""
file="Development\Interactive Page Properties.htm" />
```

4. The `dw.popupAction()` method only inserts the function code for the specified behavior, but it returns the proper function call. Therefore, your `objectTag()` function has to construct and return the event handler and function call using that returned information.

   To insert an unformatted piece of text that says **Click here** and contains the function call, revise your `objectTag()` function like this:

```
function objectTag() {
myCall = dw.popupAction("Development/Set Page Properties.htm");
returnString = '<a href="#" onClick="'+myCall+'">Click here<\/a>';
return returnString;
}
```

5. Try it out! Launch Dreamweaver and open a new document. From the Development category of the Insert bar, click your new Interactive Page Properties object and see what happens.

6. If you want to give the user the chance to determine the text to be inserted, you need to add a simple form to your object file's <body> section:

```
<body>
<form name="myForm">
<input type="text" name="linkname">
</form>
</body>
```

And revise the objectTag() function to look like this:

```
function objectTag() {
linkname = document.myForm.linkname.value;
myCall = dw.popupAction("Development/Set Page Properties.htm");
returnString = '<a href="#" onClick="'+myCall+'">'+linkname+'<\/a>'
return returnString;
}
```

7. Try out the new object. Your object should call up its own dialog box and then the behavior's dialog box. Your results should look like those shown in Figure 8.5.

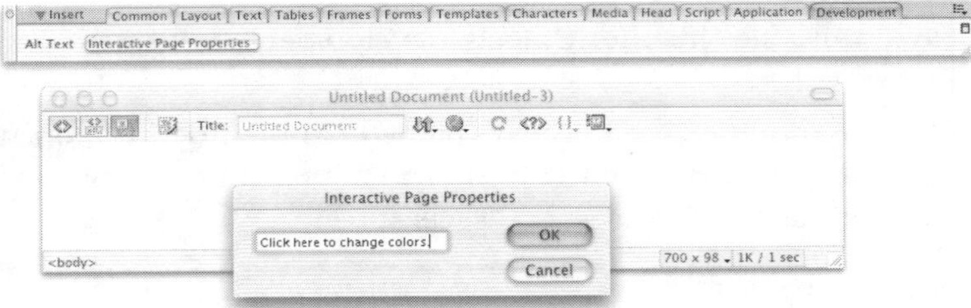

FIGURE 8.5 *An object that inserts a text link already attached to a behavior.*

You may have noticed a problem that is common when you ask Dreamweaver to perform more than one extension task at a time, like this. If the user clicks Cancel in the object's dialog box (the first one that appears), the operation is completely canceled; but if the user clicks Cancel from the behavior's dialog box, an incomplete portion of the intended code gets inserted.

8. To address this, tweak the objectTag() function so it looks like this:

```
function objectTag() {
linkname = document.myForm.linkname.value;
myCall = dw.popupAction("Development/Set Page Properties.htm");
if (myCall) {
returnString = '<a href="#" onClick="'+myCall+'">'+linkname+'<\/a>';
}else{
returnString = "";
}
return returnString;
}
```

There you go! Your object should now insert HTML code plus a behavior. The new behavior will even show up in the Behaviors panel after it's inserted, so the user can edit it from there. Can you see the difference between this sample, using `dw.popupAction()`, and the workings of the `dom.addBehavior()` method? The `dom.addBehavior()` method does not call up the behavior's own dialog box, so it requires you to assemble the function call yourself. The `dw.popupAction()` does call up the behavior's dialog box, but it still requires you to construct the exact function call as appropriate.

Summary

If you worked through the practice exercises here, you should be getting a good idea about how flexible the extension types can be, how to use them to take advantage of each other and build on each other, and how the same task can often be accomplished in many different ways. You should also have a good grasp of the major building blocks that go into Dreamweaver extensibility—the most commonly used types of extensions as well as the API methods available for your extension-writing tasks.

The following chapter covers a different side of Dreamweaver extensibility—writing extensions specifically for use with the Dreamweaver Live Data features.

CHAPTER 9

Server Behaviors

So far, all of the extension types covered in this book have related to Dreamweaver tasks that work for static, as well as dynamic, web sites. But if you're into databases, you know that there's a whole other world of Dreamweaver functionality beyond that—the world of ASP, ASP.NET, JSP, PHP, and ColdFusion. This world is also extensible. The Dreamweaver API allows for creation of custom server models, data sources, and server-side scripting; translation of custom server markup to display in Dreamweaver Design view; opening up communication between Dreamweaver and databases, and between Dreamweaver and web servers; and more. This part of the API is complex and different in many respects from the rest of the API. It has to be, to accommodate the different language structures that server markup can have. This chapter covers the most accessible kind of live data extensibility, and probably the main type of extension you'll want to create for your dynamic pages: the server behavior.

Server Behavior API

This part of the API is complex and is distinctly different from anything you've seen before—to accommodate the different languages and structures the server markup can have. The good news is that unless you want to do something fancy, you don't have to code your server behavior extensions by hand. Dreamweaver provides a special interface, the Server Behavior Builder (SBB), to do the coding for you. In this chapter, we'll take a look at working with the builder; then we'll see what's really going on "under the hood" for those occasions when you want to tweak the coding yourself.

note

Standard extensions such as objects and commands can be used to insert server markup. The advantage of coding your custom markup snippets as server behaviors is that you take advantage of the Dreamweaver management system. For instance, your behavior will appear as a menu choice only if the user is working with the appropriate server model and language (for example, ASP/JavaScript).

Server Behavior Builder

Even fairly complex server-side code can be built into an extension without hand-coding, by using the SBB. The basic procedure is simple:

1. Determine exactly what code you want to insert (and make sure it works!), and which portions if any should be user-specified through a dialog box.
2. In the Server Behaviors panel, click the + button to show the actions list, and choose New Server Behavior (see Figure 9.1). This activates the SBB.

FIGURE 9.1 *Accessing the New Server Behavior command from the Server Behaviors panel.*

3. Follow the instructions in the dialog boxes that follow, and Dreamweaver will build the extension for you.

Some Basic Server Behavior Concepts

Even if you're using the Server Behavior Builder to do all the dirty work, you need to know a few fundamentals of how server behaviors work. These fundamentals will be even more important if you decide to code your own behaviors directly. The following list describes some of these elements, and Figure 9.2 shows how these elements will be added to the SBB main dialog box.

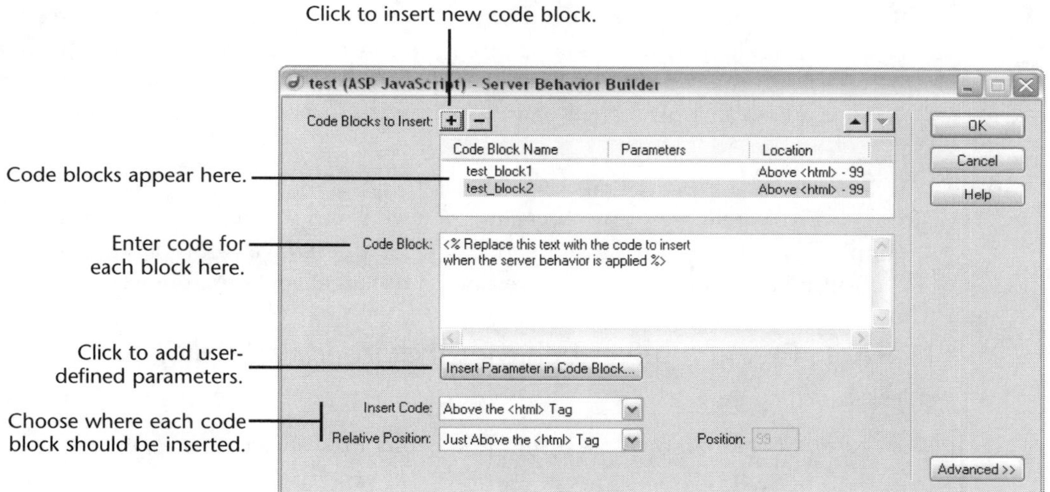

FIGURE 9.2 *The SBB dialog box. Multiple code blocks, parameters, and position/weighting are set here.*

- **Multiple code blocks.** The server markup that comprises a server behavior can consist of several individual blocks of code to be entered in different places in the document. Variables may be set above the `<html>` tag, for instance, and then used in the `<body>`. When defining the behavior, each block must be specified separately.
- **Position and weighting.** The various code blocks in a behavior may need to be positioned at the top of the document, above the opening `<html>` tag; at the bottom, beneath the closing `</html>` tag; or before, after, or surrounding the user's current selection. For code blocks placed above the `<html>` tag, certain blocks may need to precede others. Dreamweaver uses a weighting system, from

1–99, to determine how to order these blocks. The higher a block's weight is, the further down the list it can be placed. A block with a weight of 99 will be added after all other code blocks, directly preceding the `<html>` tag. A block with a weight of 1 will be inserted as the very first piece of code in the document—after the language declaration. For each code block you create, you'll be asked where to position it; if the block should be positioned above the `<html>` tag, you'll also need to specify a weight to determine how it should be placed relative to other above-the-tag elements.

- **Parameters.** If you want your server behavior to include customizable elements that will be determined by user input, you can add parameter placeholders. If the behavior includes one or more parameters, Dreamweaver will automatically generate a dialog box to collect the user input for those parameters. Dreamweaver stores parameter values in the code as `@@parameter_name@@`, so it knows to replace them with user input.

Building Server Behaviors: Practice Session

To see how the SBB works, we'll create a few very simple server behaviors. For the examples shown here, we'll insert various pieces of ASP/JavaScript markup. Feel free to substitute code from another server model or language, if you prefer.

Task 1: Create a server behavior that inserts a "Hello, world" message

For our first behavior, we'll use a simple statement that inserts a line of code:

```
<%="Hello, world!"%>
```

To make things simple, we won't allow for any user input—this behavior will always insert exactly the same hello message.

Before you can proceed with this task, you need to activate the Server Behaviors panel by defining a dynamic site and opening a dynamic document. Take a moment to do that now, using ASP/JavaScript as your server model. (If you want to, follow the example code shown here.)

1. In the Server Behaviors panel, click the + button to access the Behaviors menu. From the menu, choose New Server Behavior. In the dialog box that follows, choose your language (ASP/JavaScript, if you're using the code as shown here), and give your behavior the name **Hello world** (as shown in Figure 9.3). When you're done, click OK to close the dialog box.

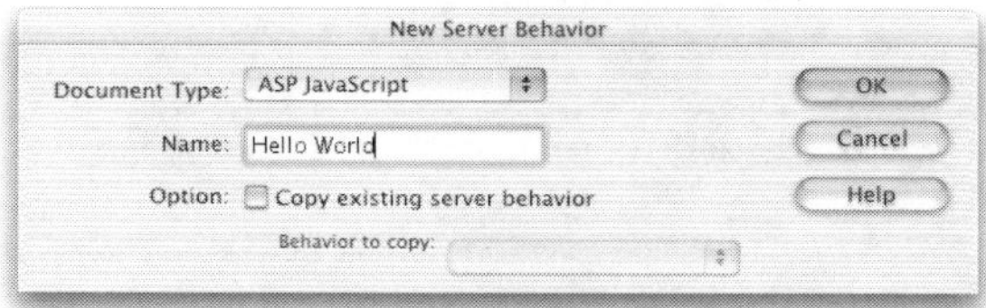

FIGURE 9.3 *Naming the new server behavior, and specifying a language for it.*

2. Next, you're presented with the SBB dialog box. The rest of your behavior building will take place in this interface.
3. Click the + button in the upper left corner to add a new code block. The Create a New Code Block dialog box appears, giving your new code block the default name of `Hello_World_block_1`. That's a fine code block name, so click OK to accept it. Figure 9.4 shows this happening.

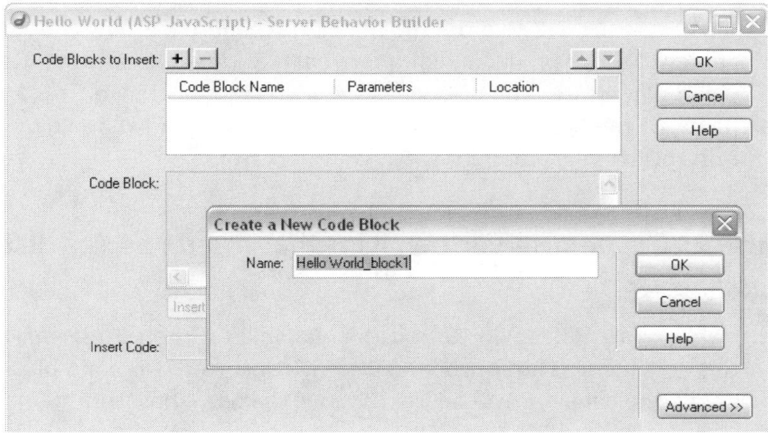

FIGURE 9.4 *Creating a new code block for the Hello World server behavior.*

4. Back in the SBB dialog box, the top information field shows your new code block in place. The middle field now contains some default code for the block. Replace that code with the code chosen earlier in this Task (`<%="Hello, world!"%>`). At the bottom of the dialog box, from the first popup menu choose to insert the code block `Relative to Selection`; from the second popup menu, choose to Replace Current Selection. Figure 9.5 shows this happening.

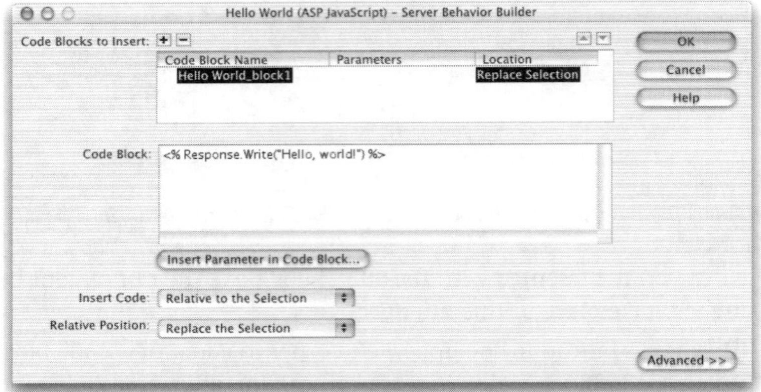

FIGURE 9.5 *The SBB dialog box, showing settings for the Hello World behavior.*

3. That's it! Click OK to close the dialog box, and try it out. As long as you have an ASP/JavaScript document (or whatever kind of document you specified when you created the behavior) open, your new behavior will appear in the + menu of the Server Behavior panel. Inserting it will plug your specified code into the active document, wherever the cursor is.

Task 2: Create a server behavior that inserts a user-defined message

Next, we'll create a behavior that uses a variable to insert a user-specified message into the document. The finished code will consist of two code blocks. Above the `<html>` tag, the behavior will add the following code (shown in ASP/JavaScript):

```
<% var myVar="@@param1@@" %>
```

(The `@@param1@@` value will be replaced by the custom message the user chooses when he inserts the behavior.) At the cursor, the behavior will insert the following:

```
<%=myVar%>
```

1. Start as you did in the previous task, by clicking + in the Server Behaviors panel and choosing New Server Behavior. Name the new behavior **Custom Message**, and choose the appropriate server model and language (ASP/JavaScript to match the examples here).
2. In the SBB dialog box, click + to add a new code block. Leave the code block name at the default (`Custom_Message_block_1`) and click OK to close the dialog box.

3. For the code block, enter the variable declaration shown previously, but without the @@-defined parameter, like this:

```
<% var myVar= %>
```

4. Position the cursor where the parameter should be inserted (after the =) and click the Insert Parameter button. A dialog box opens, asking you to name the parameter. Leave the name at its default (param1) and click OK to close the dialog box (see Figure 9.6). Back in the SBB dialog box, Dreamweaver has entered the parameter code for you.

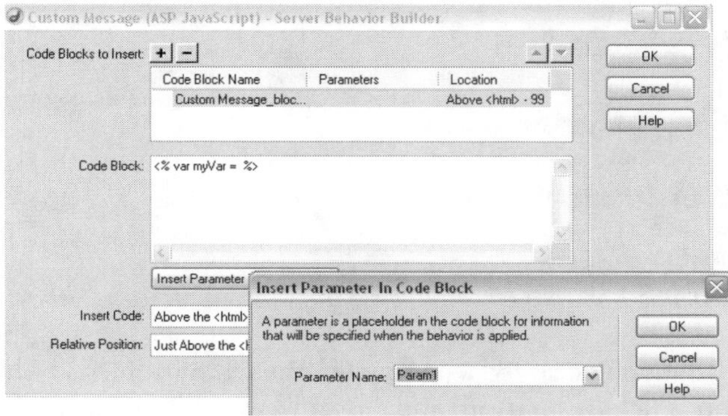

FIGURE 9.6 *Adding a user-defined parameter to a server behavior code block.*

5. For the positioning and weighting of your code block, use the two popup menus to enter the code block just above the <html> tag. (Its relative position above the tag won't matter because the server won't be accessing the variable until the <body> tag has loaded.) Figure 9.7 shows the dialog box as it should appear when you're done.

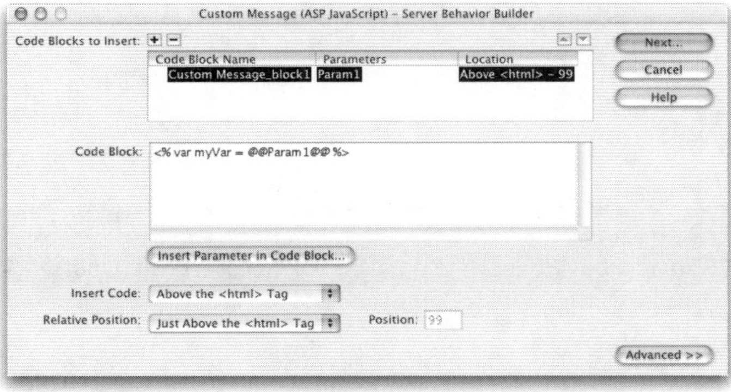

FIGURE 9.7 *The SBB dialog box, with settings in place for the first code block of the Custom Message behavior.*

6. Repeat the previous procedure to create the second code block of your behavior. You won't need to assign any parameters, and the position should be relative to the selection, replacing the current selection. Figure 9.8 shows the finished SBB dialog box.

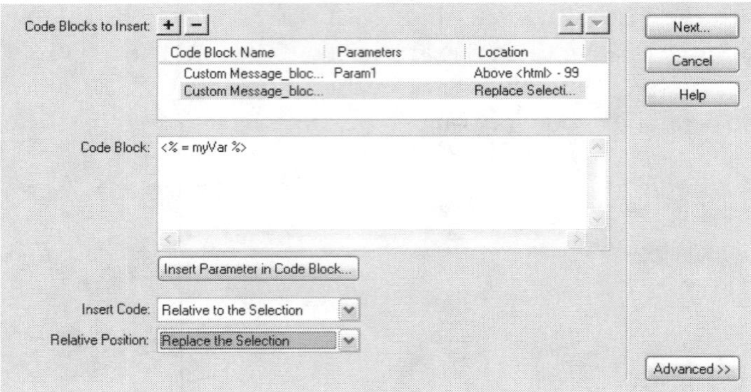

FIGURE 9.8 *The SBB dialog box with all settings for the Custom Message behavior in place.*

7. Now that you've added a parameter, the OK button has been replaced by a Next button. Click this button, and Dreamweaver asks what sort of dialog box should ask for the parameter (see Figure 9.9). For this behavior, leave the input type at **Text Field**, and click OK. Your behavior is finished. Try it out! Figure 9.10 shows the new server behavior being chosen and inserted.

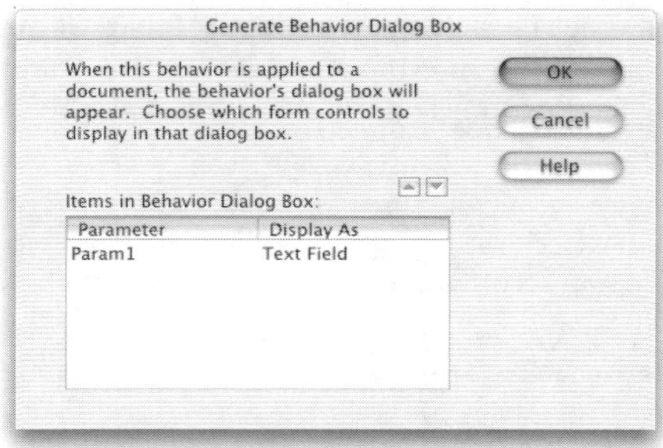

FIGURE 9.9 *The SBB dialog box for creating a dialog box to collect user input.*

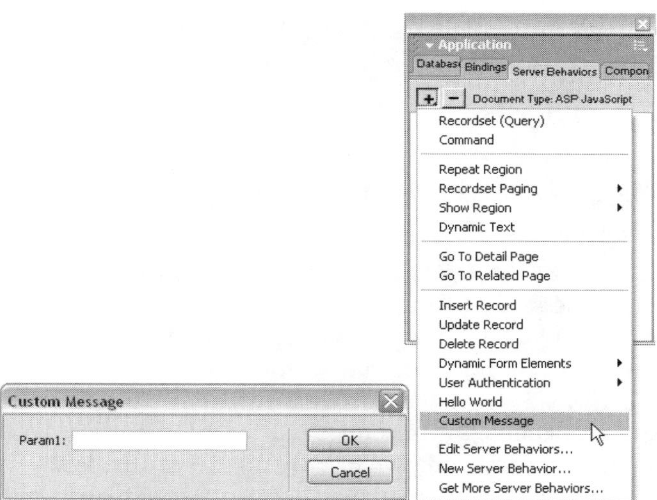

FIGURE 9.10 *The Custom Message server behavior being applied.*

Beyond the SBB: How Server Behaviors Are Constructed

When you use the SBB, extension files are being manipulated and created for you. If you want to move beyond the confines of the SBB—or if you just enjoy knowing what's happening "under the hood" as you work—you'll want to examine the server behavior API in more detail.

Server Behaviors in the Configuration Folder

Each server behavior is constructed from three or more files stored in the Configuration/Server Behaviors folder, in the subfolder corresponding to the appropriate markup language (ASP, JSP, ColdFusion, and so forth).

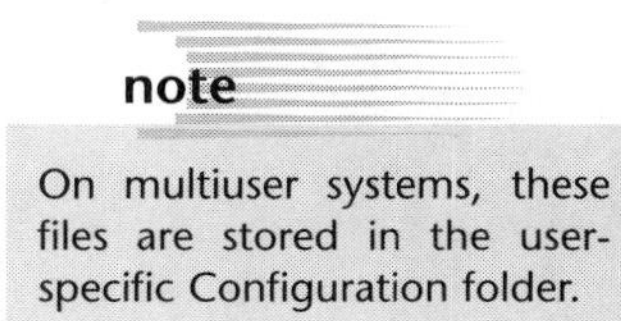

On multiuser systems, these files are stored in the user-specific Configuration folder.

HTML/JS

Like all extensions covered so far, server behaviors begin with an HTML file. The HTML file, with an optional linked JS file, contains instructions for constructing and inserting the server markup into the user's document.

XML

Unlike other extension types covered so far, the API for server behaviors separates the actual content to be inserted—the code blocks—from the instructions on how to insert them. This content is stored in XML files with the .edml filename extension. For each behavior, the following exist:

- One *group file*, containing information for the behavior as a whole
- One *participant file* for each code block, containing the contents of that code block

Why put the code in XML files? Separating form from content like this allows Dreamweaver to efficiently manage similar server behaviors in each of the multiple server languages it supports.

Figure 9.11 shows the Server Behaviors/ASP_JS folder with the various Hello World and Custom Message files in place. Note that each behavior consists of one HTML file (Hello world.htm and Custom Message.htm). In addition, the first behavior consists of two XML files: a group file for the behavior as a whole (Hello World.edml) and one participant file named after the only code block the behavior inserts (Hello World_block_1.edml). The second behavior consists of three files: a group file (Custom Message.edml) and two participant files for the behavior's two code blocks (Custom Message_block_1.edml and Custom Message_block_2.edml).

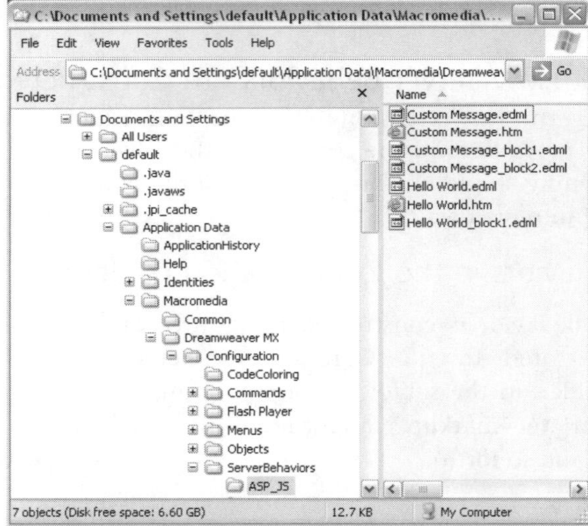

FIGURE 9.11 *The Configuration/Extension Data folder showing the XML data files for the Hello World and Custom Message behaviors.*

Structure of a Server Behavior (XML)

The actual code to be inserted in the behavior is specified through custom tags and attributes in the group and participant XML files. To see the tags in action, examine the XML files for Hello World and Custom Message. For a complete listing of what the tags and attributes mean, check out Chapter 13 of the *Extending Dreamweaver* manual.

Structure of a Server Behavior (HTML/JS)

A server behavior's HTML/JS files must contain various functions and other API elements in order to work properly. (To see these elements at work, examine the files created by the SBB for Hello World and Custom Message.)

Page Title

Whatever appears in the document's `<title>` tag will become the + menu entry for the behavior and the title for any dialog box the behavior calls up.

canApplyServerBehavior(sbObj) Function

This function, which is part of the API and is called automatically, determines whether the behavior can be inserted into the user's document. It requires one argument—a JavaScript object representing the behavior to be inserted—which Dreamweaver passes to it automatically. It returns `true` or `false`.

applyServerBehavior(sbObj) Function

This function, also part of the API and called automatically, inserts whatever code is specified in the XML files into the appropriate places in the user's document. It, too, is automatically passed one argument—a JavaScript object representing the behavior to be inserted. It relies on the `applySB()` helper function to perform the actual code insertion. (See the explanation of helper functions later in this chapter.)

findServerBehaviors() Function

This function is called automatically whenever a document containing an instance of the server behavior is opened. It returns an array of JavaScript objects representing all instances of the current behavior in the document. It relies on the `findSBs()` helper function to perform the actual search. (See explanation of helper functions later in this chapter.)

deleteServerBehavior(sbObj) Function

This API function is called automatically when the user clicks the – button in the Server Behaviors panel. It is automatically passed a JavaScript object representing the behavior as it appears in the document. Its purpose is to delete the behavior. It relies on the `deleteSB()` helper function to perform the actual deletion. (See explanation of helper functions later in this chapter.)

analyzeServerBehavior(sbObj,allRecs) Function

This optional API function, if present, is called automatically, in conjunction with `findServerBehaviors()`, to populate the list of applied behaviors in the Server Behaviors panel. When called, it is automatically passed two parameters: a JavaScript object representing the behavior and an array of records that constitute the data sources for the document. Its purpose is to remove duplicates and other unnecessary items from the behaviors list.

Form

As with any extension, the dialog box for collecting user input is created from a form in the HTML file. The OK and Cancel buttons will be supplied automatically. The form is optional.

inspectServerBehavior(sbObj) Function

This optional API function, if present, is called automatically when the user double-clicks on a behavior in the Server Behaviors panel's list. It is automatically passed a JavaScript object representing the behavior as it appears in the document. Its purpose is to repopulate the behavior's dialog box so the user can edit any parameters.

displayHelp() Function

If this optional API function is present, any dialog box will include a Help button.

Helper Functions

Back in Chapter 2, "Creating Custom Objects," in introducing the Dreamweaver API, we distinguished between functions that are part of an extension type's API procedure and those that are part of the extension-writing API, but not an automatic part of any process. The former type of function is called automatically, but must be individually scripted to return the required values. The latter type must be explicitly called, but is already scripted to return appropriate values. All of the API functions listed previously are of the former type. But several of them call on helper functions of the latter type.

The helper functions allow you to encode server behaviors with functions that are automatically called, which then call helper functions that are already scripted, and return their values. This can leave very little for you to do. The following code, for instance, finds all instances of a particular behavior in a document, without you doing much more than passing control to a helper function and returning its value:

```
function findServerBehaviors() {
var sbObj=findSBs();
return sbObj;
}
```

Helper functions are unique in that each works only within the API function whose name it matches—`findServerBehaviors()` and `findSBs()`, for instance. Table 9.1 lists the specifications of the helper functions.

Table 9.1 Server Behavior Helper Functions

Function	`applySB()`
Description	Inserts or updates the markup code for the server behavior. Must be explicitly called from `applyServerBehavior()`.
Syntax	`applySB(paramObj,sbObj)`
Arguments	`paramObj`—An object representing any user-defined parameters as collected from a dialog box. This object must have a property matching each defined `@@param@@` in the relevant XML file. It is the job of `applyServerBehavior()` to construct this object. `sbObj`—An object representing the server behavior instance that is to be added to the document. This is the same object that Dreamweaver passes to `applyServerBehavior()` when it calls that function.
Returns	True if the code was successfully inserted; false if not.

Example	`function applyServerBehavior(sbObj) {`
	`//create parameter object`
	`paramObj=new Object();`
	`//collect values from dialog box`
	`paramObj.msg=document.myForm.msg.value;`
	`//call the helper function`
	`applySB(paramObj,sbObj);`

Function	`findSBs()`
Description	Finds all instances of the current server behavior in the current document. Must be explicitly called from `findServerBehaviors()`.
Syntax	`findSBs(`*`serverBehaviorTitle`*`);`
Arguments	*`serverBehaviorTitle`* (optional)—Title string used to override the XML title.
Returns	An array of objects, one for each instance of the current behavior found in the document. Object properties contain all behavior information, as well as user-defined parameters (see example following).

Example	`function findServerBehaviors() {`
	`listSBs=findSBs();`
	`return listSBs;`
	`}`
	
	Assuming the document contains one instance of the Custom Message behavior, this function will return the following array:

continues

Function	`findSBs()`

	`listSBs[0].title="Custom Message (@@myVar@@)";`
	`listSBs[0].type="CustomMessage";`
	`listSBs[0].selectedNode=null;`
	`listSBs[0].incomplete=false;`
	`listSBs[0].participants[0]=someAspNodePointer;`
	`listSBs[0].weights[0]=aboveHTML+99;`
	`listSBs[0].types[0]="CustomMessage_block1";`
	`listSBs[0].participants[1]=someAspNodePointer;`
	`listSBs[0].weights[1]=replaceSelection;`
	`listSBs[0].types[1]="CustomMessage_block2";`
	`listSBs[0].parameters.Param1="This is my message.";`
	
	(Compare the results here with the specifications in the Custom FMessage XML files.)

Function	`deleteSB()`
Description	Deletes all code blocks relating to the selected instance of the current behavior. Must be explicitly called from `deleteServerBehaviors()`.
Syntax	`findSBs(`*`sbObj`*`);`
Arguments	`sbObj`—An object representing the server behavior instance that is to be added to the document. This is the same object that Dreamweaver passes to `deleteServerBehavior()` when it calls that function.
Returns	Nothing

Example	`function deleteServerBehavior(sbObj) {`
	`deleteSB(sbObj);`
	`}`

API Procedure for Server Behaviors

Figure 9.12 diagrams the API procedure for processing server behaviors. As the diagram shows, various processes can occur, initiated by the user adding, editing, duplicating, or deleting behaviors, or opening documents containing behaviors. The diagram also shows the importance of the JavaScript object array, created by `findServerBehaviors()` and accessed by other functions. It also shows the interrelationship between the main API functions and their helper functions, and how all processes depend on JavaScript objects representing behavior instances in the document.

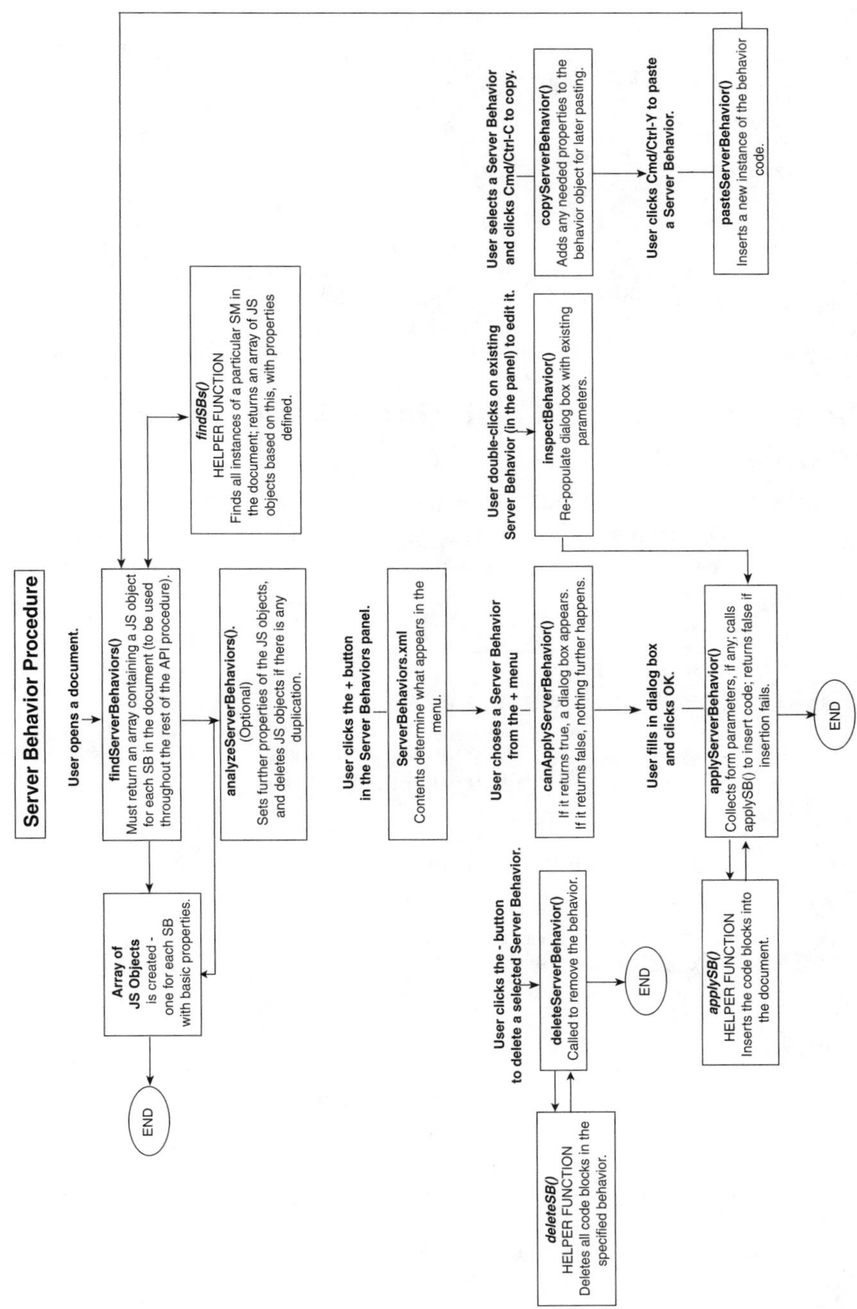

FIGURE 9.12 *The API procedure for processing server behaviors. User actions are indicated by text outside boxes.*

We'll finish up this look at Server Behaviors with two workshops that will show you how to build behaviors with the SBB and beyond. For the projects and code written here, we'll be using the ASP/JavaScript server model. To develop and test them, you'll need access to an ASP server and a simple database.

note

You can download some sample ASP and database files to play with from this book's companion web site, `www.newriders.com` (see Appendix F, "Contents of the Extensions Workshop Companion Web Site" for full details).

Workshop #1: Inserting Conditional Page Content with an If-Then Statement

For this workshop, we'll build a behavior that accomplishes a simple but incredibly useful task: displaying certain page content only if a particular field in a data source has a certain value. Our behavior will insert the if-then conditional statement that will wrap around some piece of page content, allowing that content to be hidden or shown as needed.

Task 1: Create the code to insert

As with any extension, a server behavior is only as good as the code it inserts. Also, with server behaviors as with regular behaviors, the code must be scripted according to certain formats, or it won't fit into the SBB's model, and it won't work.

Your conditional statement, written using the ASP/JavaScript model, might look like this:

```
<% if (Recordset.Fields.Item("fieldName").Value==testValue) {
Response.Write("conditional content here");
}
%>
```

But you wouldn't be able to wrap this code around complex existing content. So instead, you'll write it like this (conditional content to be hidden or shown is displayed here in italic):

```
<%
if (Recordset.Fields.Item("fieldName").Value==testValue) {
%>
<h1>conditional content here</h1>
<%
}
%>
```

Splitting up the code like this lets you create a server behavior in two code blocks—one before the user's current selection and one after. Thus, when using this server behavior, the user will select an image or table or text block, choose the server behavior, and that object will become conditional—a procedure similar to defining a repeating region. (If you're not sure of this code or how it will work, test it out in its hand-coded form before building it into the behavior.)

Task 2: Create the behavior with hard-coded values

After you have code that works, open the Server Behavior panel and choose New Server Behavior... from the + menu. Call your new behavior **If-Then**, choose the server model you want to use (ASP/JavaScript to match the examples here), and click OK to access the New Server Behavior dialog box. Here's where the building really happens.

1. In the New Server Behavior dialog box, click + to create the first code block. Leave the name at its default (`If-Then_block1`) and click OK to return to the New Server Behavior dialog box. In the code field, enter the first portion of the code discussed in Task 1:

```
<%
if (Recordset.Fields.Item("fieldName").Value==testValue) {
%>
```

For positioning, choose Relative to Selection and Before Selection.

note

Why not use one code block set to Wrap Around the Selection, instead of two code blocks? The wrap feature works only for tag pairs, such as `<cfm></cfm>`.

2. Now click + to create the second code block. Again, accept the default name for the code block. In the code field, enter the second portion of code discussed in the previous task:

```
<%
}
%>
```

   For positioning, choose Relative to Selection and After Selection.

3. Figure 9.13 shows how the completed dialog box should look with the first code block selected. When you have both code blocks in place, click OK to finish.

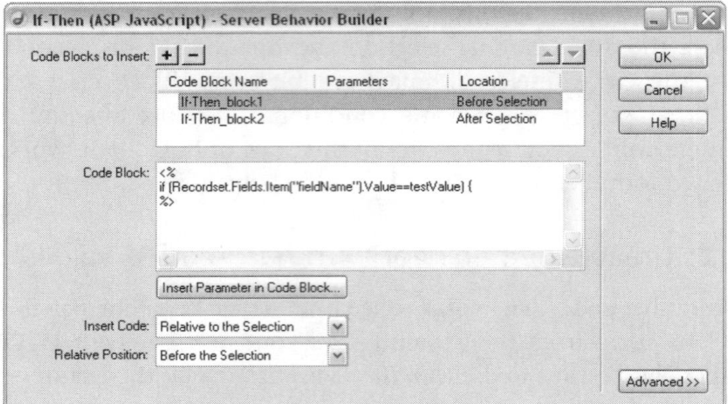

FIGURE 9.13 *The SBB main dialog box with code blocks assigned for the If-Then server behavior.*

4. Test your behavior. Open a dynamic document (ASP/JavaScript, if you're following the examples here) and enter some simple content, like a line of text or a heading. Select the content and insert your server behavior. It should wrap around your content, turning it into conditional content. The code should look exactly the same as the code you created by hand in Task 1. If it doesn't, tweak it until it does.

Task 3: Replace hard-coded values with parameters

The trickiest part of using the SBB can be figuring out how to add parameters to the code, how to treat quotation marks, and so on. Remember that each parameter will become a field in the behavior's dialog box. Also be aware of a few parameter-entering gotchas:

- If a value appears in quotes in the final code, those quotes must be present surrounding the parameter.
- No + concatenation operators are necessary between parameters and nonparameter code.
- If the parameters refer to a recordset field, the recordset must be set in a separate parameter from the recordset field. This will become clear as you work.

With these dangers in mind, proceed to replace the hard-coded recordset and field name in your server behavior with user-specified parameters.

1. In the Server Behaviors panel, click +, and choose Edit Server Behavior from the menu. From the dialog box that appears, find the If-Then behavior and click Edit. This brings you back to the SBB main dialog box.

2. Select the first code block and take a look at its code. The hard-coded values you'll be replacing appear here in bold:

```
<% if (Recordset.Fields.Item("fieldName").Value == testValue) {
%>
```

3. Select and delete the word `Recordset`. Then click the Insert Parameter button. Call the parameter `testRS`. It will appear in the code surrounded by @@ signs.
4. Repeat the process with `fieldName`, being careful to select only the word and not its surrounding quotes. Call this parameter `testField`.
5. Finally, replace `testValue` with a parameter called `testVal`. Your code should now look like this (replaced values appear in bold):

```
<% if (@@testRS@@.Fields.Item("@@testField@@").Value == @@testVal@@) {
%>
```

6. The OK button now says Next.... Click that button to set up your dialog box. You want the `testRS` form input element to be a Recordset menu, `testField` to be a Recordset Field menu, and `testVal` to be a regular text field. Figure 9.16 shows these options being chosen. You can also use the up and down arrows in this dialog box to rearrange the parameters, which will determine how they appear in the behavior's dialog box.

FIGURE 9.14 *Setting up the input elements for the If-Then behavior's dialog box.*

7. After you've done this, close all dialog boxes and test out your revised behavior. Make sure it still inserts the same code structure that you determined in Task 1. (Note that because you've included a Recordset Menu as one of your If-Then parameters, you'll have to be working in a dynamic document that already contains at least one recordset before Dreamweaver will let you apply this server behavior.) Figure 9.15 shows the dialog box for inserting the If-Then behavior, and the resulting code inserted into a document.

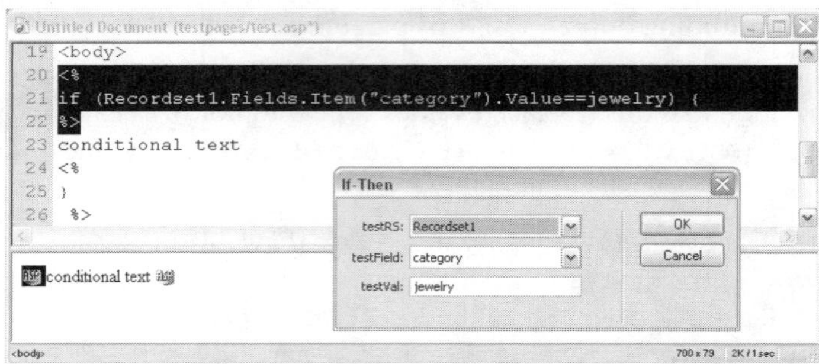

FIGURE 9.15 *The If-Then dialog box with values chosen, and the resulting server markup the behavior inserts into a document.*

Task 4: Refine the behavior's appearance in the Server Behaviors panel

After the behavior has been inserted into a document, do you like the way it is titled as it appears in the Server Behaviors panel? More importantly, what happens when you select the applied behavior from the behaviors list? Doing that should select one of the code blocks in the document. For this behavior, it should select the first code block because that's where the main if-then statement exists.

If either of these things isn't to your liking, go to Edit Server Behavior again, and this time click the Advanced button to expand the main dialog box. Choose the code block to select, and change the title if you like. Figure 9.16 shows this happening.

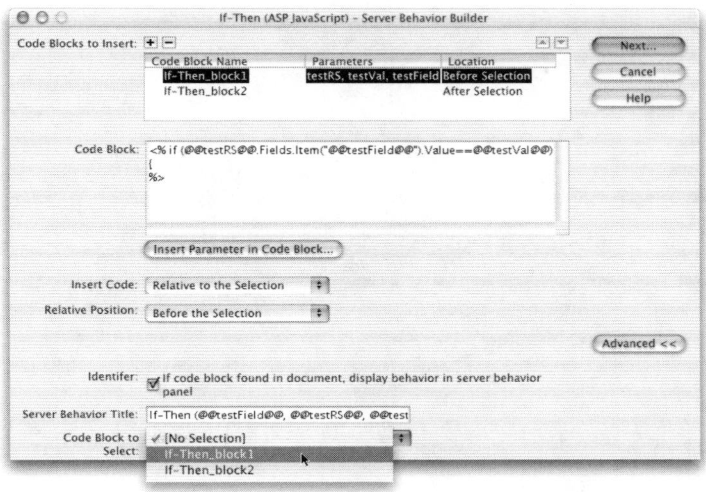

FIGURE 9.16 *The SBB dialog box with Advanced options showing.*

Task 5: Refine the If-Then Server Behavior's dialog box

We've gone about as far as we can with the SBB. It's time to dip into the extension files to make the dialog box look a little more user-friendly.

1. Either in Dreamweaver or your text editor, find and open Configuration/ServerBehaviors/ASP_JS/If-Then.htm. This is your behavior's main extension file, which contains the code for the dialog box.
2. What can you safely do in this file? For one thing, you can rename the interface elements so they have friendlier names than `test_RS` and so forth. You can also adjust how the form elements are laid out, if you don't find the default positioning intuitive. Figure 9.17 shows the dialog box being revised in Dreamweaver Design view, and the resulting dialog box created by these changes.

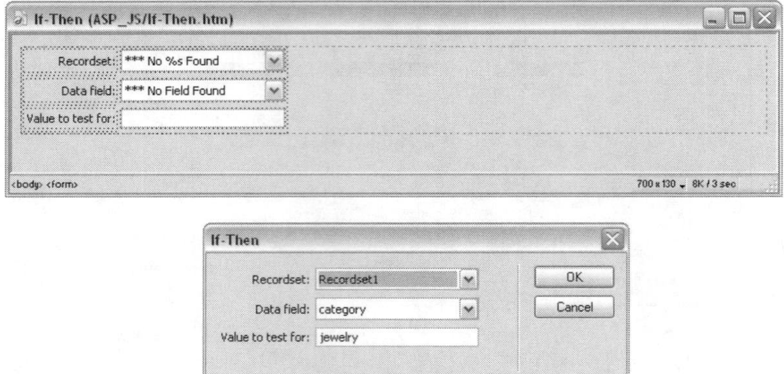

Figure 9.17 *The If-Then dialog box layout being edited in Dreamweaver, and the resulting interface changes.*

Task 6: Add an Expression option to the dialog box

One possible source of confusion for your users is that some test values need to be in quotes (strings), and others don't (expressions and numbers). We can easily add a checkbox to the dialog box to let users choose which kind of information they want to enter. Based on that checkbox, we'll add or remove quote marks from the value in the `testVal` field. All we need to do is create a function that reads the checkbox value and adjusts the field contents; then call that function when the user clicks OK to insert the behavior.

1. Still in the If-Then.htm extension file, add a row to the bottom of the table, with a check box and Expression label, like that shown in Figure 9.18.

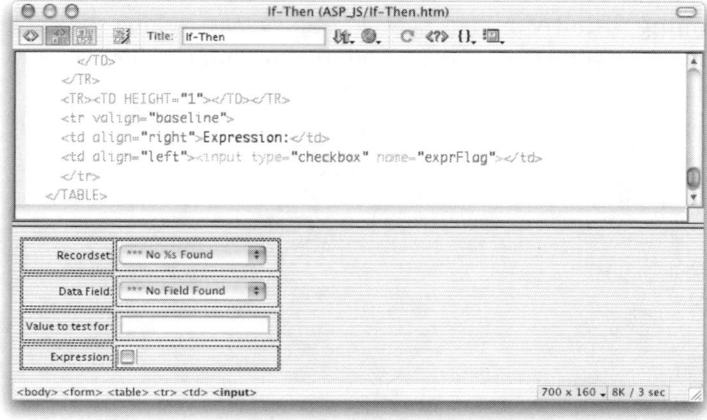

Figure 9.18 *The If-Then dialog box with an Expression option checkbox at the bottom.*

2. Now add a new function to the <head> section to account for this new input. Like this:

```
1 function checkQuotes() {
2 var testVal=document.theForm.testVal.value;
3 var exprFlag=document.theForm.exprFlag.checked;
4 var regexp=/^["'].*["']$/; //look for quotes at beginning and end
5 if (testVal.search(regexp) <0) { //if there are no quotes
6    document.theForm.testVal.value=(exprFlag)?testVa1:'"'+testVal+'"';
7    }else{ //if there are quotes
8    document.theForm.testVal.value=(exprFlag)?testVal.substring
     ➥(1,testVal.length-1):testVal;
9    }
10 }
```

What is this function doing? In line 2, it creates a variable (`testVal`) to collect the information entered into the text field. Then in line 3, it creates another variable (`exprFlag`) to determine whether the checkbox is selected or not. And it sets up a regular expression (`regexp`) to easily find quotes that might already be surrounding the text field value. Starting in line 5, then, a conditional tests to see if the text field contains no quotes. If line 5 finds no quotes, line 6 processes `testVal`, adding quotes if `exprFlag` is not selected. If line 5 finds quotes, line 8 processes `testVal`, removing quotes if `exprFlag` is selected.

In short, if the user has selected the `exprFlag` check box, the function makes sure there are no quotes surrounding `testVal`; if the user has not selected the check box, the function makes sure there are quotes.

3. Finally, you need to call this the `checkQuotes()` function. You want it to execute when the user clicks OK to apply the server behavior, but before any of the standard API functions execute. Because the OK button isn't coded into the If-Then.htm file, you can't use a standard event handler to trigger it. But if you know your way around the API procedure for server behaviors, you can piggyback it onto one of the functions that Dreamweaver calls automatically when the user clicks OK.

   Check out the API procedure diagram in Figure 9.12, and you'll see that the first API function to be executed when the user clicks OK is the `applyServerBehavior()` function. This function's job is to prepare data and pass it to `applySB()` for insertion.

   In the If-Then.htm file, find the `applyServerBehavior()` function. Call `checkQuotes()` at the very beginning of this function, so it executes before the behavior is processed (new code is in bold):

```
function applyServerBehavior(sbObj)
{
checkQuotes();
  var paramObj = new Object();
  var errStr = "";
etc
}
```

4. Try it out! Back in Dreamweaver, try inserting the If-Then server behavior into a dynamic document with various different values in the `testVal` field, with and without the `exprFlag` checkbox selected. The If-Then server behavior is now complete.

Workshop #2: Inserting Dynamically Determined Images

This behavior comes from one of my favorite database tricks: using an ID field from a database record to construct names and pathnames of images to insert in documents. An online catalog, for instance, might give each inventory item a unique ID such as `CW-11`. The manufacturer of that item might have the unique ID `CW`. Given those IDs, if I save a picture of the product as **CW-11.jpg,** and store it in a folder with all my other images, I can construct image paths for my documents without having to add an extra database field to store the image name or path. Although it's certainly possible to use the dynamic attributes available in Dreamweaver to accomplish this same thing, there's a lot less typing and thinking involved if it can be packaged up into a nice neat server behavior.

Task 1: Create the code to insert

This particular task highlights the limitations that the Dreamweaver API puts on syntax for server markup. One way to code the dynamic image tag is as a series of dynamic attributes, like this:

```
<img src= "Images/" + <% Stuff.Fields.Item("itemID").Value %> + ".jpg"
alt="<%Stuff.Fields.Item("itemID").Value%>">
```

But this would require either inserting one code block that consists of multiple tags, or multiple code blocks of incomplete tags, and the SBB doesn't allow for these. But we can write the code like this:

```
<%
var folderpath="images/";
var basename=Inventory.Fields.Item("itemID").Value;
var fileExt=".jpg";
var altLabel=Inventory.Fields.Item("itemname").Value;
%>

<img<%=' src="'+folderpath+basename+fileExt+'" alt="'+altLabel+'"' %>>
```

Because this code consists of two complete tags (the `<% %>` pair and the `<img>` tag itself), it can be inserted as a two-block server behavior. So that's the code we'll choose to insert. (Again, test it if you're not sure what it's doing, or not sure that you have it coded correctly.)

Task 2: Create the behavior with hard-coded values

Repeating the procedure from the previous workshop, choose the New Server Behavior command and create a behavior called Dynamic Image. Create two code blocks for it, based on the code shown in Task 1, and test it out to make sure it works. Figure 9.19 shows the SBB dialog box with code block entries completed.

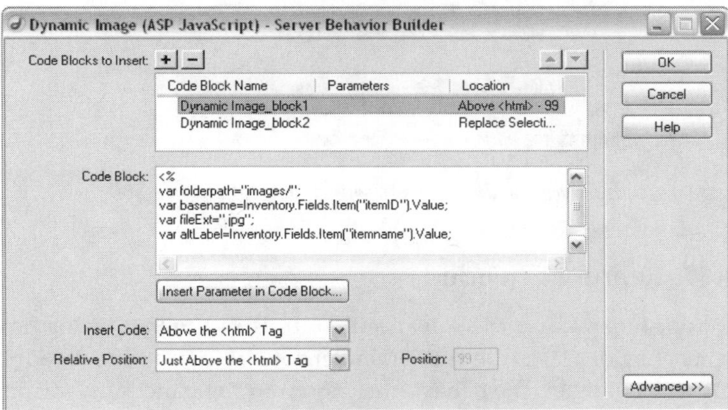

FIGURE 9.19 *The SBB dialog box for the Dynamic Image server behavior.*

Task 3: Replace hard-coded values with parameters

This also is the same as in the previous workshop. Be careful, though, with your quotes! There are a lot of them to watch out for in this bit of concatenating. The final code for your second code block won't have any parameters added to it. The code for your first code block should have the following parameters inserted in place of hard-coded entries (parameters are shown in bold):

```
<%
var folderpath="@@folderpathParam@@";
var basename=@@rsSrcParam@@.Fields.Item("@@fieldSrcParam@@").Value;
var fileExt="@@fileExtParam@@";
var altLabel=@@rsAltParam@@.Fields.Item("@@fieldAltParam@@").Value;
%>
```

When you're done adding the parameters, make sure you set the dialog box up so that the proper input elements are used for each one. As before, you'll have a mixture of text fields, Recordset menus, and Recordset Field menus. Figure 9.20 shows the proper assignment of element types.

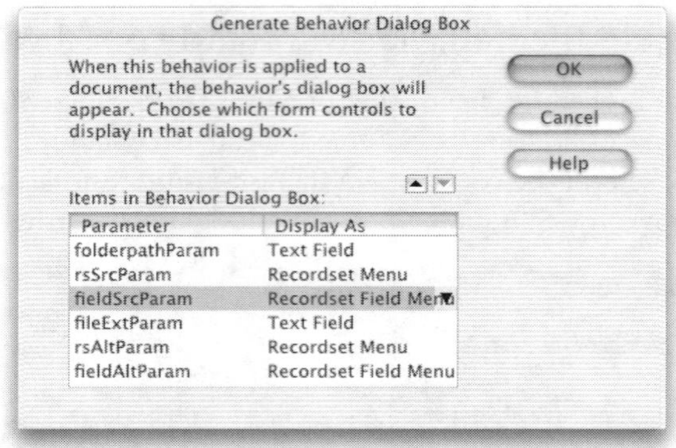

FIGURE 9.20 *Setting up the Dynamic Image behavior dialog box in the SBB.*

Task 4: Refine as needed

As in Workshop #1, use the Advanced controls in the SBB dialog box to determine how the behavior appears in the Server Behaviors panel and to determine which code block is selected when the behavior is chosen in the panel's list of applied behaviors. Open Dynamic Image.htm (in Configuration/Server Behaviors/ASP_JS) and tweak the form layout as desired, relabeling the form elements for user-friendliness. Figure 9.21 shows what the refined dialog box might look like.

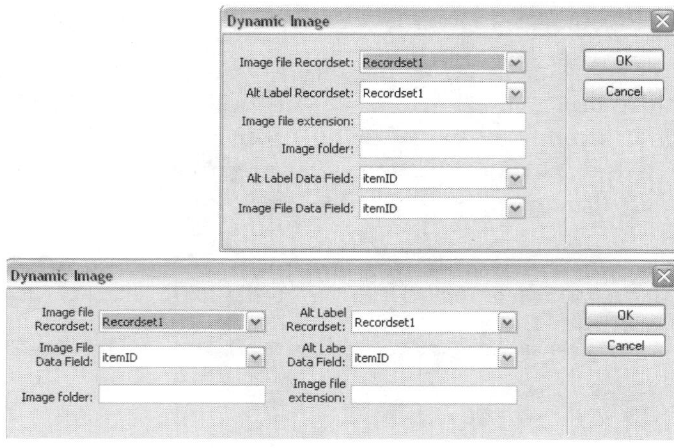

FIGURE 9.21 *The Dynamic Image dialog box with a slightly revised layout.*

Task 5: Add error-checking

Here's where you need to dip a little further into the extension files. What if the user forgets to add the trailing / after the folder name? What if the user specifies a `.jpg` or `.gif` file extension, but forgets the opening `.`? This sort of validation and fixing-up is a nicety of good interface design. Adding it means revising the `applyServerBehavior()` function.

1. Open the Dynamic Image.htm file in your text editor and find its `applyServerBehavior()` function. You should see the following code:

```
function applyServerBehavior(sbObj) {
  var paramObj = new Object();
  var errStr = "";
  if (!errStr)
    errStr = _folderpathParam.applyServerBehavior(sbObj, paramObj);
  if (!errStr)
    errStr = _rsSrcParam.applyServerBehavior(sbObj, paramObj);
  if (!errStr)
    errStr = _fieldSrcParam.applyServerBehavior(sbObj, paramObj);
  if (!errStr)
    errStr = _fileExtParam.applyServerBehavior(sbObj, paramObj);
  if (!errStr)
    errStr = _rsAltParam.applyServerBehavior(sbObj, paramObj);
  if (!errStr)
    errStr = _fieldAltParam.applyServerBehavior(sbObj, paramObj);
  if (!errStr) {
    fixUpSelection(dw.getDocumentDOM(), true, true);
    applySB(paramObj, sbObj)
  }
  return errStr;
}
```

   What's happening here? Before the behavior can be inserted, all data must be collected into an object representing the behavior's main code—`sbObj`—and an object representing the user-defined parameters—`paramObj`. Those two objects are then passed to the `applySB()` helper function. In order to create the parameter object, each of the dialog box's input elements has been defined as an instance of a custom class, and a class method is being called that retrieves the user's input and turns it into a property of the `paramObj` object. Assuming you named your parameters the same as in the example code, your `paramObj` will end up having the following properties assigned to it:

```
paramObj.folderpathParam;
paramObj.rsSrcParam;
paramObj.fieldSrcParam;
paramObj.fileExtParam;
paramObj.rsAltParam;
paramObj.fieldAltParam;
```

Can you see where these names came from? By the time `applySB()` is called at the bottom of the main function, all of these properties will have data in them. You can use those properties for error-checking.

2. Add the following lines of code directly above the `applySB()` function call (new code is in bold):

```
1  function applyServerBehavior(sbObj) {
etc
18 //begin error-checking
19 var extString=paramObj.fileExtParam;
20 if (extString.search(/\./)<0) {
21    paramObj.fileExtParam="."+extString;
22    }//end if
23 var folderString=paramObj.folderpathParam;
24 if (folderString.search(/\/$/)<0) {
25    paramObj.folderpathParam+="/";
26    }//end if
27 //end error-checking
28    applySB(paramObj, sbObj)
29  }
30  return errStr;
31 }
```

What is this code doing? Lines 19–22 collect the value the user has entered as a file extension (`fileExtParam`), and use a conditional to determine if a `.` needs to be added at the beginning. Lines 23–26 collect the folder path (`folderPathParam`) and use a conditional to determine if a `/` needs to be added at the end.

3. When your error-checking is in place, try out your new behavior. Can you enter parameters in the Dynamic Image dialog box that will break it? If so, come back to the `applyServerBehavior()` function and expand your error-checking as needed. Keep tinkering until you have a nice, robust server behavior.

That's the end of the workshop. Is it the end of what you can do with server behaviors? Certainly not! You can go much further than this in customizing the `applyServerBehavior()` and other API functions, though it's a difficult undertaking because the server behavior API is built from so many diverse, interrelated modules. But as long as you don't interfere with the main workings of the behavior, as set up by the SBB, you can still add data preparation and error-checking to fine-tune your behaviors.

Summary

In this chapter, you looked at the most commonly used and easily accessible means of extending dynamic data functions: creating custom server behaviors. Believe it or not, you have barely scratched the surface of what's possible with dynamic data-related extension projects. other extension types in this area include translators, data sources, connections, server formats, and server models. Custom objects in the API that relate to dynamic data include `MMDB` (for communicating with databases), `MMHttp` (for communicating with web servers), `dw.serverBehaviorInspector`, and `dw.dbi`. Read all about them in the *Extending Dreamweaver* manual.

CHAPTER 10

Into the Great Beyond

Here we are, at the last chapter. If you've worked your way through the previous nine chapters, doing all the exercises and building all the projects, you're in pretty good shape to go off extending on your own. You don't know everything there is to know, but you've worked with objects, behaviors, commands, menus, inspectors, floating panels, and even server behaviors. Think of this chapter as the ice cream at the end of the meal, the cherry on top. Instead of learning how to make different kinds of extensions, this chapter rounds off the book by looking at how to make the extensions we can make better, prettier, and with more powerful interfaces. The chapter also introduces an amazing set of resources for creating efficient interfaces: shared class files and image files tucked away in the Configuration/Shared folder.

The Nature of Class Files

The Dreamweaver API, as you should know by now, includes a wide range of custom JavaScript objects for handling different scripting tasks. From the `dw` and `dom` objects, which we've been using throughout this book, to the `site` object, to much more specialized objects such as `SWFFile` and `FWLaunch`, there are dozens of custom objects comprising thousands of methods and properties to help us extend Dreamweaver functionality.

In addition to these objects that are built into the API, however, the Macromedia engineers have used JavaScript to write a whole series of custom object classes that build on the API. These classes are defined in JavaScript files in the Configuration/Shared folder, with the most commonly used files being found in the Configuration/Shared/Common subfolder. The dwscripts.js file, for instance—which we have used throughout this book—defines the `dwscripts` class to hold its utility functions. Link your extension file to this file, and access the `dwscripts` utilities at will.

This chapter focuses on using classes that extend our ability to control the interfaces of our extensions. These include ListControls, ImageButtons, and TabControls.

SHARE-IN-MEMORY and Shared JavaScript Files

Some of Macromedia's shared JavaScript files—such as dwscripts.js and most of the class files—include a directive as the first line of the file: `//SHARE-IN-MEMORY=true`. This directive means that, once any HTML extension file links to that file and uses any of its contents, that JavaScript file is stored in memory until the next time the user quits Dreamweaver. Any other HTML extension file can then reference functions and variables stored in that JavaScript file without explicitly linking to it (without having to include the <script src="...etc..."></script> tag in its code). So, strictly speaking, you don't have to link to commonly used shared files like dwscripts.js or ListControlClass.js before using their utility functions or implementing ListControl elements. Just remember, though—every time the user launches Dreamweaver, the first HTML extension to need the shared JavaScript file must explicitly link to it; just in case your extension is first in line to use the shared functionality, it's safer to always add the <script src="etc"></script> tag to your extension files whenever you want to use shared files. The purpose of the SHARE-IN-MEMORY directive is to speed up Dreamweaver rather than to save you the trouble of creating links.

ListControl Items

ListControl interface elements are found throughout the Dreamweaver interface. Any time the interface presents multiple selection lists that interact with each other, those are ListControls. Any time a panel or dialog box displays a selection list that includes + and – buttons (and maybe up and down arrows), that's another ListControl. Figure 10.1 shows just a few of the many examples of ListControl elements Dreamweaver provides for its users.

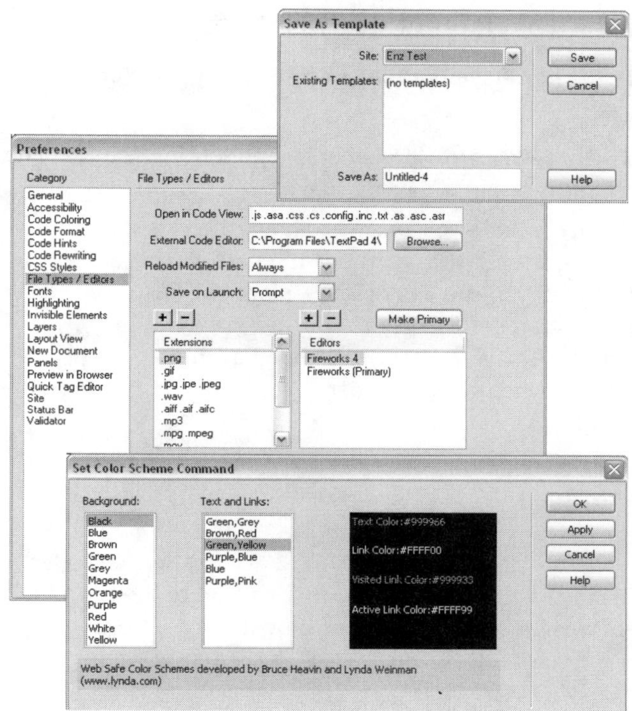

FIGURE 10.1 *Several ListControl elements at work in the Dreamweaver interface.*

How are ListControls created? Unlike tree structures or color buttons, ListControls are not custom form elements. There's nothing official in the API about them. They're nothing more than `<select>` input elements (form lists or menus) with some extra coding to govern their functionality. That extra coding is not built into the API. Rather, it's tucked away in the ListControlClass.js file, in the Shared/Common/Scripts folder. To take advantage of that extra coding, all you have to do is link your extension file to ListControlClass.js.

Specifications

Using a ListControl involves making changes to both the interface layout and the scripting of an extension file.

The ListControl Element in the Interface

To add a ListControl element to your interface, your `<form>` code should include the following:

- A named `<select>` form element, representing the list. The `<select>` element can occur in or out of layers.
- (Optional) A table cell or layer above the one containing the list that contains the buttons at the list's head. In this cell or layer, place the following shared images (found in the Shared/MM/Images/ folder), all coded as image button form elements, in order:
  1. btnAdd.gif
  2. btnDelete.gif
  3. btnUp.gif
  4. btnDown.gif

> **note**
>
> To create multiple button states (grayed out, normal, and so on), you'll need to access the `ImageButton` class, discussed in the following section.

If your ListControl includes images, this portion of the layout table will look like the one shown in Figure 10.2. (The form shown is from Commands/Insert Nav Bar.htm. Note that the `<select>` element itself has been assigned a pixel width using the `style` property.)

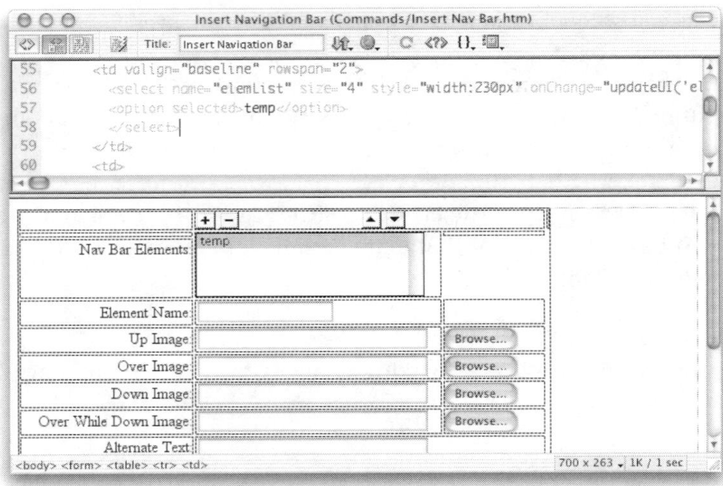

FIGURE 10.2 *A form including a ListControl element, shown in Dreamweaver Code and Design view.*

Scripting a ListControl Element

Before you can add a ListControl element to an extension file, you must link to ListControlClass.js. Add the following script tag to the `<head>` section:

```
<script src="../Shared/Common/Scripts/ListControlClass.js"></script>
```

Depending on where in the Configuration folder your extension file is stored, the relative path in this `<script>` tag will vary.

Next, the ListControl element should be added to the `<script>` section of the extension file like this:

- At the top of the head's `<script>` section, declare a global variable to be used as the name of the ListControl—but don't give it a value:

  ```
  var MyList;
  ```

- In the `initializeUI()` function, use a constructor statement (a line of code that generates a new instance of a class, like the ListControl class) to create a new ListControl from the global variable, referring to the name of your `<select>` form element:

  ```
  MyList = new ListControl(selectName);
  ```

The name of the new ListControl must be the same as the global variable created in the previous step. The constructor has one argument, the name of the `<select>` element to be connected to this new ListControl. All the ListControl methods, as described in ListControlClass.js, are now available to you! Table 10.1 details the specifications of these methods.

note

It's important to remember that the visual element is the HTML `<select>` menu. The ListControl object is a JavaScript object, which has its own properties and methods but has no visual interface of its own. That's why the `<select>` element and the ListControl object must be created separately, and then joined so that they function together.

Table 10.1 Methods of the ListControl Object Class. To Access These Methods, Your Extension File Must Be Llinked to the Class File.

Creating and Managing ListControl Structures

Syntax	*Description*
`list.refresh()`	Captures the current selection
`list.enable()`	Enables control if not already enabled
`list.disable()`	Disables control if not already disabled

Putting Information into a List

Syntax	*Description*
`list.init()`	Sets the list to the current HTML text and values
`list.setAll (labelList,valueList)`	Sets the entire list at once
`list.add()`	Adds a new blank line after the selected line
`list.add (labelString)`	Adds text
`list.add (labelString, valueString)`	Adds text and an associated value
`list.append()`	Appends a new blank line to the end of the list
`list.append (valueString)`	Appends default text
`list.append (valueString, value)`	Appends text and an associated value
`list.del()`	Deletes the selected line
`list.set (textstring)`	Sets the text of the current selection
`list.set (textString, `*n*`)`	Sets the text of the *n*th item
`list.init()`	Sets the entire list to the current HTML text and values
`list.setValue (value)`	Sets the value of the current selection
`list.setValue (value, `*n*`)`	Set the value of the *n*th item
`list.setIndex(`*n*`)`	Sets the selection to the number given as *n*

Getting Information from a List

Syntax	*Description*
`list.get()`	Returns the current selection text
`list.get(n)`	Returns the text of item *n* (starts at zero)
`list.get('all')`	Returns an array of all text items
`list.getValue()`	Returns the current selection value
`list.getValue(n)`	Returns value item *n* (starts at zero)
`list.getValue ('all')`	Returns an array of all value items
`list.getValue ('multiple')`	Returns an array of all selected value items
`list.getIndex()`	Returns the selected index
`list.getLen()`	Returns the list length
`list.pickValue (value)`	Sets the selection to the item with the given value

ListControl Practice

Nervous about using ListControl elements? There's no need to be. ListControls are remarkably simple—and lots of fun to work with. This practice session will help you get comfortable with this wonderful interface tool.

Task 1: Build a basic command file to play with

ListControl lists can be used anywhere a standard popup menu or list is possible—in dialog boxes for commands, objects, and behaviors, or in Property inspectors or floating panels. For this practice session (and the rest of the practice sessions throughout this chapter), we'll practice on the easiest kind of extension to set up—the command. Our first task is to create the command. We'll build the framework and create a very simple dialog box with a `<select>` list form element.

1. Start by creating a simple command file to practice with. In your text editor, create a new file. Enter the following framework code:

```
<html>
<head>
<title>ListControl Practice</title>
<script language="JavaScript">
function myCommand() {
//command statements here
}
```

```
</script>
</head>
<body>
</body>
</html>
```

When the code is in place, save the file in the Configuration/Commands folder as ListControl Practice.htm.

2. It's not important what this command does (at the moment, it does nothing). But you want it to have a dialog box that includes a `<select>` element you can play with and a set of OK and Cancel buttons so that you can close the dialog box with or without executing the command's main function (`myCommand()`). To accomplish this, add the following code to your command file (new code shown in bold):

```
<html>
<head>
<title>ListControl Practice</title>
<script language="JavaScript">
function myCommand() {
}
function commandButtons() {
return new Array("Apply","myCommand()","Close","window.close()");
}
</script>
</head>
<body>
<form name="myForm">
<select name="mySelect" size="5" style="width:150px">
   <option>**nothing yet**</option>
</select>
</form>
</body>
</html>
```

Why does the `<select>` element contain only one option, `**nothing yet**`? Because the list will be populated (filled with entries) dynamically after it has been turned into a ListControl element. Note also that the `commandButtons()` function defines Apply and Close, instead of OK and Cancel, buttons. As you'll see in the following tasks, this makes running diagnostics easier.

3. To make sure your command works, try it out in Dreamweaver. The resulting dialog box should look like the one shown in Figure 10.3.

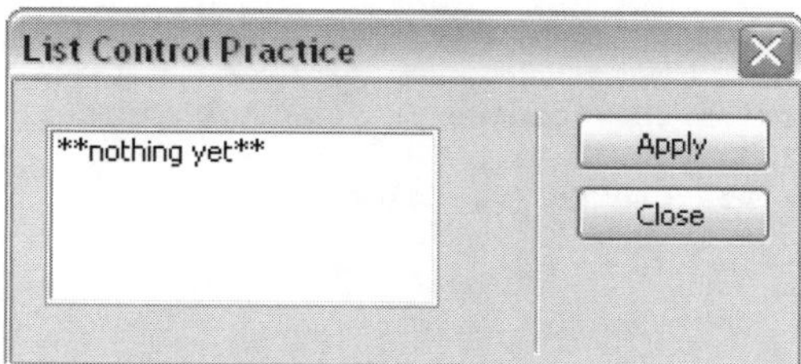

FIGURE 10.3 *The ListControl Practice dialog box.*

Task 2: Create a ListControl object and attach it to the *<select>* element

Okay, you have a `<select>` form element in place. Now it's time to officially turn that `<select>` menu into a ListControl element, or list. This involves following the steps outlined in the earlier section "The ListControl Element in the Interface."

1. First, you must be linked to the shared file that defines the ListControl class. To establish this link, revise your command file's `<head>` section by adding the following code (shown in bold):

   ```
   <head>
   <title>ListControl Practice</title>
   <script src="../Shared/Common/Scripts/ListControlClass.js"></script>
   <script language="JavaScript">
   ```

   This code links your command file to the Macromedia shared file where the ListControl class is defined. Note how the relative path to the shared file is constructed. (Up one folder, and then down into the Shared/MM/Scripts/Class folder to find the ListControlClass.js file.)

2. Add a global variable to your command file's main `<script>` section, like this (new code is in bold):

   ```
   <script language="JavaScript">

   var myList;

   function myCommand() {
   //command statements here
   }
   etc
   </script>
   ```

3. Now you need an `initializeUI()` function, set to create a new ListControl element when the document loads (new code is in bold):

```
<script language="JavaScript">
var myList;
//thisfunction creates the ListControl element
function initializeUI(){
myList=new ListControl('mySelect');
}

etc other functions

</script>
</head>
<body onLoad="initializeUI()">
```

That's it! Believe it or not, that's all you have to do to create a ListControl element. Of course, if you try out your command in Dreamweaver right now, the `<select>` won't behave any differently because you haven't used any ListControl methods to control it. But you're on the road!

Task 3: Initialize the ListControl list

One of the prime purposes of ListControl elements is to allow easy creation of dynamically populated popup menus—in other words, popup menus whose entries will be created based on conditions in the user's computer at runtime. (If you did the exercises in Chapter 5, remember the Automatic Alt Text command—its dialog box included a popup menu of images in the user's document.) In this task, we'll add the `list.setAll()` method to our `initializeUI()` function to generate entries for the list.

1. To generate all entries for a ListControl element, use the `list.setAll()` method. Check the syntax requirements for this method in Table 10.1 and you'll see that it takes two arguments: *`list`* and *`valueList`*. The first is an array of strings that will become the labels of items in the ListControl element; the second is an array of strings that will become the values of items. So, start by adding two arrays to the `initializeUI()` function (new code is in bold):

   ```
   function initializeUI(){
   myList=new ListControl('mySelect');
   var listArray = new Array("A Night at the Opera","A Day at the
   Races","Duck Soup","Horse Feathers","Animal Crackers","Monkey
   Business");
   var valArray = new
   Array("opera","races","soup","horse","animal","monkey");
   }
   ```

   What you've done here is create six menu items for the `<select>` list, each complete with a label (the contents of `listArray`) and a value (the contents of `valArray`).

2. Now that you have what you need for the `list.setAll()` methods' required parameters, add the method to your `initializeUI()` function (new code is in bold):

```
function initializeUI(){
myList=new ListControl('mySelect');
var listArray = new Array("A Night at the Opera","A Day at the
Races","Duck Soup","Horse Feathers","Animal Crackers","Monkey
Business");
var valArray = new
Array("opera","races","soup","horse","animal","monkey");
myList.setAll(listArray,valArray);
}
```

3. Try it out. Reload extensions in Dreamweaver and choose Commands > ListControl Practice. The command calls up a dialog box like that shown in Figure 10.4.

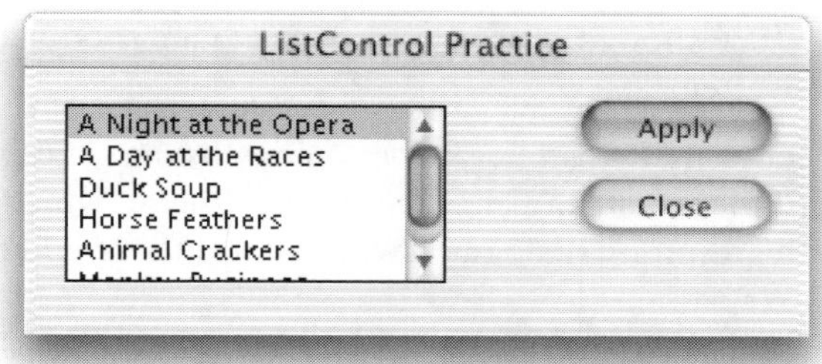

FIGURE 10.4 *The ListControlListControl Practice dialog box, with its `<select>` list initialized.*

Note that ListControl elements must be initialized in this way. If you fill the `<select>` list with entries by hard-coding each `<option>` element into the HTML of your extension file, instead of using `list.setAll()`, Dreamweaver won't recognize those entries for scripting purposes, and you won't be able to control them using ListControl methods entries.

Task 4: Examine the list

Now that you have a fully populated list in your dialog box, you want to quickly learn about it—including what entries it contains and which entry (or entries) the user has selected. You can do this with the various `get`-related methods of the ListControl object. For this practice session, you'll program the ListControl Practice command to get information when the user clicks OK, which means adding new code to the `myCommand()` function.

1. Revise the `myCommand()` function to determine how many items are in the list, like this:

```
function myCommand() {
var myMessage=myList.getLen();
window.alert(myMessage);
}
```

2. After this code is in place, try it out. In Dreamweaver, reload extensions and choose Commands > ListControl Practice. In the dialog box, click OK. An alert window should open with the number 6 showing as its message. That's because there are six items in the list.

3. Now ask about the selection. Revise your `myCommand()` function to look like this:

```
function myCommand() {
var myMessage=myList.get();
window.alert(myMessage);
}
```

   As Table 10.1 showed you, the `list.get()` method accesses the label of the selected list item.

4. Try this code out. Reload Dreamweaver extensions, choose the command, select an item from the list, and click OK. Depending on which item you choose from the list, the resulting dialog box will look something like Figure 10.5.

FIGURE 10.5 *The ListControl Practice command, displaying the currently selected list item.*

5. Take a few moments now to explore the other get methods. For each method, use the `myCommand()` function to put your collected information into the alert window that this command calls up.

Task 5: Add and remove list items

After a ListControl list has been initialized, you might want to add or remove individual entries, one at a time, as the user interacts with the dialog box or panel that contains the list. To do this, use one of the `list.add()` or `list.remove()list.add()` or `list.remove()` methods shown in Table 10.1.

1. To add a new list item when the user clicks OK, revise your `myCommand()` function like this (new code is in bold):

   ```
   function myCommand() {
   myList.add("A Night in Casablanca");
   }
   ```

2. When this code is in place, reload extensions in Dreamweaver and try it out. Choose Commands > ListControl Practice. In the dialog box that appears, select the first item in the list and click OK. Then select the last item in the list and click OK. Every time you click OK, another menu item named `A Night in Casablanca` appears.
3. To remove any list item when the user clicks OK, revise your `myCommand()` function like this (new code is in bold):

   ```
   function myCommand() {
   myList.del();
   }
   ```

4. When you're done, try this one out. In the ListControl Practice dialog box, select any menu item and click OK. It's gone!
5. After you have the hang of this, explore some of the other methods that have to do with adding and removing entries. Tinker until you have a good idea what each method does that is unique.

Task 6: Move items up (and down) in the list

Rearranging the list is not quite as easy as adding and removing elements, because there is no `list.rearrange()` method. To rearrange items in the list, you need to use one of the `list.get()` methods to collect the labels and values from the list, rearrange those values, and then use one of the `list.set()` methods to re-insert those items.

1. Because this is a more complex operation, you'll create two new functions in your command file to hold the instructions for moving an item up and down. Start by adding the framework code for the `moveUp()` function to your `<script>` tag:

```
function moveUp(){
//get selected item (name, value, and index)
//determine if it's the first item
//get the item above the item (name and value)
//put the selected item into the position above (index - 1)
//put the other item into the current position (index)
//change selection to the position above (index - 1)
}
```

   Can you see what logic the framework is following? In each function, you want to collect the information from the currently selected item and the item above it. Then you want to put that information in the proper slot—in other words, the slot above and the current slot. And finally, you want the selection in the list to change, so now the slot above is selected.

2. Now add the code to the framework (new code is in bold):

```
function moveUp(){
//get selected item (name, value, and index)
var myName=myList.get();
var myValue=myList.getValue();
var myIndex=myList.getIndex();
//determine if it's the top item
if (myIndex==0) {
   return;
   }
//get the item above the item (name and value)
var upName=myList.get(myIndex-1);
var upValue=myList.getValue(myIndex-1);
//put the selected item into the position above (index - 1)
myList.set(myName,myIndex-1);
myList.setValue(myValue,myIndex-1);
//put the other item into the current position (index)
myList.set(upName,myIndex);
myList.setValue(upValue,myIndex);
//select the position above
myList.setIndex(myIndex-1);
}
```

   As you can see, after the logic has been laid out, writing the code is fairly simple. It just involves several trips to Table 10.1, to take advantage of the various ListControl methods.

3. After you have the moveUp() function in place, revise the myCommand() function to call the moveUp() function:

```
function myCommand() {
moveUp();
}
```

The myCommand() function, remember, gets executed when the user clicks OK. By calling moveUp() from here, you're turning the OK button into a sort of Up button.

4. Try it out. When you get the ListControl Practice dialog box open, select the item at the bottom of the list (Monkey Business) and click OK to move it up. If it doesn't work, tinker with your code until it does.

5. After you have the moveUp() function in place, the moveDown() function is quick and straightforward—just a matter of duplicating the moveUp() function and changing a few directional items within. In your code, select the entire moveUp() function and duplicate it so that you have two in your <script> tag. Then make the following changes (shown in bold):

```
function moveDown(){
//get selected item (name, value, and index)
var myName=myList.get();
var myValue=myList.getValue();
var myIndex=myList.getIndex();
//determine if it's the last item
if (myIndex==(myList.getLen()-1)) {
   return;
   }
//get the item below the item (name and value)
var downName=myList.get(myIndex+1);
var downValue=myList.getValue(myIndex+1);
//put the selected item into the position below (index + 1)
myList.set(myName,myIndex+1);
myList.setValue(myValue,myIndex+1);
//put the other item into the current position (index)
myList.set(downName,myIndex);
myList.setValue(downValue,myIndex);
//select the position below
myList.setIndex(myIndex+1);
}
```

6. To see how this function works, change the myCommand() function so that it calls this function (new code is in bold):

```
function myCommand() {
moveDown();
}
```

7. Try it out. In the ListControl Practice dialog box, select the first item and use OK as a down button to scoot the item down the list.

That's all there is to coding a simple `ListControl` element. Now let's see how to spiff things up a little by adding some graphic appeal.

Task 7: Add button graphics to the interface

As shown earlier in Figure 10.2, a common arrangement of buttons for ListControls is to have a + and – button on the left, and up and down buttons on the right. Each of those buttons is a graphic from the Shared/MM/Images folder. In this task, we'll access the shared graphics and add those four images to the ListControl Practice file.

1. Start by refining the layout of your dialog box, creating a table to contain the image buttons in its top row and the `<select>` element into its bottom row. Figure 10.6 shows what the revised layout should look like. The revised code for your `<body>` section should look like this (new code is in bold):

```
<body onLoad="initializeUI()">
<form name="myForm">
<table>
  <tr>
      <td align="left">
      </td>
      <td align="right">
      </td>
  </tr>
  <tr>
      <td colspan="2">
        <select name="mySelect" size="5" style="width:150px">
          <option>**nothing yet**</option>
      </select>
    </td>
  </tr>
</table>
</form>
</body>
```

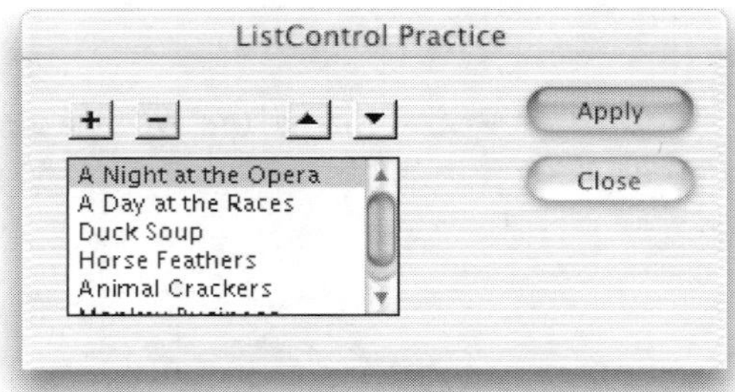

Figure 10.6 *The ListControl Practice command file, with the layout adjusted to fit image buttons at the top.*

2. Now add all four buttons (add, remove, up, down) to the top row of the table—two to each cell. It's easiest to do this in Dreamweaver Design view, but you can code it by hand if you like.

   If you're working in Design view, to insert each button choose Insert > Form Objects > Image Field. In the Select Image Source dialog box, navigate to the Configuration/Shared/MM/Images folder and place btnAdd.gif and btnDel.gif in the top left cell and btnUp.gif and btnDown.gif in the top right cell. Name each button to match its filename, minus the extension (for instance, `btnAdd` for the btnAdd.gif graphic).For accessibility, also add alt text to each button, such as **Add Item** or **Move Item Up in List**. Figure 10.7 shows this happening.

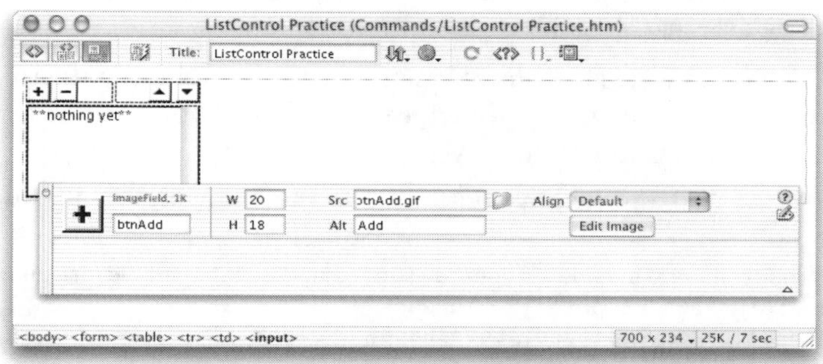

FIGURE 10.7 *Using Dreamweaver Design view to add the four buttons to the ListControl Practice dialog box.*

If you're creating the code by hand, the code for the top row of your table should end up looking like this:

```
<tr>
  <td>
    <input name="btnAdd" type="image" src="../Shared/MM/Images/btnAdd.gif"
    ➥width="20" height="18" border="0" alt="Add Item">
    <input name="btnDel" type="image" src="../Shared/MM/Images/btnDel.gif"
    ➥width="20" height="18" border="0" alt="Remove Item">
  </td>
  <td align="right">
    <input name="btnUp" type="image" src="../Shared/MM/Images/btnUp.gif"
    ➥width="20" height="18" border="0" alt="Move Item Up in List">
    <input name="btnDown" type="image" src="../Shared/MM/Images/btnDown.gif"
    ➥width="20" height="18" border="0" alt="Move Item Down in List">
  </td>
</tr>
```

Task 8: Add event handlers to the images

As long as you have the images in there, you might as well put them to work. By attaching event handlers to the images, you can use them to trigger the ListControl methods you've been working with.

1. For the Up and Down buttons, add event handlers that include function calls for the `moveUp()` and `moveDown()` functions (new code is in bold):

```
<input name="btnUp" type="image" src="../Shared/MM/Images/btnUp.gif"
➥width="20" height="18" border="0" alt="Move Item Up in List"
➥onClick="moveUp()">
<input name="btnDown" type="image" src="../Shared/MM/Images/btnDown.gif"
➥width="20" height="18" border="0"alt="Move Item Down in List"
➥onClick="moveDown()">
```

2. Try it out. In the ListControl Practice dialog box, clicking the Up and Down buttons should move the selected list item up and down in the list. Just like all of the other lists in Dreamweaver.
3. For the Add and Remove buttons, add the following event handlers (shown in bold):

```
<input name="btnAdd" type="image" src="../Shared/MM/Images/btnAdd.gif"
➥width="20" height="18" border="0"alt="Add Item"
➥onClick="myList.add('Love Happy','happy')">
<input name="btnRemove" type="image"
➥src="../Shared/MM/Images/btnDel.gif" width="20" height="18"
➥border="0"alt="Remove Item" onClick="myList.del()">
```

4. Try out this functionality. Clicking the + button adds `Love Happy` to the menu; clicking the – button removes the selected menu item.

note

Of course, in the real world, an Add button that kept adding the same menu item over and over would be fairly useless. Instead of this limited functionality, you would probably call up a dialog box to ask the user what menu item she would like to add. For purposes of this practice, however, we're keeping things simple and adding hard-coded information only.

ImageButtons

You already know how to add images to your interfaces, as icons and image buttons in forms. By taking advantage of the `ImageButton` object class, defined in ImageButtonClass.js, you can take those images to the next level of sophistication, adding multiple states like normal, selected, highlighted, and disabled. You can create graphic toggles, radio buttons, and push buttons, and have them behave on cue, with just a little scripting setup.

Specifications

Creating a scriptable ImageButton involves linking to the ImageButtonClass.js file, creating and correctly naming the desired button graphics, and adding an ImageButton constructor statement to the code of your extension file.

The ImageButton Element in the Interface

A selection of standard interface icons can be found in Configuration/Shared/MM/Images. Whether you use those graphics or create your own, you must follow certain naming conventions for the multiple states of a button image to work properly. All images must be stored in the same folder so that their pathnames are identical. Their filenames must also be built from a basename with specific alterations (see Table 10.2 in the next section). Not all states need be present, although the constructor statement for the image button object should specify which states exist.

Place the graphics in your layout using either the `<img>` tag or `<input type="image">`. Each image must be given a name so that you can refer to that name when attaching the ImageButton object to the image.

Scripting an ImageButton Element

Before you can add an ImageButton element to an extension file, you must link to ImageButtonClass.js. Add the following script tag to the `<head>` section:

```
<script src="../Shared/Common/Scripts/ImageButtonClass.js"></script>
```

Depending on where in the Configuration folder your extension file is stored, the relative path in this `<script>` tag will vary.

After that, like ListControl elements, each ImageButton must be added to the main `<script>` tag in two stages:

- Declare a global variable to hold the button, like this:
  ```
  var IBTN_thisBtn;
  ```
- In the `initializeUI()` function, use a constructor statement to create a new ImageButton from the global variable, referring to the name you have given the image. The syntax for this statement looks like this:
  ```
  IBTN_thisBtn=new ImageButton(theObjName, theVarName, theStateMask,
  theIsToggle, theIsRadio, theInitialValue, theIsDisabled)
  ```

The name of the new ImageButton must be the same as the global variable created in the previous step. The constructor has seven possible arguments, but only the first is required. Table 10.2 lists the specifications for each of these parameters. Here are some sample button constructor statements:

```
IBTN_minusBtn = new
ImageButton("minusBtn","IBTN_minusBtn","sSd",false,false,false,true);

IBTN_rightAlignBtn = new ImageButton("rightAlignBtn");
```

Table 10.2 Specifications for the *ImageButton* Constructor Statement

Parameter	*Description [(R)= Required]*
`theObjectName`	The name attribute of the `<img>` this button is built on. (R)
`theVarName`	The variable name that will be used to refer to the object. If this parameter isn't present, the name defaults to `'IBTN_<objName>'`. This is used to hook up the necessary events to the class.
`theStateMask`	The list of image types available for this button. The possible image types are `sShHdD` where `s` stands for standard, `h` stands for highlight, and `d` stands for disabled. Capitals indicate the selected state. Construct this parameter from the following mask types (each shown with its corresponding required filename addition):
	s *basename*.ext
	S *basename*_sel.ext
	h *basename*_hlt.ext
	H *basename*_sel_hlt.ext
	d *basename*_dis.ext
	D *basename*_sel_dis.ext
`theIsToggle`	Indicates that this image button should operate as a toggle switch, versus a push button. Defaults to `true`.
`theIsRadio`	Indicates that this image button should operate like a radio button. Defaults to `false`.
`theInitialValue`	Indicates which state the image button should start in; `true` indicates selected. Defaults to `false`, or unselected.
`theIsDisabled`	Indicates whether the image button should start in the disabled state or not. Defaults to `false`.

Controlling the ImageButton

After the image has been instantiated using the constructor, you'll have access to all the properties and methods shown in Tables 10.3 and 10.4, each of which swaps the image source for an appropriately named alternate image as needed. You'll also be able to use the `onMouseUp` event handler with the image itself to execute code statements.

Table 10.3 ImageButton Properties

Syntax	*Value*	*Description*
`button.initialValue`	True/false	The starting value of the image button
`button.value`	True/false	The current value of the image button
`button.startDisabled`	True/false	The starting disabled value
`button.disabled`	True/false	The current disabled state of the button
`button.isToggle`	True/false	If `true`, the button functions as a toggle (otherwise, the button is a pushbutton)
`button.isRadio`	True/false	If `true`, the button operates as a radio button

Table 10.4 ImageButton Methods

Syntax	*Description*
`button.reset()`	Resets the button to its initial state
`button.enable()`	Enables the button if it is disabled
`button.disable()`	Disables the button if it is enabled
`setDisabled(`*`isDisabled`*`)`	Sets the disabled state of the button
`setValue(`*`value`*`)`	Sets the value of the button
`setIsToggle(`*`isToggle`*`)`	Sets the button to be a toggle or pushbutton

ImageButton Practice

The main benefit of setting your extensions' images up as ImageButton elements is that you can swap one image for another as needed: creating enabled and disabled states, toggled on and off states, and so forth. In this practice session, we'll experiment with a simple but useful toggle image.

Task 1: Build a basic command file containing an image

1. In your text editor, create a new file. Save it in the Commands folder as Imagebutton Practice.htm, and enter the following framework code:

```
<html>
<head>
<title>ImageButton Practice</title>
<script language="JavaScript">
function myCommand(){
//command statements go here
```

```
}
function commandButtons() {
return new Array("Apply","myCommand()","Close","window.close()");
}
</script>
</head>
<body>
<form name="myForm">
</form>
</body>
</html>
```

2. An ImageButton requires an image. For this task, you'll use bold.gif, which is what the image Dreamweaver uses to indicate bold text (see Figure 10.8). Add the following code to your command file's `<form>`:

```
<input type="image" name="boldBtn" src="../Shared/MM/Images/bold.gif">
```

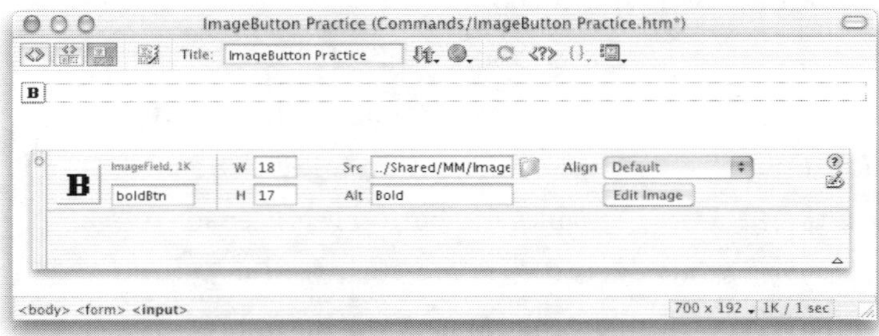

FIGURE 10.8 *Adding the bold.gif image to the practice file, as seen in Dreamweaver Design view.*

This inserts the shared image file bold.gif into the layout as a form element and gives it the name `boldBtn`.

3. Just to make sure everything's working properly, try out your command. Choosing Commands > ImageButton Practice should open a simple dialog box like the one shown in Figure 10.9. Of course, so far the button is only a static graphic—clicking on it doesn't toggle it between selected and deselected states, as you'd expect it to. Adding that effect comes next.

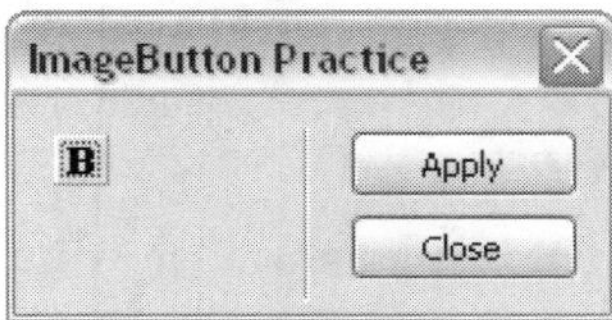

FIGURE 10.9 *The bold button in the ImageButton Practice dialog box.*

Task 2: Create an ImageButton script object and attach it to the image

Now that you have an image, your next job is to make the image scriptable by connecting it to an ImageButton.

1. Start by linking your command file to the file that defined the ImageButton class of objects. Add the following `<script>` tag to your `<head>` section (new code shown in bold):

   ```
   <head>
   <title>ImageButton Practice</title>
   <script src="../Shared/Common/Scripts/ImageButtonClass.js"></script>
   <script language="JavaScript">
   ```

2. Add a global variable to the main `<script>` section, like this (new code is in bold):

   ```
   <script language="JavaScript">

   var IBTN_boldBtn;
   function myCommand() {
   //command statements here
   }
   etc
   ```

3. Next, add an `initializeUI()` function, containing a constructor statement for the ImageButton:

   ```
   function initializeUI() {
   IBTN_boldBtn = new ImageButton("boldBtn","IBTN_boldBtn","sSd");
   }
   ```

   If you compare the parameters in this constructor to the specifications in Table 10.2, you'll see that this ImageButton consists of three states (`sSd`): normal, selected, and disabled. Its lack of optional parameters means that it is a toggle and that it will initially display in is normal state (not selected or disabled).

4. The `initializeUI()` function must be called `onLoad`, so add the following code to your `<body>` tag:

   ```
   <body onLoad="initializeUI()">
   ```

   There you go! The bold.gif graphic is now functioning as an ImageButton in the layout.

5. Try it out. Reload extensions and choose the ImageButton Practice command to access your dialog box. In the dialog box, click the Bold button a few times—even with no additional scripting work on your part, it's already toggling on and off, just as it should. Pretty nice!

Task 3: Use scripting to change the button state

The on/off toggle effect happens automatically, but that doesn't mean you can't use extra scripting to control your button's appearance. What if, for instance, you want the button to display differently depending on whether the user has something bold selected? What if you want the button to display its deselected state if the user doesn't have text selected? In this task, you'll get a chance to add this functionality.

1. To see how easy it is to disable the button, add the following code to the `myCommand()` function:

   ```
   function myCommand() {
   IBTN_boldBtn.disable();
   }
   ```

   As specified in your `commandButtons()` function, this function will execute when the user clicks the Apply button. Try the command and see! When the ImageButton Practice dialog box opens, the image shows in its normal state. Click Apply, and it switches to a grayed-out version of itself.

2. Now turn the button to its selected state. Revise `myCommand()` like this:

   ```
   function myCommand() {
   IBTN_boldBtn.setValue(true);
   }
   ```

   How does setting the button's value change its state? The value is a true/false toggle. If it's true, the button is selected; if it's false, the button is deselected. Try it and see. When you click Apply and trigger `myCommand()` to execute, the result should look like Figure 10.10.

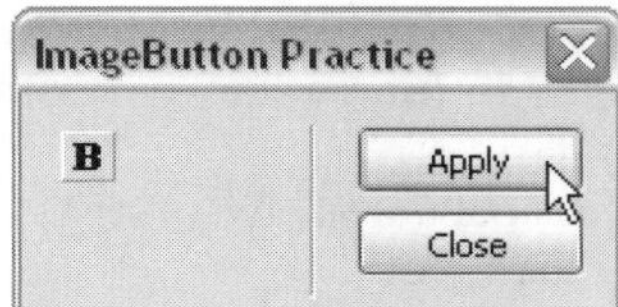

FIGURE 10.10 *The ImageButton Practice dialog box, with the button displaying as selected.*

3. Now that you know how to disable and select the button through scripting, getting it to function more like a true bold button—displaying differently depending on user selection—is just a matter of adding a little DOM-detection to the mix. To see how this can work, add the following (very crude) function framework to your <script> tag:

```
function amIBold() {
//access the currently selected object
//is the selected object text?
//if so, is it bold? select the button
//if not, disable the button
}
```

   Can you see the logic that's outlined here? If the currently selected object is text and is bold, the button should be set to its selected state. If the object is not text, the button should be set to its disabled state. If the object is text that isn't bold, the button should remain in its normal state.

4. After you understand the logic, fill in the framework, like this (new code is in bold):

```
function amIBold() {
//access the currently selected object
var myDOM=dw.getDocumentDOM();
var myObject=myDOM.getSelectedNode();
//is the selected object text?
if (myObject.nodeType==3) {
   //if so, is it bold? select the button
   if (myObject.parentNode.tagName=="B" ||
   ➥myObject.parentNode.tagName=="STRONG") {
      IBTN_boldBtn.setValue(true);
      }
//if not, disable the button
   }else{
   IBTN_boldBtn.disable();
   }
}
```

5. To get this function to execute when the dialog box opens, call it from your `initializeUI()` function (new code is in bold):

```
function initializeUI() {
IBTN_boldBtn=new ImageButton("boldBtn","IBTN_boldBtn","sSd");
amIBold();
}
```

6. To test your bold button's functionality, reload Dreamweaver extensions and create a new document. In the document, insert a table (any size or shape of table will do). In one of the table cells, enter the following sentence:

   This is a test of the bold button in my practice command.

   Select the table. Choose your command. When the dialog box appears, the bold button is disabled! That's because the table isn't a text object.

   Select the word `practice`. Choose your command. The bold button is in its normal state. That's because you have text selected, but not bold text.

   Select your entire sentence and make it bold. Then select the word `practice` and choose the command again. The bold button is selected! That's because your selected word is inside a `<b>` or `<strong>` tag.

7. Challenge: Note that this is a pretty crude bit of coding you've done here, suitable only as a starting point for true bold-detecting. What happens, for instance, if you select the entire sentence, after it's bold? When you choose the command, the bold button appears as disabled because the selected object is a tag (`<b>` or `<strong>`), not text. What happens if you select an entire paragraph or heading that is bold? Again, the button shows as disabled, because the selected object is `<p>`, `<h1>`, or some other tag. Expanding the `amIBold()` function to accommodate all circumstances is a good exercise in DOM-scripting. Are you up to the challenge?

Don't try a complex bit of DOM work like this without first investigating all the helper functions that are available in Shared/Common/Scripts/dwscript.js and other shared files.

Layered Interfaces

If your interface won't fit properly in a reasonably sized dialog box, you can break it into two or more dialog boxes, or you can create one multipart dialog box that is essentially several dialog boxes' worth of interface sharing one space. Multipart dialog boxes are used throughout the Dreamweaver interface. They're created by putting different form elements on different layers, and using JavaScript to alternately show and hide each layer. In some dialog boxes, the layered effect is done almost invisibly—the Preferences and Site Definition interfaces, for instance,display different contents depending on which category is chosen—an effect easily created by showing and hiding layers (see Figure 10.11). In other dialog boxes, such as the Drag Layer behavior and Clean Up Word HTML command, the layers are a graphic presence, appearing like a stack of tabbed note cards (see Figure 10.12). In this section of the chapter, we'll be focusing mainly on the tabbed layer interface because it's more graphically challenging; but similar scripting techniques are involved in both kinds of interfaces.

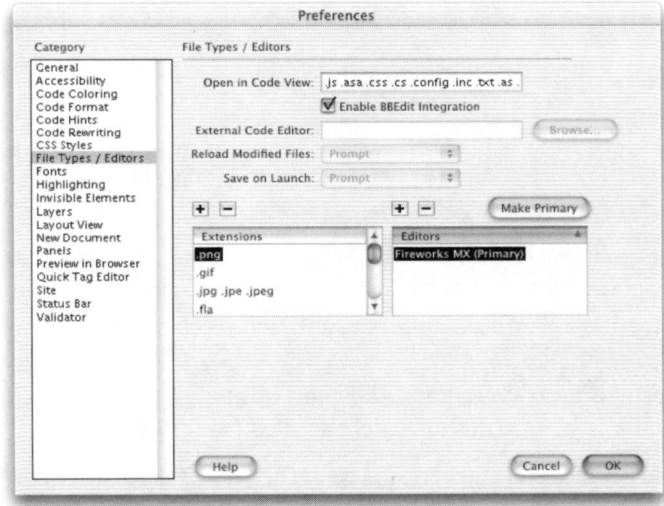

FIGURE 10.11 *Subtle layer-swapping can create interfaces like that seen in the Preferences dialog box.*

note

Because neither the Preferences nor the Site Definition dialog box is written as an extension, it's impossible to tell for sure how their content-swapping interfaces have been created. However, it seems logical to assume that some sort of layer scripting is involved.

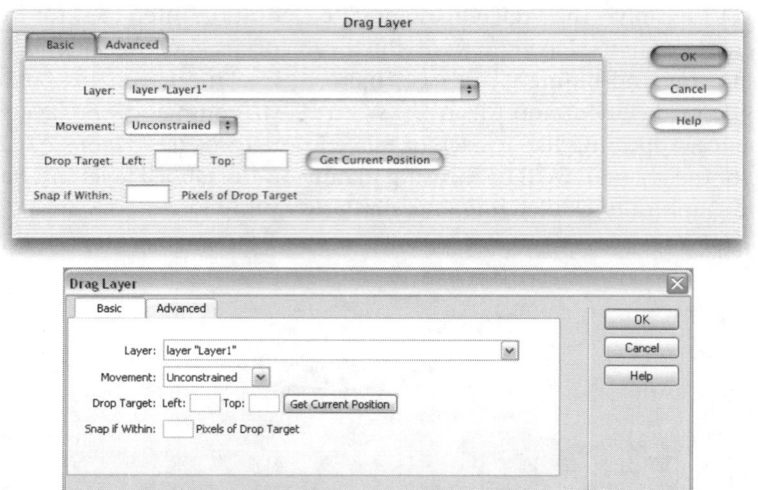

FIGURE 10.12 *The graphically presented "tabbed" layer interface as seen in other parts of the interface. (Mac OS X and Windows XP versions shown.)*

Specifications

There really are no special API tools for working with layered interfaces; there are only common sense and some slightly sneaky scripting.

There are two general ways to approach the tabbed layer interface: the easy way and the hard way. Although the basic layer setup is the same for both, the scripting setup is drastically different, as are the structural requirements for how the layers are put together. The simple way is quick and easy to set up, but it offers only a fraction of the power and flexibility of the hard way. We'll look at both, beginning with the simpler.

Layers the Simple Way

A simple tabbed layer interface is created from a layout built with layers and a JavaScript function controlling layer visibility.

Creating the Layers

The first step in creating a tabbed interface is assembling various interface elements into layers. As with any layered extension interface, it's not crucial how the layers are coded. Both `<div>` and `<span>` tags will work, and there are no special restrictions except the general warning that layers may not display exactly the same across platforms.

If you're creating a tabbed layer interface, the structure of your layers gets a bit more complicated. The "tabbed" look of a layered interface is created from the graphics employed in the various layers. Figure 10.13 shows a diagram of the layer structure utilized in the Macromedia extensions (such as the Drag Layer dialog box shown in Figure 10.12). From this diagram, you can see that a large layer containing a background graphic creates the main 3D note card effect. In front of this layer, each "page" of interface elements consists of five layers: the contents layer and four smaller layers creating the tab effect. These four layers consist of one layer to hold the "unselected" tab graphic, one to hold the "selected" tab graphic, one to hold the title that appears in the tab, and one to hold an invisible image field form element. The JavaScript for showing and hiding the layers is called `onClick` from that invisible button. Image files are available for all of these graphic needs, all stored in the Configuration/Shared/MM/Images folder. Table 10.5 lists the different images available, along with their uses. (Note that most are platform-specific, so you must target your tabbed layer interface to one platform or another.)

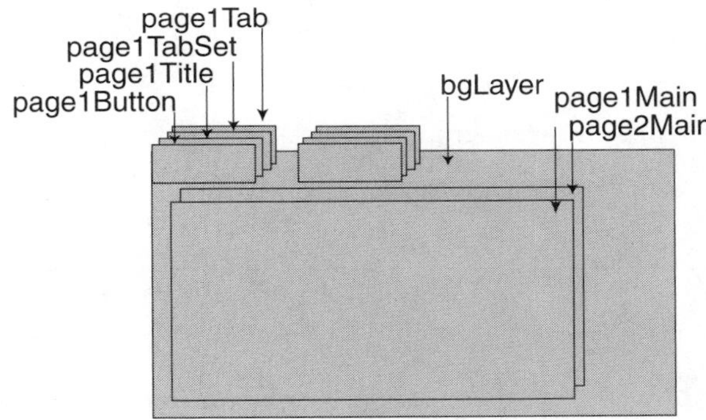

Figure 10.13 *The tabbed layer interface effect, diagrammed to show layer stacking.*

Table 10.5 Macromedia Images Available for Use with Tabbed Layer Interfaces (All Can Be Found in Configuration/Shared/MM/Images)

Image	*Usage*	*Target Platform*
tabBg.gif	Non-selected tab	Generic
tabBgSel.gif	Selected tab	
tabBgWin.gif	Non-selected tab	Win
tabBgSmallWin.gif	Background	
tabBgWin335x290.gif	Background	
tabBgWin500x160.gif	Background	

continues

Table 10.5 Continued

Image	*Usage*	*Target Platform*
tabBgOSX.gif	Non-selected tab	Mac OS X
tabBgSelOSX.gif	Selected tab	
tabBgOSX335x290.gif	Background	
tabBgOSX435x334.gif	Background	
tabBgOSX500x160.gif	Background	
tabBgOSX500X162.gif	Background	
tabBgOSX505x410.gif	Background	
tabBgXP.gif	Non-selected tab	Win XP
tabBgSelXP.gif	Selected tab	
tabBgSmallWinXP.gif	Background	
tabBgWinXP.gif	Background	
tabBgWinXP335x290.gif	Background	
tabBgWinXP500x160.gif	Background	
tabBgXP.gif	Selected tab	

note

Although you are free to use any graphics you choose if you want your tabbed layers to blend seamlessly with the rest of the Dreamweaver interface, you should use the Macromedia standard graphics. If you find that the dimensions of any of these graphics don't suit your interface needs, you can make duplicates and tweak them in an image-editing program, or you can just stretch and squash the originals by changing their width and height attributes in your extension file. (Warning: This may result in visual distortions.)

How you create the layers is not crucial as long as you follow certain conventions in naming them (covered in the next section) and stick to the general structure diagrammed in Figure 10.13. You can create your layered page layout by hand-coding or by working in Dreamweaver Design view.

Scripting the Layered Interface

The key to a good, layered interface (tabbed or plain) is the scripting that hides and shows the various layers. Ultimately, it's up to you to create a script that works best for you; but you can start from the sample code here.

Generally, only one layer (or one set of content) is visible at a time. The key to accomplishing this is to create a global variable that holds the name of the visible layer; and to create a function for showing one layer and hiding all others. Because any layer in the interface should be able to call this function, each layer must pass its name to the function as a parameter so that Dreamweaver knows which layer to make visible when the function runs. The basic code structure is like this:

```
var gCurrentLayer="page1";//this is the name of the currently visible
➥page

function bringMeForward(myName) {//each layer passes its own name as a
➥parameter
//if the layer that called the function (myName) is already visible,
➥stop
//otherwise, make that layer (myName) visible
//make the layer that's currently visible (gCurrentLayer) invisible
//set gCurrentLayer to myName
}
```

For a non-tabbed layered interface (like the Preferences or Site Definition dialog box), the fleshed-out version of the code looks like this:

```
var gCurrentLayer="page1";

function bringMeForward(myName) {
//if the layer that called the function (myName) is already visible,
➥stop
if (gCurrentLayer==myName) {
   return;
   }
//otherwise, make that layer (myName) visible
eval("document."+myName+".visibility=visible");
//make the layer that's currently visible (gCurrentLayer) invisible
eval("document."+gCurrentLayer+".visibility='hidden'");
//set gCurrentLayer to myName
gCurrentLayer=myName;
}
```

The `eval()` function helps you construct the DOM accessing statement (`document.myForm.myLayer.visibility=visible`) to accommodate whatever layers have been defined as `myName` and `gCurrentLayer`. As long as the names of your layers are legal (no special characters, and so forth), it doesn't matter what you have named them for this to work.

For a tabbed layer interface, the code has to be more complex because several layers are being shown and hidden at a time (the content layer, the layer containing the selected tab graphic, and so forth). To accommodate this complexity and make your scripting task much easier, name the layers according to a set naming scheme that incorporates a base name and consistent prefixes or suffixes. If the layers that comprise the first tabbed layer are named `page1Main`, `page1Tab`, `page1TabSel`, `page1Title`, and `page1Button`, for instance, the fleshed-out function will look like this:

```
var gCurrent="page1";
function bringMeForward(myShortName){
//if the layer that called the function (myShortName) is already
➥visible, stop
if (gTab == myShortName) {
   return;
   }
//otherwise, make that layer (myShortName) visible
eval("document."+myShortName+"Main.visibility='visible'");
eval("document."+myShortName+"TabSel.visibility='visible'");
//make the layer that's currently visible (gCurrentLayer) invisible
eval("document."+gCurrent+"Main.visibility='hidden'");
eval("document."+gCurrent+"TabSel.visibility='hidden'");
//set gCurrent to myShortName
gCurrent=myShortName;
}
```

note

Don't forget: Whenever you design an interface in layers, you'll need to use `findObject()`—or some other equivalent function—to access the form elements. Link to UI.js or another shared file containing `findObject()`, or copy the function into your extension file.

note

Thanks to Andrew Wooldridge's QuickTime object extension, from which I adapted this function code.

Each function call to this function must then pass only its base name (for example, `page1`) to the function. The function will construct all other names by adding various suffixes (`Main`, `Tab`, `TabSel`, and so forth) to this base; and the `eval()` statement will hide or show all layers associated with the same base name.

note

The layer terminology can get confusing here. Because, in a tabbed interface, multiple <div> or <span> elements go to make up each tab, Macromedia's convention is to refer to each <div> or <span> element as a layer, and each tabbed unit as a page. Thus, page1 refers to five layers.

Layers the Fancy Way

Now for the more complex and powerful way to set up the tabbed interface. This is the method used in the standard Dreamweaver extensions. It involves utilizing custom `TabControl` class objects, as well as custom page objects defined according to a specific set of rules. Setting up to use this system is much more of an undertaking than just writing the simple script shown above. But you get a payoff in the form of much more flexible functionality if you're willing to put some work in up front.

Creating the Layers

Because the layers in this kind of interface must work with predefined `TabControl` objects, the requirements for constructing them are more exact. This is especially true of the layers that create the tabbed effect. You have much more freedom in constructing the content layers (the layers containing the actual form elements). The safest way to begin constructing the interface is to copy the existing code for the tab layers from one of the standard extensions. These include Commands/Clean Up Word HTML.htm, Behaviors/Actions/Drag Layer.htm, and Commands/Insert Nav Bar.htm. You can also retype the code from here, if you like. The following style information should be added to your extension file's `<head>` section:

```
<style type="text/css">
.pageBg { position:absolute; left:18px; top:21px; width:10px;
➥height:10px; z-index:1; visibility:hidden; }
.tabLayer { position:absolute; top:0px; width:70px; height:20px; z-
➥index:8; visibility:hidden ;}
.tabInnerLayer { position:absolute; width:75px; height:23px; z-index:8;
➥left: 0px; top: 0px; visibility:inherit ;}
.tabLabelLayer { position:absolute; width:69px; height:1px; z-index:8;
➥left: 0px; top: 5px; visibility:inherit; text-align:center }
</style>
```

And the following code to create the tab layers should be added to the `<body>` section:

```
<div class="pageBg" style="visibility:visible; left:4px; ">
  <img name="tabBgWin" width="335" height="290"
  ➥src="../Shared/MM/Images/tabBgWin335x290.gif">
</div>
<div id="Tab0" class="tabLayer" style="left: 8px; ">
  <div class="tabInnerLayer"> <img src="../Shared/MM/Images/tabBg.gif">
  ➥</div>
  <div id="Tab0Sel" class="tabInnerLayer" style="visibility:hidden">
    <img src="../Shared/MM/Images/tabBgSel.gif"> </div>
  <div name="Tab0Label" class="tabLabelLayer"></div>
  <div class="tabInnerLayer">
    <input type="image" src="../Shared/MM/Images/transparent.gif"
    ➥width="69" height="21"> </div>
```

```
</div>
<div id="Tab1" class="tabLayer" style="left: 78px; ">
  <div class="tabInnerLayer"> <img src="../Shared/MM/Images/tabBg.gif">
➥</div>
  <div id="Tab1Sel" class="tabInnerLayer" style="visibility:hidden">
    <img src="../Shared/MM/Images/tabBgSel.gif"> </div>
  <div name="Tab1Label" class="tabLabelLayer"></div>
  <div class="tabInnerLayer">
    <input type="image" src="../Shared/MM/Images/transparent.gif"
    ➥width="69" height="21"> </div>
</div>
```

You can substitute different graphics as needed, as well as adjust the size of the background layer. You may also need to adjust the path to the image files, depending on where your extension is stored. But it's easiest and safest not to change any other names.

As noted, you can create the page content layers without such coding restrictions, in Dreamweaver Design view or elsewhere. There are no special naming restrictions on content layers, either.

note

You can find a copy of the basic framework code for this tabbed layer interface on the book's companion web site: www.newriders.com.

Scripting the Layers

Here's how this system works, in brief: You create a custom page class for each different kind of page in your interface, based on a model `PageControl` class provided in the shared files. You then link to the TabControlClass.js shared file, which defines a custom class for `TabControl` objects. In your extension file, you create an instance of a `TabControl` object, passing it your custom pages. You can then call on the various `TabControl` methods, each of which in turn will call on your custom page class's methods. You can also put custom functionality into the page class methods. Get it? If not, you will when you've seen it in action.

First, you'll create the custom page classes.

1. From the Macromedia Class folder, in the Shared folder, find and open the PageControlClass.js file. This file contains a template for defining page objects to be used with TabControls.
2. Copy the code from this file, and paste it into your extension file.
3. Throughout the new code in your extension file, wherever the name `PageControl` appears, replace it with a class name suitable to your project—`Pg1`, for instance, or `BasicOptionsPage` if you like to type long names.

4. Repeat steps 2 and 3 for each type of "page" or set of content your interface will require. For a simple two-tab interface, for instance, you'll need to copy, paste, and rename two times. If you called the first class `Pg1`, you might call the second `Pg2`.

   Now you're ready to create an instance of the `TabControl` object and instantiate the custom page classes. This all needs to happen `onLoad`.

5. Create an `initializeUI()` function, called from the `<body>` tag. Enter the following code (names that can vary from file to file are shown in italic):

```
function initializeUI() {

//Initialize the TabControl
//Pass the prefix used for the tab layers
T = new TabControl('Tab');

//Add tab pages
//by creating instances of your custom page objects
//Pass the layer name, and the page object)
T.addPage('basicPage', new Pg1("Basic"));
T.addPage('advPage', new Pg2("Advanced"));

//Initialize and display the tabs.
//(Optional: pass the name of a page to start on)
T.start('basicPage');

}
```

   What does this code do? It creates a new `TabControl` object, called `T` here—this could be any name. Then, using the `TabControl's addPage()` method, it creates instances of your custom page objects. Finally, using the `start()` method, it sets up the tabs.

   Table 10.6 lists the methods of the `TabControl` object. Examining the `addpage()` method will reveal that in the previous code you're defining a content layer called `basicPage` as an instance of the `Pg1` object and a content layer called `advPage` as an instance of the `Pg2` object, and that the user will see the titles `Basic` and `Advanced` in the tabs for these layers.

Table 10.6 Methods of the TabControl Object

Syntax	*Description*
`tab.getPageNum (thePageName)`	Returns the index in the `pageList` of the given page (starting from 0; returns –1 if the page can't be found).
`tab.getCurPageNum()`	Returns the index in the `pageList` of the current page (starting from 1).

continues

Table 10.6 Continued

Syntax	*Description*
`tab.getTotalPages()`	Returns the total number of pages in the current group.
`tab.getPageObject (pageName)`	Returns the page object for the current page.
`tab.start(startpage)`	Initializes the tabs (`startPage` is an optional parameter, indicating the page that should be loaded to start).
`tab.finish()`	Unloads the current page, and sends the `lastUnload` event to each of the pages in the current group.
`tab.addGroup (groupName, groupArray)`	Adds a group of pages to the list of possible groups (`theGroupArray` is an array of page names). Returns `true` if successful; `false` if not.
`tab.showGroup (groupName)`	Selects a group to display (call `refresh` or `showPage` to view the new group).
`tab.addPage(pagename, pageObject)`	Adds a page and its corresponding object to the list of possible pages (`thePageName` is the div id of the page).
`tab.showPage (pageName)`	Shows the page with the given name in the current group. (Calls the `unload()` method of the current page. Calls the `canLoad()` and `load()` methods of the new page.)
`tab.showPageNum (thePageNum)`	Shows the page with the given index in the current group.
`tab.nextPage()`	Shows the next page in the current group.
`tab.previousPage()`	Shows the previous page in the current group.
`tab.refresh()`	Refreshes the tab display.
`tab.insertPage (thePageName, insertBeforeName, allowDuplicates)`	Dynamically inserts a page in the current group; `insertBeforeName` specifies the page to insert after, null = insert at end. (Calls `refresh` or `showPage` to view the new page.)
`tab.removePage (thePageName)`	Dynamically removes a page from the current group. (Calls `refresh` or `showPage` to remove the page from the display.)
`tab.update (theItemName)`	Calls the `update()` method in the page object for the current page.

Now that there's a `TabControl` object and pages for it to act on, any of the methods shown in Table 10.6 can be used to create interface functionality.

6. To create the basic show/hide behavior, for instance, just attach the `showPage()` method to the transparent image in the appropriate tab layer, passing the name of the layer to make visible, like this:

```
<input type="image" src="../Shared/MM/Images/transparent.gif"
➥width="69" height="21" onClick="T.showPage('basicPage')"> </div>
```

If you examine the custom page classes you created, you'll see a variety of defined methods in each, most of which currently have no content. These methods are called by the `TabControl` object. Whatever code you place here will execute on cue. For instance, form data entered on one page can cause changes to occur in another page by setting those changes into motion as part of the new page's `load()` method. Like this (very simple) example, passing input from a text field on one page, to a text field on another:

```
function Pg2_load() {
findObject("outputField").value=findObject("inputField").value;
}
```

To get an idea when each of these page class methods executes, uncomment the alerts in each; then try tabbing through the interface.

Simple versus Fancy Layers

As you can tell just from looking at the `TabControl` methods, interfaces created with the more complex method have much greater flexibility than those created the simple way. In addition to tabbing between content pages, pages can be dynamically generated, pages can be grouped to create customized content for every situation, and pages can act on one another.

Layered Interface Practice

This practice session will help familiarize you with tabbed layer interfaces. At the end of the session, you'll also have a handy framework file to use as stationery for other layered interfaces you want to build.

Task 1: Create a command file with one tabbed layer

Probably the hardest part of building a layered interface is keeping track of all those groups of layers, or pages. For this task, you'll create a command with a dialog box that consists of one page only. That involves one content layer and four layers to hold the graphics for the tabbing effect.

1. In your text editor, create a new file. Save it in the Commands folder as Layer Practice.htm, and enter the following framework code:

   ```
   <html>
   <head>
   <title>Layer Practice</title>
   <script language="JavaScript">
   function myCommand() {
   //command statements go here
   }
   function commandButtons() {
   return new Array("OK","myCommand()","Close","window.close()");
   }
   </script>
   </head>
   <body>
   <form name="myForm">
   </form>
   </body>
   </html>
   ```

   This creates a simple command with a very basic dialog box. Before proceeding to add layers, take a moment and try this command out, to make sure it works.

2. Each tab of a tabbed layer interface looks like it's sitting on a notecard or other embossed rectangle. To create this effect, you need to place one of the tab images on a layer. Working either in Dreamweaver Design view or in your text editor, create a layer containing this graphic. The code for your <body> should now look like this (substitute whichever background graphic you choose, sizing your layer to match):

   ```
   <form name="myForm">
   </form>
   <div id="bgLayer" style="position:absolute; left:10px; top:50px;
   ➥width:335; height:290; z-index:1">
      <img src="../Shared/MM/Images/tabBgOSX335x290.gif" width="335"
      ➥height="290">
   </div>
   ```

   If you try your command out at this point, the dialog box will look something like the one shown in Figure 10.14. (Note that the <form> tag must remain! As you learned back in Chapter 5, command files display dialog boxes only if the body contains a form—whether or not the form is used for anything.)

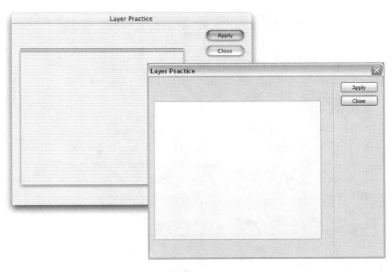

FIGURE 10.14 *Layer Practice dialog box, with background layer (and graphic) in place.*

2. Now add another layer, containing a selected tab graphic (see Table 10.5 to choose the appropriate graphic for the job). Position the layer so that it looks like it's attached to the background layer along the top edge (like a tabbed note-card). Name the layer **page1TabSel**. Figure 10.15 shows what the layout might look like in Dreamweaver Design view.

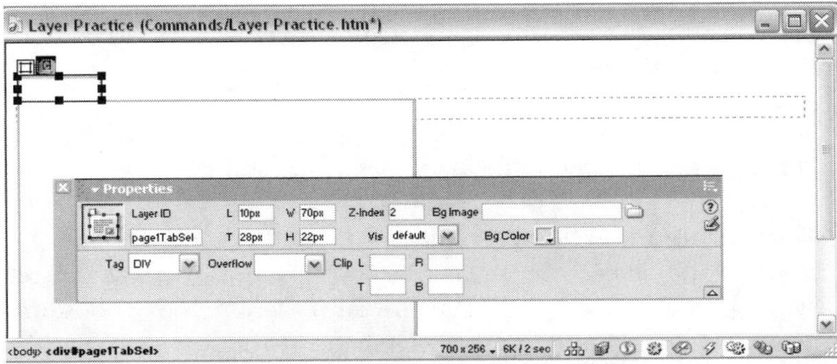

FIGURE 10.15 *Layer Practice dialog box, with selected tab layer in place, as seen in Dreamweaver Design view.*

3. The layer for the non-selected tab should be exactly the same size and placement as the layer holding the selected tab. Create a new layer, identical to the `page1TabSel` layer. Replace the graphic with the appropriate non-selected tab graphic, and name the layer **page1Tab**. Adjust the `z-index` so that `page1Tab` is behind `page1TabSel`. (If you're working Dreamweaver Design view as you do this, you should now be able to use the visibility icons in the Layers panel to switch `page1TabSel` on and off, quickly checking the selected and non-selected states of this "page" of the dialog box.)
4. For the title layer, create another layer. Name it **page1Title**. Position and size it to hold the title that you want to sit in your layer tab, and set its `z-index` to be in front of the other layers.Type **PageOne** in this layer. Figure 10.16 shows what this looks like in Dreamweaver Design view.

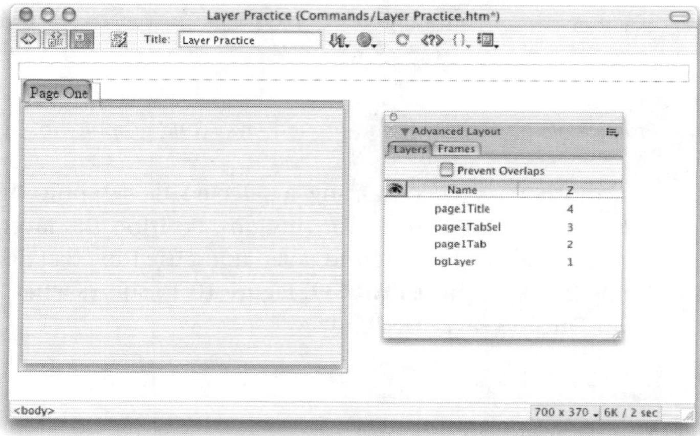

FIGURE 10.16 *The `page1Title` layer being added to the Layer Practice dialog box, as seen in Dreamweaver Design view.*

5. For the button layer, create another layer the same size and position as your selected and unselected tab layers. Name it **page1Button**. To create the button itself, if you're working in Dreamweaver Design view choose Insert > Form > Image Field and insert the space.gif image.If you're coding by hand, add the following code inside the button layer:

```
<input type="image" src="../Shared/MM/Images/space.gif" width="7"
➥height="7">
```

   Resize this image to match the size of the tab graphics.
6. Finally, put some contents in your first page. Create another new layer, sized to fit within the area of the background image. Name this layer **page1Main**. Type a few words in it, or place a few form elements to simulate a working dialog box.

7. There's your first page! Make sure all of your layers are visible, and then try it out. Figure 10.17 shows approximately what the resulting dialog box will look like. Figure 10.18 shows the various layers that went into making this tab, as they appear in the Dreamweaver Layers panel.

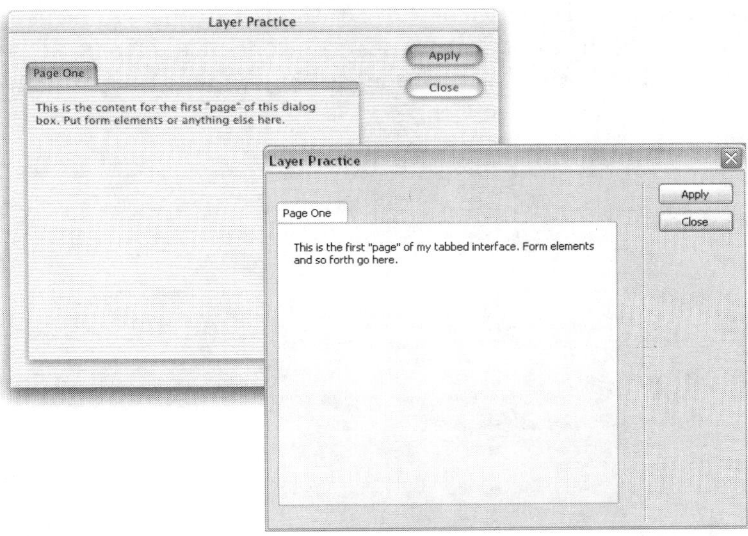

FIGURE 10.17 *The Layer Practice dialog box, with* `page1` *in place.*

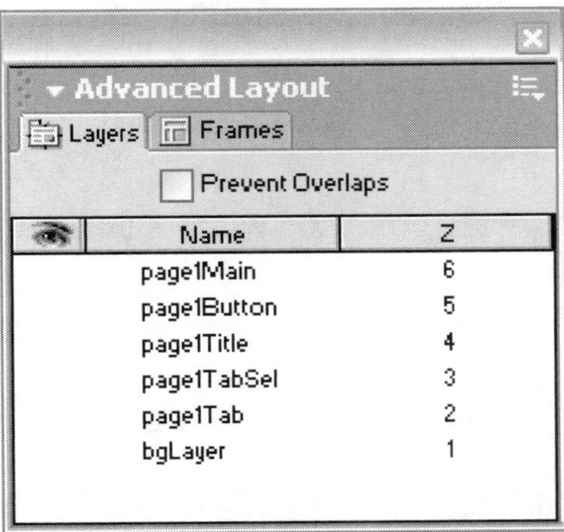

FIGURE 10.18 *The Layers panel showing all of the layers that make up* `page1` *of this interface.*

Task 2: Create the second "page" of the interface

The steps for creating the second page, or tabbed layer, are the same as those for the first page, with the exception that the base name should be `page2`, various tab layers should be moved over to the right to create that stack-of-notecards look, and the title and content should be different. Go ahead and create that second page now. If you're working in Dreamweaver, make life easy on yourself and temporarily hide the layers that belong to `page1` so that they don't get in your way. Your resulting layout should look like the one shown in Figure 10.19.

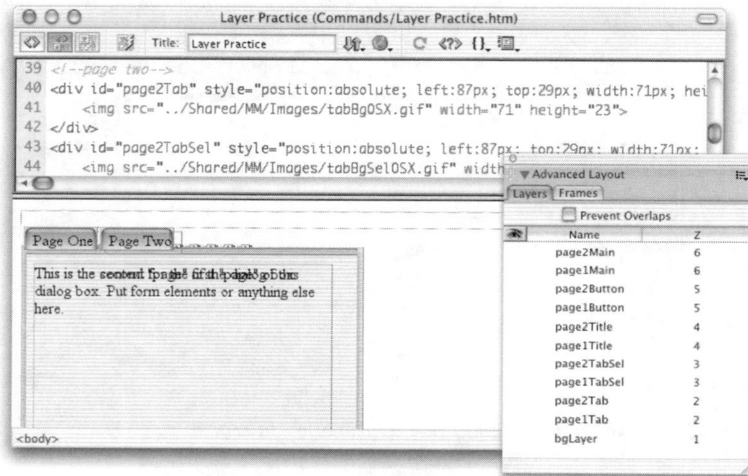

FIGURE 10.19 *The two-page interface of the Practice Layers command, in DreamweaverCode and Design view.*

Task 3: Add the scripting to switch between layers

Okay, you have two pages to your dialog box, and they look good when the right layers are visible and hidden. It's time to build that visibility control into the extension.

1. Take a look at your layers one more time, to make sure they follow the naming convention. (If you're in Dreamweaver Design view, you can use the Layers panel for that.)
2. When the dialog box first opens, `page1` should be visible. Using the `visibility` attribute (if you're hand-coding) or the Layers panel (if you're working in Design view), hide `page2Main` and `page2TabSel`. Everything else should be visible. (Food for thought: Can you tell, after having worked with your multipage dialog box for a while, why only a few layers need to be shown and hidden to create the tabbed effect?)

3. Add the following code to the <script> tag in the head section of your command file (new code is in bold):

```
<script language="JavaScript">
function myCommand() {
//command statements go here
}
function commandButtons() {
return new Array("OK","myCommand()","Close","window.close()");
}
var gCurrent="page1";
function bringMeForward(myShortName){
//if the layer that called the function (myShortName) is already
➥visible, stop
if (gCurrent == myShortName) {
   return;
   }
//otherwise, make that layer (myShortName) visible
eval("document."+myShortName+"Main.visibility='visible'");
eval("document."+myShortName+"TabSel.visibility='visible'");
//make the layer that's currently visible (gCurrentLayer) invisible
eval("document."+gCurrent+"Main.visibility='hidden'");
eval("document."+gCurrent+"TabSel.visibility='hidden'");
//set gCurrent to myShortName
gCurrent=myShortName;
}
</script>
```

4. Now you just need to call the new function. Users expect the tabs to change when they click on a tab; so you'll add an event handler and function call to each of the two transparent buttons you created for each tab. The code should look like this:

```
<div id="page1Button" ... etc ... >
<input type="image" src="../Shared/MM/Images/space.gif" width="70"
➥height="23" border="0" onClick="bringMeForward('page1')">
</div>

<div id="page2Button" ... etc ... >
  <input type="image" src="../Shared/MM/Images/space.gif" width="70"
➥height="23" border="0" onClick="bringMeForward('page2')">
</div>
```

5. Try it out. In the Layer Practice dialog box, clicking either tab should appear to bring its page to the front, as shown in Figure 10.20.

   If it doesn't work, carefully check how you named your layers; how carefully you typed the various single and double quotes in the `eval()` statements; and whether the correct graphics are indeed placed within the correct layers. Keep tinkering until your layers work. What a handy file to build on for future projects!

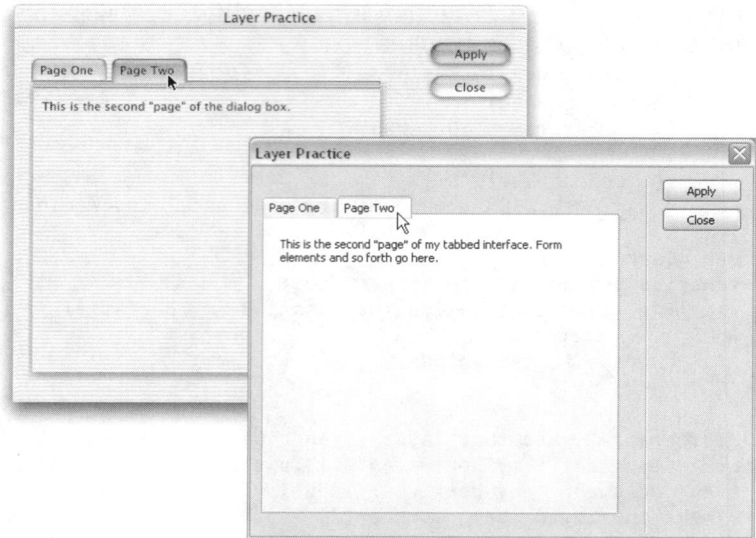

Figure 10.20 *Hiding and showing layers to create the tabbed interface, in the Layer Practice command.*

Other Custom Classes

In this final chapter, we have seen how to create some of the complex interfaces that the Dreamweaver API allows for. We learned about the wonderful graphic resources available in the Shared/MM/Images folder for dressing up our extensions. And we dipped our toes into the power of custom classes, such as ListControl, ImageButton, PageControl, and TabControl. You can take a look at Tables 10.6 and 10.7 for information on other custom classes related to interface development and specifications of custom form elements available for use.

Table 10.6 Custom Form Elements for Use in Dreamweaver Extension Interfaces (see Chapter 3 of the *Extending Dreamweaver* manual for full information on these)

Element Name	*Syntax*	*Description*
Color button (introduced in Chapter 2)	HTML: <input type= "mmcolorbutton" name="myColor" value= "#FFFFFF" onChange="myFunction()">	Adds the standard Macromedia color button to a form; clicking on the button opens the color palette. (Used throughout the Dreamweaver interface.)

Element Name	*Syntax*	*Description*
	JavaScript: var myColor = document.myForm. myColor.value;	
Combobox (editable <select> element)	HTML: <select name="mySelect" editable="true" editText="any text"> JavaScript: var userChoice = document.myForm. mySelect.editText;	Combines the functionality of an editable text field and a popup menu. Users can type in values or choose from predefined lists. (Used throughout the Dreamweaver interface.)
Database controls (<select> element with special features)	HTML: <select name="myDBTree" type="mmdatabasetree" connection="myConn" noexpandbuttons showHeaders></select> JavaScript: document.myForm.myDBTree. connection=myNewConn;	Useful for displaying database can also be added, to handle different numbers and widths of columns in the display grid.
Tree control	HTML: <mm:treecontrol name="myTree"> <mm:treecolumn name= "col1" width="100" value="Items"> <mm:treenode name= "item1" value="One" selected></mm:treenode> <mm:treenode name= "item2" value="Two"> </mm:treenode> <mm:treenode name= "item3" value="Three"> </mm:treenode>	Displays data in a hierarchical or grid format, with expanding/collapsing nodes. (Used in the Keyboard Shortcuts editor and Tag Inspector, for instance.)

continues

Table 10.6 Continued

Element Name	*Syntax*	*Description*

	</mm:treecolumn>
	</mm:treecontrol>
	JavaScript:
	//add a node
	document.myForm.
	myTree.col1.innerHTML+
	='<mm:treenode name=
	"Item4" value="Four">
	<\/mm:treenode>'
	//change a value
	document.myForm.myTree.
	col1.item1.value=
	"First Choice";	

Table 10.7 Custom Classes for Working with Extension Interfaces (see the programmers' notes in the class files for full information on using these)

Class	*Description*	*Methods*
GridControl (GridControlClass.js)	This control manages an editable grid control class (related to the custom <treecontrol> form element).	setAll(), getAll(), setIndex(), getIndex(), setColumnNames(), getColumnNames(), append(), del(), delAll(), add(), moveUp(), moveDown()
RadioGroup (RadioGroupClass.js)	This control manages a group of radio buttons.	getSelectedIndex(), getSelectedValue(), setSelectedIndex(), setSelectedValue()
TreeControl (TreeControlClass.js)	This control manages a <treecontrol> form element.	setAllRows(), addRow(), addRows(), delRow(), setRow(), initTreeControl(), setRowValue(), getRow(), getRowValue(), setRowIndex(), pickRowValue(), getRowIndex(), getRowLen(), refresh(), getColumnNames(), getItem(), setItem()

Class	*Description*	*Methods*
TreeControlWithNavControls (TreeControlClass.js)	This control manages a `<treecontrol>` form element that includes navigation buttons (add, remove, move up, move down).	`initButtons()`, moveRowDown(), `moveRowUp()`
NameValuePair(MM—NameValuePairClass.js)	Creates and manages a list of name/value pairs.	`set()`, `get()`, `getName()`, `del()`, `changeName()`, `length()`, `getNames()`, `getAll()`
CheckboxSet(MM—classCheckbox.js)	Manages a set of checkbox form elements.	`addCheckbox()`, `clicked()`, `isChecked()`, `check()`
Checkbox(MM—classCheckbox.js) `isChecked()`, `getName()`	Manages a graphic three-state checkbox.p	`check()`, `clicked()`,

Summary

In the chapters leading up to this one, we learned how to create the most popular extension types, and got a lot of practice manipulating the Dreamweaver DOM, exploring the methods and properties available through the API, and just generally brushing up our scripting skills.

Is this the end of the story? Not by a long shot! Even after all this work, we've only delved a little way into the wide world of Dreamweaver extensibility. There are hundreds more API methods to take advantage of; half a dozen extension types not covered here, including reports, toolbars, translators and server models. There are more custom interface elements, and more things to be done with those interface elements we already know.

Want to learn more? Study the *Extending Dreamweaver* manual. Examine the code and comments in the files of The Dreamweaver Configuration folder. Appendix E, "Online Resources for Dreamweaver Extensibility," lists various web resources, including the Macromedia Developers' Forum, an excellent source of support and information. Pretty soon, you'll be taking it for granted that you can make Dreamweaver do just about anything you want it to do—and you'll wonder why all software isn't written this way.

Part III

Appendixes

A JavaScript Primer 413

B Macromedia User Interface Guidelines 437

C Packaging Extensions for Use with the Extension Manager 455

D Submitting Extensions to the Macromedia Dreamweaver Exchange 477

E Online Resources for Dreamweaver Extensibility 487

F Contents of the Dreamweaver MX Extensions Book Companion Web Site 493

APPENDIX A

JavaScript Primer

How are your scripting skills? You don't have to be the world's greatest JavaScript guru to work through the projects in this book, but you do need to have a good grasp of how JavaScript works, including how to create simple scripts that use functions, expressions, and logical constructs such as if-statements and loops; how to build HTML forms and collect information from them; and how to work with JavaScript objects such as strings and documents. For those of you who maybe need a little refresher course or a quick once-over of the basics, this appendix will take you through everything you need to know. The explanations here aren't meant as a substitute for reading a really good JavaScript book—like Danny Goodman's *JavaScript Bible* or any of the O'Reilly JavaScript books—but they do cover the basics, focusing on just what you'll need to know to get your extending career started. The exercises can be done using any text editor, or using Dreamweaver Code view, and previewing in any version 4.0 or higher browser. Good luck!

How JavaScript and HTML Work Together

The JavaScript language was developed to work with HTML—to be written into an HTML document and interpreted by a browser. JavaScript statements can be inserted into an HTML document using the <script> tag, like this:

```
<script language="JavaScript">
[JavaScript statements go here]
</script>
```

The <script> tag can go just about anywhere in the HTML code, in the <head> or <body> section, and will be executed as soon as the browser loads the <script> tag. The following exercise shows how this works.

Practice Session #1

In this exercise, you'll insert a <script> tag containing a simple JavaScript statement into an HTML document, experimenting with placing the tag in various places in the document. The JavaScript statement, when executed, causes an alert window to appear.

1. In the text editor of your choice, or in Dreamweaver Code view, open a new document. Save the document as practice1.htm.
2. Enter the basic HTML framework code (unless your program enters it for you). Your code should look like this:

```
<html>
<head>
<title>Practice Session 1</title>
</head>
<body>
</body>
</html>
```

3. Enter a block of JavaScript code in the <body> section of the document (new code is in bold):

```
<html>
<head>
<title>Practice Session 1</title>
</head>
<body>
<script language="JavaScript">
alert("Hello world!");
</script>
</body>
</html>
```

4. Open this page in a browser. As soon as the browser loads the page, an alert window should pop up with the "Hello world!" message showing (see Figure A.1). If this doesn't happen, double-check your code—it must look exactly like the code shown here. JavaScript doesn't allow typos!

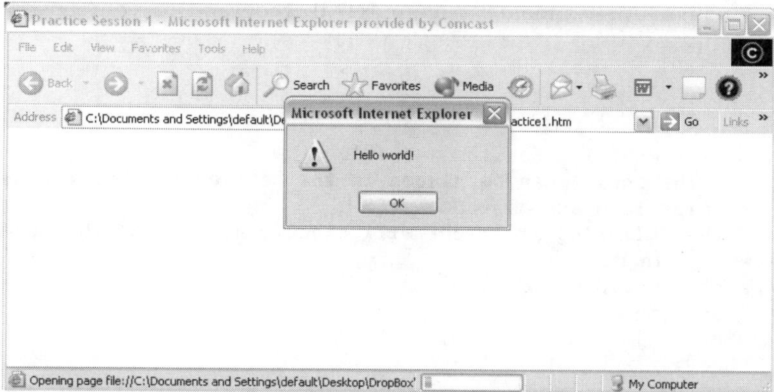

FIGURE A.1 *The practice1.htm file, containing a JavaScript alert statement set to execute when the* `<body>` *loads.*

note

When you're extending Dreamweaver, it will be the Dreamweaver application itself that interprets your JavaScript code. For the purpose of learning JavaScript, though, it's easier to test your code in a browser. That's what you'll be doing throughout this appendix.

5. Now move the `<script>` tag from the `<body>` to the `<head>` of your HTML document. Your code should look like this (new code in bold):

```
<html>
<head>
<title>Practice Session 1</title>
<script language="JavaScript">
alert("Hello world!");
</script>
</head>
<body>
</body>
</html>
```

6. View the page in a browser again. You'll see that the result isn't much different from what you had before. The `alert` statement is actually being executed slightly sooner than it was before, because it's occurring slightly earlier in the code—but the entire page is loaded so quickly that there is essentially no difference.

7. Finally, add comments to your HTML code and to your JavaScript code for future reference:

```
<html>
<head>
<title>Practice Session 1</title>
<!--The script can be placed in the head or body of the document -->
<script language="JavaScript">
//The following statement will execute as soon as this part of the
➥page loads
alert("Hello world!");
</script>
</head>
<body>
</body>
</html>
```

Remember, everything outside the `<script>` tag is normal HTML. HTML comments are coded using the `<!--` and `-->` characters. Everything inside the `<script>` tag must be in JavaScript syntax. In JavaScript, the `//` characters indicate that the rest of the line (until the next hard return) is a comment.

Variables and Expressions

A *variable* is a container that holds a piece of data (called the *value*). An *expression* is the part of a JavaScript statement that evaluates the variable, substituting the value for the variable where necessary. In JavaScript, we use the keyword `var` to create a variable, and the equal sign (=) to assign a value to a variable. Here is a typical group of statements using variables:

```
var x = 6;
var y = 3;
var z = x + y;
x = x + 1;
y = y + 1;
var a = x + y;
```

At the end of this group of statements, the variable `z` is equal to (contains) 9; `a` is equal to 11.

A variable can contain different types of information, including numbers, pieces of text called *strings*, and true/false values called *Booleans*. Depending on the kind of information contained in a variable, the JavaScript interpreter evaluates the expression containing it differently. When variables contain numbers, for instance, as in the preceding example, the + operator means to perform a mathematical addition operation. When variables contain text strings, the + operator means to join the two strings together, as follows:

```
var a = "inter";
var b = "mediate";
var c = a + b;
```

At the end of this group of statements, the variable c is equal to the text string "intermediate." This process of joining text strings is called *concatenation*. Variables can be concatenated with each other and with other text strings, like this:

```
var d = "Fred";
var e = "Barney";
var f = d + " and " + e;
```

At the end of this group of statements, the variable f is equal to the text string "Fred and Barney". The word and, as well as the spaces on either side of this word, are contained in the text string that is joined to, or concatenated with, the two variables.

Practice Session #2

In this exercise, you'll build on the practice file you created in the previous exercise, using variables to construct the message that appears in the alert window.

1. In your text editor, open practice1.htm and save it as practice2.htm.
2. Change the contents of the <script> tag to look like this (new code is in bold):

```
<script language="JavaScript">
var person = "Fred";
var greeting = "Hello, " + person + "!";
alert(greeting);
</script>
```

3. Save the file and try it out in a browser. The resulting alert window should look like the one shown in Figure A.2. Can you see how the extra space at the end of the Hello, text string creates the space between the words in the final message?

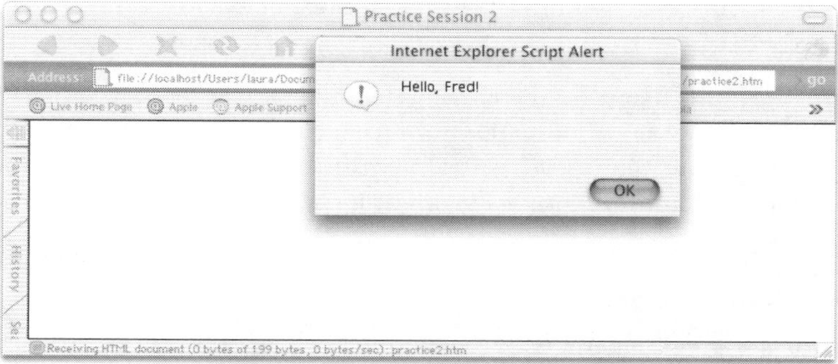

FIGURE A.2 *The alert window for practice2.htm, concatenating variables to create the alert message.*

Functions

Before you can work with Dreamweaver extensions, you need to know about more than variables. You must also know your way around JavaScript functions. This includes defining functions, using function calls, adding parameters to your functions, and returning values from functions.

Functions and Function Calls

When code statements are placed inside a `<script>` tag, they are executed as soon as the tag loads. A more powerful and efficient way to write JavaScript code is to put the statements inside functions. A function is like a recipe for action. It contains all the script statements that need to be executed, but it won't be executed until it's called by a function call statement. Functions are usually placed inside `<script>` tags in the `<head>` of an HTML document. Function call statements can be placed anywhere, but are often placed in the `<body>` section, attached to page elements like text links or form buttons and set to execute when certain events take place, like when the user clicks on or mouses over the page element.

A `<script>` tag containing a simple function looks like this:

```
<script language="JavaScript">
function addMe() {
var a = 3;
var b = 6;
var c =  a + b;
alert("The sum of these numbers is " + c + ".");
}
</script>
```

Any one-word name can be used as the function's name (`testMe`, `myFunction`, and so forth). All function names must end with the opening and closing parentheses `( )`. The statements contained in the function must be enclosed in the opening and closing curly braces `{ }`.

A function call, like other JavaScript statements, can be placed anywhere within a `<script>` tag. When it's attached to a page element, it is used in conjunction with an event handler that specifies the event that will trigger the function call. Typical event handlers and function calls might look like this:

```
<a href="#" onClick="addMe()">Click here</a>
```

```
<img src="myImage.gif" onMouseOver="addMe()">
```

```
<body onLoad="addMe()">
```

Different page elements can have different event handlers attached to them. Only the `<body>` tag can be used with `onLoad`, for instance. Only certain form elements can use the `onChange` and `onBlur` event handlers. Some page elements (such as plain text) can't have any event handlers attached.

Function Parameters

Information can be passed to a function from its function call by using a parameter. A parameter is a special kind of variable that gets defined between the parentheses of the function name when it's defined, and can be used within the function. The value that should go into the parameter is put between the parentheses of the function name when it's called. The `<script>` tag is where the function is defined and looks like this:

```
<script language="JavaScript">
function addMe(a) {
var b = 6;
var c =  a + b;
alert("The sum of these numbers is " + c + ".");
}
</script>
```

If you compare this and the previous example of a function definition, you'll see that the parameter replaces the line of code where the variable was defined and assigned a value.

The function call, complete with parameter, then looks like this:

```
<a href="#" onClick="addMe(3)">Click me</a>
```

Like other variables, parameters can hold numbers, strings, and other kinds of data. Note that when the parameter value is a text string, it must be enclosed within single or double quotes so that the JavaScript interpreter will know that it is a string. If the function call itself is enclosed in double quotes (as in the preceding example), the string inside the function call must be enclosed in single quotes. This is so that the interpreter can determine which quotes belong with which string.

A function can also accept more than one parameter. Multiple parameters are specified in the function's definition as items separated by commas, like this:

```
<script language="JavaScript">
function addMe(a,b) {
var c =  a + b;
alert("The sum of these numbers is " + c + ".");
}
</script>
```

Multiple parameters must be similarly specified in the function call:

```
<a href="#" onClick="addMe(3,6)">Click me</a>
```

All expected parameters should be present, in the same order as they are specified in the function definition, in the function call. If a particular parameter isn't present in the call, a null or empty value is passed to the function.

Practice Session #3

In this exercise, you'll build on the same practice file you've been creating. This time you'll put the alert statement in a function and call it from a function call. Then you'll practice adding parameters to the function and its call.

1. Open the practice2.htm file and save it as practice3.htm.
2. Change the script statements in your document `<head>` into a function by adding a few lines to your code, like this (new code is in bold):

   ```
   <script language="JavaScript">
   function greetMe() {
   var person = "Fred";
   var greeting = "Hello, " + person + "!";
   alert(greeting);
   }
   </script>
   ```

3. Try viewing your page in a browser now. All you'll see is a blank page. No alert window will appear, because the script statements aren't being executed. Code within a function will not execute until the function is called.
4. Revise your document's `<body>` section to include the following (new code is in bold):

   ```
   <body>
   <a href="#" onClick="greetMe()">Click here for a greeting.</a>
   </body>
   ```

5. Preview in a browser again. Your page includes a text link. Click the text link, and the alert window should appear (see Figure A.3). If the page doesn't work as expected, check your code against the code shown here. Are there any minor misspellings in the function's defined name and the name you used in the function call?

FIGURE A.3 *The practice3.htm file, with a text link containing an event handler and function call triggering the* `greetMe()` *function.*

6. Back in your text editor, try rewriting the function to accept a parameter. Revise the function definition to look like this (new code is in bold):

```
<script language="JavaScript">
function greetMe(person) {
var greeting = "Hello, " + person + "!";
alert(greeting);
}
</script>
```

   Note that the parameter has been added between the function name's parentheses and the statement assigning a value to the `person` variable has been removed from the code.

7. Preview your page in a browser now. When you click the text link, a message window appears but with an undefined value where the person parameter should be used (see Figure A.4).

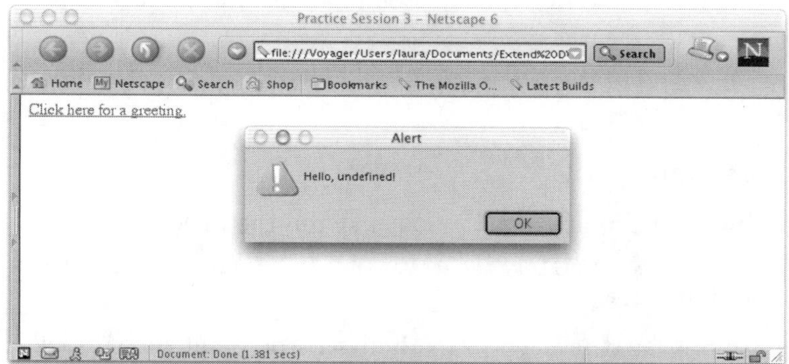

FIGURE A.4 *The practice3.htm file, showing what happens when an expected parameter hasn't been defined.*

   Not all parameter situations have happy endings like this. Depending on how your parameter is used in the function's statements, trying to execute the function without defining the parameter may result in a syntax error.

8. Now revise the function call so that it passes the correct parameter to the function (new code is in bold):

```
<body>
<a href="#" onClick="greetMe('Fred')">Click here for a greeting.</a>
</body>
```

   Pay attention to the double and single quotes in this statement, or your code won't work. Because the function call is in double quotes, the enclosed text string must be in single quotes.

9. Preview your page in a browser and try clicking the text link. If all is well, your result will look just like the one shown in Figure A.3.

   To experiment a little bit more with this, try altering the function call slightly by playing with the quotes, like this:

   ```
   <a href="#" onClick="greetMe("Fred")">Click here for a greeting.</a>
   ```

   and this:

   ```
   <a href="#" onClick='greetMe("Fred")'>Click here for a greeting.</a>
   ```

   You'll see that the second code change works fine, but the first doesn't. This demonstrates that double and single quotes must be alternated when one text string is nested inside another—but it doesn't matter whether double or single quotes are used for the outermost string.

10. Try rewriting the function and its call to use multiple parameters. Revise the <script> tag so that the function looks like this (new code is in bold):

    ```
    <script language="JavaScript">
    function greetMe(person,salutation) {
    var greeting = salutation + ", " + person + "!";
    alert(greeting);
    }
    </script>
    ```

    Rewrite the function call to look like this (new code is in bold):

    ```
    <a href="#" onClick="greetMe('Fred','Hello')">Click here for a
    greeting.</a>
    ```

11. Try this latest revision in the browser. The result should look exactly like the alert window you created earlier.

12. Finally, learn the flexibility of functions and function calls by adding a second function call to your page. Revise the <body> section of your document like this (new code is in bold):

    ```
    <body>
    <a href="#" onClick="greetMe('Fred','Hello')">Click here for a
    ➥greeting.</a>
    <br>
    <a href="#" onClick="greetMe('Barney','Good-bye')">Click here for
    ➥another greeting.</a>
    </body>
    ```

13. Test this page in a browser. You now have two text links. Clicking each link calls up an alert window with a different message inside (see Figure A.5).

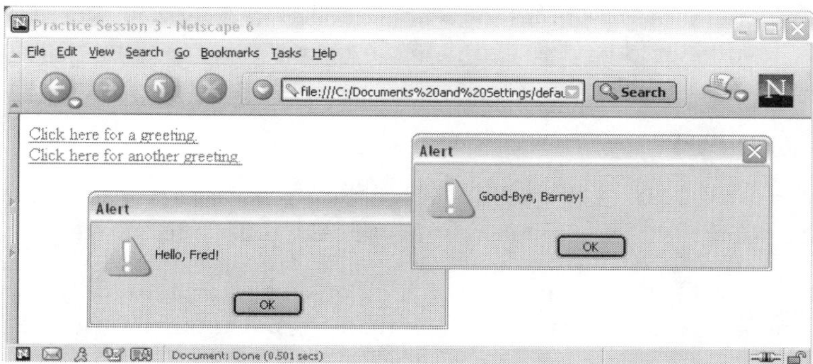

FIGURE A.5 *The practice3.htm file with two text links, both calling the same function but with different parameters.*

Logical Structures (Conditionals and Loops)

Logical structures allow us to determine whether certain statements are going to execute, and how many times they'll execute. The two most commonly used kinds of logical structures are if-then statements and for-loops. Other kinds of logical structures, not covered here, include switch statements, while-loops, and do-loops.

Conditional Statements

A conditional statement evaluates a specified condition and determines which other statements to execute based on whether the condition evaluates as true or false. These are also sometimes called *if-then* statements. The basic syntax for a conditional can be one of the following:

```
if (condition) {
statements to execute;
}
or
if (condition) {
statements to execute;
} else {
other statements to execute;
}
```

Conditional statements use conditional operators to evaluate whether a condition is true or false. These include:

```
==   is equal to
=>   is equal to or greater than
>    is greater than
=<   is equal to or less than
<    is less than
!=   is not equal to
```

If more than one condition must be evaluated to determine whether a set of code statements should be executed, Boolean operators are used to combine the expressions. These include:

`&&` both conditions must be true

`||` one of the conditions must be true

`&!` one of the conditions must be true; the other must be false

Here is a sample function that will bring up an alert window only if two conditions are met—one variable must be larger than 10, and another must be equal to 6.

```
function addMe(a,b) {
var c =  a + b;
if (c >10 && a == 6) {
   alert("The sum of these numbers is " + c + ".");
   }
}
```

The indented lines here are simply to make the code more readable by us humans. It doesn't affect how the JavaScript interpreter treats the statements.

Practice Session #4

In this exercise, you'll build on the practice file you've been creating. You'll add a conditional statement to govern what message appears in the alert window.

1. Open the practice3.htm file. Save it as practice4.htm.
2. To test the basic workings of conditionals, revise the main function so that it contains an `if-then` statement that always evaluates to true (new code is in bold):

   ```
   <script language="JavaScript">
   function greetMe(person,salutation) {
   if (true) {
      var greeting = salutation + ", " + person + "!";
      alert(greeting);
      }
   }
   </script>
   ```

3. Save the file and try viewing it in a browser. Because the conditional is always true, the greeting window will always appear.
4. Change the condition so that it is always false:

   ```
   <script language="JavaScript">
   function greetMe(person,salutation) {
   if (false) {
      var greeting = salutation + ", " + person + "!";
      alert(greeting);
      }
   }
   </script>
   ```

5. Save the file and try viewing it in a browser again. Because the conditional is always false, no greeting will ever appear.
6. Now rewrite the statement so that it tests one of the variables and executes (or not) based on that (new code is in bold):
```
<script language="JavaScript">
function greetMe(person,salutation) {
if (person == "Fred") {
   var greeting = salutation + ", " + person + "!";
   alert(greeting);
   }
}
</script>
```
7. Save again and preview in a browser. If you click on the first link in your page (the one that passes "Fred" as a parameter), the alert will appear. If you click on the second link (the one that passes "Barney" as a parameter), no alert will appear.
8. Now add an `else` clause to your `if-then` statement so that alternate code will be executed if the condition is false (new code is in bold):
```
<script language="JavaScript">
function greetMe(person,salutation) {
if (person == "Fred") {
   var greeting = salutation + ", " + person + "!";
   alert(greeting);
   } else {
   alert("You aren't Fred!");
   }
}
</script>
```
9. Try this in a browser. Clicking on the second link should cause the message "You aren't Fred!" to appear in the alert window. Clicking on the first link causes the original greeting to appear.

For-Loops and Arrays

Loop statements specify that certain other code statements, those contained within the loop, should be executed a certain number of times. The syntax for a for-loop looks like this:

```
for (var a=0; a < 10; a++) {
[statements to be executed]
}
```

The opening statement of the for-loop does the following:

- Creates a counter variable and assigns that variable a starting value
- Specifies an ending condition, when the counting variable reaches a certain number
- Increments the counting variable

The JavaScript interpreter will execute the statements enclosed within the loop over and over, incrementing the counting variable each time, until the counting variable reaches the ending condition. Then the loop will stop.

Loop statements are often used in conjunction with arrays. An *array* is a special kind of variable that, instead of holding a single value, holds a series of values. Arrays are created like this:

```
var myArray = new Array();
```

The individual slots in an array can be filled with values by referring to them by number:

```
myArray[0] = 16;
myArray[1] = 7;
myArray[2] = 23;
```

Note that the numbering always begins with 0. To refer to an individual value within the array, the array name and slot number are used together, like this:

```
var x = myArray[0] + myArray[2];
```

To find out how many slots an array has, access its length property:

```
var x = myArray.length;
```

Practice Session #5

In this exercise, you'll use an array to hold a series of names. Then you'll use a loop to access all the names in the array, adding each to the final greeting to be displayed in the alert window.

1. In your text editor, create a new file. Enter the basic HTML code framework, unless your editor has done so for you. Save the file as practice5.htm.
2. Enter the framework code for a function called `listNames()` in the document `<head>`. The code for your `<head>` section should look like this:

```
<head>
<title>Practice Session 5</title>
<script language="JavaScript">
function listNames() {
}
</script>
</head>
```

3. Enter a function call for this function in the document `<body>`. The code for your `<body>` section should look like this:

```
<body>
<a href="#" onClick = "listNames()">Click here for a list of names.</a>
</body>
```

4. In your function, create an array and populate it (fill its slots) with four names (new code is in bold):

```
function listNames() {
var myNames = new Array();
myNames[0] = "Fred";
myNames[1] = "Barney";
myNames[2] = "Wilma";
myNames[3] = "Betty";
}
```

5. Now create an alert message that displays the contents of a variable called list (new code is in bold):

```
function listNames() {
var myNames = new Array();
var myList = "";
myNames[0] = "Fred";
myNames[1] = "Barney";
myNames[2] = "Wilma";
myNames[3] = "Betty";
alert(myList);
}
```

Note that the `myList` variable starts out as an empty string, indicated by two quote marks side-by-side.

6. Finally, add the for-loop that will create a display list from the members of the array (new code is in bold):

```
function listNames() {
var myNames = new Array();
var list = "";
myNames[0] = "Fred";
myNames[1] = "Barney";
myNames[2] = "Wilma";
myNames[3] = "Betty";
for (var a=0;a<myNames.length;a++) {
  list+=myNames[a]+"\n";
  }
alert(list);
}
```

This loop starts with the counting variable a equal to `0`. It adds the value stored in `myNames[0]` to the list, followed by a new line character (`\n`). Then it keeps adding `1` to the counting variable and collecting the value from the next slot in the array, until it comes to the end of the array.

7. Save the page and try it out in a browser! If your syntax has been correct throughout, clicking the text link will call the `listNames()` function and generate an alert window like that shown in Figure A.6.

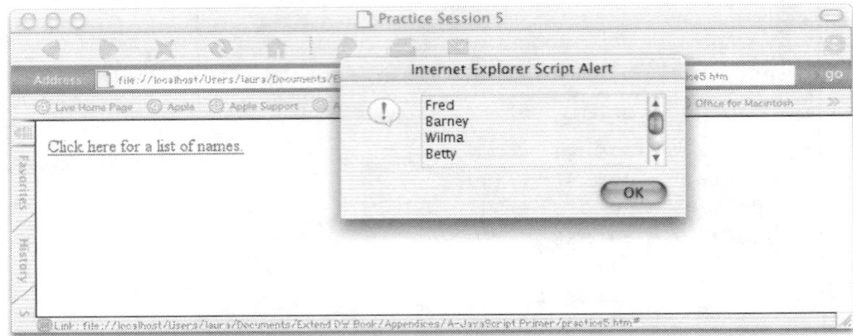

FIGURE A.6 *The practice5.htm file, showing an alert window generated by looping through the values stored in an array.*

Working with Form Elements

Almost every extension you make will involve collecting and processing user input using HTML forms. It's important that you know how to code the standard form elements and how to access each element to collect its value. Note that each form and each form element in a document must have a unique name before its value can be accessed—except radio buttons, which must be named as a group.

note

Experienced scripters know that forms and form elements can also be referred to as members of arrays in the document. The first form in a document is `form[0]`, the first input element in a form as `form.elements[0]`, and so forth. The exercises and projects in this book all use names to access form elements, so accessing them as array members is not covered here.

Form

The form itself has the following syntax:

```
<form name="myForm">
[form elements go here]
</form>
```

For use within extensions, the `<form>` tag doesn't require a method or action attribute.

Text Fields

The basic required code for a text field looks like this:

```
<input type = "text" name = "myTextField">
```

To specify the width of the text field, use one of the following methods (new code is in bold):

```
<input type = "text" name = "myTextField" size = "10">
```

```
<input type = "text" name = "myTextField" style = "size:10px">
```

The first method measures how many characters will show in the field; the second measures its size in pixels.

The JavaScript expression that collects a text field's value looks like this:

```
document.myForm.myTextField.value
```

The following function collects the value stored in a text field called `username`, in a form called `myForm`, and puts it in an alert window:

```
function greetMe() {
var greeting = "Hello, " + document.myForm.username.value + "!";
alert(greeting);
}
```

Checkboxes

The code for a checkbox looks like this:

```
<input type = "checkbox" name = "myCheckBox"  value="myValue">
```

To specify that a checkbox is selected by default, add the following optional attribute (shown in bold):

```
<input type = "checkbox" name = "myCheckBox" value="myValue" checked>
```

The JavaScript expression that determines whether a checkbox has been selected or not looks like this:

```
document.myForm.myCheckBox.checked
```

If the checkbox has been selected, this expression will evaluate as true; if not, it will evaluate as false.

Listing A.1 show the code for a document with a form containing a checkbox and input button. Clicking the button calls a function that determines whether the checkbox has been selected, and if it has been, it displays an alert window:

Listing A.1 A Document with a Form Containing a Checkbox and Input Button

```
<html>
<head>
<title>Checkbox Test</title>
<script language="JavaScript">
function greetMe() {
if (document.myForm.greeting.checked) {
  alert("Greetings!");
  }
}
</script>
</head>
<body>
<form name="myForm">
<input type="checkbox" name="greeting">
<input type="button" value="Click" onClick="greetMe()">
</form>
</body>
</html>
```

Radio Buttons

Unlike other form elements, radio buttons come in groups. Each group has a unique name. Only one member of the group at a time is allowed to be selected. The code for a group of two radio buttons looks like this:

```
<input type = "radio" name = "myRadioGroup" value = "Fred">
<input type = "radio" name = "myRadioGroup" value = "Barney">
```

To indicate that one of the members in the group should be selected by default, add the following optional attribute (shown in bold):

```
<input type = "radio" name = "myRadioGroup" value = "Barney" checked>
```

In JavaScript, the radio button group is treated like an array. The JavaScript expression that determines whether a particular member of a radio button group has been selected looks like this (using 0 to test the first member of the group):

```
document.myForm.myRadioGroup[0].checked
```

The following function steps through an array of radio buttons looking for the one that is selected; when it finds the selected radio button, it displays an alert window and stops looking:

```
function greetMe() {
for (var a=0;a<document.myForm.myRadioGroup.length;a++) {
  if (document.myForm.myRadioGroup[a].checked) {
    alert("Greetings, " + document.myForm.myRadioGroup[a].value);
    break;
    }
  }
}
```

Listing A.2 shows the code for a document with a form containing two radio buttons and an input button. Clicking the button calls a function that determines which radio button has been selected and displays an appropriate greeting in an alert window:

Listing A.2 A Document with a Form Containing Two Radio Buttons and an Input Button

```
<html>
<head>
<title>Radio Button Test</title>
<script language="JavaScript">
function greetMe() {
for (var a=0;a<document.myForm.myRadioGroup.length;a++) {
  if (document.myForm.myRadioGroup[a].checked) {
    alert("Greetings, " + document.myForm.myRadioGroup[a].value);
    break;
    }
  }
}
</script>
</head>
<body>
<form name="myForm">
<input type = "radio" name = "myRadioGroup" value = "Fred" checked>
<input type = "radio" name = "myRadioGroup" value = "Barney">
<input type="button" value="Click" onClick="greetMe()">
</form>
</body>
</html>
```

Popup Menus

The popup menu (sometimes called the dropdown menu) is the most complex of the standard form elements to create. The HTML code looks like this:

```
<select name="myMenu">
    <option value="Fred">Fred</option>
    <option value="Barney">Barney</option>
    <option value="Wilma">Wilma</option>
    <option value="Betty">Betty</option>
</select>
```

To specify a particular option as selected by default, add the following optional attribute (shown in bold):

```
<option value="one" selected>First Item</option>
```

Accessing the value of a menu involves two steps—determining which option in the menu has been selected, and accessing the value of that option. The JavaScript code looks like this:

```
myChoice = document.myForm.myMenu.selectedIndex;
myValue = document.myForm.myMenu.options[myChoice].value;
```

As with radio buttons, the menu's options form an array that is accessed by number.

The following function looks through an array called `myMenu`, in a form called `myForm`, to find the selected option and greets the person named in that option:

```
function greetMe() {
myChoice = document.myForm.myMenu.selectedIndex;
myName = document.myForm.myMenu.options[myChoice].value;
window.alert("Greetings, " + myName + "!");
}
```

Listing A.3 shows the code for a document with a form containing a popup menu and an input button. Clicking the button calls a function that determines which menu option has been selected and displays a greeting in an alert window:

Listing A.3 A Document with a Form Containing a Popup Menu and an Input Button

```
<html>
<head>
<title>Select Menu Test</title>
<script language="JavaScript">
function greetMe() {
myChoice = document.myForm.myMenu.selectedIndex;
myName = document.myForm.myMenu.options[myChoice].value;
window.alert("Greetings, " + myName + "!");
}
</script>
</head>
<body>
<form name="myForm">
  <select name="myMenu">
    <option value="Fred">Fred</option>
    <option value="Barney">Barney</option>
    <option value="Wilma">Wilma</option>
    <option value="Betty">Betty</option>
  </select>
</form>
</body>
</html>
```

Buttons

When creating forms for use with Dreamweaver extensions, you don't have to create your own buttons for basic functions like OK and Cancel. But you might want to create buttons for other purposes. The HTML code for a button looks like this:

```
<input type = "button" value = "Click Me">
```

The `value` attribute determines what text will appear in the button. The button can also have a name, but it isn't necessary for most form uses because buttons don't store user input.

Form Elements and Event Handlers

Most form elements can have event handlers (and therefore function calls) attached to them.

Buttons, radio buttons, and checkboxes can have the `onClick` event handler attached to them, like this:

```
<input type = "button" value = "Click Me" onClick="greetMe()">
```

Popup menus, radio buttons, and checkboxes can have the `onChange` event handler attached to them—this handler triggers a function to execute whenever the user chooses a new option from the list:

```
<select name="myMenu" onChange = "greetMe()">
```

Text fields can have the `onBlur` event handler attached to them—this handler triggers a function to execute whenever the user enters text in the field and then moves on to interact with another form element:

```
<input type = "text" name= "myTextField" onBlur = "greetMe()">
```

Listing A.4 shows the code for a document that contains an HTML form with two radio buttons and one text field. Clicking either of the radio buttons changes the value of the text field to match its own value.

Listing A.4 A Document That Contains an HTML Form with Two Radio Buttons and One Text Field

```
<html>
<head>
<title>Form Test</title>
<script language="JavaScript">
function setMe() {
for (var a=0;a<document.myForm.myRadioGroup.length;a++) {
  if (document.myForm.myRadioGroup[a].checked) {
```

continues

Listing A.4 Continued

```
document.myForm.myTextField.value=document.myForm.myRadioGroup[a].value;
    break;
      }
   }
}
</script>
</head>
<body>
<form name="myForm">
   <input type="radio" name="myRadioGroup" value="Fred"
onChange="setMe()">
   <input type="radio" name="myRadioGroup" value="Barney"
onChange="setMe()">
    <input type="text" name="myTextField">
</form>
</body>
</html>
```

To get some practice using form elements and calling on their values, create files using the code in the previous listings and try them out in a browser. You'll be getting the hang of coding forms in no time.

JavaScript and Objects

JavaScript is an object-oriented scripting language, which means it thinks in terms of objects, properties, and methods. Although you can do a lot of work in JavaScript without being aware of its object-oriented nature, you're always using JavaScript objects when you work in this language; and the more you know about them, the more the language will make sense.

In scripting terms, an *object* is a collection of attributes that describe it and actions that it can perform. The attributes are called *properties*; the actions are called *methods*. Properties are similar to variables, only they're always associated with a particular object. Methods are similar to functions. An object and its properties and methods are referred to in JavaScript using dot syntax, like this:

```
object.property
```

```
object.method()
```

For a real-world analogy, think of your dog as an object. He has various attributes—breed, fur color, size, and so forth. He also has actions that he is capable of performing—barking, running, jumping, whining. If your dog's name is Fido, his properties and methods would be referred to like this:

```
fido.breed = schnauzer;
fido.color = gray;
fido.bark();
fido.run();
```

Objects can also contain other objects—again, just like your dog contains a tail and four instances of the paw object. In dot syntax, objects contained within other objects are referred to like this:

```
parent_object.child_object
```

Just like your dog's tail would be referred to as

```
fido.tail
```

JavaScript comes with a set of built-in objects ready for your use. These include the `Date` object, `String` object, `window` object, `document` object, and others. Each object has its own properties and methods. When you use the `window.alert()` statement, you're actually calling on the `alert()` method of the `Window` object. When you use `document.myForm.myTextField.value` to collect the value of a text field, you're actually collecting the value property of an object named `myTextField`, which is the child of an object called `myForm`, which is the child of the `document` object. (The hierarchical structure of elements within a document is called the DOM, or Document Object Model, in JavaScript. Chapter 4 covers using the DOM for extension writing.)

When you start working with Dreamweaver extensions, you'll discover that Dreamweaver provides a whole series of objects specifically for writing extensions. These include the `dreamweaver` or `dw` object, the `site` object, and the `dom` object.

Linking JS and HTML Files

Some web authors prefer not to mix JavaScript and HTML code in one document. For tidiness and efficient authoring, they move the JavaScript code to an external document, named with the .js file extension, and link that file to the HTML file. When a JS file is linked to an HTML document, the JavaScript interpreter treats the two files as one. Any JavaScript functions in the JS file can be called on from the HTML file and executed. To link an HTML file to a JS file, use the `<script>` tag with the following syntax and with no contents:

```
<script language="JavaScript" src="MyScripts.js"></syntax>
```

Listing A.5 shows an HTML file with embedded JavaScript functions. Listing A.6 and Listing A.7 show the same file with JavaScript code removed to a linked JS file.

Listing A.5 Contents of the MyDoc.html File with All JavaScript Code Contained in the Document (Script Tag Shown in Bold)

```
<html>
<head>
<title>JavaScript Test</title>
<script language="JavaScript">
function testMe() {
alert("Hello, world!");
```

Listing A.5 Continued

```
}
</script>
</head>
<body>
<a href="#" onClick="testMe()">Click here</a>
</body>
</html>
```

Listing A.6 Contents of the MyDoc.html File with JavaScript Function Removed to a Linked JS File (Script Tag Shown in Bold)

```
<html>
<head>
<title>JavaScript Test</title>
<script language="JavaScript" src="MyScripts.js">
</script>
</head>
<body>
<a href="#" onClick="testMe()">Click here</a>
</body>
</html>
```

Listing A.7 Contents of the MyScripts.js file

```
function testMe() {
alert("Hello, world!");
}
```

Summary

Although this appendix in no way aspires to reveal all the mysteries of JavaScript, it covers all the very basic bases that you need to know to get started writing Dreamweaver extensions. If you can easily go through all the tasks in the practice sessions, your scripting skills are definitely ready for some extension writing. If you need further help, try the wonderful JavaScript tutorials in *Teach Yourself JavaScript in 24 Hours* (SAMS), or read through Danny Goodman's *JavaScript Bible* (IDG). You can also learn more scripting online for free, by visiting tutorial and informational sites like `www.webmonkey.com`.

Appendix B

Macromedia User Interface Guidelines

If you want to submit your extensions to the Macromedia Exchange (read more on that in Appendix D, "Submitting Extensions to the Macromedia Dreamweaver Exchange"), you won't get a Macromedia-approved rating unless you follow the official User Interface Guidelines for any extensions that include an interactive component (that is, dialog boxes, Property inspectors, floating panels). Even if you're not planning to submit to the Exchange, the guidelines offer good advice on creating interfaces that blend well with the rest of Dreamweaver, work across platforms, and are intuitive to use and difficult to mess up. In addition to the official required guidelines, this appendix looks at some suggested guidelines from Macromedia for writing good extensions. It covers learning about layout; using buttons; providing help; working with fonts, colors, and graphics; and providing error-checking and bulletproofing.

Fonts and Colors

When it comes to specifying fonts and colors, the advice is simple: Just say no. Don't specify any background colors for your pages, table cells, or layers. Don't specify font colors, sizes, typefaces, or styles. Plain default vanilla is the required flavor, which allows Dreamweaver to assign values that will mesh with the rest of the program's interface across Mac and Windows platforms.

note

The one exception to this is when providing a short online help paragraph within a dialog box. In this situation, a specific background table cell color (#D3D3D3) is required. See the section on Online Help later in this appendix for details.

Graphics

Your interface might require graphics for functional purposes (navigation using a folder icon, for instance), illustrative purposes (icons in Property inspectors, for instance, or icons for common functions such as alignment, make bold, and so on), or branding purposes (your company logo, to identify the author of the extension).

Inserting Images

You get images into a dialog box, inspector, or panel the same way you get an image into a Web page—by linking to it using a relative pathname. If the image is for illustrative or branding purposes, use the `<img>` tag. If it is intended to be functional (that is, a button in a form), use the `<input>` tag to create an image button.

File Formats

Although Macromedia nowhere specifies this as a requirement, all images in the standard extensions are GIFs. GIF images work nicely for the crisp, clean, simple requirements of icons and other tiny pictures, which is mainly what your interface should be using. For the icon displayed in the Insert bar, only a GIF image will work (JPG and other formats are ignored, and substituted with the default icon). For icons displayed in dialog boxes, inspectors, and floating panels, JPG images will work but probably won't look as clean as you need them to. In addition, JPG images don't support transparency, and transparency helps images blend into the interface. (Figure B.1 shows an example of GIF versus JPG images.)

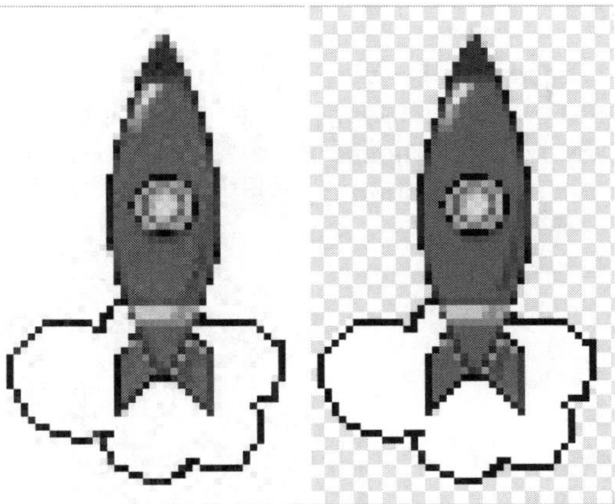

FIGURE B.1 *A GIF and a JPG image compared for displaying a small icon image.*

Navigational/Illustrative Images (Icons)

Macromedia doesn't give any size recommendations for icons, but it does recommend restricting the size of dialog boxes and floating panels, and Property inspectors have their own size restrictions. So it makes sense to keep icons small and only use them when they actually enhance the interface more than a simple text label would. Figure B.2 shows some examples of icons in the Macromedia standard interface. Though tiny, their meaning and purpose is clear, and they serve to make the interface less crowded, not more so.

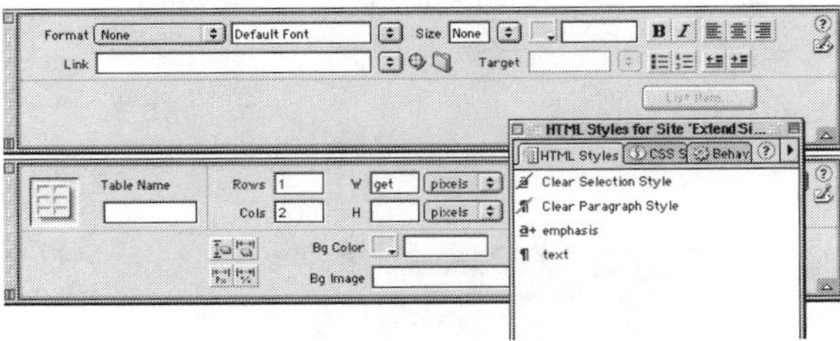

FIGURE B.2 *Illustrative and navigational icons in some Macromedia standard inspectors and panels.*

note

Icon design is an art and a skill. It's not easy creating meaningful pictures out of just a handful of pixels! It takes practice and knowledge of symbology. If your skills aren't up to it, either don't use icons or get help with them.

Shared Images

Many of the little icon images you might want to use are available in the Configuration/Shared/MM/Images folder, ready for your dialog boxes or other interfaces. Figure B.3 shows this folder and its partial contents. If you do use any of these images, make sure you don't undermine the Dreamweaver interface—use them for their intended purpose only.

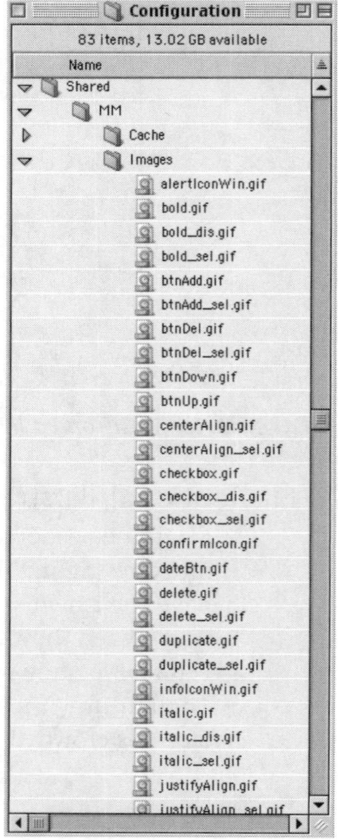

FIGURE B.3 *Icons ready for use, in the Configuration/Shared/MM/Images folder.*

Branding Images (Logos)

Macromedia's user interface guidelines allow you to place your company logo in your interfaces, as long as you follow these rules:

- **Dialog boxes.** Logos must be placed at the bottom of dialog boxes or made available by adding an About button to the dialog box.
- **Property inspectors.** Logos must be placed in the upper-right corner of the inspector, and must fit above the horizontal divider.
- **Floating panels.** Macromedia does not specifically mention requirements for logos in floating panels other than the Property inspector.

Figure B.4 shows the Macromedia recommended placement for logos.

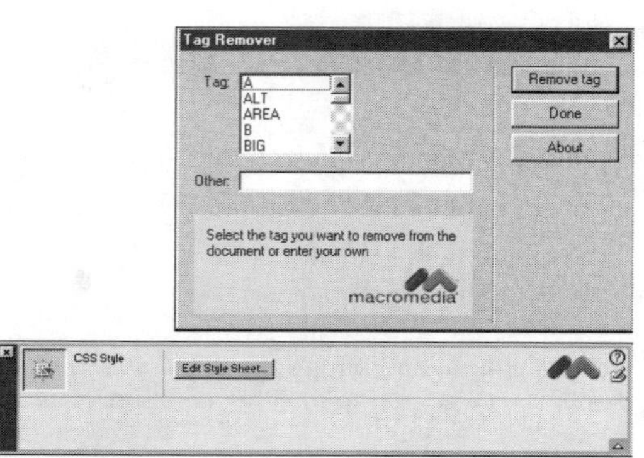

FIGURE B.4 *From the online user interface guidelines, Macromedia's examples of correct branding.*

Layout

In general, the requirement is that layouts be clean, easy to read, and not take up more space than necessary. Scrolling (that is, interfaces that don't completely fit on the user's screen) is a no-no. Macromedia gives separate instructions for laying out dialog boxes and Property inspectors, and gives no instructions for floating panels.

Dialog Box Layout

Dialog box layout should be controlled by using tables. If a dialog box contains too much information to fit in a reasonable size, the content can be organized into tabbed layers, each of which uses a table for its layout.

Tables for Layout

Tables created for dialog box layout should have the following characteristics:

- Don't set width, height, cellspacing, or cellpadding attributes. Dreamweaver determines height and width, as needed by your contents and the user's platform (see Figure B.5).

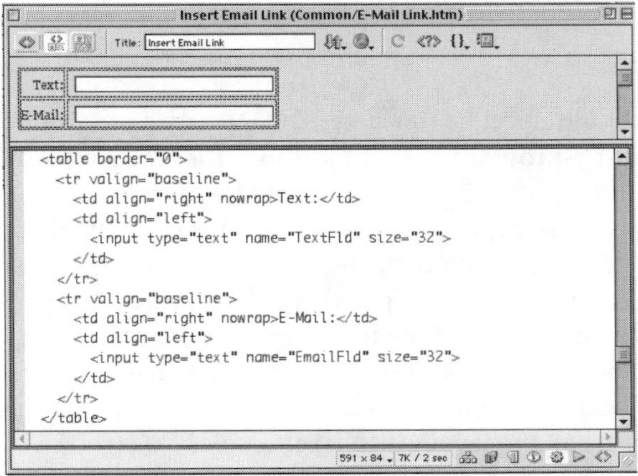

FIGURE B.5 *Proper table formatting for a dialog box layout.*

- With the exception of any online help (see the later section "Online Help"), don't use background colors for the table or its cells.
- To vertically align the contents of cells, use `valign=baseline`. (In the standard extensions, this is applied to the `<tr>` tag.)
- When text labels are used, they should appear to the left of the input elements they refer to. Text should be right-aligned by adding `align="right"` to the `<td>` tag. Labels should have each first word capitalized, and should end with a colon. Labels should never wrap, so use the `nowrap` attribute for these cells (see Figure B.6).

- If a form element consists of more than one line (such as a multiline text field), align the label with the top of the text label. This can be done by using `valign="baseline"` in the `<td>` tag for both adjoining cells. (Figure B.6 shows the proper presentation of multiline controls.)

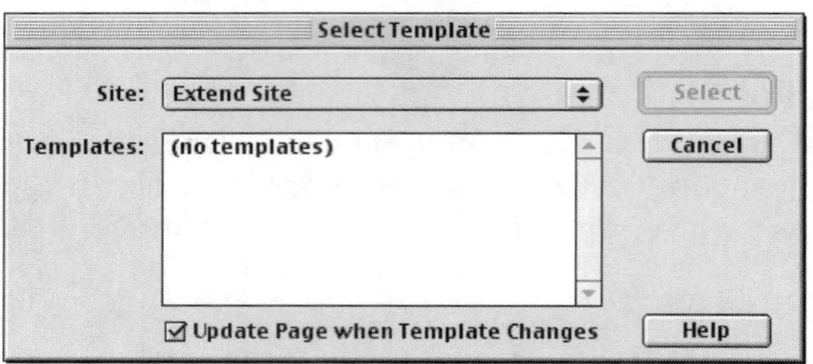

FIGURE B.6 *Proper presentation of multiline controls.*

- If a browse button is to be used, either with the Browse… label or a folder icon, it should appear to the right of the text field its results will display in.

Dialog Box Size

Dialog boxes should never be too large. The Dreamweaver Application Programming Interface (API) provides a function for setting dialog box size—`windowDimensions()`—however, Macromedia instructs you not to use this function. If you don't specify a size for the dialog box or for the table that contains the layout, Dreamweaver determines the correct size based on content. The minimum content area for a dialog box is 200×50 pixels; the maximum area is 511×434. If content would cause the size to exceed the maximum in width or height, Dreamweaver automatically provides scrollbars to the dialog box to make it functional—but this is bad design, and is a definite no-no. If your dialog box contains this much content, reduce the content, or break the layout into layers.

Organizing Content with Layers

It is acceptable to use tabbed layers to present chunks of options in a dialog box. Although Macromedia offers no specific instructions on the construction of layers in its user interface guidelines, you can learn from seeing how layered interfaces are implemented in the standard extensions.

Figure B.7 shows a sample layered dialog box. Figure B.8 shows the document that created this dialog box as it appears in Dreamweaver design and code views. From these figures, you can learn the following:

- Each set of content is in its own layer. (The interface shown has two content layers: Main and Options.) A background graphic, in this case tabBigWin500×160.gif, creates the 3D beveled appearance.
- Each layer's tab comes from two graphics, each stored in its own layer: tabBg.gif and tabBgSel.gif.
- Clicking on one of the tab images changes layer visibility as needed.

Macromedia's guidelines do not specifically mention this, but it is standard in interface design that the name of a button or menu command that opens a dialog box should end with an ellipsis (...). The only place where this convention isn't observed is in the main buttons to the right of a dialog box.

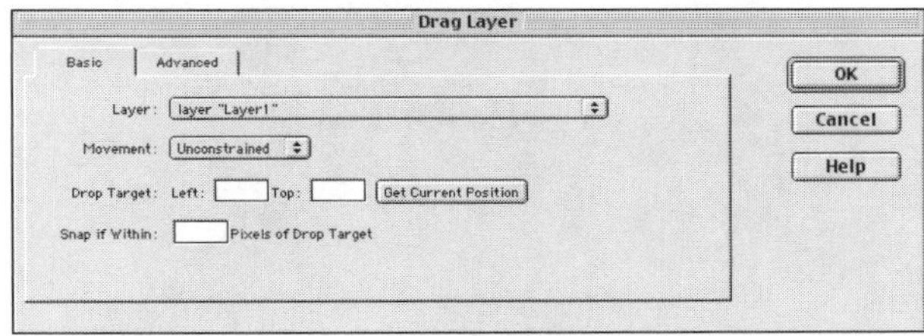

Figure B.7 *Dialog box for the Drag Layer behavior, showing a tabbed interface.*

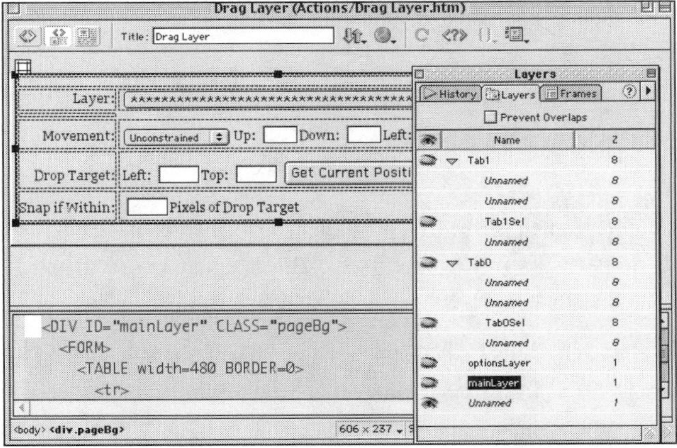

Figure B.8 *The Drag Layer behavior file, as it looks in Dreamweaver Design and Code views. The Layers panel shows how the content is divided into layers. The code shows images being used to create the tabbed look.*

Property Inspector Layout

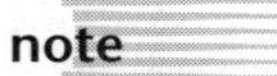

note

Refer to Chapter 10, "Into the Great Beyond," for a complete discussion of creating and working with tabbed layouts like this.

The user interface guidelines don't specify how Property inspector layouts should be created, but all the standard inspectors use layers to position layout elements. Macromedia warns that inspector layouts will look different on Windows and Macintosh platforms, and you are therefore encouraged to check your custom inspector layouts carefully for cross-platform compatibility. Inspectors aren't required to look exactly the same across platforms, but to be readable and functional on both. Figure B.9 shows an example of this inconsistency at work.

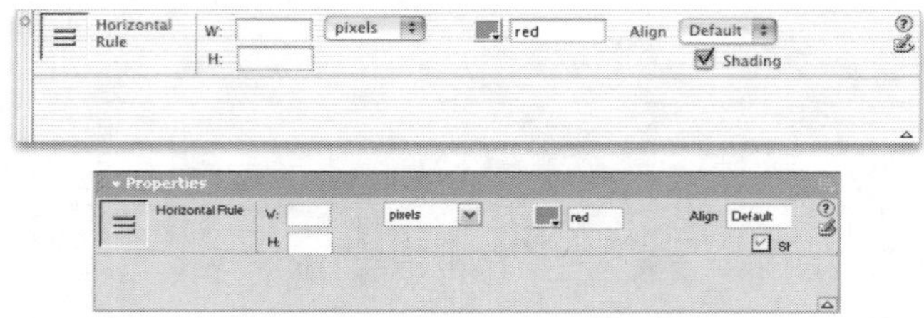

FIGURE B.9 *A custom Property inspector as it looks in Dreamweaver/Mac and Dreamweaver/Windows.*

Form Elements

There are few specific requirements for form elements, but there are several suggestions and observations to help you use them to their best.

Text Fields

According to the official guidelines, you shouldn't use the size attribute with text fields, as it doesn't display correctly on the Macintosh platform. Instead, you should use inline styles such as these:

- `style="width:230px"` for wide text fields (to hold URLs, for instance)
- `style="width:135px"` for narrower text fields

This having been said, however, it should be noted that many of the standard Macromedia extensions do use the size attribute. (See the dialog box analyzed in Figure B.6, as an example of this.) For fields holding numbers, `size="8"` is often used (or sometimes `size="6"`). For fields holding color names, the common width is `size="10"`.

Checkboxes and Radio Buttons

Use checkboxes for controls that can be selected and deselected independently (see Figure B.10). Use radio buttons when a group of controls works as a set, where only one may be selected at a time (see Figure B.11). When using radio buttons, always have one button selected as the default.

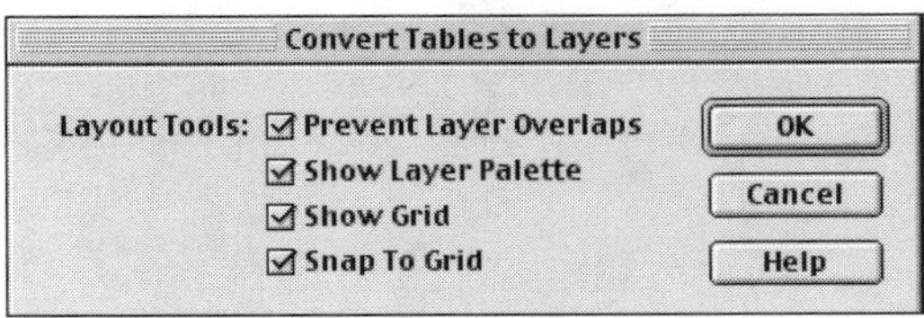

FIGURE B.10 *Using checkboxes for choices that can be set independently of one another.*

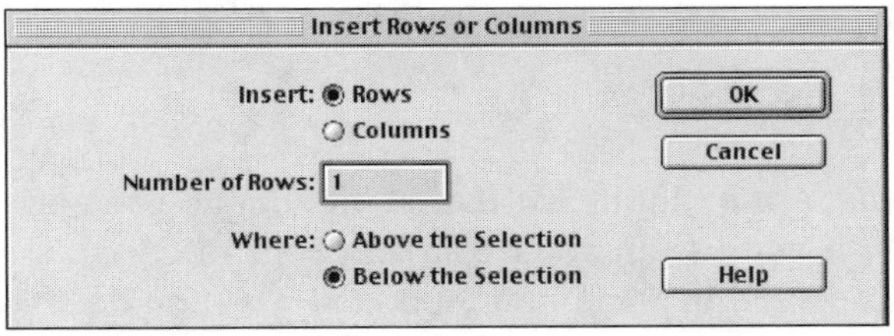

FIGURE B.11 *Using groups of radio buttons for groups of options that can have only one selection each.*

Lists and Popup Menus

You can use multiline lists or popup menus to provide users with a list of choices. Use popup menus when the user must select one choice only from the set of options (see Figure B.12). Use multiline lists when the user is allowed to select more than one item (see Figure B.13).

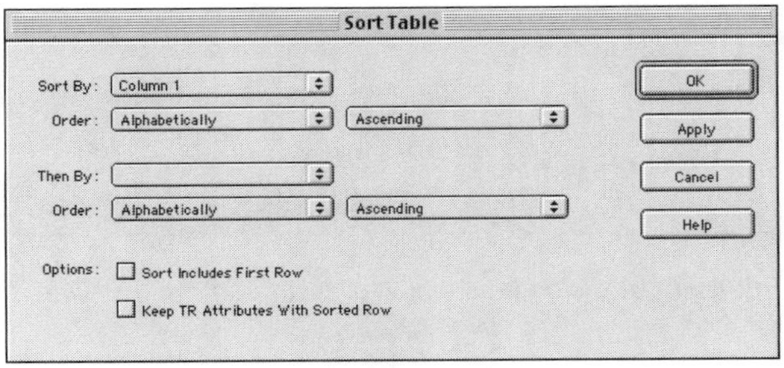

FIGURE B.12 *Using popup menus to allow the user to choose one from each set of options.*

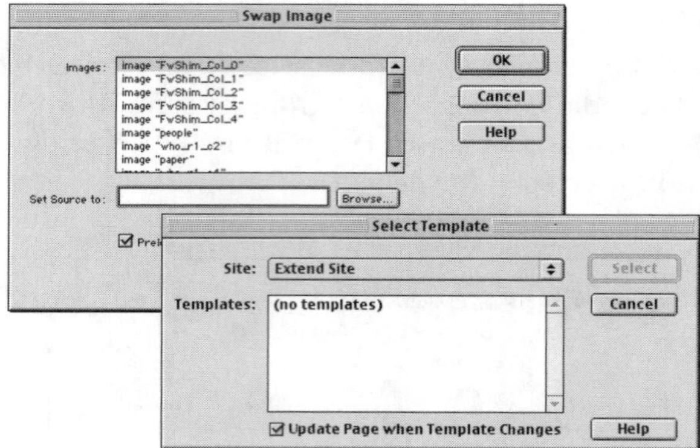

FIGURE B.13 *The Swap Image and Apply Template dialog boxes, showing two different uses of selection lists/menus.*

Additive Lists

An *additive list* is a multiline list that allows the user to add or subtract items (see Figure B.14). If you use an additive list in your interface, use + and - buttons for adding and subtracting items, and (optionally) up and down arrows for rearranging items. Dim any button when its function is no longer operable (for example, when no more items can be added to the list, dim the + button). The images for all these buttons are available in the Configuration/Shared/MM/Images folder (refer to Figure B.4).

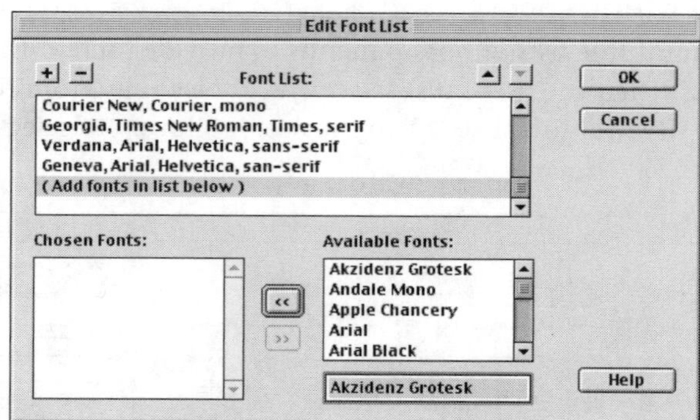

FIGURE B.14 *The Edit Font List dialog box, which uses an additive multiline list.*

Color Buttons

Although the Macromedia UI guidelines don't specifically mention color buttons, you should take note of how this Dreamweaver-specific form element is used in the standard extensions. The color button always appears in conjunction with a text field for displaying or manually entering color values. The color button is on the left, and the text field is on the right. The two form elements should be linked so that choosing a color in one will reveal a value or color swatch in the other. Figure B.15 shows this happening.

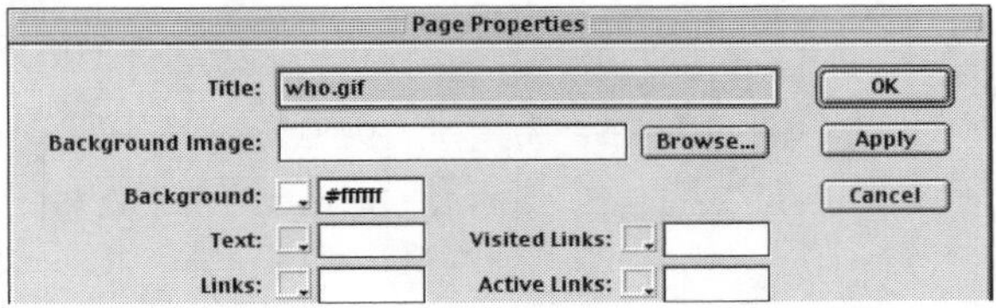

FIGURE B.15 *A portion of the Page Properties dialog box, showing standard use of the* `<mmcolorbutton>` *form element.*

Note also that if a user types a color into the color field, you should make sure your script adds the **#**, if necessary. This is how the standard color controls work.

note

See Workshop #3 of Chapter 2, "Creating Custom Objects," for a complete discussion of creating and working with color buttons.

Tree Controls

Another Dreamweaver-specific form element—tree controls—are also not covered in the UI guidelines. From their appearance in the Keyboard Shortcuts Editor (see Figure B.16), you can see that they give users the ability to navigate through hierarchies of choices for situations that require complex input choices. A tree structure in a dialog box necessitates some sort of scrolling within the tree control itself when the tree is fully expanded. This is an acceptable part of this interface element. Scrolling the dialog box around the tree is still not acceptable.

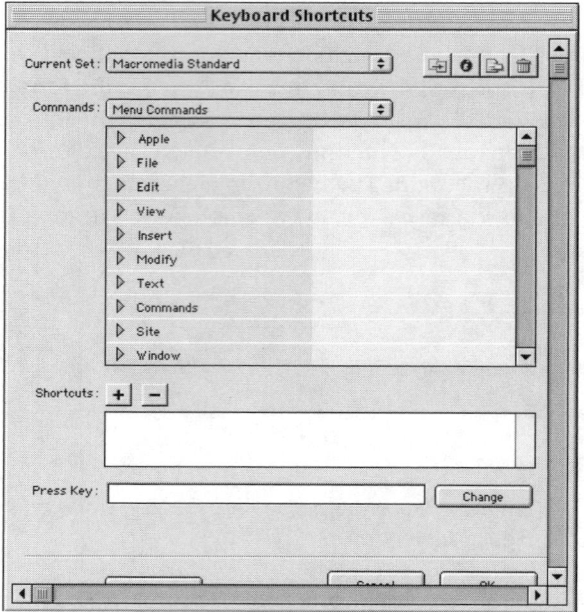

FIGURE B.16 *The Keyboard Shortcuts Editor, showing the use of tree controls.*

Buttons

The buttons referred to here are those that Dreamweaver inserts into dialog boxes for objects, behaviors, and commands. You have no control over how these buttons look, other than to specify the text labels that appear in command buttons.

Buttons In Objects and Behaviors

For dialog boxes belonging to objects and behaviors, OK and Cancel buttons are supplied automatically by Dreamweaver. A Help button will be supplied automatically if you include the `displayHelp()` function in your code. Because you have no control over any of these, there are no user interface guidelines for them.

Buttons In Commands

For commands, Dreamweaver places whatever buttons you specify along the right edge of the dialog box. Because you determine which buttons appear and in which order, they are subject to interface requirements and suggestions. In particular:

- The OK button should always come first, at the top of the dialog box. The OK button doesn't have to actually say OK—if a different name is more appropriate, use it—but there should always be an OK button.
- If there's an Apply button, it should come next. (This button executes all or part of the command, but does not close the dialog box.) If there is more than one apply-type button for applying different parts of the command, they should all come immediately after the OK button.
- The Cancel button should come next. There should always be a Cancel button.
- If there's a Help button, it should come last.

note

It can be tempting to create fun-sounding alternate names for buttons, but don't do so lightly! Everyone knows what OK, Save, Done, Open, Import, and such mean; and they're transparent enough to be useful without being annoying. Do It, Go For It, Go Get It, and the like may be confusing to some users and will probably annoy others after a while.

Any button whose purpose is to help the user set values in the form (for instance, a Browse button) should be defined as part of the form, and should appear next to the field it's associated with. Figure B.17 shows various buttons in command dialog boxes. (Note that `OK` is not always the appropriate value for the OK button.)

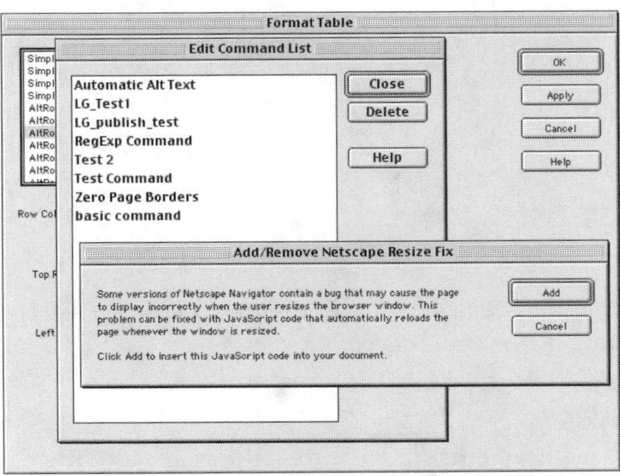

FIGURE B.17 *Several command dialog boxes, showing the types of buttons appropriate to this extension type.*

Buttons In Property Inspectors/Floating Panels

No buttons are automatically created for either Property inspectors or floating panels. All buttons must therefore be defined as part of the form, using the `<input>` tag. If a button is associated with a particular form element, such as a text field, place it next to that item. If the button is to be created from an image, use `<input type="image">`.

Online Help

Macromedia does not approve any extension that doesn't include some sort of online help as part of its interface. Help text must contain at least an explanation of each field or value the user can control, and/or a procedure describing how to use the extension. If the extension is relatively simple, a few sentences can be added to the bottom of the dialog box. If the dialog box uses tabbed layers, the Help can exist in a special Help layer. Otherwise, there must be a Help button.

Short Help

If the amount of help a user needs can fit at the bottom of your dialog box, place it there. To do this, adjust your dialog box's layout table as follows:

1. Create a table cell at the bottom of the dialog box to contain the help text.
2. Assign the cell a `bgcolor` of #D3D3D3 (a slightly darker shade of gray than the rest of the dialog box will be given).

Figure B.18 shows short online help at the bottom of a dialog box.

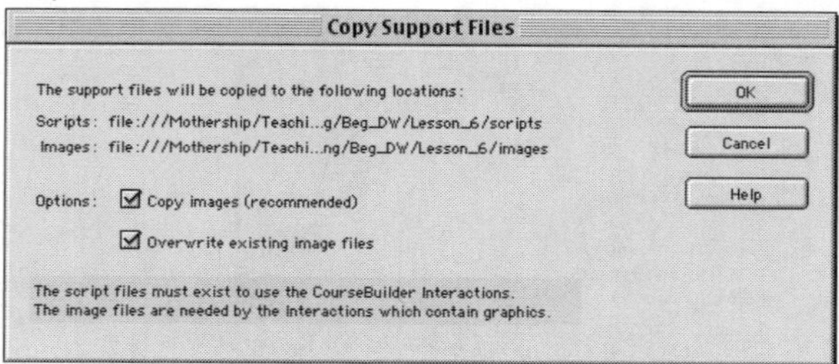

FIGURE B.18 *The dialog box for the CourseBuilder extension, showing short help text (in addition to a Help button) added to the dialog box layout.*

Tabbed Help Layer

There are no requirements for creating help in a layer, other than the requirements and suggestions for creating tabbed layouts in general (see preceding). If the help is placed here rather than at the bottom of the dialog box, it must be more substantial than a few sentences' worth of information.

Help Button

For objects and behaviors, Help buttons are automatically added to dialog boxes when you define the `displayHelp()` function. For commands, you create a local function to display help, and include a Help button in the `commandButtons()` function. When a user clicks a Help button, one of three things must happen:

- An alert window appears, containing the help text.
- An HTML page containing help opens in the user's browser. This page can be on the Internet, accessed using an absolute URL, or it can be stored locally in a custom folder you have created in the Configuration/Shared folder.
- A hidden layer appears, containing the help text. (This is slightly different from using a tabbed Help layer. The dialog box needn't use the tabbed layer interface to have a Help layer appear.)
- Dreamweaver activates the operating system's built-in Help application, which displays one or more pages of help text.

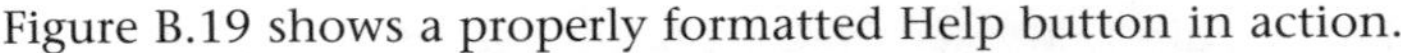

Figure B.19 shows a properly formatted Help button in action.

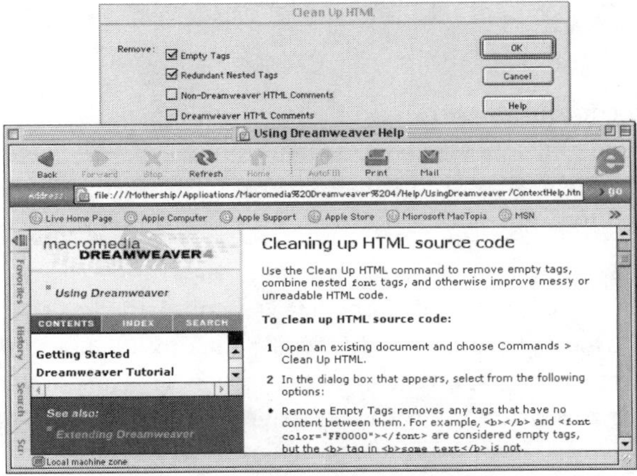

FIGURE B.19 *A dialog box containing a Help button, and the actions that will occur if it is clicked.*

Error-Checking, Default Values, and More

Error-proof handling of input is not necessarily part of the visible interface, but it's still part of the interface. You want to make sure that dialog boxes are ready to receive input, that they include default values when appropriate, and that they stay out of the user's way but stop him from making disastrous coding mistakes. Macromedia suggests the following:

Focus and Selection

If the dialog box includes one or more text fields, the first of these should have keyboard focus so that the user can immediately start typing without having to click in the field first.

Also, if the dialog box comes up with default contents in the text field, contents should be selected so that the user doesn't have to select and delete them before typing.

Both of these functions are handled by the two lines of code you've been entering in the locally defined `initializeUI()` function:

```
document.myForm.firstTextField.focus();
document.myForm.firstTextField.select();
```

By defining this function and calling it by using the `onLoad` event handler, you accomplish this interface requirement.

Error-Checking

What happens if the user supplies bad information or no information in a dialog box? An attribute requires a numeric value, but the user enters a filename by mistake. A required attribute for a certain tag is left blank. What should a good interface do?

Hands-Off Philosophy

The Macromedia philosophy is this: Do nothing unless the mistake will actually "break" the page in a browser—in other words, if it will cause visitors' browsers to crash or display the page disastrously wrong. If the error causes some page element to "fail gracefully," you shouldn't interfere with it.

Why such a hands-off approach? One of the reasons web designers love Dreamweaver is that it stays out of their way, not insisting that it knows coding better than the user does. Users might not be making mistakes; they may be applying newly evolving coding standards or creating effects the software authors could not expect as they're writing the software. Therefore, you must assume users know what they're doing until they absolutely prove otherwise.

Preventing Disasters

It's all about form validation—using event handlers to check user input as soon as it's entered and before it becomes part of the document. Luckily, you only have to interfere when certain input (or lack of input) will break the page, and, surprisingly, it's not that easy to truly break a Web page. A table formatted with `width="fred"` probably won't display quite as the user intended, but it probably won't ruin the display of the entire page. Therefore, in its Table object, Dreamweaver won't interfere if a user enters this value. However, just try adding a Swap Image behavior without specifying an image to use as the rollover state. Dreamweaver won't let that happen because rollover code without a source image specified will generate a JavaScript error in a browser.

What should you do if some user input will cause a disaster, and must be prevented? The appropriate response is to show an alert dialog box, explaining the reasons why the input is invalid and returning the values to their previous, or default, settings. Figure B.20 shows this happening with the Swap Image behavior.

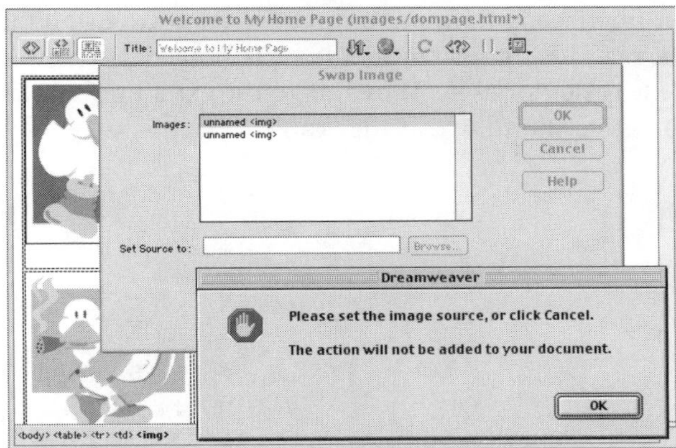

FIGURE B.20 *A dialog box showing the interface response to invalid user input.*

Default Values

Dialog boxes should not only function with strange user input; they should also function with no user input. Creating this situation isn't always possible, but you should take advantage of those situations in which it is possible. This can be accomplished in various ways, depending on the circumstances.

If the input value is for an optional parameter, obviously omitting to fill in the value should remove the parameter from the code. In this case, `field` can default to `empty` every time the dialog box appears, or a value can appear by default. The document code won't actually suffer in either case. The operative question here is the following: In most cases, do you think users will want a value there or not? And if so, what is probably the most likely value they'll want?

If the input value is required, it makes sense to have a default value always appear. Remember, though, that by "required," you mean the following: Will the page be ruined without a value here? If a missing value will cause one page element to display improperly but won't affect the rest of the page, this could be considered to fall under the non-interference policy. Your judgment is required to determine how much damage a page can suffer without being "broken."

Summary

A good user interface is an important part of your extension's usability and success. After all, the main reason you're adding extensions to Dreamweaver in the first place is to make life easier for users. Why not go the extra mile and make your extensions as approachable and intuitive as they can be?

Appendix C

Packaging Extensions for Use with the Extension Manager

Just as the Macromedia Extensions Manager has become the accepted way to install and manage Dreamweaver extensions, creating installation packages is the way to prepare your files to share with others. Instead of handing over several separate HTML, JavaScript, and GIF files, along with instructions on what files to put where, you package everything up in an MXP file, and the Extensions Manager takes care of the rest. This appendix describes the procedure for creating an MXP file for easy sharing.

Packaging Extensions

An MXP file is nothing more than a package containing all the separate files that constitute an extension, along with a set of instructions on where each file should go and what changes should be made to menus.xml to support the extension. Creating an MXP involves collecting all the files, coding the instructions as an XML file, and using the Extension Manager to generate the package. Aside from a brief dip into some new XML, all the hard work is done by the time you're ready to package.

Task 1: Collect your materials

This sounds easy. Create a folder, somewhere outside the Configuration folder, and copy all the various files that constitute your extension into this folder. If your extension consists of only one or two files, and you're not creating any custom subfolders, it's a no-brainer. For more complex extensions, it takes a little bit of planning to assure that no one gets left out. Some tips:

- If your extension involves custom folders (a custom objects, behaviors category, or a shared folder, for instance), you don't need to copy those folders to the staging area—though if it helps you keep your organization straight, it doesn't hurt to copy them.
- If your extension consists of several files—especially if they need to be stored in several different folders inside the Configuration folder—make a list of files (and where each should be stored) before you start collecting them.
- If your extension requires changes to menus.xml, make a note of those changes. Add them to the list of files you're already creating.
- If your extension includes different files with the same names (an object, command, and inspector all named Flash Detector.htm, for instance), you need to put them in different subfolders inside your collection folder. Whether you use subfolders or not doesn't matter, as far as the MXP-making process goes. It's just a way of allowing files with identical names to share space in preparation for packaging.

note

Technically, collecting the files is optional. It is possible to create an MXP package while your various extension files are still in their Development folders, scattered throughout the Dreamweaver Configuration folder. It's much easier, however, and safer to keep track of the files to be packaged if they're all in one place.

Collecting Materials for a Simple Extension: Set Page Properties Behavior (Chapter 3, Workshop #2)

This simple behavior consists of only two files (HTML and JS), creates no special folders, and doesn't make any changes to the menus. The materials list is simple:

- Set Page Properties.htm
- Set Page Properties.js

Collecting Materials for a Multifile Extension: Custom Horizontal Rule Object (Chapter 3, Workshop #3, and Chapter 6, Workshop #2)

The list of materials to assemble for this extension includes the following:

- Objects: Custom HR.js
- Inspectors: Custom HR.htm
- Inspectors: Customhr.gif

Figure C.1 shows the collection folder for this extension.

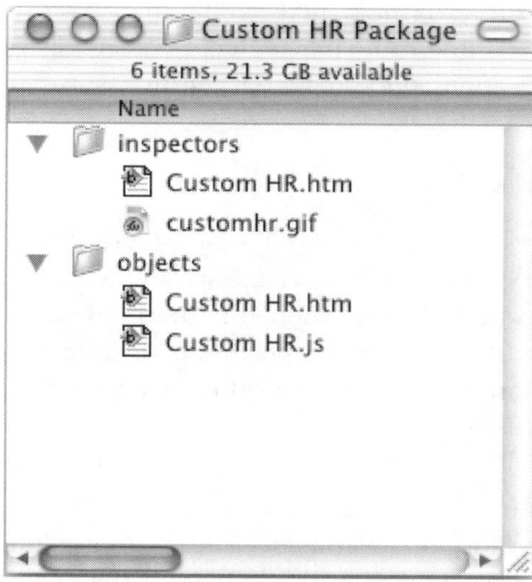

FIGURE C.1 *The files comprising the Custom Horizontal Rule object, assembled in a collection folder and ready for packaging.*

Collecting Materials for an Extension with Menu Changes: Table Helper Floating Panel (Chapter 7, Workshop #1)

This extension consists of only one file, so that part of the job is easy. But the checklist of materials also includes the menu changes:

- TableHelper.htm
- menu change: In the `id="DWMenu_Window"` menu, after this menu entry:

```
<menuitem name="Rest_ore All" … id="DWMenu_Window_RestoreAll" />
```

  add this:

```
<separator />
<menuitem name="Table Helper" enabled="true"
➥command="dw.toggleFloater('TableHelper')"
➥checked="dw.getFloaterVisibility('TableHelper')"
➥id="RocketLaura_TableHelper_Floater"/>
```

Task 2: Create the MXI (instructions) file

This is the most painstaking part of the packaging process. The package requires an XML file, with the extension .mxi, containing instructions on where to put files, how to change menus, and what folders to create; as well as information on what the extension is supposed to do, who its author is, and so forth. The XML syntax for this file is very exacting.

Saving the MXI File

The installer file is simply an XML file saved with the .mxi extension. Its filename, however, must be valid on both Windows and Macintosh platforms, and can have no spaces. It can be saved anywhere on your hard drive, but because all pathnames to the extension files must be relative to the MXI file, it makes the most sense to save it in the collection folder with your other extension files.

Structure of an MXI File

Lucky for you, the Macromedia Extension Manager comes with detailed documentation, a sample file, and a blank template file to use in creating the MXI document. To find them, locate the application folder for the Extension Manager on your computer, and look inside. Inside the Samples/Dreamweaver subfolder, you see the following:

- **Sample.htm**—A very simple command file.
- **Sample.mxi**—An MXI instruction sheet for packaging the Sample.htm command file extension.
- **Blank.mxi**—A blank MXI template to use in constructing your own MXI files. This file is nicely commented to help you fill it out.

The contents of Sample.mxi, a simple but properly structured MXI file, are shown here:

```
<macromedia-extension
      name="Hello, World"
      version="1.0"
      type="Command">

      <!-- List the required/compatible products -->

      <products>
            <product name="Dreamweaver" version="3" primary="true" />
      </products>

      <!-- Describe the author -->

      <author name="Macromedia" />

      <!-- Describe the extension -->

      <description>
      <![CDATA[
      This is a sample extension.<br><br>
      It displays a javascript alert that says "Hello, World!".
      ]]>
      </description>

      <!-- Describe where the extension shows in the UI of the product -->

      <ui-access>
      <![CDATA[
      Access from the 'Hello, World' entry in the Commands menu.
      ]]>
      </ui-access>

      <!-- Describe the files that comprise the extension -->

      <files>
            <file name="Sample.htm"
            ➥destination="$dreamweaver/configuration/commands" />
      </files>

      <!-- Describe the changes to the configuration -->

      <configuration-changes>

            <!-- Add an entry to the commands menu -->

            <menu-insert insertAfter="DWMenu_Commands_SortTable"
            ➥skipSeparator="true">
```

```
                <menuitem name="Hello, World"
                ➥file="Commands/Sample.htm" id="Sample_HelloWorld" />
                <separator id="Sample_HelloWorld_Separator" />
            </menu-insert>

        </configuration-changes>
</macromedia-extension>
```

Unfortunately, both Sample.mxi and Blank.mxi are limited in only providing options for relatively simple extensions. Tables C.1 through C.16 provide more detailed specifications for the possible contents of the MXI file, along with syntax requirements. Use these tables in conjunction with the Blank.mxi template to construct your instruction file.

note

Note that the tables do not present an exhaustive list of elements—they cover only those elements used for creating extension types covered in this book.

A much more detailed set of instructions and syntax requirements is available in PDF form on the Macromedia Exchange Web site (`http://www.macromedia.com/exchange/dreamweaver`).

Table C.1 describes `<macromedia-extension>`, which is the main tag for extension installation files.

Table C.1 MXI File: *<macromedia-extension>*

Attributes	*Contents*	*Container*	*Examples*
`id`—A unique extension ID to be created by Macromedia after you submit your extension. Never add or modify this attribute yourself.	`<description>` —required `<ui-access>` —required `<products>` —required	None (this is the parent tag for the document)	`<macromedia-extension name = "My Object" version = 1.0" type = "object" > <description> <ui-access> <products> </macromedia-extension>`
`version`—The version number of the extension, in the format a[.b[.c]]. Valid entries include `1, 2.5, 3.0.2`	`<configuration-changes>`—required only if the extension changes the menus or shortcuts files		`<macromedia-extension name = "Automatic Alt Text" version = 2" type = "command" > <description> <ui-access> <products> <configuration-changes> </macromedia-extension>`

Attributes	*Contents*	*Container*	*Examples*
`type`—Indicates the kind of extension. Valid entries are `object`, `command`, `behavior` or `action`, `browserProfile`, `translator`, `dictionary`, `encoding`, `floater`, `propertyInspector`, `jsExtension`, `query`, `template`, `thirdPartyTags`, `plugin`, `report`, `flashbuttonstyle`, `suite`* `[requires-restart]` —Indicates whether Dreamweaver must be restarted after the extension is installed. Valid entries are `true` and `false`. If omitted, this defaults to `false`. (For Dreamweaver 3, this attribute is ignored, and the program must always be restarted.)			

*A suite is a group of extensions installed as a unit.

Table C.2 describes `<products>`. This tag is the container for one or more `<products/>` tags.

Table C.2 MXI File: *<products>*

Attributes	*Contents*	*Container*	*Examples*

None	One or more `<products />` tags	`<macromedia-extension>`	`<products>`
			`<product />`
			`<product /`
			`</products>`

Table C.3 describes <product />. Each instance of this tag specifies a Macromedia product(s) with which the extension is compatible. At least one <product/> tag must be defined.

Table C.3 MXI File: *<product />*

Attributes	*Contents*	*Container*	*Examples*
`name`—The name of a product. Valid entries are `Dreamweaver`, `Fireworks`, `Flash`, `UltraDev` `[version]`—The minimum version number that the extension should be used for. `[primary]`—Indicates whether the specified product is the one the extension was primarily intended for. `[required]`—Indicates whether the specified product is required for the extension to work properly.	None (empty tag)	`<products>`	`<product name = "Dreamweaver" version = "4" primary = "true" />`

Table C.4 describes <author />, which contains the extension author's name. This information will appear in the Extension Manager window.

Table C.4 MXI File: *<author />*

Attributes	*Contents*	*Container*	*Examples*
`name`—The author's name	None (empty tag)	`<macromedia-extension>`	`<author name = "Rocket Laura" />`

Table C.5 shows `<description>`. This tag describes what the extension does or is used for. This information will appear in the Extension Manager window.

Table C.5 MXI File: *<description>*

Attributes	*Contents*	*Container*	*Examples*
None	`<![CDATA[` *Put the descriptive text here. You can use and to format the information.* `]]>`	`<macromedia-extension>`	`<description> <![CDATA[This command automatically inserts ALT text based on link or file name information to all images in the document. Images which already have ALT text are ignored.]]</description>`

Table C.6 describes `<ui-access>`. This tag specifies where to find the extension in the Dreamweaver user interface. This information will appear in the Extension Manager window.

Table C.6 MXI File: *<ui-access>*

Attributes	*Contents*	*Container*	*Examples*
None	`<![CDATA[` *Put the descriptive text here. You can use and to format the information.* `]]>`	`<macromedia-extension>`	`<ui-access><![CDATA[Run this command by choosing Modify: Add Automatic Alt Text.]] </ui-access>`

Table C.7 describes `<files>`, which is the container for one or more `<file/>` tags.

Table C.7 MXI File: *<files>*

Attributes	*Contents*	*Container*	*Examples*

None	One or more `<file/>` tags.	`<macromedia-extension>`	`<files>`
			`<file />`
			`<file />`
			`</files>`

Table C.8 describes `<file />`. Each instance of this tag provides information about a specific file to be installed as part of the extension.

Table C.8 MXI File: *<file />*

Attributes	*Contents*	*Container*	*Examples*
`source`—The nameof other file. It can include a path relative to the location of the installation file (the extension's files don't all have to be in the same folder). Use color, slash, or backslash to separate folder names and before the filename in the path. Don't use the same filenames as MM extensions unless your extension is intended as a substitute for the MM extension. `destination`—The name of the folder that the file will be copied to. If the folder doesn't exist, it will be created during installation. Valid entries begin with `$dreamweaver`, which refers to the DW Configuration folder. This attribute is not case-sensitive. Use a color, slash, or backslash between folder names in the path. `[platform]`—Indicates what platform the file	None (empty tag)	`<files>`	`<file name="Automatic Alt Text.htm" destination="$dreamweaver/commands" />`

Attributes	*Contents*	*Container*	*Examples*
is intended for. If a platform is specified, the extension is installed only on that platform. Valid entries are `mac` and `win`. `[shared]`—Indicates whether the file is used by more than one extension. (If the extension is uninstalled, shared files won't be removed.) Valid entries are `true` and `false`. `[systemfile]`—Indicates whether the file is used by anything other than extensions.			

Table C.9 describes `<configuration-changes>`. This tag is the container for tags specifying changes to menus, shortcuts, server behaviors, server formats, and data sources.

Table C.9 MXI File: *<configuration-changes>*

Attributes	*Contents*	*Container*	*Examples*

None	Any combination of `<menu-remove>`, `<menu-insert>`, `<shortcut-remove>`, `<shortcut-insert>`, `<server-behavior-changes>`, `<server-format-changes>`, `<server-format-definition-changes>`, `<data-source-changes>` tags.	`<macromedia-extension>`	`<configuration-changes>`
			`<menu-insert >`
			`<menuitem />`
			`</menu-insert>`
			`</configuration-changes>`

Table C.10 describes <menu-remove />. Each instance of this tag specifies a menu bar, menu, menu item, or format to remove from the interface.

Table C.10 MXI File: *<menu-remove />*

Attributes	*Contents*	*Container*	*Examples*
id—Unique ID of the item to be removed. Note that menu bars and menus won't be removed unless they're empty.	None (empty tag)	Any of the following: <configuration-changes>, <server-behavior-changes>, <server-format-changes>, <server-format-definition-changes>, <data-source-changes>	<menu-remove id ="DWContext_RemoteSite_Checkout" />

Table C.11 describes <menu-insert >. Each instance of this tag specifies where to insert a menu bar, menu, menu item, or format.

Table C.11 MXI File: *<menu-insert >*

Attributes	*Contents*	*Container*	*Examples*
Use only one of the following four attributes, determining the relationship of the new item to an existing menu item: insertAfter*, insertBefore, appendTo, prePendTo Value must be an existing item's unique ID. *[skipSeparator] —If the insertAfter attribute is specified, assign true or false to this attribute to	Contents of this tag will be inserted as a block into menus.xml file. When used When used When used format-definition> parent tag, contents must include one or more <format> tags. Elsewhere, contents must include one or more <menu> and/or <menuitem> tags.*	Any of the following: configuration-changes>, <server-behavior-changes>, <server-format-changes>, <server-format-definition-changes>, <data-source-changes>	<menu-insert insertAfter="DWMenu_Happy"> <menu name="Campers" id="Menu_1"> </menu-insert>

Attributes	*Contents*	*Container*	*Examples*
indicate whether the newly inserted item should be placed after any separator that follows the existing item.			

*See the discussion on menus.xml entries in Chapter 7, "Creating Custom Floating Panels," for details of how to format menu entries.

Table C.12 describes `<shortcut-remove />`. Each instance of this tag specifies a keyboard to remove from the menus.xml file.

Table C.12 MXI File: *<shortcut-remove />*

Attributes	*Contents*	*Container*	*Examples*
`id`—Unique ID of the shortcut to be removed.	None (empty tag)	`<configuration-changes>`	`<shortcut-remove id="DWFroggie">`

Table C.13 describes `<shortcut-insert >`. Each instance of this tag specifies a keyboard shortcut to be added to a particular location in the menus.xml file.

Table C.13 MXI File: *<shortcut-insert >*

Attributes	*Contents*	*Container*	*Examples*
`listId`—Unique ID of the shortcut list in which to insert the new shortcut	`<shortcut>` tag Contents of this tag will be inserted as a block into menus.xml file.	`<configuration-changes>`	`<shortcut-insert listId="DWFrogList">` `<shortcut>` `</shortcut-insert>`

*See the discussion on menus.xml entries in Chapter 7 for details of how to format shortcuts.

Table C.14 describes `<ftp-extension-map-changes>`. This container tag specifies a change to the FTPExtensionMap.txt file. (This file defines whether the file is downloaded/uploaded to an FTP server as ASCII or binary.)

Table C.14 MXI File: *<ftp-extension-map-changes>*

Attributes	*Contents*	*Container*	*Example*

None	May contain one `<ftp-extension-insert>` tag; and/or one `<ftp-extension-remove>` tag.	`<configuration-changes>`	`<ftp-extension-map-changes>`
			`<ftp-extension-insert>`
			`<ftp-extension-remove />`
			`</ ftp-extension-map-changes >`

Table C.15 describes < `ftp-extension-remove` />. This tag specifies the extension to be removed from the SourceFormat.txt file.

Table C.15 MXI File: *< ftp-extension-remove />*

Attributes	*Contents*	*Container*	*Examples*
`extension`—The file extension, such as `GIF` or `JPG`, to be removed.	None (empty tag)	`<ftp-extension-map-changes>`	`<ftp-extension-remove extension="JPG" />`

Table C.16 describes <`ftp-extension-insert` />. This tag specifies a change to the FTPExtensionMap.txt file.

Table C.16 MXI File: <ftp-extension-insert />

Attributes	*Contents*	*Container*	*Examples*
`extension`—The file extension, such as GIF or JPG. `type`—Format to use when uploading. Accepted values are `ASCII` and `Binary`. `mac-creator`—Macintosh creator code. If you don't know the code, use `????`.	None (empty tag)	`<ftp-extension-map-changes>`	`<ftp-extension-insert extension="GIF" type="ASCII" mac-creator="MKBY" mac-file-type="GIFf">`

Attributes	Contents	Container	Examples
mac-file-type— If you don't know this, use ????			

The following is an alternate blank MXI template file, including many more specialized options that can be used in place of Blank.mxi.

```
<!--remove this comment -- for each tag attribute, assign a value or
➥remove the attribute-->
<!--remove this comment -- not all tags will be required for all
➥extensions some tags may be present more than once for a given
➥extension-->

<macromedia-extension name version type requires-restart>
      <products>
            <product name version primary required />
      </products>

      <author name />

      <description>
      <![CDATA[
      <!--remove this comment and add your descriptive text here-->
      ]]>
      </description>

      <ui-access>
      <![CDATA[
      <!--remove this comment and add user access information here-->
      ]]>
      </ui-access>

      <files>
            <file name destination platform shared systemfile win-
            ➥extension/>
      </files>

      <configuration-changes>
            <menu-remove id />
            <menu-insert insertAfter insertBefore appendTo prependTo
            ➥skipSeparator>
                  <menu name id platform>
                        <menuitem name id key platform file command
                        ➥enabled checked dynamic arguments />
                  </menu>
            </menu-insert>
```

```
        <shortcut-remove id>

        <shortcut-insert listId>
              <shortcut key id command file platform />
        </shortcut-insert>

        <ftp-extension-map-changes>
              <ftp-extension-insert extension type mac-creator mac-
              ➥file-type />
              <ftp-extension-remove extension />
        </ftp-extension-map-changes>

</configuration-changes>
</macromedia-extension>
```

note

You can download the alternate blank template shown above from the book's companion web site, www.newriders.com.

Creating a Simple MXI: Set Page Properties Behavior

With all the above resources to work from, creating this installation file shouldn't be too difficult. An example of what the completed MXI file might look like is shown as follows. In particular, take note of the following:

- **`<product>` specification**—Unless you're sure an extension will work with a particular version of Dreamweaver or UltraDev, don't specify it here.
- **`<file>`**—Each file in the extension requires its own entry here. The destination attribute determines where the file will be installed. It's not case-sensitive, but must begin with `$dreamweaver`.

```
<macromedia-extension name="Set Page Properties" version="1.0"
➥type="behavior" requires-restart="true">
     <products>
          <product name="Dreamweaver" version="6" primary="true"  />
     </products>

     <author name="RocketLaura" />

     <description>
     <![CDATA[
     Create a JavaScript that lets page visitors change page and text
     ➥colors.<br>
     All default page, text, link colors can be specified.
```

```
        ]]>
        </description>

        <ui-access>
        <![CDATA[
        Access from the Behaviors menu.
        ]]>
        </ui-access>

        <files>
             <file name="Set Page Properties.htm"
             ➥destination="$dreamweaver/configuration/behaviors/actions" />
             <file name="Set Page Properties.js"
             ➥destination="$dreamweaver/configuration/behaviors/actions" />
        </files>

</macromedia-extension>
```

Creating an MXI for a Multifile Extension: Custom Horizontal Rule Object

An example of what the MXI file for this extension might look like is shown as follows. In particular, note the various `<file>` entries. Note the following:

- **files**—Every file in the extension must be given an entry, including each GIF.
- **filenames**—Because the files for this extension have collected into various subfolders for the packaging process, we must specify a relative pathname for each. (The pathname must be relative to the installation file. These names assume that the MXI file is being stored at the root level of the collection folder.)
- **destinations**—This extension requires a custom folder (in the Objects folder). By specifying a folder in the destination path that doesn't yet exist in the user's Configuration folder, you instruct the installer to create that folder.

```
<macromedia-extension name="Custom Horizontal Rule" version="1.0" type="object"
➥requires-restart="true">
     <products>
          <product name="Dreamweaver" version="4" primary="true"
          ➥required="true" />
     </products>

     <author name="RocketLaura" />

     <description>
     <![CDATA[
     This object inserts a horizonatal rule, with an insertion dialog
     ➥box for setting attributes, and an inspector that displays the
     ➥color attribute.
     <br><br>
```

```
   ]]>
   </description>

   <ui-access>
   <![CDATA[
   Access from the My Stuff category of the Insert bar.
   ]]>
   </ui-access>

   <files>

      <file name="objects/Custom HR.htm"
      destination="$dreamweaver/configuration/objects/My Stuff" />
      <file name="objects/Custom HR.js"
      destination="$dreamweaver/configuration/objects/My Stuff" />
      <file name="inspectors/Custom HR.htm"
      destination="$dreamweaver/configuration/inspectors" />
      <file name="inspectors/customhr.gif"
      destination="$dreamweaver/configuration/inspectors" />

   </files>

</macromedia-extension>
```

Creating an MXI for an Extension with Menu Changes: Table Helper Floating Panel

An example of what the installer file for the Table Helper might look like is shown as follows. In particular, pay attention to the following:

- **`<configuration-changes>`**—Because this extension changes the menus, you must include this set of tags.
- **`<menu-insert>`**—The alternate blank MXI template (shown in the section titled "The Structure of an MXI File") shows all the options you have for specifying exactly where your new menuitem should go. The MXI shown for Table Helper is set to insert the new menuitem after the existing menu entry that has the ID value of `DWMenu_Window_RestoreAll`.
- **`<menuitem>`**—This line is a re-creation of the syntax you originally developed for Table Helper. It will be placed exactly as it appears here, in the user's menus.xml file. Again, the alternate blank template shown previously shows the various options you could use in this line.

```
<macromedia-extension name="Table Helper" version="1.0" type="floater"
➥requires-restart="true">
      <products>
            <product name="Dreamweaver" version="4" primary="true"/>
            <product name="UltraDev"/>
      </products>

      <author name="RocketLaura" />

      <description>
      <![CDATA[
      This panel provides comprehensive information about the cell
      ➥dimensions and
      structure of a selected table.
      ]]>
      </description>

      <ui-access>
      <![CDATA[
      Access from the 'Table Helper' entry in the Window menu.
      ]]>
      </ui-access>

      <files>
            <file name="TableHelper.htm"
            ➥destination="$dreamweaver/configuration/floaters" />
      </files>

      <configuration-changes>
            <menu-insert insertAfter="DWMenu_Window_RestoreAll">
                        <menuitem name="Table Helper"
                        ➥id="RocketLaura_TableHelper_Floater"
                        ➥command="dw.toggleFloater('TableHelper')" enabled="true"
                        ➥checked="dw.getFloaterVisibility('TableHelper')"  />
            </menu-insert>

      </configuration-changes>
</macromedia-extension>
```

note

It's important to understand what's happening in the MXI file. If you don't want to spend time hand-coding every MXI file you need, try out Public Domain's MXI File Creator extension, available from the Macromedia Dreamweaver Exchange. This extension creates a Dreamweaver command that allows you to enter all the relevant information for your MXI file (in plain old English) and then writes the MXI file for you.

Task 3: Package the Extension Into an MXP (Installer) File

After you've assembled all your bits and pieces into the folder you've designated as your staging area, and you've created the MXI file with instructions for turning those pieces into an extension, it's time to create the installer package. Follow these steps:

1. Launch the Macromedia Extension Manager.
2. Go to File > Package Extension.
3. In the dialog box that appears, select your MXI file.
4. Click Open.
5. Assign a name to the MXP file. Make sure the name contains no special characters or spaces, and ends with the .mxp extension.
6. Click Save.

   If there's any problem with the MXI file, you'll get an explanatory error message. (Usually, errors have to do with incorrect syntax or incorrectly referenced extension files.) Leave the Extension Manager, remedy the problem, and try again.

   If everything is correctly set up, you'll get a lovely message telling you the file was created successfully. Congratulations! You made your first installer file. Figure C.2 shows the completed installer files for the Set Page Properties, Flash Detector, and Table Helper extensions.

FIGURE C.2 *The completed MXP files for your three sample extensions.*

Summary

Just because you didn't generate any errors in creating the MXP file doesn't mean your extension is ready for sharing. There's many a slip twixt the cup and the happy, stable cross-platform user experience. Be sure to test your packaged-up extension before inflicting it on unsuspecting users. The basic tests performed by the quality control techs at the Macromedia Exchange are a good model for testing. These tests include the following:

- **Does the extension install correctly?** Try your MXP installer file out, on both Macintosh and Windows platforms if possible. Make sure all the files get installed in all the proper places, and that all configuration changes are successfully made, as well. (Note that, if you're installing onto the same copy of Dreamweaver where you developed your extension, you'll want to manually remove the development files from your Configuration folder before installing.)
- **Does the installed extension work properly?** Presumably, at this stage of development you've already done your error checking (see Appendix D, "Submitting Extensions to the Macromedia Dreamweaver Exchange," for advice on this). But does the installed extension work the same as the development version you created? Does it work cross-platform? Does it disturb any of the functionality of other Dreamweaver extensions, including other third-party extensions?
- **Is the installer file (the MXP) virus-free?** Although this has nothing to do with the inherent quality, stability or usefulness of the extension, you'll certainly affect the user experience if you pass a virus along with it.

An extension that passes these tests qualifies for basic approval at the Macromedia Exchange. See Appendix B, "Macromedia User Interface Guidelines," for information on user interface guidelines, if you want your extension to qualify as a Macromedia Approved extension. More information on both of these topics is available online at the Exchange.

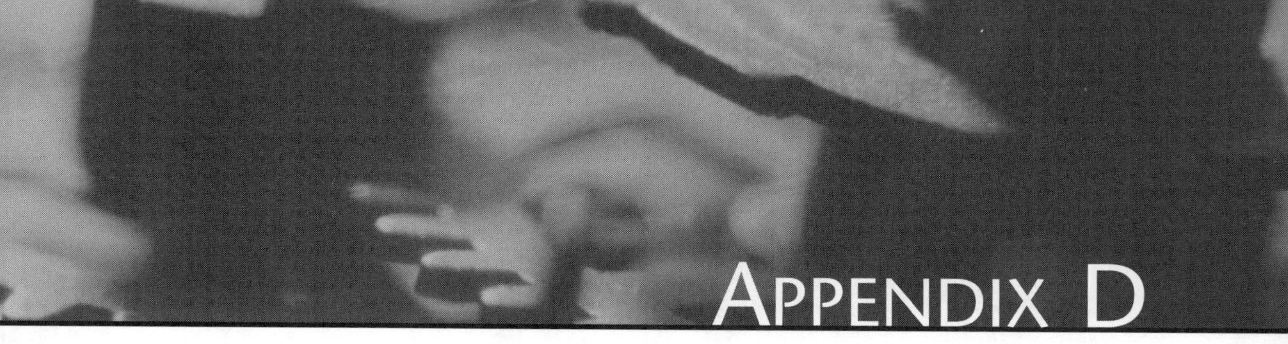

Submitting Extensions to the Macromedia Dreamweaver Exchange

If you're interested enough in extensions to be reading this book, you're undoubtedly already familiar with Macromedia's Dreamweaver Exchange and all the extensions there. After you've written your own extension, tested it, and packaged it up, you may want to share it with other users. Submitting to the Exchange is an obvious way to do that. You can find detailed information at the Exchange on how to submit extensions and how to prepare them for submission. This appendix offers a checklist, condensed from the Exchange instructions, for testing and preparing your extensions for submission. Although the information is geared specifically toward Macromedia's requirements and advice, it's good advice regardless of how you plan to put your extension out into the world.

Guidelines for Submission

This section contains requirements and suggestions for creating extensions that will be submitted to the Exchange.

Follow these guidelines regarding file location:

- **Put no more than three files in the standard extension folders—** Macromedia requires that each extension can add up to only three files in the standard extension folders (that is, Objects, Commands, and so on). This allows for an HTML file, a linked JavaScript file, and an optional GIF file.
- **Place extra files in a folder in the Shared folder—** Any files other than the 2–3 files of the extension itself should go in the Shared folder—in a subfolder identified with your name or your company's name.
- **Separate the extension into HTML and JavaScript files—**This is for all but the simplest extensions. The HTML file should include only local variables, the HTML for the user interface, and links to any needed JavaScript files.

Follow these guidelines regarding scripting:

- Comment your code.
- Declare all variables.
- Give variables informative names.
- Don't give variables similar names.
- Use semicolons at the ends of statements.
- Use curly braces ({}) for clarity.
- Use consistent indentation. Two spaces per indentation level is Macromedia's default.
- Spin off small tasks into separate functions.

Make note of these requirements for borrowing Macromedia JavaScript code:

- **Remove any unused material—**This includes variables, comments that are no longer relevant, and debugging routines. (Don't just comment out the debugging routines—remove them.)
- **Rename variables—**Change variable names to fit the context in which you're using the variables.
- **Rename Macromedia functions if you modify them—**In particular, don't retain the `MM_` prefix for the name of a modified Macromedia function from a behavior.

Recommended Test Plan

The following testing guidelines help you debug your extensions. Although you may not have access to both a Macintosh and Windows system, have different versions of Netscape, and so on, follow as much of the test plan as you can. Always perform the installation and compatibility tests, no matter what kind of extension you're testing.

Be sure to test your extension in a variety of scenarios. It may work in exactly the case it was designed for, but fail miserably in any other case. Due to the scope and variety of possible extensions, this test plan does not thoroughly cover every way in which an extension can be tested, nor does it necessarily reflect the testing process that is performed at Macromedia. Treat this plan as a starting point, a minimum standard that your extension should be able to pass, and perform further tests as appropriate.

After you submit your extension to Macromedia for certification, it will be further tested by Macromedia Quality Assurance. QA will send you a list of any problems encountered; you can then fix the problems and resubmit the extension. However, you're expected to do thorough testing before submitting the extension.

After you perform the steps listed in "Preparing to Test" and "Testing Installation," follow the appropriate test plan for your extension type. If your extension can operate on an entire site, follow the test plan for "Testing Site-Wide Extensions."

All Extensions: Preparing to Test

After completing an extension or fixing a bug, prepare to test your extension:

1. Back up your Configuration folder.
2. Install the extension in either of the following ways:
   - Use the Extension Manager.
   - Place the files in the appropriate subfolder in the Configuration folder.
3. Quit and relaunch Dreamweaver if you installed without the Extension Manager, or if you are prompted to do so by the Extension Manager.

All Extensions: Testing Installation

To make sure that you can install your extension on all platforms, perform these tests for all extensions:

1. Install on both Windows and Macintosh.
2. Verify that the installation worked correctly. In particular:
   - Make sure all files, including Help files (if any), are installed in the proper folders.
   - Check the Dreamweaver user interface for anything that might be affected by installation, including Property inspectors, the Insert bar, and relevant menus.

3. Run virus-checking software to verify lack of infection before and after using the extension.

Testing Objects

Perform these tests if your extension is an object.

Test the Object's User Interface

1. Launch Dreamweaver, and open the Insert bar.
2. Make sure the object has an icon in the Insert bar. (Every object in Dreamweaver should have a unique 18×18 pixel GIF icon.)
3. Make sure the name of the object in the Insert menu is correct and makes sense.
4. Move the pointer over the object icon in the Insert bar, and make sure the ToolTip indicates what the object does.

Insert the Object

1. Insert the object using the Insert menu. If a parameter-entry dialog box appears, verify the following:
   - Default values for all fields make sense.
   - The insertion point is in the first text field by default (and the default value, if any, is selected).
   - Layout is readable and makes sense visually and logically (see "UI Guidelines for Extension Developers," available for download from Exchange).
   - Pressing Tab moves through the fields in a reasonable order.
2. If there is a Help button in the parameter-entry dialog box, click it and verify that it does the right thing (opens an appropriate page in the Windows or Mac help utility, for example).
3. Back in the parameter-entry dialog box, click OK to insert the object with default values.
4. Verify that no error occurs when the default-valued object is inserted.
5. Insert the object again, and enter nondefault values in the dialog box. Click OK to insert the object. Verify that these values are reflected in the HTML code and in the Property inspector (if there is an inspector for the object).
6. Insert the object again, and enter invalid data in each field. Try leaving the field blank, using large or negative numbers, using invalid characters (such as /, ?, :, *, and so on), and using letters in numeric fields. Generally, you should allow the user to enter an invalid value or blank field, and doing so shouldn't cause a display problem and shouldn't crash Dreamweaver. For more information, see "UI Guidelines for Extension Developers."

Check HTML and Browser Display

1. Using the HTML Source inspector, verify that the correct HTML was inserted.
2. Click the object's icon in the Insert bar, and verify that the correct HTML was inserted.
3. Drag and drop the object out of the Insert bar, and verify that the correct HTML was inserted.
4. Preview in the following browsers, on both Windows and Macintosh (or as many of these browsers and platforms as you have access to). All objects should work properly in any 4.0 or later browser, and should either work properly or fail gracefully on any 3.0 browser.

Using the Object

Spend 10–15 minutes using the object. Make sure your testing includes these tasks:

- Run the Property inspector tests on any object that has a Property inspector.
- Use the object with other Dreamweaver objects (insert it in a layer, a table, and so on).
- Verify that the object's user interface is relatively intuitive and that the object works when previewed in a browser.

Testing Property Inspectors

Perform these tests if your extension is a Property inspector.

1. Verify that the Property inspector appears when the correct kind of item is selected in either the Document window or the HTML Source inspector (and that the Property inspector doesn't appear when other items are selected).
2. Make sure the Property inspector is visually acceptable (follow the "UI Guidelines for Extension Developers"). In particular, ensure the following:
   - The ordering and layout of items makes visual and logical sense.
   - The text is readable and large enough.
   - The text fields are long enough to accommodate the information they'll hold (for example, you should be able to see all seven characters in a text field for a color value).
3. Make sure all important attributes of a given tag are included in the Property inspector.
4. Click each of the Property inspector's buttons, and verify the following:
   - The color picker icons work.
   - The File browse icons work.
   - The Help button (if there is one) works.

5. Edit values in the Property inspector, and verify that the changes are reflected in both the Document window and the HTML Source inspector.
6. Edit values in the HTML Source inspector, and verify that the changes are reflected in both the Document window and the Property inspector.
7. Verify that other custom Property inspectors (such as those for `<head>` area items such as `Title`) still work. If any inspector fails to appear when it should, check your `canInspectSelection()` function—it's probably not specific enough.

Testing Commands

Perform these tests if your extension is a command.

For commands that are specific to an object or tag (such as Format Table):

1. Select an appropriate object, and make sure the command is enabled in the Commands menu.
2. Select an object that the command doesn't apply to, and make sure the command is disabled in the Commands menu.
3. Verify that the command is enabled when the insertion point is inside the object (for objects such as layers and tables), even when not all of the object is selected.

For commands that use dialog boxes:

1. Select an appropriate object. Choose the command from the Commands menu.
2. Verify the following:
   - Default values for all fields make sense.
   - The insertion point appears in the first text field (and the default value, if any, is selected) by default.
   - Layout is readable and makes sense visually and logically (follow the "UI Guidelines for Extension Developers").
   - Pressing Tab moves through the fields in a reasonable order.
3. If there is a Help button, click it, and verify that it does the right thing (opens an appropriate page in a browser, for example).
4. Back in the dialog box, click OK to use the command with default values.
5. Verify that no error occurs when the default-valued object is inserted.

6. Choose the command again, and enter non-default values in the dialog box. Click OK to run the command. Verify that the values you entered are reflected in the HTML code and in the Property inspector (if there is an inspector for the object), as appropriate.
7. Choose the command again, and enter invalid data in each field of the dialog box. Try leaving the field blank, using large or negative numbers, using invalid characters (such as /, ?, :, *, and so on), and using letters in numeric fields. Generally, you should allow the user to enter an invalid value or blank field, and doing so shouldn't cause a display problem and shouldn't crash Dreamweaver. See the user interface guidelines document for more information.

To check the command and browser display:

1. Run the command, and verify that the command does what you expect it to.
2. Preview as many browsers and platforms as you have access to.

Any changes made by a command should appear properly in any 4.0 or later browser, and should either appear properly or fail gracefully in any 3.0 browser.

Testing Behaviors

Perform these tests if your extension is a behavior.

1. Make sure the behavior is available in the Behavior panel and has the correct name. Also, do the following:
   - Make sure the behavior is enabled only for the appropriate browser versions in the Behavior panel's Events For pop-up menu. (For example, a layer behavior should be dimmed when Events For Netscape 3.0 is selected.)
   - If the behavior is tag-specific, make sure the behavior is enabled in the Behavior panel whenever the tag/object is selected, and that the behavior is dimmed otherwise. For example, the Go To URL behavior is enabled only if an image or layer is selected.
   - If the behavior isn't tag-specific, make sure the behavior is enabled and dimmed at the appropriate times. For example, the timeline behaviors are enabled only when there's a timeline on the page.
2. Choose the behavior from the Behavior panel (with the proper object selected). If there's a dialog box, do the following:
   - Verify that default values for all fields make sense.
   - Verify that the insertion point appears in the first text field (and the default value, if any, is selected) by default.

- Verify that the layout is readable and makes sense visually and logically (follow the "UI Guidelines for Extension Developers").
- Verify that pressing Tab moves through the fields in a reasonable order.
- If there is a Help button, click it, and verify that it does the right thing (opens an appropriate page in a browser, for example).
- Back in the dialog box, click OK to use the behavior with default values.
- Verify that no error occurs when the default-valued behavior is applied.
- Verify that the default event for the behavior (such as `onClick` or `onMouseOver`) makes sense.
- Verify that the behavior appears in the HTML Source inspector.
- If the behavior is added to the `<head>` section of the document, verify that it includes the Dreamweaver version number that the behavior was created for.
- Choose the behavior again, and enter invalid data in each field of the dialog box. Try leaving the field blank, using large or negative numbers, using invalid characters (such as /, ?, :, *, and so on), and using letters in numeric fields. Generally, you should allow the user to enter an invalid value or blank field, and doing so shouldn't cause a display problem and shouldn't crash Dreamweaver. For more information, see "UI Guidelines for Extension Developers."

3. Select the object you attached the behavior to, and verify in the Behavior panel that the Events and Actions columns are correctly populated.
4. Preview as many browsers and platforms as you have access to.

   Any behavior should behave properly in any 4.0 or later browser, and should either behave properly or fail gracefully in any 3.0 browser.
5. Remove the behavior from the Behavior panel, and verify that the behavior is removed from the list and from the document's code.

Testing Floating Panels

Perform these tests if your extension is a floating panel.

note

Floating panels can have a wide range of purposes; the main idea of these tests is to make sure the floating panel works as it was designed.

1. Launch Dreamweaver, and open your floating panel.
2. If the floating panel is supposed to be tabbed with another floating panel upon the initial launch only, verify that it is. (This doesn't happen automatically; you must code it that way yourself.)
3. Verify the floating panel's layout:
   - The floating panel's title makes sense on the floating panel's tab and title bar, and in the Windows menu.
   - The floating panel's layout makes sense visually and logically, and conforms to the "UI Guidelines for Extension Developers."
   - Any appropriate controls resize when you resize the floating panel.
   - The context-menu arrow (top-right corner) is disabled (you can't have a context menu in a custom floating panel).
4. The floating panel's name is checked or unchecked in the Window menu, depending on whether the floating panel is visible or not. (This doesn't happen automatically; you must code it that way yourself.)
5. Floating panels can respond to either selection changes or document edits, so make sure the floating panel responds to the appropriate action depending on its purpose. For example:
   - Both the HTML Source inspector and the Frame panel change with both selection changes and document edits.
   - The Behavior panel changes only when you make document edits.
6. Make changes in the floating panel (for example, if you were testing the Layer panel, you could change a layer's visibility), and verify that the changes are reflected in the Document window.
7. If there are any buttons on the floating panel, verify that they work. If a button on the floating panel opens a dialog box:
   - Verify that default values for all fields make sense.
   - Verify that the insertion point is in the first text field (and the default value, if any, is selected) by default.
   - Verify that the layout is readable and makes sense visually and logically (follow the "UI Guidelines for Extension Developers").
   - Verify that pressing Tab moves through the fields in a reasonable order.
   - If there is a Help button, click it, and verify that it does the right thing (opens an appropriate page in a browser, for example).
   - Back in the dialog box, click OK to use the floating panel with default values.
   - Verify that no error occurs when the default-valued dialog is accepted.
   - Verify that an appropriate action occurs.

- Click the button to display the dialog box again, and enter invalid data in each field of the dialog box. Try leaving the field blank, using large or negative numbers, using invalid characters (such as /, ?, :, *, and so on), and using letters in numeric fields. Generally, you should allow the user to enter an invalid value or blank field; doing so shouldn't cause a display problem, shouldn't cause a JavaScript error, and shouldn't crash Dreamweaver. For more information, see the "UI Guidelines for Extension Developers."

8. Open a large document, and verify that the floating panel doesn't slow down performance. (If it does reduce performance, one possible reason could be that the script's running time is proportional to the size of the document—for example, it might count the number of characters in the document each time you edit the document.)

Testing Site-Wide Extensions

Perform these tests if your extension features site-wide functionality.

1. Follow the normal testing procedures for extensions of that type (commands, objects, behaviors, and so on) as detailed previously.
2. If the extension can operate on different categories of files—such as Current Document, All Open Documents, and Entire Site—verify that the extension works with each category.
3. Verify that the extension provides a log that shows which files have been operated on and which haven't.
4. Verify that the extension shows a wait cursor while running.
5. Verify that the extension warns the author that any action run on unopened files cannot be undone.
6. Verify that the extension handles locked files appropriately.
7. Verify that the extension handles checked out files appropriately.

APPENDIX E

Online Resources for Dreamweaver Extensibility

There's a thriving community of extension developers out there. They submit to the Macromedia Dreamweaver Exchange, they have their own Web sites, they participate in online discussions, and they hold conferences. This appendix lists some extension-writing help you can find online.

Web Sites

Some old, some new. Most are devoted primarily to already-written extensions for downloading. All those included here have at least some how-to information as well.

- **http://www.macromedia.com/support/dreamweaver/extend.html** and **http://www.macromedia.com/support/ultradev/behaviors/create_extensions/**—The official Macromedia help sites for developing extensions.
- **http://www.udzone.com**—The UltraDev zone. Includes brief tutorials on writing extensions, along with some helpful tips.
- **http://hotwired.lycos.com/webmonkey/99/11/index2a.html**—WebMonkey's guide to Extending Dreamweaver, by Nadav and Taylor. An excellent, in-depth look at writing extensions. From WebMonkey's home page, go to Programming: JavaScript: Extending Dreamweaver.
- **http://www.basic-ultradev.com/building_extensions/index.asp**—Online companion site to Building Dreamweaver 4 and Dreamweaver UltraDev 4 Extensions, by Tom Muck and Ray West.
- **http://www.andrewwooldridge.com/dreamweaver/**—Andrew Wooldridge's Dreamweaver Depot. Andrew and his site have been staples of the extensibility community for quite awhile. Check the Tutorials link for a few project-specific tutorials.
- **http://www.massimocorner.com/**—Massimo Foto's Dreamweaver site. Massimo was voted Best Extension Developer at the Macromedia Dreamweaver Conference 2000 in Monterey, California. Includes a Tips & Tricks section.
- **http://home.att.net/~JCB.BEI/Dreamweaver/**—The Excellent Dreamweaver Supply Bin. Mostly devoted to offering third-party extensions, this site includes a very basic overview of how "inserting stuff in Dreamweaver" works.
- **http://www.arrakis.es/~andrewc/downloads/dream.htm**—Andrew Castle's Dreamweaver site. An oldie, but a goodie. Includes a few tutorials on specific projects and an overview of how objects and behaviors work.
- **http://www.extending-dreamweaver.com/**—This site is devoted to extension developers. Resources include shared scripts, shared C libraries, user interface and general extending guidelines, and some utilities.
- **http://www.geocities.com/rabi.s.raj/dreamweaver/**—Rabi Sunder Raj's Dreamweaver Extensions site. Rabi's Menu Builder won the Best Extension award at the Macromedia Dreamweaver Conference 2000. No tutorials, but a How-To link to the WebMonkey article on extension development.

Forums

Forums allow Dreamweaver developers to share tips and ask questions online. Remember, before participating in any forum, to read the forum guidelines and to be a good and polite forum citizen.

- **Macromedia DEVFORUM newsgroup**—The main online forum for extensibility help and discussions. Chat with the big names here! Sign up at the Macromedia Dreamweaver Exchange—you'll need a login and password to get in.

Tools

Various utilities exist to help you build better extensions. The ones listed here are available online and are free.

- **Dreamweaver Platform SDK Extension**—Develop extensions for the Dreamweaver platform. Created by Macromedia. Package contains samples of all the major extension types (see Figure E.1), along with some really wonderful utilities (see Figure E.2).

FIGURE E.1 *The SDK sample objects category, part of Macromedia's SDK for Dreamweaver.*

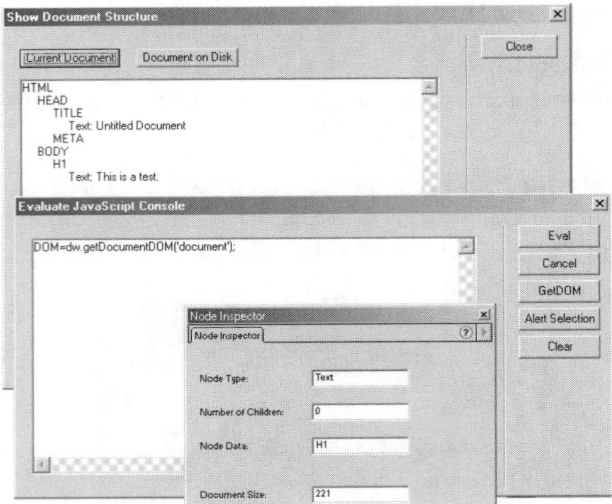

FIGURE E.2 *The Evaluate JavaScript Console, Show Document Structure window, and Node Floater at work, also part of Macromedia's SDK for Dreamweaver.*

- **Create Behavior Extension**—Create your own behaviors quickly and easily. By Ruairi Conor McComb. Available on the Macromedia Dreamweaver Exchange.
- **EditPlus**—By ES-Computing. A shareware text editor for Windows. Dreamweaver files for EditPlus are aimed at Dreamweaver extension development using the EditPlus editor, including Dreamweaver DOM-specific syntax highlighting. Available at `http://www.extending-dreamweaver.com/`.
- **JSExtensionBrowser**—By ES-Computing. A small application for Windows that opens shared C libraries for Windows and browses its functions. Available at `http://www.extending-dreamweaver.com/`.
- **Extension Debug Suite Extension**—By Public Domain. Windows only. Allows for more control and cleaner debugging when developing DW/UltraDev/FW extensions. Contains a debug code viewer that captures output from the debug commands entered into the extension being developed, alleviating the need for JavaScript alert boxes to see the value of variables, evaluated JavaScript expressions, or string messages (see Figure E.3). Available on the Macromedia Dreamweaver Exchange.

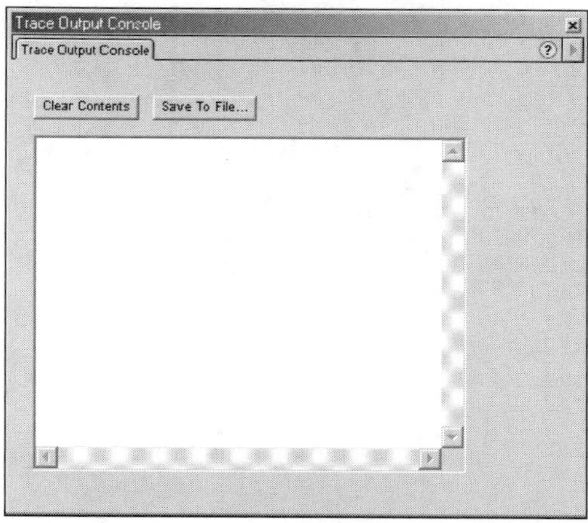

FIGURE E.3 *The Trace Output Console, part of Public Domain's Extension Debug Suite.*

- **MXI File Creator**—By Public Domain. A Windows-only Dreamweaver extension that automatically creates the MXI information document necessary to make MXP installer files (see Figure E.4). Available on the Macromedia Dreamweaver Exchange.

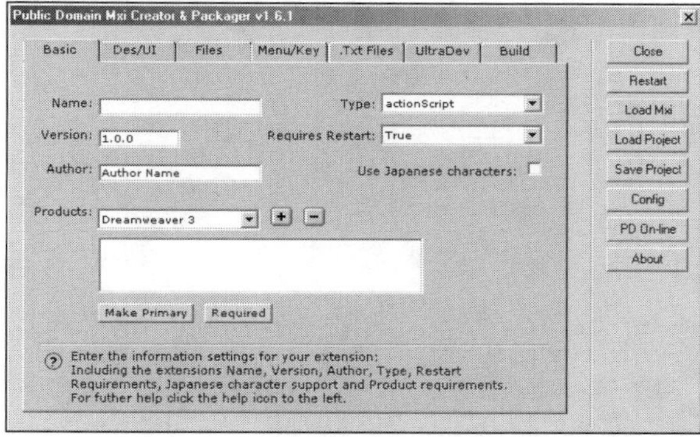

FIGURE E.4 *The MXI Creator & Packager extension by Public Domain.*

- **OSA for Dreamweaver**—By Late Night Software, Ltd. This freeware package provides the tools required to integrate AppleScript (or any other OSA scripting system) with Macromedia Dreamweaver. Use AppleScript as part of any Dreamweaver custom Object, Behavior, Command, or Translator. Available at `http://www.latenightsw.com/freeware/OSADreamweaver/index.html`.

Appendix F

Contents of the Dreamweaver MX Extensions Book Companion Web Site

You'll find the companion web site to this book at www.newriders.com. What will you find on the web site? Lots of stuff! Including the following:

- Supporting files for all the practice, workshop, and project exercises, and sample files to practice on
- Framework code for each extension type covered here
- Icons for all inspector and object file exercises
- Completed versions of each exercise
- Active links to all online resources mentioned throughout the book.

Each chapter's files are available in a ZIP file. Here's a detailed rundown:

Chapter 2: "Creating Custom Objects"

Object Framework.htm: HTML framework file with script tag in the `<head>`, `objectTag()`, `displayHelp()`, and `initializeUI()` function frameworks, with comments.

Workshop #1: Centering Table

Centering Table.htm: Object file inserts a 100%×100% borderless table, with contents centered. Same as completed workshop exercise.

Centering Table.gif: Object icon for use with `Centering Table` object.

Workshop #2: Block Spacer Tag

Block Spacer.htm: Object file inserts a `<spacer>` tag with user-defined height and width. Same as completed workshop exercise.

Block Spacer.gif: Object icon for use with `Block Spacer` object.

Workshop #3: Custom Horizontal Rule

Custom HR.htm: Main object file inserts a horizontal rule, allowing a user to set attributes, including color. Same as completed workshop exercise.

Custom HR.js: JavaScript for Custom HR object file.

Custom HR.gif: Object icon for use with `Custom HR` object.

Chapter 3: "Creating Custom Behaviors"

Behavior Framework.htm: HTML framework file with script tag in the `<head>`, `canAcceptBehavior()`, `behaviorFunction()`, `applyBehavior()`, `inspectBehavior()`, `displayHelp()`, and `initializeUI()` functions, with comments.

Workshop #1: Back/Forward Behavior

Back or Forward.htm: Behavior file that inserts a JavaScript for creating "back" and "forward" links into user documents. Same as completed workshop exercise.

Workshop #2: Set Page Properties

Set Page Properties.htm: Behavior file that inserts a JavaScript for changing default background and text colors into user documents. Same as completed workshop exercise.

Set Page Properties.js: JavaScript for Set Page Properties behavior file.

Chapter 4: "The Dreamweaver DOM"

Command_Test.mxp: Installs a floater that allows direct typing of DOM-related and other command statements. The floater will appear in the Window menu as Command Tester.

Test Files

dompage.htm, duck1.gif, duck2.gif: A simple HTML document and supporting files for practicing DOM access commands. This is the same file used in the chapter examples.

Chapter 5: "Creating Custom Commands and Menu Commands"

Command Framework.htm: HTML framework file with script tag in the `<head>`, including `canAcceptCommand()`, `mainCommand()`, `commandButtons()`, `receiveArguments()`, `displayHelp()`, and `initializeUI()` functions, with comments.

Menu Command Framework.htm: HTML framework file with script tag in the `<head>`, including `mainCommand()`, `setMenuText()`, `getDynamicContent()`, `isCommandChecked()`, `receiveArguments()`, `commandButtons()`, `displayHelp()`, and `initializeUI()` functions, with comments.

Workshop #1: Automatic Alt Text

Automatic Alt Text.htm: Command inserts `alt` text for all images in a document, except shim files and images that already have `alt` text. Same as completed workshop exercise.

AutomaticAltHelp.htm: Help file to be called from the `Automatic Alt Text` command.

Workshop #2: Make Uppercase

Make Uppercase.htm: Command that changes selected text to uppercase. Same as completed workshop exercise.

Workshop #3: Change Case

Change Case.htm: Command that can be used with two menu entries, Make Uppercase and Make Lowercase, changing the case of selected text as specified. Same as completed workshop exercise.

Menu Commands Practice

Set_Menu_Text.htm: Menu command file that generates a menu entry with dynamically determined text. Same as completed practice file.

Toggle_Check.htm: Menu command file that dynamically determines whether to include a check mark next to its menu entry. Same as completed practice file.

Select_Check.htm: Menu command file that creates a submenu of selections, one of which will be checked, depending on user selection. Same as completed practice file.

Dynamic_Test.htm: Menu command that creates a dynamically generated submenu, depending on the contents of the user document. Same as completed practice file.

Workshop #4: Select Images

Select_Images.htm: Menu command that creates a dynamically generated submenu that lists all the images in the current document, includes a check mark if one of those images is selected, and selects the appropriate image if the user chooses it from the submenu. Same as completed workshop exercise.

Chapter 6: "Creating Custom Property Inspectors"

Inspector Framework.htm: HTML framework file with opening comment line, script tag in the `<head>`, including `canInspectSelection()`, `inspectSelection()`, and `displayHelp()` functions.

Blank Inspector.png: Picture of a blank Property inspector, for use as a tracing image in planning and constructing inspector layout.

Blank Inspector Icon.png: Image file containing the background elements (inset beveling) for an inspector icon.

Inspector Practice

mood.htm: Inspector file for inspecting the fictitious `<mood>` tag and its contents. Same as completed practice file.

mood.gif: Inspector icon for use with mood inspector.

Workshop #1: Block Spacer Inspector

Block Spacer.htm: Inspector for examining and editing the `<spacer>` tag created in Chapter 2.

Block Spacer.gif: Inspector icon for use with the Block Spacer inspector.

Workshop #2: Custom Horizontal Rule Inspector

Custom HR.htm: Inspector for examining and editing the custom `<hr>` tag created in Chapter 2.

Custom HR.gif: Inspector icon for use with the Custom HR inspector.

Chapter 7: "Creating Custom Floating Panels"

Floater Framework.htm: HTML framework file with script tag in the `<head>`, including `initialPosition()`, `isDockable()`, `getDockingSide()`, `isAvailableInCodeView()`, `displayHelp()`, `documentEdited()`, and `selectionChanged()` functions, with comments.

Sample and Resource Files

duck floater.htm: Sample of a floater using images, rollovers, and layers.

workshop.swf: SWF file to be placed in a floater.

smiley.gif: Animated GIF image to be placed in a floater.

duck01.gif: GIF image to be placed in a floater.

duck02.gif: GIF image to be placed in a floater.

click.gif: GIF image to be used creating a rollover effect in a floater.

click_over.gif: GIF image to be used creating a rollover effect in a floater.

click_down.gif: GIF image to be used creating a rollover effect in a floater.

Workshop #1: Table Helper

Table Helper.htm: Floater that examines a selected table in the user document, and reports on its dimensions and structure.

Chapter 8: "Mixing Extension Types"

Alt Text.htm: Object that causes the Automatic Alt Text command file to execute.

Alt Text.gif: Object icon to be used with the Alt Text object.

Create Table.htm: Object that inserts a table and then launches the Table Helper floater.

Create Table.gif: Object icon to be used with the Create Table object.

Interactive Page Properties.htm: Object file that creates a text link, and adds the Insert Page Properties behavior to it.

Interactive Page Properties.gif: Object icon to be used with the Insert Page Properties object.

Chapter 9: "Server Behaviors"

This chapter's files contain the HTML and XML files for each server behavior workshop. To find out where each of these files must be stored in the Configuration folder, read the section in Chapter 9 on "Server Behaviors in the Configuration Folder."

Workshop #1: If-Then Statement (Conditional Content)

If-Then.htm: Main file for a server behavior that inserts an If-Then statement into an ASP/JavaScript document.

If-Then.edml: XML "group" file containing supporting data for the If-Then behavior.

If-Then_block_1.edml and If-Then_block_2.edml: XML "participant" files for the If-Then behavior.

Workshop #2: Dynamically Determined Image

Dynamic Image.htm: Main file for a server behavior that constructs an `<img>` tag from database fields for an ASP/JavaScript document.

Dynamic Image.edml: XML "group" file containing supporting data for the Dynamic Image behavior.

Dynamic Image_block_1.edml: XML "participant" file containing supporting data for the Dynamic Image behavior.

Dynamic Image_block_2.edml: XML "participant" file containing supporting data for the Dynamic Image behavior.

Chapter 10: "Into the Great Beyond"

Practice Files

ListControl Practice.htm: Completed command file for the ListControl practice session.

ImageButton Practice.htm: Completed command file for the ImageButton practice session.

Layer Practice.htm: Completed command file for the layers practice session.

Resource and Framework Files

Bold-Italic-Align.htm: Command file containing code for creating fully functional bold, italic, and align ImageButtons.

Layer Framework.htm: Command file containing a working set of code for a layered interface that uses `TabControl` class objects.

Appendixes

Blank.mxi: Alternate template of the MXI installer file, as discussed in Appendix C, "Packaging Extensions for Use with the Extension Manager."

Index

Symbols

+ operators, 416

1-10 rating, as Property inspector file requirement, 232

A

accessing
- document elements (DOM), 126-129
- DOM objects, dw.getDocumentDOM( ) function, 113
- inspectors and floaters, dw.setFloaterVisibility( ) function, 318-319
- selections, 121

Add Popup Behavior command (Window menu), 327

addAlt( ) function
- creating basic code (adding alt parameters to document images), 143-145
- refining (adding alt parameters to document images), 145-147

adding
- button graphics to interface (ListControl), 378-379
- event handlers to images (ListControl), 380
- forms, creating custom objects, 24-25
- ListControl elements to interface, 366
- ListControl list items, 375

additive lists, User Interface Guidelines, 446

addpage( ) function, 397

alt parameters, adding to all images in document (creating custom commands), 142, 167
- addAlt( ) function code, 143-145
- adding browsing capability to dialog box, 152-154
- adding canAcceptCommand( ) function, 147-148
- adding dialog box and commandButtons( ) function, 149-152
- adding online help, 164-167
- creating a fancier dialog box, 155-163
- creating command file document, 143
- refining addAlt( ) function, 145-147

altering page elements (DOM), 130

analyzeServerBehavior( ) function, HTML files (server behaviors), 343

API (Application Programming Interface), 8-10, 229
- custom form input tags, 9
- custom objects, 8-9
- extension-specific functions and procedures, 8
- functions
  - *creating custom floating panels, 283-284*
  - *mixing extension types, 313-319*
  - *setting and manipulating the selection, 118-122*
  - *working with objects, 114-116*
  - *working with selection offsets, 117-118*
  - *working with selections, 116-117*
- procedure
  - *behavior constuction, 60*
  - *creating custom commands, 140*
  - *creating custom floating panels, 279-280*
  - *creating custom objects, 19*
  - *creating custom Property inspectors, 236-237*
  - *creating custom server behaviors, 346-348*
  - *inspecting behaviors, 61-62*
  - *menu command construction, 198-199*

applications (DOM), 123
- accessing different document elements, 126-129
- altering page elements, 130
- creating practice command file, 124
- examining practice command file, 125-126
- selecting page elements, 130-132
- using string functions on page elements, 132-134

Application Programming Interface. *See* API

Apply Template dialog box, 446

applyBehavior( ) function, 62
- as behavior file requirement, 58
- rewriting, custom behavior construction, 72-74, 83-84

applySB( ) helper function, 343

applyServerBehavior( ) function, HTML files (server behaviors), 343

arrays, 425-428

author tags, 462

Automatic Alt Text dialog box, 150

B

Back/Forward behavior (creating simple behaviors), 68
- creating a form to collect user input, 72
- inserting code into behavior file framework, 70-71
- JavaScript code insert, 68-69
- rewriting applyBehavior( ) function, 72-74

basic files
- behavior files, custom behavior construction, 63-66
- command files
  - *ImageButtons, 383-384*
  - *layered interfaces, 399-403*
  - *ListControl elements, 369-370*
- floaters, creating custom floating panels, 280-283
- object files
  - *creating custom objects, 22-24*
  - *creating user input objects, 34-35*
  - *horizontal rule object construction, 40-41*

behaviorFunction( ) function, 62, 71

behaviors
- buttons (User Interface Guidelines), 448
- creating custom behaviors, 55-62
  - *API procedure, 60*
  - *basic behaviors folder, 63-66*
  - *Configuration folder, 57-58*
  - *creating custom behaviors folder, 62*
  - *full-featured behaviors, 75-87*
  - *optional elements, 59-60*
  - *passed parameters, 66-67*
  - *required elements, 58*
  - *simple behaviors, 67-74*
- enhancing with DOM, 122-123
- inserting, 315-318
- inspecting, 90
  - *API procedure, 61-62*
  - *inspectBehavior( ) function, 90, 95-96*
  - *practice file, 90-93*
  - *Set Page Properties behavior, 96-98*
  - *shared files, 94-95*
- server. *See* server behaviors
- Set Page Properties
  - *collecting materials for simple extension packaging, 457*
  - *creating simple MXI files (packaging extensions), 470*
- testing, submitting extensions to Macromedia Dreamweaver Exchange, 483-484

Blank.mxi file, 458

body content
- as behavior file requirement, 58
- as command file optional element, 139
- as floater file required element, 277

body elements, as Property inspector file requirement, 233

Booleans, 416

borrowing code guidelines, submitting extensions to Macromedia Dreamweaver Exchange, 478

branding images, User Interface Guidelines, 440

browseForShim( ) function, 152

browser display, object testing, submitting extensions to Macromedia Dreamweaver Exchange, 481

browsing capability, adding to dialog boxes, 152-154

built-in objects (JavaScript), 435

buttons, 433
- adding graphics to interface (ListControl), 378-379
- Insert Behavior, 327
- User Interface Guidelines, 448
  - *behaviors, 448*
  - *commands, 449*
  - *floating panels, 450*
  - *objects, 448*
  - *Property inspectors, 450*

C

C programming language, 4

canAcceptBehavior( ) function, 60
- as behavior file optional requirement, 59
- as command file optional element, 139
- enhancing objects and behaviors with DOM, 123

canAcceptCommand( ) function, 140
- adding alt parameters to document images, 147-148

converting text to uppercase, creating custom string access command, 172-178
revising (creating custom menu commands), 220

canApplyServerBehavior( ) function, HTML files (server behaviors), 343

canInspectSelection( ) function, 236
as Property inspector file requirement, 233
creating Netscape Block Spacer inspector, 251
replacing default inspectors, 259-272

changeCase( ) function, 176
revising to accommodate arguments, 192-193

character offsets, accessing selections, 121

checkboxes, 429
User Interface Guidelines, 445

checkQuotes( ) function, 355

class files, 364
ImageButtons, 380-388
applying scripting to change the button state, 386-388
basic command files, 383-384
controlling, 382
creating and attaching to an image, 385
functions, 383
properties, 382
scripting, 381
specifications, 381-382
layered interfaces, 388
basic command files, 399-403
complex tabbed layer interfaces, 395-399
creating second pages, 404
simple tabbed layer interfaces, 390-394
specifications, 390
switching between layers, 404-405
ListControl elements, 364-365
adding and removing list items, 375
adding button graphics to interface, 378-379
adding elements to interface, 366
adding event handlers to images, 380
building basic command files, 369-370
creating an object and attaching select element, 371-372
examining the list, 373-374
initializing ListControl list, 372-373
rearranging list items, 375-378
scripting ListControl elements, 367
specifications, 365

code
blocks (SBB), positioning and weighting, 335
strings of code (DOM), 122

collecting materials for packaging extensions, 456
Flash Detector object, 457
Set Page Properties behavior, 457
Table Helper floating panel, 458

color buttons (User Interface Guidelines), 447

color control button, 9

color input, refining (creating custom full-featured objects), 47-48

coloring outside lines, as reason to mix extension types, 312-313

colors (User Interface Guidelines), 438

command files
creating custom menu commands, 215-216
documents, converting text to uppercase, 169
ImageButtons, 383-384
layered interfaces, 399-403
ListControl elements, 369-370

commandButtons( ) function, 140, 386, 451
adding alt parameters to document images, 149-152
as command file optional element, 139

commands
buttons (User Interface Guidelines), 449
creating custom commands, 135-137
API procedure, 140
command files' structure, 137-140
Configuration folder, 137
DOM, 141-167
string access commands, 167-178
creating custom menu commands, 180-214
API procedure, 198-199
applying isCommandChecked( ) function, 204-208
Configuration folder, 193
controlling command's appearance in menus, 187
creating custom folder to hold menu commands, 200
creating menu item name with setMenuText( ) function, 201-204
creating submenus with getDynamicContent( ) function, 209-213

displaying images in a document, 214-228
manipulating menu entry for a command, 189-193
Menu Command files' structure, 194-196
menus.xml file, 181-186
passing parameters to commands using receiveArguments( ) function, 187-188
setting up development submenu to hold test commands, 200
dw.runCommand( ) function, mixing extension types, 313
File menu, Package Extension, 474
Insert menu, Form Objects, Image Field, 379
object-based selection commands, accessing selections, 121
testing, submitting extensions to Macromedia Dreamweaver Exchange, 482-483
Window menu, Add Popup Behavior, 327

Comments (COMMENT_NODE objects), 110

competing inspectors, creating custom Property inspectors, 248

complex behaviors. *See* full-featured behaviors

complex object files. *See* full-featured object files

complex tabbed layer interfaces, 395
creating layers, 395-396
scripting layers, 396-399
TabControl class object functions, 397-398

concatenation, 417

conditional page content, inserting with if-then statements (custom server behaviors), 348
adding Expression option to dialog box, 354-356
creating code to insert, 348
hard-coded values, 349-350
refining behavior appearance (Server Behaviors panel), 352
refining If-then server behavior dialog box, 353
replacing hard-coded values with parameters, 350-352

conditional statements, 423-425

Configuration folder, 3-5
behaviors, 57-58
commands, command file structure, 137-140
files, 5-6
HTML files, 5
previously installed versions, 6
user-specific files, 7
XML files, 6
floating panels, Floaters folder files, 275-279
menu commands, 193
objects, 12-13
Property inspectors, Inspector folder files, 230-235
server behaviors, 341
HTML files, 341-344
XML files, 341-342
subfolders, 4

configuration-changes tag, 465

content organization (dialog box layout), User Interface Guidelines, 442

controlling ImageButtons, 382

converting text to uppercase, custom string access commands, 168-178

Create a New Code Block dialog box, 337

Create Behavior Extension, 490

creating
custom behaviors, 55-62
API procedure, 60
basic behaviors folder, 63-66
Configuration folder, 57-58
custom behaviors folder, 62
full-featured behaviors, 75-87
optional elements, 59-60
passed parameters, 66-67
required elements, 58
simple behaviors, 67-74
custom commands, 135-178
API procedure, 140
command files' structure, 137-140
Configuration folder, 137
DOM, 141-167
string access commands, 167-178
custom floating panels, 273-295
API functions, 283-284
API procedure, 279-280
basic floaters, 280-283
Configuration folder, 275
documentEdited( ) function, 294-295
Floater files' structure, 276-279
form elements, 291-293
layout, 284-286
rollover images, 286-288
selectionChanged( ) function, 293-294
SWF movies, 289-290
table-editing utility, 296-308

custom menu commands, 180-214
API procedure, 198-199
applying isCommandChecked( ) function, 204-208
Configuration folder, 193
controlling command's appearance in menus, 187
creating custom folder to hold menu commands, 200
creating menu item name with setMenuText( ) function, 201-204
creating submenus with getDynamicContent( ) function, 209-213
displaying images in a document, 214-228
manipulating menu entry for a command, 189-193
Menu Command files' structure, 194-196
menus.xml file, 181-186
passing parameters to commands using receiveArguments( ) function, 187-188
setting up development submenu to hold test commands, 200
custom objects, 11-53
adding forms, 24-25
API procedure, 19
basic object files, 22-24
Configuration folder, 12-13
custom object categories, 20-22
full-featured object files, 16-18, 39-53
Insert bar objects, 14
Insert menu objects, 14
simple object files, 14-16, 27-38
custom Property inspectors, 229-272
adding forms and inspectBehavior( ) function, 239-240
adding local functions and event handlers, 241-242
API procedure, 236-237
bare-bones mood inspector, 238-239
competing inspectors, 248
Configuration folder, 230-232
Inspector files' structure, 232-235
Netscape Block Spacer inspector, 248-255
re-creating the interface with layers, 242-247
replacing default inspectors, 255-272
custom server behaviors, 341-360
API procedure, 346-348
Configuration folder, 341-344
helper functions, 344-346
inserting conditional page content with an if-then statement, 348-356
inserting dynamically determined images, 356-360
SBB, 336-341
layers
complex tabbed layer interfaces, 395-396
simple tabbed layer interfaces, 390-392
ListControl object, attaching select element, 371-372
MXI files (packaging extensions), 458
Flash Detector object, 471
saving MXI file, 458
Set Page Properties behavior, 470
structure of MXI file, 458-470
Table Helper floating panel, 472-473
object icons (creating table objects), 31-32
practice command file (DOM), 124
second pages, layered interfaces, 404
table objects (simple object construction), 27
adding an entry for the object in insertbar.xml file, 30
creating an icon for the object, 31-32
HTML code, 27-28
placing code in object file framework, 28-29
testing and troubleshooting new object, 30-31

Ctrl-clicking (Windows) icon, 22

custom behaviors, creating, 55-62
API procedure, 60
basic behaviors folder, 63-66
Configuration folder, 57-58
custom behaviors folder, 62
full-featured behaviors, 75-87
optional elements, 59-60
passed parameters, 66-67
required elements, 58
simple behaviors, 67-74

custom commands, creating, 135-178
API procedure, 140
command files' structure, 137-140
Configuration folder, 137
DOM, 141-167
string access commands, 167-178

custom floating panels, creating, 273-295
API functions, 283-284
API procedure, 279-280
basic floaters, 280-283
Configuration folder, 275
documentEdited( ) function, 294-295
Floater files' structure, 276-279
form elements, 291-293

layout, 284-286
rollover images, 286-288
selectionChanged( ) function, 293-294
SWF movies, 289-290
table-editing utility, 296-308

custom form input tags (API), 9

Custom Horizontal Rule object, replacing default inspectors, 256-257

custom menu commands, creating, 180-214
API procedure, 198-199
applying isCommandChecked( ) function, 204-208
Configuration folder, 193
controlling command's appearance in menus, 187
creating custom folder to hold menu commands, 200
creating menu item name with setMenuText( ) function, 201-204
creating submenus with getDynamicContent( ) function, 209-213
displaying images in a document, 214-228
manipulating menu entry for a command, 189-193
Menu Command files' structure, 194-196
menus.xml file, 181-186
passing parameters to commands using receiveArguments( ) function, 187-188
setting up development submenu to hold test commands, 200

Custom Message behavior, 338-341

custom objects (API), 8-9
creating, 11-53
adding forms, 24-25
API procedure, 19
basic object files, 22-24
Configuration folder, 12-13
custom object categories, 20-22
full-featured object files, 16-18, 39-53
Insert bar objects, 14
Insert menu objects, 14
simple object files, 14-16, 27-38
methods, 8

custom Property inspectors, creating, 229-272
adding forms and inspectBehavior( ) function, 239-240
adding local functions and event handlers, 241-242
API procedure, 236-237
bare-bones mood inspector, 238-239
competing inspectors, 248
Configuration folder, 230-232
Inspector files' structure, 232-235
Netscape Block Spacer inspector, 248-255
re-creating the interface with layers, 242-247
replacing default inspectors, 255-272

custom server behaviors, creating, 341-360
API procedure, 346-348
Configuration folder, 341-344
helper functions, 344-346
inserting conditional page content with an if-then statement, 348-356
inserting dynamically determined images, 356-360
SBB, 336-341

D

debugging extensions, submitting extensions to Macromedia Dreamweaver Exchange, 479
behavior testing, 483-484
command testing, 482-483
floating panel testing, 484-486
installation testing, 479-480
object testing, 480-481
preparing to test, 479
Property inspector testing, 481-482
side-wide extension testing, 486

default inspectors, replacing when creating custom Property inspectors, 255
canInspectSelection( ) function, 259
Custom Horizontal Rule object, 256-257
inspectSelection( ) function, 259-262
local functions, 263-266
priorities, 267-272

default values, User Interface Guidelines, 453-454

deleteSB( ) helper function, 343

deleteServerBehavior( ) function, HTML files (server behaviors), 343

description tag, 463

determined images, inserting in custom server behaviors, 356
adding error-checking, 359-360
creating the code to insert, 356
hard-coded values, 357
refining behavior appearance (Server Behaviors panel), 358
replacing hard-coded values with parameters, 357

development subfolder, setting up to hold test commands, 200

diagramTable( ) function, 299

dialog boxes
- Apply Template, 446
- Automatic Alt Text, 150
- Create a New Code Block, 337
- Edit Font List, 446
- ImageButton Practice, 384
- Insert Table, 28
- Keyboard Shortcuts, 9, 447
- Layer Practice, 400-401
- layout, User Interface Guidelines, 441-442
- ListControl Practice, 373
- logos, 440
- New Server Behavior, 349
- Page Properties, 447
- refining (creating custom full-featured objects), 48-50
- SBB, 335
- Select Image Source, 379
- Set Page Properties, 86
- Swap Image, 446

disaster prevention, error checking (User Interface Guidelines), 452-453

displayDiagram( ) function, 324-326

displayHelp( ) function, 451
- as behavior file optional requirement, 60
- as floater file optional element, 278
- full-featured object files, 17
- HTML files (server behaviors), 344

displaying images in a document, creating custom menu commands, 214
- collecting arguments with receiveArguments( ) function, 220-221
- creating the command file, 215-216
- creating the main function, 221-222
- creating the menu entry, 214
- filling in the getDynamicContent( ) function, 216-220
- revising isCommandChecked( ) function, 222-228
- revising the canAcceptCommand( ) function, 220

document elements, accessing (DOM), 126-129

Document Object Model. *See* DOM

document structure, Level 1 DOM, 111

documentEdited( ) function
- as floater file optional element, 279
- creating custom floating panels, 294-295

DOCUMENT_NODE objects, 107-108

DOM (Document Object Model)
- applications, 123
  - *accessing different document elements, 126-129*
  - *altering page elements, 130*
  - *creating practice command file, 124*
  - *examining practice command file, 125-126*
  - *selecting page elements, 130-132*
  - *using string functions on page elements, 132-134*
- creating custom commands, 141
  - *adding alt parameters to all images in document, 142-167*
  - *wrapping up automatic Alt command, 167*
- DOM object, 112
  - *accessing, 113*
  - *API functions for setting and manipulating the selection, 118-122*
  - *API functions for working with objects, 114-116*
  - *API functions for working with selection offsets, 117-118*
  - *API functions for working with selections, 116-117*
  - *strings of code, 122*
- enhancing objects and behaviors, 122-123
- JavaScript, 101-102
- Level 0 DOM, specifications, 103, 107
- Level 1 DOM, 102-103, 107
  - *document structure, 111*
  - *nodes, 107-111*

dom.addBehavior( ) function
- creating a floater that inserts a behavior, 326-328
- mixing extension types, 315-318

dom.getElementsByTagName( ) function, 143, 148

dom.getSelectedNode( ) function, 121

dom.getSelection( ) function, 121, 170

dom.insertObject( ) function
- creating command for inserting objects, 322-323
- mixing extension types, 314-315

dom.setSelectedNode( ) function, 121

Dreamweaver Depot, 488

Dreamweaver Platform SDK Extension, 489

dw.browseForFileURL( ) function, 152-153

dw.getConfigurationPath( ) function, 165

dw.getDocumentDOM( ) function
creating custom floating panels, table-editing utility, 297-299
specifications, 113

dw.PopupAction( ) function, creating an objet that inserts behaviors and HTML code, 329-331

dw.popupAction( ) function, mixing extension types, 315-318

dw.runCommand( ) function
creating an Insert Alt Text object, 319-320
mixing extension types, 313

dw.setFloaterVisibility( ) function, 276
creating command for opening floating panels, 322-323
mixing extension types, 318-319

dw.toggleFloater( ) function, 276

DWFile object, 8

Dynamic Image behavior, 357

dynamically determined images, inserting in custom server behaviors, 356
adding error-checking, 359-360
creating the code to insert, 356
hard-coded values, 357
refining behavior appearance (Server Behaviors panel), 358
replacing hard-coded values with parameters, 357

E

Edit Font List dialog box, 446

editing behaviors, 90
inspectBehavior( ) function, 90
practice file, 90-93
revising inspectBehavior( ) function to call extractArgs function, 95-96
Set Page Properties behavior, 96-98
shared files, 94-95

EditPlus, 490

ELEMENT_NODE objects, 108-109

enhancing objects and behaviors (DOM), 122-123

error-checking, adding to determined images (custom server behaviors), 359-360

error-proof handling (User Interface Guidelines), 451
default values, 453-454
error-checking, 452-453
focus and selection, 452

errorChecking( ) function, 253-254

eval( ) function, 393

event handlers, 433-434
adding to images (ListControl), 380
as Property inspector file requirement, 233
creating custom Property inspectors, 241-242

exactOrWithin tag, as Property inspector file requirement, 232

Excellent Dreamweaver Supply Bin, 488

Exchange (Macromedia Dreamweaver Exchange), submitting extensions, 477-478
borrowing code guidelines, 478
file location guidelines, 478
recommended test plan, 479-486
scripting guidelines, 478

expressions, 416-417

Extending Dreamweaver manual, 8

Extension Debug Suite Extension, 490

extension interfaces, custom form elements, 406-408

extension-specific functions, 8

extension types, mixing, 311-313
coloring outside lines, 312-313
jump menus, 312
navigation bars, 312
rollovers, 312

extractArgs( ) function, inspecting behaviors, 95

F

file formats (User Interface Guidelines), 438

file location guidelines, submitting extensions to Macromedia Dreamweaver Exchange, 478

File menu commands (Package Extension), 474

filenames
as command file requirement, 138
as floater file required element, 276
simple object files, 15

files
configuration files, 5-6
HTML files, 5
previously installed versions, 6
user-specific files, 7
XML files, 6
linking JavaScript and HTML, 435-436
files tag, 463
findObject( ) function, 235-236, 394
findSBs( ) helper function, 343
findServerBehaviors( ) function, 346
HTML files (server behaviors), 343
Flash Detector object
collecting materials for packaging extensions, 457
creating an MXI file for multifile extensions (packaging extensions), 471
Floaters folder, floating panels files, 275
floating panels
accessing, dw.setFloaterVisibility( ) function, 318-319
buttons, User Interface Guidelines, 450
creating custom floating panels, 273-295
API functions, 283-284
API procedure, 279-280
basic floaters, 280-283
Configuration folder, 275
documentEdited( ) function, 294-295
Floater files' structure, 276-279
form elements, 291-293
layout, 284-286
rollover images, 286-288
selectionChanged( ) function, 293-294
SWF movies, 289-290
table-editing utility, 296-308
creating custom Property inspectors, Configuration folder, 275
logos, 440
Table Helper
collecting materials for extensions with menu changes, 458
creating an MXI file for an extension with menu changes (packaging extensions), 472-473
final code, 306
testing, submitting extensions to Macromedia Dreamweaver Exchange, 484-486
fnCall parameter, 93
focus, error-proof handling (User Interface Guidelines), 452
folders, creating custom folders to hold menu commands, 200
fonts (User Interface Guidelines), 438
for-loops, 425-428
form elements, 428
buttons, 433
checkboxes, 429
creating custom floating panels, 291-293
event handlers, 433-434
forms, 428
popup menus, 431-432
radio buttons, 430-431
text fields, 429
Form Objects, Image Field command (Insert menu), 379
form tags, full-featured object files, 16-17
forms, 428
adding, creating custom objects, 24-25
as floater file optional element, 277
as Property inspector file requirement, 233
custom form input tags (API), 9
custom Property inspectors, 239-240
designing a form to collect user input
custom behavior construction, 72-82
horizontal rule objects, 40
user input objects, 33
HTML files (server behaviors), 344
interactivity, creating user input objects, 35-37
replacing default inspectors, 256-257
User Interface Guidelines, 444
checkboxes, 445
color buttons, 447
lists, 445-446
popup menus, 445-446
radio buttons, 445
text fields, 444
tree controls, 447
forums (online resources), 489
Forward/Back behavior (creating simple behaviors), 68
creating a form to collect user input, 72
inserting code into behavior file framework, 70-71
JavaScript code insert, 68-69
rewriting applyBehavior( ) function, 72-74
ftp-extension-insert tags, 468
ftp-extension-map-changes tags, 467
ftp-extension-remove tags, 468
full-featured behaviors (Set Page Properties behavior), 75
adding local functions, 84-86
designing form to collect user input, 82

placing code into basic behavior file framework, 80-81
rewriting applyBehavior function, 83-84
splitting code into HTML and JavaScript files, 87
writing the JavaScript function, 75-79

full-featured object files, 16, 39
displayHelp( ) function, 17
form tags, 16-17
horizontal rule object
adding an entry for the object in insertbar.xml file, 42
adding online help, 48-50
basic object files, 40-41
building objectTag( ) function's return statement, 44-47
designing the form to collect user input, 40
HTML code, 39
refining color input, 47-48
refining the dialog box, 48-50
revising objectTag( ) function to collect user input, 43-44
splitting code into separate HTML and JS files, 52-53
isDomRequired( ) function, 17
local functions, 18

function calls, 418

function parameters, 419-422

functions
addAlt( )
creating basic code, 143-145
refining addAlt( ) function, 145-147
addpage( ), 397
analyzeServerBehavior( ), HTML files (server behaviors), 343
applyBehavior( ), 62
as behavior file requirement, 58
custom behavior construction, 72-74, 83-84
applyServerBehavior( ), HTML files (server behaviors), 343
behaviorFunction( ), 62, 71
as behavior file requirement, 58
browseForShim( ), 152
canAcceptBehavior( ), 60
as behavior file optional requirement, 59
as command file optional element, 139
enhancing objects and behaviors with DOM, 123
canAcceptCommand( ), 140
adding alt parameters to document images, 147-148
converting text to uppercase (custom string access commands), 172-178
creating custom menu commands, 220
canApplyServerBehavior( ), HTML files (server behaviors), 343
canInspectSelection( ), 236
as Property inspector file requirement, 233
creating Netscape Block Spacer inspector, 251
replacing default inspectors, 267-272
changeCase( ), 176
revising to accommodate arguments, 192-193
checkQuotes( ), 355
commandButtons( ), 140, 386, 451
adding alt parameters to document images, 149-152
as command file optional element, 139
deleteServerBehavior( ), HTML files (server behaviors), 343
diagramTable( ), 299
displayDiagram( ), making a floater updatable from outside itself, 324-326
displayHelp( ), 278, 451
as behavior file optional requirement, 60
full-featured object files, 17
HTML files (server behaviors), 344
documentEdited( ), 279
creating custom floating panels, 294-295
DOM object functions
objects, 114-116
selection offsets, 117-118
selections, 116-117
setting and manipulating selections, 118-122
dom.addBehavior( ), creating a floater that inserts a behavior, 326-328
dom.getElementsByTagName( ), 143, 148
dom.getSelectedNode( ), accessing selections, 121
dom.getSelection( ), 170, applying character offsets to gain access to selections, 121
dom.insertObject( ), creating command for inserting objects, 322-323
dom.setSelectedNode( ), accessing selections, 121
dw.browseForFileURL( ), 152-153
dw.getConfigurationPath( ), 165
dw.getDocumentDOM( )
creating custom floating panels, 297-299
specifications, 113
dw.PopupAction( ), creating an objet that inserts behaviors and HTML code, 329-331
dw.runCommand( ), creating an Insert Alt Text object, 319-320

dw.setFloaterVisibility( ), 276
creating command for opening floating panel, 322-323
dw.toggleFloater( ), 276
errorChecking( ), 253-254
eval( ), 393
extension-specific, 8
extractArgs( ), inspecting behaviors, 95
findObject( ), 235, 394
as Property inspector file optional requirement, 236
findServerBehaviors( ), 346
function calls, 418
function parameters, 419-422
getDockingSide( ), 278
getDynamicContent( ), 195-196
creating custom menu commands, 216-220
creating submenus, 209-213
getElementsByTagName( ), 129
helper functions, server behaviors, 343-346
ImageButtons, 383
initializeUI( ), 367, 371, 452
initialPosition( ), 277
inspectBehavior( ), 61, 90
adding to practice file, 92-93
as behavior file optional requirement, 59
creating custom Property inspectors, 239-240
inspecting behaviors, 90
revising to call extractArgs function, 95-96
inspectSelection( )
as Property inspector file semi-requirement, 234
creating Netscape Block Spacer inspector, 251
replacing default inspectors, 259-262
inspectServerBehavior(sbObj), HTML files (server behaviors), 344
isAvailableInCodeView( ), 278
isCommandChecked( )
creating a command with a checkmark toggle, 204-206
creating an options submenu, 206-208
creating custom menu commands, 222-228
isDockable( ), 278
isDomRequired( )
as command file optional element, 139
enhancing objects and behaviors with DOM, 123
full-featured object files, 17
list.add( ), 375
list.remove( ), 375
list.setAll( ), 372
ListControl elements, 368
creating and managing list control structures, 368
getting information from a list, 369
putting information into a list, 368
load( ), 399
local functions
as behavior file optional requirement, 60
custom behavior construction, 84-86
full-featured object files, 18
replacing default inspectors, 263-266
mixing extensions, 313
dom.addBehavior( ), 315-318
dom.insertObject( ), 314-315
dw.popupAction( ), 315-318
dw.runCommand( ), 313
dw.setFloaterVisibility( ), 318-319
MM_reloadPage( ), 244
moveDown( ), 377
moveUp( ), 376
myCommand( ), 374
newBehavior( ), 91
objectTag( ), 312, 320
building return statement (horizonatal rule object construction), 44-47
revising to collect user input (horizonatal rule object construction), 43-44
simple object files, 15-16
onBlur, 233
receiveArguments( ), 140
adding to command document, 192
as command file optional element, 140
creating custom menu commands, 220-221
passing parameters to commands, 187-188
runCommand( ), 126, 169
selectionChanged( ), 279
creating custom floating panels, 293-294
setColorButton( ), 48, 85
setColorField( ), 48, 85
setColorText( ), 48
setDimensions( ), creating Netscape Block Spacer inspector, 251-252
setMenuText( ), 194-195
creating menu item names, 201-204
setProperties( ), 77
setTitleTag( ), 233
showPage( ), 399
substring( ), 145
TabControl class objects, 397-398
testGeneration( ), 175
toUpperCase( ) string, 168

FWLaunch object, 8

G

generic function, as behavior file requirement, 58

getDockingSide( ) function, as floater file optional element, 278

getDynamicContent( ) function, 195-196
- creating submenus, 209-213
- filling in (creating custom menu commands), 216-220

getElementsByTagName( ) function, 129

GIF file
- object construction, 13
- Property inspector construction, 231

GIF images, 438

graphics (User Interface Guidelines), 438
- file formats, 438
- icons, 439-440
- inserting images, 438
- logos, 440

group files, server behaviors, 342

gTesting variable, 175

guidelines
- submitting extensions to Macromedia Dreamweaver Exchange, 478
- User Interface Guidelines, 437
  - *buttons, 448-450*
  - *colors, 438*
  - *error-proof handling, 451-454*
  - *fonts, 438*
  - *form elements, 444-447*
  - *graphics, 438-440*
  - *layout, 441-444*
  - *online help, 450-451*

H

hands-off philosophy, error checking (User Interface Guidelines), 452

help, online
- adding to custom commands, 164-167
- adding to custom full-featured objects, 48-50

Help buttons (User Interface Guidelines), 451

helper functions, server behaviors, 343-346

hiding floater means, as floater file required element, 276

History panel, 124

hline parameter, as Property inspector file requirement, 232

horizontal rule objects (creating custom full-featured objects), 39
- adding an entry for the object in insertbar.xml file, 42
- adding online help, 48-50
- basic object files, 40-41
- building objectTag( ) function's return statement, 44-47
- designing the form to collect user input, 40
- HR object, 39-42
- HTML code, 39
- refining color input, 47-48
- refining the dialog box, 48-50
- revising objectTag( ) function to collect user input, 43-44
- splitting code into separate HTML and JS files, 52-53

HTML
- code
  - *converting text to uppercase, 169-172*
  - *creating for table object construction, 27-29*
  - *custom horizontal rule objects, 39*
  - *spacer object construction, 33*
- comments, COMMENT_NODE objects, 110
- elements, ELEMENT_NODE objects, 108-109
- files
  - *behavior construction, 57*
  - *Configuration folder, 5*
  - *floating panel construction, 275*
  - *object construction, 13*
  - *Property inspector construction, 231*
  - *server behavior construction, 341-344*
- how JavaScript works with HTML, 414
  - *linking files, 435-436*
  - *script tags, 414-416*
- object testing, submitting extensions to Macromedia Dreamweaver Exchange, 481

I

icons
- as Property inspector file optional requirement, 236
- User Interface Guidelines, shared images, 439-440

if-then statements, 423-425
inserting conditional page content (custom server behaviors), 348
adding Expression option to dialog box, 354-356
creating code to insert, 348
hard-coded values, 349-350
refining behavior appearance (Server Behaviors panel), 352
refining If-Then server behavior dialog box, 353
replacing hard-coded values with parameters, 350-352

illustrative icons (User Interface Guidelines), 439

image files, Property inspector construction, 232

ImageButton Practice dialog box, 384

ImageButtons, 380-388
applying scripting to change the button state, 386-388
basic command files, 383-384
controlling, 382
creating and attaching to an image, 385
functions, 383
properties, 382
scripting, 381
specifications, 381-382

images
creating custom floating panels, 284-286
inserting dynamically determined images in custom server behaviors, 356
adding error-checking, 359-360
creating the code to insert, 356
hard-coded values, 357
refining behavior appearance (Server Behaviors panel), 358
replacing hard-coded values with parameters, 357
User Interface Guidelines, 438

inactive folders, previously installed versions (Configuration folder files), 7

initializeUI( ) function, 367, 371, 452

initializing ListControl list, 372-374

initialPosition( ) function, as floater file optional element, 277

Insert Alt Text object, creating by mixing extension types, 319-320

Insert bar objects, 14

Insert Behavior button, 327

Insert menu
commands, Form Objects, Image Field, 379
objects, 14

Insert Rollover object file, 312

Insert Table dialog box, 28

inserting
behaviors, 315-318
conditional page content with an if-then statement (custom server behaviors), 348
adding Expression option to dialog box, 354-356
creating code to insert, 348
hard-coded values, 349-350
refining behavior appearance (Server Behaviors panel), 352
refining If-Then server behavior dialog box, 353
replacing hard-coded values with parameters, 350-352
dynamically determined images (custom server behaviors), 356
adding error-checking, 359-360
creating the code to insert, 356
hard-coded values, 357
refining behavior appearance (Server Behaviors panel), 358
replacing hard-coded values with parameters, 357
images, User Interface Guidelines, 438
lines of code (server behaviors), 336-338
Netscape Spacer tag (creating simple objects), creating the spacer object, 32-38
objects
dom.insertObject( ) function, mixing extension types, 314-315
object testing, submitting extensions to Macromedia Dreamweaver Exchange, 480
single-celled centering tables (creating simple objects), 27
user-defined messages (server behaviors), 338-341

inspectBehavior( ) function, 61
adding to practice file, 92-93
as behavior file optional requirement, 59
creating custom Property inspectors, 239-240
inspecting behaviors, 90
revising to call extractArgs function, 95-96

inspecting behaviors, 90
API procedure, 61-62
inspectBehavior( ) function, 90

practice file, 90-92
revising inspectBehavior( ) function to call extractArgs function, 95-96
Set Page Properties behavior, 96-98
shared files, 94-95

Inspector folder
file structure, 232, 276
optional elements, 235, 277-279
required elements, 232-233, 276-277
semi-required elements, 234-235
Property inspector files, 231-232

inspectSelection( ) function
as Property inspector file semi-requirement, 234
creating Netscape Block Spacer inspector, 251
replacing default inspectors, 259-262

inspectServerBehavior( ) function, HTML files (server behaviors), 344

installation testing, submitting extensions to Macromedia Dreamweaver Exchange, 479-480

interactivity
form elements, creating custom floating panels, 291-293
forms, creating user input objects, 35-37

interfaces
class files. *See* class files
ImageButtons, 380-383
applying scripting to change the button state, 386-388
basic command files, 383-384
controlling, 382
creating and attaching to an image, 385
functions, 383
properties, 382
scripting, 381
specifications, 381-382
layered interfaces, 388
basic command files, 399-403
complex tabbed layer interfaces, 395-399
creating second pages, 404
simple tabbed layer interfaces, 390-394
specifications, 390
switching between layers, 404-405
ListControl elements, 364-365
adding and removing list items, 375
adding button graphics to interface, 378-379
adding elements to interface, 366
adding event handlers to images, 380
building basic command files, 369-370
creating an object and attaching select element, 371-372
examining the list, 373-374
initializing ListControl list, 372-373
rearranging list items, 375-378
scripting ListControl elements, 367
specifications, 365

isAvailableInCodeView( ) function, as floater file optional element, 278

isCommandChecked( ) function
creating a command with a checkmark toggle, 204-206
creating an options submenu, 206-208
revising (creating custom menu commands), 222-228

isDockable( ) function, as floater file optional element, 278

isDomRequired( ) function
as command file optional element, 139
enhancing objects and behaviors with DOM, 123
full-featured object files, 17

J

JavaScript
code insert, Back/Forward behavior (creating simple behaviors), 68-69
DOM, 101-102
files
behavior construction, 58
floating panel construction, 275
object construction, 12
Property inspector construction, 231
how JavaScript works with HTML, 414
linking files, 435-436
script tags, 414-416
objects, 434-435

JPG images, 438

JSExtensionBrowser, 490

jump menus, as reason to mix extension types, 312

K-L

Keyboard Shortcut Editor dialog box, 9, 447

Layer Practice dialog box, 400-401

layered interfaces, 388
basic command files, 399-403
complex tabbed layer interfaces, 395
creating layers, 395-396
scripting layers, 396-399
TabControl class object functions, 397-398

creating second pages, 404
Macromedia images, 391-392
scripting, switching between layers, 404-405
simple tabbed layer interfaces, 390
creating layers, 390-392
scripting, 392-394
specifications, 390

layers
as Property inspector file optional requirement, 235
creating
complex tabbed layer interfaces, 395-396
simple tabbed layer interfaces, 390-392
creating custom floating panels, 284-286
dialog box layout, User Interface Guidelines, 442
re-creating custom Property inspector interfaces, 242-247
scripting, complex tabbed layer interfaces, 396-399

layout
creating custom floating panels, images and layers, 284-286
elements, replacing default inspectors, 256-257
User Interface Guidelines, 441
dialog box layout, 441-442
Property inspector layout, 444

Level 0 DOM, 103, 107

Level 1 DOM, 102-111
document structure, 111
nodes, 107-111
COMMENT_NODE objects, 110
DOCUMENT_NODE objects, 107-108
ELEMENT_NODE objects, 108-109
TEXT_NODE objects, 110-111

lines of code, inserting (building server behaviors), 336-338

linking files, JavaScript and HTML, 435-436

list.add( ) function, 375

list.remove( ) function, 375

list.setAll( ) function, 372

ListControl elements, 364-365
adding button graphics to interface, 378-379
adding event handlers to images, 380
building basic command files, 369-370
creating an object and attaching select elements, 371-372
functions, 368
creating and managing list control structures, 368
getting information from a list, 369
putting information into a list, 368
initializing ListControl lists, 372-373
adding and removing list items, 375
examining the list, 373-374
rearranging list items, 375-378
specifications, 365
adding ListControl element to interface, 366
scripting ListControl elements, 367-369

ListControl Practice dialog box, 373

lists (User Interface Guidelines), additive lists, 445-446

load( ) function, 399

local functions
as behavior file optional requirement, 60
creating custom Property inspectors, 241-242
custom behavior construction, 84-86
full-featured object files, 18
replacing default inspectors, 263-266

logical structures, 423
conditional statements, 423-425
loop statements, 425-428

logos (User Interface Guidelines), 440

loop statements, 425-428

Lower Case command, adding change to Text menu, 190-191

M

Macromedia DEVFORUM newsgroup, 489

Macromedia Dreamweaver Exchange, submitting extensions, 477-478
borrowing code guidelines, 478
file location guidelines, 478
recommended test plan, 479-486
scripting guidelines, 478

Macromedia images, tabbed layer interfaces, 391-392

Macromedia User Interface Guidelines, 437
buttons, 448
behaviors, 448
commands, 449
floating panels, 450
objects, 448
Property inspectors, 450

colors, 438
error-proof handling, 451
default values, 453-454
error-checking, 452-453
focus and selection, 452
fonts, 438
form elements, 444
checkboxes, 445
color buttons, 447
lists, 445-446
popup menus, 445-446
radio buttons, 445
text fields, 444
tree controls, 447
graphics, 438
file formats, 438
icons, 439-440
inserting images, 438
logos, 440
layout, 441
dialog box layout, 441-442
Property inspector layout, 444
online help, 450
Help buttons, 451
short help, 450
tabbed layouts, 450

macromedia-extension tags, 460

Make Upper Case command
adding entry to menus.xml file, 189-190
changing menu placement, 189
code listing, 178

manipulating menu entry for a command, 189
adding change to Lower Case command to Text menu, 190-191
adding entry for Make Upper Case to menus.xml file, 189-190
adding receiveArguments( ) function to command document, 192
changing menu placement of Make Upper Case command, 189
revising changeCase function( ), 192-193

menu change extensions, collecting materials for packaging extensions (Table Helper floating panel), 458

Menu Command files, structure, 194
getDynamicContent( ) function, 195-196
setMenuText( ) function, 194-195

menu commands
API procedure, 198-199
applying isCommandChecked( ) function, 204-208
Configuration folder, 193
controlling command's appearance in menus, 187
creating custom folder to hold menu commands, 200
creating menu item name with setMenuText( ) function, 201-204
creating submenus with getDynamicContent( ) function, 209-213
displaying images in a document, 214
collecting arguments with receiveArguments( ) function, 220-221
creating the command file, 215-216
creating the main function, 221-222
creating the menu entry, 214
filling in the getDynamicContent( ) function, 216-220
revising isCommandChecked( ) function, 222-228
revising the canAcceptCommand( ) function, 220
manipulating menu entry for a command, 189
adding change to Lower Case command to Text menu, 190-191
adding entry for Make Upper Case to menus.xml file, 189-190
adding receiveArguments( ) function to command document, 192
changing menu placement of Make Upper Case command, 189
revising changeCase function( ), 192-193
Menu Command files' structure, 194
getDynamicContent( ) function, 195-196
setMenuText( ) function, 194-195
menus.xml file, 181-186
passing parameters to commands using receiveArguments( ) function, 187-188
setting up development submenu to hold test commands, 200

menu tags, 201

menu-insert tags, 466

menu-remove tags, 466

menus.xml file, 181-186

methods, 434. *See also* functions
COMMENT_NODE objects, 110
custom API objects, 8
DOCUMENT_NODE objects, 108
ELEMENT_NODE objects, 109
TEXT_NODE objects, 111

mixing extension types, 311-319
API functions, 313
dom.addBehavior( ), 315-318
dom.insertObject( ), 314-315
dw.popupAction( ), 315-318
dw.runCommand( ), 313
dw.setFloaterVisibility( ), 318-319
creating an Insert Alt Text object, 319-320
dom.addBehavior( ) function, creating a floater that inserts a behavior, 326-328
dom.insertObject( ) function, creating command for inserting objects, 322-323
dw.PopupAction( ) function, creating an objet that inserts behaviors and HTML code, 329-331
dw.setFloaterVisibility( ) function, creating command for opening floating panels, 322-323
making a floater updatable from outside itself, 324-326
reasons, 312-313

mm:treecolumn tags, 9

mm:treecontrol tags, 9

mm:treenode tags, 9

mmcolorbutton tags, 9

MMHttp objects, 8

MMNotes objects, 8

MM_reloadPage( ) function, 244

mood inspector, creating custom Property inspectors, 238-239

mood.htm code listing, 245

moveDown( ) function, 377

moveUp( ) function, 376

multifile extensions, collecting materials for packaging extensions (Flash Detector object), 457

multiple code blocks, SBB (Server Behavior Builder), positioning and weighting, 335

MXI (instruction) files
author tags, 462
configuration-changes tags, 465
creating when packaging extensions, 458
Flash Detector object, 471
saving MXI file, 458
Set Page Properties behavior, 470
structure of MXI file, 458-470
Table Helper floating panel, 472-473
description tags, 463
files tag, 463-465
ftp-extension-insert tags, 468
ftp-extension-map-changes tags, 467
ftp-extension-remove tags, 468
macromedia-extension tags, 460
menu-insert tags, 466
menu-remove tags, 466
products tags, 461-462
shortcut-insert tags, 467
shortcut-remove tags, 467
ui-access tags, 463

MXI File Creator, 491

MXP (installer) files, packaging extensions, 455-456
collecting materials, 456-458
creating the MXI (instructions) file, 458-473
packaging into MXP (installer) files, 474
tests, 474

myCommand( ) function, 374

N

navigation bars, as reason to mix extension types, 312

navigational icons (User Interface Guidelines), 439

Netscape Block Spacer inspector, creating custom Property inspectors, 248
basic inspector files, 249
canInspectSelection( ) function, 251
new layout and form, 249-250
refining, 253-255
revising inspectSelection( ) function, 251
setDimensions( ) function, 251-252

Netscape Spacer tags, inserting (creating simple objects), creating the spacer object, 32-38

New Server Behavior dialog box, 349

newBehavior( ) function, 91

nodes, Level 1 DOM, 107, 111
COMMENT_NODE objects, 110
DOCUMENT_NODE objects, 107-108
ELEMENT_NODE objects, 108-109
TEXT_NODE objects, 110-111

O

object access, creating custom floating panels, table-editing utility, 301-304

object testing, submitting extensions to Macromedia Dreamweaver Exchange, 480-481
HTML checks, 481
inserting objects, 480
user interface, 480

object-based selection commands, accessing selections, 121

objects
- buttons, User Interface Guidelines, 448
- creating custom objects, 11-53
  - *adding forms, 24-25*
  - *API procedure, 19*
  - *basic object files, 22-24*
  - *Configuration folder, 12-13*
  - *custom object categories, 20-22*
  - *full-featured object files, 16-18, 39-53*
  - *HR, 39-42*
  - *Insert bar objects, 14*
  - *Insert menu objects, 14*
  - *simple object files, 14-16, 27-38*
- custom objects (API), methods, 8-9
- DOM object, 112
  - *accessing, 113*
  - *API functions for setting and manipulating the selection, 118-122*
  - *API functions for working with objects, 114-116*
  - *API functions for working with selection offsets, 117-118*
  - *API functions for working with selections, 116-117*
  - *strings of code, 122*
- enhancing with DOM, 122-123
- Flash Detector
  - *collecting materials for multifile extension packaging, 457*
  - *creating an MXI file for multifile extensions (packaging extensions), 471*
- inserting, dom.insertObject( ) function, 314-315
- JavaScript, 434-435

objectTag( ) function, 312, 320
- building return statement (horizonatal rule object construction), 44-47
- revising to collect user input (horizonatal rule object construction), 43-44
- simple object files, 15-16

onBlur event handlers, 241

onBlur function, 233

online help
- adding (creating custom full-featured objects), 48-50
- adding to custom commands, 164-167
- User Interface Guidelines, 450-451

online resources, 487
- forums, 489
- tools/utilities, 489-490
- Web sites, 488

opening line/comment, as Property inspector file requirement, 232

Option( ) constructor (JavaScript), 157

Option-clicking (Mac) icon, 22

optional elements
- behavior constuction, 59-60
- command files, 138-140
- floating panel files, 277-279
- Property inspector files, 235

optional files
- object construction, 13
- Property inspector construction, 231

OSA for Dreamweaver, 491

P

Package Extension command (File menu), 474

packaging extensions, 455-456
- collecting materials, 456
  - *Flash Detector object, 457*
  - *Set Page Properties behavior, 457*
  - *Table Helper floating panel, 458*
- creating the MXI (instructions) file, 458
  - *Flash Detector object, 471*
  - *saving MXI file, 458*
  - *Set Page Properties behavior, 470*
  - *structure of MXI file, 458-470*
  - *Table Helper floating panel, 472-473*
- packaging into MXP (installer) files, 474
- tests, 474

page elements (DOM)
- altering, 130
- applying string functions, 132-134
- selecting, 130-132

Page Properties dialog box, 447

Page title
- as behavior file requirement, 58
- as command file requirement, 138
- as floater file required element, 277
- HTML files (server behaviors), 343

parameters
- alt parameters, adding to all images in document, 142-167
- fnCall, 93
- function parameters, 419-422
- passing to commands, receiveArguments( ) function, 187-188
- SBB, 336

paramObj object, 359

participant files, server behaviors, 342

passed parameters
- custom behavior construction, 66-67
- receiveArguments( ) function, 187-188

popup menus, 431-432
User Interface Guidelines, 445-446
positioning SBB code blocks, 335
preparing to test, submitting extensions to Macromedia Dreamweaver Exchange, 479
previous installations (Configuration folder files), 6
priorities
creating custom Property inspectors, 248
replacing default inspectors, 267-272
procedures, 10
extension-specific, 8
products tag, 461-462
properties
COMMENT_NODE objects, 110
DOCUMENT_NODE objects, 107
ELEMENT_NODE objects, 108
ImageButtons, 382
TEXT_NODE objects, 110
Property inspectors
accessing, dw.setFloaterVisibility( ) function, 318-319
buttons (User Interface Guidelines), 450
creating custom Property inspectors, 229-272
adding forms and inspectBehavior( ) function, 239-240
adding local functions and event handlers, 241-242
API procedure, 236-237
bare-bones mood inspector, 238-239
competing inspectors, 248
Configuration folder, 230-232
Inspector files' structure, 232-235
Netscape Block Spacer inspector, 248-255
re-creating the interface with layers, 242-247
replacing default inspectors, 255-272
layout, User Interface Guidelines, 444
logos, 440
testing, submitting extensions to Macromedia Dreamweaver Exchange, 481-482

Q-R

radio buttons, 430-431
User Interface Guidelines, 445
Raj, Rabi Sunder, Web site, 488
rearranging ListControl list items, 375-378
receiveArguments( ) function, 140
adding to command document, 192
as command file optional element, 140
collecting arguments (creating custom menu commands), 220-221
passing parameters to commands, 187-188
re-creating custom Property inspector interfaces, layers, 242-247
removing ListControl list items, 375
replacing default inspectors, custom Property inspectors, 255
Custom Horizontal Rule object, 256-257
layout and form elements, 259-272
required elements
behavior constuction, 58
command files, 138
floating panel files, 276-277
Property inspector files, 232-233
required files
behavior construction, 57-58
object construction, HTML files, 13
Property inspector construction, HTML files, 231
resources, online, 487
forums, 489
tools/utilities, 489-490
Web sites, 488
rewriting applyBehavior( ) function, custom behavior construction, 72-74, 83-84
rollover images, creating custom floating panels, 286-288
rollovers, as reason to mix extension types, 312
rowspan attributes (creating custom floating panels), table-editing utility, 305-308
runCommand( ) function, 126, 169

S

Sample.htm (simple command file), 458
Sample.mxi file, 458
saving MXI files (packaging extensions), 458
SBB (Server Behavior Builder), 334-341
dialog box, 335
inserting a line of code, 336-338
multiple code blocks, 335

parameters, 336
positioning and weighting of code blocks, 335
user-defined messages, 338-341

script tags, 414-416

scripting
guidelines, submitting extensions to Macromedia Dreamweaver Exchange, 478
ImageButtons, 380-388
layers, complex tabbed layer interfaces, 396-399
ListControl elements, 367-369
simple tabbed layer interfaces, 392-394

second pages, creating layered interfaces, 404

select element, attaching to ListControl object, 371-372

Select Image Source dialog box, 379

selecting page elements (DOM), 130-132

selection offsets, applying DOM, API functions for using selection offsets with objects, 117-118

selectionChanged( ) function
as floater file optional element, 279
creating custom floating panels, 293-294

selections
accessing, 121
applying DOM
API functions for getting information about current selection, 116-117
API functions for setting and manipulating selections, 118-122

semi-required elements, Property inspector files, 234-235

separator tags, 201

Server Behavior Builder. *See* SBB

server behaviors, 333
creating custom server behaviors, 341
API procedure, 346-348
Configuration folder, 341-344
helper functions, 344-346
inserting conditional page content with an if-then statement, 348-356
inserting dynamically determined images, 356-360
SBB, 334-336
dialog box, 335
inserting a line of code, 336-338
multiple code blocks, 335
parameters, 336
positioning and weighting of code blocks, 335
user-defined messages, 338-341

Set Page Properties behavior, 75
adding local functions, 84-86
collecting materials for packaging extensions, 457
creating simple MXI files (packaging extensions), 470
designing form to collect user input, 82
inspecting, 96-98
placing code into basic behavior file framework, 80-81
rewriting applyBehavior function, 83-84
splitting code into HTML and JavaScript files, 87
writing the JavaScript function, 75-79

Set Page Properties dialog box, 86

setColorButton( ) function, 48, 85

setColorField( ) function, 48, 85

setColorText( ) function, 48

setDimensions( ) function, creating Netscape Block Spacer inspector, 251-252

setMenuText( ) function, 194-195
creating menu item names, 201-204

setProperties( ) function, 77

setTitleTag( ) function, 233

shared files, 10
inspecting behaviors, 94-95

shared images (User Interface Guidelines), 440

short help (User Interface Guidelines), 450

shortcut-insert tags, 467

shortcut-remove tags, 467

showing floater means, as floater file required element, 276

showPage( ) function, 399

side-wide extensions, testing, submitting extensions to Macromedia Dreamweaver Exchange, 486

simple behaviors, creating Back/Forward behavior, 67-74
creating a form to collect user input, 72
inserting code into behavior file framework, 70-71
JavaScript code insert, 68-69
rewriting applyBehavior( ) function, 72-74

simple extensions, collecting materials for packaging extensions (Set Page Properties behavior), 457

simple object files, 14-16, 27-38
creating table objects, 27
adding an entry for the object in insertbar.xml file, 30
creating an icon for the object, 31-32
HTML code, 27-28
placing code in object file framework, 28-29
testing and troubleshooting new object, 30-31
inserting single-celled centering tables, 27
objectTag( ) function, 15-16
recognizable filenames, 15
title tags, 15
user input objects, inserting a Netscape Spacer tag, 32-38

simple tabbed layer interfaces, 390
creating layers, 390-392
scripting, 392-394

single-celled centering tables, creating simple objects, 27

site object, 8

size, dialog box layout (User Interface Guidelines), 442

spacer tags, inserting (creating simple objets), 32-38

specifications
dom.addBehavior( ) function, 315-318
dom.insertObject( ) function, 314-315
dw.browseForFileURL( ) function, 153
dw.getDocumentDOM( ) function, 113
dw.popupAction( ) function, 315-318
dw.runCommand( ) function, 313
dw.setFloaterVisibility( ) function, 318-319
ImageButtons, 381-382
layered interfaces, 390
Level 0 DOM, 103, 107
ListControl elements, 365

string access
custom floating panels, table-editing utility, 299-301
custom commands, converting selected text to uppercase, 167-169
adding canAcceptCommand( ) function, 172-175
command file document, 169
creating basic code for the main function, 169-172
refining canAcceptCommand( ) function, 175-178

string functions, page elements (DOM), 132-134

strings
code,applying DOM, 122
concatenation, 416-417

structure
command files, 137
optional elements, 138-140
required elements, 138
Floater files, 276
optional elements, 277-279
required elements, 276-277
Inspector files, 232
optional elements, 235
required elements, 232-233
semi-required elements, 234-235
MXI files (packaging extensions), 458-470

Subfolders (Configuration folder), 4

submitting extensions, Macromedia Dreamweaver Exchange, 477-478
borrowing code guidelines, 478
file location guidelines, 478
recommended test plan, 479-486
scripting guidelines, 478

substring( ) function, 93, 145

supporting media files, floating panel construction, 275

Swap Image dialog box, 446

SWF movies, creating custom floating panels, 289-290

switching between layers, layered interfaces, 404-405

T

tabbed help (User Interface Guidelines), 450

tabbed layer interfaces. *See* layered interfaces

TabControl class objects, creating complex tabbed layer interfaces, 395
creating layers, 395-396
functions, 397-398
scripting layers, 396-399

Table Helper floating panel
collecting materials for packaging extensions, 458
creating an MXI file for an extension with menu changes (packaging extensions), 472-473

Table Helper. *See* table-editing utility

table objects, creating (simple object construction), 27
adding an entry for the object in insertbar.xml file, 30
creating an icon for the object, 31-32
HTML code, 27-28
placing code in object file framework, 28-29
testing and troubleshooting new object, 30-31

table-editing utility, creating custom floating panels, 296
basic floater, 296-297
dw.getDocumentDOM( ) function, 297-299
object access, 301-304
rowspan and colspan attributes, 305-308
string access, 299-301

tables
dialog box layout (User Interface Guidelines), 441
single-celled centering tables, creating simple objects, 27

tagNameOrKeyword tags, as Property inspector file requirement, 232

tags
author, 462
configuration-changes, 465
custom form input tags (API), 9
description, 463
exactOrWithin, as Property inspector file requirement, 232
files, 463-465
form tags
adding forms to custom objects, 24-25
full-featured object files, 16-17
ftp-extension-insert, 468
ftp-extension-map-changes, 467
ftp-extension-remove, 468
macromedia-extension, 460
menu tags, 201
menu-insert, 466
menu-remove, 466
menuitem tags, 182
products, 461-462
script tags, 414-416
separator tags, 201
shortcut-insert, 467
shortcut-remove, 467
spacer tags, inserting in simple objects, 32-38
tagNameOrKeyword, as Property inspector file requirement, 232
title tags, simple object files, 15
ui-access, 463

test plan, submitting extensions to Macromedia Dreamweaver Exchange, 479
behavior testing, 483-484
command testing, 482-483
floating panel testing, 484-486
installation testing, 479-480
object testing, 480-481
preparing to test, 479
Property inspector testing, 481-482
side-wide extension testing, 486

testGeneration( ) function, 175

testing objects, creating table objects, 30-31

tests, packaging extensions, 474

text
converting to uppercase, creating custom string access commands, 168-178
fields, 429
objects, TEXT_NODE objects, 110-111

title tags, simple object files, 15

tools/utilities (online resources), 489-490

toUpperCase( ) string function, 168

tree controls
structure, 9
User Interface Guidelines, 447

troubleshooting objects, creating table objects, 30-31

U-V

ui-access tags, 463

UldraDev zone, 488

user input objects (creating simple objects), inserting a Netscape Spacer tag, 32-38

User Interface Guidelines, 437
buttons, 448
behaviors, 448
commands, 449
floating panels, 450
objects, 448
Property inspectors, 450
colors, 438
error-proof handling, 451
default values, 453-454
error-checking, 452-453
focus and selection, 452
fonts, 438
form elements, 444
checkboxes, 445
color buttons, 447

lists, 445-446
popup menus, 445-446
radio buttons, 445
text fields, 444
tree controls, 447
graphics, 438
file formats, 438
icons, 439-440
inserting images, 438
logos, 440
layout, 441
dialog box layout, 441-442
Property inspector layout, 444
online help, 450
Help buttons, 451
short help, 450
tabbed layouts, 450

user interface testing, object testing, submitting extensions to Macromedia Dreamweaver Exchange, 480

user-defined messages, inserting (building server behaviors), 338-341

user-specific files, Configuration folder, 7

utilities/tools (online resources), 489-490

values, 416

variables, 416-417

vline parameter, as Property inspector file requirement, 232

W-Z

Web site resources, 488

WebMonkey's guide to Extending Dreamweaver, 488

Weighting SBB code blocks, 335

Window menu commands, Add Popup Behavior, 327

window.alert( ) statement, 171

within inspectors, 236

Workshops
Command that Uses Object Access, 141-167
Command that Uses String Access, 167-180
Creating a Full-Featured Behavior, 75-89
Creating a Menu Command, 214-228
Creating a More Complex Object, 39-53
Creating a Simple Behavior, 67-74
Creating a Simple Object with User Input, 32-38
Creating a Simple Object, 27-32
Floating Panel Utility, 295-308
Inserting Conditional Page Content with an If-Then Statement, 348-356
Inserting Dynamically Determined Images, 356-360
Inspecting the Set Properties Behavior, 96-97
Manipulating the Menu Entry for a Command, 189-193
Replacing a Default Inspector, 255-272
Simple Property Inspector, 248-255

XML files
Configuration folder, 6
server behavior construction, tags and attributes, 341-342

VOICES THAT MATTER

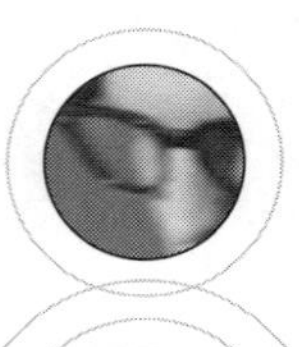
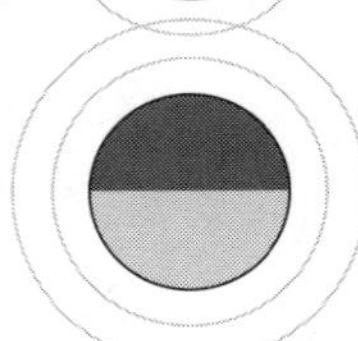

HOW TO CONTACT US

VISIT OUR WEB SITE

WWW.NEWRIDERS.COM

On our web site, you'll find information about our other books, authors, tables of contents, and book errata. You will also find information about book registration and how to purchase our books, both domestically and internationally.

EMAIL US

Contact us at: **nrfeedback@newriders.com**

- If you have comments or questions about this book
- To report errors that you have found in this book
- If you have a book proposal to submit or are interested in writing for New Riders
- If you are an expert in a computer topic or technology and are interested in being a technical editor who reviews manuscripts for technical accuracy

Contact us at: **nreducation@newriders.com**

- If you are an instructor from an educational institution who wants to preview New Riders books for classroom use. Email should include your name, title, school, department, address, phone number, office days/hours, text in use, and enrollment, along with your request for desk/examination copies and/or additional information.

Contact us at: **nrmedia@newriders.com**

- If you are a member of the media who is interested in reviewing copies of New Riders books. Send your name, mailing address, and email address, along with the name of the publication or web site you work for.

BULK PURCHASES/CORPORATE SALES

The publisher offers discounts on this book when ordered in quantity for bulk purchases and special sales. For sales within the U.S., please contact: Corporate and Government Sales (800) 382-3419 or **corpsales@pearsontechgroup.com**. Outside of the U.S., please contact: International Sales (317) 581-3793 or **international@pearsontechgroup.com**.

WRITE TO US

New Riders Publishing
201 W. 103rd St.
Indianapolis, IN 46290-1097

CALL/FAX US

Toll-free (800) 571-5840
If outside U.S. (317) 581-3500
Ask for New Riders
FAX: (317) 581-4663

WWW.NEWRIDERS.COM